D1789333

Non-refoulement under the European Convention on Human Rights and the UN Convention against Torture

International Refugee Law Series

Editor-in-Chief

David James Cantor

Editorial Board

VOLUME 6

The titles published in this series are listed at *brill.com/irls*

Non-refoulement under the European Convention on Human Rights and the UN Convention against Torture

The Assessment of Individual Complaints by the European Court of Human Rights under Article 3 ECHR and the United Nations Committee against Torture under Article 3 CAT

By

Fanny de Weck

BRILL

NIJHOFF

LEIDEN | BOSTON

Based on the author's thesis (doctoral University of Lucerne), 2014.

The Library of Congress Cataloging-in-Publication Data is available online at http://catalog.loc.gov
LC record available at http://lccn.loc.gov/2016036657

Typeface for the Latin, Greek, and Cyrillic scripts: "Brill". See and download: brill.com/brill-typeface.

ISSN 2213-3836
ISBN 978-90-04-31148-0 (hardback)
ISBN 978-90-04-31149-7 (e-book)

Für Joël

∵

Contents

Preface

The idea for this study emerged while I was working at the International Human Rights Unit of the Swiss Federal Office for Justice in Bern. With regard to the principle of non-refoulement, my own country, Switzerland, was seldom confronted with individual complaints introduced before the European Court of Human Rights in Strasbourg, but frequently had to deal with cases submitted to the United Nations Committee against Torture in Geneva. I observed that the United Nations complaint mechanism in Geneva appeared to be becoming more and more attractive for asylum lawyers and human rights advocates. I wanted to know why. I therefore decided to compare the practice and case law of the European Court of Human Rights with that of the United Nations Committee against Torture in the assessment of individual complaints concerning the principle of non-refoulement.

This book is based on my doctoral thesis, which I successfully completed at the University of Lucerne in 2014. It includes the case law published up to February 2016. I would not have been able to conduct this study without the support of several persons and institutions. A special thanks goes to my doctoral supervisor Professor Martina Caroni from the University of Lucerne for her unfailing support during these years of research. I would also like to express my gratitude to Professor Frank Schürmann. The legal knowledge and trust given to me by these two excellent scholars have provided me with the expertise and confidence I needed to conduct this research. Particular thanks also goes to Professor Alberto Achermann from the University of Bern.

I want to thank the Swiss National Science Foundation, which enabled me to deepen my research as a Visiting Fellow at the Irish Centre of Human Rights in Galway and the Refugee Studies Centre at the University of Oxford. I had important exchanges with numerous scholars during the months I spent at these institutions.

Although I cannot mention all the individuals who have supported me in one way or another, I would like to note my particular appreciation for the legal expertise, critical reviews and other support from the following persons: Gwen Clayton, Dr Babak Fargahi, Christian Puricel, Dr Thomas Forster, Dennis Guggenheim, Stephanie Motz, Gregor Münch, Liliane Blum, Laura and Joseph de Weck and in particular Margaux de Weck. For believing in my projects and me, I want to thank my parents and Frederic Steck.

Fanny de Weck
Zurich, Galway, Oxford, Bern, Kinshasa, Geneva, Sent
February 2016

Table of Abbreviations and Acronyms

CAT	Convention against Torture and Other Cruel, Inhuman or Degrading Treatment or Punishment
CCPR	see ICCPR
CIA	(US) Central Intelligence Agency
CJEU	Court of Justice of the European Union
ComAT	Committee against Torture
DRC	Democratic Republic of the Congo
ECHR	European Convention for the Protection of Human Rights and Fundamental Freedoms
ECJ	European Court of Justice
EComHR	European Commission on Human Rights
ECRE	European Council on Refugees and Exiles
ECtHR	European Court of Human Rights
ELENA	European Legal Network on Asylum
ETS	European Treaty Series (*Council of Europe*)
EU	European Union
FGM	Female genital mutilation
HRC	Human Rights Committee
ICC	International Criminal Court
ICCPR	International Covenant on Civil and Political Rights
ICJ	International Court of Justice
ICTR	International Criminal Tribunal for Rwanda
ICTY	International Criminal Tribunal for the former Yugoslavia
IDP	Internally Displaced Person
LGBTI	Lesbian, gay, bisexual, transgender, intersex
LTTE	Liberation Tigers of Tamil Eelam
NGO	Non-Governmental Organisation
OHCHR	United Nations Office of the High Commissioner for Human Rights
OJ L	Official Journal of the European Union
PKK	*Partiya Karkerên Kurdistan* (Kurdistan Workers' Party)
TFEU	Treaty on the Functioning of the European Union
UN	United Nations
UNHCR	United Nations High Commissioner for Refugees
UK	United Kingdom
US/USA	United States of America

Table of Cases

International Court of Justice

ICJ, *Ahmadou Sadio Diallo (Republic of Guinea v. DRC)*, 30 November 2010, IJC Reports 2010, p. 639

International Criminal Tribunal for the Former Yugoslavia

ICTY, *Prosecutor v. Furundzija*, 10 December 1989, no. IT-95-17/1-T,
ICTY, *Prosecutor v. Delacic and Others*, 16 November 1998, no. IT-96-21-T
ICTY, *Prosecutor v. Kunarac*, 22 February 2001, no. IT 96-23-T and IT-96-23/1-T

(former) European Court of Justice/ Court of Justice of the European Union

ECJ, C-465-07, *Meki Elgafaji and Noor Elgafaji v. Staatssecretaris van Justitie*, 17 February 2009
CJEU, Joined Cases C-411/10 and C-493/10, *N.S. v. Secretary of State for the Home Department and M.E. and Others v. Refugee Applications Commissioner & Minister for Justice, Equality and Law Reform*, 21 December 2011
CJEU, Joined Cases C-71/11 and C-99/11, *Y and Z v. Bundesrepublik Deutschland*, 5 September 2012
CJEU, Joined Cases C-199/12, C-200/12, C-201/12, *X, Y and Z v Minister voor Immigratie, Integratie en Asiel*, 7 November 2013
CJEU, C-4/11, *Kaveh Puid v. Bundesrepublik Deutschland*, 14 November 2013
CJEU, C-542/13, *Mohamed M'Bodji v. Etat belge*, 18 December 2014

(former) European Commission of Human Rights

EComHR, *X. v. Belgium*, 29 May 1961, no. 984/61
EComHR, *Denmark, Norway, Sweden and Netherlands v. Greek* (the Greek case), report of 5 November 1969, Yearbook 12 (1969), p. 186
EComHR, *East African Asians v. UK*, 14 December 1973, nos. 4403/70 and further
EComHR, *Y. v. UK*, 8 October 1991, no. 14229/88
EComHR, *M. v. Denmark*, 14 October 1992, no. 17392/90

ECtHR, *Dzhaksybergenov v. Ukraine*, 10 February 2011, no. 12343/10

ECtHR, *Elmuratov v. Russia*, 3 March 2011, no. 66317/09

ECtHR, *Rahimi v. Greece*, 5 April 2011, no. 8687/08

ECtHR, *Toumi v. Italy*, 5 April 2011, no. 25716/09

ECtHR, *Soedji v. Switzerland*, 7 April 2011, no. 21714/11 (striking out)

ECtHR, *Izevbekhai and Others v. Ireland*, 17 May 2011, no. 43408/08 (decision)

ECtHR, *E.G. v. UK*, 31 May 2011, no. 41178/08

ECtHR, *Anam v. UK*, 7 June 2011, no. 21783/08 (decision)

ECtHR, *R.U. v. Greece*, 7 June 2011, no. 2237/08

ECtHR, *S.P. v. Belgium*, 14 June 2011, no. 12572/08 (decision)

ECtHR, *Dobrov v. Ukraine*, 14 June 2011, no. 42409/09 (decision)

ECtHR, *Diallo v. Czech Republic*, 23 June 2011, no. 20493/07

ECtHR, *Sufi and Elmi v. UK*, 28 June 2011, nos. 8319/07 and 11449/07

ECtHR, *Shakor and 48 other applications v. Finland*, 28 June 2011, no. 10941/10 (decision)

ECtHR, *Al-Skeini and Others v. UK*, 7 July 2011 [GC], no. 55721/07

ECtHR, *Baltaji v. Bulgaria*, 12 July 2011, no. 12919/04

ECtHR, *Z.K. and 27 other applications v. Denmark*, 23 August 2011, no. 37199/10 (decision)

ECtHR, *Ameh and Others v. UK*, 30 August 2011, no. 4539/11 (decision)

ECtHR, *M. v. Finland*, 6 September 2011, no. 48933/09 (striking out)

ECtHR, *Omeredo v. Austria*, 20 September 2011, no. 8969/10 (decision)

ECtHR, *H.R. v. France*, 22 September 2011, no. 64780/09

ECtHR, *Ali Gedi v. Austria and 3 other applications*, 4 October 2011, no. 61567/10 (decision)

ECtHR, *Genovese v. Malta*, 11 October 2011, no. 53124/09

ECtHR, *Auad v. Bulgaria*, 11 October 2011, no. 46390/10

ECtHR, *Husseini v. Sweden*, 13 October 2011, no. 10611/09

ECtHR, *Samina v. Sweden*, 20 October 2011, no. 55463/09

ECtHR, *Ahorugeze v. Sweden*, 27 October 2011, no. 37075/09

ECtHR, *Yakubov v. Russia*, 8 November 2011, no. 7265/10

ECtHR, *Agalar v. Norway*, 8 November 2011, no. 55120/09 (decision)

ECtHR, *Al Hanchi v. Bosnia and Herzegovina*, 15 November 2011, no. 48205/09

ECtHR, *Barnic v. Austria*, 13 December 2011, no. 54845/10 (decision)

ECtHR, *Ergashev v. Russia*, 20 December 2011, no. 12106/09

ECtHR, *Mwanje v. Belgium*, 20 December 2011, no. 10486/10

ECtHR, *J.H. v. UK*, 20 December 2011, no. 48839/09

ECtHR, *Habib v. Sweden*, 4 January 2012, no. 11152/09 (decision)

ECtHR, *Abu Qatada v. UK*, 17 January 2012, no. 8139/09

ECtHR, *Harkins and Edwards v. UK*, 17 January 2012, nos. 9146/07 and 32650/07

ECtHR, *Popov v. France*, 19 January 2012, no. 39472/07

ECtHR, *S.S. v. UK*, 24 January 2012, no. 12096/10 (decision)

ECtHR, *Ahmed Ali v. Netherlands and Greece*, 24 January 2012, no. 26494/09 (decision)

Committee against Torture

Human Rights Committee

Non-refoulement Cases Assessed on the Merits

This table enumerates the judgments of the European Court of Human Rights and the decisions of the United Nations Committee against Torture, published up to 29 February 2016, in which these institutions have assessed *on the merits* whether there is a violation of the principle of non-refoulement under Article 3 ECHR or Article 3 CAT. The idea behind this list is to offer a useful overview on Strasbourg and Geneva non-refoulement jurisprudence on the merits.[1]

Also attached is the Committee's General Comment No. 1 on the 'Implementation of article 3 of the Convention in the context of article 22' CAT. The Committee adopted this first General Comment at its 19th session in November 1997 in order to give guidelines for the implementation of Article 3 CAT in the context of individual complaints. It summarizes its own approach in the assessment of individual complaints under that provision. At its 55th session in summer 2015, the Committee decided to revise its General Comment No. 1 on Article 3 CAT.[2]

Judgments of the European Court of Human Rights with Regard to the Principle of Non-refoulement under Article 3 ECHR

1989

ECtHR, *Soering v. United Kingdom*, 7 July 1989, no. 14038/88* (US)

1991

ECtHR, *Cruz Varas and Others v. Sweden*, 20 March 1991, no. 15576/89 (Chile)

ECtHR, *Vilvarajah and Others v. United Kingdom*, 30 October 1991, nos. 13163/87 (Sri Lanka)

---

1 This symbol (*) marks the judgments (Court) and decisions (Committee) in which a *violation* of the principle of non-refoulement in Art. 3 ECHR or Art. 3 CAT was found. I have enumerated all judgments (Court) and decisions (Committee) on the merits with regard to non-refoulement that were accessible and found by me on the Court's and the UN database up to the 29 February 2016. In this list, I have not included inadmissibility decisions adopted in Strasbourg and Geneva and those judgments in which the Court has struck out cases or in which it assessed an alleged violation of Art. 13 ECHR in conjunction with Art. 3 ECHR only.

2 Statement of the Chairperson of the Committee Against Torture to the 70th session of the General Assembly, New York, 20 October 2015, accessible on the Committee's website [15.2.2016].

1996
ECtHR, *Chahal v. United Kingdom*, 15 November 1996, no. 22414/93* (India)
ECtHR, *Ahmed v. Austria*, 17 December 1996, no. 25964/94* (Somalia)

1997
ECtHR, *H.L.R. v. France*, 29 April 1997, no. 24573/94 (Colombia)
ECtHR, *D. v. United Kingdom*, 2 May 1997, no. 30240/96* (St. Kitts)

2000
ECtHR, *Jabari v. Turkey*, 11 July 2000, no. 40035/98* (Iran)

2001
ECtHR, *Bensaid v. United Kingdom*, 6 February 2001, no. 44599/98 (Algeria)
ECtHR, *Hilal v. United Kingdom*, 6 March 2001, no. 45276/99* (Tansania/Zanzibar)

2004
ECtHR, *Venkadajalasarma v. Netherlands*, 17 February 2004, no. 58510/00 (Sri Lanka)
ECtHR, *Thampibillai v. Netherlands*, 17 February 2004, no. 61350/00 (Sri Lanka)

2005
ECtHR, *Mamatkulov and Askarov v. Turkey*, 4 February 2005 (Grand Chamber) nos. 46827/99 and 46951/99 (Uzbekistan)
ECtHR, *Shamayev and Others v. Georgia and Russia*, 12 April 2005, no. 36378/02* (Russia)
ECtHR, *Müslim v. Turkey*, 26 April 2005, no. 53566/99 (Iraq)
ECtHR, *Said v. Netherlands*, 5 July 2005, no. 2345/02* (Eritrea)
ECtHR, *N. v. Finland*, 26 July 2005, no. 38885/02* (DRC)
ECtHR, *Bader and Kanbor v. Sweden*, 8 November 2005, no. 13284/04* (Syria)

2006
ECtHR, *Aoulmi c. France*, 17 January 2006, no. 50278/99 (Algeria)
ECtHR, *D. and others v. Turkey*, 22 June 2006, no. 24245/03* (Iran)
ECtHR, *Cahuas v. Spain*, 10 August 2006, no. 24668/03 (Peru)

2007
ECtHR, *Salah Sheekh v. Netherlands*, 11 January 2007, no. 1948/04* (Somalia)
ECtHR, *Garabayev v. Russia*, 7 June 2007, no. 38411/02* (Turkmenistan)
ECtHR, *Sultani v. France*, 20 September 2007, no. 45223/05 (Afghanistan)

2008
ECtHR, *Saadi v. Italy*, 28 February 2008 (Grand Chamber), no. 37201/06* (Tunisia)

ECtHR, *Garayev v. Azerbaijan*, 10 June 2010, no. 53688/08* (Uzbekistan)

ECtHR, *Kolesnik v. Russia*, 10 June 2010, no. 26876/08* (Turkmenistan)

ECtHR, *S.H. v. United Kingdom*, 15 June 2010, no. 19956/06* (Bhutan)

ECtHR, *M.B. and Others v. Turkey*, 15 June 2010, no. 36009/08* (Iran)

ECtHR, *Isakov v. Russia*, 8 July 2010, no. 14049/08* (Uzbekistan)

ECtHR, *Yuldashev v. Russia*, 8 July 2010, no. 1248/09* (Uzbekistan)

ECtHR, *Dbouba v. Turkey*, 13 July 2010, no. 15916/09* (Tunisia)

ECtHR, *A v. Netherlands*, 20 July 2010, no. 4900/06* (Libya)

ECtHR, *N. v. Sweden*, 20 July 2010, no. 23505/09* (Afghanistan)

ECtHR, *Karimov v. Russia*, 29 July 2010, no. 54219/08* (Uzbekistan)

ECtHR, *Y.P. and L.P. v. France*, 2 September 2010, no. 32476/06* (Belarus)

ECtHR, *Iskandarov v. Russia*, 23 September 2010, no. 17185/05* (Tajikistan)

ECtHR, *Gaforov v. Russia*, 21 October 2010, no. 25404/09* (Tajikistan)

ECtHR, *Sultanov v. Russia*, 4 November 2010, no. 15303/09* (Uzbekistan)

ECtHR, *B.A. v. France*, 2 December 2010, no. 14951/09 (Chad)

2011

ECtHR, *N.S. v. Denmark*, 20 January 2011, no. 58359/08 (Sri Lanka)

ECtHR, *P.K. v. Denmark*, 20 January 2011, no. 54705/08 (Sri Lanka)

ECtHR, *S.S. and Others v. Denmark*, 20 January 2011, no. 54703/08 (Sri Lanka)

ECtHR, *T.N. and S.N. v. Denmark*, 20 January 2011, no. 36517/08 (Sri Lanka)

ECtHR, *T N. v. Denmark*, 20 January 2011, no. 20594/08 (Sri Lanka)

ECtHR, *M.S.S. v. Belgium and Greece*, 21 January 2011 (Grand Chamber), no. 30696/09* (Greece/Afghanistan)

ECtHR, *Dzhaksybergenov v. Ukraine*, 10 February 2011, no. 12343/10 (Kazakhstan)

ECtHR, *Elmuratov v. Russia*, 3 March 2011, no. 66317/09 (Uzbekistan)

ECtHR, *Toumi v. Italy*, 5 April 2011, no. 25716/09* (Tunisia)

ECtHR, *E.G. v. United Kingdom*, 31 May 2011, no. 41178/08 (Sri Lanka)

ECtHR, *Sufi and Elmi v. United Kingdom*, 28 June 2011, nos. 8319/07 and 11449/07* (Somalia)

ECtHR, *H.R. v. France*, 22 September 2011, no. 64780/09* (Algeria)

ECtHR, *Auad v. Bulgaria*, 11 October 2011, no. 46390/10* (Lebanon)

ECtHR, *Sharipov v. Russia*, 11 October 2011 no. 18414/10 (Kazakhstan)

ECtHR, *Husseini v. Sweden*, 13 October 2011, no. 10611/09 (Afghanistan)

ECtHR, *Samina v. Sweden*, 20 October 2011, no. 55463/09 (Pakistan)

ECtHR, *Ahorugeze v. Sweden*, 27 October 2011, no. 37075/09 (Rwanda)

ECtHR, *Yakubov v. Russia*, 8 November 2011, no. 7265/10* (Uzbekistan)

ECtHR, *Al Hanchi v. Bosnia and Herzegovina*, 15 November 2011, no. 48205/09 (Tunisia)

ECtHR, *Ergashev v. Russia*, 20 December 2011, no. 12106/09* (Uzbekistan)

ECtHR, *J.H. v. United Kingdom*, 20 December 2011, no. 48839/09 (Afghanistan)

ECtHR, *Mwanje v. Belgium*, 20 December 2011, no. 10486/10 (Cameroon)

Decisions on the Merits of the UN Committee against Torture with Regard to the Principle of Non-refoulement under Article 3 CAT

1997

ComAT, *X v. Switzerland*, 28 April 1997, no. 27/1995 (Sudan)

ComAT, *Paez v. Sweden*, 28 April 1997, no. 39/1996* (Peru)

ComAT, *Mohamed v. Greece*, 28 April 1997, no. 40/1996 (Ethiopia)

ComAT, *Aemei v. Switzerland*, 9 May 1997, 34/1995* (Iran)

ComAT, *X. v. Switzerland*, 9 May 1997, no. 38/1995 (Sudan)

ComAT, *E.A. v. Switzerland*, 10 November 1997, no. 28/1995 (Turkey)

ComAT, *P.Q.L. v. Canada*, 17 November 1997, no. 57/1996 (China)

1998

ComAT, *X. Y. and Z. v. Sweden*, 6 May 1998, no. 61/1996 (RDC)

ComAT, *I.A.O. v. Sweden*, 6 May 1998, no. 65/1997 (Djibouti)

ComAT, *A.F. v. Sweden*, 8 May 1998, no. 89/1997* (Iran)

ComAT, *G.R.B. v. Sweden*, 15 May 1998, no. 83/1997 (Peru)

ComAT, *A.L.N. v. Switzerland*, 19 May 1998, no. 90/1997 (Angola)

ComAT, *K.N. v. Switzerland*, 19 May 1998, no. 94/1997 (Sri Lanka)

ComAT, *J.U.A. v. Switzerland*, 10 November 1998, no. 100/1997 (Nigeria)

ComAT, *Chipana v. Venezuela*, 10 November 1998, no. 110/1998* (Peru)

ComAT, *Ayas v. Sweden*, 12 November 1998, no. 97/1997* (Turkey)

ComAT, *A. v. Netherlands*, 13 November 1998, no. 91/1997* (Tunisia)

ComAT, *Korban v. Sweden*, 16 November 1998, no. 88/1997* (Jordan/Iraq)

ComAT, *Haydin v. Sweden*, 20 November 1998, no. 101/1997* (Turkey)

1999

ComAT, *H:D. v. Switzerland*, 30 April 1999, no. 112/1998 (Turkey)

ComAT, *S.M.R. and M.M.R. v. Sweden*, 5 May 1999, no. 103/1998 (Iran)

ComAT, *M.B.B. v. Sweden*, 5 May 1999, no. 104/1998 (Iran)

ComAT, *N.P. v. Australia*, 6 May 1999, no. 106/1998 (Sri Lanka)

ComAT, *Elmi v. Australia*, 14 May 1999, no. 120/1998* (Somalia)

ComAT, *Arana v. France*, 9 November 1999, no. 63/1997* (Spain)

ComAT, *A.D. v. Netherlands*, 12 November 1999, no. 96/1997 (Sri Lanka)

ComAT, *K.M. v. Switzerland*, 16 November 1999, no. 107/1998 (Turkey)

ComAT, *G.T. v. Switzerland*, 16 November 1999, no. 137/1999 (Turkey)

ComAT, *K.T. v. Switzerland*, 19 November 1999, no. 118/1998 (RDC)

2000

ComAT, *N.M. v. Switzerland*, 9 May 2000, no. 116/1998 (RDC)

ComAT, *H.A.D. v. Switzerland*, 10 May 2000, no. 126/1999 (Turkey)

ComAT, *S.C. v. Denmark*, 10 May 2000, no. 143/1999 (Ecuador)

ComAT, *V.X.N. and H.N. v. Sweden*, 15 May 2000, no. 130 and 131/1999 (Vietnam)

ComAT, *T.P.S. v. Canada*, 16 May 2000, no. 99/1997 (India)

ComAT, *A.M. v. Switzerland*, 14 November 2000, no. 144/1999 (Chad)

ComAT, *M.R.P. v. Switzerland*, 24 November 2000, no. 122/1998 (Bangladesh)

ComAT, *A.S. v. Sweden*, 24 November 2000, no. 149/1999* (Iran)

2001

ComAT, *M.K.O. v. Netherlands*, 9 May 2001, no. 134/1999 (Turkey)

ComAT, *S.S. and S.A. v. Netherlands*, 11 May 2001, no. 142/1999 (Sri Lanka)

ComAT, *S.L. v. Sweden*, 11 May 2001, 150/1999 (Iran)

ComAT, *S.V. et al. v. Canada*, 15 May 2001, no. 49/1996 (Sri Lanka)

ComAT, *Z.Z. v. Canada*, 15 May 2001, no. 123/1998 (Afghanistan)

ComAT, *X.Y. v. Switzerland*, 15 May 2001, no. 128/1999 (Syria)

ComAT, *Y.S. v. Switzerland*, 15 May 2001, no. 147/1999 (Turkey)

ComAT, *M.S. v. Switzerland*, 13 November 2001, no. 156/2000 (Sri Lanka)

ComAT, *H.O. v. Sweden*, 13 November 2001, no. 178/2001 (Iran)

ComAT, *B.S. v. Switzerland*, 14 November 2001, no. 166/2000 (Iran)

ComAT, *M.S. v. Australia*, 23 November 2001, no. 154/2000 (Algeria)

ComAT, *Y.H.A. v. Australia*, 23 November 2001, no. 162/2000 (Somalia)

ComAT, *S.T. v. Netherlands*, 23 November 2001, no. 175/2000 (Sri Lanka)

2002

ComAT, *M.P.S. v. Australia*, 30 April 2002, no. 138/1999 (Sri Lanka)

ComAT, *E.T.B. v. Denmark*, 30 April 2002, no. 146/1999 (Georgia)

ComAT, *B.M. v. Sweden*, 30 April 2002, no. 179/2001 (Tunisia)

ComAT, *F.F.Z. v. Denmark*, 30 April 2002, no. 180/2001 (Libya)

ComAT, *H.M.H.I. v. Australia*, 1 May 2002, no. 177/2001 (Somalia)

ComAT, *Karoui v. Sweden*, 8 May 2002, no. 185/2001* (Tunisia)

ComAT, *L.M.T.D. v. Sweden*, 15 May 2002, no. 164/2000 (Venezuela)

ComAT, *V.N.I.M. v. Canada*, 12 November 2002, no. 119/1998 (Honduras)

ComAT, *H.K.H. v. Sweden*, 19 November 2002, no. 204/2002 (Iran)

2003

ComAT, *H.B.H., T.N.T., H.J.H., H.O.H., H.R.H. and H.G.H. v. Switzerland*, 29 April 2003, no. 192/2001 (Syria)

ComAt, *A.A. v. Netherlands*, 30 April 2003, no. 198/2002 (Sudan)

ComAT, *U.S. v. Finland*, 1 May 2003, no. 197/2002 (Sri Lanka)

ComAT, *M.V. v. Netherlands*, 2 May 2003, no. 201/2002 (Turkey)

ComAT, *S.S. v. Netherlands*, 5 May 2003, no. 191/2001 (Sri Lanka)

ComAT, *G.K. v. Switzerland*, 7 May 2003, no. 219/2002 (Spain)

ComAT, *K.S.Y. v. Netherlands*, 15 May 2003, no. 190/2001 (Iran)

ComAT, *Z.T. v. Australia*, 11 November 2003, no. 153/2000 (South Africa/Algeria)

ComAT, *K.K. v. Switzerland*, 11 November 2003, no. 186/2001 (Sri Lanka)

ComAT, *J.A.G.V. v. Sweden*, 11 November 2003, no. 215/2002 (Columbia)

ComAT, *A.R. v. Netherlands*, 13 November 2003, no. 203/2002 (Iran)

ComAT, *E.J.V.M. v. Sweden*, 14 November 2003, no. 213/2002 (Costa Rica)

ComAT, *Attia v. Sweden*, 17 November 2003, no. 199/2002 (Egypt)

ComAT, *V.R. v. Denmark*, 17 November 2003, no. 210/2002 (Russia)

ComAT, *T.M. v. Sweden*, 18 November 2003, no. 228/2003 (Bangladesh)

ComAT, *M.O. v. Denmark*, 23 November 2003, no. 209/2002 (Algeria)

2004

ComAT, *A.K. v. Australia*, 5 May 2004, no. 148/1999 (Sudan)

ComAT, *S.G. v. Netherlands*, 12 May 2004, no. 135/1999 (Turkey)

ComAT, *A.I. v. Switzerland*, 12 May 2004, no. 182/2001 (Sri Lanka)

ComAT, *B.S.S. v. Canada*, 12 May 2004, no. 183/2001 (India)

ComAT, *M.A.K. v. Germany*, 12 May 2004, no. 214/2002 (Turkey)

ComAT, *M.A.M. v. Sweden*, 14 May 2004, no. 196/2002 (Bangladesh)

ComAT, *S.U.A. v. Sweden*, 22 November 2004, no. 223/2002 (Bangladesh)

ComAT, *Rios v. Canada*, 23 November 2004, no. 133/1999* (Mexico)

2005

ComAT, *David v. Sweden*, 2 May 2005, no. 220/2002 (Bangladesh)

ComAT, *Diaz v. France*, 3 May 2005, no. 194/2001 (Spain)

ComAT, *M.M.K. v. Sweden*, 3 May 2005, no. 221/2002 (Bangladesh)

ComAT, *Elahi v. Switzerland*, 3 May 2005, no. 222/2002 (Pakistan)

ComAT, *T.A. v. Sweden*, 6 May 2005, no. 226/2003* (Bangladesh)

ComAT, *Brada v. France*, 17 May 2005, no. 195/2002* (Algeria)

ComAT, *Agiza v. Sweden*, 20 May 2005, no. 233/2003* (Egypt)

ComAT, *S.P.A. v. Canada*, 7 November 2005, 282/2005 (Iran)

ComAT, *M.S.H. v. Sweden*, 14 November 2005, no. 235/2003 (Bangladesh)

ComAT, *M.C.M.V.F. v. Sweden*, 14 November 2005, no. 237/2003 (El Salvador)

ComAT, *Z.T. (No. 2) v. Norway*, 14 November 2005, no. 238/2003 (Ethiopia)

ComAT, *S.S.S. v. Canada*, 16 November 2005, no. 245/2004 (India)

ComAT, *Dadar v. Canada*, 23 November 2005, no. 258/2004* (Iran)

ComAT, *S.N.A.W. et al. v. Switzerland*, 24 November 2005, no. 231/2003 (Sri Lanka)

ComAT, *S.S.H. v. Switzerland*, 25 November 2005, no. 254/2004 (Pakistan)

2006

ComAT, *Elmansoub v. Switzerland*, 8 May 2006, no. 278/2005 (Sudan)

ComAT, *Zare v. Sweden*, 12 May 2006, no. 256/2004 (Iran)

ComAT, *El Rgeig v. Switzerland*, 15 November 2006, no. 280/2005* (Libya)

ComAT, *A.A.C. v. Sweden*, 16 November 2006, no. 227/2003 (Bangladesh)

ComAT, *A.H. v. Sweden*, 16 November 2006, no. 265/2005 (Azerbaijan)

ComAT, *A.A. v. Switzerland*, 17 November 2006, no. 251/2004 (Iran)

ComAT, *M.N. v. Switzerland*, 17 November 2006, no. 259/2004 (Bangladesh)

ComAT, *C.T. and K.M. v. Sweden*, 17 November 2006, no. 279/2005* (Rwanda)

ComAT, *M.R.A. v. Sweden*, 17 November 2006, no. 286/2006 (Iraq)

ComAT, *V.L. v. Switzerland*, 20 November 2006, no. 262/2005* (Belarus)

ComAT, *N.Z.S. v. Sweden*, 22 November 2006, no. 277/2005 (Iran)

2007

ComAT, *E.R.K. and Y.K. v. Sweden*, 30 April 2007, no. 270 & 271/2005 (Azerbaijan)

ComAT, *A.A. v. Switzerland*, 1 May 2007, no. 268/2005 (Pakistan)

ComAT, *Pelit v. Azerbaijan*, 1 May 2007, no. 281/2005* (Turkey)

ComAT, *E.V.I. v. Sweden*, 1 May 2007, no. 296/2006 (Azerbaijan)

ComAT, *Tebourski v. France*, 1 May 2007, no. 300/2006* (Tunisia)

ComAT, *Ahmad Dar v. Norway*, 11 May 2007, no. 249/2004 (Pakistan)

ComAT, *C.A.R.M. et al. v. Canada*, 18 May 2007, no. 298/2006 (Mexico)

ComAT, *Sogi v. Canada*, 16 November 2007, no. 297/2006* (India)

ComAT, *Iya v. Switzerland*, 16 November 2007, no. 299/2006* (RDC)

2008

ComAT, *Z.K. v. Sweden*, 9 May 2008, no. 301/2006 (Azerbaijan)

ComAT, *J.A.M.O. v. Canada*, 9 May 2008, no. 293/2006 (Mexico)

ComAT, *R.K. et al. v. Sweden*, 16 May 2008, no. 309/2006 (Azerbaijan)

ComAT, *A.A. et al. v. Switzerland*, 10 November 2008, no. 285/2006 (Algeria)

ComAT, *L.J.R. v. Australia*, 10 November 2008, no. 316/2007 (USA)

ComAT, *M.M. et al. v. Sweden*, 11 November 2008, no. 332/2007 (Azerbaijan)

ComAT, *E.J. et al. v. Sweden*, 14 November 2008, no. 306/2006 (Azerbaijan)

ComAT, *M.F. v. Sweden*, 14 November 2008, no. 326/2007 (Bangladesh)

2009

ComAT, *X. v. Australia*, 30 April 2009, no. 324/2007 (Lebanon)

ComAT, *Minani v. Canada*, 5 November 2009, no. 331/2007 (Burundi)

ComAT, *F.A.B. v. Switzerland*, 17 November 2009, no. 348/2008 (Cote d'Ivoire)

2010

ComAT, *A.M. v. France*, 5 May 2010, no. 302/2006 (RDC)

ComAT, *N.S. v. Switzerland*, 6 May 2010, no. 356/2008 (Turkey)

ComAT, *Njamba and Balikosa v. Sweden*, 14 May 2010, no. 322/2007* (RDC)

ComAT, *C.M. v. Switzerland*, 14 May 2010, no. 355/2008 (Republic Congo)

ComAT, *Güclü v. Sweden*, 11 November 2010, no. 349/2008* (Turkey)

ComAT, *A.M.A. v. Switzerland*, 12 November 2010, no. 344/2008 (Togo)

ComAT, *T.I. v. Canada*, 15 November 2010, no. 333/2007 (Uzbekistan)

ComAT, *Amini v. Denmark*, 15 November 2010, no. 339/2008* (Iran)

ComAT, *Aytulun and Guclu v. Sweden*, 19 November 2010, no. 373/2009* (Turkey)

2011

ComAT, *Jahani v. Switzerland*, 23 May 2011, no. 357/2008* (Iran)

ComAT, *Mondal v. Sweden*, 23 May 2011, no. 338/2008* (Bangladesh)

ComAT, *Khalsa et al. v. Switzerland*, 26 May 2011, no. 336/2008* (India)

ComAT, *E.C.B. v. Switzerland*, 26 May 2011, no. 369/2008 (Republic Congo/Cote d'Ivoire)

ComAT, *T.D. v. Switzerland*, 26 May 2011, no. 375/2009 (Ethiopia)

ComAT, *Ktiti v. Morocco*, 26 May 2011, no. 419/2010* (Algeria)

ComAT, *Chahin v. Sweden*, 30 May 2011, no. 310/2007* (Syria)

ComAT, *Singh v. Canada*, 30 May 2011, no. 319/2007* (India)

ComAT, *M.S.G. v. Switzerland*, 30 May 2011, no. 352/2008 (Turkey)

ComAT, *R.T-N. v. Switzerland*, 3 June 2011, no. 350/2008 (RDC)

ComAT, *Bakatu-Bia v. Sweden*, 3 June 2011, no. 379/2009* (RDC)

ComAT, *Boily v. Canada*, 14 November 2011, no. 327/2007* (Mexico)

ComAT, *N.B.-M. v. Switzerland*, 14 November 2011, no. 347/2008 (DRC)

ComAT, *E.L. v. Switzerland*, 15 November 2011, no. 351/2008 (DRC)

ComAT, *S.M., H.M. and A.M. v. Sweden*, 21 November 2011, no. 374/2009* (Azerbaijan)

ComAT, *Faragollah et al. v. Switzerland*, 21 November 2011, no. 381/2009* (Iran)

ComAT, *Eftekhary v. Norway*, 25 November 2011, no. 312/2007* (Iran)

ComAT, *Kalinichenko v. Morocco*, 25 November 2011, no. 428/2010* (Russia)

2012

ComAT, *M.D.T. v. Switzerland*, 14 May 2012, nc. 382/2009 (DRC)

ComAT, *N.T.W. v. Switzerland,* 16 May 2012, no. 414/2010 (Ethiopia)

ComAT, *Kalonzo v. Canada*, 18 May 2012, no. 343/2008* (DRC)

ComAT, *E.L. v. Canada*, 21 May 2012, no. 370/2009 (Haiti)

ComAT, *M.Z.A. v. Sweden*, 22 May 2012, no. 424/2010 (Azerbaijan)

ComAT, *M.A.M.A. et al. v. Sweden*, 23 May 2012, no. 391/2009* (Egypt)

ComAT, *E.T. v. Switzerland*, 23 May 2012, no. 393/2009 (Ethiopia)

ComAT, *A.A.M. v. Sweden*, 23 May 2012, no. 413/2010 (Burundi)

ComAT, *J.L.L. v. Switzerland*, 18 May 2012, no. 364/2008 (DRC)

ComAT, *Gbadjavi v. Switzerland*, 1 June 2012, no. 396/2009* (Togo)

ComAT, *Abdussamatov and 28 Others v. Kazakhstan*, 1 June 2012, no. 444/2010* (Uzbekistan)

ComAT, *Ke Chun Rong v. Australia*, 5 November 2012, no. 416/2010* (China)

ComAT, *A.A. v. Denmark*, 13 November 2012, no. 412/2010 (Iraq)

ComAT, *G.B.M. v. Sweden*, 14 November 2012, no. 435/2010 (Tanzania)

ComAT, *R.A. v. Switzerland*, 20 November 2012, no. 389/2009 (Turkey)

ComAT, *M.A.F. et al v. Sweden*, 23 November 2012, no. 385/2009 (Libya)

ComAT, *S.M. v. Switzerland*, 23 November 2012, no. 406/2009 (Ethiopia)

ComAT, *Y.Z.S. v. Australia*, 23 November 2012, no. 417/2010 (China)

ComAT, *H.K. v. Switzerland*, 23 November 2012, no. 432/2010 (Ethiopia)

ComAT, *K.H. v. Denmark*, 23 November 2012, no. 464/2011* (Afghanistan)

2013

ComAT, *Abichou v. Germany*, 21 May 2013, no. 430/2010* (Tunisia)

ComAT, *Y. v. Switzerland*, 21 May 2013, no. 431/2010 (Turkey)

ComAT, *D.Y. v. Sweden*, 21 May 2013, no. 463/2011 (Uzbekistan)

ComAT, *R.S.M. v. Canada*, 24 May 2013, no. 392/2009 (Togo)

ComAT, *M.B. v. Switzerland*, 31 May 2013, no. 439/2010 (Iran)

ComAT, *Y.B.F., S.A.Q. and Y.Y. v. Switzerland*, 31 May 2013, no. 467/2011 (Yemen)

ComAT, *M.A.H. and F.H. v. Switzerland*, 17 November 2013, no. 438/2010 (Tunisia)

ComAT, *R.D. v. Switzerland*, 8 November 2013, no. 426/2010 (Ethiopia)

ComAT, *Sivagnanaratnam v. Denmark*, 11 November 2013, no. 429/2010 (Sri Lanka)

ComAT, *Dewage v. Australia*, 14 November 2013, no. 387/2009* (Sri Lanka)

ComAT, *Y.G.H. et al v. Australia*, 14 November 2013, no. 434/2010 (China)

2014

ComAT, *X.Q.L. v. Australia*, 2 May 2014, no. 455/2011 (China)

ComAT, *Mr. X and Mr. Z v. Finland*, 12 May 2014, no. 483/2011 and 485/2011* (Iran)

ComAT, *Alp v. Denmark*, 14 May 2014, no. 466/2011 (Turkey)

ComAT, *Nasirov v. Kazakhstan*, 14 May 2014, no. 475/2011* (Uzbekistan)

ComAT, *R.A.Y. v. Morocco*, 16 May 2014, no. 525/2012 (Algeria)

ComAT, *K.N., F.W. and S.N. v. Switzerland*, 19 May 2014, no. 481/2011* (Iran)

ComAT, *Fadel v. Switzerland*, 14 November 2014, no. 450/2011* (Yemen)

ComAT, *Mopongo and Others v. Morocco*, 7 November 2014, no. 321/2007* (Algeria)

ComAT, *Khademi et al. v. Switzerland*, 14 November 2014, no. 473/2011* (Iran)

ComAT, *T.M. v. Republic of Korea*, 21 November 2014, no. 519/2012 (Myanmar)

ComAT, *R.S. et al. v. Switzerland*, 21 November 2014, no. 482/2011 (Kosovo[3])

ComAT, *X. v. Switzerland*, 24 November 2014, no. 470/2011* (Iran)

ComAT, *W.G.D. v. Canada*, 26 November 2014, no. 520/2012 (Ethiopia)

ComAT, *Tahmuresi v. Switzerland*, 26 November 2014, no. 489/2012* (Iran)

ComAT, *Azizi v. Switzerland*, 27 November 2014, no. 492/2012* (Iran)

ComAT, *X. v. Denmark*, 28 November 2014, no. 458/2011 (Ethiopia)

---

3 All reference to Kosovo in this book should be understood in full compliance with Security Council resolution 1244(1999), without prejudice to the status of Kosovo.

2015

ComAT, *E.C. v. Switzerland*, 21 April 2015, no. 476/2011 (Gambia)

ComAT, *G.A.B. v. Switzerland*, 4 May 2015, no. 440/2010 (Guinea)

ComAT, *E.K.W. v. Finland*, 4 May 2015, no. 490/2012* (RDC)

ComAT, Z. v. Switzerland, 5 May 2015, no. 468/2011 (Algeria)

ComAT, *E.E.E. v. Switzerland*, 8 May 2015, no. 491/2012 (Ethiopia)

ComAT, *Tursunov v. Kazakhstan*, 8 May 2015, no. 538/2013* (Uzbekistan)

ComAT, *C.S. v. Switzerland*, 8 May 2015, no. 540/2013 (Turkey)

ComAT, *X. v. Russia*, 8 May 2015, no. 542/2013* (Uzbekistan)

ComAT, *A.K. v. Switzerland*, 8 May 2015, no. 544/2013* (Turkey)

ComAT, *S.K. and Others v. Sweden*, 8 May 2015, no. 550/2013 (Russia)

·   ComAT, *Z. v. Sweden*, 8 May 2015, no. 556/2013 (Russia)

ComAT, *A.B. v. Sweden*, 11 May 2015, no. 539/2013 (Russia)

ComAT, *M.A. and M.N. v. Sweden*, 30 July 2015, no. 566/2013 (Russia)

ComAT, *X. v. Kazakhstan*, 3 August 2015, no. 554/2013* (Russia)

ComAT, *X, Y and their daughter Z v. Sweden*, 4 August 2015, no. 530/2012 (Belarus)

ComAT, *Z. v. Denmark*, 10 August 2015, no. 555/2013 (China)

ComAT, *M.S. v. Denmark*, 10 August 2015, no. 571/2013 (Afghanistan)

ComAT, *P.S.B. and T.K. v. Canada*, 13 August 2015, no. 505/2012 (India)

With regard to the Committee's *56th session* (9 November to 9 December 2015) the following non-refoulement decisions on the merits were accessible when this book was completed by the end of February 2016:

ComAT, *F.B. v. Netherlands*, 20 November 2015, no. 613/2014* (Guinea)

ComAT, *J.K. v. Canada*, 23 November 2015, no. 562/2013* (Uganda)

ComAT, *F.K. v. Denmark*, 23 November 2015, no. 580/2014* (Turkey)

ComAT, *S.A.P. v. Switzerland*, 25 November 2015, no. 565/2013 (Russia)

ComAT, *R.G. et al. v. Sweden*, 25 November 2015, no. 586/2014* (Russia)

ComAT, *K. v. Australia*, 25 November 2015, no. 591/2014 (Sri Lanka)

ComAT, *B.M.S. v. Sweden*, 25 November 2015, no. 594/2014 (Algeria)

General Comment No. 01: Implementation of Article 3 of the Convention in the Context of Article 22 CAT (21 November 1997)[4]

In view of the requirements of article 22, paragraph 4, of the Convention against Torture and Other Cruel, Inhuman or Degrading Treatment or Punishment

---

4   The Committee adopted this General Comment at its 19th session in November 1997. It is
    contained in the Committee's 'Annual Report 1998' (UN Doc. A/53/44, annex IX). At its 55th

that the Committee against Torture 'shall consider communications received under article 22 in the light of all information made available to it by or on behalf of the individual and by the State party concerned,'

In view of the need arising as a consequence of the application of rule 111, paragraph 3, of the rules of procedure of the Committee (CAT/C/3/Rev.2), and

In view of the need for guidelines for the implementation of article 3 under the procedure foreseen in article 22 of the Convention,

The Committee against Torture, at its nineteenth session, 317th meeting, held on 21 November 1997, adopted the following general comment for the guidance of States parties and authors of communications:

1. Article 3 is confined in its application to cases where there are substantial grounds for believing that the author would be in danger of being subjected to torture as defined in article 1 of the Convention.

2. The Committee is of the view that the phrase 'another State' in article 3 refers to the State to which the individual concerned is being expelled, returned or extradited, as well as to any State to which the author may subsequently be expelled, returned or extradited.

3. Pursuant to article 1, the criterion, mentioned in article 3, paragraph 2, of 'a consistent pattern or gross, flagrant or mass violations of human rights' refers only to violations by or at the instigation of or with the consent or acquiescence of a public official or other person acting in an official capacity.

Admissibility

4. The Committee is of the opinion that it is the responsibility of the author to establish a prima facie case for the purpose of admissibility of his or her communication under article 22 of the Convention by fulfilling each of the requirements of rule 107 of the rules of procedure of the Committee.

Merits

5. With respect to the application of article 3 of the Convention to the merits of a case, the burden is upon the author to present an arguable case. This means that there must be a factual basis for the author's position sufficient to require a response from the State party.

---

session in summer 2015, the Committee decided to revise its General Comment No. 1 on Art. 3 CAT; Statement of the Chairperson of the Committee Against Torture to the 70th session of the General Assembly, New York, 20 October 2015, accessible on the Committee's website [15.2.2016].

6. Bearing in mind that the State party and the Committee are obliged to assess whether there are substantial grounds for believing that the author would be in danger of being subjected to torture were he/she to be expelled, returned or extradited, the risk of torture must be assessed on grounds that go beyond mere theory or suspicion. However, the risk does not have to meet the test of being highly probable.

7. The author must establish that he/she would be in danger of being tortured and that the grounds for so believing are substantial in the way described, and that such danger is personal and present. All pertinent information may be introduced by either party to bear on this matter.

8. The following information, while not exhaustive, would be pertinent:

(a) Is the State concerned one in which there is evidence of a consistent pattern of gross, flagrant or mass violations of human rights (see art. 3, para. 2)?

(b) Has the author been tortured or maltreated by or at the instigation of or with the consent or acquiescence of a public official or other person acting in an official capacity in the past? If so, was this the recent past?

(c) Is there medical or other independent evidence to support a claim by the author that he/she has been tortured or maltreated in the past? Has the torture had after-effects?

(d) Has the situation referred to in (a) above changed? Has the internal situation in respect of human rights altered?

(e) Has the author engaged in political or other activity within or outside the State concerned which would appear to make him/her particularly vulnerable to the risk of being placed in danger of torture were he/she to be expelled, returned or extradited to the State in question?

(f) Is there any evidence as to the credibility of the author?

(g) Are there factual inconsistencies in the claim of the author? If so, are they relevant?

9. Bearing in mind that the Committee against Torture is not an appellate, a quasi-judicial or an administrative body, but rather a monitoring body created by the States parties themselves with declaratory powers only, it follows that:

(a) Considerable weight will be given, in exercising the Committee's jurisdiction pursuant to article 3 of the Convention, to findings of fact that are made by organs of the State party concerned; but

(b) The Committee is not bound by such findings and instead has the power, provided by article 22, paragraph 4, of the Convention, of free assessment of the facts based upon the full set of circumstances in every case.

Introduction

1.1   *Introduction*

It is a well-established principle of international law that states have the right to decide whether to allow a foreign national to enter or remain in their territory. This principle finds its origins in the concept of state sovereignty. The freedom for states to decide who is allowed to stay on their territory, however, is restricted by human rights, among them the *principle of non-refoulement*. Generally speaking, this principle obliges states not to return a person to another state where there is a risk he may face persecution, or be subject to torture or other inhuman treatment.[1]

The principle of non-refoulement is the cornerstone of international refugee protection. It was first enshrined internationally in the 1951 Convention Relating to the Status of Refugees (the 'Refugee Convention').[2] Article 33 of the Refugee Convention states that no 'Contracting State shall expel or return (*"refouler"*) a refugee in any manner whatsoever to the frontiers of territories where his life or freedom would be threatened on account of his race, religion, nationality, membership of a particular social group or political opinion.'

Alongside the 1951 Refugee Convention, the principle of non-refoulement has also been established in more general international human rights treaties at the universal and regional levels, notably relating to the prohibition of torture or cruel, inhuman or degrading treatment or punishment.

At the United Nations level, the principle of non-refoulement is contained in the prohibition on torture and cruel, inhuman or degrading treatment or punishment in Article 7 of the International Covenant on Civil and Political Rights.[3] A protection against refoulement based on the prohibition of torture is further explicitly guaranteed by Article 3 of the United Nations Convention

---

1 When referring to a person or an individual in general, I use the male form.

2 The Convention relating to the Status of Refugees was adopted on 25 July 1951 in Geneva and entered into force on 22 April 1954. It should be read together with the additional Protocol relating to the Status of Refugees that was adopted on 31 January 1967 in New York. The additional Protocol entered into force on 4 October 1967 and removed the geographic and temporal limits of the 1951 Refugee Convention.

3 For more information on the International Covenant on Civil and Political Rights (ICCPR) see Chapter 1 Section 5.

against Torture and Other Cruel, Inhuman or Degrading Treatment or Punishment, which will be discussed in detail.[4]

At the regional level, the principle of non-refoulement is guaranteed within the prohibition of torture and inhuman or degrading treatment or punishment in Article 3 of the European Convention for the Protection of Human Rights and Fundamental Freedoms. This provision will be discussed in detail in this study. In Europe, a prohibition on refoulement is further explicitly enshrined in Article 19(2) of the Charter of Fundamental Rights of the European Union.[5] Other regional human rights treaties outside Europe that prohibit refoulement are the American Convention on Human Rights,[6] the Inter-American Convention to Prevent and Punish Torture,[7] the African Charter of Human Rights and People's Rights[8] and the Convention Governing the Specific Aspects of Refugee Problems in Africa.[9]

The great majority of the world's states have implemented the principle of non-refoulement in their national legislation and are bound by one or more regional or universal conventions.[10] The principle of non-refoulement is regarded as a norm of customary international law.[11] In accordance with that, states are bound by the principle whether or not they have ratified the conventions mentioned above. It is argued that the principle of non-refoulement has achieved the status of a *jus cogens* norm.[12] According to Article 53 of the 1969 Vienna Convention on the Law of Treaties, a norm achieves this status if it is 'accepted and recognized by the international community of States as a whole as a norm from which no derogation is permitted and which can be modified only by a

---

4   At the universal level, the principle of non-refoulement is further guaranteed in the context of armed conflicts through international humanitarian law; see on this Droege 2008.

5   See on this Chapter 1 Section 6.

6   See Art. 22(8) American Convention on Human Rights (ACHR), which was inspired by the Refugee Convention. The prohibition of torture and other inhuman treatment in Art. 5 ACHR also contains an obligation of non-refoulement. The ACHR entered into force on 18 July 1978.

7   See Art. 13(4) of this Convention, which entered into force on 28 February 1987.

8   See Art. 5 and 12(3) of this Convention, which entered into force on 21 October 1986.

9   See Art. 2(3) of this Convention, which entered into force on 20 June 1974.

10   See Lauterpacht & Bethlehem 2003, pp. 93 and 147 and annexes.

11   Goodwin-Gill & McAdam 2007, pp. 345–354; Lauterpacht & Bethlehem 2003, pp. 146–164.

12   Allain 2001, pp. 538–558; Nowak & McArthur 2008, p. 147 (§ 70); Rosati 1998, p. 550; also Judge Pinto de Albuquerque in his Concurring Opinion to ECtHR, *Hirsi Jamaa and Others v. Italy*, 23 February 2012 [GC], no. 27765/09.

subsequent norm of general international law having the same character.' It is recognized that the prohibition of torture has achieved *jus cogens* character.[13] The point has correctly been made that it is inconsistent to recognize the status of *jus cogens* for the prohibition on torture but not for the principle of non-refoulement, which is an integral part of that prohibition.[14] However, the *jus cogens* character of the protection from refoulement based on an alleged harm that is less severe than torture, such as certain forms of persecution or inhuman or degrading treatment, is more contentious.[15] In general, as will also be apparent from this study, there is no unique worldwide interpretation of the character and limits of the principle of non-refoulement. This makes the question of its *jus cogens* character particularly challenging.

1.2 Objective, Sources and Scope of This Study

This study elaborates and compares the scope and content of the principle of non-refoulement under Article 3 of the European Convention for the Protection of Human Rights and Fundamental Freedoms (the European Convention on Human Rights or the ECHR) and Article 3 of the United Nations Convention against Torture and Other Cruel, Inhuman or Degrading Treatment or Punishment (the Convention against Torture or the CAT), as it is guaranteed in individual complaint proceedings before the European Court of Human Rights and the United Nations Committee against Torture.

The European Court of Human Rights in Strasbourg and the United Nations Committee against Torture in Geneva both produced an important body of case law on the principle of non-refoulement in the last 25 years. The Court adopted its first judgment on that principle in 1989 in the famous case *Soering v. United Kingdom*.[16] The Committee against Torture adopted its first decision on non-refoulement in 1994 in the case *Mutombo v. Switzerland*.[17] Up to February 2016, the Court in Strasbourg had adopted 215 judgments on the

---

13 As a source of authority see, in particular, ICTY, *Prosecutor v. Furundzija*, 10 December 1989, no. IT-95-17/1-T, §§ 153–157; ICTY, *Prosecutor v. Delacic and Others*, 16 November 1998, no. IT-96-21-T, § 454; ICTY, *Prosecutor v. Kunarac*, 22 February 2001, no. IT 96-23-T and IT-96-23/1-T, § 466. Also ECtHR *Al-Adsani v. UK* 21 November 2001[GC], no. 35763/97, § 61.

14 See in this sense ICTY, *Prosecutor v. Furundzija*, 10 December 1989, no. IT-95-17/1-T, § 144. Further Alleweldt 1996, p. 102; Delas 2011, p. 98; Wouters 2009, p. 30. Goodwin-Gill 2011, p. 444, notes that non-refoulement 'is an inherent aspect of the absolute prohibition of torture, even sharing perhaps in some of the latter's *jus cogens* character.'

15 Alleweldt 1996, p. 101; Goodwin-Gill & McAdam 2007, p. 348; Wouters 2009, p. 30.

16 ECtHR, *Soering v. UK*, 7 July 1989, no. 14038/88.

17 ComAT, *Mutombo v. Switzerland*, 27 April 1994, no. 13/1993.

merits with regard to the principle of non-refoulement under Article 3 ECHR.[18] The Committee in Geneva has published 234 decisions on the merits with regard to Article 3 CAT.[19] As a result, they are the two international human rights adjudicators with the greatest experience in the assessment of individual complaints concerning the principle of non-refoulement.[20] The analysis and comparison of their case law and practice provides a particularly substantial insight into the principle of non-refoulement as interpreted under international human rights treaties and provides practical knowledge of and guidance on how and under what circumstances individuals might be protected against refoulement at the international level. This study has two main objectives:

1.   To give a comprehensive overview on the European Court of Human Rights' and the United Nations Committee against Torture's case law and practice with regard to the assessment of individual complaints in which a violation of the principle of non-refoulement is invoked.
2.   To delineate the main similarities and differences between the practice and case law of these two international institutions with regard to the principle of non-refoulement.

This book is based on the analysis of the judgments and decisions on the merits adopted by the Court and the Committee with regard to complaints in which a violation of the principle of non-refoulement under Article 3 ECHR or Article 3 CAT has been alleged.[21] With regard to admissibility decisions, the study is limited to the analysis of those decisions adopted by the Court in Strasbourg and

---

18   See XXXII.

19   See XXXIX.

20   Another international monitoring body that has dealt with non-refoulement in the context of an individual complaint mechanism is the UN Human Rights Committee. On its practice see Section 5 of this chapter. At the international level, the American Convention on Human Rights and the African Charter of Human Rights do also provide for individual complaint mechanisms. On the rather scant case law developed under these two regional human rights conventions see Kälin 2013, pp. 54–57; Rieter 2010, pp. 144–170, 273–279, 817 and 833.

21   The judgments of the Court and decisions of the Committee are available on their websites. See the Court's database HUDOC at <http://hudoc.echr.coe.int/>. All documents issued by the UN Committee against Torture including its decisions on individual complaints can be found at the UN database under <http://juris.ohchr.org> and the Committee's website <http://www.ohchr.org/en/hrbodies/cat/pages/catindex.aspx>.

the Committee in Geneva that are published *and* are of particular relevance for the understanding of the protection against refoulement.[22] I have taken into account the case law that was published up to 29 February 2016.[23]

This monograph provides a comprehensive analysis and comparison of the Court's and the Committee's case law and practice in individual complaint proceedings concerning the principle of non-refoulement. Complete records of either the Strasbourg or the Geneva case law and practice in the assessment of individual complaints under the principle of non-refoulement are rare,[24] and comparative studies even rarer.[25] With the fast-growing body of international case law, these records become both increasingly challenging to assemble in full, and increasingly important. Against this background, I have chosen to focus on a systematisation and comparison of the case law. I believe this should

---

22   In contrast to the Court, the Committee against Torture usually publishes all its decisions on admissibility; see on this Chapter 2 Section 1.1.1.

23   This book is based on the updated version of my doctoral thesis successfully completed at the University of Lucerne in 2014.

24   Oliver Thurin has published an in-depth analysis of the case law on the principle of non-refoulement under Art. 3 ECHR: 'Der Schutz des Fremden vor rechtswidriger Abschiebung, Das Prinzip des Non-refoulement nach Artikel 3 EMRK,' second edition, Vienna 2012. For another discussion of the issue see Nuala Mole's and Catherine Meredith's, 'Asylum and the European Convention on Human Rights,' Strasbourg 2010. With regard to the case law under Article 3 CAT, a helpful basis for my research was Manfred Nowak's and Elizabeth McArthur's comprehensive work, 'The United Nations Convention Against Torture, A Commentary,' Oxford 2008.

25   A comprehensive publication on the principle of non-refoulement under the 1951 Refugee Convention, the ECHR, the ICCPR and the CAT is Kees Wouters' *International Legal Standards for the Protection from Refoulement*, published in 2009. This excellent book will often be referred to. See also Jane McAdam's *Complementary Protection in International Refugee Law*, Oxford 2007.

     In addition, the articles cited in the bibliography of the following authors have focused on the principle of non-refoulement under the ECHR and the CAT: Walter Suntinger (1995), David Weissbrodt and Isabel Hörtreiter (1999), Vincent Chetail (2006) and the article of my former supervisors at the Swiss Federal Office for Justice Frank Schürmann and Adrian Scheidegger (2009). These articles have been important pillars for my research. However, while they focus on the Committee against Torture's practice under Art. 3 CAT rather than on the Court's case law under Art. 3 ECHR, this study does not concentrate on either norm or institution. With regard to the Committee's practice, I would also like to mention my own article published in 2011, 'Die Praxis des Ausschusses der Vereinten Nationen gegen die Folter in Individualmitteilungsverfahren zum Non-refoulement-Prinzip,' *Schweizerische Zeitschrift für Asylrecht und – Praxis* 2/2011, pp. 4–11.

provide a precious resource for both practitioners and scholars, and hope it will provide a better understanding of the scope and content of the principle of non-refoulement under international human rights law and an insight into the protection against refoulement at the international level in practice. However, this study is more than a *résumé* – it provides a critical analysis of the practice and case law and as such aims to offer a useful reference for further discussion, development and improvement with regard to the protection from refoulement through individual procedures before the Court in Strasbourg and the Committee in Geneva.

It should be noted that the United Nations Committee against Torture has also provided guidelines on how the principle of non-refoulement in Article 3 CAT should be interpreted in the context of its state reporting procedure under Article 19 CAT.[26] I will make references to the Committee's observations with respect to this state reporting system. However, this study focuses on the Committee's findings taken in individual complaint proceedings under Article 22 CAT. In concentrating on complaint proceedings, this study is of particular relevance to practitioners acting on every aspect of proceedings before the European Court of Human Rights in Strasbourg or the Committee against Torture in Geneva: be they potential complainants and human rights lawyers, state parties to the ECHR and the CAT, or even the Court and the Committee themselves. Consistent with this practical approach, this study will not only analyse the Court's and the Committee's case law on the merits with regard to the principle of non-refoulement; it will also discuss main procedural issues with regard to the complaint proceedings.[27]

Before the United Nations Committee against Torture, the great majority of individual complaints under the prohibition on non-refoulement have been submitted against European states. Since this study compares a universal complaint mechanism with a European protection mechanism, it is of

---

26   On the UN Committee against Torture's supervisory powers see Chapter 1 Section 3.1.2.

27   For the procedural aspects of this study, I was able to draw on several years of practical experience with international individual complaints proceedings: first, in 2007, as an intern at the Court in Strasbourg; from 2008 to 2013 at the International Human Rights Unit of the Swiss Federal Office for Justice that dealt with individual complaints submitted against Switzerland before the European Court of Human Rights and the Committee against Torture; today as a jurist in a law firm specialised on migration law. I was further privileged to be able to speak about procedural issues with Sophie Piquet, from the European Court of Human Rights Registry, as well with Marie-Eve Friedrich and Antoanela Pavlova from the United Nation's Committee against Torture petitions section within the Office of the High Commissioner for Human Rights (OHCHR) in Geneva.

particular interest from a European perspective. Section 6 of this chapter will also give an introduction on the prohibition on refoulement under European Union law and references will be made throughout the study. However, in light of the fact that the provisions of the CAT including the principle of non-refoulement are binding for 158 states today and that the prohibition on refoulement is regarded as a norm of customary law, the relevance of this study goes beyond the European context.

In addition to the European Court of Human Rights in Strasbourg and the Committee against Torture in Geneva, there is a third international human rights law regime offering protection against refoulement through an individual complaint mechanism applicable in many European states, but which I have only briefly considered in my research: the complaint mechanism before the United Nations Human Rights Committee, based on the International Covenant on Civil and Political Rights (ICCPR) and its First Optional Protocol. However, section 5 of this chapter will give an overview on the principle of non-refoulement as guaranteed under the ICCPR, and there are references to the Human Rights Committee's practice throughout this study. The UN Human Rights Committee's practice on individual complaints concerning the principle of non-refoulement is not as rich as the Court's or the Committee's, although it has also grown remarkably in the last five years.[28] Individuals threatened with refoulement have preferred to address complaints to the Committee against Torture than to the Human Rights Committee if a choice was available.[29] As a consequence, the Committee against Torture has become the most experienced monitoring body with regard to the assessment of individual complaints concerning the principle of non-refoulement within the United Nations human rights treaty bodies.

Section 4 of this chapter will give an overview on the principle of non-refoulement as guaranteed under Article 33 of the 1951 Refugee Convention. Further references to the Refugee Convention will be made throughout this study. While the principle of non-refoulement contained in the 1951 Refugee Convention is aimed at protecting refugees, the prohibition on refoulement in the European Convention on Human Rights and the Convention against Torture is aimed at preventing any individual from being subjected to torture or inhuman and degrading treatment or punishment. Protection against refoulement that is not based on the Refugee Convention but on other international human rights treaties of a more general nature, such as the ECHR and the CAT,

---

28   See Chapter 1 Section 5.

29   Nowak & McArthur 2008, p. 730 (§ 24).

is often referred to as 'complementary protection.'[30] This study will provide detailed analysis of how and when this form of protection should be attributed according to the practices of the Court in Strasbourg and the Committee in Geneva.

As will be apparent from this book, in substance there is considerable over-lap between the protection offered under the prohibition on refoulement in Article 33 of the Refugee Convention and that offered under Article 3 ECHR and Article 3 CAT. Claims reaching Strasbourg or Geneva have usually been made within the terms of the Refugee Convention at the national level. How-ever, since the 1951 Refugee Convention does not offer an individual complaint mechanism at international level, applicants taking the international path have to rely on general human rights law in order to be protected against re-foulement. Mole and Meredith note that the role previously played by the 1951 Refugee Convention is now in many respects performed in the European con-text by general human rights instruments and, in particular, by the ECHR.[31] Indeed, the Court and the Committee have both developed important prin-ciples and minimal standards for states with regard to the determination of the refugee status in general.[32] Their case law therefore includes important aspects of refugee law. However, despite the evident overlap between the prin-ciple of non-refoulement under refugee law and general human rights law, it should not be forgotten that it is not within the Court and the Committee's competence nor within their field of expertise to verify how states honour their obligations under the 1951 Refugee Convention. The Refugee Convention contains particularities and obligations for state parties under the principle of non-refoulement and beyond that are not covered by the rights and freedoms guaranteed through the ECHR or the CAT.[33]

1.3   *Terminology*

The *principle of non-refoulement* obliges states not to return a person to anoth-er state where there is a risk that he may face persecution, or may be subject to torture or other inhuman treatment. The term *refoulement* is adopted from the French, and literally means repression, rejection, expulsion or deportation. It is used in legal literature on international refugee protection and human rights in a more general manner to include all measures by which a person is

---

30   For a detailed description of the term and concept of 'complementary protection' see McAdam 2007, pp. 1–4 and 20–28.

31   Mole & Meredith 2010, pp. 10–11.

32   Gorlick, 1999, p. 483; McAdam 2007, p. 125.

33   See on this Chapter 1 Section 4.

physically transferred from one state to another where he fears persecution, torture or other ill treatment. More specifically for the purposes of this study, the term is applied as shorthand for the expulsion, extradition or any kind of formal or informal handover of a person from one state to another in violation of the principle of non-refoulement under Article 3 ECHR and/or Article 3 CAT.

The terms *refoulement case* or *non-refoulement case* are used in this study for any cases submitted or assessed by the European Court of Human Rights in Strasbourg or the Committee against Torture in Geneva in which a violation of the principle of non-refoulement under Article 3 ECHR or Article 3 CAT has been invoked. The term *domestic case* is used in contrast for cases assessed in Strasbourg or Geneva that do not concern an alleged violation of the principle of non-refoulement. The term *ill treatment* is used to indicate torture or inhuman or degrading treatment or punishment.

The term *expulsion* is used independent of definitions provided by domestic legislation to mean any measure compelling the departure of an alien from a state's jurisdiction to another, with the exception of extraditions.[34] The term *extradition* refers to 'the obligatory departure of a person from one State to another, at the request of the latter State, for the purpose of bringing him or her to justice or of implementing a judgment, if the person has already been sentenced and convicted.'[35] The terms *removal* or *deportation* as used in this study refer to any kind of transfer of a person from one state to another, be it through extradition, expulsion, or any other formal or informal transfer.[36]

The term *respondent state* or *contracting state* refers to the state against which a complaint is submitted either before the Court in Strasbourg or the Committee in Geneva. The state to which an applicant might be deported is designated as the *receiving state* or the *state of destination*.[37]

The term *asylum* is occasionally referred to in the Court's and the Committee's judgments and decisions. Goodwin-Gill and McAdam rightly note that the meaning of this word tends 'to be assumed by those who use it, but its

---

34   See the definition used in ECtHR, *Nolan and K. v. Russia*, 12 February 2009, no. 2512/04, § 112 under Article 1 of Protocol No. 7 to ECHR. This term is used in this manner by the Court and the Committee in their case law on non-refoulement.

35   Nowak & McArthur 2008, p. 376 (§ 25).

36   These terms are used in this manner by the Court and the Committee in their decisions and judgments on non-refoulement in various contexts, whether for expulsions or extraditions.

37   Where this is useful, the name of the receiving state will be added in brackets to the judgment or decision cited in the footnote: see, for example, ECtHR, *Sufi and Elmi v. UK*, 28 June 2011, nos. 8319/07 and 11449/07 (Somalia).

content is rarely explained.'[38] This might be related to the fact that this term has 'no common meaning in international law.'[39] Very generally, it refers to the status provided by national law to formally recognized refugees in the sense of the 1951 Refugee Convention.[40] This appears to be the Court's and the Committee's understanding of that term, too.[41]

The European Court of Human Rights will be referred to as *the Court* throughout this study and the United Nations Committee against Torture as *the Committee*. The findings of the Court in Strasbourg are called *judgments*. Its findings on admissibility are called *decisions*.[42]

The Committee is not an international Court but 'a monitoring body with declaratory powers only.'[43] Its findings on individual cases are not legally binding. This is reflected in the terms used in the CAT. Article 22 CAT designates the Committee's findings on individual cases as *views* and the complaints submitted as *communications*. Individuals submitting their claims to the Committee against Torture have been designated as *authors*.[44] However, over the course of the years, the Committee has changed its terminology: in 2002, it made clear that its findings are to be known as *decisions* rather than as *views*.[45] Already prior to this, the Committee began to use the terms *complaint* instead of *communication*[46] and *complainant* instead of *author*.[47] Being the current terminology used by the Committee, the terms *decision, complaint* and *complainant* are used in this study.[48] Generally, whether with regard to Strasbourg or in Geneva,

---

38   Goodwin-Gill & McAdam, 2007, p. 355. See their analysis of the concept of asylum in pp. 355–417.

39   Wouters 2009, p. 23.

40   Kälin 2013, p. 598 (§ 1409).

41   See, for example, ECtHR, *Müslim v. Turkey*, 26 April 2005, no. 53566/99, § 72; ComAT, *Aemei v. Switzerland*, 9 May 1997, 34/1995, § 11.

42   When a *decision on admissibility* of the Court in Strasbourg is cited, the term 'decision' is added in brackets to the case cited; for example, ECtHR, *T.I. v. UK*, 7 March 2000, no. 43844/98 (decision).

43   ComAT, General Comment No. 1 on Art. 3 CAT (1997), § 9.

44   See, for example, ComAT, *Mutombo v. Switzerland*, 27 April 1994, no. 13/1993 and ComAT, General Comment No. 1 on Art. 3 CAT (1997), § 9.

45   UN doc. CAT/C/SR.518/Add.1.

46   For example, ComAT, *Chipana v. Venezuela*, 10 November 1998, no. 110/1998, § 6.1.

47   For example, ComAT, *V.N.I.M. v. Canada*, 12 November 2002, no. 119/1998.

48   These are also the terms used in the Committee's Rules of Procedure; see ComAT (CAT/C/3/Rev.6). The Committee also uses the terms *case law* or *jurisprudence* to describe its practice in the assessment of individual complaints; see, for example, ComAT, *Kalonzo v. Canada*, 18 May 2012, no. 343/2008, § 9.7.

the terms *complaint* or *complainant* are used interchangeably with the terms *application* or *applicant*.

1.4   *Structure of This Study*

This study consists of five chapters. The first, chapter 1, presents the European Convention on Human Rights and the United Nations Convention against Torture as well as the enforcement mechanisms to these Conventions. This chapter will further provide a general introduction to the principle of non-refoulement under Article 3 ECHR and Article 3 CAT. It will also give an overview on the prohibition on refoulement contained in the 1951 Refugee Convention, the International Covenant on Civil and Political Rights and within European Union law with a focus on the main differences to the ECHR and the CAT.

Chapter 2 focuses on procedural issues. It will explain the individual complaint mechanisms before the Court in Strasbourg and the Committee in Geneva, and consider questions of particular relevance to the principle of non-refoulement. This chapter will also look at the legal nature, effects and enforcement of the Court's and the Committee's judgments and decisions. It will discuss the admissibility requirements for submitting complaints to the Court or the Committee, with a focus on issues of particular interest in the context of non-refoulement.

Chapter 3 will analyse and compare the harm that triggers the application of the principle of non-refoulement under the ECHR and the CAT. It will compare the scope of Article 3 ECHR with that of Article 3 CAT and determine the practical impact of the fact that the principle of non-refoulement as defined in Article 3 CAT is limited to the protection against acts of torture, while the prohibition on refoulement contained in Article 3 ECHR includes a protection against torture and inhuman or degrading treatment or punishment.

Chapter 4 will discuss the elements taken into account by the Court and the Committee in their risk assessment under the principle of non-refoulement. The structure of this central part mirrors the structure of the Court's and the Committee's judgments and decisions on non-refoulement: first, an introduction is given to the standard and burden of proof as well as the role of the actors in proceedings. This is followed by the discussion of the time at which the risk assessment is made in Strasbourg and in Geneva. Subsequently, the three main elements that are important in the Court's and the Committee's risk assessment under the principle of non-refoulement are discussed:

1.   The question of whether the case has been properly assessed at national level. This section will also look at the right to an effective remedy under the principle of non-refoulement.

2.   The analysis of the human rights situation in the receiving state.

3.   The applicant's personal circumstances.

Finally, chapter 4 presents an analysis of three further issues that might be relevant in the assessment of individual complaints: (1) the possibility of an internal flight alternative for the applicant in the receiving country; (2) the existence of diplomatic assurance with regard to the complainant's security in the receiving country; and (3) the risk of an indirect removal.

Chapter 5 concludes this book with a summary of the findings obtained through the various comparisons, considerations on the mutual influence that the Court and the Committee have had on each other and a critical look at the impact and persuasiveness of their judgments and decisions.

I have chosen to arrange my discussions of the Court's and the Committee's case law, followed by comparisons between them, by subject title.[49] This might produce an element of repetition. Nevertheless, it enables readers to inform themselves about the case law of each institution individually and examine the comparative considerations selectively. It also allows the reader to concentrate on specific subjects under the principle of non-refoulement separately.

2   The European Convention on Human Rights (ECHR)

2.1   *Introduction to the Convention System*

2.1.1   The ECHR

The European Convention for the Protection of Human Rights (ECHR) is an international treaty through which 47 European states have agreed to secure a range of fundamental rights and freedoms. The ECHR was drawn up within the Council of Europe. This institution was established in the aftermath of the Second World War with the aim of promoting human rights, democracy, the rule of law and social development. The ECHR was opened for signature on 4 November 1950 in Rome and entered into force on 3 September 1953. The drafters of the ECHR took their inspiration from the Universal Declaration of Human Rights proclaimed by the General Assembly of the United Nations on 10 December 1948. Accordingly, the ECHR contains mainly civil and political rights. However, the European Court of Human Rights has developed a rich and multifaceted case law. It has thereby treated the ECHR as a 'living

---

49   Only the conditions for admissibility of complaints are described together in Chapter 2 Section 3. Important differences in their handling in practice are discussed within the subsections and in Chapter 2 Section 3.3.

instrument,' which must be interpreted in light of present-day conditions.[50] Today, the rights and freedoms guaranteed by the ECHR sometimes go beyond what are understood to be classic civil or political rights, and may imply positive obligations for states including guarantees of a social nature.[51]

According to Article 1 of the ECHR, each contracting state has the obligation to secure for everyone within its jurisdiction the rights and freedoms defined in the Convention. A catalogue of substantive rights and freedoms follows in the Articles 2 to 14 ECHR: Article 2 ECHR guarantees the right to life. Article 3 ECHR prohibits torture and inhuman or degrading treatment or punishment. As will be shown in detail, the principle of non-refoulement is inherent to this prohibition.

The contracting parties have further adopted amending and additional protocols to the ECHR. The additional Protocols Nos. 1,[52] 4,[53] 6,[54] 7,[55] 12[56] and 13[57] added further substantial rights and liberties to those guaranteed by the ECHR.

The amending Protocols concern the organisation and procedure of the Convention's control system. They complete the second section of the ECHR that contains the provisions governing the structure and procedure before the European Court of Human Rights (Articles 19–51 ECHR). The functioning and organisation of the Court is further set out in more detail in the Court's Rules of Procedure.[58]

---

50   Amongst others, ECtHR, *Soering v. UK*, 7 July 1989, no. 14038/88, § 102.

51   As an example in the context of the treatment of asylum seekers in Europe: ECtHR, *M.S.S. v. Belgium and Greece*, 21 January 2011 [GC], no. 30696/09, §§ 249–264.

52   Entry into force on 18 May 1954: protection of property (Art. 1), right to education (Art. 2), right to free elections (Art. 3).

53   Entry into force on 2 May 1968: prohibition on imprisonment for debt (Art. 1), freedom of movement (Art. 2), prohibition on expulsion of nationals (Art. 3), prohibition on collective expulsion of aliens.

54   Entry into force on 1 March 1985: abolition of the death penalty except in times of war or imminent threat of war.

55   Entry into force on 1 November 1988: procedural safeguards relating to the expulsion of aliens (Art. 1), right of appeal in criminal matters (Art. 2), right to compensation for a wrongful conviction (Art. 3), right not to be punished twice (Art. 4), equality between spouses (Art. 5).

56   Entry into force on 1 April 2005: general ban on discrimination.

57   Entry into force on 1 July 2003: abolition of the death penalty in all circumstances.

58   The most recent version of the Court's Rules of Procedure dates from 1 January 2016. It is available on the Court's website at: <http://www.echr.coe.int/>.

Of particular importance are amending Protocols Nos. 11[59] and 14[60] to the ECHR. Protocol No. 11 came into force on 1 November 1998 and radically reformed the supervisory system, creating a single full-time Court to which individuals have direct recourse. Prior to this, two part-time organs dealt with applications introduced by states or individuals: the European Commission of Human Rights and the European Court of Human Rights. The European Commission of Human Rights first considered the admissibility of any submitted complaint. If it declared the complaint admissible, it examined the merits of the case. It then submitted a report to the Committee of Ministers and the parties concerned, expressing its opinion as to whether there had been a violation of the ECHR. Within three months of the submission to the Committee of Ministers, the Commission or the respondent state could refer this report to the Court. The applicant himself could only ask for referral to the Court if the state against which the complaint was introduced had ratified Protocol 9 to the ECHR.[61] Cases taken to the Court were decided in a full judicial procedure. The Committee of Ministers, a political organ, decided on cases that were not referred to the Court. The Committee of Ministers usually fully adopted the Committee's report without any further investigation.

Protocol No. 14 to the ECHR amended the permanent Court's control system. It entered into force in June 2010. Its main purpose was to give the dramatically overburdened Court 'the procedural means and flexibility it needs to process all applications in a timely fashion, while allowing it to concentrate on the most important cases which require in-depth examination.'[62] Protocol No. 14 introduced three main changes: (1) It reinforced the Court's filtering capacity with respect to the huge volume of unmeritorious applications by making a single judge competent to declare applications inadmissible or strike them out.[63] (2) A new admissibility criterion for individual applications was inserted to empower the Court to declare inadmissible applications where the applicant had not suffered a 'significant disadvantage.'[64] (3) The Protocol further introduced measures for dealing with repetitive cases.[65] These and other changes brought

---

59   Adopted 11 May 1994. Entry into force on 1 November 1998.

60   Adopted 13 May 2004. Entry into force on 1 June 2010.

61   This additional Protocol has been repealed with the entry into force of Protocol No. 11 to the ECHR.

62   'Explanatory Report to Protocol No. 14 to the ECHR,' ETS No. 194, § 35.

63   See Art. 27 ECHR and 'Explanatory Report to Protocol No. 14 to the ECHR,' ETS No. 194, §§ 36 and 38.

64   See Art. 35(3)b ECHR.

65   See Art. 28 § 1 b) ECHR.

by Protocol No. 14[66] have enhanced the efficiency of the Court – above all due to the remarkable impact of the single-judge procedure.[67] However, despite these efforts, the Court is still overburdened, as will be discussed in the next section. Member states and the Court are hence continuing in their efforts to unburden the Court and make it more efficient.[68]

2.1.2   The European Court of Human Rights ('the Court') and the Individual Complaint Mechanism

The ECHR provides two types of mechanisms for enforcement: inter-state applications under Article 33 ECHR and individual applications under Article 34 ECHR. Inter-state complaints are rare.[69] The primary feature of the enforcement system is the right to submit individual applications to the Court. Originally conceived as an option that states could recognise at their discretion, it was turned into a compulsory right under the ECHR by Protocol No. 11 in 1998.

However, it must be kept in mind that according to Article 1 ECHR, the primary responsibility for ensuring that the ECHR is applied effectively at national level lies with the state parties. Only if national authorities fail to supervise the safeguarding of the rights contained in the ECHR will the mechanism before the Court as set up in Article 34 ECHR come into play. The supervision of the respect of Convention rights by the Court is of a subsidiary nature. This concept is also referred to as the principle of subsidiarity.

The Court is composed of a number of judges equal to the number of contracting states,[70] which are currently 47. The Parliamentary Assembly of the Council of Europe elects the judges from a shortlist of three candidates put

---

66   For all amendments see 'Explanatory Report to Protocol No. 14,' ETS No. 194.

67   ECtHR, 'Annual Report 2012,' p. 12; 'Annual Report 2014,' pp. 63 and 65.

68   One such effort is Protocol No. 15 to the ECHR (ETS 213), which will enter into force when all the states parties to the ECHR have ratified it. It amends the ECHR and introduces, *inter alia*, an explicit reference to the principle of subsidiarity in the Preamble of the Convention. It also reduces from six to four months the time limit within which an application may be made to the Court following a final domestic decision. Protocol No. 16 to the ECHR (ETS 214) will allow the highest national courts to request advisory opinions on the interpretation of the ECHR by the Court, to resolve cases more speedily at the national level. It will enter into force once 10 parties to the ECHR have ratified it. For further actions taken see the Court's annual reports published on its website.

69   A prominent example is the case ECtHR, *Ireland v. UK*, 18 January 1978 [GC], no. 5310/71 relating to security measures in Northern Ireland.

70   Art. 20 ECHR.

forward by each of the national governments.[71] The judges are elected for a single term of nine years.[72] The judges do not represent any state but sit on the Court in their individual capacity. They have to 'be of high moral character and must either possess the qualifications required for appointment to high judicial office or be jurisconsults of recognised competence.'[73]

To consider individual applications brought before it, the Court sits in either a single-judge formation, in committees of 3 judges, in chambers of 7 judges or in the Grand Chamber of 17 judges.[74] The assignment to one or the other decision body depends on the well-foundedness of a complaint and whether it raises a serious issue of general importance. Chapter 2 section 1.1 will take a closer look at the potential paths of individual complaints submitted in Strasbourg.

The Court's judgments are binding on the state party concerned.[75] If the Court finds that there has been a violation of the ECHR, the judgment is transmitted to the Committee of Ministers, responsible for supervising the execution of judgments.[76] The Committee of Ministers verifies whether the state in respect of which a violation of the ECHR has been found has taken adequate remedial measures to comply with the Court's judgment. Those measures may be specific and/or of general nature. In most refoulement cases, the respondent state simply has the duty to revoke a decision to expel or extradite the applicant.[77]

In the early years of the ECHR, the number of applications lodged before the Strasbourg institutions were low. Since the 1980s, the number of cases has been growing steadily, and this has made it increasingly difficult for the Court to keep the length of proceedings within acceptable time limits. The rapid increase in the number of contracting states after the fall of the Berlin wall from 1990 onwards exacerbated the problem. The Court has become the victim of its own success. As has been mentioned, Protocol No. 14 to the ECHR has raised the Court's efficiency in the handling of complaints. It is, however, still overwhelmed by individual applications. By the end of 2014,

---

71   Art. 22 ECHR.

72   Art. 23(1) ECHR.

73   Art. 21 ECHR.

74   Art. 26(1) ECHR.

75   Art. 46(1) ECHR. See on this Chapter 2 Section 1.3.

76   Art. 46(2) ECHR. The Committee of Ministers is made up of the Ministers for Foreign Affairs of each member state. On a day-to-day basis, the Committee of Ministers acts through the ministers' permanent representatives in Strasbourg; see also Chapter 2 Section 1.3.

77   See Chapter 2 Section 1.3.

69,900 complaints were pending.[78] Individual procedures may take years, which, as will also become apparent in this study, has worrying effects on the efficiency and credibility of the protection system. Still, the system is considered one of the most successful international human rights systems in the world.[79]

2.2 *The Principle of Non-refoulement under Art. 3* ECHR

2.2.1   The Principle of Non-refoulement Inherent to Article 3 ECHR
The principle of non-refoulement is not explicitly guaranteed in the ECHR. It is inherent to Article 3 ECHR, which provides that 'no one shall be subjected to torture or to inhuman or degrading treatment or punishment.' It is

> ... the settled case law of the Court that the decision by a Contracting State to remove a fugitive and, *a fortiori*, the actual removal itself – may give rise to an issue under Article 3, and hence engage the responsibility of that State under the Convention, where substantial grounds have been shown for believing that the person in question would, if expelled or extradited, face a real risk of being subjected to treatment contrary to Article 3 in the receiving country.[80]

Where an individual has established such a real risk of ill treatment in case of removal, Article 3 ECHR implies an obligation on the state concerned not to deport that individual. This obligation constitutes an exception to the Court's general principle, according to which the ECHR does not guarantee the right of non-nationals to enter or remain in the territory of a member state. As the Court constantly repeats, 'States have the right, as a matter of well-established international law and subject to their treaty obligations, including the Convention, to control the entry, residence and expulsion of aliens.'[81]

The *traveaux préparatoires* to the ECHR neither confirm nor reject the possibility that the drafters of Article 3 ECHR intended this provision to include a prohibition on refoulement.[82] It is clear, however, that the drafters wished the prohibition of ill treatment to be comprehensive and open to further

---

78   ECtHR, 'Annual Report 2014,' p. 63.

79   Leach 2011, p. 6.

80   ECtHR, *El-Masri v. Former Yugoslav Republic of Macedonia*, 13 December 2012 [GC], no. 39630/09, § 212.

81   For example, ECtHR, *Saadi v. Italy*, 28 February 2008 [GC], no. 37201/06, § 124.

82   Thurin 2012, pp. 12–14.

developments.[83] In 1961 the former European Commission of Human Rights stated for the first time that 'the deportation of a foreigner to a particular country might in exceptional circumstances give rise to the question whether there had been 'inhuman treatment' within the meaning of Article 3 of the Convention.'[84] The Commission reaffirmed this approach in subsequent decisions; however, it never found a violation of Article 3 ECHR based on that principle.[85]

It was only in July 1989 in the famous case *Soering v. United Kingdom*[86] that the European Court of Human Rights for the first time analysed a complaint in which a violation of the principle of non-refoulement was alleged. The case concerned a young German citizen who was accused of murdering his girl-friend's parents in the United States of America. He had fled to the United Kingdom where he was arrested for extradition to the state of Virginia. He submitted a complaint to the Court claiming that his extradition would violate Article 3 ECHR, because he risked being subjected to the death penalty. He maintained that in suffering from the so-called death row phenomenon he would be subjected to treatment contrary to Article 3 ECHR. The death row phenomenon may be described as the emotional distress that prisoners facing a capital charge have to endure before being executed. At the time, the Court did not consider that the death penalty *as such* was a treatment prohibited by Article 3 ECHR.[87] However, in the Court's view, in consideration of the long period of time spent in extreme conditions on death row with the ever-mounting anguish of awaiting execution, as well as the personal circumstances of the applicant, especially his young age and mental state at the time of the offence, the applicant's extradition would have exposed him to a real risk of treatment that went beyond the threshold set by Article 3 ECHR.[88] This was the first time' the Court had found a violation of Article 3 ECHR based on the consequences of a removal.

Before reaching this finding, the Court had asked the question of whether the extradition of a fugitive to another State where he would likely be subjected to torture or to inhuman or degrading treatment or punishment would *itself* engage the responsibility of a contracting state under Article 3 ECHR.

83   *Ibid.*
84   EComHR, *X. v. Belgium*, 29 May 1961, no. 984/61.
85   For analyses of the Commission's case law on the prohibition on refoulement see Einarsen 1990, pp. 364–375; Kälin 1982, pp. 167–188.
86   ECtHR, *Soering v. UK*, 7 July 1989, no. 14038/88.
87   This is no longer the case today; see on this Chapter 3 Section 2.2.5.
88   *Ibid.*, § 111.

The Court held that Article 3 ECHR makes no provision for exceptions and no derogation from it is permissible in time of war or other national emergency.[89] It noted that the absolute prohibition of ill treatment shows that Article 3 ECHR enshrines one of the fundamental values of the democratic societies making up the Council of Europe.[90] The Court further held that a prohibition on refoulement based on the prohibition of torture is recognised in Article 3 CAT, and added that the fact that a specialised treaty spelled out in detail a specific obligation attaching to the prohibition of torture did not mean that an essentially similar obligation was not already *inherent* in the general terms of Article 3 ECHR. It then added:

> It would hardly be compatible with the underlying values of the Convention, that 'common heritage of political traditions, ideals, freedom and the rule of law' to which the Preamble refers, were a Contracting State knowingly to surrender a fugitive to another State where there were substantial grounds for believing that he would be in danger of being subjected to torture, however heinous the crime allegedly committed. Extradition in such circumstances, while not explicitly referred to in the brief and general wording of Article 3, would plainly be contrary to the spirit and intention of the Article, and in the Court's view this inherent obligation not to extradite also extends to cases in which the fugitive would be faced in the receiving State with a real risk of exposure to inhuman or degrading treatment or punishment proscribed by that Article.[91]

In sum, the Court held that the decision to extradite a fugitive might give rise to an issue under Article 3 ECHR and hence engage a member state's responsibility. These considerations contained two novelties: it was the first time the Court had recognised a certain 'extraterritorial application' of Article 3 ECHR;[92] it was also the first time the Court assessed the existence of a possible future human rights violation instead of a past one. The judges held:

---

89 See Art. 15 ECHR. On the absolute nature of the protection against ill treatment under Art. 3 ECHR see Chapter 3 Section 2.4.

90 ECtHR, *Soering v. UK*, 7 July 1989, no. 14038/88. § 88.

91 *Ibid.*

92 See the Grand Chamber's statement in ECtHR *Al-Adsani v. UK*, 21 November 2001 [GC], no. 35763/97, § 39: 'In *Soering*, cited above, the Court recognised that Article 3 has some, limited, extraterritorial application ... .'

> It is not normally for the Convention institutions to pronounce on the existence or otherwise of potential violations of the Convention. However, where an applicant claims that a decision to extradite him would, if implemented, be contrary to Article 3 by reason of its foreseeable consequences in the requesting country, a departure from this principle is necessary, in view of the serious and irreparable nature of the alleged suffering risked, in order to ensure the effectiveness of the safeguard provided by that Article.[93]

The issue in most refoulement cases is thus not a violation of the ECHR that has already taken place, but a hypothetical violation that could take place if the state concerned proceeded with the expulsion or extradition.[94] Suntinger speaks of a 'preventive approach to human rights.'[95] The establishment of such a possible human rights violation 'inevitably involves an assessment of conditions in the requesting country against the standards of Article 3 of the Convention.'[96] Nonetheless, according to the Court, there is no question of establishing the responsibility of the receiving country, whether under general international law, under the Convention or otherwise. Insofar as any liability under the ECHR may be incurred, it is liability incurred by the extraditing contracting state 'by reason of its having taken action which has as a direct consequence the exposure of an individual to proscribed ill-treatment.'[97]

In 1991, the Court confirmed the *Soering* principles with regard to the expulsion of failed asylum seekers in two judgments.[98] The Court made clear that the principle of non-refoulement inherent to Article 3 ECHR is applicable to all kinds of transfers of persons from one jurisdiction to another, be it through expulsion, extradition, repatriation or any other means. The Court has recently summarized its approach on that matter and considered that 'the question whether there is a real risk of treatment contrary to Article 3 in another State cannot depend on the legal basis for removal to that State.'[99] With regard to extraditions it has made clear that the ECHR 'does not prevent cooperation between States, within the framework of extradition treaties or in

---

93   ECtHR, *Soering v. UK*, 7 July 1989, no. 14038/88, § 90.

94   Danelius 1993, p. 270.

95   Suntinger 1995, pp. 204 and 224.

96   `ECtHR, *Soering v. UK*, 7 July 1989, no. 14038/88, § 91.

97   *Ibid.* On the nature of the prohibition on refoulment see also Chapter 3 Section 1.

98   ECtHR, *Cruz Varas and Others v. Sweden*, 20 March 1991, no. 15576/89; ECtHR, *Vilvarajah and Others v. UK*, 30 October 1991, nos. 13163/87 and further.

99   ECtHR, *Babar Ahmad and Others v. UK*, 10 April 2012, nos. 24027/07, 11949/08, 36742/08, 66911/09 and 67354/09, § 168.

matters of deportation, for the purpose of bringing fugitive offenders to justice, provided that it does not interfere with any specific rights recognised in
the Convention.'[100] Accordingly, the obligation under Article 3 ECHR *not* to
surrender a fugitive to another state where there are substantial grounds for
believing that he would be in danger of being subjected to torture or inhuman treatment overrides the expelling state's obligations under the extradition
treaties it has concluded.[101]

2.2.2   The Court's Case Law on Non-refoulement

As at February 2016, the Court had released 215 judgments on the merits with
regard to the principle of non-refoulement inherent to Article 3 ECHR. A violation was found in 125 of these judgments.[102] Out of the 215 judgments on the
merits, around 70 concerned extraditions, the others expulsions.

All other complaints concerning refoulement that have been submitted
to the Court have either been declared inadmissible in accordance with
Article 35 ECHR or have been struck out of the Court's list in accordance
with Article 37 ECHR.[103] Unfortunately, the Court does not provide exact data
on the character of complaints introduced under Article 3 ECHR. However,
from the information published on the requests for interim measures, it can
be observed that the number of non-refoulement complaints submitted must
have exceeded 5,000.[104]

It has been explained that the Court adopted the first judgment concerning non-refoulement in 1989 in the famous case of *Soering*.[105] Between 1989
and 2007, it released 24 judgments on the merits that concerned refoulement
(that is, approximately 1.3 judgments per year). The number rapidly increased
after 2007. From 2008 until 2011, the Court adopted 73 judgments (around 18
judgments per year). In 2012, the Court adopted 23 judgments concerning refoulement. In 2013, it was 38 judgments and in 2014, the Court released 31 judgments. In 2015, it had adopted 19 judgments.

The rising number of complaints with which the Court has been confronted in the last years explains the rising number of judgments concerning

---

100   ECtHR, *Calovskis v. Latvia*, 24 July 2014, no. 22205/13, § 129.

101   ECtHR, *Al-Saadoon and Mufdhi v. UK*, 2 March 2010, no. 61498/08, § 128, referring to the
      Soering judgment.

102   See the table of 'non-refoulement cases assessed on the merits' (XXXII).

103   See on this Chapter 2 Section 3.

104   See Chapter 2 Section 1.2 on interim measures and the thematic statistics on interim mea-
      sures 2008 to 2012 on the Court's website [3.1.2014, copy in possession of the author] and
      2012 to 2015 <http://www.echr.coe.int/Pages/home.aspx?p=reports> [11.2.2016].

105   ECtHR, *Soering v. UK*, 7 July 1989, no. 14038/88.

non-refoulement. Between 2006 and 2010, the Court saw an increase of over 4,000 per cent in the number of requests it received for interim measures in the context of refoulement.[106] In this respect, Bossuyt's observation that the Court has become more lenient with regard to refoulement complaints since 2005 seems to be at odds with the figures.[107] Unfortunately, Bossuyt is relying on the absolute numbers of judgments released by the Court without placing them in the context of the rising number of complaints submitted.[108]

Since there is no exact data on all the complaints handled by the Court concerning the principle of non-refoulement, it is impossible to determine the success rate of such complaints. The known data nevertheless indicates that it must be extremely low. As has been mentioned, the Court has dealt with thousands of requests for interim measures but it is only in 125 judgments to date that it has found that the principle of non-refoulement has been violated.[109]

The member state of the Council of Europe that has, to date, been condemned most often for the violation of the principle of non-refoulement is Russia (46 violations, mostly concerning extraditions), followed by Italy (17 violations, mostly concerning the deportation of suspected terrorists to Tunisia before the 'Arab Spring'), France (13 violations), Turkey (9 violations), the United Kingdom (9 violations) and Sweden (6 violations).

2.2.3   The Protection against Refoulement under Other Rights
          of the ECHR

In principle, there is no hierarchy between the various rights and freedoms guaranteed by the ECHR. Article 3 ECHR nevertheless has a key importance in the eyes of the Court: together with the right to life in Article 2 ECHR, the prohibition of torture and inhuman or degrading treatment in Article 3 ECHR is considered as 'one of the core rights under the Convention.'[110] In the famous *Soering* judgment, the Court recognised the 'extraterritorial application' of Article 3 ECHR because of the fundamental importance and absolute nature of the prohibition of torture and inhuman treatment.[111] For similar reasons, the

---

106   ECtHR, statement issued on 11 February 2011 by the President of the Court concerning requests for interim measures, doc. GT-GDR-C(2012)005. See also Chapter 2 Section 1.2.

107   See Bossuyt 2010, pp. 127–128.

108   See the critique also in Delas 2011, pp. 407–408.

109   However, it should be noted that many complaints are also struck out of the Court's registry; see on this Chapter 2 Section 3.2.7.c.

110   ECtHR, *Mamatkulov and Askarov v. Turkey*, 4 February 2005 [GC], nos. 46827/99 and 46951/99, § 108.

111   See ECtHR, *Soering v. UK*, 7 July 1989, no. 14038/88, § 88 and Chapter 1 Section 2.2.1.

Court recognized the extraterritorial application of the right to life in Article 2 ECHR.[112]

According to the Court, issues under Articles 2 and 3 ECHR in the context of refoulement are indissociable. Correspondingly, the Court deals with refoulement complaints based on Article 2 ECHR under Article 3 ECHR.[113] With that, the right to life in Article 2 ECHR has not offered any additional protection against refoulement than that already provided by Article 3 ECHR in practice. There are refoulement cases in which the Court referred to Articles 3 *and* 2 ECHR. However, in these cases, the Court still relied solely on the principles developed under Article 3 ECHR.[114] The prohibition on refoulement based on the right to life is therefore not further analysed in this study.

The prohibition on refoulement inherent to Articles 2 and 3 ECHR remains exceptional as it is based on the fundamental importance and absolute character attached to these guarantees.[115] According to the Court, a prohibition on refoulement does not automatically apply under the other provisions of the ECHR. The judges have made clear that on 'a purely pragmatic basis, it cannot be required that an expelling Contracting State only return an alien to a country which is in full and effective enforcement of all the rights and freedoms set out in the Convention.'[116] The Court has, however, recognized a certain extraterritorial application for two further guarantees provided by the ECHR: the right to a fair trial in Article 6 ECHR and the right to liberty and security in Article 5 ECHR. It has not excluded developments with regard to other rights.[117]

---

112   See, among others, ECtHR, *Al-Saadoon and Mufdhi v. UK*, 2 March 2010, no. 61498/08, § 143. According to Art. 15 ECHR, no derogation shall be made in times of war or other public emergency from Art. 3, or from Art. 2 (right to life), except with respect to deaths resulting from lawful acts of war.

113   See, for example, ECtHR, *H.N. v. Sweden*, 15 May 2012, no. 30720/09, §§ 32 and 36; ECtHR, *H. and B. v. UK*, 9 April 2013, nos. 70073/10 and 44539/11, § 64.

114   See, for example, ECtHR, *Bader and Kanbor v. Sweden*, 8 November 2005, no. 13284/04; ECtHR, *S.A. v. Sweden*, 27 June 2013, no. 66523/10; ECtHR, *L.M. and Others v. Russia*, 15 October 2015, nos. 40081/14, 40088/14 and 40127/14. The Court's approach with regard to Art. 2 ECHR in the context of refoulement is not fully convincing since the scopes of Art. 2 and Art. 3 ECHR are not congruent.

115   It is arguable that the other ECHR guarantees from which no derogations are allowed under Art. 15 ECHR also contain a prohibition on refoulement. Those are Art. 4(1) ECHR (prohibition on slavery or servitude) and Art. 7 ECHR (no punishment without law); see in this sense Wouters 2009, p. 346.

116   ECtHR, *F. v. UK*, 22 June 2004, no. 17341/ 03 (decision).

117   In his concurring opinion to ECtHR, *Hirsi Jamaa and Others v. Italy*, 23 February 2012 [GC], no. 27765/09 Judge Pinto de Albuquerque notes that any Convention right can trigger the

Article 6 ECHR guarantees the right to a fair trial in civil or criminal proceedings. It does not apply to asylum or extradition procedures.[118] In *Soering*, the Court has, however, indicated that, 'an issue might exceptionally be raised under Article 6 ECHR by an extradition decision in circumstances where the fugitive has suffered or risks suffering a flagrant denial of a fair trial in the requesting country.'[119] The Court has reiterated this principle on several occasions.[120] In *Abohurgeze v. France* adopted in October 2011,[121] it shed light on the meaning of the phrase 'flagrant denial of a fair trial' in the extradition setting, as compared to the notion of a fair trial as guaranteed by Article 6 ECHR in the domestic context. The case concerned the extradition of a man of Hutu origin to Rwanda, where he was charged with genocide and crimes against humanity. The Court explained 'flagrant denial of a fair trial' as follows:

> A flagrant denial of justice goes *beyond mere irregularities* or lack of safeguards in the trial procedures such *as might result in a breach of Article 6* if occurring within the Contracting State itself. What is required is a breach of the principles of fair trial guaranteed by Article 6 which is *so fundamental as to amount to a nullification, or destruction of the very essence, of the right guaranteed* by that Article.[122] (Emphasis added)

With regard to the applicant, the Court noted that in 2008 and 2009, the International Criminal Tribunal for Rwanda (ICTR) and several countries had refused to extradite genocide suspects to Rwanda due to fair trial concerns. However, the Court observed that the Rwandan laws and practice had meanwhile improved. It noted, *inter alia*, that the applicant's concern not to be able to adduce witness testimony was not justified, that he could benefit from the assistance of experienced state-paid lawyers and that in general, the Rwandan judiciary could not be considered to lack independence and impartiality. The Court also took into account that that the applicant would be tried by

---

non-refoulement obligation. However, this has yet to be substantiated by the Court's case law. See on this also Wouters, pp. 351–353.

118   ECtHR, *Maaouia v. France*, 5 October 2000 [GC], no. 39652/98, §§ 33–41.

119   ECtHR, *Soering v. UK*, 7 July 1989, no. 14038/88, § 113.

120   For example, ECtHR, *Mamatkulov and Askarov v. Turkey*, 4 February 2005 [GC], nos. 46827/99 and 46951/99, §§ 90–91; ECtHR, *Babar Ahmad and Others v. the UK*, 6 July 2010, nos. 24027/07, 11949/08 and 36742/08, §§ 132–133 (decision).

121   ECtHR, *Ahorugeze v. Sweden*, 27 October 2011, no. 37075/09.

122   *Ibid.*, § 115. With that the Court had assumed the definition of the judges Bratza, Bonello and Hedigan in their partly dissenting opinion (§ 16) in ECtHR, *Mamatkulov and Askarov v. Turkey*, 4 February 2005 [GC], nos. 46827/99 and 46951/99.

Rwanda's High Courts and *not* by the community-based *gacaca* tribunals set up in 2002. It also indicated that in June 2011, the ICTR had for the first time transferred an indicted genocide suspect for trial to Rwanda. For all these reasons, it concluded that the applicant would not risk a flagrant denial of a fair trial if extradited and that Article 6 ECHR would hence not be violated in that event.[123]

The test for the existence of a 'flagrant denial of a fair trial' is a particularly stringent one.[124] There are only three cases in which the Court has recognized the existence of a real risk of 'flagrant denial of fair trial':[125] one is the case *Abu Qatada v. United Kingdom* decided in January 2012.[126] It concerned the deportation of Omar Othman, known as Abu Qatada, to Jordan, where he had been convicted *in absentia* for involvement in terrorist conspiracies. Abu Qatada claimed that if deported to Jordan, he would be retried, which would put him at risk of torture and a grossly unfair trial based on evidence obtained by the torture of his codefendants.[127] With regard to the question of whether there was a real risk for the applicant to be tried in flagrant denial of the guarantees set by Article 6 ECHR in Jordan, the Court first indicated which forms of unfairness could amount to a flagrant denial of justice prohibiting a removal. It enumerated the following circumstances:

- conviction *in absentia* with no subsequent possibility of obtaining a fresh determination of the merits of the charge;
- a trial which is summary in nature and conducted with a total disregard for the rights of the defence;
- detention without any access to an independent and impartial tribunal to have the legality of the detention reviewed;
- deliberate and systematic denial of access to a lawyer, especially for an individual detained in a foreign country.[128]

---

123   ECtHR, *Ahorugeze*, §§ 117–129.

124   *Ibid.*, § 115. However, for complainants alleging a flagrant denial of fair trial in case of deportation, the same standard and burden of proof should apply as in the examination of extraditions and expulsions under Article 3 ECHR; § 116.

125   ECtHR, *Abu Qatada v. UK*, 17 January 2012, no. 8139/09; ECtHR, *Al Nashiri v. Poland*, 24 July 2014, no. 28761/11; ECtHR, *Abu Zubaydah v. Poland*, 24 July 2014, no. 7511/13.

126   ECtHR, *Abu Qatada v. UK*, 17 January 2012, no. 8139/09.

127   The complainant *Qatada* also claimed a violation of the principle of non-refoulement under Art. 3 ECHR, which was rejected since the UK had obtained diplomatic assurances for the complainant's security. For a discussion of this part of the judgment and the Court's general practice with regard to diplomatic assurances see Chapter 4 Section 3.4.2.a.

128   ECtHR, *Abu Qatada*, § 259.

The Court then assessed whether the use of evidence obtained by torture would also amount to a flagrant denial of justice. Referring to international law, in particular Article 15 CAT, the Court held that the prohibition on the use of evidence obtained by torture is one of the most fundamental norms of international criminal justice. It then observed that evidence obtained by torture of third persons would be admitted at the applicant's retrial. In those circumstances, there was a real risk of flagrant denial of justice for Abu Qatada in Jordan. The Court hence concluded that his deportation would violate the prohibition on refoulement inherent to Article 6 ECHR.[129]

In the *Abu Qatada* judgment, the Court also assessed whether the right to liberty and security as guaranteed in Article 5 ECHR could apply in the refoulement context. Article 5 ECHR protects individuals against arbitrary detentions. The Court considered that, despite the doubts it expressed in its earlier case law,[130] it was possible for that provision to apply in an expulsion case, where an applicant was at real risk of a flagrant breach. However, as with Article 6 ECHR, a high threshold should be applied. According to the Court, a flagrant breach of Article 5 ECHR would occur only if, for example, the receiving state arbitrarily detained an applicant for many years without any intention of bringing him or her to trial. Another example would be if an applicant were at risk of being imprisoned for a substantial period in the receiving state, having previously been convicted after a flagrantly unfair trial.[131] The Court considered that it would be illogical if an applicant who faced imprisonment in a receiving state after a flagrantly unfair trial could rely on Article 6 ECHR to prevent his expulsion to that State, but an applicant who faced imprisonment without any trial whatsoever could not rely on Article 5 ECHR to prevent his expulsion. Equally, there may well be a situation where an applicant has already been convicted in the receiving state after a flagrantly unfair trial and is to be extradited to that state to serve a sentence of imprisonment. If there were no possibility of those criminal proceedings being reopened on his return, he could not rely on Article 6 ECHR because he would not be at risk of a further flagrant denial of justice. According to the Court, it would hence be unreasonable if that applicant could not then rely on Article 5 ECHR to prevent his extradition.[132] With regard to the situation of *Abu Qatada* if convicted in Jordan, the Court found that the applicant's main complaints under Article 5 ECHR were more

---

129   *Ibid.*, §§ 263–287.

130   The Court referred to ECtHR, *Tomic v. UK*, 14 October 2003, no. 17837/03 (decision).

131   ECtHR, *Abu Qatada*, § 233.

132   *Ibid.*, § 232.

appropriately examined under Article 6 ECHR so that no separate assessment under Article 5 ECHR was necessary.[133]

In the cases *Al Nashiri* and *Abu Zubaydah v. Poland* decided in July 2014, the Court found a violation of the principle of non-refoulement inherent to the Articles 3 and 6 ECHR, and, for the first time, of Article 5 ECHR.[134] They concerned two men suspected of terrorism who were secretly detained in Poland by the US Central Intelligence Agency (CIA) in 2002, and transferred from there to Guantanamo Bay with the acquiescence of Polish authorities.[135] Under Article 6 ECHR, the Court held that the Polish authorities were aware that it was a military commission that would try any suspect held in Guantanamo. Having regard to the fact that this commission (i) did not offer guarantees of impartiality of independence (ii) that, as confirmed by the US Supreme Court, it had no proper legitimacy under US and international law and (iii) that there was a high probability of admission of evidence obtained under torture, the Court concluded that, at the time of the applicant's transfer from Poland, there was a real risk that their trial before this military commission would amount to a 'flagrant denial of justice.' Accordingly, their transfers had violated Article 6 ECHR.[136]

With respect to the right to liberty in Article 5 ECHR, the judges observed that 'the unacknowledged detention of an individual is a complete negation' and a 'most grave violation' of Article 5 ECHR.[137] According to the Court, the secret detention of terrorist suspects was a fundamental feature of the CIA rendition programme, the aim of which was to remove persons from any legal protection against ill treatment and arbitrary detention. The Court hence found violations of Article 5 ECHR with respect to both the complainant's detention on Polish territory and their transfer from Poland to other secret detention facilities, and eventually Guantanamo.[138] The Court recently confirmed

---

133 *Ibid.*, § 234.

134 ECtHR, *Al Nashiri v. Poland*, 24 July 2014, no. 28761/11; ECtHR, *Abu Zubaydah v. Poland*, 24 July 2014, no. 7511/13.

135 On these 'extraordinary renditions' see also Chapter 2 Section 3.2.1.a.

136 ECtHR, *Al Nashiri*, §§ 565–569; ECtHR, *Abu Zubaydah*, §§ 555–561.

137 ECtHR, *Al Nashiri*, § 529.

138 ECtHR, *Al Nashiri*, §§ 527–532; ECtHR, *Abu Zubaydah*, §§ 521–526. On the 'extraterritorial' application of Art. 5 ECHR see also ECtHR, *Al-Moayad v. Germany*, 20 February 2007, no. 35865/03 (decision) and ECtHR, *Babar Ahmad and Others v. UK*, 6 July 2010, nos. 24027/07, 11949/08 and 36742/08 (decision). In these decisions, the Court indicated there would have been a violation of Art. 3, 5 and 6 ECHR if the complainants, whose extradition had been requested by the United States, were designated as 'enemy combatants' or detained in Guantanamo Bay or prosecuted by a military tribunal or any extraordinary court. Since

the approach taken with regard to Article 5 ECHR in *Nasr and Ghali v. Italy*, concerning the abduction by the CIA of an Egyptian applicant in Italy and his subsequent transfer to Egypt, where he was held in secret for several months.[139]

2.2.4   Other Provisions Relevant in the Context of Migration

The ECHR and its additional protocols do not differentiate between nationals and non-nationals. In principle, all individuals living under the jurisdiction of the Court are protected equally.[140] However, there are exceptions: Article 16 ECHR explicitly allows states to impose restrictions on the exercise of political activities by foreigners. Article 3 of Protocol No. 4 to the ECHR prohibits the expulsion of nationals only. In addition, where it is justified by the needs of public safety or economic well-being, the freedoms in Articles 8 to 11 ECHR may be applied more restrictively to foreigners.

However, there are also guarantees that have been of particular relevance for immigrants. One such guarantee is the right to respect for family and private life in Article 8 ECHR, which may act as a barrier to a removal. When the Court assesses whether an expulsion is compatible with Article 8 ECHR, it follows a case-by-case approach in which it tries to strike a balance between the public interests served by the expulsion and the interests of the individuals concerned.[141] The Court has developed several criteria to be taken into account in this proportionality test, such as the length of the stay and the integration of the individual concerned in the contracting state, his family ties and the best interests of any children involved, and the seriousness of offences committed by the person in question.[142] In cases of extradition, 'it will only be in exceptional circumstances that an applicant's private or family life in a Contracting State will outweigh the legitimate aim pursued by his or her extradition.'[143]

---

the US authorities had given assurances that the applicants would not be designated as 'enemy combatants' or detained in Guantanamo and that they would be tried before ordinary courts, the complaints were rejected.

139   See ECtHR, *Nasr and Ghali v. Italy*, 23 February 2016, no. 44883/09, §§ 296–309. The Court further found violations of Art. 3, 8 and 13 ECHR. On the subject of these 'extraordinary renditions' see Chapter 2 Section 3.2.1.a.

140   See Art. 1 ECHR: 'The High Contracting Parties shall secure to everyone within their jurisdiction the rights and freedoms defined in Section 1 of the Convention.'

141   Such a balancing test is impermissible under the principle of non-refoulement in Art. 3 ECHR, which is absolute, see on this Chapter 3 Section 2.4.

142   See, amongst others, ECtHR, *Boultif v. Switzerland*, 2 August 2001, no. 54273/00, § 48.

143   ECtHR, *Babar Ahmad and Others v. UK*, 10 April 2012, nos. 24027/07, 11949/08, 36742/08, 66911/09 and 67354/09, § 252.

It is not unusual for complainants to claim that their expulsion would violate both the principle of non-refoulement inherent to Article 3 ECHR *and* the right to family life as protected by Article 8 ECHR. When the Court considers such complaints, it first assesses whether there would be a violation of Article 3 ECHR in the event of removal. If this is the case, it will not proceed to an additional assessment of Article 8 ECHR.[144] However, if the Court first concludes that the removal would *not* violate Article 3 ECHR, it will assess as a second step whether it might violate the applicant's rights under Article 8 ECHR.[145]

Article 5 ECHR protects individuals against arbitrary detentions. According to this provision, 'no one shall be deprived of his liberty' if this is not in accordance with a 'procedure prescribed by law.' Paragraph 1 provides an exhaustive list of permissible grounds for detention such as the conviction by a court or 'the lawful arrest or detention of a person to prevent his effecting an unauthorized entry into the country or of a person against whom action is being taken with a view to deportation or extradition.'[146] A detention on that ground must meet the condition of being necessary to prevent the individual from committing an offence or fleeing.[147] It will only be justified for as long as deportation or extradition proceedings are in progress. If such proceedings are not 'actively and diligently pursued,' the detention will cease to be permissible.[148] Article 5(1) ECHR does not contain maximum time limits; the question of whether the length of deportation proceedings affects the lawfulness of detention depends on the circumstances of each case.[149]

Conditions in which immigrants are lawfully detained must also comply with the standards of Article 3 ECHR. The conditions in reception centres and for aliens held in detention for immigration control purposes must be adequate and include appropriate food, hygiene and health care.[150]

---

144   See, for example, ECtHR, *Saadi v. Italy*, 28 February 2008 [GC], no. 37201/06, § 170. As an exception ECtHR, *El-Masri v. Former Yugoslav Republic of Macedonia*, 13 December 2012 [GC], no. 39630/09, §§ 247–250.

145   For example, ECtHR, *Bensaid v. UK*, 6 February 2001, no. 44599/98; ECtHR, *Nacic and Others v. Sweden*, 15 May 2012, no. 16567/10.

146   Art. 5(1)f ECHR.

147   See, among others, ECtHR, *Ahmed v. Malta*, 23 July 2013, no. 55352/12, § 139.

148   ECtHR, *Auad v. Bulgaria*, 11 October 2011, no. 46390/10, § 134.

149   *Ibid.*, § 128.

150   See, for example, ECtHR, *Mwanje v. Belgium*, 20 December 2011, no. 10486/10, §§ 91–99; ECtHR, *Ahmed v. Malta*, 23 July 2013, no. 55352/12, §§ 85–100.

Particular attention must be given to the rights and needs of children.[151] There are several cases in which the Court has found a violation of Article 3 ECHR because asylum seekers were detained in inhuman or degrading conditions.[152]

As stated before, the right to a fair trial in Article 6 ECHR does not in principle apply to asylum or extradition procedures.[153] However, Article 1 of Protocol No. 7 to the ECHR guarantees certain procedural safeguards relating to the expulsion of aliens. It requires that any expulsion order be based on national legislation that is sufficiently accessible, foreseeable and that offers adequate guarantees against arbitrariness.[154] With the exception of extraditions, any measure compelling an alien's departure from the territory where he was lawfully resident constitutes 'expulsion' for the purposes of this provision.[155] The applicability of Article 1 of Protocol No. 7 is, however, limited to aliens who are considered 'lawful residents' in the contracting state.[156] Asylum seekers whose request has been denied fall outside this scope.[157] Equally, foreigners whose status in the territory of the state party has not yet been regularised or who have been admitted to the territory for a limited period cannot rely on the provision.[158] A right to review is further not applicable when an 'expulsion is necessary in the interest of public order or is grounded on reasons of national security.'[159] With these limitations, Article 1 of Protocol No. 7 to the ECHR has not been of particular importance so far; especially in the context of non-refoulement, in which most of the complaints concern either the expulsion of failed asylum seekers or extraditions. However, there are a few cases in which the Court has found that this provision had been violated because the expulsion of former residents had not been in pursuance of a decision reached

---

151   See, for example, ECtHR, *Muskhadzhiyeva v. Belgium*, 19 January 2010, no. 41442707 §§ 55–63; ECtHR, *Rahimi v. Greece*, 5 April 2011, no. 8687/08, §§ 62 and 81–96; ECtHR, *Popov v. France*, 19 January 2012, no. 39472/07, §§ 62–78.

152   See, among others, ECtHR, *M.S.S. v. Belgium and Greece*, 21 January 2011 [GC], no. 30696/09, § 222 with further references.

153   See, among others, ECtHR, *Maaouia v. France*, 5 October 2000 [GC], no. 39652/98, §§ 33–41. Exceptionally, the presumption of innocence in Article 6(2) ECHR is applicable where extradition proceedings are a 'direct consequence, and the concomitant, of the criminal investigation pending against the applicant in the receiving state'; see ECtHR, *Ismoilov v. Russia*, 24 April 2008, no. 2947/06, §§ 160–170.

154   ECtHR, *Baltaji v. Bulgaria*, 12 July 2011, no. 12919/04, § 55.

155   ECtHR, *Nolan and K. v. Russia*, 12 February 2009, no. 2512/04, § 112.

156   Art. 1(1) of Protocol No. 7 to the ECHR.

157   ECtHR, *Immanovic and Immanovic v. Sweden*, 13 November 2012, no. 57633/10 (decision).

158   'Explanatory Report on Protocol No. 7 to the ECHR,' ETS No. 117, §§ 9 and 10.

159   Art. 1(2) of Protocol No. 7 to the ECHR.

in accordance with proper legislation or/and the individual concerned was not given the chance to submit reasons against their expulsion.[160]

With regard to procedural guarantees in expulsion or extradition proceedings, the right to an effective remedy in Article 13 ECHR has been of greater importance.[161] This provision obliges states to provide an effective remedy in domestic law with respect to any 'arguable claim' under one of the rights guaranteed by the ECHR. It is applicable to asylum and extradition cases or any other removal proceedings that could be problematic under Article 3 or Article 8 ECHR. To be considered effective, a remedy must meet particular standards. Section 3.1.1 of chapter 4 will discuss these standards as they are required under the principle of non-refoulement inherent to Article 3 ECHR.[162]

According to the prohibition of discrimination in Article 14 ECHR, the rights and freedoms set forth in the ECHR shall be secured without discrimination on any grounds such as sex, race, colour, language, religion, political or other opinion, national or social origin, association with a national minority, property, birth or other status. Although the application of Article 14 ECHR does not necessarily presuppose a *breach* of other substantive provisions of the ECHR, it can only be applied if the issue falls within the ambit of one of the rights set forth in the Convention.[163] The prohibition on discrimination can be of relevance in the immigration context.[164] As a rule, differential treatment of individuals based on their nationality must be justified by 'very weighty reasons.'[165] However, the prohibition on discrimination in Article 14 ECHR must always be invoked in conjunction with a substantive provision of the Convention and the ECHR does not contain a right to nationality or

---

160 See, for example, ECtHR, *Lupsa v. Romania*, 8 June 2006, no. 10337/04, §§ 47–61; ECtHR, *Bolat v. Russia*, 5 October 2006, no. 14139/03, §§ 76–83; ECtHR, *Baltaji v. Bulgaria*, 12 July 2011, no. 12919/04, §§ 54–59; ECtHR, *Takush v. Greece*, 17 January 2012, no. 2853/09, §§ 52–63.

161 See Lambert 2007, p. 59, noting that Art. 13 ECHR has proven to be a key provision in terms of guaranteeing procedural rights to aliens.

162 For the minimum requirements of Art. 8 combined with Art. 13 ECHR in expulsion cases, see ECtHR, *De Souza Ribeiro v. France*, 13 December 2012 [GC], no. 22689/07.

163 Protocol No. 12 to the ECHR provides a *general ban* on discrimination. It entered into force on the 1 April 2005 and has been ratified by 19 states so far.

164 The Court has for instance held that legislation making it easier for a man than for a woman to obtain permission for the non-national spouse to settle in the UK constitutes discrimination in breach of Art. 14 in conjunction with Art. 8 ECHR; ECtHR, *Abdulaziz, Cabales and Balkandali v. UK*, 28 May 1985, nos. 9214/80, 9473/81 and 947481, §§ 74–83.

165 ECHR, *Poirrez v. France*, 30 September 2003, no. 40892/98, § 46.

citizenship.[166] In addition, contracting states have the right to control the entry, residence and expulsion of aliens.[167] Hence, a difference in treatment of nationals and non-nationals with regard to entry, expulsion, residence status or citizenship will usually either fall outside the scope of the Convention or will likely be considered as justified for the public interest.[168]

The only *explicit* prohibitions on removing individuals can be found in Protocol No. 4 to the ECHR.[169] This Protocol prohibits the expulsion of nationals (Article 3) and the collective expulsion of aliens (Article 4). By collective expulsion, the Court means any measure 'compelling aliens as a group to leave the country, except where such a measure is taken after and on the basis of a reasonable and objective examination of the particular cases of each individual alien of the group.'[170] The purpose of Article 4 of Protocol No. 4 is to prevent states from removing aliens without examining their personal circumstances and without enabling them to put forward their arguments against the measure.[171] However, the fact that a number of aliens are subject to similar decisions 'does not in itself lead to the conclusion that there is a collective expulsion if each person concerned has been given the opportunity to put arguments against his expulsion to the competent authorities on an individual basis.'[172] So far, there are only few individual complaints in which the Court found that Article 4 of Protocol No. 4 had been violated:[173] In *Conka and Others v. Belgium*, the Court held that an expulsion procedure against Slovakian nationals of Roma origin had not afforded 'sufficient guarantees demonstrating that the personal circumstances of each of those concerned had been genuinely and individually taken into account.'[174] The case *Hirsi Jamaa and Others v. Italy* concerned the return of Somalian and Eritrean migrants intercepted on the Mediterranean Sea by an Italian naval vessel.[175] The Italian authorities

---

166   ECtHR, *Genovese v. Malta*, 11 October 2011, no. 53124/09, § 30.

167   For example, ECtHR, *Mohammed v. Austria*, 6 June 2013, no. 2283/12, § 91.

168   See illustrative ECtHR, *Moustaquim v. Belgium*, 18 February 1991, no. 12313/86, §§ 48–49. See also § 19 of the 'Explanatory Report to Protocol No. 12 to the ECHR,' ETS No. 177. However, an arbitrary denial of citizenship might raise an issue under Art. 8 ECHR; ECtHR, *Genovese v. Malta*, 11 October 2011, no. 53124/09, §§ 29–49.

169   This Protocol entered into force on 2 May 1968 and has been ratified by 43 states.

170   ECtHR, *Hirsi Jamaa and Others v. Italy*, 23 February 2012 [GC], no. 27765/09, § 166.

171   ECtHR, *M.A. v. Cyprus*, 23 July 2013, no. 41872/10, § 245.

172   ECtHR, *Hirsi Jamaa and Others v. Italy*, 23 February 2012 [GC], no. 27765/09, § 184.

173   See also inter-state application ECtHR, *Giorgia v. Russia* (I), 3 July 2014 [GC], no. 13255/07; and ECtHR, *Khlaifia and Others v. Italy*, 1 September 2015, no. 16483/12 (not in force yet – referral to GC).

174   ECtHR, *Conka and Others v. Belgium*, 5 February 2002, no. 51564/99, § 63.

175   ECtHR, *Hirsi Jamaa and Others v. Italy*, 23 February 2012 [GC], no. 27765/09.

restricted themselves to embarking all the migrants onto military ships and disembarking them on Libyan soil. The personnel aboard the military ships were not trained to conduct individual interviews and were not assisted by interpreters or legal advisers. In the Court's view this was sufficient to rule out the existence of appropriate guarantees ensuring that the individual circumstances of each of the intercepted migrants were actually the subject of a detailed examination.[176] In *Sharifi and Others v. Italy and Greece*, the Afghan applicants were immediately deported back to Greece by Italian authorities without any form of individual examination, after they had arrived with an illegal vessel from Greece at the ports of Bari, Ancona and Venice.[177] The Court found that the Italian authorities' action had violated Article 4 of Protocol No. 4. It emphasized that no form of collective and indiscriminate returns or other violations of the Convention could be justified by reference to the EU cooperation through the Dublin system[178] or to problems related with the handling of migration flows (*'flux migratoires'*) or the reception of asylum seekers.[179]

3   The United Nations Convention against Torture (CAT)

3.1   *Introduction to the Convention System*
3.1.1   The CAT
The United Nations Convention against Torture (CAT) was adopted by the United Nations General Assembly in resolution 39/46 of 10 December 1984 and entered into force on 26 June 1987. At this time, torture was already addressed by important international human rights treaties such as the 1966 United Nations International Covenant on Civil and Political Rights. The establishment of the CAT was hence not motivated by the objective to enshrine another prohibition on torture on a universal level but, as stated in the CAT's preamble, 'to make more effective the struggle against torture and other cruel, inhuman or degrading treatment or punishment throughout the world.' In January 2016 there were 158 state parties to the CAT.[180]

Article 1 CAT constitutes the first definition of torture in an international treaty. As will be discussed in detail in chapter 3, this definition contains four main elements that characterize torture: an act may only be classified as

---

176   *Ibid.*, §§ 166–186 and ECtHR, *M.A. v. Cyprus*, 23 July 2013, no. 41872/10, § 251.

177   ECtHR, *Sharifi and Others v. Italy and Greece*, 21 October 2014, no. 16643/09.

178   On this topic under Art. 3 ECHR see Chapter 4 Section 3.4.3.a.

179   ECtHR, *Sharifi and Others v. Italy and Greece*, §§ 223 and 224.

180   See the UN Treaty Collection <https://treaties.un.org>.

torture if it (1) causes *severe pain or suffering*, (2) is inflicted *intentionally*, (3) for *certain purposes* such as obtaining information, a confession, or punishing, intimidating or coercing the individual concerned, and (4) is conducted by or at the instigation of or with the consent or acquiescence of a *public official*. According to the definiton, 'lawful sanctions' are excluded from acts of torture.[181]

Articles 2 to 16 CAT contain the substantial obligations that the contracting states have. According to Article 2 CAT, 'each State Party shall take effective legislative, administrative, judicial or other measures to prevent acts of torture in any territory under its jurisdiction.' Paragraph 2 of this provision enshrines the absolute character of the prohibition on torture. It says that 'no exceptional circumstances whatsoever, whether a state of war or a threat of war, internal political instability or any other public emergency, may be invoked as a justification of torture.' This includes threats of terrorism as well as armed conflicts.[182] In 2008, the Committee released a General Comment No. 2 on Article 2 CAT, which gives important explanations to this provision and the Committee's general understanding of the state's obligation to prevent torture and other inhuman treatment or punishment under the CAT.[183]

Article 3 CAT enshrines the principle of non-refoulement. It explicitly states that no 'State Party shall expel, return (*"refouler"*) or extradite a person to another State where there are substantial grounds for believing that he would be in danger of being subjected to torture.' This provision will be analysed in detail.

According to Article 4 CAT, each state shall ensure 'that all acts of torture are offences under its criminal law' and 'punishable by appropriate penalties which take into account their grave nature.' According to Articles 5 to 7 CAT, state parties must establish a system of universal jurisdiction in order to make 'safe-havens' for torturers impossible.[184] According to Article 10 CAT, state parties shall ensure that any law enforcement personnel are educated about the prohibition on torture. Article 11 CAT obliges member states to systematically review their interrogation rules or methods of treatment of persons in detention, in order to prevent any cases of torture. According to Article 12 CAT,

---

181   However, it is not clear whether this exclusion has an impact; see on this the Sections 3.2.3
        and 4.2.2 in Chapter 3.

182   ComAT, General Comment No. 2 on Art. 2 (2008).

183   See ComAT, General Comment No. 2 on Art. 2 (2008).

184   Burger & Danelius 1988, p. 3. Art. 8 CAT contains specific provisions with regard to extraditions of the perpetrators of torture. According to Art. 9 CAT, state parties shall afford one another assistance in connection with criminal proceedings brought with respect to the offences of torture.

authorities have the obligation to proceed to an investigation *ex officio*, wherever there are reasonable grounds to believe that acts of torture or ill treatment have been committed under their jurisdiction. According to Article 13 CAT, any individual who alleges that he has been subjected to torture has the right to have his case promptly and impartially examined by the authorities. According to Article 14 CAT, state parties shall ensure that, under their legal system, victims of torture obtain redress and have an enforceable right to adequate compensation.

Article 15 CAT prohibits the use of evidence obtained through torture in any proceedings. This provision also applies to extradition proceedings.[185] The case *Ktiti v. France*[186] concerned the extradition of a French national from Morocco to Algeria. He claimed that the arrest warrants issued by the Algerian judiciary and his sentencing *in absentia* to life imprisonment there were based on statements made under torture. The Committee found that the applicant's extradition would violate Article 3 CAT. In addition, by not verifying the complainant's allegation with regard to the evidentiary basis of the Algerian extradition request, the authorities had violated Article 15 CAT. The Committee held that the questions under Articles 3 and 15 CAT were closely linked.[187]

Article 16 CAT obligates each state party to prevent 'other cruel, inhuman or degrading treatment or punishment' in any territory under its jurisdiction. However, there is no prohibition on refoulement based on this provision. The difference between torture and inhuman treatment and the fact that the prohibition on refoulement under the CAT does *not* in principle encompass inhuman treatment will be discussed in detail in chapter 3. It will further be explained that even though Article 16 CAT does not contain a prohibition on refoulement, it can be of relevance in the context of immigration. This might be the case if immigrants are detained in inhuman conditions[188] or if the act of the forced removal *itself* is executed in an inhuman manner.[189]

---

185   ComAT, *P.E. v. France*, 21 November 2002, no. 193/2001, § 6.3; ComAT, *G.K. v. Switzerland*, 7 May 2003, no. 219/2002, § 6.10.

186   ComAT, *Ktiti v. Morocco*, 26 May 2011, no. 419/2010, § 8.8.

187   See the comparable case ECtHR, *Abu Qatada v. UK*, 17 January 2012, no. 8139/09, discussed in Section 2.2.3 of this chapter. In this case, the Court found that the applicant's deportation would amount to a flagrant breach of the applicant's right to a fair trial in Art. 6 ECHR, because he risked being sentenced in a trial based on evidence obtained by the torture of his co-defendants. However, relying on assurances provided by the receiving state Jordan, the Court rejected the applicant's claim under Art. 3 ECHR.

188   See Chapter 3 Section 3.2.2.

189   See Chapter 3 Section 3.2.5.

The second part of the CAT (Articles 17–24) provides for different control mechanisms by which the Committee against Torture supervises the member states' implementation of the substantive obligations just described. The next section will introduce the Committee against Torture and its supervisory powers.

It should be added that the UN General Assembly adopted an Optional Protocol to the CAT on 18 December 2002, by which it established a system of regular visits undertaken by international and national bodies to places where people are deprived of their liberty in order to *prevent* torture and other inhuman treatment or punishment. The Optional Protocol was adopted on 18 December 2002 and entered into force on 22 June 2006.[190]

3.1.2 The Committee against Torture ('the Committee') and Its Supervisory Functions

First of all, it is up to the national authorities and tribunals of states having ratified the CAT to ensure its enforcement. The Committee against Torture's function to ensure that the CAT is implemented and observed is subsidiary.

The Committee's supervisory functions are mainly modelled on those of the UN Human Rights Committee.[191] Articles 19 to 22 CAT provide four different enforcement mechanisms: (1) a state reporting system; (2) the possibility of investigatory procedures; (3) the assessment of inter-state complaints; and (4) the assessment of individual complaints. The latter will be looked at in more detail in section 3.1.3 of this chapter.

(1) In common with all principal UN human rights conventions, the CAT provides for a state reporting system. According to Article 19 CAT, state parties to the CAT are obliged to submit, every four years, reports on the measures they have taken to give effect to their undertakings under the CAT. The Committee analyses the reports and responds to them by the issue and publication of 'Concluding Observations.' Those Observations consist of a section in which the Committee notes the positive aspects of the state's observance of the obligations under the CAT and another with subjects of concern and related recommendations. The state reporting procedure is considered the key supervisory mechanism exercised by the Committee.[192] Being mandatory for all state parties to the CAT, it represents the most extensive output of the Committee and

---

190   By the time this book was completed, the Protocol had been ratified by 70 states.
191   Burger & Danelius 1988, p. 81.
192   Burns 2001, p. 404.

demands the great majority of its work time.[193] The Committee has provided important guidelines on how the principle of non-refoulement in Article 3 CAT should be implemented by the national authorities in Concluding Observations.[194] However, the Committee's observations within the state reporting procedure focus on general state practices and legislation, rather than the state's responsibilities in individual cases.

(2) Based on Article 20 CAT, the Committee may start *ex officio* inquiries in the event of well-founded indications that torture is systematically practised by a state party to CAT. Such inquiries can include fact-finding missions in the country concerned.[195]

(3) Under Article 21 CAT, the Committee may be responsible for examining inter-state complaints. According to this provision, a state party may claim before the Committee that another state party is not fulfilling its obligations under the CAT. As with similar provisions under other international human rights conventions, this has shown to be an instrument that states are extremely reluctant to use. No such complaint has been lodged to date.

Article 17 and 18 CAT set out the requirements for the composition and functioning of the Committee. Pursuant to Article 17(1) CAT, the Committee shall consist of 10 'experts of high moral standing and recognized competence in the field of human rights.' All members must be nationals of a state party to the CAT and there should be an equitable geographical distribution within the Committee.[196] Corresponding to an informal agreement, the Committee usually has two members from the African Continent, two from Latin America, one from Asia, one or two from Eastern Europe, two or three from Western Europe and one from North America or Canada.[197] The members shall serve in their personal capacity, independent of the interests of their state of origin.[198] They may neither seek nor accept instructions from anyone concerning the performance of their duties.[199] According to Article 17(1) CAT, consideration shall be given 'to the usefulness of the participation of some persons having

---

193   Information received from OHCHR, 3 October 2013.

194   See on this Nowak & McArthur 2008, pp. 147–156. As has been mentioned, the 'Concluding Observations' will occasionally be referred to in this study.

195   See on this Nowak & McArthur 2008, pp. 660–700. The supervision through *ex officio* inquiries had no precedent in the other UN human rights treaties.

196   Art. 17(1) CAT.

197   See on this also Nowak & McArthur 2008, pp. 591 to 592 (§ 29).

198   Art. 17(1) CAT.

199   Rule 15(1) ComAT (CAT/C/3/Rev.6).

legal experience.' In practice, the majority of the Committee members have legal professional backgrounds, be it as professors, lawyers, prosecutors or civil servants. However, there are also doctors, psychologists and journalists.[200]

The 10 members of the Committee are nominated by the state parties and elected at biennial meetings of the state parties.[201] According to Article 17(5) CAT, members shall be elected for a term of four years. They can, however, be re-elected. The Committee members elect the chairperson.[202] So far, the chairperson always had a legal background. Article 18(2) CAT empowers the Committee against Torture to adopt its own Rules of Procedure. These Rules give more details about the Committee against Torture, its monitoring functions and the respective procedures.[203]

The Committee is not a permanent organ: the members meet usually twice a year for sessions of three weeks. The sessions are held at the UN Office in Geneva.[204] One session is in April/May and the other in November. Because of 'serious difficulties' for the Committee due to the brevity of the meeting time, it has been enabled by the UN General Assembly to hold longer and more sessions per year.[205] However, the Committee is still overburdened.[206]

The Committee has stated itself that it 'is not an appellate, a quasi-judicial or an administrative body, but rather a monitoring body created by the State parties themselves with declaratory powers only.'[207] Its recommendations or decisions on individual cases are not legally binding for the state concerned.[208] The Committee has to rely on the political and moral force of its declarations for the enforcement of them.[209]

---

200 See also Nowak & McArthur 2008, p. 597 (§ 46), who note that the diverse composition 'better corresponds to the multi-disciplinary task of combating and preventing torture.'

201 Art. 17(3) CAT.

202 Rule 16 ComAT (CAT/C/3/Rev.6). For the Chairperson's powers see further Rule 37.

203 The most recent version of the Committee's Rules of Procedure dates from 13 August 2013; see UN doc. ComAT, CAT/C/3/Rev.6.

204 Rule 4 ComAT (CAT/C/3/Rev.6).

205 See ComAT, 'Annual Report 2011/2012,' p. 6 (A/67/44); ComAT, 'Annual Report 2012/2013,' p. 5 (A/68/44); ComAT, 'Annual Report 2014/2015,' p. 22 (A/70/44); in 2015 and 2016, there are *three* regular sessions.

206 See on this also the next Section 3.1.3 and Chapter 5 Section 3.2.

207 ComAT, General Comment No. 1 on Art. 3 CAT (1997), § 9.

208 On the legal status of the decisions and their implementation see Chapter 2 Section 2.3.

209 Burns 2001, p. 411; Goodwin-Gill & McAdam 2007, p. 300.

3.1.3 The Optional Individual Complaint Mechanism

There are no mandatory individual complaint mechanisms under the UN human rights treaties. They are all optional. According to Article 22(1) CAT, 'a State Party to this Convention may at any time declare under this article that it recognizes the competence of the Committee to receive and consider communications from or on behalf of individuals subject to its jurisdiction who claim to be victims of a violation by a State Party of the provisions of the Convention.'[210] The paragraph further states that 'no communication shall be received by the Committee if it concerns a State Party which has not made such a declaration.' States are hence free to ratify the CAT without accepting the Committee's competence to assess individual complaints under Article 22 CAT.[211]

There are 66 state parties to the CAT that have declared that they recognize the competence of the Committee to receive and consider complaints under Article 22 CAT.[212] With the exception of the United Kingdom, all Western European states have accepted the individual complaints procedure. Of the 47 states subordinated to the jurisdiction of the European Court of Human Rights, only the following 9 have not accepted the Committee's competence to assess individual complaints: Albania, Armenia, Estonia, Latvia, Lithuania, the Former Yugoslav Republic of Macedonia, Romania, San Marino and the United Kingdom. After the European states, it is mostly Latin American states that have accepted the individual complaint mechanism under Article 22 CAT. Canada and Australia have also made the declaration. A state party can

---

210 According to Art. 22(8) CAT, five declarations are needed for the complaint procedure to come into force. Since there were five such declarations within the first 20 states which ratified the CAT, the complaint mechanism came into force on the same date as the CAT itself on 26 June 1987; Nowak & McArthur 2008, p. 779 (§ 160).

211 This is in contrast to the complaints mechanism before the Court, which is mandatory for states that have ratified the ECHR.

212 The following state parties to the CAT have made the declaration: Algeria, Andorra, Argentina, Australia, Austria, Azerbaijan, Belgium, Bolivia, Bosnia and Herzegovina, Brazil, Bulgaria, Burundi, Cameroon, Canada, Chile, Costa Rica, Croatia, Cyprus, Czech Republic, Denmark, Ecuador, Finland, France, Georgia, Germany, Ghana, Greece, Guatemala, Guinea-Bissau, Hungary, Iceland, Ireland, Italy, Kazakhstan, Liechtenstein, Luxembourg, Malta, Mexico, Monaco, Montenegro, Morocco, Netherlands, New Zealand, Norway, Paraguay, Peru, Seychelles, Poland, Portugal, Republic of Korea, Republic of Moldova, Russian Federation, Senegal, Serbia, Slovakia, Slovenia, South Africa, Spain, Sweden, Switzerland, Togo, Tunisia, Turkey, Ukraine, Uruguay and Venezuela; see ComAT, 'Annual Report 2013/2014,' annex III (A/69/44).

withdraw the declaration at any time by notification to the Secretary-General.[213] No state has done this so far.

The individual complaints submitted under Article 22 CAT are assessed in closed meetings during the Committee's sessions in Geneva.[214] According to Article 18(2)a CAT, six members must be present so that the Committee is able to adopt decisions. The decisions of the Committee are taken by majority vote of the members present, even though the Committee should first try to reach decisions by consensus before voting,[215] which is usually the case in practice.[216] A Committee member shall not take part in the examination of an individual complaint if he has a personal interest or any implication in the case, or if he is either a national or is employed by the state party concerned.[217]

The life of complaints submitted in Geneva will be discussed in more detail in chapter 2 section 2.1.1. It has been mentioned that the Committee is over-burdened. With regard to individual complaints this is very apparent. In 2012, the Committee's chairperson addressed the issue at the UN General Assembly and held that the current backlog of cases pending before the Committee 'severely weakens the system as justice cannot be provided to States and individuals within a reasonable time, thus diminishing the credibility of a system that was created by the Member States of the UN.'[218] In October 2015, there was a backlog of 160 complaints pending before the Committee.[219]

3.2   *The Principle of Non-refoulement under the CAT*

3.2.1   The Principle of Non-refoulement in Article 3 CAT

Article 3 CAT explicitly codifies the principle of non-refoulement. It stipulates:

1.   No State Party shall expel, return (*'refouler'*) or extradite a person to another State where there are substantial grounds for believing that he would be in danger of being subjected to torture.

---

213   Art. 22(8) CAT.

214   Art. 22(6) CAT and Rule 107(1) ComAT (CAT/C/3/Rev.6).

215   Art. 18(2)(b) CAT and Rule 50 ComAT (CAT/C/3/Rev.6).

216   Information obtained by the OHCHR, 3 October 2013.

217   Rule 109 ComAT (CAT/C/3/Rev.6).

218   Statement by Claudio Grossman, 67th session of the General Assembly, New York, 23 October 2012. See on this also Chapter 5 Section 3.2.

219   Statement of the Chairperson of the Committee Against Torture to the 70th session of the General Assembly, New York, 20 October 2015, accessible on the Committee's website under <http://www.ohchr.org/EN/NewsEvents/Pages/DisplayNews.aspx?NewsID =16624& LangID=E> [15.2.2016].

2.   For the purpose of determining whether there are such grounds, the
      competent authorities shall take into account all relevant considerations
      including, where applicable, the existence in the State concerned of a
      consistent pattern of gross, flagrant or mass violations of human rights.

The CAT is the first treaty 'to formulate an explicit ban on refoulement in
the event of a threat of torture.'[220] The drafters of Article 3 CAT were influenced by the former European Commission of Human Rights' case law under
Article 3 ECHR and the prohibition on refoulement in Article 33 of the 1951
Refugee Convention.[221] The prohibition on refoulement under 3 CAT 'covers
all forms of obligatory departure of a human being (aliens as well as citizens)
from one jurisdiction to another.'[222] This includes any kind of expulsion and
extradition. The term *return* ('*refouler*'), which is taken from the Refugee Convention, was introduced to make clear that persons who have entered a state
illegally or are intercepted at the border are protected as well.[223]

According to the second paragraph of Article 3 CAT, state authorities must
take into account whether there is a consistent pattern of gross, flagrant or
mass violation of human rights in the receiving state when assessing whether
there is a risk of torture in the sense of the first paragraph or not. During the
drafting process, the Soviet delegation proposed the listing of specific situations where the risk of torture would be particularly high, such as, *inter alia*,
apartheid, racial discrimination, genocide or the occupation of foreign territory. However, the working group eventually agreed not to include these specific
situations and to request the states generally to take into account consistent
patterns of violation of human rights.[224]

The principle of non-refoulement in Article 3 CAT is principally limited to
the protection against acts of torture in the sense of Article 1 CAT.[225] It does
not extend to inhuman or degrading treatment or punishment in the sense of
Article 16 CAT. This was decided in order to achieve consensus.[226] During the

---

220   Ingelse 2001, p. 291.
221   Burger and Danelius 1988, pp. 125–162. On the *traveaux préparatoires* on Art. 3 CAT see,
      detailed, Nowak & McArthur 2008, pp. 130–146.
222   Nowak 2008, p. 113.
223   Goodwin-Gill & McAdam 2007, p. 201; Nowak & McArthur 2008, pp. 195–196 (§§ 172 and
      173); Weissbrodt & Hörtreiter 1999, p. 7.
224   Suntinger, p. 209.
225   See on this and the difficulty to separate torture from inhuman treatment, particularly in
      refoulement cases, Sections 3.1, 3.2 and 4.2.1 of Chapter 3.
226   Nowak & McArthur 2008, p. 539 (§ 2). The original draft, which had included inhuman
      and degrading treatment, was changed; Burgers and Danelius 1988, pp. 49, 74 and 150.

drafting of the CAT, many representatives were of the opinion that the concept of inhuman treatment was too vague and could not be defined in terms favourable to all legal systems worldwide.[227] It was hence decided that not all obligations under the CAT should refer to inhuman or degrading treatment.[228]

3.2.2   The Committee's Case Law on Non-refoulement
In May 2015, after 54th session, the Committee had registered 679 complaints concerning 36 state parties since 1989.[229] At this moment, it had adopted a final *decision on the merits* on 265 complaints and found violations of the Convention in 101 of them. Of the registered complaints 198 had been discontinued and 68 had been declared inadmissible.[230]

By the end of August 2015, the Committee had published 281 decisions on complaints in which individuals alleged that their deportation would violate the principle of non-refoulement inherent to Article 3 CAT (decisions on inadmissibility included).[231] A violation of this provision was found in 67 of these cases.[232] This makes for a success rate of more than 20 per cent for refoulement complaints assessed by the Committee.[233] Most refoulement complaints assessed by the Committee concerned expulsions.[234]

---

227   Boulesbaa 1990, pp. 296–297.

228   Burger & Danelius 1988, pp. 47 and 70–71; Ingelse 2001, p. 77–78.

229   ComAT, 'Annual Report 2014/2015,' p. 19 (A/70/44).

230   *Ibid.* A total of 148 complaints were pending.

231   Counted by the author on the basis of the information on individual complaints as published in the Committee's annual reports and the UN database (today <http://juris .ohchr.org>).

232   See the table of 'non-refoulement cases assessed on the merits' (XXXIX).

233   According to information obtained by the OHCHR on 3 October 2013, it is rare for complaints concerning the principle of non-refoulement not to be registered. On the life of a complaint in Geneva see Chapter 2 Section 2.1.2.

234   The following cases concern extraditions: ComAT, *Arana v. France*, 9 November 1999, no. 63/1997; ComAT, *Chipana v. Venezuela*, 10 November 1998, no. 110/1998; ComAT, *P.E. v. France*, 21 November 2002, no. 193/2001; ComAT, *G.K. v. Switzerland*, 7 May 2003, no. 219/2002; ComAT, *Diaz v. France*, 3 May 2005, no. 194/2001; ComAT, *Pelit v. Azerbaijan*, 1 May 2007, no. 281/2005; ComAT, *L.J.R. v. Australia*, 10 November 2008, no. 316/2007; ComAT, *Ktiti v. Morocco*, 26 May 2011, no. 419/2010; ComAT, *Boily v. Canada*, 14 November 2011, no. 327/2007; ComAT, *Kalinichenko v. Morocco*, 25 November 2011, no. 428/2010; ComAT, *Abdussamatov and 28 Others v. Kazakhstan*, 1 June 2012, no. 444/2010; ComAT, *S.A.C. v. Monaco,* 13 November 2012, no. 346/2008; ComAT, *Abichou v. Germany*, 21 May 2013, no. 430/2010; ComAT, *Nasirov v. Kazakhstan,* 14 May 2014, no. 475/2011; ComAT, *R.A.Y. v. Morocco*, 16 May 2014, no. 525/2012; ComAT, *Tursunov v. Kazakhstan*, 8 May 2015, no. 538/2013; ComAT, *X. v. Kazakhstan*, 3 August 2015, no. 554/2013.

The first decision on refoulement was adopted in 1994 in *Mutombo v. Switzerland*.[235] In this case, the Committee found that Article 3 CAT would be violated if the complainant were deported to the former Zaire. From then on, the complaints submitted concerning refoulement rose remarkably. The overwhelming majority of the complaints handled by the Committee concern allegations of a violation of the principle of non-refoulement in Article 3 CAT (more than 80 per cent of all cases concluded by a decision) and not allegations of acts of torture that would have occurred within the territory of the respondent state.

Nowak and McArthur explain this by referring to the fact that the great majority of states that have accepted the competence of the Committee to assess individual complaints are European or other industrialized countries in which torture is not as common as in other states. They further observed that in states with systematic practices of torture, the individuals concerned often lack effective access to international institutions or are afraid to submit complaints. However, they also point to the increasingly restrictive asylum and immigration laws in Europe and other states as a reason for the numerous complaints.[236]

It can further be observed that out of all the states that have made a declaration under Article 22 CAT, only a few are actually confronted with individual complaints. In fact, at August 2015, the states against which most of the complaints had been submitted were Switzerland (168 registered complaints) followed by Sweden (135 registered complaints) and Canada (124 registered complaints).[237] Those are also the states against which most violations of the principle of non-refoulement have been found (Sweden: 20 violations; Switzerland: 16 violations; Canada: 8 violations).[238] Other states that have been confronted with five or more complaints concerning the principle of non-refoulement are Australia, Denmark, France, the Netherlands and Norway.[239] This concentration on particular countries is mostly explained by the high level of awareness and/or means and capacity among legal professionals and NGOs in those states.[240] Burns observes that states that have developed a legal system 'that can be characterized as human rights sensitive' and that have

---

235   ComAT, *Mutombo v. Switzerland*, 27 April 1994, no. 13/1993.

236   Nowak & McArthur 2008, pp. 127–128 (§ 1) and 723 (§. 5).

237   See statistical survey 'Status of the Cases Dealt with under Art. 22 CAT,' 15 August 2015, accessible on the Committee's website [15.2.2016] under <http://www.ohchr.org/en/hrbodies/cat/pages/catindex.aspx>.

238   *Ibid.*

239   *Ibid.*

240   Nowak & McArthur 2008, pp. 127–128 (§ 1); Rieter 2010, p. 266.

demonstrated 'the highest commitment to the objects and ideals' of the CAT have been the most concerned with Article 3 CAT complaints.[241]

Originally, the complaints mechanism was established to make the world-wide struggle against torture more effective. Through the assessment of a large number of individual complaints concerning an alleged risk of torture in case of deportation from Western states, the Committee has unwittingly become an international authority specialising in the principle of non-refoulement.[242] Nowak and McArthur note that this development has led to a certain criticism that the Committee is acting as a 'kind of fourth instance in asylum proceedings in the North rather than concentrating its efforts on denouncing torture in those States where it actually is practised.'[243] It is clear that the drafters of the CAT, and Article 22 CAT in particular, did not actually intend to create an international complaints mechanism specialising in issues under Article 3 CAT.

4   The Principle of Non-refoulement in the Refugee Convention

The Convention relating to the Status of Refugees was adopted on 25 July 1951 and entered into force on 22 April 1954.[244] The principle of non-refoulement is the core provision of the Refugee Convention. It is anchored in Article 33, which states the following:

1.   No Contracting State shall expel or return (*'refouler'*) a refugee in any manner whatsoever to the frontiers of territories where his life or freedom would be threatened on account of his race, religion, nationality, membership of a particular social group or political opinion.
2.   The benefit of the present provision may not, however, be claimed by a refugee whom there are reasonable grounds for regarding as a danger to the security of the country in which he is, or who, having been convicted by a final judgment of a particularly serious crime, constitutes a danger to the community of that country.

---

241   Burns 2001, p. 407 and fn. 30, referring to Australia, Canada, France, Netherlands, Sweden and Switzerland.
242   Goodwin-Gill & McAdam 2007, p. 301.
243   Nowak & McArthur 2008, pp. 127–128 (§ 1).
244   Read together with the additional protocol adopted on 31 January 1967, which entered into force on 4 October 1967. The additional protocol extends the Refugee Convention's temporal and geographical application. By the time this research was completed the Refugee Convention had been ratified by 145 states.

In contrast to the ECHR and the CAT, this prohibition of refoulement does not have its source in the prohibition of torture or inhuman treatment, but in the status of an individual as a refugee as defined in Article 1A(2) of the Refugee Convention. According to this provision, a refugee is a person who 'owing to well-founded fear of being persecuted for reasons of race, religion, nationality, membership of a particular social group or political opinion, is outside the country of his nationality and is unable or, owing to such fear, is unwilling to avail himself of the protection of that country.'[245] The Refugee Convention protects against persecution aimed at the individual's life or freedom on account of one of the five grounds enumerated in Article 1: race, religion, nationality, membership of a particular social group or political opinion. Under the ECHR and the CAT, the reason for which a person might be threatened with torture or inhuman treatment is immaterial.

According to the UNHCR *Handbook on Procedures and Criteria for Determining Refugee Status* (hereinafter the UNHCR *Handbook*), there is no universally accepted definition of *persecution*, and various attempts to formulate such a definition have met with little success.[246] According to Article 33 of the Refugee Convention, a threat to life or freedom on account of the five enumerated grounds is persecution. According to the UNHCR Handbook, 'other serious violations of human rights – for the same reasons – would also constitute persecution.'[247] Whether other prejudicial actions or threats would amount to persecution will depend on the circumstances of each case, including the subjective character of the fear of persecution of the person concerned.[248] The protection under the Refugee Convention can encompass both public and private forms of persecution.[249] According to the UNHCR *Handbook*, where serious discriminatory or other offensive acts are committed by the local populace, they can be considered persecution if they are knowingly tolerated by the authorities, or if the authorities refuse, or prove unable, to offer effective protection.[250]

Persecution must be distinguished from punishment for a common law offence. Persons fleeing from prosecution or punishment for such an offence are

---

245   Art. 1A(2) further refers to a person who, 'not having a nationality and being outside the country of his former habitual residence as a result of such events, is unable or, owing to such fear, is unwilling to return to it.'

246   UNHCR *Handbook* 1992, § 51.

247   *Ibid.*, § 51.

248   *Ibid.*, § 52.

249   McAdam 2007, p. 114.

250   UNHCR *Handbook*, 1992, § 65.

not normally refugees.[251] However, a person guilty of a common law offence may be liable to excessive punishment, which may amount to persecution. In addition, there may be cases in which a person, besides fearing prosecution or punishment for a common law crime, may also have 'well founded fear of persecution.'[252] It is, however, necessary to consider in such cases that persons who are serious criminals are excluded from refugee status. According to Article 1F, the provisions of the Refugee Convention *shall not apply* to any person with respect to whom there are serious reasons for considering that:

(a)   he has committed a crime against peace, a war crime, or a crime against humanity, as defined in the international instruments drawn up to make provision in respect of such crimes;
(b)   he has committed a serious non-political crime outside the country of refuge prior to his admission to that country as a refugee;
(c)   he has been guilty of acts contrary to the purposes and principles of the United Nations.

In addition, according to Article 33(2) Refugee Convention, refugees are excluded from the protection against refoulement 'if there are reasonable grounds for regarding them as a danger to the security of the country in which they are, or who, having been convicted by a final judgment of a particularly serious crime, constitute a danger to the community of that country.' However, these exceptions to the protection offered under the Refugee Convention must be applied restrictively.[253] The exclusion of certain individuals from the protection against refoulement under the Refugee Convention is the main difference in the protection against refoulement offered by the ECHR, the CAT and the ICCPR.[254] The principle of non-refoulement under these three treaties is absolute: they protect each and every human being from refoulement irrespective of the circumstances and the conduct of the individual, however undesirable or dangerous it might be and no matter what state interests are involved in a deportation.[255] It should further be noted that according to the definition in Article 1A(2) of the Refugee Convention, the protection against refoulement is limited to individuals who are outside their country of

---

251   *Ibid.*, § 56.
252   *Ibid.*, §§ 57 and 58.
253   Lauterpacht & Bethlehem 2003, p. 179; Wouters 2009, p. 183.
254   Wouters 2009, pp. 563–564.
255   On this absolute protection under the ECHR and the CAT see the Sections 2.4, 3.4 and 4.4 of Chapter 3.

nationality or habitual residence. There is no such limitation under Article 3 ECHR and Article 3 CAT.[256]

While the non-refoulement obligations under the ECHR and the CAT are broader with respect to individuals with a certain criminal background or those considered to pose a threat to the community of the host state, it should be noted that the protection against refoulement under the Refugee Convention may be broader in other respects. For example, there are forms of persecution recognised by the Refugee Convention that do not necessarily amount to torture or inhuman or degrading treatment in the sense of the ECHR or the CAT. Examples are detention for political reasons[257] or the cumulative violation of different human rights that does not amount to torture or other inhuman or degrading treatment.[258] Individuals threatened with such harms may be protected against refoulement under the Refugee Convention, but not necessarily under the ECHR or the CAT. The principle of non-refoulement under the Refugee Convention is thus both broader and narrower than the protection offered under the ECHR or the CAT.[259]

However, it is clear that there is considerable overlap between the protection against refoulement offered under the Refugee Convention and that afforded by the ECHR, the CAT and the ICCPR.[260] Torture and other inhuman treatment will usually qualify as persecution in the sense of the Refugee Convention, and persecution will often imply a risk of torture or other ill treatment. Lauterpacht and Bethlehem note that 'in practice the distinction is likely to be more apparent than real given the potential overlap of the two types of risk.'[261] Goodwin-Gill and McAdam note that protection, as guaranteed by Article 3 CAT, may provide relief for those unable to demonstrate a link between the feared ill treatment and one of the five Refugee Convention grounds, those who are excluded from the Refugee Convention's protection and finally those who have been overlooked as refugees due to narrow interpretations of the Refugee Convention at the domestic level.[262]

In that context, it must be noted that the Refugee Convention does not provide for an international judicial or quasi-judicial body that supervises

---

256 On this Wouters 2009, pp. 531–533.

257 Kälin 1982, p. 2000; Wouters 2009, p. 242, citing the example of a detention lasting several months for a political and nonviolent protest.

258 Chetail 2004, pp. 180–181; Wouters 2009, p. 179.

259 Nowak & McArthur 2008, p. 195 (§ 171); Trechsel 1996, p. 92.

260 See Chetail 2006, p. 102; Nowak & McArthur 2008, pp. 209 (§ 199) and 212 (§ 204). With regard to the ECHR and CAT, see Chapter 4 Sections 3.3.1.c, 3.3.2.c and 3.3.3.c.

261 Lauterpacht & Bethlehem 2003, p. 160.

262 Goodwin-Gill & McAdam 2007, p. 303; McAdam 2007, pp. 118 and 134.

its implementation. The United Nations High Commissioner for Refugees (UNHCR) has a supervisory function when it comes to the interpretation and application of the Refugee Convention at the national level.[263] However, it is not provided with formal tools or enforcement mechanisms. In Europe, its role is mainly advisory and consultative.[264] Since domestic actors are responsible for the implementation of the Refugee Convention and discretion is given to the state parties, the degree of protection varies a great deal depending on political will.[265] The understanding of the concept of persecution may vary considerably between states.[266] As Wouters states, the international meaning of the prohibition on refoulement contained in the Refugee Convention is far more difficult to determine than for instance under the ECHR and the CAT.[267]

The Refugee Convention does not 'contain an obligation to be granted residence permit or legal status in any form, but it does question the long-term responsibility of States to find a durable solution to the situation of refugees, including the responsibility to regularise their presence in the host State.'[268] The applicability of the principle of non-refoulement under the Refugee Convention leads ineluctably to the attribution of the legal status as a recognized refugee to the individual concerned with the rights attributed to that status.[269] In contrast, a violation of the principle of non-refoulement under the ECHR and the CAT does not imply the right to any legal status whatsoever for the individual concerned. It only infers an obligation on the state concerned not to deport the individual in question.[270]

5   The Principle of Non-refoulement in the ICCPR

The International Covenant on Civil and Political Rights (ICCPR) was adopted on 16 December 1966 and entered into force on 23 March 1976.[271] The United

---

263   According to Art. 35 of the Refugee Convention, state parties have to cooperate with the UNHCR to facilitate its duty of supervising such application.

264   The office of the UNHCR acts through a wide range of advocacy activities including the publication of various documents to convince state parties of its views on interpretation; on the supervisory functions of the UNHCR see Wouters 2009, pp. 39–42.

265   Weissbrodt & Hörtreiter 1999, p. 27.

266   Ibid., p. 21. See on this also Pirjola 2007, pp. 645–648.

267   Wouters 2009, p. 528.

268   Ibid., p. 184.

269   Chetail 2006, p. 104. On the rights attributed to the refugee status, see Kälin 2013, p. 601 (§ 1496), referring to the Articles 13 and 14, 17 to 24 and 28 Refugee Convention.

270   See on this Chapter 2 Sections 1.3.2 and 2.3.2.

271   By the time this research had been completed, the ICCPR had been ratified by 168 states.

Nations Human Rights Committee, a body of 18 independent experts appointed by the UN General Assembly, supervises its enforcement.

The ICCPR provides a similar supervisory mechanism before the Human Rights Committee to the one the CAT provides with the Committee against Torture. While the submission of periodic country reports is mandatory under Article 40 ICCPR, the Human Rights Committee may only assess individual complaints where the state against which the individual wishes to claim has ratified the First Optional Protocol to the ICCPR.[272] The procedure under this Optional Protocol is similar to that under the CAT. Article 22 CAT was in fact modelled on the provisions of the First Optional Protocol to the ICCPR.[273] Like the decisions of the Committee against Torture, the Human Rights Committee's views on individual complaints are not legally binding.[274]

As the name of the Convention suggests, the ICCPR contains a range of civil and political rights.[275] As under the ECHR, the principle of non-refoulement is not explicitly guaranteed in the ICCPR. It is inherent to the prohibition against torture or cruel, inhuman or degrading treatment or punishment in Article 7 ICCPR.[276] The right to life in Article 6 ICCPR also contains a prohibition on refoulement. State parties have the obligation

> ... not to extradite, deport, expel or otherwise remove a person from their territory where there are substantial grounds for believing that there is a real risk of irreparable harm, such as that contemplated by articles 6 and 7 of the Covenant, either in the country to which removal is to be effected or in any country to which the person may subsequently be removed.[277]

The Human Rights Committee has further indicated that other provisions of the ICCPR may also contain a prohibition on refoulement.[278]

As of November 2015, the Human Rights Committee had published 46 views on the merits concerning the principle of non-refoulement.[279] The great

---

272   At the time of completion of this book 115 states were party to this Optional Protocol.

273   Nowak & McArthur 2008, p. 726 (§ 9).

274   On the legal status of the Committee's decisions see Chapter 2 Section 2.3.

275   See the rights in Art. 6 to 27 ICCPR.

276   See HRC, General Comment No. 20 on Art. 7 (1992), § 9.

277   HRC, General Comment No. 31 on the nature of the general legal obligation imposed on state parties to the Covenant (2004), § 12.

278   See HRC, *Z. v. Australia*, 18 July 2014, no. 2049/2011, §§ 8.3 and 10 with regard to Art. 18 ICCPR (freedom of religion) and Art. 19 ICCPR (freedom of expression).

279   HRC, *Kindler v. Canada*, 30 July 1993, no. 470/1991 (US); HRC, *Ng v. Canada*, 5 November 1993, no. 469/1991 (US); HRC, *Cox v Canada*, 31 October 1994, no. 539/1993 (US); HRC, *A.R.J. v Australia*, 28 July 1997, no. 692/1996 (Iran); HRC, *G.T. v Australia*, 4 November 1997,

majority of these views were adopted after 2010: there has been a considerable increase of non-refoulement cases treated in the last five years. The majority concern removals from Canada followed by Denmark, Australia and Sweden.

Several communications dealt with by the Human Rights Committee concerned persons who feared the death penalty in case of extradition or expulsion.[280] The death penalty is *not* prohibited by the ICCPR,[281] but according

no. 706/1996 (Malaysia); HRC, *Judge v. Canada*, 5 August 2002, no. 829/1998 (US); HRC, *C. v. Australia*, 28 October 2002, no. 900/1999 (Iran); HRC, *Ahani v Canada*, 29 March 2004, no. 1051/2002 (Iran); HRC, *Byahuranga v. Denmark*, 1 November 2004, no. 1222/2003 (Uganda); HRC, *Alzery v. Sweden*, 25 October 2006, no. 1416/2005 (Egypt); HRC, *Pirmatov and Others*, 16 July 2008, nos. 1461/2006, 1462/2006, 1476/2006 and 1477/2006 (Uzbekistan); HRC, *Kwok v. Australia*, 23 October 2009, no. 1442/2005 (China); HRC, *Hamida v. Canada*, 18 March 2010, no. 1544/2007 (Tunisia); HRC, *Kaba v. Canada*, 25 March 2010, no. 1465/2006 (Guinea); HRC, *Pillai et al. v. Canada*, 25 March 2011, no. 1763/2008 (Sri Lanka); HRC, *Warsame v. Canada*, 21 July 2011, no. 1959/2010 (Somalia); HRC, *X.H.L. v. Netherlands*, 22 July 2011, no. 1564/2007 (China); HRC, *Israil v. Kazakhstan*, 31 October 2011, no. 2024/2011 (China); HRC, *X v. Sweden*, 1 November 2011, no. 1833/2008 (Afghanistan); HRC, *G.K. v. Netherlands*, 22 March 2012, no. 1801/2008 (Armenia); HRC, *Lin v. Australia*, 21 March 2013, no. 1957/2010 (China); HRC, *M.I. v. Sweden*, 25 July 2013, no. 2149/2012 (Bangladesh); HRC, *Shakeel v. Canada*, 24 July 2013, no. 1881/2009 (Pakistan); HRC, *Choudhary v. Canada*, 28 October 2013, no. 1898/2009 (Pakistan); HRC, *Thuraisamy v. Canada*, 31 October 2013, no. 1912/2009 (Sri Lanka); HRC, *Valetov v. Kazakhstan*, 17 March 2014, no. 2104/2011 (Kyrgyzstan); HRC, *Ostavari v. Republic of Korea*, 25 March 2014, no. 1908/2009 (Iran); HRC, *X. v. Denmark*, 26 March 2014, no. 2007/2007 (Eritrea); HRC, *Z. v. Australia*, 18 July 2014, no. 2049/2011 (China); HRC, *Aarrass v. Spain*, 21 July 2014, no. 2008/2010 (Morocco); HRC, *B.L. v. Australia*, 16 October 2014, no. 2053/2011 (Senegal); HRC, *Mr. X and Ms. X v. Denmark*, 22 October 2014, no. 2186/2012 (Russia); HRC, *A.H.G. and M.R. v. Canada*, 25 March 2015, no. 2091/2011 (Jamaica, health issue); HRC, *N.S. v. Russia*, 27 March 2015, no. 2192/2012 (Kyrgyzstan); HRC, *P.T. v. Denmark*, 1 April 2015, no. 2272/2013 (Sri Lanka); HRC, *Z. v. Denmark*, 15 July 2015, no. 2329/2014 (Iran); HRC, *A.H. v. Denmark*, 16 July 2015, no. 2370/2014 (Afghanistan); HRC, *K. v. Denmark*, 16 July 2015, no. 2393/2014 (Afghanistan); HRC, *Y. v. Canada*, 22 July 2015, no. 2280/2013 (Sri Lanka); HRC, *Jasin v. Denmark*, 22 July 2015, no. 2360/2014 (Dublin-transfer, Italy); HRC, *X v. Denmark*, 22 July 2015, no. 2389/2014 (Iran); HRC, *Omo-Amenaghawon v. Denmark*, 23 July 2015, no. 2288/2013 (Nigeria); HRC, *H.E.A.K. v. Denmark*, 23 July 2015, no. 2343/2014 (Egypt); HRC, *F.M. v. Canada*, 5 November 2015, no. 2284/2013 (Chad); HRC, *X. v. Canada*, 5 November 2015, no. 2366/2014 (Afghanistan); HRC, *X. v. Norway*, 5 November 2015, no. 2474/2014 (Afghanistan).

280   See HRC, *Kindler v. Canada*, 30 July 1993, no. 470/1991; HRC, *Ng v. Canada*, 5 November 1993, no. 469/1991; HRC, *Cox v Canada*, 31 October 1994, no. 539/1993; HRC, *A.R.J. v Australia*, 28 July 1997, no. 692/1996; HRC, *G.T. v Australia*, 4 November 1997, no. 706/1996; HRC, *Judge v. Canada*, 5 August 2002, no. 829/1998; HRC, *Kwok v. Australia*, 23 October 2009, no. 1442/2005; HRC, *Israil v. Kazakhstan*, 31 October 2011, no. 2024/2011. See also HRC, *Shakeel v. Canada*, 24 July 2013, no. 1881/2009, § 8.5; HRC, *Choudhary v. Canada*, 28 October 2013, no. 1898/2009, § 9.8.

281   Art. 6 ICCPR permits the death penalty in limited circumstances.

to the Human Rights Committee, cruel methods of execution may amount to inhuman treatment in violation of Article 7 ICCPR. An example would be execution by gas asphyxiation,[282] whereas the death penalty carried out by lethal injection is *not* considered a prohibited treatment or punishment.[283] The Human Rights Committee has further made clear that any imposition of a death sentence after an unfair trial is a violation of Article 7 ICCPR.[284] For those states that have ratified the Second Optional Protocol to the ICCPR, the death penalty is generally prohibited.[285] In addition, the Human Rights Committee has established that a state party that has itself abolished the death penalty would violate an individual's right to life under Article 6 ICCPR if it were to remove a person to a country where there was a real risk of that person being sentenced to death.[286]

Other than the death penalty, which is today generally prohibited by Article 3 ECHR,[287] Article 7 ICCPR has a similar scope to Article 3 ECHR.[288] Both provisions prohibit removal where 'there are substantial grounds for believing that there is a real risk of either torture or cruel, inhuman or degrading treatment or punishment.'[289] According to the Human Rights Committee, it is not necessary to 'establish sharp distinctions' between torture and other inhuman or degrading treatment. It has nevertheless indicated that 'the distinctions depend on the nature, purpose and severity of the treatment applied.'[290] As under Article 3 ECHR, there is no obstacle in the ICCPR to an act being qualified as torture or inhuman treatment if carried out by private actors.[291] Indeed, General Comment No. 20 on Article 7 ICCPR stipulates that it is the duty of states to afford everyone protection through legislative and such other measures as may be necessary against the acts prohibited by Article 7 ICCPR, whether inflicted by people acting in their official capacity or in a private

---

282   HRC, *Ng v. Canada*, 5 November 1993, no. 469/1991, § 16.4.

283   HRC, *Kindler v. Canada*, 30 July 1993, no. 470/1991; confirmed in HRC, *Cox v Canada*, 31 October 1994, no. 539/1993.

284   HRC, *Kwok v. Australia*, 23 October 2009, no. 1442/2005, § 9.4.

285   The Second Optional Protocol to the ICCPR on the abolition of the death penalty was adopted on 15 December 1989 and entered into force on 11 July 1991. By the time this research was completed it had been ratified by 81 states.

286   Established in HRC, *Judge v. Canada*, 5 August 2002, no. 829/1998, §§ 10.3–11.

287   See on this Chapter 3 Section 2.2.5.

288   Thurin 2012, p. 134; Weissbrodt & Hörtreiter 1999, p. 44.

289   HRC, 'General Comment No. 31 on the Nature of the General Legal Obligation Imposed on State Parties to the Covenant' (2004), § 12.

290   HRC, 'General Comment No. 20 on Art. 7' (1992), § 4.

291   As will be explained in Chapter 3 Section 3.3, the Committee's practice under Art. 3 CAT with regard to the protection against harms emanating from private actors is ambivalent.

capacity.[292] The Human Rights Committee has further made clear in a recent view that, similarly to Article 3 ECHR, Article 7 ICCPR may apply in refoulement cases in which the risk in the receiving state is extreme precarity, if particularly vulnerable individuals are concerned.[293] It has also made clear that this provision applies to cases in which a deportation has severe consequences on an applicant's health.[294]

To describe the standard of risk required, the Human Rights Committee speaks, similarly to the Court in Strasbourg, of a 'necessary and foreseeable consequence' that must be demonstrated.[295] It has specified in recent views that the risk of ill treatment 'must be personal, and that there is a high threshold for providing substantial grounds to establish that a real risk of irreparable harm exists. Thus, all relevant facts and circumstances must be considered, including the general human rights situation in the author's country of origin.'[296]

What stands out in the Human Rights Committee's practice in the assessment of individual complaints on the principle of non-refoulement is that it attaches *particular weight to the question of whether there has been a proper risk assessment at national level.*[297] According to the Human Rights Committee, as a general rule, it is for the national organs to review or evaluate facts and

---

292   HRC, 'General Comment No. 20 on Art. 7' (1992), § 2. See further HRC, *Kaba v. Canada*, 25 March 2010, no. 1465/2006, §§ 10–10.4, in which the HRC held that subjecting a woman to genital mutilation amounts to treatment prohibited under Article 7 ICCPR. Also HRC, *Omo-Amenaghawon v. Denmark*, 23 July 2015, no. 2288/2013, § 7.5 (violation), concerning the removal of a victim of human trafficking to Nigeria.

293   See HRC, *Jasin v. Denmark*, 22 July 2015, no. 2360/2014, concerning the transfer of a Somali woman with her three minor children based on the EU Dublin system to Italy, where they risked being left without shelter or means of subsistence. The HRC endorsed to a large extent the Strasbourg case law adopted in the similar case ECtHR, *Tarakhel v. Switzerland*, 4 November 2014 [GC], no. 29217/12, discussed in Chapter 3 Section 2.3.2.b.

294   See HRC, *A.H.G. and M.R. v. Canada*, 25 March 2015, no. 2091/2011, discussed in Chapter 3 Section 4.2.4, concerning the deportation of a mentally ill person to Jamaica. Interestingly, the Human Rights Committee appears to take a less strict approach in this case under Art. 7 ICCPR then the Court does in comparable cases under Art. 3 ECHR; see on this Chapter 3 Section 2.3.2.a.

295   See, for example, HRC, *A.R.J. v Australia*, 28 July 1997, no. 692/1996, §§ 6.10.

296   See, among others, HRC, *K. v. Denmark*, 16 July 2015, no. 2393/2014, § 7.2; HRC, *Y. v. Canada*, 22 July 2015, no. 2280/2013, § 7.2 and HRC, *H.E.A.K. v. Denmark*, 23 July 2015, no. 2343/2014, 8.2 with reference to earlier views.

297   Wouters 2009, pp. 395 and 422. For cases in which procedural deficiencies appear to be the major reason for the HRC's finding of a violation see, for example, HRC, *Ahani v Canada*, 29 March 2004, no. 1051/2002; HRC, *Byahuranga v. Denmark*, 1 November 2004,

evidence and 'significant weight should be given to the assessment conducted by the authorities of State parties, unless it is found that the evaluation was clearly arbitrary or amounted to a denial of justice.'[298] In recent cases, this approach was applied quite firmly.[299] However, the Human Rights Committee is not thoroughly consistent in applying it.[300] It appears in fact that there is an ongoing debate within the Committee members on the question of how active they are allowed (or obliged) to be, when evaluating facts and evidence.[301] However, in recent decisions, as a consequence of its focus on procedural deficiencies at the national level, when finding a violation of the principle of non-refoulement, the Human Rights Committee does request the state party to provide the author with an effective remedy, including full reconsideration of the claim regarding the risk of treatment contrary to Article 7 ICCPR and to refrain from expelling the author while this request for asylum is under reconsideration.[302] The state party must thereby take into account the view adopted on the case by the Human Rights Committee.[303] However, the Human Rights Committee gives no order as to the substantive outcome of the reconsideration required at the national level. Hence, on this aspect, the Court's and the Committee against Torture's approach appears more attractive for applicants. Once they find a violation of the principle of non-refoulement (even if it is mainly for procedural reasons), they simply advise the contracting state concerned not to deport the applicant.[304]

Since it is absolute, as under the ECHR and the CAT, the prohibition on refoulement under the ICCPR is applicable to any kind of removal (be it

---

no. 1222/2003; HRC, *Pillai et al. v. Canada*, 25 March 2011, no. 1763/2008, HRC, *X v. Sweden*, 1 November 2011, no. 1833/2008; HRC, *Shakeel v. Canada*, 24 July 2013, no. 1881/2009.

298 See, among others, HRC, *A.H. v. Denmark*, 16 July 2015, no. 2370/2014, § 8.4; HRC, *P.T. v. Denmark*, 1 April 2015, no. 2272/2013, § 7.3.

299 See, in particular, HRC, *Mr. X and Ms. X v. Denmark*, 22 October 2014, no. 2186/2012; HRC, *N.S. v. Russia*, 27 March 2015, no. 2192/2012; HRC, *P.T. v. Denmark*, 1 April 2015, no. 2272/2013; HRC, *Z. v. Denmark*, 15 July 2015, no. 2329/2014; HRC, *K. v. Denmark*, 16 July 2015, no. 2393/2014; HRC, *X. v. Canada*, 5 November 2015, no. 2366/2014; HRC, *X. v. Norway*, 5 November 2015, no. 2474/2014.

300 See also Wouters 2009, p. 397, who rightly notes that this principle is not always strictly applied.

301 See the individual opinions on HRC, *Thuraisamy v. Canada*, 31 October 2013, no. 1912/2009; HRC, *Shakeel v. Canada*, 24 July 2013, no. 1881/2009; HRC, *Choudhary v. Canada*, 28 October 2013, no. 1898/2009 and HRC, *X v. Denmark*, 22 July 2015, no. 2389/2014.

302 See, for example, HRC, *M.I. v. Sweden*, 25 July 2013, no. 2149/2012, § 9; HRC, *Omo-Amenaghawon v. Denmark*, 23 July 2015, no. 2288/2013, § 9.

303 *Ibid.*

304 See on this Chapter 2 Sections 1.3.2 and 2.3.2.

expulsion or extradition) and irrespective of the legal status or criminal background of the individual concerned. No derogation or exception of the prohibition on refoulement under the Articles 6 and 7 is permitted, even in times of emergency.[305] As the Committee has made clear, the principle of non-refoulement 'is not subject to any balancing with considerations of national security or the type of criminal conduct of which an individual is accused or suspected.'[306]

During the *traveaux préparatoires* to Article 22 CAT, some delegation members mentioned that there could be a risk of duplication or even conflicts between the individual complaints procedures before the Human Rights Committee and the Committee against Torture.[307] It is clear that there is common ground between the CAT and the ICCPR, in particular as regards the protection offered against torture including the principle of non-refoulement.[308] However, there is no institutional coordination between the two committees.[309]

In cases in which an individual complaint is directed against a state that has recognised both complaint mechanisms, the complainant is asked by the Secretariat to choose between the two bodies.[310] Even though it has become richer in the last five years, the jurisprudence of the Human Rights Committee with regard to non-refoulement is still scant compared to that of the Committee against Torture. This is astonishing since the protection against refoulement offered under Article 7 ICCPR is in principle broader than that offered by Article 3 CAT: As will be discussed in this research, the prohibition on refoulement under the CAT principally only applies to acts of torture and not to other less severe forms of inhuman treatment. However, as will also be shown, in a large number of non-refoulement cases, this restriction of protection to those at risk of torture under Article 3 CAT makes no material difference.[311] Nowak and McArthur note that 'generally, complainants who face deportation are more likely to submit their complaints to the Committee

---

305 See Art. 4(2) ICCPR and HRC, General Comment No. 20 on Art. 7 (1992), § 3. Also, for example, HRC, *Ahani v Canada*, 29 March 2004, no. 1051/2002, § 10.10.

306 HRC, *Israil v. Kazakhstan*, 31 October 2011, no. 2024/2011, § 9.4.

307 Nowak & McArthur 2008, p. 726 (§ 9).

308 See Ingelse 2001, p. 115, who notes that all the material considered by the Committee against Torture is also relevant for the Human Rights Committee.

309 Ingelse 2001, p. 116.

310 Nowak & McArthur 2008, p. 730 (§ 23). See Rule 103(2) ComAT (CAT/C/3/Rev.6).

311 See Chapter 3 Sections 3.2.2 and 4.2.1.

against Torture because of the particularly strong protection' offered by Article 3 CAT.[312]

6   The Principle of Non-refoulement in European Union Law

The European Union (EU) comprises 28 member states. The law of the EU is composed of treaties – namely the Treaty on European Union and the Treaty on the Functioning of the European Union – and secondary EU law. The EU rules concerning asylum and immigration are complex. Several legal instruments constitute together what is called the Common European Asylum System.

The Charter of Fundamental Rights of the EU became legally binding with the entering into force of the Treaty of Lisbon in December 2009 and is now playing an important role in the development of EU asylum law.[313] It provides in Article 18 that 'the right to asylum' shall be guaranteed with due respect for the rules of the 1951 Refugee Convention. According to Article 19(2) of the Charter 'no one may be removed, expelled or extradited to a State where there is a serious risk that he or she would be subjected to the death penalty, torture or other inhuman or degrading treatment or punishment.' This article incorporates the relevant case law of the Strasbourg Court under Article 3 ECHR.[314]

Article 78 of the Treaty on the Functioning of the European Union (TFEU) states that the Union shall develop a common policy on asylum, subsidiary protection and temporary protection with a view to offering appropriate status to any third-country national requiring international protection and ensuring compliance with the principle of non-refoulement. This system of protection must be in accordance with the 1951 Refugee Convention and 'other relevant treaties,'[315] such as the ECHR, the ICCPR or the CAT. Numerous legislative instruments have been adopted to implement this provision at the national level, namely the Qualification Directive,[316] the Directive on

---

312   Nowak & McArthur 2008, p. 730 (§ 24). See also Ingelse 2001, p. 308.

313   Peers, Moreno-Lax, Garlick & Guild 2015, p. 28.

314   'Explanation Relating to Art. 19 EU Charter of Fundamental Rights,' 2007/C 303/02.

315   Art. 78(1) TFEU.

316   Directive 2011/95/EU of the European Parliament and of the Council of 13 December 2011 on Standards for the Qualification of Third-Country Nationals or Stateless Persons as Beneficiaries of International Protection, for a Uniform Status for Refugees or for Persons Eligible for Subsidiary Protection, and for the Content of the Protection Granted (Recast), OJ L 337/9 (hereinafter 'Qualification Directive').

Reception Conditions[317] and Asylum Procedures[318] and the Regulations on the Dublin System.[319,320]

The EU Qualification Directive is of particular interest with regard to the principle of non-refoulement among this secondary EU legislation. It was adopted on 29 April 2004[321] and its recast was adopted with Directive 2011/95/EU in December 2011.[322] The deadline for the member states to comply with this Recast Directive expired in December 2013. The main objective of the Qualification Directive is to ensure that member states apply common criteria for the identification of refugees and other persons in need of international protection, and to ensure that a minimum level of benefits is available for those persons.[323]

According to Article 21 of the Directive, member states shall respect the principle of non-refoulement in accordance with their international obligations. Member states shall grant refugee status to third-country nationals or stateless persons if they face an act of persecution within the meaning of

---

317   Directive 2013/33/EU of the European Parliament and of the Council of 26 June 2013 Laying Down Standards for the Reception of Applicants for International Protection (Recast), OJ L 180/96 (hereinafter 'Reception Conditions Directive').

318   Directive 2013/32/EU of the European Parliament and of the Council of 26 June 2013 on Common Procedures for Granting and Withdrawing International Protection (Recast), OJ L 180/60.

319   On the so-called Dublin system see, in particular, Chapter 4 Section 3.4.3.a. The basic legal instrument for the so-called Dublin system is Regulation No 604/2013 of the European Parliament and of the Council of 26 June 2013 establishing the criteria and mechanisms for determining the member state responsible for examining an application for international protection lodged in one of the member states by a third-country national or a stateless person (recast), OJ L 180/31 (hereinafter 'Dublin III Regulation'). Most cases referred to in this study concern the previous version: Council Regulation No 343/2003 of 18 February 2003 establishing the criteria and mechanisms for determining the member state responsible for examining an asylum application lodged in one of the member states by a third-country national OJ L 50/1 (hereinafter 'Dublin II Regulation').

320   For an overview and analysis of EU immigration and asylum law including these and further directives and regulations see Peers, Moreno-Lax, Garlick & Guild 2015.

321   Council Directive 2004/83/EC of 29 April 2004 on Minimum Standards for the Qualification and Status of Third Country Nationals or Stateless Persons as Refugees or as Persons Who Otherwise Need International Protection and the Content of the Protection Granted, OJ 2004 L 304/12.

322   Fully cited in fn. 316 above.

323   Recital No. 12 and Art. 1 EU Qualification Directive. For an overall analysis of the Qualification Directive see Peers, Moreno-Lax, Garlick & Guild 2015, pp. 65–210.

Article 1 A of the 1951 Refugee Convention. According to Article 9 of the Directive, such an act of persecution must:

(a)   be sufficiently serious by its nature or repetition as to constitute a severe violation of basic human rights, in particular the rights from which derogation cannot be made under Article 15 (2) of the ECHR; or

(b)   be an accumulation of various measures, including violations of human rights which is sufficiently severe as to affect an individual in a similar manner as mentioned in point (a).[324]

The different forms of persecution and the acts listed in Article 9 must be attributable to one of the five reasons for persecution derived from the 1951 Geneva Convention (race, nationality, religion, membership of a particular social group and political opinion).[325]

   In addition to regulating refugee status within the EU legal order, the Qualification Directive makes provision for granting subsidiary protection status to those who do not qualify as refugees but who are in need of international protection: pursuant to Articles 2(e) and 15 of the directive, a person eligible for subsidiary protection is a third-country national who is not a refugee according to the 1951 Refugee Convention, but who would face a real risk of suffering serious harm if returned to his country of origin and who is unable, or, owing to such risk, unwilling to avail himself of the protection of that country. The notion of *serious harm* is defined in Article 15 as consisting of:

(a)   death penalty or execution; or

(b)   torture or inhuman or degrading treatment of an applicant in the country of origin; or

(c)   serious and individual threat to a civilian's life or person by reason of indiscriminate violence in situations of international or internal armed conflict.

The notion of a 'person eligible for subsidiary protection' and the establishment of a legal status for those entitled to it have no precedent in international

---

324   Art. 9(1) EU Qualification Directive. Art. 9(2) further indicates that persecution can take other forms, including acts of physical, mental or sexual violence and measures which are discriminatory, as well as 'acts of a gender-specific or child-specific nature.'

325   Art. 10 EU Qualification Directive.

law.[326] However, the standards for the definition and content of subsidiary protection have been drawn 'from international obligations under human rights instruments and practices existing in Member States.'[327] They are largely derived from Article 3 ECHR, but also from Article 3 CAT and Article 7 ICCPR and seek, among others, 'to give effect to Member States' obligations under those instruments.'[328]

The definition of *serious harm* in Article 15(a) and (b) reflects closely the wording and scope of Article 3 ECHR and the Strasbourg case law is of direct relevance for interpreting and applying this provision.[329] The Luxembourg Court held that while Article 15(b) of the directive corresponds, in essence, to Article 3 ECHR, Article 15(c) had an independent scope and 'covered a more general risk of harm.'[330] Article 15(c) was adopted with the aim to protect persons fleeing indiscriminate violence in armed conflicts and is not based on an international human rights treaty.[331] However, as will also be addressed in light of the current Strasbourg case law in severe conflict zones, there is an important overlap between 15(c) and Article 3 ECHR – and with that between 15(b) and 15(c) of the directive.[332] Yet, the exact overlap of these provisions remains unclear.[333]

Unlike Article 3 ECHR (and unlike Articles 3 CAT and 7 ICCPR), Article 15 on subsidiary protection is subject to an exclusion clause in Article 17 of the directive. However, taking into consideration the widely congruent scope of subsidiary protection with the scope of protection offered under Article 3 ECHR, it 'may be argued that people demonstrating exposure to any of the three forms of serious harm described in Article 15 of the Directive are entitled to unqualified protection from refoulement.'[334] As mentioned, Article 19 of the EU Charter of Fundamental Rights, which is meant to have the same scope as Article 3 ECHR, further guarantees an absolute protection against refoulement.[335]

---

326   Peers, Moreno-Lax, Garlick & Guild 2015, p. 133.

327   Recital No. 34 EU Qualification Directive.

328   Peers, Moreno-Lax, Garlick & Guild 2015, p. 133.

329   Peers, Moreno-Lax, Garlick & Guild 2015, p. 135. Art. 15(a) refers to the death penalty, which is today prohibited under Art. 3 ECHR; see Chapter 3 Section 2.2.5.

330   ECJ, C-465-07(2009), *Meki Elgafaji and Noor Elgafaji v. Staatssecretaris van Justitie*, 17 February 2009, §§ 28 and 33.

331   Peers, Moreno-Lax, Garlick & Guild 2015, pp. 135–136.

332   See Chapter 4 Section 3.2.1.

333   Peers, Moreno-Lax, Garlick & Guild 2015, pp. 139–143.

334   *Ibid.*, p. 154 and pp. 150–155.

335   Explanation Relating to Art. 19 EU Charter of Fundamental Rights, 2007/C 303/02.

The EU Charter further provides in Article 52(3) that where it contains rights which correspond to rights guaranteed by the ECHR, the 'meaning and scope' of those rights shall be the same as those laid down by that said Convention. Like the Refugee Convention, the ECHR is also 'a parameter of legitimacy for secondary legislation, which must be interpreted in the light of its provisions.'[336] Protection from refoulement within the EU should hence comply with the standards set by Article 3 ECHR.[337]

As for the relationship between EU legislation and other sources of human rights law, such as the CAT or the ICCPR, Article 53 of the EU Charter provides that nothing in the Charter 'shall be interpreted as restricting or adversely affecting human rights and fundamental freedoms' recognized by EU law or international agreements to which the EU or all Member States are parties. All 28 EU member states are state parties to the ECHR, the CAT and the ICCPR.

How is EU law implemented? The national courts have the duty to ensure that EU legislation is correctly applied and enforced. In case of doubt regarding the interpretation of a EU provision, national courts can, and even must in certain circumstances, seek guidance from the European Court of Justice in Luxemburg, using the preliminary reference procedure under Article 267 TFEU.[338] Until the entry into force of the Treaty of Lisbon in December 2009, the EU Court in Luxembourg was known as the European Court of Justice (ECJ). Since then, its name has changed to the Court of Justice of the European Union (CJEU).[339] The CJEU has the competence to ensure the correct application and interpretation of EU law by national courts. In that context, it has

---

336 Cherubini 2015, p. 177 and Article 78 TFEU. The Court in Luxembourg looks to the ECHR and the Strasbourg jurisprudence when determining the scope of human rights protection under EU law; Peers, Moreno-Lax, Garlick & Guild 2015, p. 35.

337 In addition, the Lisbon Treaty mandates the EU to join the ECHR as a party so that in future, individuals wishing to complain about the EU's failure to guarantee human rights should be entitled to bring an application against the EU before the Court in Strasbourg (see Art. 6(2) TEU). The accession process is ongoing but has proved to be complicated. A draft treaty was agreed in 2013, but in an opinion delivered in 2014, the Court of Justice of the EU concluded that it is not compatible with EU law; see Opinion 2/13 of the Court, 18 December 2014.

338 Access to this Luxembourg Court for *individuals* pursuant to Article 263(4) TFEU is narrow; it is not comparable to the individual complaints procedure in Strasbourg.

339 This book refers to the ECJ for decisions and judgments issued before December 2009 and to the CJEU for those adopted since 1 December 2009.

adopted important judgments on the principle of non-refoulement, to which reference will be made later in this study.[340]

---

340   See, in particular, ECJ, C-465-07, *Meki Elgafaji and Noor Elgafaji v. Staatssecretaris van Jus-titie*, 17 February 2009; CJEU, Joined Cases C-411/10 and C-493/10, *N.S. v. Secretary of State for the Home Department and M.E. and Others v. Refugee Applications Commissioner & Minister for Justice, Equality and Law Reform*, 21 December 2011; CJEU, Joined Cases C-71/11 and C-99/11, *Y and Z v. Bundesrepublik Deutschland*, 5 September 2012; CJEU, Joined Cases C-199/12, C-200/12, C-201/12, *X, Y and Z v Minister voor Immigratie, Integratie en Asiel*, 7 November 2013; CJEU, C-4/11, *Kaveh Puid v. Bundesrepublik Deutschland*, 14 November 2013; CJEU, C-542/13, *Mohamed M'Bodji v. Etat belge*, 18 December 2014.

The Individual Complaint Mechanisms in Light of the Non-refoulement Principle

This chapter gives an overview of procedural questions with regard to the individual complaint mechanisms before the Court in Strasbourg and the Committee in Geneva with a particular focus on the issues relevant in the context of non-refoulement. A comprehensive analysis and comparison of the complaint mechanisms, in particular the handling of admissibility criteria, would be beyond the scope of this study. Since the Court does not publish most of its inadmissibility decisions, it would actually be impossible.

It is nevertheless important to give an overview of the most important procedural features to fully understand how the Court and the Committee supervise the implementation of the principle of non-refoulement in individual cases. As is the case in asylum proceedings at the national level, procedural questions, in particular the manner in which the admissibility of complaints is handled, may have considerable impact on the protection offered in practice.

1 Procedure under Article 34 ECHR

1.1 *The Complaint Mechanism*

1.1.1　　The Life of an Application in Strasbourg

According to Article 34 ECHR, the Court may receive applications from any person, non-governmental organisation or group of individuals claiming to be the victim(s) of a violation by one of the contracting parties of the rights set forth in the Convention. Applications must be submitted in writing by regular post or fax and will first be received by the Registry, which is staffed by lawyers from all member states.[1] The task of the Registry 'is to provide legal and administrative support to the Court in the exercise of its judicial functions.'[2]

1　Applications *must* be made on the application form provided by the Registry on the Court's website; see Rule 47 ECtHR (1 January 2016).

2　See on the Court's website: 'Registry' [16.2.2016]. Currently, there are some 640 staff members of the Registry: 270 lawyers and 370 other support staff.

There are four different decision bodies within the Court to which an application may be assigned for decision: the single-judge formation, the committee of 3 judges, the chamber of 7 judges and the Grand Chamber of 17 judges.[3]

An individual application that clearly fails to meet one of the admissibility criteria set out in Article 35 ECHR and can therefore be rejected 'without further examination' will be referred to either a single judge or a committee of three judges.[4] These judicial formations may then declare a case inadmissible or strike it out of the Court's list of cases. The committee of three judges may also render a judgment on the merits in cases in which the underlying question is already the subject of well-established case law.[5] The single-judge formation was introduced by Protocol No. 14 to the ECHR to deal more efficiently with the backlog of cases resulting from the large number of inadmissible applications. It provides a filtering function for such cases.[6] Before Protocol No. 14 came into force on 1 June 2010, the committee of three judges dealt with all complaints that appeared to be clearly inadmissible.[7] Today, applications that are clearly inadmissible are usually dealt with by the newly introduced single judge rather than by a three-judge committee.[8] The great majority of the applications submitted to the Court have been rejected in a non-contradictory procedure for being manifestly inadmissible by the committee of three judges and, since the entering into force of Protocol No. 14 to the ECHR, the single judge (which means without the involvement of the state concerned).[9] Inadmissibility decisions by single judges or the committee of three judges are final. If the single judge does not declare an application inadmissible or strike it out, he must forward it to a committee or to a chamber for further examination.[10]

Applications that are *not* clearly inadmissible are initially referred to a chamber for decision. These chambers consists of seven judges, of which one has the nationality of the respondent state party.[11] All applications that are referred to a chamber are communicated to the state party concerned for written observations. The complainant is then given a certain amount of time to

---

3   Art. 26(1) ECHR.

4   Art. 27 and 28 ECHR.

5   Art. 28(1) ECHR.

6   ECtHR, 'Annual Report 2012,' p. 33.

7   See former Art. 28 ECHR.

8   Court's 'Practical Guide on Admissibility Criteria,' 2014, p. 11 (§ 2).

9   See the statistical information in the Court's annual reports: ECtHR, 'Annual Report 2012,' p. 149; ECtHR, 'Provisional Annual Report 2015,' pp. 65 and 66.

10   Art. 27(3) ECHR.

11   Rule 26 ECtHR (1 January 2016).

reply to the government's observations.[12] The chamber adopts its decisions or judgments by majority vote.[13] As a rule, the chamber determines on both the admissibility and the merits of a complaint in a single judgment, although it can, where appropriate, take a separate decision on admissibility.[14]

Where a case pending before a chamber raises

> ... a serious question affecting the interpretation of the Convention or the Protocols thereto, or where the resolution of a question before the Chamber might have a result inconsistent with a judgment previously de-livered by the Court, the Chamber may, at any time before it has rendered its judgment, relinquish jurisdiction in favour of the Grand Chamber, un-less one of the parties to the case objects.[15]

Within three months after delivery of a chamber judgment, the parties to the procedure may also request that a case be referred to the Grand Chamber of 17 judges.[16] If the three-month period expires without any request having been made or if a request is refused (by a Grand Chamber panel of five judges), the chamber judgment becomes final.[17] Grand Chamber judgments are final upon delivery.

When the Court adopts a judgment according to which the state concerned has failed to respect a right enshrined in the ECHR, this state is legally obliged under Article 46 ECHR to abide by the Court's findings.[18] The judgment is transmitted to the Committee of Ministers, which supervises its execution. All judgments and admissibility decisions except those adopted by single-judge formations are published in the Court's database (HUDOC).[19] Applicants whose complaint is rejected for being manifestly inadmissible by a single judge receive a brief standard letter indicating that their application has been rejected. The reason for which the complaint is declared inadmissible is not indicated.[20]

---

12   Rule 54(2)b ECtHR (1 January 2016).

13   Rules 23 and 56 ECtHR (1 January 2014).

14   Art. 29(1) ECHR.

15   Art. 30 ECHR.

16   Art. 43 ECHR.

17   Art. 44 ECHR.

18   See on this Section 1.3 of this chapter.

19   ECtHR, 'Annual Report 2012,' p. 64. Before Protocol No. 14 came into force, the decisions of the committee of three judges were not published.

20   See on this frustrating practice for applicants, Keller, Fischer & Kühne 2010, p. 1046.

Finally, it should be added that at any stage of the proceedings, the Court may suggest that the parties reach a friendly settlement according to Article 39 ECHR. If a settlement can be reached (which requires an agreement on compensation from both parties; this can be of a pecuniary or other nature), the Court strikes the case out of the Registry's list and publishes the solution reached.[21]

1.1.2   Hearings, Confidentiality, Languages, Costs, Legal Representation, Third Party and Length of Procedure

The procedure before the Court is primarily in written form. Oral hearings take place in cases decided by the Grand Chamber or if a chamber considers that further clarification is needed in the presence of the parties.[22] Hearings are the exception.

As a general rule, hearings and any information contained in the documents submitted to the registry are accessible to the public unless the Court decides otherwise.[23] The Court can decide *ex officio* or upon request by the complainant to disclose the complainant's identity to the public,[24] which is frequently done in non-refoulement cases. Applications and requests for interim measures may be submitted in any of the official languages of the state parties to the ECHR. Once the Court decides to give notice of an application to the respondent government for observations, one of the Court's official languages, which are English and French, must be used for subsequent submissions.[25]

The individual complaint procedure before the Court is free of charge. Applicants may present their cases themselves, but once their application has been communicated to the respondent government for observations, they have to be legally represented by an advocate authorised to practise in any of the contracting parties or any other person approved by the president of the chamber.[26] The Court might provide *legal aid* for applicants if it is necessary for the proper conduct of the case and the applicant has insufficient means for the costs entailed.[27] If the Court finds that there has been a violation of

21   Art. 39 ECHR. See also Rule 62A ECtHR (1 January 2016) on the respondent government's possibility to make a unilateral declaration.

22   The political importance of a case may also be of significance in the chamber's decision to hold a hearing; Leach 2011, p. 75.

23   Art. 40(2) ECHR.

24   Rule 33(2) (1 January 2016).

25   Unless the president of the chamber grants leave for the continued use of the official language of a contracting party; see Rule 34(3)a ECtHR (1 January 2016).

26   Rule 36 ECtHR (1 January 2016).

27   Rules 100–105 ECtHR (1 January 2016).

the ECHR, it may award 'just satisfaction' to the applicant according to Article 41 ECHR. This may include compensation for pecuniary and non-pecuniary damages and legal costs and expenses. In non-refoulement cases, the Court does not usually grant any compensation other than for the coverage of legal costs.[28]

Once a complaint has been notified to the respondent state for observations, the Court can authorise third parties to intervene by submitting their own observations on the matter.[29] In refoulement cases with potentially broader impact, NGOs such as Amnesty International, Human Rights Watch and the AIRE Centre as well as international organisations like the UNHCR regularly make use of the possibility to intervene with their opinion.[30] Member states to the ECHR that are not a party in the procedure may also be allowed to submit written comments or participate in a hearing. In the context of refoulement, states have mainly made use of this in cases concerning the deportation of individuals charged for serious crimes, in particular terrorism,[31] and in cases concerning the functioning of the EU Dublin system.[32]

The duration of the proceedings before the Court is variable; it may take a few months or several years.[33] Inadmissibility decisions are usually taken more quickly.[34] On average, procedures concerning non-refoulement that are concluded by a judgment on the merits take between one and three years.

---

28 See on this Section 1.3 of this chapter.

29 Art. 36(2) ECHR.

30 See, for example, ECtHR, *Hirsi Jamaa and Others v. Italy*, 23 February 2012 [GC], no. 27765/09 (UNHCR, Human Rights Watch, Columbia Law School Human Rights Clinic, AIRE Centre, Amnesty International, International Federation for Human Rights).

31 See, in particular, ECtHR, *Saadi v. Italy*, 28 February 2008 [GC], no. 37201/06 (UK); ECtHR, *Ramzy v. Netherlands*, 20 July 2010, no. 25424/05 (Lithuania, Portugal, Slovakia and UK; struck out of the list); ECtHR, *A v. Netherlands*, 20 July 2010, no. 4900/06 (Lithuania, Portugal, Slovakia and UK); ECtHR, *Ahorugeze v. Sweden*, 27 October 2011, no. 37075/09 (Netherlands; extradition of genocide suspect to Rwanda).

32 See, in particular, ECtHR, *M.S.S. v. Belgium and Greece*, 21 January 2011 [GC], no. 30696/09 (UK, the Netherlands); ECtHR, *Tarakhel v. Switzerland*, 4 November 2014 [GC], no. 29217/12 (Italy, the Netherlands, Sweden, Norway and UK).

33 For a procedure taking almost ten years see ECtHR, *S.S. v. Netherlands*, 12 January 2016, no. 39575/06.

34 Here as well there are disparities: for an extremely short procedure see ECtHR, *Kaldik v. Germany*, 22 September 2005, no. 28526/05 (decision), decided within two months. For a long procedure see, for example, ECtHR, *Al-Moayad v. Germany*, 20 February 2007, no. 35865/03 (decision), decided within more than three years. Today, where a request for interim measures under the principle of non-refoulement is refused, that decision is increasingly combined with a inadmissibility decision so the procedure can be quite short;

The Court has the option of granting priority to applications under Rule 41 of the Rules of the Court, which it usually does in cases in which it has granted interim measures.[35] Applications that are granted priority are usually decided within one or two years.[36] However, in those cases as well, proceedings may take longer.[37]

1.2   *Interim Measures*

When there is an imminent risk to the applicant's life or where there is a substantial risk of ill treatment, the Court may, at the request of a complainant or of its own motion, indicate to the parties any interim measure which it considers should be adopted in the interests of the parties or of the proper conduct of the proceedings before it.[38] In the context of refoulement, *interim measures* (also referred to as *provisional measures*) are sought by the applicant and granted by the Court to preserve the status quo pending the Court's determination on the case.[39] This means that the Court may ask the respondent member state not to deport the applicant until it adopts a final decision on the case.

In principle, interim measures are only granted in cases concerning the right to life in Article 2 or the prohibition of torture and inhuman treatment in Article 3 ECHR.[40] The Court uses interim measures almost exclusively to ensure the protection of individuals against refoulement under Article 3 ECHR.[41] Interim

---

Steering Committee for Human Rights (CDDH), 'Draft CDDH Report on Interim Measures under Rule 39 of the Rules of the Court,' 2 February 2013, CDDH(2013)R77, p. 5 (§ 14).

35   See the Court's note on its priority policy in which it has indicated that applications in which interim measures are granted or that raise issues under Art. 2 and 3 ECHR are considered as urgent. The note is available on the Court's <http://www.echr.coe.int/Documents/Priority_policy_ENG.pdf> [16.2.2016].

36   See Steering Committee for Human Rights (CDDH), 'Draft CDDH Report on Interim Measures under Rule 39 of the Rules of the Court,' 2 February 2013, CDDH(2013)R77, p. 5 (§ 14) fn. 22.

37   See, for example, ECtHR, *Harkins and Edwards v. UK*, 17 January 2012, nos. 9146/07 and 32650/07.

38   Rule 39 ECtHR (1 January 2016).

39   ECtHR, *Mamatkulov and Askarov v. Turkey*, 4 February 2005 [GC], nos. 46827/99 and 46951/99, § 108.

40   On rare occasions, the Court has granted interim measures where a violation of the right to respect for family life according to Art. 8 ECHR was alleged; see, for example, ECtHR, *Neulinger and Shuruk v. Switzerland*, 6 July 2010 [GC], no. 41615/07, concerning child abduction.

41   Rieter 2010, p. 265.

measures are only indicated in 'truly exceptional cases,'[42] where it appears to the Court that there is an imminent risk of a serious and irremediable violation of the ECHR.[43] In the years 2008 to 2011, the Court rejected about 70 per cent of requests for interim measures. In 2012, this proportion rose to 90 per cent.[44]

There is no provision in the ECHR itself empowering the Court to order interim measures but a provision is found in Rule 39 of the Court's Rules of Procedure.[45] In the judgment *Cruz Varas and Others v. Sweden* adopted in 1991, the Court held that state parties are not legally bound to respect the Court's indication of interim measures.[46] In 2005, the Grand Chamber overruled this finding in the judgment *Mamatkulov and Askarov v. Turkey*.[47] It held that the extradition of two Uzbek applicants despite the order by the Court of interim measures under Rule 39 had violated their right to effectively submit an individual application to the Court under Article 34 ECHR. With that, the Court made clear that there is a legal obligation under Article 34 ECHR on states to comply with an interim measures order.

The Court justified this by pointing to the particular importance of Article 3 ECHR, as 'one of the core rights of the Convention.'[48] It further relied on two arguments: first, the effective exercise of an individual applicant's right to submit applications under Article 34 ECHR, and second, general principles of international law including the view expressed on this subject by other international bodies. The Court referred to principles established on that matter by the International Court of Justice, the Inter-American Court of Human Rights, the UN Human Rights Committee and the Committee against Torture.[49] The Court further held that indications of interim measures

---

42 ECtHR, *Dzhurayev v. Russia,* 25 April 2013, no. 71386/10, § 213.

43 Steering Committee for Human Rights (CDDH), 'Draft CDDH Report on Interim Measures under Rule 39 of the Rules of the Court,' 2 February 2013, CDDH(2013)R77, p. 2 (§§ 2 and 3).

44 See the Court's factsheet on interim measures of January 2013 [accessible on the Court's website, 3.1.2014, copy in possession of author].

45 This rule has been introduced following the reform of the Strasbourg supervisory system through Protocol No. 11 to the ECHR. Before this reform, the former European Commission on Human Rights and the Court also had the practice of granting interim measures; Delas 2011, p. 342.

46 ECtHR, *Cruz Varas and Others v. Sweden,* 20 March 1991, no. 15576/89, §§ 94–105.

47 ECtHR, *Mamatkulov and Askarov v. Turkey,* 4 February 2005 [GC], nos. 46827/99 and 46951/99, §§ 108–129.

48 *Ibid.,* § 108.

49 *Ibid.,* §§ 110–124.

... permit it not only to carry out an effective examination of the application but also to ensure that the protection afforded to the applicant by the Convention is effective; such indications also subsequently allow the Committee of Ministers to supervise execution of the final judgment. Such measures thus enable the State concerned to discharge its obligation to comply with the final judgment of the Court, which is legally binding by virtue of Article 46 of the Convention.[50]

The judges Caflish, Türmen and Kovler dissented with regard to the obligatory nature of the measures arguing 'that the matter examined here is one of legislation rather than of judicial action.' They held that neither 'the constitutive instrument of this Court nor general international law' would empower the Court to issue binding provisional measures.[51] However, the Court's approach adopted in *Mamatkulov and Askarov* according to which interim measures are legally binding has been confirmed since then. In *Dzhurayev*, the Court recently emphasized that any laxity on the binding legal effect of interim measures would be 'inconsistent with the fundamental importance of the right to individual petition and, more generally, undermine the authority and effectiveness of the Convention as a constitutional instrument of European public order.'[52]

Generally, interim measures indicated by the Court are respected, particularly in expulsion cases.[53] Interestingly, this was already the custom before the Court adopted *Mamatkulov and Askarov* in 2005.[54] In recent years, there has, however, been an increase in cases in which the Court found violations of Article 34 ECHR because interim measures had not been respected.[55] Particularly

---

50   *Ibid.*, § 125.

51   They pointed out that contrary to the ACHR and the ICJ Statute, the ECHR itself does not contain any provision concerning interim measures.

52   ECtHR, *Dzhurayev v. Russia*, 25 April 2013, no. 71386/10, § 213.

53   ECRE/ELENA 'Research on ECHR Rule 39 Interim Measures,' April 2012, p. 17.

54   See the Court's statement in ECtHR, *Mamatkulov and Askarov v. Turkey*, 4 February 2005 [GC], nos. 46827/99 and 46951/99, § 105. See also the Court's indication in ECtHR, *Cruz Varas and Others v. Sweden*, 20 March 1991, no. 15576/89, § 55, according to which in some cases concerning extraditions states had failed to comply.

55   The Court found a violation of Art. 34 ECHR for the non-observance of interim measures in the following non-refoulement cases: ECtHR, *Mamatkulov and Askarov v. Turkey*, 4 February 2005 [GC], nos. 46827/99 and 46951/99; ECtHR, *Shamayev and Others v. Georgia and Russia*, 12 April 2005, no. 36378/02; ECtHR, *Aoulmi c. France*, 17 January 2006, no. 50278/99; ECtHR, *Cahuas v. Spain*, 10 August 2006, no. 24668/03; ECtHR, *Mostafa and Others v. Turkey*, 15 January 2008, no. 16348/05; ECtHR, *Khemais v. Italy*, 24 February 2009, no. 246/07; ECtHR, *Al-Saadoon and Mufdhi v. UK*, 2 March 2010, no. 61498/08;

worrisome are the repeated incidents of disappearance of applicants in Russia, in respect of whom interim measures had been indicated by the Court.[56]

The Court has made clear that when it assesses whether the respondent government has complied with Article 34 ECHR, 'it will not re-examine whether its decision to apply interim measures was correct.'[57] The Court hence may find a breach of Article 34 ECHR for the failure to respect provisional measures independently of the question of whether it has been established, in a particular case, that there is a real risk of ill treatment in case of deportation in breach of Article 3 ECHR.[58]

If a contracting state has taken all steps that could reasonably be taken to comply with the order but was not able to prevent the deportation, Article 34 ECHR will not be breached. It is, however, for the respondent government to demonstrate that there was an 'objective impediment' that

---

ECtHR, *Trabelsi v. Italy,* 13 April 2010, no. 50163/08; ECtHR, *Kamaliyevy v. Russia,* 3 June 2010, no. 52812/07; ECtHR, *Toumi v. Italy,* 5 April 2011, no. 25716/09; ECtHR, *Mannai v. Italy,* 27 March 2012, no. 9961/10; ECtHR, *Rrapo v. Albania,* 25 September 2012, no. 58555/19; ECtHR, *Abdulkhakov v. Russia,* 2 October 2012, no. 14743/11; ECtHR, *Zokhidov v. Russia,* 5 February 2013, no. 67286/10; ECtHR, *Ermakov v. Russia,* 7 November 2013, no. 43165/10; ECtHR, *Kasymakhunov v. Russia,* 14 November 2013, no. 29604/12; ECtHR, *Trabelsi v. Belgium,* 4 September 2014, no. 140/10; ECtHR, *Mamazhonov v. Russia,* 23 October 2014, no. 17239/13; ECtHR, *Mukhitdinov v. Russia,* 21 May 2015, no. 20999/14. See also Haeck, Burbano Herrera & Zwaak 2011, pp. 380–403.

56   See ECtHR, *Iskandarov v. Russia,* 23 September 2010, no. 17185/05; ECtHR, *Abdulkhakov v. Russia,* 2 October 2012, no. 14743/11; ECtHR, *Dzhurayev v. Russia,* 25 April 2013, no. 71386/10; ECtHR, *Nizomkhon Dzhurayev v. Russia,* 3 October 2013, no. 31890/11, ECtHR, *Ermakov v. Russia,* 7 November 2013, no. 43165/10; ECtHR, *Kasymakhunov v. Russia,* 14 November 2013, no. 29604/12, §§ 122–128. In these cases, the complainants had been kidnapped and transferred into the custody of Tajik or Uzbek authorities with the knowledge and either passive or active involvement of the Russian authorities. See also the Committee of Ministers' decision on various Russian cases CM/Del/Dec(2013)1176/H46-2 adopted on 10 July 2013 at the 1176th meeting of the Minister's Deputies. See similar ECtHR, *Mamazhonov v. Russia,* 23 October 2014, no. 17239/13; ECtHR, *Mukhitdinov v. Russia,* 21 May 2015, no. 20999/14.

57   ECtHR, *Al-Saadoon and Mufdhi v. UK,* 2 March 2010, no. 61498/08, § 161; ECtHR, *Rrapo v. Albania,* 25 September 2012, no. 58555/19, § 82; ECtHR, *Zokhidov v. Russia,* 5 February 2013, no. 67286/10, § 206.

58   In *Mamatkulov and Askarov,* the Court found a violation of Art. 34 ECHR but noted that it was not able to conclude that, at the date of the complainants' extradition, substantial grounds existed for believing that the applicant faced a real risk of treatment proscribed by Art. 3 ECHR. See also ECtHR, *Cahuas v. Spain,* 10 August 2006, no. 24668/03, § 81, according to which 'the State's decision as to whether it complies with the measure cannot be deferred pending the hypothetical confirmation of the existence of a risk.'

prevented compliance.[59] National legislation or agreements with the receiving country, such as diplomatic assurances obtained after the Court's indication of provisional measures, as well as reasons of state security are not considered to be such 'objective impediments' justifying non-compliance with interim measures.[60] In two cases, the Court accepted that the respondent state's authorities were simply not given enough time to respect the indication by the Court.[61] The Court may also find a breach of Article 34 ECHR if it is made impossible for the complainant to effectively submit a request for interim measures before he is expelled.[62]

The Court assesses each request on an individual and priority basis through a written procedure. It tries to decide on the requests within one working day.[63] Applicants or their representatives should specify the grounds on which their particular fears are based and the nature of the alleged risk.[64] According to Rule 39, a judge appointed for that task has the power to grant interim measures. In practice, the Registry's preparation of the decision is of particular importance in this urgent decision-making.[65] Since September 2011, all requests for interim measures are considered by a centralised Rule 39 unit against a standard checklist.[66] The Court does not publish its decisions on interim measures and does not give reasons to the parties concerned on its decision to grant or refuse them.[67] There is no possibility to appeal against a

---

59   ECtHR, *Al-Saadoon and Mufdhi v. UK*, 2 March 2010, no. 61498/08, § 161.

60   ECtHR, *Al-Saadoon and Mufdhi*, §§ 160–165; ECtHR, *Rrapo v. Albania*, 25 September 2012, no. 58555/19, §§ 84–88.

61   ECtHR, *Muminov v. Russia*, 11 December 2008, no. 42502/06, §§ 132–138 and ECtHR, *M.B. and Others v. Turkey*, 15 June 2010, no. 36009/08, § 48. In these two cases, the deportations in question took place only a few minutes before or after the respondent governments were informed of the measures.

62   ECtHR, *D.B. v. Turkey*, 13 July 2010, no. 33526/08, §§ 61–67.

63   Steering Committee for Human Rights (CDDH), 'Draft CDDH Report on Interim Measures under Rule 39 of the Rules of the Court,' 2 February 2013, CDDH(2013)R77, p. 6 (§§ 20 and 21).

64   See the Practice direction issued by the president of the Court in accordance with Rule 32 of the Rules of Court on 5 March 2003 as amended on 16 October 2009 and on 7 July 2011. Accessible on the Court's website under <http://www.echr.coe.int/pages/home.aspx?p=basictexts/rules&c> [16.2.2016].

65   See in this sense also Haeck, Burbano Herrera & Zwaak 2008, p. 57 fn. 5.

66   This system was designed to improve efficiency and consistency within the Court: see Steering Committee for Human Rights (CDDH), 'Draft CDDH Report on Interim Measures under Rule 39 of the Rules of the Court,' 2 February 2013, CDDH(2013)R77, p. 4 (§ 11). The checklist can be found in the appendix of this report.

67   For a critique of this practice see Haeck, Burbano Herrera & Zwaak 2008, pp. 57–59.

refusal. It is hence difficult to anticipate the circumstances under which they might be granted.[68]

As stated above, the great majority of requests for interim measures are rejected. The Court only issues them in exceptional cases where it considers that the applicant faces a real risk of serious, irreversible harm if the measure is not applied. Frequently, requests are rejected because the applicant has failed to substantiate the risk of ill treatment in the receiving state.[69] Applicants do not have to establish a 'real risk' of ill treatment to be granted provisional measures, as they are required in the regular procedure, but must establish a *prima facie* arguable claim to benefit from provisional measures.[70] The Court applies a lower threshold with regard to the establishment of a risk of ill treatment in case of removal when it decides on interim measures than it does when it decides on whether the application should be declared inadmissible for being 'manifestly ill-founded.'[71] This, however, only gives a vague idea of the standard of proof required in the interim measures procedure. As in the ordinary assessment of refoulement complaints, it is the particular circumstances of the case that are decisive. However, it appears that the human rights situation is of particular importance in the Rule 39 procedure.[72] The Court further attaches great importance to the reasons set out by the national authorities for rejecting an asylum application or an objection to removal.[73] Reasons for the rejection may also include the fact that the risk of deportation is not imminent[74] or that the harm expected in the receiving country does not appear to fall within the kind of harm prohibited by Article 3 ECHR.[75] It is extremely rare for cases in which the request has been denied to be successful on the merits.[76]

---

68 Rieter 2010, pp. 180–181.

69 ECtHR, 'Annual Report 2005,' p. 60.

70 Mole & Meredith 2010, p. 218.

71 Rieter 2010, p. 831. On this inadmissibility criterion see Section 3.2.6 of this chapter.

72 Rieter 2010, p. 871.

73 Steering Committee for Human Rights (CDDH), 'Draft CDDH Report on Interim Measures under Rule 39 of the Rules of the Court,' 2 February 2013, CDDH(2013)R77, p. 6 (§ 19).

74 This might be the case when the applicant has not exhausted available domestic remedies with suspensive effect. However, the Court will not refrain from applying interim measures where the remedies available at the national level are non-suspensive; see Steering Committee for Human Rights (CDDH), 'Draft CDDH Report on Interim Measures under Rule 39 of the Rules of the Court,' 2 February 2013, CDDH(2013)R77, p. 11 (§ 38).

75 Rieter 2010, p. 272.

76 As exceptions see ECtHR, *M.S.S. v. Belgium and Greece*, 21 January 2011 [GC], no. 30696/09; ECtHR, *Auad v. Bulgaria*, 11 October 2011, no. 46390/10. Also ECtHR, *Ryabikin v. Russia*, 19 June 2008, no. 8320/04, §§ 34, 87 and 115, in which the measure had been lifted.

If a request is accepted, the correspondent government is immediately informed by fax or electronically and has the duty to report as soon as possible which measures it has taken to fulfil the Court's indication not to deport the applicant.[77] Usually, interim measures are valid until the Court has taken a final decision or judgment on the case.[78] However, the Court might reevaluate its decisions on interim measures and lift them.[79]

The number of requests for interim measures has increased substantially over the last ten years. Up to 1989, the Court had received 182 requests for interim measures in expulsion cases. In 31 of these cases the measures had been granted.[80] Between 1974 and 2000, there were a total of 2,219 requests.[81] Between 2006 and 2010, the Court saw an increase of over 4,000 per cent in the number of requests. While in 2006 the Court received 112 requests, that figure had risen to 4,786 in 2010.[82] When looking at those numbers, it should be taken into account that many requests are directed against the same countries or concern similar issues.[83] The statistics from 2008 to 2012 show that the United Kingdom, France, the Netherlands and Sweden are the states against which most requests for interim measures have been made.[84]

---

77   On the divergent practices of European states see ECRE/ELENA 'Research on ECHR Rule 39 Interim Measures,' pp. 80–84.

78   If a chamber adopts a judgment, interim measures are valid for three more months after the judgment's delivery or until a request for referral to the Grand Chamber is denied. If such a request is accepted, the measures remain valid until the Grand Chamber has adopted its judgment; see Art. 44 ECHR and ECtHR, *F.H. v. Sweden*, 20 January 2009, no. 32621/06, §§ 106 and 107.

79   See, for example, ECtHR, *Ameh and Others v. UK*, 30 August 2011, no. 4539/11 (decision). The Court has occasionally granted interim measures for a specified period, in order to obtain more information from the respondent government or the applicant; see, for example, ECtHR, *F.H. v. Sweden*, 20 January 2009, no. 32621/06, §§ 40 and 44.

80   ECtHR, *Cruz Varas and Others v. Sweden*, 20 March 1991, no. 15576/89, § 55.

81   Leach 2011, p. 33.

82   ECtHR, statement issued on 11 February 2011 by the president of the Court concerning requests for interim measures, doc. GT-GDR-C(2012)005.

83   See Resolution 1788(2011) of the Parliamentary Assembly of the Council of Europe of January 2011, § 12: 'Notwithstanding the rise in the number of requests for Rule 39 measures addressed to the Court, the majority of these requests are directed against a handful of the 47 member States.' Between October 2010 and January 2011 alone, the Court received around 2,500 requests concerning returns to Iraq. At the same time, there were a large number of requests concerning returns under the Dublin Regulation.

84   See the Court's factsheet on interim measures of January 2013 [accessible on the Court's website, 3.1.2014, copy in possession of author]. In 2010 for instance, more than 2,000 were made in respect of the United Kingdom, 400 against the Netherlands and more than 300

The statistics from 2012 to 2015 show a similar picture with Russia added to the list.[85]

The rise of requests and the implications for the already overburdened Court led former president of the Court Jean-Paul Costa to issue a statement in February 2011, reminding 'both Governments and applicants of the Court's proper but limited role in immigration and asylum matters and emphasising their respective responsibilities to co-operate fully with the Court.'[86] He reminded potential applicants and their representatives that the Court is 'not an appeal tribunal from asylum tribunals in Europe' and that it should 'only be required to intervene in truly exceptional cases.' Addressing the member states, he held that they should provide 'national remedies with suspensive effect which operate effectively and fairly.' He further requested that 'where a lead case concerning the safety of return to a particular country of origin is pending before the national courts or the Court itself, removals to that country should be suspended.'[87] The former president also stated that Rule 39 proceedings 'often confront the Court with a difficult or indeed impossible task. Decisions have to be taken as a matter of urgency, on the basis of a rudimentary case file, on whether to allow or refuse the expulsion or extradition of people to countries where they are at risk of serious violations of their rights.'[88] It is evident from this statement that the Court itself is not wholly at ease with the fact that it has to take so many important decisions in haste.

In 2011, requests under Rule 39 dropped for the first time to approximately 2,750. In 350 of these cases the measures were granted.[89] In 2012 the numbers dropped again: there were 1,972 requests, of which only 103 were granted.[90]

---

against France; ECtHR, statement issued on 11 February 2011 by the president of the Court concerning requests for interim measures, doc. GT-GDR-C(2012)005.

85   See the Court's thematical statistics on interim measures 2012–2015; accessible on the Court's website under <http://www.echr.coe.int/Pages/home.aspx?p=reports> [16.2.2016].

86   ECtHR, statement issued on 11 February 2011 by the President of the Court concerning requests for interim measures, doc. GT-GDR-C(2012)005.

87   *Ibid.*

88   ECtHR, 'Annual Report 2011,' p. 40.

89   *Ibid.*, p. 15. Some 600 requests were considered to be outside the scope of Rule 39 of the Rules of Court. Requests that are captured in the 'out of scope' section of the Court's statistics include applications that are either incomplete or too late or fall below the threshold of real risk of serious, irreversible harm; see Steering Committee for Human Rights (CDDH), 'Draft CDDH Report on Interim Measures under Rule 39 of the Rules of the Court,' 2 February 2013, CDDH(2013)R77, p. 8 (§ 28).

90   See the Court's statistical information on Rule 39 – requests granted and refused in 2008, 2009, 2010, 2011 and 2012 by responding state [accessible on the Court's website, 3.1.2014, copy in possession of author]; 666 requests were considered 'out of scope.'

In 2013 there were 1,588 requests, of which 108 were granted. In 2014, there were 1,929 requests, of which 216 were granted. And finally in 2015, there were 1,458 requests, of which 161 were granted.[91] The Court has become increasingly reluctant to attribute interim measures in recent years. In this context, it must be noted that states had also expressed their concerns about the rising number of applications concerning asylum matters and the interim measures applied. They stressed that the Court is not meant to be a fourth-instance asylum court.[92] The Court responded to these concerns and began to adopt a different approach, which has contributed to the fact that, in the past two years, the number of interim measures indicated has fallen to under 10 per cent of all requests.[93]

1.3   *Legal Nature, Effects and Enforcement of Judgments*
1.3.1   In General
The judgments of the Court are legally binding on the state party concerned. Article 46 ECHR imposes on the respondent state a legal obligation to implement appropriate general and/or individual measures to secure the right of the applicant which the Court found to be violated.[94] However, it is primarily for the state to choose the means to be used to discharge its legal obligation under Article 46 ECHR, provided that those means are compatible with the judgment.

Which individual measures have to be taken depends on the Court's indication in the judgments and the circumstances of the case. They may include

---

91   Court's thematical statistics on interim measures 2012–2015; accessible on the Court's website under <http://www.echr.coe.int/Pages/home.aspx?p=reports> [16.2.2016].

92   On these developments see Steering Committee for Human Rights (CDDH), 'Draft CDDH Report on Interim Measures under Rule 39 of the Rules of the Court,' 2 February 2013, CDDH(2013)R77, pp. 2 (§ 3) and the Declaration adopted on 27 April 2011 at the Izmir High-level Conference on the future of the European Court of Human Rights, (preamble § 12 and follow-up plan § 3).

93   See Steering Committee for Human Rights (CDDH), 'Draft CDDH Report on Interim Measures under Rule 39 of the Rules of the Court,' 2 February 2013, CDDH(2013)R77, p. 12 (§ 44); the measures taken by the Court, among them the creation of a centralised Rule 39 unit, are described in this report. See also ECtHR, 'Annual Report 2012,' p. 33. See further the Declaration adopted on 27 April 2011 at the Izmir High-level Conference on the future of the European Court of Human Rights, (follow-up plan § 3). See also the Court's thematical statistics on interim measures 2012–2015; accessible on the Court's website under <http://www.echr.coe.int/Pages/home.aspx?p=reports> [16.2.2016].

94   ECtHR, *Dzhurayev v. Russia*, 25 April 2013, no. 71386/10, § 247.

specific actions or, according to Article 41 ECHR, compensation for the cost of the procedure at the national level and just satisfaction for pecuniary or non-pecuniary damages. The next section will discuss which measures are required under the principle of non-refoulement.

In particular situations, the Court may find it useful to indicate to the respondent state *general measures* that should be taken to put an end to the situation that gave rise to the finding of a violation, in particular if the violation is of a systematic nature. In *Auad v. Bulgaria* for instance, the Court stated that to fully respect the principle of non-refoulement as it had been breached in this particular case, the general measures in the execution of this judgment should include amendments to the Bulgarian Aliens legislation and changes to administrative and judicial practice.[95] Even though the Court's judgments in principle only address the particular case at issue, the Committee of Ministers has consistently emphasized that the measures to be taken should also be taken in respect of other persons in the applicant's position, notably by solving the problems that led to the Court's findings.[96]

The Committee of Ministers of the Council of Europe is charged with the supervision of the execution of the judgments.[97] It is a political body and is composed of one representative for each contracting state, usually the Minister of Foreign Affairs, with one vote each. The Ministers meet in person twice a year but they act throughout the year through their permanent representatives in Strasbourg (usually ambassadors). The supervision of the execution of judgments is mainly carried out at four regular meetings per year.[98]

Six months from the date on which a judgment of the Court becomes final, governments have to present 'action reports' explaining to the Committee the measures taken to implement the judgment. If the Committee of Ministers is satisfied by the measures, it will adopt a final resolution closing the examination of the case. If not, the case will remain on the Committee's agenda until the necessary actions have been taken. The Committee of Ministers regularly publishes information on the state of execution of judgments. If problems arise because of a state's failure to execute, it may issue strongly worded

---

95 ECtHR, *Auad v. Bulgaria*, 11 October 2011, no. 46390/10, §§ 136–139.

96 See the reference in ECtHR, *Dzhurayev v. Russia*, 25 April 2013, no. 71386/10, § 247.

97 Art. 46(2) ECHR.

98 For the procedure, see the Rules of the Committee of Ministers for the Supervision of the Execution of Judgments and of the Terms of Friendly Settlements, adopted by the Committee of Ministers on 10 May 2006 at the 964th meeting of the Ministers' Deputies.

interim resolutions recalling the state's legal obligations under the ECHR and urging it to take particular steps to comply with a judgment.[99]

1.3.2   In the Context of a Non-refoulement Complaint

In the great majority of non-refoulement complaints that are successful in Strasbourg, the deportation of the applicant – because of interim measures granted – has not taken place when the judgment is adopted. In these cases, the respondent state fulfils its obligation under 46 ECHR by simply not deporting the applicant. The Court may ask the respondent state to compensate the applicant for costs and expenses relating to the national and international procedure, but it does not require further compensations for any pecuniary or non-pecuniary damages to be paid, even though applicants in refoulement procedures may have lived with an uncertain legal status for years. The Court, as a principle, has considered that the finding that a deportation, if carried out, would breach Article 3 ECHR, constitutes *sufficient just satisfaction*.[100]

The Court further does not require the state party concerned to attribute a particular legal status to the applicant. It recapitulated on earlier decisions on this matter in the decision *Ahmed Ali v. Netherlands*:

> The mere fact that the applicant will not be eligible for an indefinite residence permit in 2012, which she claimed she would have been had her original asylum application been examined on its merits, is not capable of raising an issue under Article 3, either taken alone or in conjunction with Article 13. In this respect it is to be borne in mind that, although *Article 3 may in certain circumstances imply the obligation not to expel a person, the protection afforded by Article 3 cannot be construed as guaranteeing, as such, the right to a residence permit, let alone the right to a particular residence permit.* As the Court has previously held, the Convention does not lay down for the Contracting States any given manner for ensuring within their internal law the effective implementation of the Convention. Accordingly, if an applicant receives protection against being returned to a country in respect of which substantial grounds have been shown for believing that he or she would face a real risk of being subjected to treatment contrary to Article 3, the Court is *not empowered* to rule on whether the individual concerned

99   *Ibid.*
100   For example, ECtHR, *F.N. v. Sweden*, 18 December 2012, no. 28774/09, § 84.

should be granted one particular legal status rather than another, that choice being a matter for the domestic authorities alone.[101] (Emphasis added)

The Court pronounces a bar to removal rather than asking the respondent states to attribute a certain status to the applicant. As the Court is fond of repeating, the ECHR does not contain a right to political asylum.[102]

It would be beyond the scope of this study to analyse how judgments on non-refoulement are executed at the national level. State practices are diverse. However, the documents of the Committee of Ministers on the execution of non-refoulement judgments reveal that most successful applicants are granted long-term residence permits; some have even been granted refugee status.[103] Temporary protection has also been considered by the Committee of Ministers as sufficient to close execution proceedings. However, the applicant must be able to request further extension and lodge an appeal should this request be rejected.[104] It should be noted that a state may also find a further alternative to tolerating the applicant on its own territory by resettling him in a safe third country. However, in this case, it is up to the respondent state to demonstrate that this is a 'realistic alternative' and that the applicant will be safe in this third country and will not in turn be sent from there back to his country of origin.[105] In general, the majority of member states comply with the Court's

---

101   ECtHR, *Ahmed Ali v. Netherlands and Greece*, 24 January 2012, no. 26494/09, § 19 (decision).

102   For example, ECtHR, *Hirsi Jamaa and Others v. Italy*, 23 February 2012 [GC], no. 27765/09, § 113.

103   For example, CM/ResDH(98)10 on the execution of ECtHR, *D. v. UK*, 2 May 1997, no. 30240/96; CM/ResDH(2010)138 on the execution of ECtHR, *Hilal v. UK*, 6 March 2001, no. 45276/99; CM/ResDH(2010)112 on the execution of ECtHR, *Bader and Kanbor v. Sweden*, 8 November 2005, no. 13284/04; CM/ResDH(2007)35 on the execution of ECtHR, *N. v. Finland*, 26 July 2005, no. 38885/02; CM/ResDH(2011)311 on the execution of ECtHR, *D. and others v. Turkey*, 22 June 2006, no. 24245/03; DH-DD(2013)494 on the execution of ECtHR, *S.F. and Others v. Sweden*, 15 May 2012, no. 52077/10, §§ 67–71.

104   For example, CMResDH(2010)10 on the execution of ECtHR, *Salah Sheekh v. Netherlands*, 11 January 2007, no. 1948/04; CM/ResDH(2011)84 on the execution of ECtHR, *N.A. v. UK*, 17 July 2008, no. 25904/07; CM/ResDH(2013)11 on the execution of ECtHR, *Y.P. and L.P. v. France*, 2 September 2010, no. 32476/06; CH/ResDH(2013)12 on the execution of ECtHR, *H.R. v. France*, 22 September 2011, no. 64780/09.

105   See ECtHR, *Singh and Others v. Belgium*, 2 October 2012, no. 33210/11, § 83.

judgments.[106] However, there are cases in which requests for interim measures have not been respected.[107]

In cases in which the applicants *have already been deported* before the Court took its decision and in which the Court concluded that the deportation was in breach of Article 3 ECHR, it has mostly granted compensation for non-pecuniary damage.[108] However, the implementation of judgments is generally more difficult once applicants have already been deported.[109] In these cases, states should take whatever diplomatic action is possible to protect the applicant against ill treatment. In *Al-Saadoon and Mufdhi v. United Kingdom*, the Court requested the United Kingdom to take all possible steps to obtain assurance from the Iraqi authorities detaining the applicants that they would not be subjected to the death penalty.[110] In *Hirsi Jamaa and Others v. Italy*, in which the applicants were Somalian and Eritrean migrants who had been intercepted in the Mediterranean Sea by Italian authorities and returned to Libya, the Court held that the 'Italian Government must take all possible steps to obtain assurances from the Libyan authorities that the applicants will not be subjected to treatment incompatible with Article 3 of the Convention or arbitrarily repatriated.'[111] The Court has never explicitly required a member state to *bring back* an applicant whose deportation had violated Article 3 ECHR. It has, though, indicated that this may be an acceptable remedial measure.[112]

---

106 ECtHR, 'Annual Report 2012,' p. 47. So far, no case is known to the author in which an applicant was deported despite a Court's finding that his deportation *would* be in breach of Art. 3 ECHR.

107 See on this Chapter 2 Section 1.2 above on interim measures.

108 See, for example, ECtHR, *Trabelsi v. Italy*, 13 April 2010, no. 50163/08 (EUR 15,000, violation of Art. 3 and 34 ECHR); ECtHR, *M.S.S. v. Belgium and Greece*, 21 January 2011 [GC], no. 30696/09 (Belgium had to award EUR 24,900 for the distress experienced by the complainant because of his transfer to Greece); ECtHR, *Hirsi Jamaa and Others v. Italy*, 23 February 2012 [GC], no. 27765/09 (EUR 15,000 for each applicant, violation of Art. 3, 13 and Art. 4 of Protocol No. 4 to the ECHR); ECtHR, *Mannai v. Italy*, 27 March 2012, no. 9961/10 (EUR 15,000, violation of Art. 3 and 34 ECHR); ECtHR, *Kasymakhunov v. Russia*, 14 November 2013, no. 29604/12 (EUR 30,000, violation of Art. 3 and 34 ECHR).

109 This is evident from the Committee of Ministers' documents on the execution of these cases. See in particular the Interim Resolution CM/ResDH(2013)200 on the 'Garabayev group of cases' against the Russian Federation, adopted on 26 September 2013. See on this also ECtHR, *Dzhurayev v. Russia*, 25 April 2013, no. 71386/10, §§ 250–253.

110 ECtHR, *Al-Saadoon and Mufdhi v. UK*, 2 March 2010, no. 61498/08, § 171.

111 ECtHR, *Hirsi Jamaa and Others v. Italy*, 23 February 2012 [GC], no. 27765/09, § 211.

112 ECtHR, *Dzhurayev v. Russia*, 25 April 2013, no. 71386/10, § 254.

However, as the Court has itself stated, the Committee of Ministers is better placed to assess the specific measures to be taken.[113]

2 Procedure under Article 22 CAT

2.1 *The Complaint Mechanism*
2.1.1 The Life of an Application in Geneva
Article 22 CAT and the Committee's Rules of Procedure lay down how individual complaints are assessed by the Committee. Complaints must be submitted in written form by email, fax or regular post to the Secretariat of the Office of the High Commissioner for Human Rights (OHCHR) in Geneva.[114] To perform its various functions, the Committee is assisted by a full-time team of secretariat staff that consists of OHCHR professionals provided by the Secretary-General of the UN.[115] Within the secretariat staff of the OHCHR, it is the so-called Petitions Section that carries out the registration and administrative handling of the individual complaints.[116] This section also prepares the drafts of decisions that are later reviewed and adopted by the Committee.[117]

In 2002, the mandate of the rapporteur on new complaints and interim measures was established by the Committee to deal more efficiently with the rising numbers of complaints submitted, particularly concerning refoulement.[118] The Committee appoints this rapporteur from among its members. According to the Rules of Procedure, he may register cases, request further information from complainants and decide on requests for interim measures.[119]

113　*Ibid.,* § 255.

114　Nowak and McArthur recommend regular post or fax for a faster treatment (2008, p. 730 § 21).

115　Art. 18(3) CAT. In the Committee's Rules of Procedure, the secretariat staff is called the Secretary-General.

116　Rule 104(1) ComAT (CAT/C/3/Rev.6). The Petitions Section is also responsible for the administrative handling of individual complaints submitted to the Human Rights Committee, the Committee on the Elimination of Racial Discrimination and the Committee on the Elimination of Discrimination against Women (Nowak & McArthur 2008, p. 730 § 23). The unit consists of around ten international lawyers; information obtained by the OHCHR, 3 October 2013.

117　Ingelse 2001, p. 111; Nowak & McArthur 2008, p. 769 (§ 132 and fn. 268).

118　Nowak & McArthur 2008, p. 734 (§ 38). For his mandate see ComAT, 'Annual Report 2001/2002,' §§ 203, 204 and annexe VIII (A/57/44).

119　Rules 104, 105 and 114 ComAT (CAT/C/3/Rev.6).

Before the secretariat or the rapporteur on new complaints and interim measures may register a new complaint, they have to make sure that the complaint (1) is directed against a state that has made a declaration under Article 22 CAT, (2) is not anonymous and (3) is submitted by an alleged victim of the Convention or accompanied by a proper authorization.[120] The requirements for registration are identical with the admissibility conditions contained in Article 22 CAT and Rule 113 of the Rules of Procedure, but are applied less strictly.[121] Complaints might also not be registered 'if there is such an evident lack of substance in the complaint that handling it would be meaningless.'[122]

A complaint that has been registered is transmitted to the state party concerned, which will be requested to submit written observations on the case. These observations must include explanations that relate to the admissibility and the merits of the complaint as well as to any remedy that may have been provided in the matter.[123] The complainant is then given the opportunity to submit comments on the submission received from the government.[124]

Each single case is designated a special rapporteur, who – mostly together with the secretariat – will go over all documents and present his view to the Committee.[125] As has been stated, the Committee usually meets twice a year at the UN Office in Geneva for three- or four-week sessions.[126] As outlined in chapter 1 section 3.1.2, the Committee not only assesses individual complaints during these sessions; it has other supervisory functions that take up most of its meeting time. The Committee adopts its decisions on individual complaints by a simple majority at meetings where at least six members must be present.[127] Most decisions are adopted in consensus.[128] The Committee usually assesses the admissibility and merits of a complaint at the same session and

---

120   Rule 104(2) ComAT (CAT/C/3/Rev.6).

121   .Nowak & McArthur 2008, p. 732 (§§ 34 and 35) and p. 745 (§ 70).

122   Sørensen 2001, p. 174. According to information obtained by the OHCHR on 3 October 2013, this is rare for complaints concerning the principle of non-refoulement.

123   Art. 22(3) CAT and Rule 115 ComAT (CAT/C/3/Rev.6).

124   Rule 117(3) ComAT (CAT/C/3/Rev.6).

125   Sørensen 2001, p. 181. The Committee may designate rapporteurs from among its members to deal with specific complaints and make recommendations at the plenary session; see Rules 112(3) and 118(1) ComAT (CAT/C/3/Rev.6) and Nowak & McArthur 2008, p. 769 (§ 132 and fn. 268).

126   The Committee was given additional meeting time for 2015 and 2016 so that there were/ are *three* sessions in these years; see ComAT, 'Annual Report 2014/2015,' p. 22 (A/70/44).

127   Art. 18(2) CAT. See also Rule 51 ComAT (CAT/C/3/Rev.6).

128   Information obtained by OHCHR, 3 October 2013.

within the same decision.[129] It then forwards its decision to the parties concerned.[130] In case the Committee finds a violation of the CAT, it will invite the state party concerned to inform it within a specific time period of the action it has taken in conformity with the Committee's decisions.[131]

2.1.2 Hearings, Confidentiality, Languages, Costs, Legal Representation and Length of Procedure

The individual complaints procedure under the CAT is written. Closed oral meetings are possible according to 117(4) of the Rules of Procedure. So far, it is only in the framework of the assessment of the case *Abdussamatov and 28 others v. Kazakhstan* concerning the extradition of 29 complainants to Uzbekistan that the Committee has called for an oral hearing to take place in Geneva.[132]

The individual complaints procedure before the Committee is confidential. All documents associated with complaints, including the submissions of the parties, remain confidential. The complaints are assessed in closed meetings.[133] However, the decisions adopted by the Committee are public.[134] They are published in the Committee's annual report and accessible on its website. Upon request, the Secretariat will keep a complainant's identity anonymous to the public, and this is usually its practice in cases concerning non-refoulement.

According to Rule 27 of the Committee's Rules of Procedure, Arabic, Chinese, English, French, Russian and Spanish are the official languages of the Committee and, 'to the extent possible, also its working languages.' In practice its working languages are English, French, Russian and Spanish. Applicants are therefore recommended to submit complaints and requests for interim measures in one of these languages; otherwise there may be a delay in treatment.[135]

---

129   According to Rule 115(2 and 3) ComAT (CAT/C/3/Rev.6), the Committee may decide to consider the admissibility separately from the merits, something it has done rarely in the last ten years.

130   Art. 22(7) CAT.

131   Rule 118(5) ComAT (CAT/C/3/Rev.6). On the legal nature of the decisions, their effect in the context of refoulement and the follow-up mechanism established by the Committee, see Section 2.3 of this chapter.

132   ComAT, *Abdussamatov and 28 Others v. Kazakhstan*, 1 June 2012, no. 444/2010, §§ 1.3 and 9.1–10.9. Other requests for hearings in refoulement cases have been rejected; see ComAT, *Z.T. (No. 2) v. Norway*, 14 November 2005, no. 238/2003, §§ 12.1 and 12.2; ComAT, *S.N.A.W. et al. v. Switzerland*, 24 November 2005, no. 231/2003, § 7.8.

133   Art. 22(6) CAT and Rule 107(1) ComAT (CAT/C/3/Rev.6).

134   Rules 34 and 35 ComAT (CAT/C/3/Rev.6).

135   Bayefsky 2003, pp. 50 and 79; Nowak & McArthur, 2008, p. 730 (§ 21).

The individual complaint procedure before the Committee is free of charge. Article 22 CAT of the Committee's Rules of Procedure do not impose a requirement of legal representation. The Committee cannot provide legal aid or other financial assistance to complainants. In certain cases in which the Committee has found that the CAT has been violated, the Committee has instructed the respondent state to take appropriate reparation measures. In refoulement cases, the Committee usually contents itself with instructing the respondent government not to deport the complainant.[136]

In contrast to the individual complaint procedure under the ECHR, there is no formal possibility for interested third parties such as NGOs and other organisations interested in human rights to intervene.

The average time taken from the registration to the final decision on a complaint by the Committee is two and half years.[137] The Committee tries to deal with complaints in the order in which they were received.[138] However, the duration of the proceedings before the Committee is very variable. Decisions on inadmissibility are usually made more quickly.

2.2   *Interim Measures*

Following the model of the Human Rights Committee and the Strasbourg institutions, the Committee has developed the practice of granting interim measures to avoid irreparable damage to complainants threatened with refoulement.[139] As with the ECHR, there is no provision in the CAT for provisional measures. That said, the Committee has introduced a provision in its Rules of procedure: according to Article 114 of these Rules, the Committee or the rapporteur on new complaints and interim measures may, 'at any time after the receipt of a complaint, transmit to the State party concerned, for its urgent consideration, a request that it take such interim measures as the Committee considers necessary to avoid irreparable damage to the victim or victims of alleged violations.' Almost all provisional measures indicated by the Committee concern non-refoulement complaints under Article 3 CAT.[140]

---

136   See on this Section 2.3 of this chapter.

137   Report by the OHCHR, 'Strengthening the United Nations Human Rights Treaty Body System,' June 2012, p. 23.

138   Bayefsyk 2003, pp. 42 and 81.

139   Nowak & McArthur 2008, p. 722 (§ 3); pp. 733–734 (§§ 36–38) and 790–791 (§ 187).

140   As an interesting case within the few exceptions see ComAT, *P.E. v. France*, 21 November 2002, no. 193/2001, § 1.2 and 3.1 (the Committee asked the state party not to extradite the applicant based on Art. 15 because the charges in the receiving state were allegedly based on evidence obtained under torture).

The Committee has granted provisional measures in more than 70 per cent of all the refoulement complaints in which it has adopted a decision.[141]

At the end of 2015, there were 15 published cases in which provisional measures had been ignored by the respondent state in non-refoulement cases.[142] In the first cases in which this happened, the Committee reacted by expressing its deep concerns. It reminded the States in question that the failure to respect provisional measures undermined the protection of the rights enshrined in the CAT and that they had voluntarily accepted the complaint mechanism under Article 22 CAT, with the implied obligation that they would cooperate in good faith with the Committee.[143]

In 2005, in the case *Brada v. France*, the Committee for the first time found that a *state's failure to respect interim measures constituted a breach of Article 22 CAT*.[144] The Committee reaffirmed the approach in subsequent decisions; it did not follow the member states' arguments according to which provisional measures, being only based on its Rule of Procedure and not on the Convention itself, were not binding and left a certain margin of discretion for the states

---

141 According to the numbers on interim measures indicated in the last two annual reports published before completion of this book, the number has risen to almost 80 per cent in recent years, see ComAT, 'Annual Report 2013/2014,' p. 180; (A/69/44); ComAT, 'Annual Report 2014/2015,' p. 19 (A/70/44). In its early practice, the Committee granted interim measures almost automatically (Rieter 2010, p. 138).

142 ComAT, *Chipana v. Venezuela*, 10 November 1998, no. 110/1998, ComAT, *T.P.S. v. Canada*, 16 May 2000, no. 99/1997; ComAT, *Brada v. France*, 17 May 2005, no. 195/2002; ComAT, *Pelit v. Azerbaijan*, 1 May 2007, no. 281/2005; ComAT, *Tebourski v. France*, 1 May 2007, no. 300/2006; ComAT, *Ahmad Dar v. Norway*, 11 May 2007, no. 249/2004; ComAT, *Sogi v. Canada*, 16 November 2007, no. 297/2006; ComAT, *Kalinichenko v. Morocco*, 25 November 2011, no. 428/2010; ComAT, *Abdussamatov and 28 Others v. Kazakhstan*, 1 June 2012, no. 444/2010; ComAT, *R.S. et al. v. Switzerland*, 21 November 2014, no. 482/2011; ComAT, *Tursunov v. Kazakhstan*, 8 May 2015, no. 538/2013; ComAT, *X. v. Russia*, 8 May 2015, no. 542/2013; ComAT, *X. v. Kazakhstan*, 3 August 2015, no. 554/2013; ComAT, *P.S.B. and T.K. v. Canada*, 13 August 2015, no. 505/2012; ComAT, *U. v. Hungary*, 8 December 2015, no. 671/2015. See further ComAT, *X.Q.L. v. Australia*, 2 May 2014, no. 455/2011, § 1.2, in which the Australian government indicated that it might not respect the indicated interim measures. The applicant was not, however, expelled before the Committee took its decision.

143 See ComAT, *Chipana v. Venezuela*, 10 November 1998, no. 110/1998, § 8; ComAT, *T.P.S. v. Canada*, 16 May 2000, no. 99/1997, § 15.6 and the individual opinion of Committee member Guibril Camara; ComAT, *Villamar and Cancino v. Canada*, 24 November 2004, no. 163/2000, § 6.3.

144 ComAT, *Brada v. France*, 17 May 2005, no. 195/2002, § 13.4.

as to whether to respect them in a particular case.[145] In *Tebourski v. France*, the Committee noted that 'Article 18 CAT vests it with competence to establish its own Rules of Procedure, which become inseparable from the Convention to the extent they do not contradict it.' It held that today's Rule 114 'is specifically intended to give meaning and scope to Articles 3 and 22 of the Convention, which otherwise would offer asylum seekers claiming a serious risk of torture purely relative, not to say theoretical, protection.'[146]

Committee member Alessio Bruni is not convinced by this practice. In individual opinions to recent decisions, he held that, while non-compliance by a state party with interim measures 'remains a clear sign of non-cooperation undermining the Committee's effectiveness of its mandate and should clearly be blamed,' it cannot be considered a violation of Article 22 CAT, since interim measures are not mentioned in this provision, but only in the Rules of Procedure.[147] Bruni remains in the minority with this opinion. In *X v. Kazakhstan* adopted in August 2015, the state party had raised the argument that the maximum period in which the complainant could be held in extradition detention had expired and that, under domestic law, he should either have been released or extradited and that, if released, he would have posed a threat to national security.[148] The government hence decided to extradite the applicant to Russia despite the interim measures indicated in Geneva. Following its established practice, the Committee concluded that this extradition was in violation of Article 22 CAT. It referred to the absolute nature of Article 3 CAT and to Article 27 of the Vienna Convention on the Law of Treaties, according to which a party may not invoke the provisions of its national law for its failure to perform a treaty.[149] The Committee confirmed this approach a little later in *D.I.S.*

---

145   See ComAT, *Tebourski v. France*, 1 May 2007, no. 300/2006, §§ 8.6–9; ComAT, *Pelit v. Azerbaijan*, 1 May 2007, no. 281/2005, § 10.2; ComAT, *Sogi v. Canada*, 16 November 2007, no. 297/2006, §§ 1.1–1.6, 7.7 and 10.11; ComAT, *Kalinichenko v. Morocco*, 25 November 2011, no. 428/2010, §§ 1.2, 1.4 and 16.

146   ComAT, *Tebourski v. France*, 1 May 2007, no. 300/2006, § 8.6. Confirmed in ComAT, *R.S. et al. v. Switzerland*, 21 November 2014, no. 482/2011, § 7.

147   Individual opinion on ComAT, *P.S.B. and T.K. v. Canada*, 13 August 2015, no. 505/2012. See his similar opinions on ComAT, *Tursunov v. Kazakhstan*, 8 May 2015, no. 538/2013; ComAT, *X. v. Russia*, 8 May 2015, no. 542/2013; ComAT, *X. v. Kazakhstan*, 3 August 2015, no. 554/2013; ComAT, *D.I.S. v. Hungary*, 8 December 2015, no. 671/2015.

148   ComAT, *X. v. Kazakhstan*, 3 August 2015, no. 554/2013, §§ 6.1 and 10.3.

149   *Ibid.* See also HRC, *Valetov v. Kazakhstan*, 17 March 2014, no. 2104/2011, §15, according to which the non-respect of interim measures indicated by the UN Human Rights Committee is considered as a breach of the Optional Protocol to the ICCPR.

v. Hungary.[150] Here the state party had argued that if the Committee fails to reach a decision before the expiration of the deadline for the complainant's release of detention, it will have no choice but to extradite the complainant in compliance with an extradition treaty with the United States. The Committee did not show any reaction to this argument and stayed firm in its position according to which a state's obligation to respect interim measures under Article 22 CAT is part of its effective respect of Article 3 CAT, which is absolute.[151]

In *Agiza v. Sweden*, the Committee found that the state party was in breach of its obligations under Article 22 CAT because the applicant had not been given a reasonable period of time to apply to the Committee in Geneva. The Committee observed that the complainant was arrested and removed by the state party as soon as the decision to expel him was taken.[152] In the case *Dar v. Norway*, the complainant was deported to Pakistan despite interim measures being indicated. Since the complainant was later allowed to return to Norway and was granted a residence permit there for three years, Norway remedied the violation of Article 22 CAT.[153] In the case *Abichou v. Germany*, the complainant was handed over to the Tunisian authorities at Frankfurt airport around one hour after the Permanent Mission of Germany in Geneva received the Committee's request for interim measures.[154] The Committee regretted that the request for interim measures was not respected. However, it recognized the state party's efforts to transmit the request 'as expeditiously as possible, given the circumstances' and concluded that in the present instance, the state party could not be said to have failed to meet its obligations under Article 22 CAT.[155] It is essential to submit requests in a timely manner.[156]

Being confronted with a large number of complaints concerning refoulement, the Committee decided in 2002 to assign one of its members to deal

---

150   ComAT, *D.S.I. v. Hungary*, 8 December 2015, no. 671/2015.

151   *Ibid.*, §§ 6.14, 8.1, 9.2. The Committee again also referred to Article 27 of the Vienna Convention, which Bruni considers wrong, since the state party has invoked its obligations under an extradition treaty, not provisions of its internal law.

152   ComAT, *Agiza v. Sweden*, 20 May 2005, no. 233/2003, § 13.9.

153   ComAT, *Ahmad Dar v. Norway*, 11 May 2007, no. 249/2004, §§ 1.1–1.4.

154   ComAT, *Abichou v. Germany*, 21 May 2013, no. 430/2010, § 4.4.

155   *Ibid.*, § 9.1.

156   See the following cases in which the request was submitted too late ComAT, *Arana v. France*, 9 November 1999, no. 63/1997, § 4.1; ComAT, *L.O. v. Canada*, 19 May 2001, no. 95/1997, §§ 1.2 and 6.1; ComAT, *M.P.S. v. Australia*, 30 April 2002, no. 138/1999, §§ 1.2 and 4.1; ComAT, *Z.T. v. Australia*, 11 November 2003, no. 153/2000, § 1.3; ComAT, *J.A.G.V. v. Sweden*, 11 November 2003, no. 215/2002, § 1.3.

specifically with provisional measures. It established the post of rapporteur on new complaints and interim measures.[157] It is this rapporteur who decides whether to grant provisional measures. The secretariat staff provides him with the information necessary.[158] If possible, the decision is taken within 24 hours of receipt of the request.[159] If the rapporteur decides to attribute interim measures, the government concerned will be informed immediately in order to suspend the deportation.

As in Strasbourg, in Geneva there is little transparency regarding decision-making on provisional measures. The decision to grant interim measures is adopted on the basis of information contained in the complainant's submission.[160] The basic admissibility criteria set out in Article 22 CAT must be met.[161] The requirement of the exhaustion of domestic remedies need not, however, be fulfilled if the only remedies available to the applicant are without suspensive effect.[162] As for the substantive criteria, a complaint must have a reasonable likelihood of success on the merits.[163] The granting of interim measures does not imply a determination on the merits or the admissibility of the complaint. However, if a request is rejected, the complaint only has a very slim chance of success. There have so far been only very few cases in which the Court has found a violation of Article 3 CAT where it had not indicated interim measures.[164]

The Committee has been criticised by state parties, which alleged that interim measures have been granted in a too large a number of cases, particularly when the factual basis with regard to the risk of ill treatment in case of deportation was poor.[165] In the context of its observations on two cases submitted in the mid-90s, the Swiss government expressed its concerns about the fact that

---

157   UN doc. CAT/C/SR.521, 29 May 2002, §§ 21–25.

158   Nowak & McArthur 2008, p. 735 (§ 40); Rieter 2010, p. 820 fn. 122.

159   Rieter 2010, p. 138. Information confirmed by OHCHR, 3 October 2013.

160   Rule 114(3) ComAT (CAT/C/3/Rev.6).

161   ComAT, 'Annual Report 2010/2011,' § 91 (A/66/44).

162   ComAT, *S.A.C. v. Monaco*, 13 November 2012, no. 346/2008, § 7.2.

163   ComAT, 'Annual Report 2011/2012,' § 108 (A/67/44). See also ComAT, *Brada v. France*, 17 May 2005, no. 195/2002, § 13.3; the applicant must establish an 'arguable risk of irreparable harm.'

164   See ComAT, *Chahin v. Sweden*, 30 May 2011, no. 310/2007, § 1.2; ComAT, *Boily v. Canada*, 14 November 2011, no. 327/2007, §§ 1.2–1.4 (in which the Committee had withdrawn a first indication for interim measures); ComAT, *K.H. v. Denmark*, 23 November 2012, no. 464/2011.

165   See ComAT, 'Annual Report 2005/2006,' § 62 (A/61/44); recited in ComAT, 'Annual Report 2010/2011,' § 93 (A/66/44). See also Delas 2011, p. 345, noting certain states have indicated that the Committee uses interim measures excessively.

the Committee had asked for interim measures in the majority of cases transmitted to it, and applicants could use the Committee as a further appeal instance, simply allowing a suspension of the expulsion for at least six months. It noted that the possibility of demanding interim measures was not foreseen in the Convention itself but just in the Rules of Procedure. Accordingly, it should remain an exceptional remedy and the regular issuing of requests could interfere with the subsidiary nature of the procedure.[166] Bayefsky noted in 2003 that the Committee's practice has been to ask the state party to take interim measures if 'there is even a small danger that the person may be tortured if they are expelled.'[167]

The threshold for obtaining interim measures is obviously lower before the Committee then it is before the Court, where today less than 10 per cent of all requests are accepted.[168] An illustrative example of the Committee's more generous practice is the case *Abichou v. Germany*.[169] It was first submitted in Strasbourg but then withdrawn after the request for interim measures was denied and submitted in Geneva. In contrast to the Court, the Committee acceded to the applicant's request for interim measures and later even found that the principle of non-refoulement had been violated.[170] Strasbourg Judge Zupančič once advocated in an individual opinion that interim measures should be applied once there is a 'shadow of doubt' since the aim of such measures was not some kind of truth finding but to create conditions in which truth finding may yet happen.[171] This approach is more reflected in the Committee's practice than in the Court's.

The rapporteur may review his decision to grant interim measures at the initiative of the state party in light of information received to the effect that the submission was not justified and the complainant did not, in fact, face any prospect of irreparable harm.[172] However, the Committee has made clear that such requests need only be addressed if they are based on new and

---

166　See ComAT, *X v. Switzerland*, 28 April 1997, no. 27/1995, § 5.1; ComAT, *K.N. v. Switzerland*, 19 May 1998, no. 94/1997, §§ 5.1 and 5.2.

167　Bayefsky 2003, p. 80.

168　See Chapter 2 Section 1.2.

169　ComAT, *Abichou v. Germany*, 21 May 2013, no. 430/2010.

170　*Ibid.*, §§ 4.4, 8.1–8.4 and 10.1.

171　See concurring opinion of judge Zupančič in ECtHR, *Saadi v. Italy*, 28 February 2008 [GC], no. 37201/06. See in this sense also his remarks with regard to the Committee's practice in his dissenting opinion to ECtHR, *J.K. and Others v. Sweden*, 4 June 2015, no. 59166/12 (Iraq – not in force – referred to Grand Chamber).

172　Rule 114(3, 7 and 8) ComAT (CAT/C/3/Rev.6).

pertinent information that was not available to it when the initial decision was taken.[173]

2.3   *Legal Nature, Effects and Enforcement of the Decisions*

2.3.1   In General

The Committee is a monitoring body created by the state parties and holds declaratory powers only.[174] The Committee's decisions are not binding under international law.[175] The declaratory nature of the Committee's decisions is re-flected in the fact that they are considered 'views' in the Convention text.[176] However, by ratifying the CAT, state parties accept the legal obligation not to violate the obligations set out within the Convention. State parties that have made a declaration under Article 22 CAT have further given the authority to the Committee to express its view as to whether a violation of rights has occurred in an individual case.[177] In other words, they have voluntarily given the last word on the interpretation of the CAT in individual cases to the Committee.

According to the UN Human Rights Committee, its views in individual cases exhibit the 'important characteristics of a judicial decision.'[178] They represent an 'authoritative determination' by the organ established under the ICCPR it-self charged with the interpretation of that instrument.[179] The Human Rights Committee points out that the character of the views is determined by the obligation of state parties to act in good faith, both in their participation in the individual complaint procedure and in relation to the Covenant itself.[180] These considerations apply equally to the character of the Committee's decisions.[181] They demonstrate that even if decisions taken by the UN human rights treaty bodies are not legally binding in the strict sense, the question of whether they are followed is significant under international law.[182] Against this background,

---

173   ComAT, 'Annual Report 2010/2011,' § 90 (A/66/44).

174   ComAT, General Comment No. 1 on Art. 3 CAT (1997), § 9.

175   Boulesbaa 1999, p. 63; Kälin 2013, p. 259; Nowak & McArthur 2008, p. 796 (§ 199).

176   See Art. 22 CAT.

177   Bayefsky 2003, p. 33.

178   HRC, General Comment No. 33 on the Optional Protocol to the ICCPR (2008), §§ 13 and 11.

179   *Ibid.*, § 13.

180   *Ibid.*, § 15. The HRC here refers to Article 26 of the 1969 Vienna Convention on the Law of Treaties.

181   Kälin 2013, p. 657.

182   See also the International Court of Justice, according to which 'great weight' must be ascribed to the views adopted by the Human Rights Committee that was established 'spe-cifically to supervise the application of that treaty'; ICJ, *Ahmadou Sadio Diallo (Republic of Guinea v. DRC)*, Judgment of 30 November 2010, § 11, Reports 2010, p. 639.

I agree with Nowak and McArthur, who state that the Committee's decisions must be considered more than mere recommendations.[183] They and other scholars characterize the decisions as 'authoritative interpretations' of the CAT under international law.[184] However, the exact legal nature of the decisions taken by the UN human rights monitoring bodies on individual complaints remains controversial.[185]

For a long time, there was no follow-up mechanism for the supervision of compliance with the decisions of the Committee.[186] In 1999, the Committee started to request that state parties report on the action taken in conformity with the Committee's findings within 90 days.[187] In 2002, following the example of the Human Rights Committee, the Committee adopted a more formalized follow-up mechanism. At its 28th session, it established the function of a rapporteur for follow-up to decisions on complaints submitted under Article 22 CAT for the purpose of ascertaining that state parties take measures to give effect to the Committee's findings.[188] This rapporteur may send *notes verbales* to state parties enquiring about measures adopted pursuant to the decisions and recommend to the Committee action as may be necessary for follow-up.[189]

If states do not comply with a decision, the Committee will keep up a dialogue and regularly remind the state concerned of its obligations under the CAT. These follow-up dialogues are published in the Committee's annual reports until the Committee is satisfied with the measures taken by the state.[190]

---

183   Nowak & McArthur 2008, p. 777 (§ 155). See also Kälin 2013, p. 259 (§ 657).

184   Nowak & McArthur 2008, p. 797 (§ 199). Also Bayefsky 2003, p. 48; Wouters 2009, pp. 431–432. According to Nowak & McArthur, non compliance with the Committee's findings must be considered a violation of the respective obligations under the CAT.

185   For interesting reading on the discussion see, for example, Ulfstein 2012, pp. 92–100; Van Alebeek and Nollkaemper 2012, pp. 382–387. Ulfstein notes that the decisions of the UN treaty bodies entail a presumption of correctness and require states to present good reasons for any conflicting opinion. He recognizes that non-compliance with the decisions may result in 'naming and shaming' and political pressure. Nonetheless, he is of the opinion that states are 'legally free to come to the conclusion, if they have good reasons, that they will not respect these findings'; pp. 94–100 and 113.

186   Ingelse 2001, p. 192; Nowak & McArthur 2008, p. 774 (§ 147).

187   The request was made first in ComAT, *Elmi v. Australia*, 14 May 1999, no. 120/1998.

188   ComAT, 'Annual Report 2001/2002,' § 203 and annexe IX (A/57/44). See further Rule 120 ComAT (CAT/C/3/Rev.6). See also Nowak & McArthur 2008, p. 729 (§ 19) and p. 775 (§§ 148–150).

189   See Rule 120 ComAT (CAT/C/3/Rev.6).

190   See Rule 121(3) ComAT (CAT/C/3/Rev.6) and the Committee's annual reports since 2005; ComAT, 'Annual Report 2005/2006,' pp. 87–123 (A/61/44). In 2004, the Committee requested that the rapporteur provide information on follow-up to all decisions in which the

In light of this formalized follow-up mechanism, Nowak and McArthur observe that over the course of the years, the Committee has developed what was initially a 'weak procedure' into a 'fairly effective quasi judicial complaints procedure,' which is also reflected in a change of terminology.[191] In 2002 the Committee started using the term 'decision' instead of 'view' in its documents.[192] Already prior to this it had begun to use the term 'complaint' in its decisions instead of 'communication.'[193] The follow-up mechanism established by the Committee in 2002 can be compared to the Committee of Ministers' execution procedure in Strasbourg in the sense that both mainly function through reminders and, ultimately, diplomatic pressure. However, although the Committee is an organ with high political status, the Committee of Ministers in Strasbourg has far greater legal and political authority.[194]

2.3.2   In the Context of a Non-refoulement Complaint

In most cases concerning the principle of non-refoulement the complainant has not been deported at the point when the decision is adopted in Geneva because of granted interim measures. When finding a violation of the principle of non-refoulement in these cases, the Committee concludes its decision noting that the state party's decision to return the complainant would constitute a breach of Article 3 CAT. It adds that it wishes to be informed, within 90 days, of the steps taken by the state party to respond to this decision.

Which steps do state parties have to take to comply with such a decision under Article 3 CAT? In fact, the only obligation they have is *not* to remove the individual concerned. According to the Committee, Article 3 CAT 'authorizes it to determine whether return would expose a person to the danger of being subjected to torture,' but 'it is not competent to determine whether or not the author is entitled to a residence permit under a country's domestic legislation.'[195] In *Aemei v. Switzerland*, the Committee made clear that its finding of a violation of Article 3 CAT in no way affected the decisions of the national authorities

---

Committee had found that the CAT was violated, including decisions prior to the commencement of the rapporteur's mandate; see ComAT, 'Annual Report 2004/2005,' § 151 (A/60/44).

191   Nowak & McArthur 2008, p. 722 (§ 3) and p. 796 (§ 199).

192   See UN doc. CAT/C/SR.518/Add.1 and Rule 118(4) ComAT (CAT/C/3/Rev.6).

193   See for example ComAT, *Chipana v. Venezuela*, 10 November 1998, no. 110/1998, § 6.1.

194   See in this sense also Inter-committee Meeting of Human Rights Treaty Bodies, Follow-up Procedures on Individual Complaints, UN Doc. HRI/ICM/WGFU/2011/3, 7 December 2010, § 25. Art. 46 ECHR stipulates the binding force of the Court's judgments and mandates the Committee of Ministers to supervise their execution.

195   ComAT, *P.Q.L. v. Canada*, 17 November 1997, no. 57/1996, § 10.6.

concerning the granting or refusal of asylum. State authorities do, however, have the duty to find a solution to comply with the decision:

> The *finding of a violation of article 3 has a declaratory character.* Consequently, the State party is not required to modify its decision(s) concerning the granting of asylum; on the other hand, it does have a responsibility to find solutions that will enable it to take all necessary measures to comply with the provisions of article 3 of the Convention. These *solutions may be of a legal nature* (e.g. decision to admit the applicant temporarily), but also of a *political nature* (e.g. action to find a third State willing to admit the applicant to its territory and undertaking not to return or expel him in its turn).[196] (Emphasis added)

As can be seen, the legal status of the individual concerned in the country where he is allowed to stay is not relevant for the Committee.[197] Article 3 CAT, just like Article 3 ECHR, provides a bar to removal rather than a right to asylum.

As can be gleaned from its considerations on follow-up, the Committee has been quite successful with the implementation of its decisions in cases concerning the principle of non-refoulement.[198] Of the decisions in which it had found a violation of Article 3 CAT up to the end of 2012, there are *only two cases in which the state party went on to deport the applicant following the Committee's finding of a violation.* Both concerned the deportations from Canada of individuals considered a threat to national security.[199] With regard to Western European states, it can be stated that failed asylum seekers who have successfully fought their removal before the Committee appear not to have been treated any differently from those who have been successful before the Court.[200]

---

196   ComAT, *Aemei v. Switzerland*, 9 May 1997, 34/1995, § 11.

197   See also ComAT, *M.B.B. v. Sweden*, 5 May 1999, no. 104/1998, § 6.4.

198   See the Committee's considerations on follow-up activities in its annual reports beginning with ComAT, 'Annual Report 2004/2005,' (A/60/44). Information also confirmed by the OHCHR on 3 October 2013.

199   ComAT, *Dadar v. Canada*, 23 November 2005, no. 258/2004 (Iran); ComAT, *Sogi v. Canada*, 16 November 2007, no. 297/2006 (India). See ComAT, 'Annual Report 2010/2011,' pp. 162–171 (A/66/44). Australia and Canada, which are the only states outside Europe that have been confronted with complaints under Art. 3 CAT on a frequent basis, have been more reluctant than European states to simply accept and implement the Committee's findings, which can be observed in the Committee's considerations on follow-up activities in its annual reports beginning with ComAT, 'Annual Report 2004/2005,' (A/60/44).

200   Note, however, the few cases in which Western European states have disrespected interim measures: ComAT, *Brada v. France*, 17 May 2005, no. 195/2002; ComAT, *Tebourski v. France*,

A detailed analysis of the manner in which the Committee's decisions are implemented at national level would be beyond the scope of this research. However, as is apparent from the Committee's information on follow-up, most of them have been granted long-term residence permits; some have been granted refugee status. Others are granted renewable temporary residence permits.[201]

Yet, there are cases in which the complainant had already been expelled at the point when the Committee adopted its decision and found a violation of Article 3 CAT.[202] Most of these cases concern extraditions in which the Committee's request for interim measures had not been respected.[203] Instead of stating that the complainant's removal *would* violate Article 3 CAT, the Committee concluded that the deportation of the complainant *was·*in violation of Article 3 CAT. It asked the state parties to inform it of the steps taken in response to the views expressed. The Committee has further precised that the respondent state party should grant compensation for the breach of Article 3 CAT, and that it should inform it of the complainant's whereabouts

---

    1 May 2007, no. 300/2006 and ComAT, *Agiza v. Sweden*, 20 May 2005, no. 233/2003, in which the applicant was deported before he could submit his request. Note also ComAT, *Ahmad Dar v. Norway*, 11 May 2007, no. 249/2004, in which the applicant could return to Norway before the case was decided, and ComAT, *R.S. et al. v. Switzerland*, 21 November 2014, no. 482/2011, in which the non-respect was a mistake.

201   See the Committee's 'information on follow-up' published in its annual reports beginning with ComAT, 'Annual Report 2004/2005,' (A/60/44). A temporary stay might be sufficient to comply with the Committee's decision. However, the right not to be deported must at least prevail as long as the risk subsists.

202   See ComAT, *Chipana v. Venezuela*, 10 November 1998, no. 110/1998; ComAT, *Arana v. France*, 9 November 1999, no. 63/1997; ComAT, *Brada v. France*, 17 May 2005, no. 195/2002; ComAT, *Pelit v. Azerbaijan*, 1 May 2007, no. 281/2005; ComAT, *Tebourski v. France*, 1 May 2007, no. 300/2006; ComAT, *Sogi v. Canada*, 16 November 2007, no. 297/2006; ComAT, *Kalinichenko v. Morocco*, 25 November 2011, no. 428/2010; ComAT, *Abdussamatov and 28 Others v. Kazakhstan*, 1 June 2012, no. 444/2010; ComAT, *Tursunov v. Kazakhstan*, 8 May 2015, no. 538/2013; ComAT, *X. v. Russia*, 8 May 2015, no. 542/2013; ComAT, *X. v. Kazakhstan*, 3 August 2015, no. 554/2013; ComAT, *U. v. Hungary*, 8 December 2015, no. 671/2015. Worth mentioning is also ComAT, *Agiza v. Sweden*, 20 May 2005, no. 233/2003, in which the applicant was deported before he could submit his request and ComAT, *Abichou v. Germany*, 21 May 2013, no. 430/2010, § 9.1, in which the request was made too late. There are three cases in which the Committee found a breach of Art. 3 CAT but had not indicated interim measures; ComAT, *Boily v. Canada*, 14 November 2011, no. 327/2007; ComAT, *Chahin v. Sweden*, 30 May 2011, no. 310/2007; ComAT, *K.H. v. Denmark*, 23 November 2012, no. 464/2011.

203   *Ibid.* See on this also Section 2.2 of this chapter.

and assure his well-being in consultation with the country to which he was returned.[204]

In *Boily v. Canada* the complainant had been tortured upon return to a Mexican prison despite assurances provided by the Mexican authorities that his security would be guaranteed.[205] The Committee advised the respondent state to provide effective redress to the applicant in accordance with its obligations under Article 14 CAT. It requested the state party to compensate the complainant for the violation of his rights under Article 3 CAT and to provide as full a rehabilitation as possible by providing, *inter alia*, medical and psychological care including reimbursement for past expenditures, future services, and legal expenses; and to review its system of diplomatic assurances with a view to avoiding similar violations in the future.[206] It is rare that the Committee, in its findings, requests measures of a general nature to prevent future violations of Article 3 CAT.[207]

In *Kalinichenko v. Morocco*, the Committee found that the extradition of the complainant to Russia was in breach of Article 3 CAT. Two of the complainant's close business partners had either died or disappeared while in custody. The Committee urged the state party 'to provide redress for the complainant, including compensation and establishing an effective follow-up mechanism to ensure that the he is not subjected to torture or ill treatment.' It welcomed the fact 'that the authorities of the Russian Federation had undertaken to allow the Committee to visit the complainant in prison and to speak to him alone and in private' and requested that the respondent state facilitate further visits by two Committee members.[208]

---

204 See ComAT, *Brada v. France*, 17 May 2005, no. 195/2002, § 15; ComAT, *Tebourski v. France*, 1 May 2007, no. 300/2006, § 10; ComAT, *Sogi v. Canada*, 16 November 2007, no. 297/2006, § 12; ComAT, *Boily v. Canada*, 14 November 2011, no. 327/2007, § 15 and 16; ComAT, *Kalinichenko v. Morocco*, 25 November 2011, no. 428/2010, § 17; ComAT, *Abdussamatov and 28 Others v. Kazakhstan*, 1 June 2012, no. 444/2010, §§ 13.1–15; ComAT, *Tursunov v. Kazakhstan*, 8 May 2015, no. 538/2013, § 11; ComAT, *X. v. Russia*, 8 May 2015, no. 542/2013, § 13; ComAT, *X. v. Kazakhstan*, 3 August 2015, no. 554/2013, § 14.

205 ComAT, *Boily v. Canada*, 14 November 2011, no. 327/2007.

206 *Ibid.*, §§ 15 and 16.

207 As to the other exceptions see ComAT, *Agiza v. Sweden*, 20 May 2005, no. 233/2003, § 15, concerning an extraordinary rendition; ComAT, *Boily v. Canada*, 14 November 2011, no. 327/2007, § 15c, in which the Committee asked the state party to review its system of diplomatic assurances.

208 ComAT, *Kalinichenko v. Morocco*, 25 November 2011, no. 428/2010, § 17. According to Rule 120(4) ComAT (CAT/C/3/Rev.6), the rapporteur on follow-up may, with the approval of the Committee, engage in necessary visits to the state party concerned.

The case *Abdussamatov and 28 Others v. Kazakhstan* concerned 29 applicants suspected of terrorist activities who had been extradited from Kazakhstan to Uzbekistan despite the Committee's indication of interim measures.[209] The Committee concluded that Articles 3 and 22 CAT had been violated. It urged the state party to provide redress for the complainants 'including their return to Kazakhstan and adequate compensation.'[210] In the case *Abichou v. Germany*, the Committee had concluded that at the time of the complainant's extradition there was a real risk of his being subjected to torture in Tunisian custody.[211] The complainant had been acquitted, released and had not been subjected to torture subsequent to his extradition. Nevertheless, the Committee urged the state party to provide redress to the applicant including adequate compensation.[212] In *Ahmad Dar v. Norway*, the applicant had been deported to Pakistan after the Committee's request for interim measures had been made.[213] However, the state party then facilitated the applicant's return to Norway. The Committee noted that by doing so, Norway had remedied the breach of its obligations under Article 22 CAT to respect interim measures. In view of the fact that the complainant, who was not tortured during his brief stay in Pakistan, had returned to the state and had received a residence permit, the Committee considered that the issue of whether his deportation to Pakistan constituted a violation of Article 3 CAT had become a moot point.[214]

Generally, in those cases in which the complainant had already been deported when the Committee adopted its decision, the implementation of such a decision causes difficulties. Dialogues on follow-up between the Committee and the states concerned in these cases take longer than usual.[215] However, in these cases as well, states have normally shown their willingness to satisfy the Committee's demands. It can generally be observed from the Committee's information on follow-up activities, provided in its annual reports, that

---

209   ComAT, *Abdussamatov and 28 Others v. Kazakhstan*, 1 June 2012, no. 444/2010, §§ 13.1–15.

210   *Ibid.*, § 15. Similar ComAT, *X. v. Russia*, 8 May 2015, no. 542/2013, § 13.

211   ComAT, *Abichou v. Germany*, 21 May 2013, no. 430/2010.

212   *Ibid.*, §§ 11.6–13.

213   ComAT, *Ahmad Dar v. Norway*, 11 May 2007, no. 249/2004.

214   *Ibid.*, §§ 16.1–18.

215   This can be observed in the Committee's 'information on follow-up' published in its annual reports beginning with ComAT, 'Annual Report 2004/2005' (A/60/44). As explained in Section 2.3.1 of this chapter, in 2004, the Committee started to provide information on follow-up to all decisions in which the Committee had found that the CAT was violated, including decisions prior to the establishment of this follow-up system; see ComAT, 'Annual Report 2004/2005,' § 151.

ensuring compliance with its decisions in cases of domestic torture is more difficult than with those made in the context of refoulement.

3 The Admissibility of Complaints in the Context of Refoulement

3.1 *Overview of the Admissiblity Criteria under the ECHR and the CAT*

The Court and the Committee only assess complaints if all admissibility criteria as laid down in the ECHR and the CAT are fulfilled. A comprehensive analysis of the Court and Committee's practice with regard to admissibility would go beyond the scope of this study. Nonetheless, to appreciate the similarities and differences between the practices of the Court and the Committee with regard to protection against refoulement, it is essential to have an overview of the procedure as a whole – including admissibility.

The conditions for admissibility of complaints as set out in the ECHR and the CAT are almost identical. They will be described together. The admissibility criteria for complaints submitted to the Court are laid out in Article 35 ECHR and Article 34 ECHR, and those for complaints submitted to the Committee in Article 22(2) and (4) CAT and Rule 113 of the Committee's Rules of Procedure. The admissibility requirements that are common to the complaints mechanisms in Strasbourg and Geneva are the following:

- The complaint must be imputable to a state that has ratified the ECHR or the CAT (incompatibility *ratione personae; ratione loci*). With regard to the procedure under the CAT, the imputed state must further have made a declaration under Article 22 CAT according to which it accepts the Committee's competence to assess individual complaints.
- The alleged human rights violation must have occurred after ratification of the corresponding Convention (incompatibility *ratione temporis*). With regard to the Committee, the alleged human rights violation must further have occurred after the declaration under Article 22 CAT has been made.
- The same complaint shall not be pending or have been examined already by another international forum.
- All accessible effective domestic remedies must be exhausted.
- The claim must be compatible with the provisions of the relevant Convention (incompatibility *ratione materiae*).
- The complaint shall not be anonymous, abusive or manifestly ill-founded.
- The complainant must be personally affected by the violation.

There are two admissibility conditions before the Court that are not required by the Committee:

(1)   According to Article 35(1) ECHR, the Court may only deal with complaints that have been submitted within six months of the final decision taken in the domestic procedure. The Committee does not pose such an absolute limit.[216] However, according to the Court's recent practice as discussed in section 3.2.2 below, the six-month rule is not as relevant in the context of refoulement as it is with regard to complaints under other rights of the ECHR.

(2)   The Court will not assess a complaint on the merits if it considers that the applicant has not suffered a significant disadvantage in the sense of Article 35(3) b ECHR. This criterion was introduced by Protocol No. 14 to the ECHR, which came into force on 1 June 2010. So far, there have only been a few decisions on this criterion so it is difficult to make generalised statements on its impact as yet.[217] None of the published cases in which this new criterion has been applied so far have concerned the principle of non-refoulement. It is hard to imagine that this criterion would play a particular role in that context; allegations of a real risk of torture or inhuman treatment in the case of a possible deportation would probably be rejected as 'manifestly ill-founded' rather than as a 'minor' issue.[218] There is no comparable criterion before the Committee. Like the Court, it can, however, reject unfounded complaints as 'manifestly ill-founded.'[219] In sum, the two admissibility criteria that only exist in the Strasbourg procedure are not real obstacles to most non-refoulement complaints.

The Court and the Committee may declare an application inadmissible at any stage of the proceedings.[220] If an application has been declared inadmissible and then 'relevant new information' has come to light, the applicant may resubmit the case after having exhausted any domestic remedies.[221] This might

---

216   See, however, Rule 113(f) ComAT (CAT/C/3/Rev.6), discussed in Section 3.2.2 of this chapter.

217   On the criterion as applied so far see the Court's 'Practical Guide on Admissibility Criteria,' 1 January 2014, pp. 88–96.

218   See in this sense Mole & Meredith 2010, p. 231. Looking at the wording of Art. 35(3)b which uses the phrase, 'the applicant *has not* suffered a significant disadvantage,' it is questionable if the criterion is at all applicable in refoulement cases in which the applicant has not yet been deported.

219   See Section 3.2.6 of this Chapter.

220   See explicitly in Art. 35(4) ECHR.

221   Art. 35(2)b ECHR.

be the case when a complainant's case is initially declared inadmissible for non-exhaustion of domestic remedies and, after having unsuccessfully made use of those domestic remedies, the applicant submits a new complaint.[222] The Committee has the power to review a decision on admissibility, both in favour of and against the applicant.[223]

It should be noted at this point that even though the requirements for the admissibility of complaints under the ECHR and the CAT are very similar, passing the bar of admissibility is much more difficult in Strasbourg than in Geneva: While more then 95 per cent of all applications submitted to the Court (in Strasbourg) are declared inadmissible,[224] that figure is only around 20 per cent before the Committee (in Geneva).[225] The reason for this will be explained below.[226]

3.2   *A Look at Issues of Particular Interest*

This section will deal with those admissibility issues that are of particular relevance in the context of refoulement and of interest to practitioners considering the submission of an application to the Court or to the Committee.

3.2.1   Extra-territorial Jurisdiction

States may be held responsible for violations of rights carried out under their jurisdiction.[227] Any claims of Convention violations that have taken place outside the respondent state's jurisdiction are declared inadmissible for being incompatible *ratione personae* by the Court and the Committee.[228] Jurisdiction is normally exercised throughout the state's territory. However, as the following considerations will show, exceptional circumstances are capable of giving rise to the exercise of jurisdiction by a state outside its own territorial

---

222   Leach 2011, p. 147. For the Committee see ComAT, *Z.T. (No. 2) v. Norway*, 14 November 2005, no. 238/2003, § 8.4.

223   See Rule 116(2) and 117(5) ComAT (CAT/C/3/Rev.6).

224   Court's 'Practical Guide on Admissibility Criteria,' 1 January 2014, p. 11.

225   See survey 'Status of the cases dealt with under Art. 22 CAT,' 15 August 2015, accessible on the Committee's website under <http://www.ohchr.org/en/hrbodies/cat/pages/catindex .aspx> [15.2.2016].

226   See Sections 3.2.6 and 3.3 of this chapter.

227   Art. 1 ECHR; Art. 22(1) CAT and Art. 2(1) CAT in combination with ComAT, General Comment No. 2 on Art. 2 (2008), § 16.

228   Also referred to as inadmissible *ratione loci*.

boundaries. The principles of the Court and the Committee on the issue are similar even though the Court's case law is much more developed.[229]

a   *Detention by Military Forces or the ICC and Extraordinary Renditions*
Referring to the relevant principles of international law, the Court's Grand Chamber held in *Loizidou v. Turkey* that state responsibility might arise when a member state exercises effective control over an area outside its national territory.[230] The Court has confirmed this approach of *effective control* in the context of refoulement in *Al-Saadoon and Mufdhi v. United Kingdom*.[231] The case concerned two Iraqis who were arrested by British forces in 2003 and detained in Iraq in British-run detention facilities. They were suspected of various acts of violence against the coalition forces led by the United States, including the murder of two British soldiers. The British authorities decided to refer the cases to the Iraqi criminal courts and transferred the applicants to the custody of the Iraqi authorities. The applicants challenged their transfer, claiming that they risked execution by hanging. In its decision on admissibility on the case, the Court held that given the total and exclusive *de facto* and *de jure* control exercised by the British authorities over their facilities, the individuals detained there were within the United Kingdom's jurisdiction.[232] On the merits the Court found that the physical transfer of the applicants within Iraq to the custody of the Iraqi authorities despite the real risk for them of being subjected to the death penalty had violated the principle of non-refoulement under Article 3 ECHR.[233]

Looking at the Committee's practice and documents, it can be assumed that it would have reached a similar conclusion with regard to the question of state jurisdiction. In its General Comment on Article 2 CAT, the Committee has held that the state party's obligation to prevent acts of torture is not restricted to its sovereign territory, but is valid for 'any territory under its jurisdiction,' which includes all areas where the state party exercises, directly or indirectly,

---

229   For an overview of the Court's general case law on the issue see the factsheet 'Extra-territorial jurisdiction of ECHR Member States' (July 2015) accessible on the Court's website under <http://www.echr.coe.int/Documents/FS_Extra-territorial_jurisdiction_ENG.pdf>. [17.2.2016].

230   ECtHR, *Loizidou v. Turkey*, 18 December 1996 [Grand Chamber], no. 15318/89, § 52, concerning the control of Turkish authorities over northern Cyprus. On military occupation see also ECtHR, *Al-Skeini and Others v. UK*, 7 July 2011 [GC], no. 55721/07.

231   ECtHR, *Al-Saadoon and Mufdhi v. UK*, 2 March 2010, no. 61498/08.

232   ECtHR, *Al-Saadoon and Mufdhi v. UK*, 30 June 2009, no. 61498/08, § 88 (decision).

233   ECtHR, *Al-Saadoon and Mufdhi v. UK*, 2 March 2010, no. 61498/08, §§ 143–145. See on this case also Chapter 3 Section 2.2.5. on the death penalty under Art. 3 ECHR.

de jure or *de facto* control in accordance with international law.[234] The Committee has made clear that this interpretation is applicable to Article 3 CAT: In its concluding observations on Sweden's state report, it held that 'Article 3 CAT and its obligation of non-refoulement applies to a State party's military forces, wherever situated, where they exercise effective control, de jure or de facto, over an individual.'[235] It noted that any transfer of detainees within a state party's effective custody must comply fully and in all circumstances with Article 3 CAT.[236]

It is more difficult for an applicant to establish a member state's effective control and thus jurisdiction for actions taken by international organisations or multinational coalition forces.[237] The Court declared inadmissible a complaint submitted by Saddam Hussein against 21 European states that were part of the coalition forces involved in the second Iraq war.[238] Hussein complained about his arrest, detention and transfer by the coalition forces, lead by the United States, to the Iraqi authorities. He alleged that he would be sentenced to death after an unfair trial. The Court found that Hussein's arguments with regard to the jurisdiction of the European coalition partners were not substantiated. Hussein had not addressed each respondent state's role and responsibilities with regard to his arrest and handover or the division of power between them and the leading US forces. According to the Court, he had not invoked any established principle of international law according to which he would fall within any respondent states' jurisdiction on the sole basis that those states

---

234 ComAT, General Comment No. 2 on Art. 2 (2008), § 16.

235 UN Doc. CAT/C/SWE/CO/5, 4 June 2008, § 14. See further UN Doc. CAT/C/CR/33/3, 10 December 2004, § 4; UN Doc. CAT/C/USA/CO/2, 25 July 2006 § 15.

236 UN Doc. CAT/C/SWE/CO/5, 4 June 2008, § 14. Also the Committee's concluding observations on the UK state report adopted in 2013, UN Doc. 'Annual Report 2012/2013,' p. 168. See further ComAT, *J.H.A. v. Spain*, 11 November 2008, no. 323/2007, § 8.2; ComAT, *Sonko v. Spain*, 25 November 2011, no. 368/2008, § 10.3; Nowak & McArthur 2008, p. 199 (§ 181).

237 See, for example, the inadmissibility decision ECtHR, *Behrami and Behrami v. France* and *Saramati v. France, Germany and Norway*, 2 May 2007 [GC], nos. 71412/01 and 78266/01 (decision), responsibility of the UN in Kosovo. See further ECtHR, *Banković and Others v. Belgium and 16 Other Contracting States*, 19 December 2001 [GC], no. 52207/99 (decision), bombing by NATO in Serbia. However, the impact of the principles that the Court appears to have developed in this latter judgment seem to have been modified by subsequent case law; see on this, for example, Frumer 2010, pp. 966–967.

238 ECtHR, *Saddam Hussein v. Albania, Bulgaria, Croatia, Czech Republic, Denmark, Estonia, Hungary, Iceland, Ireland, Italy, Latvia, Lithuania, Netherlands, Poland, Portugal, Romania, Slovakia, Slovenia, Turkey, Ukraine and UK*, 14 March 2006, no. 23276/04 (decision).

allegedly formed part (at varying unspecified levels) of a coalition of which the United States had overall command.[239]

In October 2012, the Court declared inadmissible the application of a Congolese national detained in the UN's detention unit within Scheveningen Prison in the Netherlands.[240] The applicant had been transferred from the Democratic Republic of Congo (DRC) to the custody of the International Criminal Court (ICC) in The Hague. He alleged under Article 5 ECHR that he was being unlawfully held on Netherlands soil and denied any opportunity to seek his release. The Court declared the complaint inadmissible for being incompatible *ratione personae*. It held that 'the fact that the applicant is deprived of his liberty on Netherlands soil does not of itself suffice to bring about questions on the "jurisdiction" of the Netherlands.'[241] According to the Court, the ECHR 'did not impose on a State that had agreed to host an international criminal tribunal on its territory the burden of reviewing the lawfulness of deprivation of liberty under arrangements lawfully entered into between that tribunal and States not party to it.'[242] The judges added that the ICC's Rules of Procedure provided sufficient procedural mechanisms to ensure that the fundamental rights of detained individuals were not violated.[243] They further rejected the complainant's argument according to which the Netherlands had taken it upon itself to review the lawfulness of his detention since it had agreed to examine his asylum request.[244] As can be seen, there are exceptions to the principle that an individual's presence in the territory of a contracting party has the effect of placing that individual under the jurisdiction of the state concerned where a state hosts the headquarters of an international organisation, provided the applicant is held in conformity with certain international standards.[245]

---

239   *Ibid.*

240   ECtHR, *Djokaba Lambi Longa v. Netherlands*, 9 October 2012, no. 33917/12 (decision).

241   *Ibid.*, § 73.

242   *Ibid.*, § 80.

243   § 79.

244   *Ibid.*, §§ 81 and 82. The Court noted on that account that states are, in principle, under no obligation to allow foreign nationals to await the outcome of immigration proceedings on their territory. It must be assumed that this statement was made in ignorance of the principles the Court has developed under Art. 3 ECHR. As will be explained, in the context of non-refoulement, when a complainant alleges a risk of serious harm in case of deportation similar to the complainant in this case, the Court usually requires that member states *not* deport the individual concerned until all domestic remedies in the immigration procedure are exhausted; see on this Section 3.2.4 of this chapter and Chapter 4 Section 3.1.1.b.

245   See also the Court's 'Practical Guide on Admissibility Criteria,' 1 January 2014, p. 43 with further references.

However, in principle, contracting states are also responsible for acts performed by foreign officials on their territory with their 'acquiescence or connivance.' The Court's Grand Chamber made this clear in *El-Masri v. Former-Yugoslav Republic of Macedonia*.[246] The case concerned a German national of Lebanese origin who had been the victim of a secret 'rendition' operation carried out in Skopje with the involvement of US agents. The applicant was arrested in Skopje in December 2003, held in isolation in a hotel for 23 days and transferred to CIA agents who brought him by air to a secret detention facility in Afghanistan where he was ill-treated. While the applicant was in the hands of the US agents at Skopje Airport, he had been severely beaten, and was hooded and sodomised in the presence of state officials of the Former Yugoslav Republic of Macedonia. The Court found that the Former Yugoslav Republic of Macedonia could be held responsible for these acts of torture, since its agents actively facilitated this treatment and failed to take any measures to prevent it.[247] It further held that by transferring the applicant to the custody of the US authorities, while it was widely reported that they used practices contrary to Article 3 ECHR on persons suspected of terrorism at that time, the authorities knowingly exposed him to a real risk of ill treatment and to conditions of detention contrary to Article 3 ECHR.[248] The Court concluded that the applicant had been subjected to 'extraordinary rendition,' which it defined as 'an extra-judicial transfer of persons from one jurisdiction or State to another, for the purposes of detention and interrogation outside the normal legal system, where there was a real risk of torture or cruel, inhuman or degrading treatment.'[249] Also the Committee has made clear that such extra-judicial transfers are in breach of the principle of non-refoulement.[250]

The Court confirmed this approach in the judgments *Al Nashiri* and *Abu Zubaydah v. Poland* adopted in July 2014.[251] These cases concerned two men suspected of having played a role in several terrorist operations, including the

---

246   ECtHR, *El-Masri v. Former Yugoslav Republic of Macedonia*, 13 December 2012 [GC], no. 39630/09, § 206.

247   *Ibid.*, §§ 205–211.

248   *Ibid.*, §§ 218 and 219.

249   *Ibid.*, § 221. For this definition, the Court referred to ECtHR, *Babar Ahmad and Others v. UK*, 10 April 2012, nos. 24027/07, 11949/08, 36742/08, 66911/09, 67354/09, § 221.

250   See ComAT, *Agiza v. Sweden*, 20 May 2005, no. 233/2003, that will be discussed in Chapter 4 Section 3.4.2.b and 2.2.

251   ECtHR, *Al Nashiri v. Poland*, 24 July 2014, no. 28761/11; ECtHR, *Abu Zubaydah v. Poland*, 24 July 2014, no. 7511/13. See on those cases also Chapter 1 Section 2.2.3. Another case concerning an extrajudicial transfer is ECtHR, *Abdulkhakov v. Russia*, 2 October 2012, no. 14743/11, §§ 152–157.

11 September 2001 attacks in New York. Both complainants alleged to have been captured in Dubai and Pakistan respectively in 2002 and brought to Poland, where they were placed in a secret detention facility of the US Central Intelligence Agency (CIA). Both claimed to have been tortured and ill-treated by US agents while being held in unacknowledged detention in Poland. The complainants were later transferred to Guantanamo Bay, where they remain in detention at the time of this writing. With regard to evidence obtained through several international inquiries and reports, the Court found that the applicants' allegations were sufficiently established. The judges were further convinced that Poland had known of the CIA's activities at the time, had facilitated the whole process and had made no attempt to prevent it. Although it was unlikely that the Polish authorities had witnessed or knew exactly what happened inside US facilities, they would have been required to take measures (under Article 1 taken together with Article 3 ECHR) to ensure that individuals within their jurisdiction are neither subjected to ill treatment nor transferred to other facilities outside the country where there is a real risk of such treatment. Relying on the principles established in *El-Masri*, the Court hence found violations of Article 3 ECHR in its procedural and material aspects, including the principle of non-refoulement.[252] The Court further held that the unacknowledged detention of an individual, which was the fundamental feature of the CIA rendition programme, is 'a complete negation' and 'most grave violation' of the right to liberty in Article 5 ECHR. It hence found that the conclusions under Article 3 ECHR were likewise valid and that Poland's responsibility is also engaged under Article 5 in respect of both the applicants' detention on Polish territory and their transfer from Poland.[253] With regard to Article 6 ECHR, the Court further held that Poland knew that any terrorist suspect would be tried before a military commission in Guantanamo, where there was a foreseeable risk of facing a 'flagrant denial of justice.'[254] Accordingly, the prohibition on refoulement inherent to Article 6 ECHR was also violated.[255] The Court recently confirmed the approaches taken in the cases of *El-Masri*, *Al Nashiri* and *Abu Zubaydah* with the judgment *Nasr and Ghali v. Italy*: This case concerned the abduction by CIA agents, with the cooperation of Italian officials, of an Egyptian imam

---

252   See ECtHR, *Al Nashiri v. Poland*, 24 July 2014, no. 28761/11, §§ 507–519; ECtHR, *Abu Zubaydah v. Poland*, 24 July 2014, no. 7511/13, §§ 479–514.

253   ECtHR, *Al Nashiri*, §§ 530–532; ECtHR, *Abu Zubaydah*, §§ 521–526.

254   See on this also Chapter 1 Section 2.2.3.

255   ECtHR, *Al Nashiri*, §§ 562–569; ECtHR, *Abu Zubaydah*, §§ 552–561. The Court further found violations of Art. 8 and 13 as well as Art. 3 and 2 ECHR taken together with Protocol No. 6 (exposure to the death penalty).

granted asylum in Italy, and his subsequent transfer to Egypt, where he was held in secret for several months.[256]

The legal obligation to transfer a person to another jurisdiction through an extradition treaty or other agreement is not material to the issue of jurisdiction. The Court and the Committee will not allow states to rely on international obligations in order to deny their responsibility under the principle of non-refoulement. The Court has made clear that a contracting party 'is responsible under Article 1 ECHR for all acts and omissions of its organs regardless of whether the act or omission in question was a consequence of domestic law or of the necessity to comply with international legal obligations.'[257] According to the Court, states are 'considered to retain Convention liability in respect of treaty commitments subsequent to the entry into force of the Convention.'[258] The Committee follows the same principles.[259]

b   *Interception at Sea and Diplomatic Asylum*
In the case *Hirsi Jamaa*, the Court criticized the Italian 'pushback policy' in the Mediterranean Sea.[260] The case concerned Somalian and Eritrean migrants travelling from Libya. They had been intercepted in the Mediterranean Sea by Italian authorities and sent back to Gaddafi's Libya. The Grand Chamber assessed the question of whether this incident fell under Italy's jurisdiction. The judges reiterated the principle of international law according to which a vessel sailing on the high seas is subject to the exclusive jurisdiction of the state of the flag under which it is sailing. Hence, in the period between boarding the ships and being handed over to the Libyan authorities, the applicants had been under the continuous and exclusive *de jure* and *de facto* control of the Italian authorities. Likewise, the events had occurred within the jurisdiction of Italy.[261]

The Committee took a similar approach in *J.H.A. v. Spain*.[262] The case concerned a cargo vessel transporting 369 immigrants from various Asian and African countries, which had capsized in international waters. In response to

---

256   See ECtHR, *Nasr and Ghali v. Italy*, 23 February 2016, no. 44883/09, in which the Court also found that because of the suffering provoked as a result of her husband's disappearance, the applicant's wife Ms Ghali had also been subjected to treatment proscribed by Art. 3 ECHR.

257   ECtHR, *Al-Saadoon and Mufdhi v. UK*, 2 March 2010, no. 61498/08, § 128.

258   *Ibid.*

259   See, for example, ComAT, *Agiza v. Sweden*, 20 May 2005, no. 233/2003, § 13.1.

260   ECtHR, *Hirsi Jamaa and Others v. Italy*, 23 February 2012 [GC], no. 27765/09.

261   *Ibid.*, §§ 70–82. Confirmed in ECtHR, *Sharifi and Others v. Italy and Greece*, 21 October 2014, no. 16643/09, §§ 210–213.

262   ComAT, *J.H.A. v. Spain*, 11 November 2008, no. 323/2007.

a distress call, the ship was towed by a Spanish maritime rescue tug to the Mauritanian coast, where it remained for eight days, during which time negotiations were made concerning the repatriation of the immigrants. After the Spanish and Mauritanian governments had concluded an agreement, the passengers of the cargo were disembarked in Mauritania, and most of them were subsequently voluntarily repatriated with the assistance of the International Organization for Migration. However, some refused to sign repatriation agreements and remained in detention under Spanish control in Nouadhibou, in a former fish-processing plant. Before the Committee, it was alleged that the conditions in the ship and in detention in Nouadhibou amounted to inhuman treatment. It was further claimed that the deportation of some applicants would violate the principle of non-refoulement in Article 3 CAT.

The Spanish government argued that the authorities did not bear responsibility for the incidents that took place on the Mauritanian coast. However, the Committee did not agree. It recalled its General Comment No. 2 on Article 2 CAT and replied that jurisdictions under the CAT 'must also include situations where a State party exercises, directly or indirectly, *de facto* or *de jure control* over persons in detention.'[263] The Committee then observed that the state party maintained control over the persons on board from the time the vessel was rescued and throughout the identification and repatriation process that took place at Nouadhibou. In particular by virtue of a diplomatic agreement concluded with Mauritania, Spain had exercised constant *de facto* control over the alleged victims during their detention in Nouadhibou. The Committee hence concluded that the alleged victims were subject to Spanish jurisdiction.[264] The application·was nevertheless declared inadmissible because the NGO that had submitted the complaint was not able to demonstrate that it had the authority to act on the alleged victim's behalf before the Committee.[265]

Another interesting Committee case is *Sonko v. Spain*, concerning four African migrants, among them the applicant, who attempted to enter the autonomous City of Ceuta by swimming across the border along the coast of Morocco.[266] They were intercepted by the Spanish Civil Guard and taken onto a Spanish vessel. Having been taken to the vicinity of Bastiones Beach, in Moroccan territorial waters, they were made to jump into the water. Subsequently, one of the Civil Guards jumped into the water to save the applicant

---

263   *Ibid.*, § 8.2. See ComAT, General Comment No. 2 on Art. 2 (2008), § 16.

264   ComAT, *J.H.A. v. Spain*, 11 November 2008, no. 323/2007. § 8.2.

265   *Ibid.* § 8.3. On this admissibility criteria see Section 3.2.7a of this chapter below.

266   ComAT, *Sonko v. Spain*, 25 November 2011, no. 368/2008.

from drowning. He took him to the shore and began to perform heart massage on him but the applicant died shortly after. The Committee noted that the particular circumstances surrounding the event remained disputed but it was established that the applicant was placed in a situation that caused his death which, in this case, amounted to cruel, inhuman or degrading treatment or punishment, under the terms of Article 16 CAT.[267] As to Spain's jurisdiction for the events, the Committee recalled its General Comment No. 2 cited above and held that, 'in the present case, the Civil Guard officers exercised control over the persons on board the vessel and were therefore responsible for their safety.'[268]

In sum, the Court and the Committee have both made clear that contracting states cannot circumvent their 'jurisdiction' under the Conventions by describing interceptions at sea as rescue operations.[269]

There are further examples of the extraterritorial exercise of jurisdiction: states may be responsible for the activities of their agents abroad and on board craft.[270] The Conventions also apply to transit zones of airports.[271] According to scholars, the CAT and ECHR should also be applicable to persons who ask for protection at national borders.[272] However, neither the Court nor the Committee have dealt with such a case to date. The Court and the Committee also have yet to make clear whether states have a responsibility to ensure protection for individuals trying to seek refuge at their embassies. In *Al-Saadoon and Mufdhi*, the Court noted 'that it is not necessary in this judgment to examine generally the principles of "diplomatic asylum" or to establish when, if ever, the surrender of an individual by a Contracting State's diplomatic or consular agents could give rise to a violation of the Convention.'[273] However, it noted that the former European Commission, in an admissibility decision, 'appeared to assume, albeit without detailed reasoning, that the *Soering* principle against refoulement would apply where an individual sought and was refused refuge

---

267   *Ibid.*, §§ 10.2 and 10.3.

268   *Ibid.*, § 10.3.

269   See ECtHR, *Hirsi Jamaa and Others v. Italy*, 23 February 2012 [GC], no. 27765/09, § 79; ComAT, *J.H.A. v. Spain*, 11 November 2008, no. 323/2007, §§ 4.4, 6.1 and 8.2.

270   See ECtHR, *Öcalan v. Turkey*, 12 May 2005 [GC], no. 46221/99, § 91, concerning the arrest of Abdullah Öcalan by Turkish security forces inside an aircraft in Nairobi.

271   ECtHR, *Amuur v. France*, 25 June 1996, no. 19766/92, § 52.

272   Hörtreiter & Weissbrodt 1999, pp. 57 and 65; Lauterpacht and Bethlehem, 2003, p. 111; Moreno-Lax 2012, p. 24; Suntinger 1995, p. 10; Wouters 2009, pp. 218–219, 324, 437 and 533. See further judge Pinto de Albuquerque in his concurring opinion to *Hirsi*.

273   ECtHR, *Al-Saadoon and Mufdhi v. UK*, 2 March 2010, no. 61498/08, § 139.

in a Contracting State's embassy.'[274] The Court thus indicates that the principle of non-refoulement should apply to people who have got as far as the territory of an embassy to seek protection or who are just outside the gate.[275] McAdam notes that a particularly high threshold will be required in such cases in the sense of an 'immediate likelihood of experiencing serious injury.'[276] The question of whether the respondent state's authority has effective control over the individual will be the determinant before the Court and the Committee. In principle, effective control will only be conceded in cases in which the person concerned is physically under the respondent state's authority.[277] If a request for asylum is made by post, effective control is unlikely to be assumed.[278] The Court has made clear recently that authorities are not responsible for requests of protection under Article 3 ECHR made by individuals who are abroad, even if the person concerned has close relations to the contracting state in question and has lived there or has left that state voluntarily.[279] This is particularly so when that person is in no way under control of diplomatic or other agents of the contracting party in the third state, as was the case in *Al-Saadoon and Mufdhi* discussed above.[280] The Court held that under Article 3 ECHR, 'there is no principled reason to distinguish between, on the one hand, someone who was in the jurisdiction of a Contracting State but voluntarily left that jurisdiction and, on the other hand, someone who was never in the jurisdiction of that State.'[281] Another approach would 'create an unlimited obligation on Contracting States to allow entry to an individual who might be at real risk of ill-treatment contrary to Article 3, regardless of where in the world that

---

274   *Ibid.*, referring to EComHR, *M. v. Denmark*, 14 October 1992, no. 17392/90, concerning an applicant who, in an attempt to leave the German Democratic Republic, entered the premises of the Danish embassy but was later arrested by the East German police at the request of the Danish ambassador. On the one hand, the Commission noted that the acts 'of the Danish ambassador complained of affected persons within the jurisdiction of the Danish authorities within the meaning of Article 1 ECHR.' On the other hand, it rejected the applicability of Art. 4 Protocol No. 4 (prohibition of collective expulsion), noting that embassy premises are not part of Danish territory.

275   See in this sense also Thurin 2012, p. 11; Wouters 2009, pp. 218–219 and 324.

276   McAdam 2007, p. 171. In this sense also Thurin 2012, pp. 11–12.

277   See in this sense ECtHR, *D. v. UK*, 2 May 1997, no. 30240/96, § 48.

278   Wouters 2009, p. 219.

279   See ECtHR, *Khan v. UK*, 28 January 2014, no. 11987/11 (decision).

280   *Ibid.*, § 25.

281   *Ibid.*, § 26; the Court added that there isn't 'any support in the Court's case-law for the applicant's argument that the State's obligations under Article 3 require it to take this Article into account when making adverse decisions against individuals, even when those individuals are not within its jurisdiction.'

individual might find himself.'[282] With that, the Court made very clear that the prohibition on refoulement in Article 3 ECHR *does not provide a right to entry into a contracting state's jurisdiction.*

3.2.2 Time Limit for Submitting a Complaint

According to Article 35(1) ECHR, the Court may only deal with complaints submitted within six months of the final decision taken in the domestic procedure.[283] The purpose of this time limit is 'to promote security of the law, ensure that cases raising issues under the Convention are examined within a reasonable time, and protect the authorities and other persons concerned from being in a situation of uncertainty for a long period of time.'[284] The CAT *does not contain a time limit* for the submission of individual complaints. According to its Rules of Procedure, a case will, however, be found inadmissible if the time elapsed since the domestic remedies have been exhausted is so unreasonably prolonged as to render consideration of the claims unduly difficult by the Committee or the state party.[285] So far, this criterion has never led to the inadmissibility of a non-refoulement complaint before the Committee.[286]

In principle, the six-month period before the Court runs 'from the date of the final decision in the process of exhaustion of domestic remedies.'[287] However, in recent refoulement cases, the Court has shown to be flexible with this rule. In the judgment *M.Y.H. v. Sweden*[288] adopted in June 2013, the Court approved the practice it had applied in certain previous cases, according to which the *six-month time period only starts to run with the enforcement of a deportation.*[289]

---

282   *Ibid.,* § 27.

283   Protocol No. 15 to the ECHR, which is not in force yet, reduces the limit to *four* months.

284   Court's 'Practical Guide on Admissibility Criteria,' 31 March 2011, p. 22 (§ 66).

285   Rule 113(f) ComAT (CAT/C/3/Rev.6).

286   The Committee rejected the state's argument on this ground in ComAT, *Agiza v. Sweden,* 20 May 2005, no. 233/2003, § 9.3. It noted that the authorities had access to the relevant submissions, and thus, while the timing of submission of the complaint may have been inconvenient, it could not be said to have been made unduly difficult by the lapse of 18 months from the date of the complainant's expulsion.

287   ECtHR, *El-Masri v. Former Yugoslav Republic of Macedonia,* 13 December 2012 [GC], no. 39630/09, § 136.

288   ECtHR, *M.Y.H. v. Sweden,* 27 June 2013, no. 50859/10.

289   See ECtHR, *P.Z. and Others v. Sweden,* 29 May 2012, no. 68194/10, §§ 34–36 (decision); ECtHR, *B.Z. v. Sweden,* 29 May 2012, no. 74352/11, §§ 32–34 (decision). See further ECtHR, *Dougoz v. Greece,* 8 February 2000, no. 40907/98 (decision), in which the Court rejected

The Court justified this by the fact that in the context of refoulement, the state's responsibility under the ECHR only arises with the deportation. It held:

> While ... the date of the final domestic decision providing an effective remedy is normally the starting-point for the calculation of the period of six months, the Court reiterates ... that the responsibility of a sending State under Article 2 or 3 of the Convention is, as a rule, incurred only at the time when the measure is taken to remove the individual concerned from its territory. Specific provisions of the Convention should be interpreted and understood in the context of other provisions as well as the issues relevant in a particular type of case. The Court therefore finds that the considerations relevant in determining the date of the sending State's responsibility must be applicable also in the context of the six-month rule. In other words, the date of the State's responsibility under Article 2 or 3 corresponds to the date when the six-month period under Article 35 § 1 starts to run for the applicant. If a decision ordering a removal has not been enforced and the individual remains on the territory of the State wishing to remove him or her ... the six-month period has not yet started to run.[290]

De facto, this means that applicants who remain in the contracting state's territory have no deadline, after the final domestic decision is reached, for submitting a refoulement complaint to the Court. This makes the practice of the Court similar to that of the Committee, which does not impose a strict time limit. Before both bodies, the great majority of the complaints are submitted by applicants who are physically in the territory of the state wishing to remove them. According to the approach taken by the Court in *M.Y.H.*, it is in fact only in the rare cases in which the applicant has already been deported when he submits his complaint, that the application should be submitted at the latest six months after that deportation.[291] However, in light of the fact that the Court's practice as just cited contradicts the wording in Article 35(1) ECHR, and given that the Court's practice with regard to admissibility is sometimes unpredictable, it is more prudent to submit complaints in Strasbourg at the latest within the six months following the final decision at the national level, even

---

the government's argument that the application had been submitted out of time, noting that on the date of its introduction the applicant was still awaiting expulsion.

290   ECtHR, *M.Y.H. v. Sweden*, 27 June 2013, no. 50859/10, §§ 40 and 41.

291   See ECtHR, *Alzery v. Sweden*, 26 October 2004, no. 10786/04 (decision), which was rejected because of the six-month time limit.

if the deportation has not yet taken place.[292] However, a request for referral of *M.Y.H.* to the Grand Chamber was rejected and the approach taken in that judgment was subsequently confirmed.[293]

3.2.3   Application Submitted to Another International Body

According to Article 35(2)b ECHR, the Court may not deal with any application that 'is substantially the same as a matter that has already been submitted to another procedure of international investigation or settlement and contains no relevant new information.' Article 22(5)a CAT states that the Committee shall not consider a complaint unless it has ascertained that 'the same matter has not been, and is not being, examined under another procedure of international investigation or settlement.' The purpose of these provisions is to avoid a multiplication of international procedures on the same matter. Lawyers who decide to take the international path thus must opt for one protection mechanism or the other. However, there are two conditions for the exclusion mechanism to apply:

·   The matter of the application that has been submitted to the other international body must be substantially the same.
·   The application must have been submitted to another procedure of international investigation or settlement. Article 22(5)a CAT further details that it must be or have been examined under the other procedure.

With regard to the requirement of the same matter, the Court and the Committee have both made clear that this refers to a complaint that is submitted by the same party, concerns the same facts and invokes the same substantive rights.[294]

The Court and the Committee only consider a mechanism as another procedure of international investigation or settlement if it has a judicial or a quasi-judicial character such as the individual complaint procedures before the Court in Strasbourg and the Committee in Geneva.[295] Hence, a complaint

---

292   See also the dissenting opinion to *M.Y.H.* of judge Lemmens.
293   See ECtHR, *T.K.H. v. Sweden*, 19 December 2013, no. 1231/11, §§ 29–31; ECtHR, *A.A. and Others v. Sweden*, 24 July 2014, no. 34098/11, §§ 35–39.
294   See the Court's 'Practical Guide on Admissibility Criteria,' 1 January 2014, p. 35 For the Committee see, for example, ComAT, *D.S.I. v. Hungary*, 8 December 2015, no. 671/2015, § 10.3.
295   The Court's examination of parallel proceedings is not limited to a formal verification; it focuses on the nature of the supervisory body, the procedure it follows and the effect of its decisions; see ECtHR, *Karoussiotis v. Portugal*, 1 February 2011, no. 23205/08, §§ 62–76. For

that *is being* or *has been* assessed by the Court will in principle be declared inadmissible by the Committee and vice versa.[296] The same is true for cases submitted to other individual complaint mechanisms associated with UN human rights treaty bodies such as the Human Rights Committee.[297] The Inter-American Commission on Human Rights has this quasi-judicial character, too.[298]

In contrast, the assessment of a case by the European Committee for the Prevention of Torture and Inhuman or Degrading Treatment or Punishment is not considered to be 'another procedure of international investigation or settlement' and therefore does not prevent the Court or the Committee from assessing the same matter. This also applies to cases brought to the attention of the UN Human Rights Council and its special procedures, including the UN Special Rapporteur on torture or on extrajudicial, summary or arbitrary executions, or cases submitted under the 1503 procedure before the UN High Commissioner for Human Rights.[299] The Committee has noted that 'extra-conventional procedures or mechanisms established by the Commission on Human Rights or the Human Rights Council, whose mandates are to examine and report publicly on human rights situations in specific countries or territories or on cases of widespread human rights violations worldwide, do not constitute procedures of international investigation or settlement' within the meaning of Article 22(5)b CAT.[300] In *V.X.N. and H.N. v. Sweden*, the Committee further noted that neither the 1951 Refugee Convention nor the Statute of the UNHCR provides for the establishment of a procedure of international investigation or settlement in the sense of Article 22(5)a CAT. Confronted with a statement given by a UNHCR representative on a case pending in Geneva, the

the Committee see Nowak & McArthur 2008, p. 794 (§ 194) and ComAT, *V.X.N. and H.N. v. Sweden*, 15 May 2000, no. 130 and 131/1999, §§ 5.1 and 13.1.

296   See ComAT, *W.J. v. Australia*, 22 November 1990, no. 5/1990 (concerning the EComHR); ComAT, *A.G. v. Sweden*, 2 May 2000, no. 140/1999; ComAT, *A.A. v. Azerbaijan*, 25 November 2005, no. 247/2004; ComAT, *A.R.A. v. Sweden*, 30 April 2007, no. 305/2006; ComAT, *E.E. v. Russia*, 24 May 2013, no. 479/2011; ComAT, *M.T. v. Sweden*, 7 August 2015, no. 642/2014; ComAT, *U. v. Sweden*, 23 November 2015, no. 643/2014; ComAT, *N.B. v. Russia*, 25 November 2015, no. 577/2013; ComAT, *D.S.I. v. Hungary*, 8 December 2015, no. 671/2015, §§ 10.2–10.4 and the Court's 'Practical Guide on Admissibility Criteria,' 31 March 2011, p. 31 (§ 137).

297   *Ibid.* and ComAT, *X. v. Canada*, 20 November 1995, no. 26/1995, § 3.

298   ComAT, *X. v. Canada*, 20 November 1995, no. 26/1995, § 3.

299   Court's 'Practical Guide on Admissibility Criteria,' 31 March 2011, pp. 29–31; ComAT, *Bendib v. Algeria*, 8 November 2013, no. 376/2009, § 5.1; ComAT, *Niyonzima v. Burundi*, 21 November 2014, no. 514/2012, § 7.1.

300   ComAT, *Bendib v. Algeria*, 8 November 2013, no. 376/2009, § 5.1; ComAT, *Aarrass v. Morocco*, 19 May 2014, no. 477/2011, § 9.1.

Committee held that a written opinion or advice given by a regional or international body on a matter of interpretation of international law in relation to a particular case does not imply that the matter has been subject to international investigation or settlement.[301]

While Article 35(2)b ECHR states that the Court shall not deal with any application that has been 'submitted' to another procedure, Article 22(5)a CAT states that the Committee shall not consider a complaint unless it has ascertained that the same matter has 'not been, and is not being, examined' under another procedure. What does *has been or is being examined* mean?

Complaints that have been declared inadmissible for being manifestly ill-founded in Strasbourg have been considered as 'having been examined' and were therefore rejected by the Committee.[302] The Committee will, however, assess complaints that have been declared inadmissible by the Court for failure to observe the six-month time limit, given that the CAT does not have such a time limit.[303] Generally, the Committee is reluctant to reject complaints based on Article 22(5)a CAT if they have been rejected for procedural reasons by the other forum. This can be observed in *S.A.C. v. Monaco*.[304] Before this case had been submitted in Geneva, the same complaint had been declared inadmissible in Strasbourg. However, the Committee did not apply the exclusion mechanism, noting that the complaint 'had been rejected without an examination of the merits' in Strasbourg.[305] The Committee was hence of the opinion that the case could not be deemed to have *been examined* within the meaning of Article 22(5)a CAT.[306] Interestingly, the Committee also agreed to assess complaints

301   ComAT, *V.X.N. and H.N. v. Sweden*, 15 May 2000, no. 130 and 131/1999, §§ 5.1 and 13.1. In this case, the UNHCR Regional Representative for Baltic and Nordic Countries had informed the Swedish Minister of Justice that an expulsion of the complainants would not constitute a breach of Art. 33 of the Refugee Convention.

302   ComAT, *A.A. v. Azerbaijan*, 25 November 2005, no. 247/2004, §§ 6.6 and 6.9; ComAT, *E.E. v. Russia*, 24 May 2013, no. 479/2011, § 8.2. As to the inadmissibility criteria of 'manifestly ill-founded complaints' see Section 3.2.6 of this chapter below.

303   See ComAT, *E.E. v. Russia*, 24 May 2013, no. 479/2011, § 8.2 and Nowak & McArthur 2008, pp. 752 (§ 92) and 794–795 (§ 195). However, as explained in Section 3.2.2 of this chapter, the Court has recently adopted quite a flexible approach with regard to the six-month time limit in the context of refoulement.

304   ComAT, *S.A.C. v. Monaco*, 13 November 2012, no. 346/2008.

305   *Ibid.*, § 7.1.

306   *Ibid.* Unfortunately, we do not know which admissibility criteria Strasbourg relied on for the rejection of this complaint. The decision was not published which means that it was probably adopted in a simplified procedure (i.e., without the involvement of the respondent government; see on this Section 1.1.1 of this chapter). It is possible that neither the complainant nor the Committee know the reason for the rejection in Strasbourg, since

that had been submitted to the Court in Strasbourg but were withdrawn before they had been considered by that instance.[307] The applications had been withdrawn after the request for interim measures had been denied in Strasbourg. It is clear that this practice leaves the option for lawyers to first submit a request for interim measures to Strasbourg, and, if unsuccessful, to subsequently try the same in Geneva. Whether this is consistent with the avoidance of a multiplication of international procedures on the same matter is questionable.

The Committee's practice with regard to complaints that are submitted in Strasbourg and are *still pending* is confusing: three such complaints have been declared inadmissible by the Committee according to Article 22(5)a CAT.[308] However, in one case, the Committee rejected the state party's argument according to which the complaint should be declared inadmissible: it noted that the application was 'still pending and had not been transmitted to the State party.' In these circumstances, the Committee considered that the application could not be seen as being considered under another procedure.[309] As has been explained, the great majority of complaints submitted in Strasbourg are rejected without being transmitted to the state party of the respondent government because they are considered to be clearly inadmissible.[310] The Committee's approach in this case hence suggests that those applications pending in Strasbourg that appear clearly inadmissible in the eyes of the Court (and are therefore never reported to the respondent government) might have a second chance before the Committee. This again seems problematic from the perspective of avoiding multiplication of international procedures on the same

---

the Court does not indicate the reasons for rejection in cases dealt with in the simplified procedure. It is possible that the complaint was in fact rejected for reasons on the merits as being manifestly ill-founded, but since this does not appear in any document, it is not verifiable by the Committee without asking the Court itself. See the similar practice of the Human Rights Committee in HRC, *X. v. Norway*, 5 November 2015, no. 2474/2014, § 6.2. In contrast, however, ComAT, *D.S.I. v. Hungary*, 8 December 2015, no. 671/2015, §§ 10.2–10.4 where the exact reason of inadmissibility in Strasbourg also appears unclear but the complaint was declared inadmissible by the Committee.

307   ComAT, *J.A.G.V. v. Sweden*, 11 November 2003, no. 215/2002, §§ 4.1 and 6.1; ComAT, *Abichou v. Germany*, 21 May 2013, no. 430/2010, §§ 4.4, 8.1–8.4 and 10.1. See also ComAT, *Haro v. Argentina*, 23 May 2014, no. 366/2008, §§ 4.1 and 8.2, complaint withdrawn from Inter-American Commission of Human Rights.

308   ComAT, *W.J. v. Australia*, 22 November 1990, no. 5/1990, § 3; ComAT, *A.G. v. Sweden*, 2 May 2000, no. 140/1999, §§ 4.2 and 6.2; ComAT, *N.B. v. Russia*, 25 November 2015, no. 577/2013, § 8.2.

309   ComAT, *Keremedchiev v. Bulgaria*, 11 November 2008, no. 257/2004, § 6.1.

310   See on this Chapter 2 Section 1.1.1 above on the life of an application in Strasbourg.

matter.[311] However, in November 2015, the Committee in contrast declared a complaint inadmissible because it was pending in Strasbourg without addressing the question of whether it was reported to the responded government.[312] Also in 2015, the Committee made clear in two decisions that complaints that have been declared inadmissible by a *single judge* in Strasbourg, with the reasoning that they do 'not disclose any appearance of violation of the rights and freedoms set out in the Convention,' have been sufficiently considered on the merits so that a second assessment by the Committee in Geneva is excluded.[313] In sum, the Committee accepts the Court's simplified procedure as an examination by another forum in the sense of Article 22(5)a CAT if the complaint was or is considered on the merits in Strasbourg. However, it appears that as long as it is not evidenced for which reason exactly a complaint is declared inadmissible in Strasbourg, the Committee's handling of that complaint under Article 22(5)a CAT is quite unpredictable.[314]

It appears rare that an individual complaint is first submitted to a UN monitoring body and then to the Court.[315] Kälin notes with regard to the Human Rights Committee that this is often impossible since the proceedings before that institution regularly exceed the Court's six-month time limit.[316] This is equally valid for proceedings before the Committee. However, in light of the Court's rather flexible approach with regard to the six-month limit in the context of non-refoulement as discussed in section 3.2.3 of this chapter above, it is not impossible that a complainant might try for success in Strasbourg after he has failed in Geneva.

Finally note that in contrast to the Court and the Committee, the UN Human Rights Committee only rejects complaints submitted to another international complaint mechanism as inadmissible if they are *still pending*.[317] The Human Rights Committee may therefore assess a complaint that has already

---

311 See also the critique in de Weck 2011, p. 6 footnote 27.

312 ComAT, *N.B. v. Russia*, 25 November 2015, no. 577/2013, § 8.2.

313 ComAT, *M.T. v. Sweden*, 7 August 2015, no. 642/2014, §§ 8.3–9; ComAT, *U. v. Sweden*, 23 November 2015, no. 643/2014, §§ 6.2–6.4.

314 See also ComAT, *D.S.I. v. Hungary*, 8 December 2015, no. 671/2015, §§ 10.2–10.4, where the reason of inadmissibility in Strasbourg is not clear but the complaint was declared inadmissible under Art. 22(5)a CAT.

315 No published decision of the Court in Strasbourg is known to the author, by which a complaint has been declared inadmissible because it has already been submitted to the Committee against Torture in Geneva.

316 Kälin 2012, p. 8 footnote 35.

317 Art. 5(2)(a) ICCP Optional Protocol.

been considered by the Court. According to Kälin, this happens regularly.[318] However, in practice, many state parties to the ICCPR have made reservations under the ICCPR's Optional Protocol, according to which a similar exclusion mechanism should apply as under the ECHR or the CAT.[319]

3.2.4 Exhaustion of Domestic Remedies

a   *In General*

The primary responsibility for the protection of the rights set forth in the ECHR and the CAT lies with the contracting states. The Court and the Committee are *subsidiary to national systems safeguarding human rights*. Their subsidiary role is articulated by the rule of exhaustion of domestic remedies in Article 35(1) ECHR and Article 22(5)b CAT. This rule requires applicants first to use the remedies provided by the national legal system including appeal to the highest available court before submitting a complaint at international level. It is a general rule of international law that national courts should first have the opportunity to prevent and examine an alleged violation through their own legal system and to put the matter right themselves, *before* it is considered internationally.[320]

However, the rule of exhaustion of domestic remedies is based on the assumption that domestic legal orders provide effective remedies for violations of Convention rights. Within the ECHR, this assumption is reflected in Article 13 ECHR, which provides the right to an effective remedy for potential breaches of any right guaranteed by the ECHR.[321] The CAT does not explicitly provide a right for an effective remedy with regard to a risk of refoulement according to

---

318   Kälin 2012, p. 8. In the context of refoulement, the Human Rights Committee has proceeded in this way with regard to ECtHR, *Alzery v. Sweden*, 26 October 2004, no. 10786/04 (decision). This complaint had been rejected by the Court because of the six-month time limit and was then assessed by the Human Rights Committee; see HRC, *Alzery v. Sweden*, 25 October 2006, no. 1416/2005.

319   Bayefsky 2003, p. 137; Goodwin-Gil & McAdam 2007, p. 298. See, however, Kälin 2012, p. 8, according to which the Human Rights Committee interprets these reservations restrictively.

320   See the references to general international law in Art. 35(1) ECHR and Art. 21(1)c CAT.

321   There is a 'close affinity' between Art. 13 ECHR and the obligation to exhaust domestic remedies under Art 35(1) ECHR in the sense that if there are no effective domestic remedies at national level, an issue under Art. 13 ECHR might arise and applicants can lodge a complaint under Art. 13 ECHR in conjunction with the respective substantive provision of the ECHR; ECtHR, *Diallo v. Czech Republic*, 23 June 2011, no. 20493/07, § 55. On the right to an effective remedy according to Art. 13 ECHR in conjunction with the principle of non-refoulement in Art. 3 ECHR see Chapter 4 Section 3.1.1.b.

Article 3 CAT. However, the Committee has made clear that the prohibition on refoulement must be interpreted to encompass a remedy for its breach.[322]

Under both the Court and the Committee, the obligation to exhaust domestic remedies is limited to making use of those remedies, which are likely to be effective and available in practice and capable of redressing or, in the context of refoulement, of preventing the alleged violation.[323] If no remedies, or no *effective* remedies, are available at national level, the rule may not apply and applicants may address their petition to the Court or the Committee straight away.

According to the Court and the Committee, the adequate nature of a remedy can be undermined by its excessive duration.[324] Article 22(4)b CAT explicitly states that the rule of exhaustion of domestic remedies does not apply where the application of the remedy is unreasonably prolonged. In *C.A.R.M. et al. v. Canada*, the state party raised the fact that the complainants had not contested the decision rejecting their preremoval risk assessment application before the Federal Court of Canada.[325] However, the complainants had submitted their request for asylum in November 2002 and more than four years later their fate had still not been decided. The Committee held that in these circumstances, the proceedings as a whole had not been concluded within a reasonable time. Consequently, the communication was admissible under Article 22(5)b CAT despite the ongoing proceedings at national level.[326]

According to the Court and the Committee, the question of whether domestic remedies are available and effective and should therefore be exhausted cannot be determined *in abstracto*.[327] They both assess that question by looking at the circumstances of the case and taking into account the specific nature of the claim at issue. With regard to remedies against refoulement, they both set out minimum requirements, which will be discussed in detail in chapter 4 section 3.1 on the right to an effective remedy under the principle of

---

322 On the right to an effective remedy inherent to Art. 3 CAT see Chapter 4 Section 3.1.2.

323 See the Court's wording in ECtHR, *Salah Sheekh v. Netherlands*, 11 January 2007, no. 1948/04, § 121.

324 ECtHR, *M.S.S. v. Belgium and Greece*, 21 January 2011 [GC], no. 30696/09, §§ 292 and 320. See also ECtHR, *Mohammed v. Austria*, 6 June 2013, no. 2283/12, § 72, in which the Court notes that in the context of refoulement, a 'particularly prompt response' is required by the national authorities.

325 ComAT, *C.A.R.M. et al. v. Canada*, 18 May 2007, no. 298/2006, §§ 4.2–4.4 and 8.3.

326 *Ibid.*, § 8.4. See also ComAT, *V.N.I.M. v. Canada*, 12 November 2002, no. 119/1998, § 6.2 (proceedings of over four years).

327 ECtHR, *Muminov v. Russia*, 11 December 2008, no. 42502/06, § 100; ComAT, *Z.T. (No. 2) v. Norway*, 14 November 2005, no. 238/2003, § 8.1.

non-refoulement.[328] However, it should be noted at this stage that given the irreversible nature of the harm that might occur in refoulement cases, only remedies with suspensive effect are considered to be effective by the Court and the Committee.[329] The Committee has rightly reasoned 'that a remedy which remains pending after the act which it was designed to avert has already taken place has, by definition, become pointless, since the irreparable harm can no longer be avoided, even if a subsequent judgment were to find in favour of the complainant.'[330]

An effective remedy requires the 'independent and rigorous scrutiny of a claim.'[331] The Court and the Committee are both quite unpredictable as to their requirements on how extensive the review with regard to the substance of a case must be.[332] According to the Court, judicial review proceedings must be regarded as an effective remedy that applicants in the context of expulsion and extradition will be required to exhaust before lodging an application with the Court 'provided that the courts can effectively review the legality of executive discretion on substantive and procedural grounds and quash decisions as appropriate.'[333] In *Singh v. Canada*, the Committee noted that states should 'provide for judicial review of the merits, rather than merely of the reasonableness, of decisions to expel an individual.'[334] In this decision, the Committee set exceptionally high requirements for the thoroughness of assessments at review level.[335]

In general, the Court and the Committee both exercise the rule of exhaustion of domestic remedies with flexibility and without excessive formalism.[336] As noted in the Court's 'Practical Guide on Admissibility Criteria,' the 'rule may

---

328   See also the useful summary of the principles applicable in refoulement cases in ECtHR, *F.A. v. UK*, 10 September 2013, no. 20658/11, § 50 (decision).

329   For the Court, see for example ECtHR, *M.S.S. v. Belgium and Greece*, 21 January 2011 [GC], no. 30696/09, § 293. For the Committee see, for example, ComAT, *S.A.C. v. Monaco*, 13 November 2012, no. 346/2008, § 7.2.

330   ComAT, *Tebourski v. France*, 1 May 2007, no. 300/2006, § 7.3.

331   See, for example, ECtHR, *Isakov v. Russia*, 8 July 2010, no. 14049/08, § 136.

332   Spijkerboer 2009, p. 73, with regard to the Court.

333   ECtHR, *Isakov v. Russia*, 8 July 2010, no. 14049/08, § 137.

334   ComAT, *Singh v. Canada*, 30 May 2011, no. 319/2007, §§ 8.8 and 8.9.

335   The Committee accepted neither the review procedure before the Canadian Federal Court nor the Pre-Removal Risk assessment as effective remedies. For a critique of this decision as having overshot the mark see Chapter 4 Section 3.1.2.

336   ECtHR, *Y.P. and L.P. v. France*, 2 September 2010, no. 32476/06, § 52; Schürmann & Scheidegger 2009, p. 203.

be described as one that is golden rather than cast in stone.'[337] Unfortunately this casuistic approach renders the case law slightly unpredictable.[338]

b   *Formal Requirements, Legal Aid and Court Fees*
National courts and authorities must have the opportunity to assess all relevant allegations and related evidence establishing a risk of ill treatment in case of removal, such as past experiences of torture or political activities.[339] It is not necessary for the Convention rights, respectively Article 3 ECHR or Article 3 CAT, to be explicitly raised in domestic proceedings, provided that the applicant has 'in substance' claimed a violation of the principle of non-refoulement.

Remedies with regard to the determination of refugee status are usually considered equivalent to remedies under the principle of non-refoulement as guaranteed by Article 3 ECHR and Article 3 CAT.[340] Persons excluded from the protection under the Refugee Convention must, however, have access to an individualized risk assessment pursuant to Article 3 ECHR and Article 3 CAT in domestic legislation.[341]

The principle of exhaustion of domestic remedies requires applicants to use only remedies that are directly related to the risk of ill treatment in the country to which they would be sent, not those that might allow them to remain in the host country for reasons unrelated to that risk.[342] Consequently petitioners are not required to exhaust remedies that are given on purely humanitarian grounds, or are granted *ex gratia* rather than based on the binding obligation to respect the principle of non-refoulement.[343] Generally, applicants are not

---

337   Court's 'Practical Guide on Admissibility Criteria,' 1 January 2014, p. 23.

338   See Leach 2011, p. 19, who advises practitioners with doubts about the effectiveness of a remedy to lodge an introductory letter with the Court at the same time as pursuing the remedy in question. See also Nowak & McArthur 2008, p. 796 (§ 198).

339   See declared inadmissible for that reason: ComAT, *H.E-M. v. Canada*, 23 May 2011, 395/2009, §§ 6.3 and 6.4; ComAT, *S.K. and R.K. v. Sweden*, 21 November 2011, no. 365/2008, § 11.3; ComAT, *J.L.L. v. Switzerland*, 18 May 2012, no. 364/2008, § 7.2.

340   See illustrative ECtHR, *Y.P. and L.P. v. France*, 2 September 2010, no. 32476/06, §§ 48 and 56, in which the Court rejected the government's argument that alongside the remedies available under the Refugee Convention, the complainants could have requested a remedy with regard to Art. 3 ECHR.

341   ComAT, *Abdussamatov and 28 Others v. Kazakhstan*, 1 June 2012, no. 444/2010, § 13.9; ComAT, *Nasirov v. Kazakhstan*, 14 May 2014, no. 475/2011, § 10.4. In this sense also ECtHR, *Sidikovy v. Russia*, 20 June 2013, no. 73455/11, § 149.

342   See, for example, ComAT, *R.S.M. v. Canada*, 24 May 2013, no. 392/2009, § 6.3.

343   See ComAT, *Kalonzo v. Canada*, 18 May 2012, no. 343/2008, §§ 4.6 and 8.3, in which the Committee confirms its previous case law according to which the application for permanent residence on humanitarian and compassionate grounds under Canadian law, which

required to make use of more than one potentially effective remedy if domestic law provides for parallel remedies.[344]

Applicants must comply with formal requirements and time limits laid down in domestic law, failing which their application might be rejected under the rule of the exhaustion of domestic remedies. There is no exception to this requirement 'even in cases of expulsion to a country where there is an alleged risk of ill-treatment.'[345] In the case *A.H. v. Sweden*, the Committee held that the complainant's mental and emotional problems at the time of the expulsion order did not absolve him from the requirement to exhaust domestic remedies.[346] It has also made clear that errors of a privately retained lawyer, such as the advice not to apply for judicial review, cannot normally be attributed to the state party.[347]

However, to be effective, a remedy must be available in law as well as in practice.[348] The Court has noted that procedural rules (in particular time limits) should not be so strict or applied so inflexibly as to deny an applicant for refugee status a realistic opportunity to prove his claim.[349] The rule on the exhaustion of the domestic remedies must be applied 'to reflect the practical realities of the applicant's position in order to ensure the effective protection of the rights and freedoms guaranteed by the Convention.'[350]

The Court and the Committee both recommend that state parties undertake measures to ensure that asylum seekers are duly informed about all domestic remedies available and to establish systems by which they have access to legal aid if needed.[351] However, neither the Court nor the Committee requires states to provide free legal representation in asylum cases.[352] However, individuals

is granted depending on the discretionary authority of a minister, cannot be considered an effective remedy to be exhausted. Confirmed in ComAT, *W.G.D. v. Canada*, 26 November 2014, no. 520/2012, § 7.4; ComAT, *J.K. v. Canada*, 23 November 2015, no. 562/2013, § 9.2. The Committee's contrary statements in ComAT, *L.M.V.R.G. and M.A.B.C. v. Sweden*, 19 November 1997, no. 64/1997, §§ 3.2–5 seem not to be valid anymore.

344   ComAT, *T.P.S. v. Canada*, 16 May 2000, no. 99/1997, § 10.1.

345   ECtHR, *Bahaddar v. Netherlands*, 19 February 1998, no. 25894/94, § 45.

346   ComAT, *A.H. v. Sweden*, 15 November 2005, no. 250/2004, § 7.2.

347   See, for example, ComAT, *H.E-M. v. Canada*, 23 May 2011, 395/2009, §§ 6.3 and 6.4; ComAT, *Y. v. Canada*, 28 July 2015, no. 512/2012, § 7.3.

348   ECtHR, *M.S.S. v. Belgium and Greece*, 21 January 2011 [GC], no. 30696/09, § 290.

349   See, for example, ECtHR, *Kandomabadi v. Netherlands*, 29 June 2004, nos. 6276/03 and 6122/04 (decision); ECtHR, *I.M. v. France*, 2 February 2012, no. 9152/09, §§ 136–160. See also ComAT, *Diaz v. France*, 3 May 2005, no. 194/2001, § 6.1.

350   ECtHR, *F.A. v. UK*, 10 September 2013, no. 20658/11, § 50 (decision).

351   ComAT, *S.H. v Norway*, 19 November 1999, no. 121/1998, § 7.4; ECtHR, *M.S.S. v. Belgium and Greece*, 21 January 2011 [GC], no. 30696/09, § 319.

352   For the Court see ECtHR, *Goldstein v. Sweden*, 12 September 2000, no. 46636/99 (decision).

should be able to obtain legal aid if they are in need: in *Z.T. v. Norway n° 2* the Committee accepted that judicial review in the Norwegian asylum procedure was in principle an effective remedy that had to be exhausted.[353] In the present case, however, it was unchallenged that the complainant's language and/or legal skills were plainly insufficient to expect him to represent himself, while, at the same time, his financial means were also insufficient for him to retain private legal counsel.[354] The Committee held:

> If, in such circumstances, legal aid was denied to an individual, the Committee considered that it would run contrary to both the language of article 22, paragraph 5, as well as the purpose of the principle of exhaustion of domestic remedies and the ability to lodge an individual complaint, to consider a potential remedy of judicial review as 'available,' and thus declaring a complaint inadmissible if this remedy was not pursued. Such an approach would deny an applicant protection before the domestic courts *and* at the international level for claims involving a most fundamental right, the right to be free from torture.[355]

The Committee held that, since the complainant applied unsuccessfully for legal aid, the reasons for inadmissibility no longer applied. It noted, however, that if the complainant's financial resources exceeded the maximum level of financial means triggering the entitlement to legal aid, and he was thus able to provide for his own legal representation, then the remedy of judicial review could not have been said to be unavailable to him. Alternatively, in some circumstances, it might be considered reasonable, in light of the complainant's language and/or legal skills, that he represent himself.[356] In *Agalar v. Norway*, the Court was struck by the fact that the applicant's legal aid request was refused notwithstanding that it was clear he had at least a *prima facie* case for the existence of a real risk of facing treatment proscribed by Article 3 ECHR.[357] It held that despite the authorities' being satisfied that the applicant fulfilled the conditions of indigence for being granted free legal representation, they decided to refuse his request for such a grant. In the Court's view, the special circumstances hence absolved the applicant from his normal obligation to exhaust the national judicial remedies.[358]

---

353 ComAT, *Z.T. (No. 2) v. Norway*, 14 November 2005, no. 238/2003.
354 *Ibid.*, § 8.3.
355 *Ibid.*
356 *Ibid.*, § 8.2. See also ComAT, *Eftekhary v. Norway*, 25 November 2011, no. 312/2007, §§ 2.7 and 6.3.
357 ECtHR, *Agalar v. Norway*, 8 November 2011, no. 55120/09 (decision).
358 *Ibid.*

In *C.M. v. Switzerland*, the Committee considered that, given the complainant's personal circumstances, it was unfair to oblige him to pay the sum of 1,200 Swiss francs in order for his last application to be the reconsidered before the Swiss appeal body.[359] This view was based on the fact that the complainant was not authorized to work and that he had been denied social assistance. On this background, the Committee considered that the argument according to which the complaint was inadmissible for failure to exhaust domestic remedies did not stand.[360] In *R.S.A.N. v. Canada*, in contrast, the complainant claimed he was precluded from a remedy before the Canadian Federal Court because of his difficult financial situation.[361] The Committee noted that the complainant had not provided any information on the costs of legal representation or court fees, nor on the possibilities or any efforts on his part to obtain legal aid. The Committee hence concluded that the complainant had not adduced sufficient elements to justify his failure to avail himself of the possibility of applying for judicial review.[362] As can be seen, the Court and the Committee follow a case-by-case approach with regard to court fees and legal aid.

c   *New Evidence and Extraordinary Remedies*

In principle, the Court and the Committee do not request applicants under the exhaustion rule to use extraordinary legal remedies. However, the Court has held that where there has been significant change in either the applicant's circumstances or the conditions in his country of origin, a further submission before the national migration authorities could be required for the exhausting of domestic remedies.[363] Similarly, the Committee has rejected complaints for non-exhaustion of domestic remedies by stating that the applicant should first present new facts to the domestic authorities.[364] However, extraordinary remedies must also have suspensive effect to be considered effective.[365]

In *F.M-M. v. Switzerland* concerning an applicant from the Republic of Congo, the Committee recalled 'its case law, according to which the State

---

359   ComAT, *C.M. v. Switzerland*, 14 May 2010, no. 355/2008, §§ 4.1, 5.1 and 9.2.

360   *Ibid.*, § 9.2.

361   ComAT, *R.S.A.N. v. Canada*, 17 November 2006, no. 284/2006, § 6.4.

362   *Ibid.*

363   ECtHR, *Sufi and Elmi v. UK*, 28 June 2011, nos. 8319/07 and 11449/07, § 206.

364   ComAT, *P.M.P.K v. Sweden*, 20 November 1995, no. 30/1995, §§ 4 and 7; ComAT, *K.K.H. v. Canada*, 22 November 1995, no. 35/1999, § 5; ComAT, *K.N. v. France*, 18 November 1999, no. 93/1997, § 6.3; ComAT, *L.Z.B. and J.F.Z. v. Canada*, 8 November 2007, no. 304/2006, § 6.6; ComAT, *S.K. and R.K. v. Sweden*, 21 November 2011, no. 365/2008, §§ 7.1, 9, 11.3; ComAT, *J.L.L. v. Switzerland*, 18 May 2012, no. 364/2008, § 7.2. and 11.4; ComAT, *B.M.S. v. Sweden*, 12 November 2012, no. 437/2010, §§ 4.3 and 6.2–7.

365   ECtHR, *A.A.M. v. Sweden*, 3 April 2014, no. 68519/10, §§ 44–47.

party must have the opportunity to examine new evidence covered by Article 3 CAT before it is considered by the Committee.'366 It noted that in the instant case, the national courts had not been able to consider new and important evidence, namely proof of the complainant's political activity within the opposition movement in Switzerland and the resulting threats made against him and his family, as well as a copy of an arrest warrant. The complainant had further failed to provide any valid reason for not submitting this evidence, which he knew to exist, to the national authorities during national proceedings. The Committee hence concluded that the complaint was inadmissible. It noted that, 'in addition to the extraordinary procedure, the complainant had the right to file a new request for asylum on the basis of the new evidence' at national level.367

However, neither the Court nor the Committee will categorically exclude the assessment of complaints even though individual assertions or evidence have not been presented to national authorities. Because of the *ex nunc* assessment in cases in which the deportation has not yet taken place,368 the Court and the Committee might both take into account information or material that dates from *after* the domestic proceedings have ended.369 In *I.K. v. Austria*, the government submitted that the complaint was inadmissible for non-exhaustion of domestic remedies, since the applicant had failed to inform the domestic authorities of his deteriorating psychological health and had failed to provide them with the medical information he had submitted to the Court in Strasbourg.370 The Court first held that the new information concerning his health dated from after the domestic proceedings had ended. It then recalled its case law according to which the existence of a risk under Article 3 ECHR must be assessed at the time when the Court examines the case if the applicant has not yet been expelled.371 In light of this, the Court noted that 'it can take material and events that date from a time after the domestic proceedings had ended into account when assessing the applicant's situation in light of

---

366 ComAT, *F.M-M. v. Switzerland*, 26 May 2011, no. 399/2009, §§ 6.3–7. The Committee thereby referred to the inadmissibility decision ComAT, *A.E. v. Switzerland*, 2 May 1995, no. 24/1995.

367 ComAT, *F.M-M. v. Switzerland*, 26 May 2011, no. 399/2009, § 6.5.

368 On the 'time of the risk assessment' see Chapter 4 Section 2.

369 See the statement in ECtHR, *El-Masri v. Former Yugoslav Republic of Macedonia*, 13 December 2012 [GC], no. 39630/09, § 162. See, for example, ComAT, *C.T. and K.M. v. Sweden*, 17 November 2006, no. 279/2005, §§ 5.8 and 7.6; ComAT, *A.M. v. France*, 5 May 2010, no. 302/2006, §§ 10, 11.1, 12.2 and 12.3.

370 ECtHR, *I.K. v. Austria*, 28 March 2013, no. 2964/12, § 58.

371 *Ibid.*, §§ 61 and 63.

Article 3 pending an expulsion from the respondent State.'[372] It hence rejected the government's objection on admissibility. When newly submitted evidence indicates that the complainant has been a victim of torture in the past, the Committee also seems willing to accept late submissions.[373]

The Court and the Committee are both reluctant to accept governmental objections for non-exhaustion that refer to the fact that the human rights situation in the receiving country has changed since the case was decided at national level. As a general rule, the Court has held that, 'a full and *ex nunc* assessment is called for as the situation in a country of destination may change in the course of time' and that it is therefore necessary to take into account information that has come to light since the final decision taken by the domestic authorities.[374] The Committee follows the same approach.[375] In *Sufi and Elmi*, the Court specified that it will only declare a complaint inadmissible based on a change in the human rights situation in the receiving state if the national authority's practice has adapted in such a way that the applicant will be offered reasonable prospects of success with a new request for protection.[376] Whether there is such a reasonable prospect of success will depend on the national case law concerning individuals with comparable backgrounds as the applicant and the advice given by experienced counsel.[377]

Generally, the Court and the Committee's practice with regard to the treatment or consequences of submitting new facts or evidence at the international level is quite unpredictable. However, it should be noted that if the procedure at national level is reopened or a new asylum request is submitted by the applicant while the case is pending before the Court or the Committee, the application might be declared inadmissible for non-exhaustion for that reason,[378] unless the newly introduced remedy does not meet the criteria of effectiveness.[379]

---

372   *Ibid.*

373   ComAT, *M.M.K. v. Sweden*, 3 May 2005, no. 221/2002, § 7.5. Similar ComAT, *Z.K. v. Sweden*, 9 May 2008, no. 301/2006, § 8.4, in which although the medical reports were not presented before the national authorities they could not be 'completely disregarded as they state that the scars on the complainant's body could have occurred as a result of torture.' See further ComAT, *R.K. et al. v. Sweden*, 16 May 2008, no. 309/2006, §§ 5.3, 6.1, 6.2, 8.4 & 8.5.

374   ECtHR, *Salah Sheekh v. Netherlands*, 11 January 2007, no. 1948/04, § 136.

375   See on this also Chapter 4 Section 2.2.

376   ECtHR, *Sufi and Elmi v. UK*, 28 June 2011, nos. 8319/07 & 11449/07, §§ 215, 205–209.

377   *Ibid.*

378   See, for example, ECtHR, *L.T. v. Belgium*, 12 March 2012, no. 31201/11, § 30 (decision); ComAT, *A.K. v. Switzerland*, 8 May 2006, no. 248/2004, §§ 5, 7.1 and 7.2.

379   For example, ComAT, *M.S.G. v. Switzerland*, 30 May 2011, no. 352/2008, §§ 4.1, 4.2 and 10.2, 10.3. On the requirements of an effective remedy in extraordinary procedures see also ECtHR, *Budrevich v. Czech Republic*, 17 October 2013, no. 65303/10, §§ 77–125.

3.2.5   Compatibility with the Provisions of the Conventions

According to Article 35(3)a ECHR and Article 22(2) CAT, the Court and the Committee may only deal with complaints relating to infringements of rights set out in the ECHR or the CAT. The compatibility *ratione materiae* requires that the rights relied on by the applicant are within the scope of the Convention articles. The prohibition on refoulement under Article 3 ECHR and Article 3 CAT applies to all transfer proceedings from one jurisdiction to the other (be it through expulsion, extradition or any kind of formal or informal transfer) and to any individual under the respondent state's jurisdiction no matter his background or legal status. Hence, before the Court as well as before the Committee, it is rare for refoulement complaints to be declared inadmissible for being incompatible with the scope of Article 3 ECHR or Article 3 CAT.[380]

However, as already mentioned and as will be explained in chapter 3, the scope of protection offered under Article 3 CAT is in principle restricted to acts of torture according to the definition in Article 1 CAT. Consequently, the Committee has rejected a few claims as incompatible with the provisions of the CAT by reasoning that the harm expected in the receiving country does not appear to amount to torture.[381] According to the definition of torture in Article 1 CAT, the principle of non-refoulement under Article 3 CAT is also not applicable to acts inflicted by private actors without the consent or acquiescence of public actors. As will be explained in chapter 3, the Committee has developed a vast case law on the terms 'consent' or 'acquiescence' of public actors over the course of the years. Today, it appears that Article 3 CAT also protects against harm from private actors if the receiving state is not willing or able to offer protection against such harm. However, in autumn 2010, the Committee still declared two claims incompatible with the provisions of the CAT by reasoning that the harm expected in the receiving country emanated from private actors.[382]

In sum, the fact that the protection against refoulement under the CAT is restricted to acts of torture has had effects on the admissibility of claims.

---

380   With regard to the Court see the indication in the 'Practical Guide on Admissibility Criteria,' 1 January 2014, p. 53.

381   ComAT, *M.V. v. Netherlands*, 2 May 2003, no. 201/2002, §§ 3.1, 5.3 and 6.2; ComAT, *T.M. v. Sweden*, 18 November 2003, no. 228/2003, § 4.1 and 6.2; ComAT, *L.J.R. v. Australia*, 10 November 2008, no. 316/2007, §§ 4.3 and 6.2.

382   ComAT, *Güclü v. Sweden*, 11 November 2010, no. 349/2008, § 5.2 and ComAT, *Aytulun and Guclu v. Sweden*, 19 November 2010, no. 373/2009, § 6.2. On the issue see Chapter 3 Section 3.3.

However, looking at the case law as a whole, the criterion *ratione materiae* has not been of particular relevance in the Committee's practice.[383]

Finally, with regard to the scope of the Article 3 ECHR and Article 3 CAT, the following is worth noting: the Court is constantly repeating that the right to political asylum is not contained in the ECHR and that it is not in its competence to verify how the states honour their obligations under the Geneva Convention.[384] The Committee takes a similar position.[385] However, the declarations by the Court and the Committee have not proven to be of particular relevance in the application of the admissibility criterion *ratione materiae*.[386] As will be explained in chapter 4, it is obvious that in most cases in which individuals have asked for protection under Article 33 of the 1951 Refugee Convention at national level, they can also rely on Article 3 ECHR or Article 3 CAT in the international procedure before the Court or the Committee.[387]

3.2.6   Manifestly Ill-founded Complaints

Both the Court and the Committee reject *manifestly ill-founded* complaints. While the criterion is explicitly contained in Article 35(3)a ECHR, it cannot be found in the CAT itself, but in Rule 113(b) of the Committee's Rules of Procedure.[388] A complaint will be considered manifestly ill-founded if a *preliminary examination of its substance does not disclose any appearance of a violation* of the right guaranteed. The assessment is a preliminary test on the merits.

As is known from practice, this criterion is the reason for which 'by far most applications' are declared inadmissible before the Court.[389] Most of them

---

383   There are only few refoulement complaints in which the criterion has played a role; see
        ComAT, *L.B. v. Spain*, 18. November 1991, no. 9/1991; ComAT, *X. v. Spain*, 15 November 1995,
        no. 23/1995; ComAT, *E.H. v. Hungary*, 10 May 1999, no. 62/1996; ComAT, *I.A.F.B. v. Sweden*,
        13 November 2012, no. 425/2010; ComAT, *Z. v. Switzerland*, 25 November 2015, no. 545/2013.
        In some of these cases, it is also rather the lack of victim status that should have been ap-
        plied; the Committee appears to lack consistency and perhaps skill in the application of
        the criterion *ratione materiae*; in this sense also Bayefsky 2003, p. 47.
384   Among many others, see ECtHR, *Hirsi Jamaa and Others v. Italy*, 23 February 2012 [GC], no.
        27765/09, § 113.
385   See ComAT, *Mohamed v. Greece*, 28 April 1997, no. 40/1996, § 11.2.
386   As a rare exception see ComAT, *X v. Spain*, 15 November 1995, no. 23/1995, § 7.5, in which
        the Committee concluded that the communication was not sufficiently justified as a
        claimed violation of Art. 3 CAT but that it was a matter of political asylum, making the
        communication incompatible with Art. 22 CAT.
387   See on this Chapter 4 Sections 3.3.1.c, 3.3.2.c and 3.3.3.c.
388   See Rule 113(b) ComAT (CAT/C/3/Rev.6), using the term 'manifestly unfounded.'
389   Court's Guide on Admissibility Criteria, 1 January 2014, p. 82. See also Kälin 2013, p. 263
        (§ 665); Keller, Fischer & Kühne 2010, p. 1028.

are declared inadmissible in the *simplified procedure* by a single judge or a three-judge committee (i.e., without the respondent government being implicated in the procedure).[390] However, a chamber or even the Grand Chamber may also declare applications inadmissible for this reason. Should this be the case, the inadmissibility decision will be published and may sometimes contain lengthy and detailed reasoning, including considerations of general importance.[391]

The Court's admissibility guide states that the term 'manifestly' in Article 35(3)a ECHR may cause confusion.[392] It notes that 'if taken literally, it might be understood to mean that an application will only be declared inadmissible on this ground if it is immediately obvious to the average reader that it lacks foundation.'[393] However, as the Guide states, this is not reflected in the Court's abundant practice on the matter, from which it is clear that 'the expression is to be construed more broadly, in terms of the final outcome of the case.'[394] The criterion is essentially used by the Court to filter out weak cases.[395] As a result, the Court's handling of the criterion is rather elusive.[396]

All of the criteria that are relevant in the Court's risk assessment on the merits as discussed in this research may be relevant in deciding whether a complaint is manifestly ill-founded. A great number of complaints are considered manifestly ill-founded because of the complainant's lack of credibility and/or his failure to submit relevant evidence with regard to a risk of ill treatment in case of deportation. The Court also relies on the fact that the risk assessment conducted by the national authorities appears to have been fair and exhaustive when rejecting complaints as manifestly ill-founded.[397] It further appears that the human rights record in the receiving country plays a particularly important role in this preliminary assessment. In *K.A. v. Switzerland,* submitted to the Court in June 2009, the complainant had alleged that the Tunisian authorities persecuted him for his membership of the *Ennahda,* the Islamic party

---

390 *Ibid.*

391 See, for example, ECtHR, *T.I. v. UK,* 7 March 2000, no. 43844/98 (decision).

392 Court's 'Practical Guide on Admissibility Criteria,' 1 January 2014, p. 82.

393 *Ibid.*

394 *Ibid.*

395 Leach 2011, p. 157.

396 See Court's 'Practical Guide on Admissibility Criteria,' 1 January 2014, p. 12, in which it is stated that the concept can be broken down almost *ad infinitum.* Keller, Fischer & Kühne 2010, p. 1046, observe a danger that the category of manifestly ill-founded applications is used as a tool to control the caseload of the Court.

397 For example ECtHR, *Damla and Others v. Germany,* 26 October 2000, no. 61479/00 (decision).

opposed to the former Tunisian government.[398] During the Arab Spring, the *Ennahda* became the most powerful party in the new Tunisian government. Correspondingly, the Court noted that the complaint had lost its basis and that it must be rejected for being manifestly ill-founded.

The inadmissibility criterion of manifestly ill-founded complaints is of much more importance in the Court's practice than it is in the Committee's.[399] So far, the Committee has rejected only few complaints concerning non-refoulement for being manifestly ill-founded, most of them because insufficient evidence or no evidence at all had been adduced, or because the applicant had only made vague or contradictory allegations.[400] According to the Committee's General Comment on Article 3 CAT, it is the responsibility of the complainant to establish a *prima facie* case for the purpose of admissibility of his application.[401] Complainants must sufficiently elaborate the facts and the basis of the claim for a decision.[402] However, the level of evidence required for the purposes of admissibility appears to be low in Geneva. While before the Court, the assessment of admissibility may amount to a quite comprehensive preliminary test of the case on the merits, complaints rejected for that reason by the Committee must be more obviously lacking in foundation.[403] However, the Committee does assess certain complaints on the merits even when they appear, at least to the outsider, to be obviously unfounded.[404] It should further

---

398   ECtHR, *K.A. v. Switzerland*, 17 April 2012, no. 30352/09, §§ 27–31 (decision).

399   See also Schürmann & Scheidegger 2009, p. 203; de Weck 2011, p. 6.

400   See ComAT, *X v. Switzerland*, 17 November 1994, no. 17/1994; ComAT, *Y. v. Switzerland*, 17 November 1994, no. 18/1994; ComAT. *X and Y v. Netherlands*, 20 November 1995, no. 31/1995; ComAT, *H.I.A. v. Sweden*, 2 May 2003, no. 216/2002; ComAT, *A.T.A. v. Switzerland*, 11 November 2003, no. 236/2003; ComAT, *S.A. v. Sweden*, 6 May 2004, no. 243/2004; ComAT, *H.S.V. v. Sweden*, 12 May 2004, no. 229/2003; ComAT, *R.S. v. Denmark*, 19 May 2004, no. 225/2003; ComAT, *Chorlango v. Sweden*, 22 November 2004, no. 218/2002; ComAT, *Villamar and Cancino v. Canada*, 24 November 2004, no. 163/2000; ComAT, *R.T. v. Switzerland*, 24 November 2005, no. 242/2003; ComAT, *H.S.T. v. Norway*, 16 November 2006, no. 288/2006; ComAT, *M.K. and B.B. v. Switzerland*, 26 November 2015, no. 635/2014 (not published yet).

401   ComAT, General Comment No. 1 on Art. 3 CAT (1997), § 4. See also ComAT, *Chorlango v. Sweden*, 22 November 2004, no. 218/2002, § 5.3, in which the Committee concluded that the complaint was manifestly ill-founded by observing that the complaint did not give rise to a '*prima facie* case' under the Convention.

402   ComAT, *Sivagnanaratnam v. Dênmark*, 11 November 2013, no. 429/2010, § 9.2.

403   As exceptions see ComAT, *A.T.A. v. Switzerland*, 11 November 2003, no. 236/2003; ComAT, *R.T. v. Switzerland*, 24 November 2005, no. 242/2003.

404   For example, ComAT, *S.C. v. Denmark*, 10 May 2000, no. 143/1999; ComAT, *A.M. v. France*, 5 May 2010, no. 302/2006; ComAT, *F.A.B. v. Switzerland*, 17 November 2009, no. 348/2008; ComAT, *M.A.F. et al v. Sweden*, 23 November 2012, no. 385/2009, §§ 8.6 and 8.7; ComAT,

be noted that in certain decisions, the Committee's considerations on the merits are so scant and standardized that even if they are designated as a substantive assessment on the merits, they seem hardly worthy to be qualified as such, at least to the outside reader.[405]

Finally, note that the Court and the Committee may also reject a complaint that they consider to be an *abuse of the right to submit individual complaints*,[406] although it is rare that applications are rejected on this ground.[407] The submission of a matter must amount 'to malice or a display of bad faith or intent at least to mislead, or to be frivolous.'[408] Examples include applications containing misleading information or offensive language or that are devoid of any real purpose.[409] It does not appear that this criterion is of particular relevance in the context of refoulement. It should further be noted that the Committee might not even register a complaint if there is such an evident lack of substance that its handling would be meaningless.[410] However, this is rare for claims under the principle of non-refoulement.[411]

3.2.7   Victim Status and Loss of Victim Status
a   *Locus Standi*
According to Article 34 ECHR, the Court may receive applications from any person, NGO or group of individuals claiming to be the victim of a violation of

---

T.M. *v. Republic of Korea*, 21 November 2014, no. 519/2012, § 9.6. See also Schürmann & Scheidegger 2009, p. 203.

405   See, for example, ComAT, *S.L. v. Sweden*, 11 May 2001, 150/1999 § 6.4; ComAT, *V.R. v. Denmark*, 17 November 2003, no. 210 §§ 6.1–6.4; ComAT, *M.Z.A. v. Sweden*, 22 May 2012, no. 424/2010, §§ 8.4–8.6. See also McAdam 2011, p. 717, who notes that the Committee's negative decisions 'provide little further assistance in determining how, and against what standards of authority and corroboration, evidence is tested.'

406   Art. 35(3)a ECHR and Art. 22(2) CAT.

407   The only complaint that has been rejected for that reason by the Committee is ComAT, *P.R. v. Spain*, 23 November 2000, no. 160/2000. See further ComAT, *A.M. v. France*, 5 May 2010, no. 302/2006, §§ 4.1, 4.2, 8.2, 12.2 and 12.3, in which the Committee rejected the government's argument for abuse of rights, as the documents produced by the complainant had all the characteristics of forgeries. It is stated that it is up to the 'Committee to evaluate the good faith of the complainant in his presentation of facts and evidence, and their relevance on the inadmissibility of the communication.' See also ComAT, *T.M. v. Republic of Korea*, 21 November 2014, no. 519/2012, §§ 4.1 and 8.3. For the Court's practice see the 'Practical Guide on Admissibility Criteria,' 1 January 2014, pp. 37–40.

408   ComAT, *Ben Salem v. Tunisia*, 7 November 2007, no. 269/2005, § 8.4.

409   Nowak & McArthur 2008, p. 784 (§ 172).

410   Sørensen 2001, p. 174.

411   Information obtained by OHCHR on 3 October 2013.

the Convention. According to Article 22 CAT, the Committee considers complaints from or on behalf of individuals who claim to be victims of a violation of the provisions of the Convention.[412] The Court and the Committee only consider complaints submitted by the person *directly affected* by the alleged human rights violation. In the context of refoulement, this can only be the individual threatened with deportation. Cases brought by parties not personally affected, so-called class actions or *actio popularis*, are not accepted. NGOs or other groups interested in the protection of human rights cannot bring a claim simply because they have heard of or observed a human rights violation.

However, victims can seek assistance from NGOs, lawyers or other experts to act on their behalf. Representatives must be able to show an appropriate authorization to act on behalf of the alleged victim.[413] Neither the Court nor the Committee impose specific requirements on the manner in which the authority form must be drafted. A simple written authority signed by the applicant and his representative is valid, unless it has been shown that it was made without the applicant's understanding and consent.[414] The Court and the Committee have both rejected complaints of human rights defenders who wanted to represent migrants intercepted in the Mediterranean Sea who were immediately returned to North Africa, because they were not able to show a proper authorization.[415] Representatives must be able to demonstrate that they maintain contact with the applicant throughout the international proceeding[416] unless the loss of contact is a consequence of the defending state's action.[417] If the alleged victim has died as result of ill treatment or he is held incommunicado, the Court and the Committee might exceptionally accept complaints submitted by individuals connected with that alleged victim, in particular family members.[418]

---

412 Before the Committee, complaints that are obviously not submitted by the alleged victim or on his behalf might not even be registered: Rule 104(2)c ComAT (CAT/C/3/Rev.6).

413 Rule 45 ECtHR (1 January 2016); Rule 113(a) ComAT (CAT/C/3/Rev.6).

414 ECtHR, *Hirsi Jamaa and Others v. Italy*, 23 February 2012 [GC], no. 27765/09, §§ 52 and 53.

415 See ECtHR, *Hussun and Others v. Italy*, 19 January 2010, no. 10171/05, §§ 40–50 (striking out); ComAT, *J.H.A. v. Spain*, 11 November 2008, no. 323/2007, § 8.3.

416 ECtHR, *Sharifi and Others v. Italy and Greece*, 21 October 2014, no. 16643/09, § 134.

417 See, for example, ECtHR, *Safaii v. Austria*, 7 May 2014, no. 44689/09, §§ 35 and 36.

418 ECtHR, *Hirsi Jamaa and Others v. Italy*, 23 February 2012 [GC], no. 27765/09, § 57; Rule 113(a) ComAT (CAT/C/3/Rev.6). See ComAT, *Sonko v. Spain*, 25 November 2011, no. 368/2008, § 1.1 and ComAT, *Nasirov v. Kazakhstan*, 14 May 2014, no. 475/2011, § 1.1 in which the complaints were submitted by the applicants' siblings; ComAT, *Agiza v. Sweden*, 20 May 2005, no. 233/2003, §§ 1.1, 4.3 and 9.2, in which the authority had been submitted by

When assessing refoulement complaints submitted by families, the Committee does not consider the risk for each member individually. If it considers that the risk is established with regard to the most threatened applicant (often the father or the parents), it will advise the respondent state not to expel the whole family, even though, in some cases, the spouse or children may not face the same risk.[419] The Court normally also follows this practice.[420]

b   *Victim Status and Imminent Threat of Deportation*
As to the specific categories of cases involving expulsion or extradition measures, the Court and the Committee have made clear that individuals cannot claim to be 'victims' according to Article 34 ECHR or Article 22 CAT if they are not under an imminent threat of deportation.[421] Hence, claims under the principle of non-refoulement must be backed up with an enforceable deportation order, unless it can be demonstrated that a *de facto* threat of deportation exists without a formal order.[422]

Where the execution of the deportation or extradition order has been stayed or otherwise deprived of legal effect, or where any decision to proceed with deportation can be appealed against before the relevant courts, the complainant will not be recognized as having victim status as required.[423] The complaint is then either struck out of the register by the Court[424] or discontinued by the Committee,[425] or declared inadmissible.[426] The same will happen if the applicant submits a new request for asylum in the host state, which allows him

---

the complainant's father. The complainant himself had already been expelled to Egypt where he was held in detention.

419   For example, ComAT, *Y.B.F., S.A.Q. and Y.Y. v. Switzerland*, 31 May 2013, no. 467/2011, § 7.8.

420   See ECtHR, *Bader and Kanbor v. Sweden*, 8 November 2005, no. 13284/04, §§ 1, 34, 47–48; ECtHR, *D. and others v. Turkey*, 22 June 2006, no. 24245/03, §§ 55–56. As exception see ECtHR, *A.A. and Others v. Sweden*, 28 June 2012, no. 14499/09, § 80, in which the Court focussed on the female applicants who alleged that they were threatened with violence based on their gender in Yemen.

421   See, for example, ECtHR, *Isakov v. Russia*, 8 July 2010, no. 14049/08, § 98, with references; ComAT, *J.M.U.M. v. Sweden*, 15 May 1998, no. 58/1996, § 3.2.

422   As an example of the latter, ECtHR, *Ryabikin v. Russia*, 19 June 2008, no. 8320/04, § 115.

423   ECtHR, *Isakov v. Russia*, 8 July 2010, no. 14049/08, § 99.

424   For example, ECtHR, *Atmaca v. Germany*, 6 March 2012, no. 45293/06 (striking out).

425   The Committee does not usually publish its decision of discontinuation. As an exception see ComAT, *Khalsa et al. v. Switzerland*, 26 May 2011, no. 336/2008, § 11.1, in which the decision is visible since it only concerned one of several applicants.

426   For the Court see, for example, ECtHR, *Dobrov v. Ukraine*, 14 June 2011, no. 42409/09 (decision). For the Committee see, for example, ComAT, *B.M.S. v. Sweden*, 12 November 2012, no. 437/2010, § 6.2.

to stay legally in the host country until that new procedure is concluded.[427] Individuals benefitting from a temporary residence permit cannot in principle claim to be victims under Article 3 ECHR or Article 3 CAT.[428] In the case *Budrevich v. the Czech Republic*, the authorities had rejected the applicant's request for asylum, considering that he did not face any persecution in Belarus within the meaning of the Czech Asylum Act.[429] They did, however, consider that the applicant would face a real risk of inhuman treatment upon his return to Belarus and therefore granted him two years' subsidiary protection status. The Court noted that the applicant was able to request extension of this status and that he could lodge an appeal if this request was rejected. On this background, it concluded that the 'argument of the applicant that the protection he was afforded was only temporary is misconceived and is not relevant from the point of view of Article 3 of the Convention.' The Court recalled that the ECHR does 'not require any particular form of protection' but only that a person should not be removed to a country where he would face a real risk of treatment contrary to Article 3 ECHR.[430] In *Auad v. Bulgaria*, the Court further indicated that individuals whose 'home' receiving country does not issue travel documents enabling them to re-enter could not benefit from victim status under Article 34 ECHR.[431] However, both the Court and the Committee appear to be unpredictable on the issue of imminent threat, sometimes also assessing non-imminent deportations on the merits.[432]

c   *Striking Out and Discontinuation of the Assessment for* Loss *of Victim Status*

The applicant must be able to justify his status as a victim throughout the procedings before the Court and the Committee. According to Article 37(1) ECHR, at any time during the proceedings, the Court can strike an application from its list, where the circumstances lead to the conclusion that (a) the applicant does not intend to pursue his application; (b) that the matter has been resolved, or

---

427   See, for example, ECtHR, *Sharifi v. Switzerland*, 4 December 2012, no. 69486/11 (striking out). With regard to the Committee, this is known from practice.

428   See the explicit statement in ComAT, *E.H. v. Hungary*, 62/1996, § 6.2.

429   ECtHR, *Budrevich v. Czech Republic*, 17 October 2013, no. 65303/10, §§ 61–72.

430   *Ibid.*, § 71. See similar with regard to a temporary asylum status in ECtHR, *Tukhtamurodov v. Russia*, no. 21762/14, 20 January 2015 (decision).

431   ECtHR, *Auad v. Bulgaria*, 11 October 2011, no. 46390/10, § 92.

432   See, for example, ECtHR, *Ahmed v. Austria*, 17 December 1996, no. 25964/94, §§ 32 and 37. See also ECtHR, *Salah Sheekh v. Netherlands*, 11 January 2007, no. 1948/04, § 117 compared to ECtHR, *Kalantari v. Germany*, 11 October 2001, no. 51342/99 (striking out). For the Committee see ComAT, *A.D. v. Netherlands*, 12 November 1999, no. 96/1997, §§ 6.4 and 7.3.

(c) for any other reason if it is established by the Court that the examination of the case is not longer justified. The Court enjoys a wide discretion in identifying grounds capable of being relied upon in striking out an application on this basis[433] and unfortunately, there is no official data on this area. It may be observed from practice, however, that the Court's competence to strike out cases because their initial purpose has fallen away during the long international procedure is of particular relevance in the context of refoulement.[434]

The CAT itself does not contain a provision comparable to Article 37 ECHR. Rule 116(1) of the Committee's Rules of Procedure, however, holds that where the Committee decides that the assessment of a complaint is discontinued, it should transmit this decision to the complainant and to the state party concerned as soon as possible.[435] From the 697 complaints registered by the Committee since 1989, the assessment of 197 complaints had been discontinued up to August 2015.[436] Under the CAT as well, the discontinuation of assessment is a frequent occurrence. However, the Committee does not publish its decisions on discontinuation. It simply informs the parties concerned of the discontinuation of the assessment using a standard letter briefly indicating the reason.[437]

Why is the assessment of many refoulement complaints discontinued? There are various reasons: the Court and the Committee usually discontinue the assessment of complaints when the applicant has permanently left the contracting state against which the complaint has been submitted[438] or when contact with the applicant or his representative is lost,[439] provided that

---

433   ECtHR, *Atmaca v. Germany*, 6 March 2012, no. 45293/06 (striking out).

434   See also Mole & Meredith 2010, p. 232, noting that the Court is using the striking-out procedure in an increasing number of cases concerning asylum related issues under the Convention.

435   Rule 116(1) (CAT/C/3/Rev.6).

436   See statistical survey 'Status of the cases dealt with under Art. 22 CAT,' 15 August 2015, accessible on the Committee's website <http://www.ohchr.org/en/hrbodies/cat/pages/catindex.aspx> [23.2.2016].

437   Known from practice.

438   Such complaints might also be declared manifestly ill-founded or incompatible with the provisions of the Conventions; see ECtHR, *D.B. v. Turkey*, 13 July 2010, no. 33526/08, §§ 41–44; ComAT, *H.S.T. v. Norway*, 16 November 2006, no. 288/2006, § 6.3; ComAT, *I.A.F.B. v. Sweden*, 13 November 2012, no. 425/2010, § 7.3. See, however, ComAT, *M.S.G. v. Switzerland*, 30 May 2011, no. 352/2008, § 10.5, in which the Committee rejected the government's claim of inadmissibility for the reason that the applicant's presence in Switzerland was not established by noting that the representative was in constant contact with him.

439   See, as a famous example, ECtHR, *Ramzy v. Netherlands*, 20 July 2010, no. 25424/05, §§ 62–66. This case further shows that the Court may even strike out complaints that have already been declared admissible.

the loss of contact was not provoked by the government itself, in particular through the deportation in question.[440] The Court and the Committee may further discontinue the assessment of complaints when the applicant has explicitly and voluntarily withdrawn his application.[441] In *M.S. v. Belgium*, the Court has made clear that – if at all possible – a *de facto* renouncement from the protection against refoulement could only be accepted if the decision was clearly made freely. In this case, the complainant had decided to go back to Iraq although it was established that he ran a real risk of ill treatment there. Since he was considered a threat to Belgium's national security, he had no possibility of remaining there legally or at liberty. In these circumstances, although no deportation order was made, the Court concluded that the complainant's departure was coerced and not deliberately chosen, so that the complaint was admissible.[442]

A phenomenon that merits particular attention is that of applicants who had originally been threatened with deportation but subsequently obtain a residence permit during the international procedure, for humanitarian grounds, because of the right to family life (in particular through marriage), or because national authorities have reevaluated their initial request for protection. When a complainant obtains a residence permit for whatever reason after a case has been submitted, the Court or the Committee consider that the matter has been resolved, whether the applicant himself wants to pursue his application or not. The Court's Grand Chamber's made clear that once the applicant no longer risks being expelled, 'it considers the case to have been resolved and strikes it out of its list of cases, whether or not the applicant agrees.'[443] The reason for this is that 'the Court has consistently approached the issue as one of a potential violation of the Convention, being of the view that the threat of a violation is removed by virtue of the decision granting the applicant the right of residence in the respondent State concerned.'[444] The Court strikes such cases out

---

440   See, for example, ECtHR, *Diallo v. Czech Republic*, 23 June 2011, no. 20493/07, §§ 44–48; ECtHR, *Labsi v. Slovakia*, 15 May 2012, no. 33809/08, § 100; ComAT, *Abdussamatov and 28 Others v. Kazakhstan*, 1 June 2012, no. 444/2010, §§ 7.1 and 13.1–15.

441   See ComAT, *Gerasimov v. Kazakhstan*, 24 May 2012, no. 433/2010, §§ 5.9, 6, 7.16, 8.3–8.6, 9.1 and 11.3, in which the Committee did not abstain from assessing an individual complaint because the written withdrawal appeared to have been submitted under pressure from the respondent state party.

442   ECtHR, *M.S. v. Belgium*, 31 January 2012, no. 50012/08, §§ 91–107 and 117–120.

443   ECtHR, *M.E. v. Sweden*, 8 April 2015 [GC], no. 71398/12, § 32 (striking out).

444   *Ibid.*, § 33.

of its list on the basis of Article 37 ECHR or declares them inadmissible.[445] The Committee usually discontinues the assessment.[446]

The reason for which the applicant has been granted a residence permit is immaterial for the Court and the Committee, even if it has nothing to do with refoulement. Illustrative for that is the case *M. v. Finland*, in which the Iranian applicant claimed that even though he had been granted a continuous residence permit on the basis of family ties, this was not the same as having been granted asylum, since refugee status would ensure a much stronger and more permanent status, better rights and greater security against deportation.[447] The Court rejected the applicant's request for the maintenance of his application. It noted that the he was no longer subject to an expulsion order so that the matter could now be considered to be resolved in accordance with Article 37(1)b ECHR.

There are no official statistics from the Court and the Committee, but it is known from practice that there are many complaints that have been reassessed at national level with the subsequent attribution of a permit to stay after the case had been transmitted to the government in the context of the international procedure in Strasbourg or Geneva.[448] In this context, the communication of a refoulement complaint to the government often functions as a 'serious' – and highly effective – warning to the state authorities.[449] Of course, if a case is reassessed *ex officio* by the national authorities and a residence

---

445 See, among others, ECtHR, *M.A. v. Cyprus*, 23 July 2013, no. 41872/10, § 110 (inadmissible); ECtHR, *K.U. v. Switzerland*, 20 January 2015, no. 30349/13 (striking out).

446 Known from practice. According to information obtained by the OHCHR on 3 October 2013, a frequent reason for which the assessment of an individual complaint is discontinued is that the applicant has obtained a residence permit. As a decision of discontinuation that is visible see ComAT, *Khalsa et al. v. Switzerland*, 26 May 2011, no. 336/2008, § 11.1.

447 ECtHR, *M. v. Finland*, 6 September 2011, no. 48933/09 (striking out).

448 As examples see ECtHR, *Soedji v. Switzerland*, 7 April 2011, no. 21714/11 (decision; striking out); ECtHR, *M.Z. and N.Z. v. Switzerland*, 10 July 2012, no. 74910/11 (decision; striking out) with references; ECtHR, *M.A. v. Cyprus*, 23 July 2013, no. 41872/10, §§ 18–20, 56–57, 107–110 and 139. According to the ECRE/ELENA Research on ECHR Rule 39 Interim Measures, April 2012 pp. 77–80, lawyers from several European states have confirmed that when the Court imposes interim measures, this influences the national authirites when the case is reviewed. According to information obtained by the OHCHR on 3 October 2013, there are states in which this practice has occurred.

449 Suntinger 1995, p. 208. See also Rieter 2010, pp. 946 and 952. Also Andrysek 1997, p. 396, who notes that governments are inclined to prefer to 'compromise behind closed doors' so that 'one should not underestimate the value of individual complaint procedures just because many cases remain hidden from the public.'

permit is granted, the individual concerned will be relieved to have his situation resolved – mostly in a shorter amount of time than if he had had to wait for a judgment or decision at international level.[450] However, although the practice might help the Committee and the Court to reduce their backlog of cases, it might be, as Mole and Meredith note, 'counterproductive to this aim if issues are not dealt with by the Court in communicated cases, with the result that neither applicants nor governments know whether the Court considers that the matter raised was compatible with the Convention.'[451] While it is understandable that the Court and the Committee have no interest in assessing cases of abstract importance when there are hundreds of complainants waiting be heard, through their practice, the Court and the Committee enable governments to avoid international verdicts on issues that might raise violations of the principle of non-refoulement by unilateral decisions.

In that context, it should be recalled that at any stage of the proceedings the Court may also suggest that the parties reach a friendly settlement according to Article 39 ECHR.[452] Friendly settlements may allow governments to avoid an unwanted judgment finding a violation of the ECHR. For applicants, the procedure 'may represent an opportunity to achieve more than would be obtained from a Court's judgment itself (other than a finding of a violation).'[453] An analysis of friendly settlements reached in the context of refoulement would go beyond the scope of this study. In light of the fact that in refoulement-cases, states can unilaterally decide to resolve cases, without even having to negotiate financial or other compensation, it appears that the formal procedure of friendly settlement is of less importance than it might be with regard to other rights.[454] In contrast to the Court, the Committee does not have a formal friendly settlement procedure.

---

450   Lambert 2007, p. 54, notes: 'Thankfully, most cases never reach the final stage of judgment by the Court and are struck off because governments agree to withdraw the expulsion order and to grant some sort of status to the applicant.'

451   Mole & Meredith 2010, p. 232.

452   See, for example, ECtHR, *S.J. v. Belgium*, 19 March 2015 [GC], no. 70055/10 (striking out).

453   Leach 2011, p. 64.

454   It should be noted that in certain recent cases, the Court has started to attribute compensation for the *costs of procedures* in refoulement cases that have been discontinued because the complainant has obtained protection at national level during the international procedure; see ECtHR, *T.E. v. Switzerland*, 13 November 2014, no. 36801/13 (striking out); ECtHR, *K.U. v. Switzerland*, 20 January 2015, no. 30349/13 (striking out). In both cases, the Court attributed EUR 6,000 in compensation for the costs of the national and international procedures.

3.3   Concluding Remarks: The Court's Filter Mechanism

The individual complaint mechanisms before the Court and the Committee are constructed in a similar way. The proceedings are both free of charge and take on average between one and three years. Both attribute interim measures, even though the threshold for obtaining interim measures is much lower before the Committee. However, with regard to the procedure and treatment of inadmissible complaints, there are two major differences that should be pointed out:

(1)   The Court has a filter mechanism by which it may deal with obviously inadmissible complaints in a simplified procedure without the involvement of the government concerned. In fact, most of the cases handled by the Court are rejected as being manifestly inadmissible without the respondent state becoming involved in the procedure. The Committee does *not* have a simplified procedure. All complaints registered in Geneva are transmitted to the respondent government for observation.[455]

(2)   The formal requirements for the admissibility of complaints under the ECHR and the CAT are similar. However, while more than 95 per cent of all applications submitted to the Court are declared inadmissible, it is only around 20 per cent before the Committee.[456] The main reason that so many more complaints are declared inadmissible in Strasbourg than in Geneva is the Court's broader understanding of the concept 'manifestly ill-founded.'[457] By far the most common reason for inadmissibility in Strasbourg is that the application is considered 'manifestly ill-founded.'[458] The assessment of whether a complaint is manifestly ill-founded amounts to a preliminary assessment on the merits, which allows the Court to filter

---

455   There are a handful of complaints, in particular from the Committee's early years, that have been declared inadmissible without involvement of the respondent government; see ComAT, *X v. Switzerland*, 17 November 1994, no. 17/1994; ComAT, *Y. v. Switzerland*, 17 November 1994, no. 18/1994; ComAT, *M.A. v. Canada*, 3 May 1995, 22/1995; ComAT, *X and Y v. Netherlands*, 20 November 1995, no. 31/1995; ComAT, *N.D. v. France*, 20 November 1995, no. 32/1995; ComAT, *K.K.H. v. Canada*, 22 November 1995, no. 35/1999; ComAT, *A.T.A. v. Switzerland*, 11 November 2003, no. 236/2003. The practice was not continued.

456   Court's 'Practical Guide on Admissibility Criteria,' 1 January 2014, p. 11; statistical survey 'Status of the cases dealt with under Art. 22 CAT,' 15 August 2015, accessible on the Committee's website <http://www.ohchr.org/en/hrbodies/cat/pages/catindex.aspx> [15.2.2016].

457   See also Schürmann & Scheidegger 2009, p. 203; de Weck 2011, p. 6.

458   'Practical Guide on Admissibility Criteria,' 1 January 2014, p. 82; Keller, Fischer & Kühne 2010, p. 1028.

out the weakest cases.[459] The Committee also considers manifestly ill-founded complaints to be inadmissible, but it is much more reluctant to apply this criterion. The other admissibility criteria under the ECHR and the CAT are of a more formal character and do not leave much room for a diverse interpretation by the Court and the Committee. Hence, it must be kept in mind that while passing the bar of admissibility before the Court already represents a significant success for an applicant, it is not so significant before the Committee. This is reflected in the fact that of those cases in which a complaint has been considered admissible in Strasbourg from 1959, a violation of the ECHR by the respondent State was found in 80 per cent of them.[460] Before the Committee, it is in approximately 30 per cent of all the cases decided on the merits in which the Committee has concluded that a provision of the CAT has been violated.[461]

---

459   Leach 2011, p. 157.

460   ECtHR, 'Annual Report 2012,' p. 48.

461   Information sheet on the status of the cases dealt with under Art. 22 CAT, August 2013, obtained on request from the OHCHR; statistical survey 'Status of the cases dealt with under Art. 22 CAT,' 15 August 2015, accessible on the Committee's <http://www.ohchr.org/en/hrbodies/cat/pages/catindex.aspx> [23.2.2016].

CHAPTER 3

The Nature of the Harm Triggering the Application of the Non-refoulement Principle under the ECHR and the CAT

1   Introduction: The Harm Risked and the Act Prohibited by the Prohibition on Refoulement

What type or level of harm does an individual have to fear in a country, such that his removal to that country could raise issues under the principle of non-refoulement? Under the CAT, the harm triggering the application of the principle of non-refoulement is principally limited to torture. Under the ECHR, it is not limited to torture, but includes inhuman or degrading treatment or punishment. What do *torture* and *inhuman or degrading treatment or punishment* mean? What is the difference between torture on the one hand and inhuman or degrading treatment or punishment on the other? Can these different types of harms actually be distinguished in refoulement cases? What are the consequences of the different approaches of the Court and the Committee for complainants fearing an expulsion or extradition? These are the questions dealt with in this chapter. The following considerations do not constitute a comprehensive analysis of the definition of torture and other inhuman treatment, but will give an idea of the main characteristics of these notions as understood by the Court and the Committee, with a focus on issues pertinent in the context of non-refoulement.

However, before this analysis of the nature of the harm capable of triggering the application of Article 3 ECHR and Article 3 CAT is done, a look must be taken at the nature of the prohibition on refoulement. Where an individual has established a real risk of ill treatment or torture in case of removal, Articles 3 ECHR and 3 CAT imply an obligation on the state concerned *not to deport* that individual. As the Court has revealingly stated, the establishment of such a risk inevitably involves an assessment of the conditions in the requesting country against the standards of Article 3 ECHR.[1] This is equally valid under Article 3 CAT with regard to the standards of torture as defined under Article 1 CAT. However, it must be emphasised that under the principle of non-refoulement, there is no question of establishing the responsibility of the receiving country,

---

[1]   ECtHR, *Soering v. UK*, 7 July 1989, no. 14038/88, § 91.

whether under the CAT, the ECHR or other international provisions. The materialization of the ill treatment under another jurisdiction is not a condition for the violation of the principle of non-refoulement.[2] In other words, *the act that is prohibited under the principle of non-refoulement is not the ill treatment abroad, but the removal or decision to remove despite the real risk of ill treatment.* As made clear by the Court, the principle of non-refoulement is about the responsibility of the contracting state 'by reason of its having taken action which has as a direct consequence the exposure of an individual to proscribed ill-treatment.'[3] It is the decision of that state to remove an individual – and, *a fortiori*, the actual removal itself – that may give rise to an issue under Article 3 ECHR or Article 3 CAT, not the harm in the receiving country.[4] States having ratified the CAT or the ECHR must hence refrain from any action that could lead to the ill treatment of an individual under another jurisdiction. On this background, the prohibition on refoulement imposes first of all a negative obligation on states to refrain from causing harm by certain measures. However, there is also a positive dimension to the Articles 3 ECHR and 3 CAT, and the prohibition on refoulement in particular, as will be shown in this study.[5]

2   The Scope of Article 3 ECHR

2.1   *Introduction*
Article 3 ECHR prohibits torture as well as inhuman or degrading treatment or punishment. Based on that provision, the Court protects any individual against deportation to a country in which he would be subject to torture or inhuman or degrading treatment or punishment.

The ECHR itself contains no definition of torture or inhuman or degrading treatment or punishment. In its extensive case law on Article 3 ECHR in the domestic context, the Court has, however, identified several elements that characterize such treatments. The three prohibited forms of ill treatment – (1)

---

2   See on this also Chapter 4 Section 2.

3   ECtHR, *Soering v. UK* 7 July 1989, no. 14038/88, § 91.

4   ECtHR, *El-Masri v. Former Yugoslav Republic of Macedonia*, 13 December 2012 [GC], no. 39630/09, § 212. See illustrative for this practice ComAT, *Abichou v. Germany*, 21 May 2013, no. 430/2010, § 11.7, in which the Committee notes that the fact that the applicant was ultimately not subjected to ill treatment following his extradition cannot be justifiably used to call into question or minimize, retrospectively, the existence of such a risk at the time of his extradition.

5   States must actively take measures and provide for an adequate legal system to ensure that the principle of non-refoulement is respected in practice; see on this, in particular, Chapter 4 Section 3.1.

torture, (2) inhuman treatment or punishment and (3) degrading treatment or punishment – cannot be looked at separately but as a common concept with different levels of gravity: torture will always be inhuman and inhuman treatment will always be degrading.[6] Even though the Court attaches a 'special stigma' to acts of torture, the different forms of ill treatment are prohibited in an equal way. The classification of an act as either torture or inhuman or degrading treatment or punishment is hence not pertinent to the question of whether a state party has violated Article 3 ECHR or not. Accordingly, in its jurisprudence, the Court often does not specify whether actions taken in violation of Article 3 ECHR are to be qualified as torture or as inhuman or degrading treatment. In its judgments and decisions on non-refoulement complaints, it is particularly rare that the Court specifies whether a complainant fears acts of torture or whether he fears inhuman treatment in the event of his removal. The Court usually contents itself with stating that a person risks a 'treatment contrary to Article 3 ECHR' or risks 'being subjected to torture or to inhuman or degrading treatment or punishment' in case of removal. In *Harkin and Edwards v. United Kingdom* adopted in 2012, the judges for the first time explicitly explained their approach with regard to the different harms prohibited in the context of refoulement:

> It is correct that the Court has always distinguished between torture on the one hand and inhuman or degrading punishment on the other. However, *the Court considers that this distinction is more easily drawn in the domestic context where, in examining complaints made under Article 3, the Court is called upon to evaluate or characterise acts which have already taken place.* Where, as in the extra-territorial context, a prospective assessment is required, *it is not always possible to determine* whether the ill-treatment which may ensure in the receiving State will be sufficiently severe to qualify as torture. ...
>
> ... For this reason, whenever the Court has found that a proposed removal would be in violation of Article 3 because of a real risk of ill-treatment which would be *intentionally inflicted in the receiving State, it has normally refrained from considering whether the ill-treatment in question should be characterised as torture or inhuman or degrading treatment or punishment.*[7] (Emphasis added)

---

6 EComHR, *Denmark, Norway, Sweden and Netherlands v. Greek* (the Greek case), report of 5 November 1969, Yearbook 12 (1969), p. 186.

7 ECtHR, *Harkins and Edwards v. UK*, 17 January 2012, nos. 9146/07 and 32650/07, §§ 122 and 123. Recalled in ECtHR, *Babar Ahmad and Others v. UK*, 10 April 2012, nos. 24027/07, 11949/08, 36742/08, 66911/09 and 67354/09, §§ 170 and 171.

In cases outside the context of refoulement, the qualification or severity of an act suffered by an applicant can have consequences on the 'just satisfaction' attributed by the Court according to Article 41 ECHR. This is not the case in removal cases, where the Court in principle does not grant any compensation for non-pecuniary damage, but simply instructs the contracting state not to remove the complainant.[8] Hence, particularly in refoulement cases, as long as the judges conclude that an expected harm falls within the range of treatments contrary to Article 3 ECHR, a precise definition or classification of this harm is not imperative, since the legal consequences will be the same.[9]

The decisive question for the Court is therefore whether the harm risked by an applicant in the event of expulsion or extradition falls within the scope of Article 3 ECHR or not. The Court has stated on several occasions that the risk assessment in refoulement cases 'inevitably involves an assessment of the conditions in the receiving country against the standards of Article 3 of the Convention.'[10] To fall within the scope of Article 3 ECHR, the harm or ill treatment must attain a minimum level of severity. This minimum level of severity is relative: according to the Court's established case law, it depends on all the circumstances of the case, such as the nature or duration of the treatment, its physical and mental effects and, in some cases, the sex, age and state of health of the victim.[11] The Court follows a case-by-case approach when assessing whether an act falls within the scope of Article 3 ECHR or not. It is therefore difficult to define abstractly the minimum level of severity that leads to the application of Article 3 ECHR. The elements characterizing the standards are set out below.

2.2   The Nature of the Harm

2.2.1   Torture

Torture is the most severe form of ill treatment prohibited by Article 3 ECHR. In the landmark judgment *Ireland v. United Kingdom* decided in 1978, the Court stated that the drafters of the ECHR intended to make a distinction between the terms 'torture' and 'inhuman treatment' in the sense that a 'special stigma' should be attached to the notion of torture. The Court defined torture as 'a deliberate inhuman treatment causing very serious and cruel suffering.'[12]

---

8   See Chapter 2 Section 1.3.2.

9   Arai-Takahashi 2002, p. 16; Thurin 2012, p. 114.

10   See, amongst many others, ECtHR, *Soering v. UK*, 7 July 1989, no. 14038/88, § 91; ECtHR, *N.A. v. UK*, 17 July 2008, no. 25904/07, § 110.

11   See, amongst many others, ECtHR, *Soering v. UK*, 7 July 1989, no. 14038/88, § 100.

12   ECtHR, *Ireland v. UK*, 18 January 1978 [GC], no. 5310/71, § 167.

The distinction between torture and inhuman treatment under Article 3 ECHR derives from a difference in the intensity of the suffering inflicted.[13] In addition to the severity of a treatment, the Court has held, in referring to Article 1 CAT, that there 'is a purposive element which defines torture in terms of the intentional infliction of severe pain or suffering with the aim, *inter alia*, of obtaining information, inflicting punishment or intimidating.'[14] In 1969, the former European Commission of Human Rights stated 'that the word "torture" is often used to describe inhuman treatment which has a purpose, such as the obtaining of information or confessions, or the infliction of punishment, and it is generally an aggravated form of inhuman treatment.'[15] Accidently caused pain will hardly constitute torture. The Court clearly speaks of a deliberate treatment. But must an inflictor of severe pain always have a particular aim or purpose such as obtaining information or intimidating the victim for the harm he causes to qualify as torture? It is worth noting that the Court has not consistently required such a purposive element for the infliction of pain to be classified as torture.[16] Correspondingly, scholars specifically dealing with Article 3 ECHR see the purposive element rather as an indication of an act of torture than a condition for it.[17] However, as Schabas observes in his commentary on the ECHR, recent judgments on torture tend to refer to both the severity and the purpose of the ill treatment.[18]

Generally, there is no clear line indicating which acts have the intensity or character to amount to torture. As many scholars have noted, the best way to provide an understanding of the concept of torture is to give examples: the

---

13   See, for example, ECtHR, *Ireland v. UK*, 18 January 1978 [GC], no. 5310/71, § 167; ECtHR, *Selmouni v. France*, 28 July 1999 [GC], no. 25803/94, §§ 96–105; ECtHR, *Ilhan v. Turkey*, 27 June 2000, no. 22277/93, § 87; ECtHR, *Gäfgen v. Germany*, 1 June 2010[GC], no. 22978/05, § 108; ECtHR, *Harkins and Edwards v. UK*, 17 January 2012, nos. 9146/07 and 32650/07, § 122. See further Addo and Grief 1998, p. 512; Alleweldt 1996, p. 19; Bayefsky 2003, p. 85; Lambert 2007, p. 46; Thurin 2012, p 117; Weissbrodt & Hörtreiter 1999, p. 32.

14   See, as a recent example, ECtHR, *El-Masri v. Former Yugoslav Republic of Macedonia*, 13 December 2012 [GC], no. 39630/09, § 197.

15   EComHR, *Denmark, Norway, Sweden and Netherlands v. Greek* (the Greek case), report of 5 November 1969, Yearbook 12 (1969), p. 186.

16   See ECtHR, *Ilhan v. Turkey*, 27 June 2000, no. 22277/93, § 87, concerning severe beatings of a detainee combined with denial of medical treatment; ECtHR, *Ilaşcu and Others v. Moldova and Russia*, 8 July 2004, no. 48787/99, § 440, concerning an applicant who spent seven-and-a-half years on death row under inhuman circumstances. See also ECtHR, *Kaboulov v. Ukraine*, 19 November 2009, no. 41015/04, § 112.

17   Alleweldt 1996, p. 19; Thurin 2012, pp. 116–117.

18   Schabas 2015, pp. 177–179 with references to the case law.

first individual complaint in which the Court stated that a person had been tortured was decided in 1996 in the case *Aksoy v. Turkey*.[19] This case concerned the so-called Palestinian hanging, which means the suspension by arms tied behind the back leading to a paralysis of both arms for some time. In *Aydin v. Turkey*, the Court held that the rape of a 17-year-old detainee by a state official constituted torture.[20] The case *Selmouni v. France* is a famous example of the use against a detainee of corporal and mental violence that was considered torture.[21] The complainant was subjected to heavy blows and hits; he was urinated on and threatened with a blowlamp and a syringe. In the case *Salman v. Turkey*, the Court held that the practice of *falanga*, which means beating the soles of the feet, amounted to torture.[22] In *Yaman v. Turkey*, the Court came to the same conclusion concerning electric shocks.[23] In the case *Akkoç v. Turkey*, the complainant was also subjected to electric shocks; she was dipped into hot and cold water and was threatened with the ill treatment of her children.[24] In *Dikme v. Turkey*, the Court held that blows inflicted on the complainant amounted to torture, namely because of the duration and the purpose behind them.[25] In *El-Masri v. Former Yugoslav Republic of Macedonia*, the Court's Grand Chamber stated that the treatment suffered by the applicant at Skopje Airport at the hands of a special CIA rendition team amounted to torture.[26] The complainant had been beaten severely, stripped and sodomised with an object in the presence of Macedonian officials. He had been shackled, hooded and subjected to total sensory deprivation.

In the refoulement case *M.A. v. Switzerland* decided in 2014, the applicant was sentenced in absentia to seven years' imprisonment and 70 lashes of the whip because of his participation in anti-regime demonstrations in Iran.[27] The Court held that 'such extensive' flogging would cause deliberate and severe physical suffering of a severity that would have to be regarded as torture within

---

19   ECtHR, *Aksoy v. Turkey*, 18 December 1996, no. 21987/93, § 64.

20   ECtHR, *Aydin v. Turkey*, 25 September 1997, no. 23178/94, §§ 83 and 86.

21   ECtHR, *Selmouni v. France*, 28 July 1999, no. 25803/94, §§ 101–105.

22   ECtHR, *Salman v. Turkey*, 27 June 2000, no. 21986/93, § 115.

23   ECtHR, *Yaman v. Turkey*, 2 November 2004, no. 32446/96, §§ 11 and 47. Recalled in ECtHR, *Abu Qatada v. UK* 17 January 2012, no. 8139/09, § 270.

24   ECtHR, *Akkoç v. Turkey*, 10 October 2000, nos. 22947/93 & 22948/93, §§ 116 and 117.

25   ECtHR, *Dikme v. Turkey*, 11 July 2000, no. 20869/92, §§ 95 and 96.

26   ECtHR, *El-Masri v. Former Yugoslav Republic of Macedonia*, 13 December 2012 [GC], no. 39630/09, §§ 205–211. Similar ECtHR, *Al Nashiri v. Poland*, 24 July 2014, no. 28761/11, §§ 511–516; ECtHR, *Abu Zubaydah v. Poland*, 24 July 2014, no. 7511/13, §§ 503–511.

27   ECtHR, *M.a. v. Switzerland*, 18 November 2014, no. 52589/13.

the meaning of Article 3 of the Convention.'[28] As has been mentioned in section 2.1 of this chapter, the Court rarely specifies explicitly which kind of harm is risked in refoulement cases. The classification of the harm as torture in *M.A. v. Switerzland* hence remains exceptional. However, this does not mean to say that the judges in Strasbourg do not have torture rather than any other form of inhuman treatment in mind in certain refoulement cases, when concluding that the removal of a person would give rise to a violation of Article 3 ECHR.[29]

Generally, each case is decided on its own facts. Certain acts have either been considered as torture or as inhuman treatment depending on the circumstances and cumulative factors. In *Selmouni v. France*, the Court made clear that the concept of torture could change over time.[30]

2.2.2   Inhuman Treatment or Punishment

The Court considers a treatment or punishment inhuman or degrading when it is severe enough to fall within the scope of Article 3 ECHR, but lacks sufficient intensity or purpose to qualify as torture. Generally, most cases in which the Court has held that Article 3 ECHR has been violated have concerned inhuman or degrading treatment and not torture.[31]

The concept of inhuman or degrading treatment often comes into play when state authorities use their force for legitimate purposes but in a disproportionate way. The Court will consider treatment as being inhuman, 'if, *inter alia*, it was premeditated, was applied for hours at a stretch, and caused either actual bodily injury or intense physical and mental suffering.'[32] The Court often uses the term 'excessive use of force' in the context of inhuman treatment.[33] It made clear that 'any recourse to physical force which has not been made strictly necessary by the applicant's own conduct diminishes human dignity and is in principle an infringement of the right set forth in Article 3 ECHR.'[34]

---

28   *Ibid.*, § 58.

29   See also the corresponding conclusion of the Court in § 68 of *M.A. v. Switzerland*.

30   ECtHR, *Selmouni v. France*, 28 July 1999, no. 25803/94, § 101. See a similar statement of the Court with regard to inhuman and degrading treatment and punishment in ECtHR, *Öcalan v. Turkey*, 12 March 2003, no. 46221/99, § 194.

31   Arai-Yokoi 2003, p. 387; Thurin 2012, p. 120.

32   See, amongst many others, ECtHR, *Kudla v. Poland*, 26 October 2000 [GC], no. 30210/96, § 92.

33   For example, ECtHR, *Shamayev and Others v. Georgia and Russia*, 12 April 2005, no. 36378/02, § 380.

34   ECtHR, *El-Masri v. Former Yugoslav Republic of Macedonia*, 13 December 2012 [GC], no. 39630/09, § 207.

Most violations of Article 3 ECHR occur in the context of the treatment of arrested or detained persons.[35] In its rich case law on inhuman or degrading conditions of detention, the Court has established that 'the State must ensure that a person is detained under conditions which are compatible with respect for human dignity, that the manner and method of the execution of the measure do not subject him to distress or hardship exceeding the unavoidable level of suffering inherent in detention and that, given the practical demands of imprisonment, his health and well-being are adequately secured.'[36] There are a number of non-refoulement cases in which the Court has prohibited the extradition of complainants to countries of the former Soviet Union because of inhuman prison conditions there.[37] However, measures for punishing or depriving a person of liberty must go beyond the inevitable element of suffering or humiliation connected with a given form of legitimate treatment or punishment to amount to a treatment prohibited by Article 3 ECHR.[38]

With regard to measures of punishment, the Court considered in the refoulement case *D. and Others v. Turkey* that the sentence of 100 lashes for fornication executed publicly in Iran amounted to inhuman treatment prohibited by Article 3 ECHR.[39] As explained above, extensive flogging might even be classified as torture by the Court.[40] In *Said v. Netherlands* the complainant was a deserter from the Eritrean army. In case of expulsion he risked a punishment by, *inter alia*, being tied up in painful positions, being exposed to the sun in high temperatures or *incommunicado* detention. The Court stated that these acts constituted inhuman treatment and that the expulsion of the applicant to Eritrea would consequently violate Article 3 ECHR.[41] In the case *Elmi and Sufi* concerning a removal to parts of Somalia controlled by al-Shabaab, the Court made clear that punishments under the sharia law such as amputation, flogging and corporal punishment are in breach of Article 3 ECHR.[42]

---

35   Reidy 2002, p. 22.

36   See, for example, ECtHR, *Babar Ahmad and Others v. UK*, 10 April 2012, nos. 24027/07, 11949/08, 36742/08, 66911/09 and 67354/09, § 202.

37   See, for example, ECtHR, *Soldatenko v. Ukraine*, 23 October 2008, no. 2440/07 (extradition to Turkmenistan); ECtHR, *Kaboulov v. Ukraine*, 19 November 2009, no. 41015/04 (extradition to Kazakhstan); ECtHR, *Iskandarov v. Russia*, 23 September 2010, no. 17185/05 (extradition to Tajikistan). See more detailed Chapter 4 Section 3.2.1.b.

38   Amongst others, ECtHR, *Saadi v. Italy*, 28 February 2008 [GC], no. 37201/06, § 135.

39   ECtHR, *D. and others v. Turkey*, 22 June 2006, no. 24245/03, §§ 46–53.

40   See ECtHR, *M.A. v. Switzerland*, 18 November 2014, no. 52589/13 described in Section 2.2.1 of this chapter.

41   ECtHR, *Said v. Netherlands,* 5 July 2005, no. 2345/02, § 54.

42   ECtHR, *Sufi and Elmi v. UK*, 28 June 2011, nos. 8319/07 and 11449/07, § 276.

Imposing a life sentence without any possibility of applying for an early re-lease is also incompatible with Article 3 ECHR.[43] However, as the Court made clear in the Grand Chamber judgment *Vinter and Others v. United Kingdom*, a life sentence does not become irreducible by the mere fact that in practice it may be served in full.[44] In this respect, the Court noted that no Article 3 ECHR issue could arise if, for instance, a life prisoner had the right under domestic law to be considered for release but was refused on the ground that he contin-ued to pose a danger to society.[45] In determining whether a life sentence in a given case can be regarded as irreducible, the Court has to ascertain whether a life prisoner can be said to have any prospect of release.[46] As Judge Power-Forde summarized the Court's latest case law, Article 3 ECHR encompasses what might be described as the 'right to hope' for individuals when sentenced for life.[47]

Earlier in 2012, with *Harkins and Edwards v. United Kingdom*, the Court declared that the extradition of two men to the United States, where they risked sentences of life imprisonment without parole, did not violate Article 3 ECHR.[48] The Court observed that a mandatory sentence of life imprisonment without the possibility of parole is not *per se* incompatible with the ECHR, 'although the trend in Europe is clearly against such sentences.'[49] Following its case law in domestic cases the Court made a two-step assessment: first, it made a proportionality test between the crimes and the sentences. Second, it assessed whether there was a possibility that the applicant's continued imprisonment could, at any point, no longer be justified on any legitimate pe-nological grounds (such as punishment, deterrence, public protection or reha-bilitation) and if the sentence would be irreducible *de facto* and *de iure*. On the first point, the Court made interesting statements. It noted that,

> ... in a removal case, a violation would arise if the applicant were able to demonstrate that he or she was at a real risk of receiving a grossly

---

43   See, in particular, ECtHR *Kafkaris v. Cyprus*, 12 February 2008 [GC], no. 21906/04, §§ 97–108; ECtHR, *Vinter and Others v. the UK*, 9 July 2013 [GC], nos. 66069/09 and 130/10 and 3896/10 §§ 102–132.

44   ECtHR, *Vinter and Others v. the UK*, 9 July 2013 [GC], nos. 66069/09 and 130/10 and 3896/10, § 108.

45   *Ibid.*

46   *Ibid.*, § 109.

47   See her concurring opinion to ECtHR, *Vinter and Others v. the UK*, 9 July 2013 [GC], nos. 66069/09 and 130/10 and 3896/10.

48   ECtHR, *Harkins and Edwards v. UK*, 17 January 2012, nos. 9146/07 and 32650/07, §§ 132–142.

49   *Ibid.*, § 138.

disproportionate sentence in the receiving State. However, as the Court has recalled at paragraph 129 above, the Convention does not purport to be a means of requiring the Contracting States to impose Convention standards on other States. Due regard must be had for the fact that sentencing practices vary greatly between States and that there will often be legitimate and reasonable differences between States as to the length of sentences which are imposed, even for similar offences. The Court therefore considers that it will only be in very exceptional cases that an applicant will be able to demonstrate that the sentence he or she would face in a non-Contracting State would be grossly disproportionate and thus contrary to Article 3.[50]

The Court then looked at the circumstances of the case and observed that both complainants were charged for offences of utmost severity such as murder. It further noted that they did not possess mitigating factors that would indicate a lower level of culpability on their part such as youth or mental illness. The Court hence found that the sentences could not be considered 'grossly disproportionate.'[51] It further held that if convicted and given a life sentence, the point at which their continued incarceration would no longer serve any legitimate purpose might never arise. In view of the pardoning powers of the governors of the federal states to which the applicants were supposed to be extradited, the Court considered that the sentences were not irreducible. Accordingly there would be no violation of Article 3 ECHR in the event of the applicant's extradition.[52] The Court reaffirmed this strict approach three months later with *Babar and Ahmad and Others v. United Kingdom*, concerning the extradition of five applicants to the United States, where they were charged for terrorism offences carried out or inspired by al-Qaeda.[53] One of the complainants faced 269 counts of murder and thus multiple mandatory sentences of life imprisonment without the possibility of parole. Although the possibility of a commutation by the US president exists, it appears that, *de facto*, his eventual

---

50   *Ibid.*, § 134. The judgment will be further discussed in the Section 2.2.4 of this chapter, which addresses the question of whether there might be a different standard of protection offered under Art. 3 ECHR in domestic cases compared to non-refoulement cases.

51   *Ibid.*, §§ 139 and 141.

52   *Ibid.*, §§ 140 and 142.

53   ECtHR, *Babar Ahmad and Others v. UK*, 10 April 2012, nos. 24027/07, 11949/08, 36742/08, 66911/09 and 67354/09, §§ 243.244. See also ECtHR, *Rrapo v. Albania*, 25 September 2012, no. 58555/19.

release is barely conceivable. However, in the case *Trabelsi v. Belgium* decided in 2014, the Court – based on its more recent case law in the national context in *Vinter and Others v. United Kingdom*[54] – decided differently.[55] Mr Trabelsi was extradited to the US, where he was prosecuted on charges relating to al-Qaeda-inspired acts of terrorism with the risk of a whole-life sentence. This time, the Court considered that the provisions of US legislation governing the possibilities for reduction of life sentences and presidential pardons allowed no real possibility of review as required under Article 3 ECHR. Accordingly, the life imprisonment to which the applicant might be sentenced was not considered reducible, meaning that his extradition to the United States was considered a violation of Article 3 ECHR.[56] Looking at the fast-changing case law on extraditions to the United States with risk of life sentence, clarifying considerations by the Court on the issue would be welcome.[57]

Aside from this issue, it is clear from the case law that it is only in exceptional circumstances that, 'in a removal case, a violation would arise if the applicant where able to demonstrate that he was at a real risk of receiving a grossly disproportionate sentence in the receiving State.'[58] As the Court has stated, 'gross disproportionality' is a strict test and it will only be on 'rare and unique occasions' that it will be met.[59] So far there is in fact no extradition case in which the Court has found that the length of a sentence as such would amount to inhuman or degrading treatment or punishment.[60] Even if a punishment through detention seems politically motivated or discriminatory, this does not necessarily mean that it will fall within the scope of Article 3 ECHR.[61] In the case *M.E. v. France*, the Court indicated that the three years of prison that might await the applicant in Egypt for proselytism were *a priori* as such insufficient to

---

54 See ECtHR, *Vinter and Others v. the UK*, 9 July 2013 [GC], nos. 66069/09 and 130/10 and 3896/10 cited above.

55 See ECtHR, *Trabelsi v. Belgium*, 4 September 2014, no. 140/10, § 138.

56 *Ibid.*, §§ 121–139.

57 Schabas 2015, p. 187 notes that '*Harkins and Edwards* is probably no longer good law.'

58 ECtHR, *Babar Ahmad and Others*, § 238.

59 *Ibid.*, § 237. Recalled in ECtHR, *Calovskis v. Latvia*, 24 July 2014, no. 22205/13, § 140–149, concerning the risk of a sentence equivalent to a life sentence for cybercrime-related offences in the United States.

60 See, for example, ECtHR, *Pavlovic v. Sweden*, 23 February 1999, no. 45920/99 (decision), concerning a five-year prison sentence for desertion in Croatia: ECtHR, *Shakurov v. Russia*, 5 June 2012, no. 55822/10, concerning the extradition of an applicant charged *in absentia* in Uzbekistan for desertion, punishable by five to ten years' imprisonment.

61 See ECtHR, *Yefimova v. Russia*, 19 February 2013, no. 39786/09, § 209.

amount to an ill treatment under Article 3 ECHR.[62] Also the principle of *ne bis in idem* does not by itself raise an issue under Article 3 ECHR.[63]

Solitary confinement is not prohibited by Article 3 ECHR, but can, under specific circumstances, amount to an inhuman or degrading treatment. Whether such a measure falls within the ambit of Article 3 ECHR depends on the particular conditions, the stringency of the measure, its duration, the objective pursued and its effects on the person concerned.[64] The Court's case law and principles on that matter are well summarized in *Babar Ahmad and Others v. United Kingdom* mentioned above, concerning the extradition of suspected al-Qaeda terrorists to the United States.[65] In this case, the complainants alleged not only that the length of their sentences would be incompatible with Article 3 ECHR, but also that the conditions of detention in ADX Florence (a 'supermax' prison where they would be subjected to special administrative measures) amounted to solitary confinement in violation of Article 3 ECHR, particularly because of its indefinite duration. According to the Court, solitary confinement, even in cases entailing relative isolation, cannot be imposed indefinitely.[66] Looking at the particular circumstances of the case, the Court first observed that the complainants would not be placed at ADX without procedural safeguards and without a possible review of their placement. The Court noted that although in the special security unit in which the complainants might be detained, inmates are confined to their cells for the vast majority of the time and social interaction between inmates and staff is minimised, a great deal of in-cell simulation is provided though television and radio, frequent newspapers, books, hobby and educational programs. The inmates were further allowed to correspond with their families. Taking further into account that there was a real possibility for the applicants to be transferred to less restrictive institutions at some point in the future, the Court concluded that there would not be a violation of Article 3 ECHR in respect of their possible detention.[67]

---

62   ECtHR, *M.E. v. France*, 6 June 2013, no. 50094/10, § 51. However, the Court found that the applicant was at risk of ill treatment by Islamic groups because of his convictions.

63   See ECtHR, *M.E. v. Denmark*, 8 July 2014, no. 58363/10, § 59, in which the Court points out that even Art. 4 of Protocol No. 7 to the ECHR is limited to double punishment within the same state.

64   See ECtHR, *A.B. v. Russia,* 14 October 2010, no. 1439/06, §§ 101–113, as an example of solitary confinement as inhuman treatment; ECtHR, *Sanchez v. France*, 4 July 2006 [GC], no. 59450/00, §§ 125–150, as an example of legitimate solitary confinement.

65   ECtHR, *Babar Ahmad and Others v. UK*, 10 April 2012, §§ 205–215.

66   *Ibid.*, § 223.

67   *Ibid.*, §§ 218–224. As to the conditions in the ADX see §§ 81–103.

The protection afforded by Article 3 ECHR is not limited to cases where persons are deprived of their liberty. In the case *Salah Sheekh v. Netherlands,* the Court considered that the persecutions to which the applicant had been subjected prior to his leaving Somalia could be classified as inhuman within the meaning of Article 3 ECHR.[68] The applicant had been beaten, kicked, robbed, intimidated and harassed on many occasions by members of a majority clan and he had had to carry out forced labour. His father was killed and his sister raped by members of the same clan. In an earlier judgment also concerning a removal to Somalia, the Court considered persecution in the sense given by the Refugee Convention as an indication of a risk of ill treatment in the sense of Article 3 ECHR.[69] Under specific circumstances, the destruction of homes or property has been considered as causing suffering amounting to inhuman treatment within the meaning of Article 3 ECHR.[70] It is further worth noting that even acts of a purely non-physical nature can constitute inhuman treatment. The Court has held that 'a threat of conduct prohibited by Article 3, provided it is sufficiently real and immediate, may fall foul of that provision. Thus, to threaten an individual with torture may constitute at least inhuman treatment.'[71] The disappearance of a close family member can also incite a violation of Article 3 ECHR.[72] According to the Court, the essence of such a violation does not so much lie in the fact of the 'disappearance' of the family member, but concerns the authorities' reactions and attitudes to the situation.[73]

Next to their 'primarily negative obligation' under Article 3 ECHR to refrain from inflicting harm on persons, states also have the positive obligation to take measures to ensure that individuals under their jurisdiction are not subjected to torture or inhuman or degrading treatment, including such ill treatment administered by private individuals or foreign state actors.[74] The state's

---

68   ECtHR, *Salah Sheekh v. Netherlands,* 11 January 2007, no. 1948/04, § 146.

69   See ECtHR, *Ahmed v. Austria,* 17 December 1996, no. 25964/94, § 42. On the overlap between the protections offered against persecution by the Refugee Convention and the protection offered under Art. 3 ECHR see Chapter 4 Sections 3.3.1.c and 3.3.3.c.

70   For example, ECtHR, *Bilgin v. Turkey,* 16 November 2000, no. 23819/94 § 103; ECtHR, *Ayder and Others v. Turkey,* 8 January 2004, no. 23656/94, § 110.

71   See ECtHR, *Abu Zubaydah v. Poland,* 24 July 2014, no. 7511/13, § 501, referring to ECtHR, *Gäfgen v. Germany,* 1 June 2010 [GC], no. 22978/05, §§ 91 and 108, in which the Court notes that a 'threat of torture can amount to torture.'

72   See ECtHR, *Nasr and Ghali v. Italy,* 23 February 2016, no. 44883/09, §§ 314–317, the applicant's husband was subjected to extraordinary rendition.

73   *Ibid.,* § 314.

74   See, for example, ECtHR, *Pretty v. UK,* 29 April 2002, no. 2346/02, §§ 50 and 51; ECtHR, *El-Masri v. Former Yugoslav Republic of Macedonia,* 13 December 2012 [GC], no. 39630/09.

responsibility may be engaged where the authorities 'fail to take reasonable steps to avoid a risk of ill-treatment about which they knew or ought to have known.'[75] The Court has found a violation of Article 3 ECHR in several cases where a state party did not take effective steps to protect persons against treatments contrary to Article 3 ECHR, for example in cases of domestic violence,[76] sexual and physical abuse[77] or forced prostitution.[78] In cases concerning deportations to Nigeria, the Court made clear that female genital mutilation amounted to a treatment prohibited by Article 3 ECHR.[79] The particular significance of protection against private actors in the context of refoulement will be discussed in section 2.3.1 of this chapter.

Article 3 ECHR also contains a procedural obligation for states to investigate when an individual raises an arguable claim that he has been treated in violation of Article 3 ECHR. As an example, the case *El-Masri v. Former Yugoslav Republic of Macedonia* is worth a mention. It concerned the ill treatment of an applicant suspected of terrorism and his subsequent transfer to Afghanistan with the involvement of US and Macedonian state agents.[80] The Court found, *inter alia*, that the Macedonian authorities had been responsible for acts of torture committed by US agents in Skopje Airport and that the applicant's illegal transfer had violated the principle of non-refoulement.[81] In addition, the Court held that the summary investigation that had been carried out by the Macedonian authorities on the matter could 'not be regarded as an effective one capable of leading to the identification and punishment of those responsible for the alleged events and of establishing the truth.'[82] Against this background, the Court found that in addition to the violation of Article 3 ECHR in its substantive aspects there had been a violation of this provision 'in its procedural limb.'[83]

---

75   *Ibid.*, § 198.

76   For example, ECtHR, *Opuz v. Turkey*, 9 June 2009, no. 33401/02, § 161; ECtHR, *E.S. and Others v. Slovenia*, 15 September 2009, no. 8227/04, §§ 39–44.

77   For example, ECtHR, *Z. and Others v. UK*, 10 May 2001 [GC], no. 29392/95, §§ 74–75.

78   For example, ECtHR, *Tremblay v. France*, 11 September 2007, no. 37194/02, § 26.

79   ECtHR, *Collins and Akaziebie v. Sweden*, 8 March 2007, no. 23944/05 (decision); ECtHR, *Omeredo v. Austria*, 20 September 2011, no. 8969/10 (decision); ECtHR, *Izevbekhai and Others v. Ireland*, 17 May 2011, no. 43408/08 (decision).

80   ECtHR, *El-Masri v. Former Yugoslav Republic of Macedonia*, 13 December 2012 [GC], no. 39630/09.

81   *Ibid.*, §§ 205–223.

82   *Ibid.*, § 193.

83   *Ibid.*, §§ 182–194.

The right under Article 3 ECHR to an effective official investigation into any arguable claim of torture or other ill treatment also applies to the situation of an individual's exposure to a real and imminent risk of ill treatment through his transfer by any person to another state. Where the authorities of a state party are informed of such a real risk, they have a positive obligation, within the scope of their powers, to take preventive measures to avoid that risk and to conduct an effective investigation into any such incident.[84] In two recent cases, the applicants had been abducted in Russia and transferred to Uzbekistan against their will under unclear circumstances, but with a possible involvement of Russian state agents.[85] The Court held that there was a violation of Article 3 ECHR on account of the authorities' failure to comply with their positive obligation to protect the applicant against a real and immediate risk of forcible transfer and their failure to comply with the procedural obligation to conduct a thorough and effective investigation into his abduction and transfer.[86] As will be explained in chapter 4 section 3.1, states must provide an adequate legal system to ensure that the principle of non-refoulement is respected in practice.

2.2.3 Degrading Treatment or Punishment

Degrading treatment or punishment is the least severe form of treatment prohibited by Article 3 ECHR. However, the Court usually does not state precisely whether it considers an act as inhuman or 'only' degrading. When the Court has explicitly addressed the concept of degrading treatment or punishment, it has mostly held that it was such 'as to arouse in the victims feelings of fear, anguish and inferiority, capable of humiliating and debasing victims, or when it was such as to drive the victim to act against his will or conscience.'[87]

A famous example of degrading punishment is the case *Tyrer v. United Kingdom* concerning the corporal punishment of a young boy by a British policeman by three strokes of a birch rod.[88] In *Bouyid v. Belgium* decided in September 2015, the Grand Chamber held that 'a slap' administered by police officers to each of the applicants was found to constitute degrading treatment.[89]

---

84   ECtHR, *Ermakov v. Russia*, 7 November 2013, no. 43165/10, § 211.
85   *Ibid.*; ECtHR, *Kasymakhunov v. Russia*, 14 November 2013, no. 29604/12.
86   ECtHR, *Ermakov v. Russia*, 7 November 2013, no. 43165/10, §§ 192–230; ECtHR, *Kasymakhunov v. Russia*, 14 November 2013, no. 29604/12, §§ 120–155. See similar ECtHR, *Mamazhonov v. Russia*, 23 October 2014, no. 17239/13, §§ 166–209.
87   For example, ECtHR, *Pretty v. UK*, 29 April 2002, no. 2346/02, § 52.
88   ECtHR, *Tyrer v. UK*, 25 April 1978, no. 5856/72, §§ 28–32. See also EComHR, *Y. v. UK*, 8 October 1991, no. 14229/88, § 45, concerning the corporal punishment of a 15-year-old boy at a British private school.
89   ECtHR, *Bouyid v. Belgium*, 28 September 2015 [GC], no. 23380/09.

It recalled that when law-enforcement officers confront individuals, any recourse to physical force not strictly necessitated by the applicant's conduct is in principle an infringement of Article 3 ECHR, which is strongly linked to the concept of 'dignity.'[90] According to the judges, the term 'in principle' should thereby not be interpreted as allowing exceptions if, for example, the use of force did not meet the threshold of severity since 'any interference with human dignity strikes at the very essence of the Convention.'[91] For that reason, 'any conduct by law-enforcement officers *vis-à-vis* an individual which diminishes human dignity constitutes a violation of Article 3 of the Convention.'[92] In this particular case, the judges concluded that the applicants 'did not demonstrate that they had undergone serious physical or mental suffering,' so that their treatment could not be described as inhuman but as degrading treatment in violation of Article 3 ECHR.[93] In a joint dissenting opinion, three judges objected that they were unable to find that the minimum level of severity normally required by the Court under Article 3 ECHR was achieved. They held that the majority had departed from the well-established case law to the effect that where recourse to physical force diminishes human dignity, it would only 'in principle' constitute a violation of Article 3 ECHR. According to the dissenters, there are forms of treatment that, while interfering with human dignity, do not attain the minimum level of severity required to fall within the scope of Article 3 ECHR. In their view, the Court 'should avoid trivialising findings of a violation of Article 3 ECHR' for the sake of the authority of this norm.[94] As the abstract considerations on the concept of degrading treatment in the *Bouyid* judgment disclose, the lowermost harm falling under the scope of Article 3 ECHR is difficult to detect, which has led in fact to incoherencies in the Court's case law, particularly in the refoulement context.[95] On this background, the concerns expressed by the dissenters cannot be dismissed as unfounded.

Another remarkable case in that context is *Yankov v. Bulgaria*, in which the Court stated that the shaving off of a prisoner's hair constituted a degrading treatment, underlining, however, that there was no legal basis or valid justification for the shaving and that the applicant was already 55 years old and had to appear at a public hearing nine days later.[96] As to handcuffing, the Court has

---

90   *Ibid.*, §§ 88 and 90.

91   *Ibid.*, § 101.

92   *Ibid.*

93   *Ibid.*, § 112.

94   Joint partly dissenting opinion of judges de Gaetano, Lemmensand Mahoney.

95   See on this the next Section 2.2.4 and Sections 2.3.2 and 2.4 of this chapter.

96   ECtHR, *Yankov v. Bulgaria*, 11 December 2003, no. 39084/97, §§ 112–121.

held that it does not normally give rise to an issue under Article 3 ECHR as long as it has been imposed in connection with lawful arrest or detention and does not entail the use of force, or public exposure, exceeding what is reasonably considered necessary in the circumstances.[97] The placement of defendants presenting no security risk in a metal cage in court for trial was considered a violation of Article 3 ECHR in a case against Georgia.[98] A strip search that has no genuine relationship to security concerns or which is done in a particularly humiliating manner that goes beyond what such procedures necessarily entail can constitute a degrading treatment.[99] The humiliation of a victim and the public nature of a treatment or punishment are indicative elements of degrading treatment or punishment, but the absence of them does not rule out a violation of Article 3 ECHR.[100]

Discriminatory treatment is normally not as such an issue under Article 3 ECHR and therefore hardly triggers the application of the prohibition on refoulement.[101] However, it can be qualified as degrading or inhuman treatment by the Court if it attains a sufficient level of severity[102] and it may be considered as a relevant factor for a harm to fall within the scope of Article 3 ECHR. In the case *S.H. v. United Kingdom* concerning the removal of a complainant of Nepalese ethnicity to Bhutan, the Court held that 'acts motivated by racial discrimination will constitute an aggravating factor in considering whether treatment falls within the concept of inhuman and degrading treatment.'[103] Considering the discrimination of ethnic Nepalese in Bhutan as an important risk factor among others, the Court found a violation of Article 3 ECHR.

In the case *Pretty v. United Kingdom* the Court held that 'the suffering which flows from naturally occurring illness, physical or mental, may be covered by Article 3, where it is, or risks being, exacerbated by the treatment, whether flowing from conditions of detention, expulsion or other measures, for which

---

97 See ECtHR, *Raninen v. Finland*, 16 December 1997, no. 152/1996/771/972, § 56. See further ECtHR, *Yagiz v. Turkey*, 6 March 2007, no. 27473/02, §47, where a violation was found.

98 ECtHR, *Kokhreidze v. Georgia*, 27 January 2009, no. 1704/06, §§ 98–102.

99 See, among others, ECtHR, *Férot v. France*, 12 June 2007, no. 70204/01, §§ 35–48.

100 ECtHR, *Raninen v. Finland*, 16 December 1997, no. 152/1996/771/972, § 55; ECtHR, *Yankov v. Bulgaria*, 11 December 2003, no. 39084/97, § 117.

101 See ECtHR, *Tomic v. UK*, 14 October 2003, no. 17837/03 (decision).

102 ECtHR, *Smith and Grady v. UK*, 27 September 1999, nos. 33985/96 and 33986/96, § 121. See also EComHR, *East African Asians v. UK*, 14 December 1973, nos. 4403/70 and further, §§ 188–209.

103 ECtHR, *S.H. v. UK*, 15 June 2010, no. 19956/06, § 70. See in this sense also ECtHR, *H N. and Others v. Sweden*, 24 January 2012, no. 50043/09 (decision).

the authorities can be held responsible.'[104] The Court has made clear that there is an obligation for states to care for the basic medical needs of their inmates.[105] In 2011, the Grand Chamber judgment *M.S.S. v. Belgium and Greece* established that under particular circumstances, dire living conditions for vulnerable individuals who are wholly dependent on state support, such as asylum seekers, could amount to degrading treatment even outside the context of detention.[106] However, Article 3 ECHR cannot be interpreted as obliging states to provide everyone with a home or a certain standard of living.[107]

2.2.4   Does the Same Standard apply in the Context of Refoulement as in
          Domestic Cases with Regard to Degrading Treatment?
Scholars have raised the question whether the Court offers full protection against a removal where certain forms of degrading treatment are expected or, in other words, whether the Court protects a complainant who fears 'only' degrading treatment in the event of expulsion or extradition in the same manner as a complainant who fears inhuman treatment or torture.[108] According to the Court, Article 3 ECHR protects a person from each harm proscribed by this article equally, whether that person fears such harm from the state party in question or whether he fears it in the country to which he is supposed to be removed.[109] Any other interpretation would be contrary to the absolute character of the prohibition of ill treatment within the meaning of Article 3 ECHR.[110]

Theoretically, a real risk of a slap administered by police officers or the removal of a short-sighted person's glasses in prison[111] could be enough to trigger the application of the principle of non-refoulement. However, no such cases are known. While Wouters is of the opinion that the question is rather whether the

---

104   ECtHR, *Pretty v. UK*, 29 April 2002, no. 2346/02, § 52.

105   See, for example, ECtHR, *A.A. v. Greece*, 22 July 2010, no. 12186/08, §§ 57–65.

106   This judgment will be discussed in detail in Section 2.3.2b of this chapter.

107   ECtHR, *M.S.S. v. Belgium and Greece*, 21 January 2011 [GC], no. 30696/09, § 249; ECtHR, *Tarakhel v. Switzerland*, 4 November 2014 [GC], no. 29217/12, § 95.

108   See Arai-Takahashi 2002, pp. 16, 17 and 26, who speaks of a 'hidden double standard'; Thurin 2012, pp. 121–123; Wouters 2009, pp. 242–243 and 537.

109   ECtHR, *Soering v. UK*, 7 July 1989, no. 14038/88, §§ 88 and 93; ECtHR, *Mamatkulov and Askarov v. Turkey*, 4 February 2005, nos. 46827/99 & 46951/99 [GC], § 67; ECtHR, *Saadi v Italy*, 28 February 2008 [GC], no. 37201/06, § 127.

110   See in this sense also Arai-Yokoi 2003, p. 413; Wouters 2009, p. 243.

111   See ECtHR, *Slyusarev v. Russia*, 20 April 2010, no. 60333/00, §§ 34–44, in which the Court qualified the refusal of prison authorities to give a detainee glasses during a few months as a degrading treatment.

scope of Article 3 ECHR has not been overextended by the Court,[112] Thurin suggests that refoulement complaints concerning degrading treatment are rarely successful because it is too difficult to establish a real risk of such harms.[113] Both analyses do have a point, but neither of them can negate the impression that there is a different standard for degrading treatment in non-refoulement cases than in others.

In January 2012, the Court for the first time addressed the question explicitly in *Harkins and Edwards v. United Kingdom,* mentioned above, concerning the extradition of two men to the United States, where they expected to be imprisoned for life.[114] Relying on the reasoning of the House of Lords and the Canadian Supreme Court, the government submitted that 'a real risk of torture in the receiving State should be an absolute bar on extradition. However, for all other forms of ill-treatment, it was legitimate to consider the policy objectives pursued by extradition in determining whether the ill-treatment reached the minimum level of severity required by Article 3.'[115] The Court rejected this suggestion and reaffirmed that in domestic matters as well as in the context of refoulement including extradition, Article 3 ECHR should apply without distinction between the various forms of ill treatment proscribed by this provision.[116] It thereby referred to its own case law as well as to Article 7 ICCPR and Article 19 of the Charter on Fundamental Rights of the EU, which both prohibit torture *and* other forms of ill treatment equally in the context of refoulement.[117] However, the Court then added the following remarkable comments:

> ... in reaching this conclusion, the Court would underline that it agrees with Lord Brown's observation in Wellington that the absolute nature of Article 3 does not mean that any form of ill-treatment will act as a bar to removal from a Contracting State. As Lord Brown observed, this Court has repeatedly stated that the Convention does not purport to be a means of requiring the Contracting States to impose Convention standards on other States. This being so, treatment which might violate Article 3 because of an act or omission of a Contracting State might not attain the minimum level of severity which is required for there to be a violation of Article 3 in an expulsion or extradition case. For example,

---

112   Wouters 2009, pp. 243 and 314.

113   Thurin 2012, pp. 121–123. See likewise Einarsen 1990, pp. 371 and 372.

114   ECtHR, *Harkins and Edwards v. UK*, 17 January 2012, nos. 9146/07 and 32650/07.

115   *Ibid.,* § 105.

116   *Ibid.,* § 128.

117   *Ibid.,* §§ 124–128.

a Contracting State's negligence in providing appropriate medical care within its jurisdiction has, on occasion, led the Court to find a violation of Article 3 but such violations have not been so readily established in the extra-territorial context (compare the denial of prompt and appropriate medical treatment for HIV/AIDS in *Aleksanyan v. Russia*, no. 46468/06, §§ 145–158, 22 December 2008 with *N. v. the United Kingdom* [GC], no. 26565/05, 27 May 2008).[118]

The Court then referred to its case law in the context of the treatment of prisoners. It pointed out that in such cases, for example in the case *Yankov* (shaving of head), factors have been decisive for the violation of Article 3 ECHR that 'depend closely upon the facts of the case and so will not be readily established prospectively in an extradition or expulsion context.'[119] Looking at these considerations, they could confirm *Thurin's* approach, according to which there is in principle an equal protection against all kinds of ill treatment, but that degrading treatment will be particularly hard to establish in the context of refoulement. However, this still does not eliminate the impression of a double standard. In *Harkins and Edwards*, the Court admitted that, at the moment of the extradition of the applicants, it was hardly possible for them to establish that one day, their sentence might no longer be legitimate.[120] To this extent, they were *de facto* less protected against a life sentence amounting to ill treatment than applicants who are sentenced or imprisoned in a state subjected to the Court's jurisdiction.[121] The impression of a double standard is further strengthened by the Court's statement cited above that 'treatment which might violate Article 3 because of an act or omission of a Contracting State might not attain the minimum level of severity which is required for there to be a violation of Article 3 in an expulsion or extradition case.'[122] This statement contradicts the Court's words in the same judgment according to which Article 3 ECHR should apply without distinction between the various forms of ill treatment in domestic matters as well as in the context of refoulement.

---

118   *Ibid.*, § 129.

119   *Ibid.*, § 130.

120   *Ibid.*, §§ 137 and 140.

121   See also the concurring opinion of judge Kalaydijeva. However, in the Court's latest judgement on an extradition to the United States with risk of a life sentence, the Court found a violation of Art. 3 ECHR by applying the criteria established in the Grand Chamber judgment *Vinter and Others*; see ECtHR, *Trabelsi v. Belgium*, 4 September 2014, no. 140/10 discussed above in Section 2.2.2. See also Schabas 2015, p. 187, who notes that after *Vinter and Others*, *Harkins and Edwards* is 'probably no longer good law.'

122   ECtHR, *Harkins and Edwards*, § 129.

If the Court intended to clarify the situation in *Harkins and Edwards* discussed above, it has failed to do so.[123]

However, it would be incorrect to say that refoulement cases with regard to degrading treatment are never successful. In the aforementioned case *M.S.S. v. Belgium and Greece*, the Court explicitly held that by transferring the applicant to Greece 'the Belgian authorities knowingly exposed him to conditions of detention and living conditions that amounted to degrading treatment.'[124] That being so, there had been a violation of the principle of non-refoulement in Article 3 ECHR.[125] In addition, as stated before, particularly in refoulement cases, the Court seldom specifies the ill treatment expected in the receiving country. Judges might well have degrading treatment in mind in certain cases where they find a violation of Article 3 ECHR.

2.2.5   Death Penalty as Inhuman Treatment

Since no member state of the Council of Europe still practices capital punishment, it is almost only in refoulement cases that this issue is of practical importance.[126] Article 2(1) ECHR excludes from the right to life deaths resulting from lawful acts of war and the deprivation of life as a criminal penalty. This hindered the Court for a long time from interpreting the ECHR (in particular Article 3 ECHR) in such a way as to prohibit capital punishment.[127]

However, the removal of a person to another state where there is a real risk that the death penalty will be imposed could be a breach of Protocol No. 6 to the ECHR, concerning the abolition of the death penalty in times of peace, or Protocol No. 13 to the ECHR, concerning the abolition of the death penalty in all circumstances. The Court has confirmed the application of these Protocols in the context of refoulement as well as of Article 2 ECHR.[128] Individuals fearing a removal from states that have ratified these protocols could therefore

---

123   The Court has recalled its rather confusing statements in ECtHR, *Babar Ahmad and Others v. UK*, 10 April 2012, nos. 24027/07, 11949/08, 36742/08, 66911/09 and 67354/09, §§ 176–178; ECtHR, *Aswat v. UK*, 16 April 2013, no. 17299/12, §§ 32 and 49. See also ECtHR, *Yefimova v. Russia*, 19 February 2013, no. 39786/09, § 211.

124   ECtHR, *M.S.S. v. Belgium and Greece*, 21 January 2011 [GC], no. 30696/09, §§ 366–368.

125   This case will be discussed in more detail in Section 2.3.2b of this chapter.

126   An exception is ECtHR *Öcalan v. Turkey*, 12 May 2005 [GC], no. 46221/99.

127   See ECtHR, *Soering v. UK*, 7 July 1989, no. 14038/88, § 103; ECtHR, *Shamayev and Others v. Georgia and Russia*, 12 April 2005, no. 36378/02, § 333; ECtHR, *Öcalan v. Turkey*, 12 May 2005 [GC], no. 46221/99, § 162.

128   See, for example, ECtHR, *Al-Saadoon and Mufdhi v. UK*, 2 March 2010, no. 61498/08, § 123; ECtHR, *Rrapo v. Albania*, 25 September 2012, no. 58555/19, § 74; ECtHR, *Al Nashiri v. Poland*, 24 July 2014, no. 28761/11, §§ 576–579.

refer to them. However, as will be shown, the Court usually examines issues relating to capital punishment under Article 3 ECHR rather than under Protocols No. 6 and 13 or Article 2 ECHR.[129] In the case *Shamayev and Others v. Georgia and Russia*, the Court stated in 2005 that a 'Contracting State which has not ratified Protocol No. 6 and has not acceded to Protocol No. 13 is authorised to apply the death penalty under certain conditions, in accordance with Article 2(2) of the Convention.'[130] It recalled that 'Article 3 cannot be interpreted as generally prohibiting the death penalty since that would nullify the clear wording of Article 2 ECHR.' However, it made clear that the manner in which capital punishment is imposed or executed, the personal circumstances of the condemned and a disproportionality to the gravity of the crime committed, as well as the conditions of detention while awaiting execution, are examples of factors capable of bringing the punishment within the proscription of Article 3 ECHR.[131]

In the famous *Soering* case, the Court found that the so-called *death row phenomenon* awaiting the applicant in Virginia, which would mean a long period of time spent in custody awaiting execution, amounted to inhuman treatment. The personal circumstances of the applicant, especially his age and mental state at the time of the offence, were important factors in the decision.[132] In the case *Jabari v. Turkey*, the Court stated that the removal of the applicant to Iran, where she risked sentencing to death by stoning for adultery, would be contrary to Article 3 ECHR.[133] In the case *Ilaşcu and Others v. Moldova and Russia*, the Court considered the death penalty together with inhuman prison conditions as torture.[134] In *Bader and Others v. Sweden* in 2005, the Court stated – relying on the considerations of the Grand Chamber judgment in *Öcalan v. Turkey* earlier that year – that imposing a death sentence on someone after an unfair trial with a real risk of the sentence being carried out amounted to ill

---

129   Critical on this point is Frumer 2010, p. 985. As an exception see ECtHR, *Al Nashiri v. Poland*, 24 July 2014, no. 28761/11, §§ 576–579 (violation Articles 2 and 3 ECHR taken together with Article 1 of Protocol No. 6 to the ECHR). See also the concurring opinion of judge Barreto in ECtHR, *Bader and Kanbor v. Sweden*, 8 November 2005, no. 13284/04. In this latter case the Court exceptionally stated that the deportation of the applicants to Syria, where they risked execution after an unfair trial, would give rise to violations of Art. 3 and Art. 2 ECHR. However, in this case as well, the Court applied the principles developed in its case law under Art. 3 ECHR.

130   ECtHR, *Shamayev and Others v. Georgia and Russia*, 12 April 2005, no. 36378/02, § 333.

131   *Ibid.*

132   ECtHR, *Soering v. UK*, 7 July 1989, no. 14038/88, §§ 103, 104 and 111.

133   ECtHR, *Jabari v. Turkey*, 11 July 2000, no. 40035/98, §§ 33–42.

134   ECtHR, *Ilaşcu and Others v. Moldova and* Russia, 8 July 2004, no. 48787/99, §§ 409–442.

treatment as proscribed by Article 3 ECHR and was also in violation of the right to life in Article 2 ECHR. The Court also indicated that the abolitionist trend in Europe could one day lead to a different interpretation of Article 2 ECHR, so as to prohibit the death penalty in all circumstances.[135]

In March 2010, the Court operated as it had announced and abandoned the principle that Article 2(1) ECHR does not allow an interpretation of Article 3 ECHR prohibiting the death penalty as such. In the chamber judgment *Al-Saadoon and Mufdhi v. United Kingdom*, it stated that – given that all but two member states had signed Protocol 13 to the ECHR and all but three of the states which had signed it had also ratified it, and given further that no member state of the Council of Europe was still practicing capital punishment – *Article 2 ECHR could no longer be considered a bar to including the death penalty* in the interpretation of the words 'inhuman or degrading treatment or punishment.'[136] The case concerned a transfer of two Iraqis from the custody of the British authorities in Iraq to the Iraqi Higher Tribunal, even though there was a risk of their execution by hanging. The Court found that the applicants' well-founded fear of being executed by the Iraqi authorities had given rise to a significant degree of mental suffering and that to subject them to such suffering constituted inhuman treatment within the meaning of Article 3 ECHR.[137] The risk of an unfair trial or the conditions of their detention before an awaited execution were, in contrast to the previous judgments, not relevant factors for the violation of Article 3 ECHR. The Court considered that a well-founded fear of the death penalty in itself constituted a treatment contrary to Article 3 ECHR.[138]

Since the *Al-Saadoon and Mufdhi* judgment was released in 2010, one can say that Article 3 ECHR generally prohibits the removal of a person to a state where he fears capital punishment. This has been confirmed by subsequent verdicts, amongst them *A.L. (X.W.) v. Russia*, which was adopted unanimously by the Court in October 2015 and concerned the extradition of an applicant suspected of murder to China.[139] In this judgment, the Court held that in view

---

135 ECtHR, *Bader and Kanbor v. Sweden*, 8 November 2005, no. 13284/04, § 42. Likewise ECtHR, *Öcalan v. Turkey*, 12 May 2005 [GC], no. 46221/99, §§ 163–165.

136 ECtHR, *Al-Saadoon and Mufdhi v. UK*, 2 March 2010, no. 61498/08, § 120.

137 *Ibid.*, § 137.

138 For a discussion of that judgment and the Court's case law on the death penalty, see de Weck 2011, pp. 341–358.

139 ECtHR, *A.L. (X.W.) v. Russia*, 29 October 2015, no. 44095/14. See also ECtHR, *Rrapo v. Albania*, 25 September 2012, no. 58555/19, §§ 69–74; ECtHR, *Al Nashiri v. Poland*, 24 July 2014, no. 28761/11, §§ 576–579. See also Frumer 2010, p. 985; Mole & Meredith 2010, p. 91; de Weck 2011 p. 353.

of Russia's unequivocal undertakings to abolish the death penalty, the 'findings made in *Al-Saadoon and Mufdhi* – namely that capital punishment has become an unacceptable form of punishment that is no longer permissible under Article 2 as amended by Protocols Nos. 6 and 13 and that it amounts to 'inhuman or degrading treatment or punishment' under Article 3 – applies fully to Russia, even though it has not ratified Protocol No. 6 or signed Protocol No. 13.'[140] On this background, the Court concluded unanimously that the applicant's return to China, where there was a foreseeable risk that he be given the death penalty following trial on the capital charge of murder, would give rise to a violation of Articles 2 and 3 ECHR. As can be seen, it is not just Article 3 ECHR that is affected by the abolitionist trend. Already in *Nashiri v. Poland*, adopted in 2014, the Court had held that 'Article 2 of the Convention prohibits the extradition or deportation of an individual to another State where substantial grounds have been shown for believing that he or she would face a real risk of being subjected to the death penalty there.'[141] With that, the wording of Article 2(1) ECHR according to which the right to life excludes criminal penalty has become moot in the Strasbourg practice.

However, it is must be noted that the Court has accepted that diplomatic assurances obtained from receiving states according to which no death penalty will be imposed on the applicant may be a tool that permits states to extradite criminals to countries where this form of punishment still exists.[142]

2.2.6   Excursus: Forced Expulsion as an Ill Treatment

It is not only the circumstances in the receiving country that can raise questions under Article 3 ECHR, but also the manner in which a deportation is carried out. However, there are only a few cases in which the Court found a violation of Article 3 ECHR holding that a deportation *in itself* constituted inhuman treatment in the sense of Article 3 ECHR, irrespective of the conditions in the receiving country:

---

140   ECtHR, *A.L. (X.W.) v. Russia*, 29 October 2015, no. 44095/14, § 64.

141   ECtHR, *Al Nashiri v. Poland*, 24 July 2014, no. 28761/11, § 576, in which the Court concluded that the transfer of the applicant despite the existence of a real risk that he could be subjected to the death penalty violated Art. 2 and 3 ECHR taken together with Protocol No. 6 to the ECHR. In contrast, the Court did not refer to Protocol 6 in its conclusion on *A.L. (X.W.) v. Russia* in October 2015.

142   See on this Chapter 4 Section 3.4.2.a; the Court particularly trusts diplomatic assurances guaranteeing the non-imposition of the death penalty if US authorities give them; see, for example, ECtHR, *Rrapo v. Albania*, 25 September 2012, no. 58555/19, § 73.

In the case *Shamayev and Others v. Georgia and Russia*, the Court concluded that the applicants were treated with excessive force by the Georgian authorities during the enforcement of their extradition from Georgia to Russia, which in itself constituted inhuman treatment.[143] 'Hand-to-hand combat' between the applicants and Georgian security staff had broken out in prison in Tbilisi after the applicants had been told they were to be extradited to Russia within a few hours. Several applicants were seriously injured as a result. In the Court's opinion, the confrontation of the applicants with a *fait accompli* of their extradition after they had had to wait for weeks not knowing whether or not they would be subjected to extradition incited a riot. On this background, the recourse to physical force by the Georgian authorities could not be regarded as justified by the conduct of the applicants.[144] The case *Ghorbanov and Others v. Turkey*, decided in December 2013, is comparable.[145] The applicants were illegally deported to Iran by the Turkish police despite the fact that they were refugees recognised by the UNHCR. Twelve of the nineteen applicants were minors at the time of the events. Bearing in mind the manner in which the applicants were removed, in particular the absence of any legal procedure, and taking into account the young age of the majority of them, the Court concluded that their suffering was severe enough to be categorised as inhuman treatment within the meaning of Article 3 ECHR.[146]

The case *Mayeka and Mitunga v. Belgium* concerned the deportation of an unaccompanied five-year-old from Belgium to the DRC.[147] The Court criticized the fact that the child had to travel alone and that the Belgian authorities had not made sufficient arrangements for the child's arrival in Kinshasa. It 'was struck by the failure to provide adequate preparation, supervision and safeguards' for the deportation. The Court concluded that the Belgian state had violated its positive obligations under Article 3 ECHR to take the requisite measures and precautions.[148] In another case concerning a nine-year-old who was returned from the Netherlands to the former Zaire, the Court concluded that the child's removal did not constitute an inhuman or degrading treatment,

---

143   ECtHR, *Shamayev and Others v. Georgia and Russia*, 12 April 2005, no. 36378/02, §§ 375–386.

144   *Ibid.*

145   ECtHR, *Ghorbanov and Others v. Turkey*, 3 December 2013, no. 28127/09.

146   *Ibid.*, §§ 32–35.

147   ECtHR, *Mayeka and Mitunga v. Belgium*, 12 October 2006, no. 13178/03.

148   *Ibid.*, §§ 66–71.

since the child was constantly accompanied and looked after.[149] In *Mayeka and Mitunga*, the Court had also criticized the authorities for not taking into account the fact that the mother of the child had acquired refugee status in Canada, and that therefore a reunion of mother and child in Canada could have been possible. It found that the mother's rights under Article 3 ECHR had also been violated, because she had only been informed about her daughter's deportation after it had taken place, which caused her deep anxiety.[150] According-ing to Wouters, this demonstrates the Court's willingness to accept that 'the rights to family life could, under certain circumstances, be breached on such a level as to amount to inhuman or degrading treatment.'[151] However, the Court has regularly denied the application of Article 3 ECHR in cases concerning the separation of close family members as a result of a removal, considering that the minimum level of severity was not attained.[152] A particularity is the case *Ghali v. Italy*, concerning the abduction by CIA agents with the cooperation of Italian officials of an Egyptian imam granted asylum in Italy and his subse-quent transfer to secret detention in Egypt.[153] The Court found several viola-tions of the ECHR related to this so-called extraordinary rendition.[154] Among them, it held that the imam's wife had suffered significant damage as a result of her husband's disappearance, especially on account of the sudden inter-ruption of their married life and the damage to her psychological well-being and that of her husband.[155] With regard to the husband himself, the Court also made clear in this judgment that his abduction on the streets of Milan and his secret transfer were *as such* causing pain and suffering reaching the minimum level of severity required to fall within the scope of Article 3 ECHR, irrespective of how exactly he was treated in detention in Egypt.[156]

---

149   ECtHR, *Nsona v. Netherlands*, 28 November 1996, no. 23366/94, §§ 94–99.

150   ECtHR, *Mayeka and Mitunga*, § 70.

151   Wouters 2009, p. 237.

152   See, for example, ECtHR, *Berrehab v. Netherlands*, 21 June 1988, no. 10730/84, §§ 30 and 31. Such cases can, however, raise questions under the right to respect for private and family life under Art. 8 ECHR.

153   ECtHR, *Nasr and Ghali v. Italy*, 23 February 2016, no. 44883/09, §§ 314–317. It is further noteworthy that in ECtHR, *Tarakhel v. Switzerland*, 4 November 2014 [GC], no. 29217/12, § 121 discussed in Section 2.3.2b of this chapter, the preservation of the family unit was considered, among others, as a relevant element under Art. 3 ECHR.

154   The Court found violations of Art. 3 ECHR in its substantive as well as its procedural as-pects, as well as of the Art. 5, 8 and 13 ECHR; see on this and the comparable cases of *El-Masri*, *Al Nashiri* and *Abu Zubaydah*, Chapter 1 Section 2.2.3 and Chapter 2 Section 3.2.1a.

155   ECtHR, *Nasr and Ghali*, §§ 314–317.

156   *Ibid.*, §§ 284–287.

In the context of the inhuman or degrading nature of the deportation itself, it is also worth mentioning the admissibility decision *Conka and Others
v. Belgium*, in which the Court argued that the writing of seat numbers on the
hands of the applicants who awaited their deportation was particularly insen-
sitive, but did not amount to an illegitimate ill treatment within the meaning
of Article 3 ECHR.[157] In the case *Öcalan v. Turkey*, the Court found that the
conditions in which Öcalan had been transferred from Kenya to Turkey had
not violated Article 3 ECHR.[158] As regards the handcuffing and blindfolding of
Öcalan during his travel, the Court observed that these measures were 'means
of preventing the applicant from attempting to escape or injuring himself or
others.'[159] It further accepted the government's explanation that the purpose
of that precaution was not to humiliate the applicant but to ensure that the
transfer proceeded smoothly and that, in view of the applicant's character
and the reaction to his arrest, considerable care and proper precautions were
necessary.[160]

In several cases decided in 1999 concerning the removal of persons suffering from posttraumatic stress disorder from Sweden to Bosnia and Herzegovina, the Court raised the question of ill treatment by the removal itself.[161]
It declared all complaints inadmissible. The fact that the Swedish authorities
took into account the state of health of the complainants, who were only deported after the granting of medical permission, was an important element
in the Court's considerations. The Court has made clear in several decisions
that as long as concrete measures are provided to guarantee the security of
a complainant, such as medically supervised transport, even a serious risks
of suicide does not turn a forced deportation into an inhuman or degrading
treatment.[162] It has held that 'the fact that a person whose expulsion has been
ordered has threatened to commit suicide does not require the State to refrain

---

157   ECtHR, *Conka and Others v. Belgium*, 31 March 2001, no. 51564/99 (decision).

158   ECtHR, *Öcalan v. Turkey*, 12 May 2005 [GC], no. 46221/99, §§ 177–185.

159   *Ibid.*, § 184.

160   *Ibid.*

161   ECtHR, *Majic v. Sweden*, 23 February 1999, no. 45918/99 (decision); ECtHR, *Pavlovic v.
      Sweden*, 23 February 1999, no. 45920/99 (decision); ECtHR, *Maric v. Sweden*, 23 February
      1999, no. 45922/99 (decision); ECtHR, *Pranjko v. Sweden*, 23 February 1999, no. 45925/99
      (decision).

162   ECtHR, *Gontcharova and Alekseytsev v. Sweden*, 3 May 2007, no. 31246/06 (decision);
      ECtHR, *A.A. v. Sweden*, 2 September 2008, no. 8594/04; ECtHR, *Al-Zawatia v. Sweden*,
      22 June 2010, no 50068/08 (decision); ECtHR, *Nacic and Others v. Sweden*, 15 May 2012, no.
      16567/10, § 54; ECtHR, *Imamovic and Imamovic v. Sweden,* 13 November 2012, no. 57633/10
      (decision).

from enforcing the envisaged measure, provided that concrete measures are taken to prevent those threats from being realised.'[163] The 'same conclusion' has been reached by the Court 'regarding applicants who had a record of previous suicide attempts.'[164]

In the case *Y. v. Russia*, the Court considered whether the expulsion of an applicant in his seventies who was partially paralyzed as a consequence of a stroke entailed a breach of Article 3 ECHR.[165] The Court acknowledged that the deportation might have caused the applicant significant stress and mental anguish. However, noting that he had been examined and accompanied by a doctor and found to be fit to travel, the Court found that the high threshold set by Article 3 ECHR was not met.[166] In decisions concerning the forced deportation of complainants suffering from illnesses or at risk of suicide, the Court usually *also* takes into account the medical conditions in the receiving country and often refers to the jurisprudence developed in the context of refoulement including the high standard it has set in that domain.[167] The threshold for a violation of Article 3 ECHR in the context of health problems that might be exacerbated by a forced deportation appears particularly high.[168]

2.3   *The Source of the Harm*

2.3.1   Protection against Private Actors

According to the Court, Article 3 ECHR 'may be described in general terms as imposing a primarily negative obligation on States to refrain from inflicting serious harm on persons within their jurisdiction.'[169] Correspondingly, Article 3 ECHR is most commonly applied in cases in which the risk of ill treatment emanates from state agents or public authorities. However, as already mentioned, Article 3 ECHR does not merely require the contracting states to refrain from acts of torture or other inhuman treatment; it also imposes the positive obligation to protect persons under their jurisdiction from such acts, even if committed by private persons or performed by foreign officials on their

---

163   ECtHR, *A.S. v. Switzerland*, 30 June 2015, no. 39350/13, § 34 with references.

164   *Ibid.*

165   ECtHR, *Y. v. Russia*, 4 December 2008, no. 20113/07, §§ 43, 44, 92–95.

166   *Ibid.*, § 95. Similar ECtHR, *Senchishak v. Finland*, 18 November 2014, no. 5049/12.

167   See, for example, ECtHR, *A.A. v. Sweden, 2 September* 2008, no. 8594/04, §§ 70–73 (decision); ECtHR, *Husseini v. Sweden*, 13 October 2011, no. 10611/09, §§ 91–94; ECtHR, *Imamovic and Imamovic v. Sweden,* 13 November 2012, no. 57633/10 (decision). On the non-refoulement cases in the context of health issues see Chapter 3 Section 2.3.2.a.

168   See the critique in the comparative Section 4.2.4 of this chapter.

169   ECtHR, *Pretty v. UK*, 29 April 2002, no. 2346/02, § 50.

territory.[170] However, a complainant must be able to demonstrate that the authorities knew or should have known of the existence of a real and immediate risk of ill treatment by such actors and that they failed to take measures within the scope of their powers that might reasonably have prevented the harm.[171]

The protection of Article 3 ECHR against private actors is also effective in the context of refoulement, as the Court recognized in 1997 with the judgment *H.L.R. v. France*. It held that,

> ... owing to the absolute character of the right guaranteed, the Court does not rule out the possibility that Article 3 of the Convention may also apply where the danger emanates from persons or groups of persons who are not public officials. However, it must be shown that the risk is real and that the authorities of the receiving State are not able to obviate the risk by providing appropriate protection.[172]

Whether a receiving state is *unable* or simply *unwilling* to provide protection is immaterial.[173]

The Court raises a particularly high bar for the affirmation of a violation of the principle of non-refoulement in Article 3 ECHR in cases where threats emanate from non-state actors.[174] It has shown to be very difficult in practice for complainants to demonstrate that they would be at risk of harm from private actors and that a receiving state is not able or willing to provide protection against such risk. Until now, there have been only few cases in which the Court has stated that a removal would be contrary to Article 3 ECHR because of a threat emanating mainly from private actors.[175] The success of complaints

---

170   See, for example, ECtHR, *Z. and Others v. UK*, 10 May 2001, no. 29392/95, § 73; ECtHR, *El-Masri v. Former Yugoslav Republic of Macedonia*, 13 December 2012 [GC], no. 39630/09, § 206.

171   ECtHR, *Osman v. UK*, 28 October 1998, no 87/1997/871/1083 §§ 115 and 116; ECtHR, *Mayeka and Mitunga v. Belgium*, 12 October 2006, no. 13178/03, § 53.

172   ECtHR, *H.L.R. v. France*, 29 April 1997, no. 24573/94, § 40. This principle has been recited ever since: see, for example, ECtHR, *H. and B. v. UK*, 9 April 2013, nos. 70073/10 and 44539/11, § 91.

173   ECtHR, *N. v. Finland*, 26 July 2005, no. 38885/02, §§ 163 and 164.

174   See also Delas 2011, pp. 128 and 229–232; Goodwin-Gill& McAdam 2007, p. 314; Lambert 2005, p. 43; Thurin 2012, pp. 129–131.

175   See ECtHR, *Ahmed v. Austria*, 17 December 1996, no. 25964/94 (Somalia); ECtHR, *N. v. Finland*, 26 July 2005, no. 38885/02 (DRC); ECtHR, *Salah Sheekh v. Netherlands*, 11 January 2007, (Somalia); ECtHR, *N. v. Sweden*, 20 July 2010, no. 23505/09 (woman to Afghanistan); ECtHR, *Auad v. Bulgaria*, 11 October 2011, no. 46390/10 (stateless person of Palestinian

related to risks emanating from private actors is made even rarer because the Court is more open to accepting the possibility of an internal relocation within the receiving state in such cases.[176]

In the case *N. v. Sweden*[177] decided in 2010, the Court for the first time recognized a violation of the principle of non-refoulement relating to a risk that principally emanated from purely civilian actors, and not from powerful clans[178] or gangs associated with or acting in support of a government.[179] The case concerned the deportation of a woman to Afghanistan who feared persecution because she had separated from her husband and was 'involved' with another man. The Court stated that 'in the special circumstances of the present case ... the applicant faces various cumulative risks of reprisals which fall under Article 3 of the Convention from her husband x, his family, her own family and from the Afghan society.'[180] The Court pointed out that 80 per cent of Afghan women were affected by domestic violence and that the authorities see such violence as legitimate and do not prosecute it.[181] However, in a more recent case concerning domestic violence, the Court took a stricter approach: the case *A.A. and Others v. Sweden* concerned the expulsion of a mother and her five children to Yemen.[182] They claimed to have left their country to escape their violent husband and father. They alleged that because of their escape and the mother's attempts to divorce, the father and other male family members would subject them to honour-related crimes. The Court did not question that the mother had been subjected to marital abuse. It also accepted that one of the daughters had been forced to marry an older man when she was 14 years old and that such a marriage had been foreseen for another daughter before their departure. The judges even recognized that the complainants' allegations were corroborated by general country information on the situation of women

---

origin to a refugee camp in Lebanon). See further ECtHR, *M.E. v. France*, 6 June 2013, no. 50094/10, §§ 51–52, concerning a Christian Copt in Egypt; the Court admitted that there was a risk of ill treatment through private Islamic actors and it raised serious doubts as to the possibility that the Egyptian authorities would offer protection. However, the Court relied on the risk emanating from the authorities when concluding that the applicant's removal to Egypt would violate Art. 3 ECHR.

176   See on this Chapter 4 Section 3.4.1.a.

177   ECtHR, *N. v. Sweden*, 20 July 2010, no. 23505/09.

178   As was the case in ECtHR, *Ahmed v. Austria*, 17 December 1996, no. 25964/94 (Somalia); ECtHR, *Salah Sheekh v. Netherlands*, 11 January 2007 (Somalia).

179   As was the case in ECtHR, *N. v. Finland*, 26 July 2005, no. 38885/02 (DRC).

180   ECtHR, *N. v. Sweden*, 20 July 2010, no. 23505/09, § 62.

181   *Ibid.*, § 57.

182   ECtHR, *A.A. and Others v. Sweden*, 28 June 2012, no. 14499/09, §§ 77–96.

in Yemen. It nonetheless rejected the complaint noting, *inter alia*, that the applicants had not presented sufficient detail regarding the conditions under which they lived in Yemen and submitted too little information in order to establish the risk of ill treatment or, with regard to one minor daughter, forced marriage in case of return. The Court further noted that as a family unit, including two male sons, they would be able to support each other. It also stated that the applicants had not shown that they could not count on protection in Yemen. The Court referred to a few family members from the mother's side remaining in Yemen and added that there would be NGOs in Sana'a providing help for vulnerable women. Stating that Article 3 ECHR sets a particularly high threshold in cases 'that do not concern the direct responsibility of the Contracting State for the infliction of the harm,' the Court concluded that the applicants had not shown substantial grounds for believing that they would be exposed to a real risk of being killed or subjected to treatment contrary to Article 3 ECHR if deported to Yemen.[183] This severe judgment demonstrates that the Court is willing to accept protection by private actors or NGOs as relevant.[184]

In the context of protection against private actors, the case *Sufi and Elmi v. United Kingdom* concerning the deportation of two applicants to Somalia must be mentioned.[185] In this judgment adopted in July 2011, the Court found that the violence in Somalia's capital Mogadishu was of such a level of intensity that almost no one could be removed there under Article 3 ECHR. Stating that all parties carried out massive human rights violations and that the conflict was of an unpredictable nature in which the power balance could change from day to day, the Court found a violation of Article 3 ECHR in case of removal to Mogadishu without even addressing the question of whether the threat for the complainant was of private or public nature or whether there was a state or a 'failed State.'[186] When a conflict is of extreme general violence and the identity of the parties involved and their powers are unclear, the Court seems willing to forgo a classification of the source of the harm. It is less difficult for an

---

183   *Ibid.*

184   See the dissenting opinion of judge Power-Forde and the critique on the Court's approach with regard to gender-based violence in Chapter 4 Section 3.2.1.b. See the equally severe approach taken by the Court with regard to the removal of a woman to Mogadishu in ECtHR, *R.H. v. Sweden*, 10 September 2015, no. 4601/14 and the convincing dissenting opinion of the judges Zupančič and de Gaetano.

185   ECtHR, *Sufi and Elmi v. UK*, 28 June 2011, nos. 8319/07 and 11449/07. This case is discussed in more detail in Chapter 4 Section 3.2.1.a.

186   *Ibid.*, §§ 241–250, 293, 301, 309.

applicant to show that there is no protection against private threats in receiving states without functioning authorities.[187]

2.3.2   Harm of a Socioeconomic Nature

The Court has argued that socioeconomic and humanitarian considerations 'do not necessarily have a bearing on the question of a real risk to an applicant of ill-treatment within the meaning of Article 3 ECHR.'[188] By using the expression 'not necessarily,' the Court indicates that under particular circumstances, socioeconomic or humanitarian considerations may have a bearing under Article 3 ECHR. In the judgment *D. v. United Kingdom*, the Court made clear that under exceptional circumstances, Article 3 ECHR may extend to situations where the danger emanates neither from private nor from public actors, but from the consequences of a deportation to the applicant's health. In the cases *M.S.S. v. Belgium and Greece*, *Sufi and Elmi v. United Kingdom* and *Tarakhel v. Switzerland*, the Court further established that if refugees or asylum seekers are to expect particularly dire living conditions, the application of Article 3 ECHR might be triggered.

a   *Health Issues: The* D. v. United Kingdom *Situation*

In exceptional circumstances, the Court accepts a risk associated with the applicant's health condition as justifying the protection from a removal under Article 3 ECHR. There is, however, *only one case to date* in which the Court has found that such exceptional circumstances were at hand. It was the case *D. v. United Kingdom* decided in 1997.[189] It concerned the expulsion of an applicant in the terminal stages of AIDS to the island of St. Kitts, where no treatment for AIDS or other social welfare was available and where he had no family or resources. The Court concluded that the removal of the complainant under these 'exceptional circumstances' would constitute an inhuman treatment in violation of Article 3 ECHR. The Court held:

> ... given the fundamental importance of Article 3 ..., the Court must reserve to itself sufficient flexibility to address the application of that article

---

187   See also ECtHR, *Ahmed v. Austria*, 17 December 1996, no. 25964/94, § 44–47 (Somalia), in which the Court observed an 'absence of State authority' in Somalia in 1996. See similar ECtHR, *Salah Sheekh v. Netherlands*, 11 January 2007, no. 1948/04, § 147 (Somalia).

188   Stated, among others, in ECtHR, *N.A. v. UK*, 17 July 2008, no. 25904/07, § 122.

189   ECtHR, *D. v. UK*, 2 May 1997, no. 30240/96. See further the extradition case ECtHR, *Aswat v. UK*, 16 April 2013, no. 17299/12 discussed below, in which the Court did, however, not apply its usual approach with regard to complaints based on medical grounds.

in other contexts which might arise. It is not therefore prevented from scrutinising an applicant's claim under Article 3 ... where the *source of the risk stems from factors which cannot engage either directly or indirectly the responsibility of the public authorities of that country, or which, taken alone, do not in themselves infringe the standards of that Article.* To limit the application of Article 3 ... in this manner would be to undermine the absolute character of its protection. In any such contexts, however, the Court must subject all the circumstances surrounding the case to a rigorous scrutiny, especially the applicant's personal situation in the expelling country.[190] (Emphasis added)

However, all subsequent applications concerning the removal of HIV-positive complainants to other countries – including the Republic of Congo, Tanzania, Togo and Zambia – have been declared inadmissible, since the Court has held that the threshold set by *D. v. United Kingdom* was not reached.[191] In the case *N. v. United Kingdom*, concerning the removal of a complainant suffering from AIDS to Uganda, the Grand Chamber confirmed the strict approach in 2008. It held that:

Aliens who are subject to expulsion cannot in principle claim any entitlement to remain in the territory of a Contracting State in order to continue to benefit from medical, social or other forms of assistance and services provided by the expelling State. The fact that the applicant's circumstances, including his *life expectancy, would be significantly reduced* if he were to be removed from the Contracting State is *not sufficient in itself to give rise to a breach of Article 3.*

The decision to remove an alien who is suffering from a serious mental or physical illness to a country where the facilities for the treatment of that illness are inferior to those available in the Contracting State may

---

190   ECtHR, D. V. UK, 2 May 1997, no. 30240/96, § 49.

191   See, for example, ECtHR, *S.C.C. v. Sweden*, 15 February 2000, no. 46553/99 (decision); ECtHR, *Henao v. Netherlands*, 24 June 2003, no. 13669/03 (decision); ECtHR, *Ndangoya v. Sweden*, 22 June 2004, no. 17868/03 (decision); ECtHR, *Amegnigan v. Netherlands*, 25 November 2004, no. 25629/04 (decision); ECtHR, *M. v. UK*, 24 June 2008, no. 25087/06 (decision). However, see also ECtHR, *B.B. v. France*, 7 September 1998, no. 30930/96 (striking out), in which the EComHR had expressed the opinion that there would be a breach of Art. 3 ECHR if the complainant, suffering from HIV, was deported to the former Zaire. Since the French authorities reversed the deportation order, the Court struck the case out of the list. Similar ECtHR, *S.J. v. Belgium*, 19 March 2015 [GC], no. 70055/10 (striking out) concluded by a friendly settlement.

raise an issue under Article 3, but *only in a very exceptional case, where the humanitarian grounds against the removal are compelling.*[192] (Emphasis added)

The Court justifies a particularly high threshold set by Article 3 ECHR where health issues are at stake by the fact that in such cases, the alleged future harm does not emanate from the intentional acts or omissions of public authorities or non-State bodies, but instead from a *naturally occurring illness and the lack of sufficient resources* to deal with it in the receiving country. It reminds us in *N. v. United Kingdom* that although many of the rights in the ECHR contain implications of a social or economic nature, *the ECHR is essentially directed at the protection of civil and political rights.*[193] The Court then added the following problematical statement:

> Furthermore, inherent in the whole of the Convention is a search for a *fair balance between the demands of the general interest of the community and the requirements of the protection of the individual's fundamental rights.* Advances in medical science, together with social and economic differences between countries, entail that the level of treatment available in the Contracting State and the country of origin may vary considerably. While it is necessary, given the fundamental importance of Article 3 in the Convention system, for the Court to retain a *degree of flexibility* to prevent expulsion in very exceptional cases, Article 3 does not place an obligation on the Contracting State to alleviate such disparities through the provision of free and unlimited health care to all aliens without a right to stay within its jurisdiction. *A finding to the contrary would place too great a burden on the Contracting States.*[194] (Emphasis added)

It has rightly been criticized in the dissenting opinion of judges Tulkens, Bonello and Spielmann that in referring to 'too great a burden' for the states when defining the scope of protection under Article 3 ECHR, the Court throws into question the absolute nature of the prohibition of ill treatment, according to which no state interests whatsoever may be invoked to derogate from the prohibition of torture or other inhuman treatment.[195]

---

192   ECtHR, *N. v. UK*, 27 May 2008 [GC], no. 26565/05, § 42.

193   *Ibid.,* §§ 43 and 44.

194   *Ibid.,* § 44.

195   On the absolute nature of the prohibition of ill treatment under Art. 3 ECHR see Section 2.4 of this chapter. See also the dissenting opinion of judge Pinto de Albuquerque to

The Court has reiterated its strict approach in the case *Mwanje v. Belgium* decided in December 2011.[196] In this case, the Court found a violation of Article 3 ECHR in the domestic context because the applicant, who suffered from HIV, was not given access to medical treatment in due time while detained in Belgium on warrant on deportation to Cameroon. However, the Court rejected the complainant's claim under Article 3 ECHR with regard to the deportation, referring to the high threshold set by its case law, although it recognized that only 1.89 per cent of HIV patients have access to adequate medical treatment in Cameroon. The judges recognized that the applicant's health condition would considerably decline without medication, and that her already-reduced life expectancy would be further reduced. In referring to *N. v. United Kingdom*, they nonetheless put her current state of health in the focus of the assessment under Article 3 ECHR. The judges noted that, unlike in *D. v. United Kingdom*, the applicant's condition had been stabilized because of the medical treatment in Belgium. With regard to family support in Cameroon, they held that this element could remain open since it had not been assessed by the Belgian authorities and therefore was pure speculation.[197]

The *Mwanje* judgment can only be interpreted to mean that an applicant must be close to death at the moment of the expulsion for Article 3 ECHR to apply.[198] In a separate opinion, *six of the seven judges* held that the 'extremely high threshold' required by the Court is hardly compatible with the wording and spirit of Article 3 ECHR, which is a core right of the Convention that concerns human integrity and dignity.[199] It is clear that the harm the applicant might suffer because of her deportation to Cameroon was more serious then the harm she had suffered by the belated medical treatment in Belgian detention. The judgment therefore appears contradictory.[200] The six judges who released the separate opinion nevertheless abstained from finding a violation of Article 3 ECHR in *Mwanje*, noting that this would not be in accordance with the strict approach defined by the Grand Chamber in *N. v. United Kingdom*. They did, however, express their wish that the Court could one day review its case law.[201]

ECtHR, *S.J. v. Belgium*, 19 March 2015 [GC], no. 70055/10 (striking out), who criticizes that with this jurisprudence 'legal reasoning is abandoned in favour of politics.'

196   ECtHR, *Mwanje v. Belgium*, 20 December 2011, no. 10486/10, §§ 80–86.

197   *Ibid.*, §§ 83 and 84. See this approach also in ECtHR, *E.O. v. Italy*, 10 May 2012, no. 34724/10, §§ 38 and 39 (decision).

198   See separate opinion on *Mwanje* of the judges Tulkens, Jočiené, Popović, Karakaş, Raimondi and Pinot de Albuquerque, § 4.

199   *Ibid.*, § 6.

200   See also the critique in de Weck 2013, pp. 6–10 and the comments below in this section.

201   Separate opinion on *Mwanje* of the judges Tulkens, Jočiené, Popović, Karakaş, Raimondi and Pinto de Albuquerque, § 6.

Persons suffering from grave psychotic illness and/or at risk of suicide have also been unsuccessful when relying on arguments under Article 3 ECHR. The Court applies the same principles as developed in the HIV/AIDS cases. It has rejected the complaints submitted by either noting that the illness was not serious enough, that the applicant could rely on help by family members or that there was a chance for them to have access to medical support in the receiving state.[202] An exception is the case of *Aswat v. United Kingdom* decided in April 2013.[203] It concerned the extradition of an applicant suffering from paranoid schizophrenia to the United States. He had been indicted in respect of conspiracy to establish a jihadist training camp. Because of the applicant's serious mental health problems, the Court disjoined his case from the jointly assessed cases of *Babar Ahmad and Others v. United Kingdom*, which concerned the extradition of a group of individuals suspected of terrorism to the US.[204] Like the applicant *Aswat*, some of the applicants in *Babar Ahmad and Others* were at risk of being detained in a maximum-security facility, with a highly restrictive regime and long periods of isolation. In *Babar Ahmad and Others*, the Court did not estimate that these conditions in US detention would reach the Article 3 ECHR threshold for persons in good health with no serious mental health problems.[205] However, the Court distinguished *Aswat's* case on account of the severity of his mental condition. It noted, *inter alia*, that *Aswat's* condition could only be properly controlled with anti-psychotic medication and participation in occupational activities such that detention and treatment in a medical hospital was necessary.[206] The judges held that *Aswat* would be extradited to a country where he had no ties and where he would face an uncertain future in a potentially hostile prison environment. The Court concluded that this would result in a significant deterioration in his mental and physical health capable of reaching the Article 3 threshold.[207] It took into account the

---

202   See, for recent examples, ECtHR, *Al-Zawatia v. Sweden*, 22 June 2010, no 50068/08 (decision) §§ 50–62; ECtHR, *Anam v. the UK*, 7 June 2011, no. 21783/08 (decision); ECtHR, *H.N. and Others v. Sweden*, 24 January 2012, no. 50043/09 (decision); ECtHR, *Nacic and Others v. Sweden*, 15 May 2012, no. 16567/10, §§ 47–56; ECtHR, *Imamovic and Imamovic v. Sweden*, 13 November 2012, no. 57633/10 (decision); ECtHR, *Tatar v. Switzerland*, 14 April 2015, no. 65692/12, §§ 46–54.

203   ECtHR, *Aswat v. UK*, 16 April 2013, no. 17299/12.

204   See ECtHR, *Babar Ahmad and Others v. UK*, 10 April 2012, nos. 24027/07, 11949/08, 36742/08, 66911/09 and 67354/09.

205   Summarized as such in ECtHR, *Aswat v. UK*, 16 April 2013, no. 17299/12, § 57.

206   ECtHR, *Aswat v. UK*, 16 April 2013, no. 17299/12, § 51.

207   *Ibid.*, §§ 56–57.

fact that mental health services were available in US prisons, but it pointed to the absence of detailed information about the applicant's concrete treatment and placement there.[208] In the *Aswat* judgment, the Court *did not* refer to its principles developed in *D. v. United Kingdom* according to which 'exceptional circumstances' are required when assessing cases of mentally ill individuals threatened with deportation. It reiterated its case law developed with regard to the appropriate medical care of mentally ill persons held in detention outside the non-refoulement context and pointed out their particular vulnerability.[209]

It may be argued that since the applicant *Aswat* would have been held in detention in the United States, the responsibility for the harm he expected there lay with the receiving state's authorities, so that the case could be distinguished from the HIV/AIDS cases, in which the Court justifies the particularly high threshold set by the fact that the alleged future harm does not emanate from the public authorities' responsibility but instead from a naturally occurring illness. However, in other cases in which applicants suffering from illnesses opposed their extradition because of the inadequate medical treatment in the receiving country's prisons, the Court explicitly reiterated the strict approach developed in *N. v. United Kingdom*.[210] The Court's approach with regard to health issues and extraditions is not coherent. Looking at the case of *Aswat*, it appears that individuals suffering from illness have a better chance of being protected from extradition under Article 3 ECHR than from expulsion.[211] This might be justified in light of the argument that Article 3 ECHR may only extend to situations where the danger emanates either directly or indirectly from state authorities. However, for the individual concerned, it will hardly make a difference whether the harm he is expecting because of his deportation is somehow attributable to the receiving state.[212]

---

208 *Ibid.*, §§ 52–54.

209 *Ibid.*, § 50.

210 See ECtHR, *Ahorugeze v. Sweden*, 27 October 2011, no. 37075/09, §§ 88 and 89, concerning the extradition of a genocide suspect with heart problems to Rwanda. The Court explicitly refers to the *D. v. UK* case law and the 'very high threshold' for a medical condition to raise an issue under Art. 3 ECHR. See also ECtHR, *Yefimova v. Russia*, 19 February 2013, no. 39786/09, § 210.

211 Compare, for example, the case *Aswat* with the case ECtHR, *Bensaid v. UK*, 6 February 2001, no. 44599/98, concerning the expulsion of a schizophrenic to Algeria. See also the distinction made between extradition and expulsion with reference to *Bensaid* in ECtHR, *Aswat v. UK*, 16 April 2013, no. 17299/12, § 57.

212 See in this sense also Thurin 2012, p. 143. For a general critique of the Court's case law on that issue see also de Weck 2013, pp. 8–10.

In sum, the Court's extreme severity with regard to refoulement complaints based on medical grounds is hardly justifiable: surely, in the refoulement context, the harm feared in the receiving state must fall under the scope of Article 3 ECHR and a naturally occurring illness *as such* is not a matter of that provision. However, it is not just the applicant's illness that is relevant under Article 3 ECHR, but the *decision to remove* for which the contracting state is responsible. According to the Court's constant approach, the question under Article 3 ECHR is neither to establish the responsibility of the receiving state nor just to determine whether the applicant is fit to travel, but to establish the responsibility of the contracting state for the *direct and foreseeable consequences* of the removal, which must amount to a proscribed ill treatment.[213] It must be recalled that in the lead case *D. v. United Kingdom*, the Court made clear that the conditions in the receiving country were not in 'themselves a breach of the standards of Article 3,' but that the consequences of the removal were.[214] As the Court has further confirmed in *N.*, 'the suffering which flows from naturally occurring illness, physical or mental, may be covered by Article 3, where it is, or risks being, exacerbated by treatment, whether flowing from conditions of detention, expulsion or other measures, for which the authorities can be held responsible.'[215] In addition, in its recent case law, the Court has made very clear that states have a special responsibility under Article 3 ECHR for vulnerable individuals who are particularly dependent on the state.[216] Based on this principle, it found violations of Article 3 ECHR with regard to risks of inadequate reception conditions for asylum seekers in case of removal to Italy and Greece.[217] As the Grand Chamber stated in one of these judgments, 'the source of the risk does nothing to alter the level of protection guaranteed by the Convention or the Convention obligations of the State ordering the person's removal.'[218] Looking at this approach recently developed under Article 3 ECHR by the Court in refoulement cases and taking into consideration the low threshold

---

213   See, among many others, ECtHR, *Soering*, § 91. See on this also the dissenting opinion of judge Power-Fordeto ECtHR, *S.J. v. Belgium*, 27 February 2014, no. 70055/10 (not in force – strike out by GC on 19 March 2015). See further Section 1 of this Chapter.

214   See ECtHR, *D. v. UK*, § 53.

215   ECtHR, *N. v. UK*, 27 May 2008 [GC], no. 26565/05, § 29, referring to ECtHR, *Pretty v. UK*, 29 April 2002, no. 2346/02, § 52, which again refers to *D. v. UK*. Also recalled in the refoulement context in ECtHR, *S.J. v. Belgium*, 27 February 2014, no. 70055/10, § 118 (strike out after friendly settlement on 19 March 2015) and ECtHR, *M.T. v. Sweden*, 26 February 2015, no. 1412/12, § 46 (request for referral to the GC pending).

216   See ECtHR, *M.S.S.* and *Tarakhel* discussed in the next Section 2.3.2b.

217   *Ibid.*

218   ECtHR, *Tarakhel v. Switzerland*, 4 November 2014 [GC], no. 29217/12, § 104.

set for Article 3 ECHR to apply in certain cases in the domestic context,[219] the *extremely severe approach* developed with regard to refoulement complaints on medical grounds makes no sense no matter from which angle it is looked at – whether one puts the focus on the state's direct responsibility under Article 3 ECHR for the act of removal itself and its direct consequences or even whether one focuses on the nature of the harm in the receiving state.[220]

Against this background, it is not surprising that several judges in Strasbourg have called for a readjustment of the principles applied by the Grand Chamber in the *N.* judgment.[221] An opportunity is the case *Paposhvili v. Belgium*, which will be treated by the Grand Chamber.[222] A missed opportunity was the case *S.J. v. Belgium* concerning the expulsion to Nigeria of a mother of three children suffering from HIV.[223] Here again, the Court's chamber rejected the complaint by putting at the centre of its reasoning that the applicant is currently not 'critically ill' and 'fit to travel.'[224] The matter was referred to the Grand Chamber but then resolved by a friendly settlement. Based on 'strong humanitarian considerations,' the applicant and her children were issued residence permits.[225] No such solution was found for the applicant in the lead case *N. v. United Kingdom* described above. This complaint was rejected despite the approved fact that if

---

219 See the Court's concept of 'degrading treatment' in domestic cases as explained in the Sections 2.2.3 and 2.2.4 of this Chapter.

220 See also Chapter 3 Section 4.2.4, from which it is apparent that it is anyway difficult to classify deportation cases of applicants with health issues as classical non-refoulement cases or not. In that context, the Human Rights Committee, in its recent practice, appears to take a pragmatic and less strict approach then Strasbourg under Art. 7 ICCPR in HRC, *A.H.G. and M.R. v. Canada*, 25 March 2015, no. 2091/2011, concerning the expulsion of a person suffering a mental illness to Jamaica. The CJEU, however, appears to take an even stricter approach with regard to subsidiary protection in CJEU, C-542/13, *Mohamed M'Bodji v. Etat belge*, 18 December 2014, §§ 38–41; see on this the critique of judge Pinto de Albuquerque in his dissenting opinion on ECtHR, *S.J. v. Belgium*, 19 March 2015 [GC], no. 70055/10 (striking out).

221 See the multiple dissenting opinions on the judgments *N.*, *Mwanje* and *S.J.*.

222 See ECtHR, *Paposhvili v. Belgium*, 17 April 2014, no. 41738/10 (referral to Grand Chamber). Another opportunity is ECtHR, *M.T. v. Sweden*, 26 February 2015, no. 1412/12 (request for referral to the Grand Chamber pending).

223 See ECtHR, *S.J. v. Belgium*, 19 March 2015 [GC], no. 70055/10 (striking out) and the dissention opinion of judge Pinto de Albuquerque.

224 ECtHR, *S.J. v. Belgium*, 27 February 2014, no. 70055/10, § 124 (not in force – struck out by GC on 19 March 2015).

225 See ECtHR, *S.J. v. Belgium*, 19 March 2015 [GC], no. 70055/10 (striking out) and the dissenting opinion of judge Pinto de Albuquerque, who claims that the Court should have continued the examination based on Art. 37(1) ECHR (necessary for the respect of the Convention).

deprived of her present medication, the applicant's condition would rapidly deteriorate and she would suffer 'pain and death within a few years.'[226] The applicant *N.* in fact died some months after her removal to Uganda.[227]

b   *Living Conditions for Asylum Seekers and Refugees*
As the Court's Grand Chamber has made clear in *N. v United Kingdom*, aliens who are subject to expulsion cannot in principle claim any entitlement to remain in the territory of a contracting state to continue to benefit from medical, social or other forms of assistance and services provided by the expelling state.[228] Under Article 3 ECHR, however, the Court has not excluded 'the possibility that the responsibility of the State may be engaged in respect of treatment where an applicant, who was wholly dependent on the State, found herself faced with official indifference in a situation of serious deprivation or want incompatible with human dignity.'[229]

In the Grand Chamber judgment *M.S.S. v. Belgium and Greece* adopted in January 2011, the Court for the first time found a violation of Article 3 ECHR because of degrading living conditions.[230] The case concerned an Afghan asylum seeker. After being left homeless for months in Athens, he decided to apply for asylum in Belgium. The Belgian authorities nonetheless deported the applicant back to Greece under the European Union's Dublin II Regulation.[231] The Grand Chamber noted that Article 3 ECHR could not be interpreted as obliging the contracting parties to provide everyone within their jurisdiction with a home and neither would it entail a general obligation to give refugees a certain standard of living.[232] However, in light of the obligations incumbent on the Greek authorities under the EU's Reception Directive[233] and considering the applicant's vulnerability as a asylum seeker, the Court held the Greek authorities responsible – because of their inaction – for the situation of the applicant,

---

226   See ECtHR, *N. v. UK*, 27 May 2008 [GC], no. 26565/05, § 47.

227   See the information referred to by judge Power-Forde in her dissenting opinion on ECtHR, *S.J. v. Belgium*, 27 February 2014, no. 70055/10 (not in force – struck out by GC on 19 March 2015).

228   ECtHR, *N. v. UK*, 27 May 2008 [GC], no. 26565/05, § 42.

229   ECtHR, *Budina v. Russia*, 18 June 2009, no. 45603/05 (decision).

230   See ECtHR, *M.S.S. v. Belgium and Greece*, 21 January 2011 [GC], no. 30696/09, §§ 249–264 and 366–368.

231   On the Dublin system that applies to the member states of the EU and to Norway, Iceland, and Switzerland, see Chapter 4 Section 3.4.3.a below.

232   ECtHR, *M.S.S.*, § 249.

233   At the time EU Council Directive 2003/9/EC of 27 January 2003 laying down minimum standards for the reception of asylum seekers, OJ L31/18.

living several months in the streets without any means of providing for his essential needs. These circumstances, combined with the prolonged uncertainty in which the applicant was kept, amounted in the Court's view to degrading treatment.[234] The Court hence found that Greece had violated Article 3 ECHR. It further found that Belgium had breached the principle of non-refoulement for having transferred the applicant to Greece and thus knowingly exposed him to living conditions that amounted to degrading treatment.[235]

The Court goes a long way in its interpretation of degrading treatment in this judgment. It is the first time that it considered a state responsible under Article 3 ECHR for the living conditions of individuals outside detention. It argued similarly in the case *Elmi and Sufi v. United Kingdom* with regard to the question of whether the two Somali complainants could be expected to relocate to refugee camps in Kenya and settlements for internally displaced people in the Afgooye corridor.[236] The Court found that because of the terrible humanitarian conditions in both camps, any person forced to seek refuge there would be at real risk of treatment contrary to Article 3 ECHR.[237] It noted that internally displaced people had very limited access to food, water and shelter in the Afgooye corridor. With regard to the camps in Kenya, where the UNHCR is present, the Court observed that although humanitarian assistance is available, shelter, water and sanitary facilities were extremely limited due to severe overcrowding. The Court further considered that the inhabitants of both camps were vulnerable to violent crime, exploitation, abuse and forcible recruitment. The Court also took into account that people in both camps had very little prospect of their situation improving within a reasonable timeframe.[238]

The considerations in *M.S.S.* and *Elmi and Sufi* should not be taken to mean that the Court generally considers bad living conditions or homelessness as amounting to inhuman or degrading treatment. Both cases concerned the particular situation of individuals who were not deported to their home region

---

234   ECtHR, *M.S.S.*, §§ 263, 264 and 366. The applicant had argued that 'the Greek authorities had given him no information about possible accommodation and had done nothing to provide him with any means of subsistence even though they were aware of the precarious situation of asylum-seekers in general and of his case in particular,' § 236.

235   *Ibid.*, §§ 366–368.

236   ECtHR, *Sufi and Elmi v. UK*, 28 June 2011, nos. 8319/07 and 11449/07, §§ 278–292.

237   The Court did not specify whether that treatment would amount to inhuman or 'only' to degrading treatment.

238   ECtHR, *Sufi and Elmi*, §§ 278–292. With regard to the situation in the refugee camps in Kenya, it is problematic that the Court has assessed an 'internal' relocation alternative in Kenya, which means outside the applicants' country of origin; see on this Chapter 4 Section 3.4.1.c.

but to a place where they were either asylum seekers or displaced persons. Both cases further concerned situations in which the dire humanitarian conditions were systematic and widely known.

After *M.S.S.*, one could be tempted to think that it is *exclusively* in cases in which the deficiencies in the living or reception conditions for asylum seekers or refugees are systematic that Article 3 ECHR applies. The case *Hussein and Others v. Netherlands* appeared to confirm this interpretation.[239] It concerned the transfer of a Somali woman and her two children from the Netherlands to Italy under the Dublin II Regulation in April 2013. The Court held that 'while the general situation and living conditions in Italy of asylum seekers, accepted refugees and aliens who have been granted a residence permit for international protection or humanitarian purposes may disclose some shortcomings, it has not been shown to disclose a systematic failure to provide support or facilities catering for asylum seekers' as was the case in *M.S.S.*[240] This and similar complaints were declared manifestly ill-founded.[241] The Court of Justice of the European Union in Luxembourg (CJEU) endorsed this tendency in the judgment on the joined cases *N.S. and M.E.* adopted in December 2011.[242] It held that member states to the Dublin system may be obliged not to transfer an asylum seeker to the state originally responsible (in applying the sovereignty clause included in Article 3(2) of the Dublin Regulation), when evidence shows 'systemic deficiencies' in the asylum procedure and reception conditions in the receiving state amounting to inhuman or degrading treatment within the meaning of Article 4 of the EU Charter on Fundamental Rights.[243] However, the question remained whether it would be *exclusively* where the deficiencies in the asylum system of the receiving state are systemic that a transfer to another Dublin State may be prohibited under the principle of non-refoulement. Strasbourg answered this question in November 2014 with the Grand Chamber judgment *Tarakhel v. Switzerland.*[244] The case concerned the transfer of an

---

239 ECtHR, *Hussein and Others v. Netherlands and Italy*, 2 April 2013, no. 27725/10 (decision).

240 *Ibid.*

241 With regard to Dublin removals to Italy see, for example, ECtHR, *Abubeker v. Austria and Italy*, 18 June 2013, no. 73874/11 (decision) and ECtHR, *Halimi v. Austria and Italy*, 18 June 2013, no. 53852/11 (decision). With regard to a Dublin-transfer to Hungary see ECtHR, *Mohammadi v. Austria*, 3 July 2014, no. 71932/12, §§ 64–70.

242 CJEU, Joined Cases C-411/10 and C-493/10, *N.S. v. Secretary of State for the Home Department and M.E. and Others v. Refugee Applications Commissioner & Minister for Justice, Equality and Law Reform*, 21 December 2011.

243 *Ibid.*, §§ 86–89, 94, 106. The approach was further codified in Art. 3(2) of the Dublin III Regulation, in force since January 2014.

244 ECtHR, *Tarakhel v. Switzerland*, 4 November 2014 [GC], no. 29217/12.

Afghan family with six minor children to Italy. The applicants argued that they would be subjected to inhuman treatment because of the 'systemic deficiencies' in the reception arrangements for asylum seekers in Italy. The Court first held the following:

> It is also clear from the *M.S.S.* judgment that the *presumption* that a State participating in the 'Dublin' system will respect the fundamental rights laid down by the Convention *is not irrebuttable.*[245] For its part, the Court of Justice of the European Union has ruled that the presumption that a Dublin State complies with its obligations under Article 4 of the Charter of Fundamental Rights of the European Union is rebutted in the event of *'systemic flaws in the asylum procedure and reception conditions* for asylum applicants in the Member State responsible, resulting in inhuman or degrading treatment, within the meaning of Article 4 of the Charter, of asylum seekers transferred to the territory of that Member State.'
>
> In the case of 'Dublin' returns, the presumption that a Contracting State which is also the "receiving" country will comply with Article 3 of the Convention can therefore validly be rebutted where 'substantial grounds have been shown for believing' that the person whose return is being ordered faces a 'real risk' of being subjected to treatment contrary to that provision in the receiving country.
>
> The source of the risk does nothing to alter the level of protection guaranteed by the Convention or the Convention obligations of the State ordering the person's removal. It *does not exempt that State from carrying out a thorough and individualised examination of the situation of the person concerned and from suspending enforcement* of the removal order should the risk of inhuman or degrading treatment be established.[246] (Emphasis added)

The Court added that it 'must therefore ascertain whether, in view of the overall situation with regard to the reception arrangements for asylum seekers in Italy and the applicants' specific situation, substantial grounds have been shown for believing that the applicants would be at risk of treatment contrary to Article 3

---

245   On the aspect of the 'presumption' in the Dublin context Chapter 4 Section 3.4.3.a.

246   ECtHR, *Tarakhel v. Switzerland*, 4 November 2014 [GC], no. 29217/12, §§ 103 and 104. The Court further referred to the reasoning in a UK supreme court judgment of 19 February 2014, according to which the risk should be examined on a case-to-case basis, irrespective of whether systemic deficiencies exist in the receiving state.

if they were returned.'[247] It then cited different sources reporting a number of important failings with regard to the availability and the conditions of reception facilities for asylum seekers in Italy[248] but held that 'the current situation in Italy could in no way be compared to the situation in Greece at the time of the *M.S.S.* judgement,' so that the conditions in Italy could not 'in themselves act as a bar to all removals of asylum seekers to that country.'[249] However, since the information on Italy raised 'serious doubts as to the current capacities of the system,'[250] the Court turned to the applicants' particular situation.

It noted that, contrary to *M.S.S.*, the applicants in *Tarakhel* were not left by themselves but immediately taken charge of by the authorities when they first arrived in Italy.[251] However, the judges observed that 'the possibility that a significant number of asylum seekers removed to that country may be left without any privacy, or even in insalubrious or violent conditions, is not unfounded.'[252] In light of these shortcomings, they concluded that it is 'incumbent on the Swiss authorities to obtain assurances from their Italian counterparts that on their arrival in Italy the applicants will be received in facilities and in conditions adapted to the age of the children, and that the family will be kept together.'[253] The information that had been given by the Italian to the Swiss authorities according to which the applicants would be taken in charge of and accommodated if returned was considered too vague. The Court held that 'in the absence of detailed and reliable information concerning the specific facility, the physical reception conditions and the preservation of the family unit, the Court considers that the Swiss authorities do not possess sufficient assurances.'[254] The judgment concluded with the statement that 'were the applicants to be returned to Italy without the Swiss authorities having first obtained individual guarantees from the Italian authorities that the applicants would be taken charge of in a manner adapted to the age of the children and that the family would be kept together, there would be a violation of Article 3 of the Convention.'[255]

---

247   *Ibid.,* § 105.

248   *Ibid.,* §§ 107–113.

249   *Ibid.,* §§ 114–115.

250   *Ibid.,* § 115.

251   *Ibid.,* § 117.

252   *Ibid.,* § 120.

253   *Ibid.*

254   *Ibid.,* § 121.

255   *Ibid.,* § 122. The complaint under Art. 3 in conjunction with Art. 13 ECHR was rejected for being manifestly ill-founded.

With *Tarakhel* (adopted 14 votes to 3), the Court clarified that 'systemic breaches' in the living and reception conditions for asylum seekers were not a condition for Article 3 ECHR to apply in this context.[256] The existence of such systemic deficiencies are hence rather to be classified as an alleviation of the applicant's burden of proof with regard to the existence of a real risk of inhuman treatment.[257] The Court's approach in *M.S.S.* is actually comparable to those exceptional circumstances in which the Court has declared that a general situation of violence in a particular area could be so 'extreme,' that almost any removal thereto is prohibited under Article 3 ECHR.[258] However, the ordinary individual risk assessment under Article 3 ECHR continues to apply, even if there is no such 'extreme' situation, which is also the method the Court appears to apply in *Tarakhel*.[259] Against this background, the interpretation of Article 4 of the EU Charter on Fundamental Rights as intrinsically linked to the existence of 'systemic deficiencies' is in tension with the Strasbourg approach.[260] It seems further in tension with the UN Human Rights Committee's recent practice under Article 7 ICCPR in the case *Jasin v. Denmark* concerning the Dublin-transfer of a Somali woman with her three children to Italy, in which the *Tarakhel*-approach is widely endorsed.[261]

However, the cases *M.S.S.*, *Tarakhel* and *Sufi and Elmi* are still to be considered as rather exceptional and the principles developed in the judgments are related to the particular context of asylum seekers and refugees or displaced persons. The Court's method in these cases can be compared to its approach developed with regard to inhuman or degrading conditions for individuals in detention.[262] It appears that just like detainees, asylum seekers and refugees are, in the eyes

---

256 Confirmed in ECtHR, *V.M. and Others v. Belgium*, 7 July 2015, no. 60125/11 (not in force – referred to GC).

257 Costello & Mouzourakis 2014, p. 404.

258 See, in particular, ECtHR, *Sufi and Elmi v. UK*, 28 June 2011, nos. 8319/07 and 11449/07 with regard to the situation in Mogadishu, discussed in Chapter 4 Section 3.2.1.a.

259 See Costello & Mouzourakis 2014, p. 404. See also *Tarakhel*, § 104.

260 See Costello & Mouzourakis 2014, p. 411, who argue that the CJEU should bring its case law in line with the standards of Art. 3 ECHR.

261 See HRC, *Jasin v. Denmark*, 22 July 2015, no. 2360/2014, §§ 4.4–8.10.

262 Interestingly, before *Tarakhel*, it was only in extradition cases (or expulsion cases leading to the applicant's detention) that diplomatic assurances have played a role in the Court's practice on non-refoulement; on diplomatic assurances as a risk-reducing tool under Art. 3 ECHR see Chapter 4 Section 3.4.2.a.

of the Court, particularly vulnerable and live in particular dependence upon the authorities.[263] States therefore have special responsibilities toward them. This mode of thinking by the judges is apparent in *M.S.S.*, in which it was noted that the Court 'attaches considerable importance to the applicant's status as an asylum seeker and, as such, a member of particularly underprivileged and vulnerable population group in need of special protection.'[264]

According to the Court, there is 'a broad consensus at the international and European level concerning this need for special protection,' which is evidenced by the Geneva Convention, the activities of the UNCHR and the EU legislation, namely the Reception Directive.[265] It has further emphasised in *Tarakhel* that this special protection is particularly important when children are concerned, even if accompanied by their parents. According to the Grand Chamber, 'it is important to bear in mind that the child's extreme vulnerability is the decisive factor and takes precedence over considerations relating to the status of illegal immigrant.'[266] The *Tarakhel* judgment left open the question how the Court estimates the situation of other vulnerable asylum seekers or refugees, such as single women, disabled persons or other persons with medical problems, in Italy or other countries.[267] Nothing in the Court's considerations in *Tarakhel* indicates that the principles developed in this verdict apply only to families with children. However, as has been explained and will be addressed in the next section, the Court is particularly reluctant to accept a special state responsibility under Article 3 ECHR for individuals suffering from serious illnesses in the context of refoulement.[268]

Another question that must be clarified in the future is how the individual guarantees on the treatment of asylum seekers as required in *Tarakhel* must look, in order to be acceptable under Article 3 ECHR. The Court speaks of

---

263   See in this sense also Clayton 2011, pp. 769 and 770; see further the applicants' statement in ECtHR, *Sufi and Elmi v. UK*, 28 June 2011, nos. 8319/07 and 11449/07, § 255.

264   ECtHR, *M.S.S.*, §§ 251 and 253, see also § 232; recalled in ECtHR, *Tarakhel*, §§ 97 and 98.

265   ECtHR, *Tarakhel*, §§ 96 and 97 referring *to M.S.S.*, § 251.

266   ECtHR, *Tarakhel*, §§ 99, 118 and 119. See also ECtHR, *V.M. and Others v. Belgium*, 7 July 2015, no. 60125/11, §§ 138 and 153 (not in force – pending GC); this case concerned a Serbian family of Roma origin seeking asylum in Belgium after their request for asylum had been rejected in France. Expelled from a reception centre, the family of five children remained homeless in Brussels for four weeks. The case was referred to the Grand Chamber in December 2015 at the request of the Belgian government.

267   This question is raised in the joint partly dissenting opinion of the judges Casadevall, Berro-Lefèvre and Jäderblom.

268   In the Dublin context, see, in particular, ECtHR, *A.S. v. Switzerland*, 30 June 2015, no. 39350/13 discussed in Section 2.3.2 below.

'detailed and reliable information concerning the specific facility, the physical reception conditions and the preservation of the family unit.'[269] It must be deduced from *Tarakhel* and the Court's general practice with regard to such assurances that they should be obtained *before* a transfer decision is taken under the Dublin Regulation, so that the individuals concerned have the opportunity to ask for a comprehensive risk assessment, including the quality of the assurances, by the domestic Courts under Article 3 ECHR.[270] With that, it is clear that *Tarakhel*, after *M.S.S.*, brings to light another important obstacle to the automatic operation of the Dublin system as it was originally designed. Chapter 4 section 3.4.3.a will address this question in light of Dublin cases and the risk of 'indirect refoulement.'

c   *Distinction between Health Issues and Living Conditions*
The Court has made clear that the approach taken in *M.S.S.* with regard to living conditions is to be distinguished from that adopted in *N. v. United Kingdom* with regard to health issues.[271] It noted in *Sufi and Elmi* that in contrast to cases concerning health issues, the dire humanitarian conditions in Somalia are not 'solely or predominantly attributable to poverty or to the State's lack of resources to deal with a naturally occurring phenomenon, such as a drought.'[272] They are predominantly due to the direct or indirect actions of parties to the conflict. Consequently, the Court did not consider that the appropriate test for assessing living conditions in refugee camps in *Sufi and Elmi* was that set out in *N. v. United Kingdom*, according to which humanitarian considerations would only reach the Article 3 ECHR threshold in 'very exceptional cases' where the grounds against removal are 'compelling.' The Court instead preferred to assess *Sufi and Elmi* under the approach adopted in *M.S.S.*, 'which requires it to have regard to an applicant's ability to cater for his most basic needs, such as food, hygiene and shelter, his vulnerability to ill-treatment and the prospect of his situation improving within a reasonable time-frame.'[273]

The Court's approach is delicate: in fact, it can be extremely difficult in certain cases to differentiate between a humanitarian crisis that is predominantly due to poverty and the state's lack of resources on the one hand, and one due to the direct or indirect actions of a state or conflict parties on the other. This

---

269   ECtHR, *Tarakhel*, § 121.
270   See Matthey 2015, p. 27 and ECtHR, *Abu Qatada v. UK*, 17 January 2012, no. 8139/09, § 189 (xi).
271   See ECtHR, *Sufi and Elmi v. UK*, 28 June 2011, nos. 8319/07 & 11449/07, §§ 278–283.
272   *Ibid.*, § 282.
273   *Ibid.*, § 283.

difficulty can be observed in the judgment *S.H.H. v. United Kingdom* adopted in January 2012.[274] The case concerned an Afghan applicant who had been seriously injured during the course of a rocket launch in his home country and who had claimed asylum in the United Kingdom. His lower right leg and his penis had been amputated and he had a false limb. His left leg and right hand had been injured too. He argued that his return to Afghanistan would violate Article 3 ECHR in two ways: first, he asserted that disabled persons were particularly at risk of violence in Afghanistan, because they would be unable to remove themselves from dangerous situations swiftly and because they would be at greater risk of homelessness and thus indiscriminate violence.[275] Second, he argued that there was a real risk that he would be left in living conditions analogous to those set out in *M.S.S.*. He would be left living in the streets without any means of providing for his essential needs in Afghanistan. As a disabled person without family members, he further argued that he was part of a particularly underprivileged and vulnerable group in need of special protection.[276]

In relation to the applicant's first allegation, the Court considered that he had failed to adduce evidence to support his claim according to which disabled persons are *per se* at greater risk of violence than the general Afghan population. Since state reports from various organisations such as the UNHCR and the US State Department made no such references, the Court rejected this claim as being to a large extent speculative.[277] With regard to the applicant's claim that his living conditions would amount to a breach of Article 3 ECHR as a result of the poor provision for and ignorance surrounding persons with disabilities, the Court found that it was not the principles of *M.S.S.* that should apply, but the more severe threshold established under *N. v. United Kingdom*. It rationalised this with three reasons:

(1)   First, the Court acknowledged that, in the present case, the applicant's disability could not be considered a 'naturally' occurring illness. Nevertheless, it considered it significant that the possible future harm would emanate from a lack of sufficient resources to provide medical treatment or welfare rather than the intentional acts or omissions of the authorities of the receiving state.[278]

(2)   Second, in contrast to the present case, the case of *M.S.S.* concerned the inaction and failure of a 'fellow Contracting State,' i.e. Greece, to comply

---

274   ECtHR, *S.H.H. v. UK*, 29 January 2013, no. 60367/10.
275   *Ibid.*, § 56.
276   *Ibid.*, § 57.
277   *Ibid.*, §§ 85–87.
278   *Ibid.*, §§ 88 and 89.

with 'its positive obligations under both European and domestic legislation to provide reception facilities to asylum seekers.'[279] Central to the
Court's conclusions in *M.S.S.* was the fact that the applicant was an asylum seeker and that the Greek authorities had not yet considered his application. The Court then added the following remarkable considerations:

> By contrast, the present application concerns the living-condition and
> humanitarian situation in *Afghanistan, a non-Contracting State, which
> has no such similar positive obligations under European legislation and
> cannot be held accountable under the Convention for failures to provide ad-
> equate welfare assistance to persons with disabilities.* In that regard, it is
> recalled that the Convention does not purport to be a means of requiring
> Contracting States to impose Convention standards on other States.[280]
> (Emphasis added)

(3)   As a third point, the Court observed that the present case could be dis-
      tinguished from the situation of refugees in Somalia as considered in
      Sufi and Elmi, because there was 'clear and extensive evidence before
      the Court that the humanitarian crisis in Somalia was predominantly
      due to the direct and indirect actions of all parties to the conflict.'[281] Ac-
      cording to the Court, the situation in Afghanistan, and in particular in
      Kabul where the applicant was to be returned, was, albeit very serious,
      not comparable to Somalia where no functioning central government
      and no infrastructure at all was in place. It further noted that, unlike in
      Somalia, there remained a significant presence of international aid agen-
      cies in Afghanistan. The Court noted that although the difficulties and
      inadequacies in the provision for persons with disabilities in Afghanistan
      should not be understated, it could 'not be said that such problems are as
      a result of the deliberate actions or omissions of the Afghan authorities
      rather than attributable to a lack of resources.'[282]

The Court eventually considered that because the problems facing the applicant would be *largely a result of inadequate social provisions through a want of
resources,* the strict approach adopted by the Court in *N. v. United Kingdom* was
more appropriate. The Court had hence to determine whether the applicant's
case was 'a very exceptional one where the humanitarian grounds against

---

279   *Ibid.,* § 90.
280   *Ibid.*
281   *Ibid.*
282   *Ibid.*

removal are compelling.'[283] The judges held that they were unable to conclude that the applicant would not be able to contact his sisters who still lived in Afghanistan, and therefore did not accept his claim that he would be left without any support. However, most importantly, the Court considered that the applicant had managed to remain in Afghanistan for four years after he had been injured in 2006 and had been supported throughout that period, during which he also received medical treatment. Noting that there was no evidence that the circumstances the applicant would confront in Afghanistan would be worse than those that he had faced during that four-year period, the Court concluded that the applicant's case did not demonstrate very exceptional circumstances comparable to those referred to in *N. v the United Kingdom*.[284] Accordingly, his removal to Afghanistan would not give rise to a violation of Article 3 ECHR.

The Court's arguments in this judgment are problematic on several counts: first, the Court's reasoning that the possible future harm would emanate from a lack of sufficient resources to provide medical treatment or welfare rather than the intentional acts or omissions of the authorities of the receiving state is hard to understand in this case, in which the applicant's dire situation as a severely disabled person clearly did not result from a naturally occurring illness, but from violence within an armed conflict. As three of the seven judges stated in their dissenting opinion, the facts of the case fall somewhere in between the lines of the Court's case law.[285] Second, by differentiating between Greece, which is a member of the Council of Europe and the EU, and Afghanistan, which is not, in the scope of protection offered under Article 3 ECHR, the Court introduces a double standard that is hardly compatible with the absolute character of the prohibition on inhuman and degrading treatment. How can the Court defend the absolute prohibition of every treatment prohibited under Article 3 ECHR under any circumstances, if the scope of that prohibition depends on the legislation applicable to the individual concerned or the country to which he is sent? Third, the way the Court has distinguished the situation in Afghanistan from that in Somalia is not a convincing justification for a different approach: why should the *exact nature* of a violent conflict, which is extremely difficult to categorise, have an impact on the treatment of the individual concerned?[286]

---

283   *Ibid.*, § 92.
284   *Ibid.*, § 93.
285   See § 3, dissenting opinion of judges Ziemle, Thór Björgvinsson and de Gaetano.
286   The Court's reference to the lack of international aid agencies in Somalia to distinguish *S.H.H.* from *Sufi and Elmi* is also odd, given the assistance of the UNHCR to refugee camps to which the applicants could have been returned in *Sufi and Elmi*.

Finally, the classification of asylum seekers in Europe as a more vulnerable group than the disabled appears ill considered.[287] In this context, the question may be raised why the Court attaches so much weight to EU legislation on the treatment of asylum seekers to define inhuman treatment, but not so much to the positive obligations Afghanistan had under the UN Convention on the Rights of Persons with Disabilities. This is also remarkable in light of *Tarakhel*, which was adopted after *S.H.H.*, and in which the Court gave particular attention to the UN Convention on the Rights of the Child.[288]

The situation became even more confusing with the judgment *A.S. v. Switzerland* adopted in June 2015.[289] The case concerned a Syrian national of Kurdish origin, diagnosed with severe post-traumatic stress disorder, for which he was receiving medical treatment in Switzerland. By referring to the principles developed in *M.S.S.* and *Tarakhel*, he claimed that his Dublin transfer to Italy would violate Article 3 ECHR because of the deficiencies in housing and medical support of asylum seekers in that country. However, the Court did not apply the approach it had applied in the Dublin cases *M.S.S.* and *Tarakhel* but the particularly high threshold set in the *N.* jurisprudence on health issues. It made no reference to its considerations in *S.H.H.* and *Elmi and Sufi* as described above, but simply stated that the high threshold set in *D. v. United Kingdom* is the correct approach to apply in this case, given that the harm does not emanate from the intentional acts or omissions of the public authorities, but from a naturally occurring illness and the lack of sufficient resources.[290] The method applied by the judges in *A.S.* appears in contradiction with the Court's statement in *Tarakhel*, according to which 'the source of the risk does nothing to alter the level of protection guaranteed by the Convention or the Convention obligations of the State ordering the person's removal.'[291] In addition, in *M.S.S.*, what the applicant held against the Greek authorities was, according to the Court, that, 'because of their deliberate actions or omissions,' it had been impossible in practice for him to provide for his essential needs.[292] It was in fact based on 'their inaction' combined with the applicant's vulnerability as

---

287 See on this also the dissenting opinion to *S.H.H.* of the judges Ziemle, Thór Björgvinsson and de Gaetano, asking for a more disability-sensitive approach.

288 See ECtHR, *Tarakhel v. Switzerland*, 4 November 2014 [GC], no. 29217/12, § 99.

289 ECtHR, *A.S. v. Switzerland*, 30 June 2015, no. 39350/13.

290 *Ibid.*, § 31. The Court even reiterated its problematic statement made in *N.*, according to which another method would place a 'too great burden on the Contracting States'; see also the critique in the next section.

291 ECtHR, *Tarakhel*, § 104.

292 See ECtHR, *M.S.S.*, § 250; recalled in ECtHR, *Tarakhel*, § 96.

an asylum seeker that the Court held the Greek authorities responsible under Article 3 ECHR.[293] Against this background, it is not at all evident why the *M.S.S.* threshold should not apply in the case of *A.S.*, who did not complain about a lack of resources for medical treatment in Italy but the authorities' omissions with regard to the treatment of asylum seekers.[294] In addition – contrary to *S.H.H.* – the applicant *A.S.* was sent to a European state that has, according to the Court, particular responsibilities toward asylum seekers.

On the whole, it must be concluded that the Court's reasoning in the cases *S.H.H.* and *A.S.* is not well thought out. The only general conclusion that can be drawn, so far, is that the Court is *extremely severe* with individuals threatened with deportation who are seriously ill. Their different treatment compared to asylum seekers in the cases *M.S.S.* and *Tarakhel* is difficult to understand in light of the Court's general practice under Article 3 ECHR.

d   *Risks Accompanying the Court's Case Law on Harms of a*
       Socioeconomic Nature

According to *Bossuyt* the Court's approach taken in *M.S.S.* and *Sufi and Elmi* seems to be 'only a small step away from a future prohibition of the removal of any asylum seeker, or by extension any foreign national, to his country of origin if he is not sure to find in that country decent living conditions.'[295] This statement is polemical; it is clearly not reflected in the Court's case law, which suggests that it is only in exceptional circumstances and where the individual concerned is particularly vulnerable that living conditions may amount to a prohibited treatment. The Court has made clear that purely economic refugees do not have a claim under Article 3 ECHR.[296] However, the Court's new approach regarding living conditions makes it significantly more difficult to make general statements about where the boundaries of the protection offered by Article 3 ECHR actually are. It must be considered very dynamic.

The broadening of the scope of Article 3 ECHR to living conditions with regard to asylum seekers or certain refugees is not unproblematic. With regard to *M.S.S.*, the conclusion must be drawn that with regard to homelessness, Article 3 ECHR might offer a broader protection for asylum seekers than it does for ordinary citizens.[297] As cited, the Court speaks of 'the existence of a broad

---

293   See ECtHR, *M.S.S.*, § 263.

294   See ECtHR, *A.S. v. Switzerland*, 30 June 2015, no. 39350/13, § 19.

295   Bossuyt 2012, p. 234. He refers to judge Sajó's partly dissenting opinion to *M.S.S.*

296   Confirmed for instance in ECtHR, *Shakurov v. Russia*, 5 June 2012, no. 55822/10, § 138.

297   See in this sense also ECtHR, *S.S. v. UK*, 24 January 2012, no. 12096/10, § 74 (decision), in which a young Afghan alleged that he would be at risk of destitution in Kabul where he

consensus' at European level for the special protection of asylum seekers that is, according to the judges, evidenced in international law including the EU Reception Directive.[298] It would surmount the scope of this study to analyse whether this consensus is as 'broad' as designated by the Court's majority.[299] Apart from this question mark, it is astonishing that the Court referred to an EU Directive to indicate that states have a special responsibility for individuals under Article 3 ECHR, as it did in *M.S.S.* and *Tarakhel*.[300] A reference to obligations under EU law to determine the scope of Article 3 ECHR is not appropriate. It could be interpreted as indicating that, depending on the legal framework of the state in question, different standards are applicable.[301]

It is likely that the Court, if confronted with new complaints in which the alleged harm in the receiving state relates to dire living conditions, might take a step back and set more specific conditions or a particularly high threshold in subsequent judgments, just as it did with regard to health issues in *N. v. United Kingdom*. The cases *S.H.H.* and *A.S.* discussed above may already be interpreted as a step in this direction.[302] It is highly misleading if the Court first appears to broaden the protection available under Article 3 ECHR and then narrows its interpretation on the basis of state interests. Particularly worrying are the Court's considerations with regard to health issues in the judgment *N. v. United Kingdom* (and recently recalled in *A.S. v. Switzerland*), in which the Court somehow justified the non-violation of Article 3 ECHR by referring to

---

would be obliged to sleep in the streets. In referring to *M.S.S.*, the Court indicated that 'in the present case the applicant, a healthy male of 27 years of age, had failed to submit any evidence to indicate that he would be unable to cater for his most basic needs in Kabul or that he has any particular vulnerability.'

298   ECtHR, *M.S.S.*, § 251; ECtHR, *Tarakhel*, § 97.

299   For different opinions within the Court, see the partly dissenting opinion of judge Sajó to *M.S.S.*, who speaks of an over-broad concept of vulnerability and dependence with regard to asylum seekers. See also the dissenting opinion of judge Kjølbroto on ECtHR, *V.M. and Others v. Belgium*, 7 July 2015, no. 60125/11 (not in force – referral to GC).

300   See ECtHR, *M.S.S.*, § 263; ECtHR, *Tarakhel*, §§ 96 and 97. See also ECtHR, *S.H.H.*, § 90 and the critique in Section c. just above.

301   See similar the critiques of von Arnauld 2011; Clayton 2011, pp. 767–768; Mallia 2011, pp. 119 and 120; p. 241. See also, however, the concurring opinion of judge Rozakis to *M.S.S.*, who justifies the distinction.

302   See also ECtHR, *Hussein and Others v. Netherlands and Italy*, 2 April 2013, no. 27725/10, (decision), § 71, concerning the transfer of a Somali single mother and her two young children to Italy under the Dublin II Regulation, in which the Court held that the living conditions of asylum seekers will only be relevant under Article 3 ECHR if there are 'exceptionally compelling humanitarian grounds against removal,' which contradicts *Tarakhel*.

the excessive 'burden on the Contracting States.'[303] Equally alarming are the statements made in *S.H.H.*, according to which the scope of protection offered under Article 3 ECHR might depend on whether the receiving state is part of the Council of Europe, or whether that state has certain positive obligations under European legislation.[304] In fact, the broader the obligations of states under Article 3 ECHR are, the more the Court appears willing to take into account considerations that should not strictly have a bearing on the question of whether there is a violation of Article 3 ECHR. As Thurin rightly observes, flexibility under Article 3 ECHR is a double-edged sword: it allows for dynamic case law as well as a challenge to the absolute character of the protection under Article 3 ECHR.[305] This risks diluting the authority of Article 3 ECHR.

Observing the Court's practice with regard to harms of a socioeconomic or medical nature in the context of deportations as a whole, it appears that Strasbourg has started down a road that it is not really committed to following to the end. This has led to contradictory results and to a practice that is rather confusing: as the laborious considerations in *S.H.H.* and *A.S.* have revealed, it can be very difficult to distinguish whether the appropriate test for the risk assessment in a particular case is the stricter one as set out in *N. v. United Kingdom* or the threshold developed in *M.S.S.* and *Sufi and Elmi*. If it is already difficult for the Court to make this distinction, how much harder must it be for the national courts and authorities to follow the Court's guidance?

Finally, it should be noted that it is not unusual for the Court to assess a violation of the right to private life under Article 8 ECHR if the threshold of Article 3 ECHR is not met.[306] Article 8 ECHR foresees a balancing test between the interference in questions and opposed public interests – a test which is inadmissible under Article 3 ECHR. Before the Court starts to make – explicitly or implicitly – such balancing tests under Article 3 ECHR, it should think twice about whether Article 8 ECHR is not the more appropriate provision to apply.

2.4   *Absolute Character of the Prohibition*

As the Court has frequently stated, Article 3 ECHR enshrines one of the most fundamental values of democratic society. It prohibits in absolute terms

---

303   ECtHR, *N. v. UK*, 27 May 2008 [GC], no. 26565/05, § 44; ECtHR, *A.S. v. Switzerland*, 30 June 2015, no. 39350/13, § 31.

304   ECtHR, *S.H.H. v. UK*, 29 January 2013, no. 60367/10, § 90.

305   Thurin 2009, p. 256 and pp. 134–145. See also de Weck 2013, p. 10, and the critique in Sections 2.2.3, 2.2.4 and 2.4 of this Chapter.

306   Schabas 2015, pp. 172–173 with references to the case law.

torture or inhuman or degrading treatment or punishment, irrespective of the circumstances and the victim's behaviour.[307] Unlike most of the provisions of the Convention, Article 3 ECHR is not subject to any restriction. According to Article 15(2) ECHR, even emergency situations threatening 'the life of the nation' do not justify derogations from the prohibition of torture and inhuman or degrading treatment or punishment laid down in Article 3 ECHR. There can never be a justification for acts falling within the scope of Article 3 ECHR, irrespective of the motivation of the authorities, the conduct of the victim or the surrounding circumstances.[308]

The absolute prohibition of torture or other inhuman treatment is equally valid in refoulement cases.[309] According to the jurisprudence of the Court, neither extradition treaties nor criminal acts committed by an applicant nor other circumstances such as considerations of national security allow any exception to the application of the principle of non-refoulement. The danger emanating from an applicant or the nature of an offence committed by him is irrelevant for the protection offered by Article 3 ECHR.[310] Already in the judgment *Chahal v. United Kingdom* adopted in 1996, the Court made clear that the 'activities of the individual in question, however undesirable or dangerous, cannot be a material consideration.'[311] It specified that the protection afforded by Article 3 ECHR in this respect is wider than that provided by the 1951 Refugee Convention, which allows the exclusion of certain criminals and individuals considered to be a danger to society.[312] Therefore, regardless of a 'particularly serious crime' committed by an applicant in the sense of the exclusion clause in Article 33(2) Refugee Convention, the expulsion of that applicant can still constitute a violation of Article 3 ECHR if substantial grounds have been shown for believing that he would be at real risk of treatment contrary to that provision.[313]

---

307 See, among many others, ECtHR, *Babar Ahmad and Others v. UK*, 10 April 2012, nos. 24027/07, 11949/08, 36742/08, 66911/09 and 67354/09, § 200.

308 See, among many other judgments, ECtHR, *Ireland v. UK*, 18 January 1978 [GC], no. 5310/71, § 167; ECtHR, *Selmouni v. France*, 28 July 1999 [GC], no. 25803/94, § 95; ECtHR, *Gäfgen v. Germany*, 1 June 2010 [GC], no. 22978/05, §§ 87 and 107.

309 See, for example, ECtHR, *D. and Others v. Turkey*, 22 June 2006, no. 24245/03, § 45.

310 See, for example, ECtHR, *Bajsultanov v. Austria*, 12 June 2012, no. 54131/10, § 71.

311 ECtHR, *Chahal v. UK*, 15 November 1996, no. 22414/93, §§ 76–82.

312 *Ibid.*, § 80. See also, for example, ECtHR, *Ahmed v. Austria*, 17 December 1996, no. 25964/94, § 41; ECtHR, *Saadi v. Italy*, 28 February 2008 [GC], no. 37201/06, § 139 ECtHR, *Ryabikin v. Russia*, 19 June 2008, no. 8320/04, §§ 118 and 120; ECtHR, *Muminov v. Russia*, 11 December 2008, no. 42502/06, § 89.

313 ECtHR, *Bajsultanov v. Austria*, 12 June 2012, no. 54131/10, § 71. See on this also Chapter 1 Section 4.

In the *Soering*-judgment adopted in 1989, the Court noted that the risk of harbouring a criminal fugitive was 'a consideration which must be included among the factors to be taken into account in the interpretation and application of the notions of inhuman and degrading treatment or punishment in extradition cases.'[314] However, in *Chahal*, the Court argued that it should not be inferred from the Court's remarks in *Soering* that 'there is any room for balancing the risk of ill-treatment against the reasons for expulsion in determining whether a State's responsibility under Article 3 ECHR is engaged.'[315] The Court has confirmed this approach ever since.[316] In the case *Saadi v. Italy* decided in 2008, the applicant had been prosecuted for participation in international terrorism.[317] In Tunisia, the country seeking his extradition, he was sentenced in absentia to 20 years' imprisonment for membership of a terrorist organisation. The Grand Chamber recognized that states face immense difficulties in protecting their communities from terrorism. However, it argued:

> The concepts of 'risk' and 'dangerousness' in this context do not lend themselves to a balancing test because they are notions that can only be assessed independently of each other. Either the evidence adduced before the Court reveals that there is a substantial risk if the person is sent back or it does not. The prospect that he may pose a serious threat to the community if not returned does not reduce in any way the degree of risk of ill treatment that the person may be subject to on return.[318]

Hence, a balance of state interests with the scope of protection offered under Article 3 ECHR is contrary to the absolute protection of Article 3 ECHR, even in the most difficult situations, such as the fight against terrorism. In *Labsi v. Slovakia*, a judgment adopted in May 2012, the Court stated that terrorist violence in itself constitutes a serious threat to human rights. It noted that it considers it legitimate for states to take a firm stand against those who contribute to terrorist acts and that they must be allowed to deport non-nationals whom they

---

314   ECtHR, *Soering v. UK*, 7 July 1989, no. 14038/88, § 89.

315   ECtHR, *Chahal v. UK*, 15 November 1996, no. 22414/93, § 81.

316   See, for example, ECtHR, *Shamayev and Others v. Georgia and Russia*, 12 April 2005, no. 36378/02, § 335; ECtHR, *Auad v. Bulgaria*, 11 October 2011, no. 46390/10, §§ 95–108 and 117–123; ECtHR, *Babar Ahmad and Others v. UK*, 10 April 2012, nos. 24027/07, 11949/08, 36742/08, 66911/09 and 67354/09, § 172.

317   ECtHR, *Saadi v. Italy*, 28 February 2008 [GC], no. 37201/06, § 139.

318   *Ibid.*, § 139.

consider to be threats to national security. However, it also noted that it is 'not the Court's role to review whether an individual is in fact such a threat; its only task is to consider whether an individual's deportation would be compatible with his or her rights under the Convention.'[319] The Court has stayed firm on this principle, even though some state parties continue to oppose it.[320]

It must be noted that the Court has also relied on the absolute character of the prohibition on torture and inhuman treatment to expand the scope of harms prohibited under Article 3 ECHR.[321] In this context, it should be mentioned that it is the *ban on torture and other inhuman treatment* that is absolute, not the *concept of torture or inhuman treatment*.[322] This latter might change and evolve over time. However, as explained in section 2.3.2 of this chapter, the Court's case law on the protection against inhuman treatment of a socioeconomic nature challenges this distinction. It appears that the more the Court widens the protection under Article 3 ECHR to harms of a socioeconomic nature, the more difficult it is for it *not* to take into account considerations of a political or economic nature when defining the limits of the protection from refoulement. This challenges the absolute prohibition on inhuman or degrading treatment. The content and scope of the prohibition on torture and inhuman treatment, including the principle of non-refoulement, as a core right of

---

319   ECtHR, *Labsi v. Slovakia*, 15 May 2012, no. 33809/08, § 117.

320   See ECtHR, *Ramzy v. Netherlands*, 27 May 2008, no. 25424/05 (decision), with third-party interventions from Lithuania, Portugal, Slovakia and the UK; ECtHR, *A. v. Netherlands*, 20 July 2010, no. 4900/06, §§ 125–130, 142 and 143, with third-party interventions form Lithuania, Portugal, Slovakia and the UK. There are also critical voices within the Court; see the dissenting opinion of judge Micovićon ECtHR, *Al-Husni v. Bosnia and Herzegovina*, 7 February 2012, no. 3727/08. As further examples of the firmness of the Court in this context see ECtHR, *Dbouba v. Turkey*, 13 July 2010, no. 15916/09, § 40; ECtHR, *Auad v. Bulgaria*, 11 October 2011, no. 46390/10, §§ 101–107; ECtHR, *Labsi v. Slovakia*, 15 May 2012, no. 33809/08, §§ 108–111 and 128; ECtHR, *Mannai v. Italy*, 27 March 2012, no. 9961/10, §§ 17 and 35; ECtHR, *Al Nashiri v. Poland*, 24 July 2014, no. 28761/11, § 507.

321   The Court has relied on the absolute nature of the prohibition of torture and inhuman treatment in *Soering* to argue that this provision contains an obligation of non-refoulement. It has also referred to the absolute character to justify the applicability of Art. 3 ECHR with regard to harms of a private nature in *H.R.L. v. France*.

322   Trechsel states on this subject that, on closer examination, Art. 3 ECHR seems to be more flexible than an absolute guarantee. However, it is not the protection that is relative, but the 'elements of offence,' that is, the understanding of the notions. See also Thurin 2012, pp. 255–256. See further ECtHR, *Selmouni v. France*, 28 July 1999, no. 25803/94, § 101, in which the Court mentions that the understanding of torture can change over time. See, however, Battjes 2009, pp. 583–621, for a different approach.

the Convention, should not depend on such considerations. Otherwise, in the long run, it will lose its authority.

3   The Scope of Article 3 CAT

3.1   *Introduction*

The non-refoulement obligation in Article 3 CAT refers to torture as defined in Article 1 CAT and does not extend to situations of ill treatment envisaged by Article 16 CAT, which requires state parties to prevent 'other acts of cruel, inhuman or degrading treatment or punishment which do not amount to torture as defined in article 1.'[323] To understand the scope of Article 3 CAT, a key question to be answered is hence which acts constitute torture in the sense of Article 1 CAT, and how they can be distinguished from acts constituting cruel, inhuman or degrading treatment or punishment in the sense of Article 16 CAT. The next sections will look at how the Committee defines these different categories of ill treatment.

With regard to the confusion that could arise because of the Committee's General Comment No. 2 on Art. 2 CAT, in which it is stated 'that articles 3 to 15 are likewise obligatory as applied to both torture and ill-treatment,' Wouters rightly argues that the Committee did not mean to widen the scope of the prohibition of refoulement to inhuman treatment, which would contradict the clear wording of Article 3 CAT, but that it evoked the obligatory application of the Articles 3 to 15 CAT, whether these provisions refer to acts of torture or other forms of ill treatment.[324] Wouters' analysis has been confirmed by the Committee's practice and terminology, previous to and following to the publication of the General Comment No. 2 in January 2008.[325] However, General Comment No. 2 rightly indicates that the definitional threshold between

---

323   See the wording of Art. 3 CAT and, for example, ComAT, *T.M. v. Sweden*, 18 November 2003, no. 228/2003 § 6.2 (and the individual opinion of Committee member Mariño Menéndez). See also ComAT, General Comment No.1 on Art. 3 (1997), § 1.

324   See General Comment No. 2 on Art. 2 (2008), § 6 and Wouters 2009, pp. 519–520.

325   See, for example, ComAT, *L.J.R. v. Australia*, 10 November 2008, no. 316/2007, § 7.5; ComAT, *M.F. v. Sweden*, 14 November 2008, no. 326/2007, § 6.4; ComAT, *N.B.-M. v. Switzerland*, 14 November 2011, no. 347/2008, § 9.8; ComAT, *E.L. v. Canada*, 21 May 2012, no. 370/2009, § 8.6; *ComAT, F.B. v. Netherlands*, 20 November 2015, no. 613/2014, § 8.8.

inhuman treatment and torture is often not clear in practice,[326] a fact that is particularly visible in the non-refoulement case law.[327]

3.2 The Nature of the Harm

3.2.1 Torture

Article 3 CAT protects a person from removal to a country if he runs a real risk of being subjected to torture in that country in the sense of Article 1 CAT.[328] The definition of torture in Article 1 CAT is as follows:

1. For the purposes of this Convention, the term 'torture' means any act by which severe pain or suffering, whether physical or mental, is intentionally inflicted on a person for such purposes as obtaining from him or a third person information or a confession, punishing him for an act he or a third person has committed or is suspected of having committed, or intimidating or coercing him or a third person, or for any reason based on discrimination of any kind, when such pain or suffering is inflicted by or at the instigation of or with the consent or acquiescence of a public official or other person acting in an official capacity. It does not include pain or suffering arising only from, inherent in or incidental to lawful sanctions.

2. This article is without prejudice to any international instrument or national legislation which does or may contain provisions of wider application.

This Article constitutes the first definition of torture in an international treaty.[329] It is possible to extract four elements from the definition: (1) the causing of severe mental or physical pain or suffering, (2) the deliberate infliction of this pain for a certain purpose, (3) the involvement of a public official in causing it and (4) the exclusion of lawful sanctions. The following paragraphs will take a closer look at these elements.[330] As noted in paragraph 2 of Article 1 CAT, the definition is without prejudice to other international or national laws that recognise a wider definition.

---

326 See ComAT, General Comment No. 2 on Art. 2 (2008), § 3.
327 See on this Chapter 3 Section 4.2.1.
328 General Comment No.1 on Art. 3 (1997), § 1.
329 Ingelse 2001, p. 206.
330 For a comprehensive analysis of Article 1 CAT see Nowak & McArthur 2008, pp. 27–86.

Article 1 CAT, in defining torture, speaks of acts by which severe pain or suffering, whether physical or mental, are inflicted deliberately by officials for such purposes as, for example, obtaining information or intimidating the applicant. However, there is no definition of *severe pain or suffering*. Indicative are cases in which the Committee has identified certain acts as constituting torture in the sense of Article 1 CAT. Among these are beating of the detainee,[331] a technique known as 'dry submarine' in which the victim is tied and a polypropylene bag is placed over his head and pulled backwards,[332] rape and, under certain circumstances, other violence against women,[333] arbitrary or unlawful deprivation of life or forced disappearance.[334] The death penalty as such does not constitute torture in the sense of Article 1 CAT although certain methods of execution can amount to torture, as the example of stoning demonstrates.[335]

According to the definition in Article 1 CAT, an act is only considered as torture if it is inflicted *intentionally*. Pain or suffering resulting from an accident cannot constitute torture in the sense of Article 1 CAT. Omissions can, however, constitute acts of torture under certain circumstances if there is an intent to harm. Several scholars cite the withholding of food or drink from detainees as such an example.[336] In addition to being intentionally inflicted, Article 1 CAT requires that the 'pain or suffering' be inflicted for a *certain purpose* in order to be considered as torture. Article 1 CAT lists:

> ... such purposes as obtaining from him [the torture victim] or a third person information or a confession, punishing him for an act he or a third

---

331   ComAT, *Dimitrov v. Serbia and Montenegro*, 3 May 2005, no. 171/2000, §§ 2.1 and 7.1; ComAT, *Dimitrijevic v. Serbia and Montenegro*, 16 November 2005, no. 172/2000, §§ 2.1, 2.2 and 7.2; ComAT, *Ali v. Tunisia*, 21 November 2008, no. 291/2006, § 15.4; ComAT, *Sahli v. Algeria*, 3 June 2011, no. 341/2008, § 9.3; ComAT, *Slyusar v. Ukraine*, 14 November 2011, no. 353/2008, §§ 2.4 und 9.2.

332   ComAT, *Gerasimov v. Kazakhstan*, 24 May 2012, no. 433/2010, §§ 2.3 and 12.2.

333   ComAT, *V.L. v. Switzerland*, 20 November 2006, no. 262/2005, §. 8.10; ComAT, *Njamba and Balikosa v. Sweden*, 14 May 2010, no. 322/2007, § 9.5.

334   ComAT, *Kalinichenko v. Morocco*, 25 November 2011, no. 428/2010, §§ 15. 5 and 15.6; ComAT, *E.L. v. Canada*, 21 May 2012, no. 370/2009, § 8.6.

335   ComAT, *A.S. v. Sweden*, 24 November 2000, no. 149/1999, §§ 8.4 and 8.7. Section 3.2.4 of this chapter will have a closer look at the death penalty.

336   Boulesbaa 1999, pp. 14 and 15; Burgers & Danelius 1988, p. 118; Chetail 2006, p. 76; Ingelse 2001, p. 208; Wouters 2009, p. 440. See further ComAT, *Sahli v. Algeria*, 3 June 2011, no. 341/2008, § 9.3, in which the complainant, after have been beaten in detention, did not receive medical treatment and died as a consequence. The Committee found that this had violated Art. 1 CAT.

person has committed or is suspected of having committed, or intimidating or coercing him or a third person, or for any reason based on discrimination of any kind ...

As has been stated by *Burgers* and *Danelius*,[337] the words 'such ... as' indicate, on the one hand, that the list of purposes in Article 1 CAT is not exhaustive and, on the other hand, that other purposes must be related to those expressly listed. They note that the purpose should have a certain connection 'with the interests of policies of the State and its organs' even if it is a remote one.[338] In the case *V.L.* v. *Switzerland*, the Committee added 'retaliation, humiliation and discrimination based on gender' to the purposes listed in the definition.[339] Several scholars consider that sadistic motives will also fall within the scope of purposes listed in Article 1 CAT, since they usually contain an element of intimidation, punishment or discrimination where public officials are involved, as required by Article 1 CAT.[340] In refoulement cases, the element of purpose is barely addressed or mentioned by the Committee.[341]

The classic situation in which severe pain or suffering is caused for one of the purposes listed in Article 1 CAT occurs when a person is *deprived of his liberty*.[342] However, deprivation of liberty is not a condition for torture. In the case *V.L.* v. *Switzerland*, the Committee argued that a rape by Belarusian police agents constituted torture, 'even though it was perpetrated outside formal detention facilities.'[343] It is rather the *factual power or control* of the person inflicting the suffering, or the *powerlessness* of the victim, that are the pertinent criteria for characterizing an act as torture.[344] The causing of severe pain or suffering by state agents to individuals who are not, at the time, deprived of their liberty, for example the disproportionate use of force by a policeman to control demonstrations or hinder a flight, is more likely to be categorised as

---

337 Burgers & Danelius 1988, pp. 118–119. Confirmed in Nowak & McArthur 2008, p. 69 (§ 97).

338 Burgers & Danelius 1988, pp. 118–119.

339 ComAT, *V.L.* v. *Switzerland*, 20 November 2006, no. 262/2005, § 8.10.

340 Burgers & Danelius 1988, p.119; Chetail 2006, p. 83; Wouters 2009, p. 445. See also Rosati 1998, p. 543, stating that almost any reason for intentional harm would fall within the terms 'intimidation' and 'coercion.'

341 See also Chetail 2006, p. 83. The indication in the case ComAT, *V.L.* v. *Switzerland*, 20 November 2006, no. 262/2005, § 8.10 just cited in this section is very exceptional.

342 Boulesbaa 1999, pp. 25 and 26; Ingelse 2001, p. 211; Nowak & McArthur 2008, p. 76 (§ 114).

343 ComAT, *V.L.* v. *Switzerland*, 20 November 2006, no. 262/2005, §. 8.10. See also ComAT, *F.B.* v. *Netherlands*, 20 November 2015, no. 613/2014, § 8.8.

344 Burgers & Danelius 1988, p. 120; Nowak & McArthur 2008, p. 75 and 76; Wouters 2009, p. 458.

inhuman treatment. It is nevertheless worth bearing in mind that inhuman treatment also often occurs in the context of the treatment of detained persons. The detention or factual control is therefore not an element that can always be used to distinguish torture from other inhuman treatment.

3.2.2   Distinction from Inhuman and Degrading Treatment

Article 16(1) CAT states that each contracting state has an obligation 'to prevent in any territory under its jurisdiction other acts of cruel, inhuman or degrading treatment or punishment which do not amount to torture as defined in article 1.' It is further specified in this provision that acts are only considered inhuman or degrading if they are conducted with either the direct or indirect involvement of a government official. However, while 'torture' is defined in Article 1 CAT, there is no definition of cruel, inhuman or degrading treatment or punishment in the CAT. As stated in the 1975 United Nations Declaration on the Protection of All Persons from Being Subjected to Torture or Other Cruel, Inhuman or Degrading Treatment or Punishment, which was the primary inspiration for the drafters of the CAT, torture constitutes an aggravated and deliberate form of cruel, inhuman or degrading treatment or punishment.[345] The notion of 'cruel' in Article 16 CAT, which cannot be found in Article 3 ECHR, does not have any special significance going beyond what may be considered inhuman treatment.[346]

According to Nowak and McArthur, the decisive criteria for the distinction between torture and inhuman treatment is the *purpose* of the conduct, the *intention* of the perpetrator and the *powerlessness* of the victim.[347] The *severity* of a harm inflicted is not the main criterion in their eyes, since they consider that inhuman treatment will usually also include severe pain or suffering.[348] They state that the infliction of pain or suffering that does not reach the threshold of severe might be considered *degrading treatment* if it contains a particularly humiliating element.[349] However, other scholars refer to the severity of an inflicted harm as the main character separating torture from inhuman

---

345   See Burger & Danelius 1988, pp. 1, 16 and 33 and Art.1(2) of this Declaration adopted by UN. General Assembly resolution 3452 (XXX) on 9 December 1975.

346   Nowak & McArthur 2008, p. 558 (§ 43 footnote 76). Interestingly, the Court appears to have another understanding of the term 'cruel.' It does use it when stigmatising an act as torture by speaking of a 'deliberate inhuman treatment causing very serious and cruel suffering'; see, for example, ECtHR, *El-Masri v. Former Yugoslav Republic of Macedonia*, 13 December 2012 [GC], no. 39630/09, § 197.

347   Nowak & McArthur 2008, p. 558 (§ 43).

348   Nowak 2005, pp. 678; Nowak & McArthur 2008, pp. 69 (§ 98), 74 (§ 110) and 77 (§ 115).

349   Nowak & McArthur 2008, p. 558 (§ 44).

treatment.[350] In fact, there are situations, where the purposive element like punishment, discrimination, intimidation or coercion lay behind an official's act on a powerless individual although these actions are not ultimately considered as torture but as inhuman treatment, simply because they were not severe enough.[351] In the end, the perception depends on the understanding of the notions of 'purpose' and 'severe pain or suffering.' Nowak and McArthur seem to follow a restrictive interpretation of the purposes listed in Article 1 CAT and a broader interpretation of severe pain or suffering.[352] Since neither of these notions can be defined exhaustively,[353] they *both* have to be treated as indications of torture.[354] In any case, the Committee itself acknowledges in General Comment on Article 2 CAT that, 'in practice, the definitional threshold between ill-treatment and torture is often not clear.'[355] This is particularly true in the refoulement context as will be discussed in the comparative section 4.2.1 of this chapter.

However, what is clear is that even harm of a severe nature will not be considered torture but rather inhuman treatment if it is not inflicted *intentionally*. An illustrative case for that is *Sonko v. Spain* concerning an African migrant who attempted to enter the autonomous City of Ceuta by swimming along the coast of Morocco.[356] He was intercepted by the Spanish Civil Guard and pulled up onto their vessel. Having been taken to the vicinity of Bastiones Beach, in Moroccan territorial waters, he was made to jump into the water, at a place where, according to the applicant's representative, he was out his depth. Subsequently, one of the Civil Guards jumped into the water to save the applicant from drowning. He took him to the shore and began to perform heart massage

---

350 Boulesbaa 1990, p. 307; Chetail 2006, p. 76; Wouters 2009, p. 440. See also Committee member Menéndez 2015, p. 69, noting in an academic article, 'the Committee's jurisprudence seems to be increasingly moving towards emphasising the element of "severe pain" while attaching less significance to the purpose in causing such pain.'

351 Whether a certain form of corporal punishment may amount to torture or inhuman treatment will always depend on the severity of the act since the purposive element will *per se* be given in this context; see on this, with regard to the death penalty under the CAT, Section 3.2.4 of this chapter.

352 See in this sense the authors themselves: Nowak & McArthur 2008, p. 69 (§ 97).

353 Burger & Danelius 1988, p. 122.

354 See as illustration the case ComAT, *Sahli v. Algeria*, 3 June 2011, no. 341/2008, § 9.3, in which both criteria are assessed. See also HRC, General Comment No. 20 on Art. 7 (1992), § 4, according to which the distinctions depend on the nature, purpose and severity of the treatment.

355 ComAT, General Comment No. 2 on Art. 2 CAT (2008), § 3.

356 ComAT, *Sonko v. Spain*, 25 November 2011, no. 368/2008.

on him but the applicant died shortly after. According to the government, the incident was an accident that occurred when the Spanish patrol assisted several persons who were swimming in the sea and took them very close to shore.[357] The Committee held that the applicant was placed in a situation that caused his death. As for the legal classification of the way he was treated, it considered that while 'the subjection of Mr. Sonko to physical and mental suffering prior to his death, aggravated by the particular vulnerability as a migrant, does not constitute a violation of Article 1 of the Convention, it does exceed the threshold of cruel, inhuman or degrading treatment or punishment, under the terms of Article 16 of the Convention.'[358]

Generally, the excessive use of force by law enforcement officials in the course of arrests or other offical acts such as the suppression of demonstrations are typical examples of inhuman treatment.[359] One complaint in which the Committee found that Article 16 CAT had been violated concerned the disproportionate use of force by Bulgarian police officials during an arrest.[360] Two cases concerned the destruction of Romany houses with the acquiescence of the local police, in one case accompanied by physical violence and racial discrimination.[361]

Deplorable prison conditions are typically dealt with under Article 16 CAT.[362] This might also be relevant in the context of the treatment of migrants. The case *A.A. v. Denmark* concerned the detention in wait of expulsion of an Iraqi who suffered from post-traumatic stress disorder.[363] The Committee assessed under Article 16 CAT whether the complainant's detention as well as his solitary confinement had amounted to inhuman treatment. It rejected the claim by reasoning that the overall duration of the complainant's detention was less than three months and that he had obtained adequate medical treatment.[364] With regard to the complainant's 'exclusion from association' during his detention, it noted that this measure did not exceed four days of length

357   *Ibid.*, § 6.4.

358   *Ibid.*, §§ 10.2 and 10.3.

359   See Nowak & McArthur 2008, pp. 557–569.

360   ComAT, *Keremedchiev v. Bulgaria*, 11 November 2008, no. 257/2004, §§ 2.2 and 9.3.

361   ComAT, *Dzemajl et al. v. Yugoslavia*, 21 November 2002, no. 161/2000, § 9.2; ComAT, *Osmani v. Serbia*, 8 May 2009, no. 261/2005, §§ 10.4 and 10.5.

362   See, for example, ComAT, *L.J.R. v. Australia*, 10 November 2008, no. 316/2007, §§ 2.5, 2.6, 2.10, 4.7–4.14 and 7.5. §§ 7.3–7.6; ComAT, *Ntikarahera v. Burundi*, 12 May 2014, no. 503/2012, § 6.6; ComAT, *Kirsanov v. Russia*, 14 May 2014, no. 478/2011, § 11.2.

363   ComAT, *A.A. v. Denmark*, 13 November 2012, no. 412/2010.

364   *Ibid.*, § 7.3.

and that during that period of time, he received visits from his girlfriend, his lawyer and two doctors.[365] The Committee considered that when determining whether solitary confinement amounts to a violation of Article 16 CAT it must take into account the particular conditions, the stringency of the measure, its duration, the objective pursued and its effect on the person concerned. Given the circumstances in the present case, in particular the complainant's violent behaviour, it concluded that the measure was proportionate to the legitimate objective of preventing violence.[366] Such proportionality tests are typically applied to assess in individual cases whether the infliction of pain or suffering amounts to inhuman treatment.[367]

Finally, it should be noted that even though the prohibition on refoulement does not refer to inhuman or degrading treatment according to Article 16 CAT, this provision might nevertheless be relevant in the context of forced deportations. The Committee has for instance indicated that in exceptional circumstances, the deportation of an applicant suffering from a severe illness might *as such* amount to inhuman treatment prohibited by Article 16 CAT. The Committee's practice on that matter will be discussed in section 3.2.5 of this chapter.

3.2.3   Lawful Sanction Clause

The last sentence of Article 1(1) CAT excludes from the definition of torture 'pain or suffering only arising from, inherent in or incidental to lawful sanctions.' The clause was already controversial during the drafting of Article 1 CAT.[368] It was introduced to make the CAT palatable for states that practice corporal punishment.[369]

According to Ingelse the Committee made clear that lawful sanctions 'are punishments that must be compatible with both national and international law.'[370] Other scholars are of the opinion that the Committee itself has never clarified whether by 'lawful sanctions' it refers to international standards or to the domestic law of a state party.[371] However, as many authors have pointed out, each possible interpretation of the clause seems to be in contradiction

---

365   *Ibid.*, § 7.4. The Committee further noted that he had a television in his cell.

366   *Ibid.*

367   Nowak & McArthur 2008, p. 558 (§ 43).

368   See Boulesbaa 1999, pp. 28–35; Nowak & McArthur 2008, pp. 44 et seq and 79 to 84.

369   Ingelse 2001, pp. 78–79 and 213, who refers in particular to states practicing corporal punishments based on sharia law; Nowak & McArthur 2008, p 49 (§ 55).

370   Ingelse 2001, pp. 216, 236 and 240.

371   Goodwin-Gill 2007, p. 303; Nowak & McArthur 2008, pp. 79–84.

either with the CAT itself or with general international law.[372] To allow certain acts of torture, if legalized, would undermine the object and purpose of the CAT, which is to prevent and punish torture and other inhuman punishment in the world under any circumstances.[373] If the lawful sanctions clause addresses acts that cannot be considered torture, Article 1 CAT does not apply anyway.[374] Nowak and McArthur therefore note that the systematic interpretation 'leads to the conclusion that the lawful sanctions clause has no scope of application and must simply be ignored.'[375] Their statement is confirmed by the practice of the Committee in individual complaints and state reporting procedures.[376] There is to date no individual complaint where the lawful sanctions clause would have been – at least explicitly – relevant. There is, however, still some uncertainty about whether the lawful sanction clause could have a certain influence on the Committee members when taking their decisions.[377] It is possible that the clause leads to a certain severity on the part of the Committee in cases in which it has to consider whether a legal punishment constitutes torture or not, in particular where the legal classification of such punishment is still contentious even between Western countries, as it is with regard to the death penalty.[378]

3.2.4   The Death Penalty

Article 3 CAT applies to all forms of treatment or punishment that must be considered torture in the sense of Article 1 CAT. The death penalty is in principal not considered a form of torture. The Committee has indicated this in *L.J.R. v. Australia* decided in 2008.[379] The complainant opposed his removal from

---

372   Boulesbaa 1999, p. 31; Burger & Danelius 1988, pp. 121 and 122; Ingelse 2001, pp. 211 to 217 and 240; Nowak & McArthur 2008, pp. 81 to 84; Wouters 2009, pp. 455 to 457.

373   It should further be noted that the prohibition of inhuman treatment in Art. 16 does not contain a lawful sanction clause.

374   According to Burger & Danelius 1988, p. 123, it was not the 'intention of those who drafted the Convention that the content of the concept of torture should vary from country to country.' See also ComAT, General Comment No. 2 on Art. 2 (2008), § 5, according to which the Committee rejects 'any religious or traditional justification that would violate' the absolute prohibition of torture.

375   Nowak & McArthur 2008, p. 84 (§ 128).

376   See on that Nowak & McArthur 2006, p. 318, stating that the Committee in its state reporting procedures has never seriously employed the clause.

377   See Chetail 2006, p. 80; Delas 2011, pp. 155–168; Goodwin-Gill & McAdam 2009, p. 303; McAdam 2007, p. 117.

378   *Ibid.* See on this also Section 4.2.2 and 4.2.3 of this chapter.

379   ComAT, *L.J.R. v. Australia*, 10 November 2008, no. 316/2007.

Australia to the United States, where he was charged with murder. He alleged, *inter alia*, that despite assurances given by the US authorities, there was a risk that he would be subjected to the death penalty in California. The Committee rejected this claim at the admissibility stage as incompatible with the provisions of the CAT. It argued that the allegations fell outside the scope of the CAT in the circumstances of the case.[380] When examining further allegations on the merits, the Committee noted, however, that 'the State party considered that the United States was bound by the assurances it provided to the effect that the author, if found guilty, would not be sentenced to the death penalty.'[381] This again indicates that the Committee is not indifferent when it comes to the death penalty. In its concluding observations on state reports, the Committee regularly invites state parties to consider abolishing the death penalty.[382] However, this is usually done under the heading of the prohibition of inhuman treatment in Article 16 CAT.[383]

However, depending on the circumstances of the enforcement, the Committee may classify a death penalty as torture, even if the sentence is the result of a legal procedure. This was the case in *A.S. v. Sweden* concerning the removal of woman to Iran who had been condemned to death by stoning for adultery.[384] According to Nowak and McArthur, to determine whether the imposition of the death penalty amounts to 'torture,' it is necessary to examine the act and its surrounding circumstances under the ordinary criteria set out under Article 1 CAT.[385] Since the elements of state responsibility and purpose (punishment) can normally be taken for granted in capital punishment cases, one needs to determine whether the act in question causes the degree of pain or suffering required for it to be considered torture.

3.2.5 Excursus: Forced Expulsion as Ill Treatment

Even though the prohibition of refoulement in Article 3 CAT only refers to torture in the sense of Article 1 CAT and not to Article 16 CAT, the Committee has showed in its practice that under certain circumstances, a forced removal can *per se* constitute an inhuman or degrading treatment and therefore breach

---

380   *Ibid.*, § 6.2. See also Sørensen 2001, p. 178, noting that Art. 3 CAT does not cover capital punishment.

381   ComAT, *L.J.R. v. Australia*, 10 November 2008, no. 316/2007, § 7.5.

382   See, for example, the concluding observations of the Committee on Japan's state report UN doc. CAT/C/JPN/CO/2, 28 June 2013, § 15.

383   *Ibid.* See also Ingelse 2001, pp. 279–284 and 288.

384   ComAT, *A.S. v. Sweden*, 24 November 2000, no. 149/1999.

385   Nowak & McArthur 2008, pp. 218–219 (§ 215).

Article 16 CAT. In his individual opinion on *T.M. v. Sweden*, Committee member Menéndez notes that an expulsion 'can obviously constitute cruel, inhuman or degrading treatment or punishment' which is prohibited by the CAT and customary international law.[386]

The excessive use of force in the execution of deportations may be problematic under Article 16 CAT.[387] In this context, the Committee has found a violation of Article 16 CAT in *Sonko v. Spain* (discussed in section 3.2.2 of this chapter), concerning a migrant who was made to jump into the water at the coast of Morocco by the Spanish Civil Guard at a place out his depth.[388] The Committee further found a violation of Article 16 CAT in *Barry v. Morocco* adopted in May 2014.[389] In this case, the Moroccan gendarmes abandoned the Senegalese complainant with approximately 40 other migrants in the border area separating Morocco and Mauritania without adequate equipment and with minimal supplies of food and water. They were forced to walk some 50 kilometres through a dangerous area containing also anti-personnel mines in order to reach the next village in Mauritania. The Committee considered that the circumstances of the expulsion constituted 'the infliction of severe physical and mental suffering on the complainant by public officials' that could be considered cruel, inhuman and degrading treatment as defined in Article 16 CAT.[390] In *F.K. v. Denmark*, the applicant claimed to have suffered acts of inhuman and degrading treatment while imprisoned and through an attempt of the Danish authorities to forcibly hand him over to the Turkish embassy in Copenhagen.[391] The exact circumstances of the incidents and the intensity of the force used were disputed by the parties. However, it was decisive for the Committee that despite the appearance that the complainant had been injured and despite his subsequent complaints, no investigation was initiated, which constituted a violation of Article 12 CAT in conjunction with Article 16 CAT.[392] Noteworthy is also that in the famous case *Agiza v. Sweden* concerning the deportation from Sweden to Egypt of an Egyptian suspected of terrorist activities in December 2001 with the involvement of US agents, the Committee noted that 'immediately preceding expulsion, the complainant was subjected on the State party's territory to treatment in breach of, at least, article 16 of the Convention by foreign agents but with the acquiescence of the State

---

386   See ComAT, *T.M. v. Sweden*, 18 November 2003, no. 228/2003.

387   See on this also Nowak & McArthur 2008, pp. 566–568.

388   ComAT, *Sonko v. Spain*, 25 November 2011, no. 368/2008.

389   ComAT, *Barry v. Morocco*, 19 May 2014, no. 372/2009.

390   *Ibid*, § 7.2.

391   ComAT, *F.K. v. Denmark*, 23 November 2015, no. 580/2014.

392   *Ibid.*, §§ 3.3 and 7.7.

party's police.'[393] The applicant had been taken to a US aircraft for deportation to Egypt, where US security personnel had taken charge, fettered the applicant and applied various coercive measures on him, including prolonged hooding.[394]

In the case *G.R.B. v. Sweden*, the Committee examined for the first time whether in view of a complainant's *state of health*, the forced expulsion itself could constitute inhuman treatment in violation of Article 16 CAT.[395] The complainant was suffering from severe post-traumatic stress disorder. The Committee rejected the claim, stating that the possible aggravation of the complainant's state of health caused by her deportation would not amount to the type of cruel, inhuman or degrading treatment envisaged by Article 16 CAT.[396] The Committee has rejected several further complaints concerning applicants suffering from severe post-traumatic stress disorder under Article 16 CAT, some even as a consequence of past torture.[397] In certain cases a risk of suicide in the event of expulsion was alleged.[398] The Committee has sometimes taken into account the fact that there was access to medical treatment in the receiving state when rejecting the claim under Article 16 CAT.[399] Of interest is the recent decision *E.L. v. Canada* concerning the deportation of a Haitian applicant who alleged, *inter alia*, that his pacemaker would need to be replaced but that there was no such service in Haiti.[400] With regard to the complainant's health the Committee noted on the merits that the situation did not fall within the scope of Article 1 CAT and cannot 'on its own fall under the scope of Article 16 CAT.'[401] The Committee observed, however, that the state party had looked into the availability in Haiti of treatment appropriate for the

---

393 ComAT, *Agiza v. Sweden*, 20 May 2005, no. 233/2003, § 13.1. On this famous case in which the Committee concluded that Sweden had violated Art. 3 and 22 CAT, see in particular Chapter 4 Sections 2.2 and 3.4.2.b.

394 *Ibid.*, §§ 12.29–12.31.

395 See ComAT, *G.R.B. v. Sweden*, 15 May 1998, no. 83/1997, § 6.7.

396 *Ibid.*

397 For example, ComAT, *B.S.S. v. Canada*, 12 May 2004, no. 183/2001, § 3.1, 5.8 and 10.2; ComAT, *A.A.C. v. Sweden*, 16 November 2006, no. 227/2003, § 7.3; ComAT, *M.F. v. Sweden*, 14 November 2008, no. 326/2007, § 6.4; ComAT, *N.B.-M. v. Switzerland*, 14 November 2011, no. 347/2008, § 9.8.

398 See ComAT, *T.M. v. Sweden*, 18 November 2003, no. 228/2003, §§ 2.6, 2.8, 3.2 and 6.2; ComAT, *David v. Sweden*, 5 May 2005, no. 220/2002, §§ 3.3, 5.1 and 7.2.

399 See ComAT, *T.M. v. Sweden*, 18 November 2003, no. 228/2003, § 6.2; ComAT, *M.F. v. Sweden*, 14 November 2008, no. 326/2007, § 6.4; ComAT, *N.B.-M. v. Switzerland*, 14 November 2011, no. 347/2008, § 9.8.

400 ComAT, *E.L. v. Canada*, 21 May 2012, no. 370/2009.

401 *Ibid.*, § 8.6.

applicant and carried out necessary checks before proceeding with his remov-al.[402] Up to now, the Committee has yet to find a violation of Article 16 CAT be-cause of an expulsion or extradition itself and a complainant's state of health. It has stated that 'only in very exceptional circumstances may a removal per se constitute cruel, inhuman or degrading treatment.'[403] In most decisions, it has argued that the aggravation of the condition of an individual's physical or men-tal health by virtue of a deportation is generally insufficient, in the absence of additional factors, to amount to degrading treatment in violation of Article 16 CAT.[404] However, the Committee has never indicated what could be meant by 'additional factors' or 'very exceptional circumstances.' Thurin has rightly observed that in requiring 'additional factors' the Committee can give the im-pression that there is a particularly high standard for a violation of Article 16 CAT in situations concerning forced deportations.[405] However, there would be no basis in the prohibition of inhuman treatment for such an approach. As will be addressed in the comparative section 4.2.4 of this chapter, the Commit-tee's method is probably influenced by the Court's practice in the refoulement context. A clarification of the matter by the Committee would be desirable.[406]

3.3   *The Source of the Harm: Protection against Private Actors*

According to Article 1 CAT, severe pain or suffering can be considered torture if it is 'inflicted by or at the instigation of or with the consent or acquiescence of a public official or other person acting in an official capacity.' The term 'instigation' means incitement, inducement, solicitation, encouragement or support.[407] The terms 'consent or acquiescence' cover a wide range of actions committed by private persons of which the state is aware but does not stop or prevent.[408] The Committee has recently made clear, for example, that States

---

402   *Ibid.*

403   ComAT, *M.M.K. v. Sweden*, 3 May 2005, no. 221/2002, § 7.3.

404   ComAT, *S.S.S. v. Canada*, 16 November 2005, no. 245/2004, § 7.3; ComAT, *A.A.C. v. Sweden*, 16 November 2006, no. 227/2003, § 7.3; ComAT, *Sogi v. Canada*, 16 November 2007, no. 297/2006, § 9.3; ComAT, *M.F. v. Sweden*, 14 November 2008, no. 326/2007, § 6.4; ComAT, *Y.G.H. et al v. Australia*, 14 November 2013, no. 434/2010, § 7.4.

405   Thurin 2012, p. 152.

406   See also Chetail 2006, p. 80; Wouters 2009, p. 524.

407   Boulesbaa 1999, p. 26; Nowak & McArthur 2008, p. 78 (§ 117); Wouters 2009, p. 446.

408   Nowak & McArthur 2008, p. 78 (§ 118); Wouters 2009, p. 448 and 449. See also ComAT, *Dzemajl et al. v. Yugoslavia*, 21 November 2002, no. 161/2000, § 9.2; ComAT, *Osmani v. Ser-bia*, 8 May 2009, no. 261/2005, §§ 10.4 and 10.5 concerning the destruction of Romany houses by private actors with the acquiescence of the local police. The Committee found

have a special obligation under Article 1 CAT to prevent inmates in prisons from inflicting acts of torture on other inmates (and to prosecute such acts if they occur).[409] It derives this 'special responsibility' for acts of non-officials owing to the extent of the control that prison authorities exercise over their inmates.[410]

Hence, for an act to constitute torture in the sense of Article 1 CAT, there has to be, in principal, some form of active or passive involvement of the state.[411] Consequently, the Committee has held in several non-refoulement complaints that the issue of whether a state party has an obligation to refrain from expelling a person who might risk pain or suffering inflicted by a private person, without the consent or acquiescence of the state, falls outside the scope of Article 3 CAT.[412] In *G.R.B. v. Sweden*, the Committee considered that allegations of a risk of torture at the hands of the Shining Path (*Sendero Luminoso*), a non-state entity controlling significant portions of Peru at the time, fell outside the scope of Article 3 CAT.[413] Other examples of complaints rejected for the same reason concerned alleged risks of torture emanating from the Kurdistan Workers' Party (PKK) in Turkey[414] and the Liberation Tigers of Tamil Eelam (LTTE) in Sri Lanka.[415]

However, according to Nowak and McArthur, the term 'other person acting in an official capacity' goes beyond state officials and might include rebel, guerrilla or other groups who exercise *de facto* authority in certain regions.[416] In the case *S.S. v. Netherlands*, the Committee noted that a state party's

---

a violation of Art. 16 CAT, which contains the same requirement regarding the involvement of a public official as Art. 1 CAT.

409   ComAT, *Colmenarez and Sanchez v. Venezuela*, 15 May 2015, no. 456/2011, §§ 6.4, 6.6 and 7.

410   *Ibid.*, § 6.4.

411   Chetail 2006, p. 81.

412   ComAT, *G.R.B. v. Sweden*, 15 May 1998, no. 83/1997, § 6.5; ComAT, *V.X.N. and H.N. v. Sweden*, 15 May 2000, no. 130/1999 and 131/1999, § 13.8; ComAT, *S.V. et al. v. Canada*, 15 May 2001, no. 49/1996, § 9.5; ComAT, *M.P.S. v. Australia*, 30 April 2002, no. 138/1999, § 7.4; ComAT, *S.S. v. Netherlands*, 5 May 2003, no. 191/2001, § 6.4; ComAT, *Chorlango v. Sweden*, 22 November 2004, no. 218/2002, § 5.2; ComAT, *M.F. v. Sweden*, 14 November 2008, no. 326/2007, § 7.5; ComAT, *Güclü v. Sweden*, 11 November 2010, no. 349/2008, § 5.2; ComAT, *Aytulun and Güclü v. Sweden*, 19 November 2010, no. 373/2009, § 6.2. See also ComAT, General Comment No. 1 on Art. 3 CAT (1997), § 8.

413   ComAT, *G.R.B. v. Sweden*, 15 May 1998, no. 83/1997, § 6.5.

414   ComAT, *Aytulun and Güclü v. Sweden*, 19 November 2010, no. 373/2009, § 6.2.

415   ComAT, *S.V. et al. v. Canada*, 15 May 2001, no. 49/1996, § 9.5; ComAT, *M.P.S. v. Australia*, 30 April 2002, no. 138/1999, § 7.4.

416   Nowak & McArthur 2008, p. 78 and 79 (§ 118).

obligation to refrain from expelling a person who might risk pain or suffering inflicted by a non-governmental entity without the consent or acquiescence of the state fell outside the scope of Article 3 of the Convention, '*unless the non-governmental entity occupies and exercises quasi-governmental authority* over the territory to which the complainant would be returned' (emphasis added).[417] In this decision adopted in 2003, the Committee indicated that the LTTE could be regarded as a quasi-governmental authority, but it stated at the same time that, as long as it is possible to remove an individual to a part of a country that is not under control of the quasi-governmental authority in question, the protection of Article 3 CAT does not take effect.[418] The Committee will therefore in principle accept a risk emanating from a quasi-governmental authority as constituting a relevant risk under Article 3 CAT if there is no possibility of residing outside the realm of influence of such authority within the country of return.[419]

The only case in which the Committee has explicitly accepted the existence of a quasi-governmental authority from which the complainant could not escape is the case *Elmi v. Australia*, concerning a removal to Somalia in 1999.[420] The complainant alleged persecution by the powerful Hawiye clan. The Committee stated that 'for a number of years Somalia has been without a central government.' It noted that Mogadishu, where he was likely to reside, was 'under the effective control of the Hawiye clan, which has established quasi-governmental institutions and provides a number of public services.'[421] Since these quasi-governmental factions in Somalia would exercise certain *de facto* powers comparable to those normally exercised by legitimate governments, they could, in the Committee's view, be considered the equivalent of official authorities in the sense of Article 1 CAT.[422] Considering the complainant had established that due to his personal background as a member of a vulnerable, small and unarmed minority clan, there was a real risk of his being tortured by members of the Hawiye clan, the Committee held that his removal to Somalia would constitute a violation of Article 3 CAT.[423] However, in another case three years later, the Committee found that 'Somalia currently possesses a State

---

417   ComAT, *S.S. v. Netherlands*, 5 May 2003, no. 191/2001, § 6.4. See also ComAT, *Chorlango v. Sweden*, 22 November 2004, no. 218/2002, § 5.2.

418   ComAT, *S.S. v. Netherlands*, 5 May 2003, no. 191/2001, § 6.4.

419   See also Wouters 2009, p. 454.

420   ComAT, *Elmi v. Australia*, 14 May 1999, no. 120/1998.

421   *Ibid.*, § 6.7.

422   *Ibid.*, § 6.5.

423   *Ibid.*, §§ 6.6–7.

authority in the form of the Transitional National Government, which has relations with the international community in its capacity as central Government, though some doubts may exist as to the reach of its territorial authority and its permanence.'[424] Consequently, the Committee considered that the case did not fall 'within the exceptional situation in *Elmi*' and took the view that a risk emanating from the Hawiye clan fell outside of the scope of Article 3 CAT.[425]

In May 2010 in the case *Njamba and Balikosa v. Sweden*, the Committee found a violation of Article 3 CAT because of a risk emanating mainly from private actors without even mentioning governmental or quasi-governmental authorities.[426] The complainants in this case were a Congolese woman and her daughter. They alleged that if returned to the DRC, the mother would be tortured or killed in retaliation for her husband's former political activities by security services or other families. They further stated that the security situation in the DRC was so precarious as to make governmental protection of human rights impossible.[427] In its consideration of the merits, the Committee found that while some factual issues of the case were disputed, including the claims relating to the complainant's husband's political activities, the most relevant issue raised in the communication was the risk of danger to the complainants' security upon return.[428] The Committee cited reports by UN experts and the UNHCHR referring to alarming levels of violence against women across the whole country 'by men with guns and civilians.' It further referred to its General Comment no. 2 on Article 2 CAT, according to which the failure 'to exercise due diligence to intervene to stop, sanction and provide remedies to victims of torture facilitates and enables non-state actors to commit acts impermissible under the Convention with impunity ... .'[429] Considering the conflict situation

---

424 ComAT, *H.M.H.I. v. Australia*, 1 May 2002, no. 177/2001, § 6.4.

425 Nevertheless, the Committee did take note of the fact that the state party did not intend to return the complainant to Mogadishu, and that he would be at liberty to avail himself of the UNHCR voluntary repatriation programme and choose the area of Somalia to which he would like to return; *ibid*, § 6.6. See further ComAT, *Y.H.A. v. Australia*, 23 November 2001, no. 162/2000, §§ 7.3 and 7.4, in which the Committee rejected another complaint similar to that of *Elmi*. In this case, the Committee did not address the issue of the source of the harm in its considerations on the merits. It rejected the complaint indicating that since the complainant's Shikal clan was included in the new transitional government, he could not be considered as still being personally at risk.

426 ComAT, *Njamba and Balikosa* v. Sweden, 14 May 2010, no. 322/2007.

427 *Ibid.*, § 3.1.

428 *Ibid.*, § 9.5.

429 *Ibid.*

in the DRC as attested in the UN reports, the Committee held that it could not 'identify particular areas of the country which could be considered safe for the complainants in their current and evolving situation.'[430] The Committee concluded that 'on a balance of all of the factors in this particular case' substantial grounds existed for believing that the complainants were in danger of being subjected to torture if returned.[431]

The decision shows that the Committee accepts risks of severe pain or suffering emanating from private actors as falling under the scope of Article 3 CAT, if the receiving state does not provide protection. The term 'acquiescence' in Article 1 CAT can serve as a basis for such an approach.[432] As Ingelse notes, if a 'legal system does not prosecute private individuals who commit torture, this can be seen as acquiescence by the government.'[433] In paragraph 18 of its General Comment on Article 2 CAT adopted in 2008 (and to which it refers in *Njamba and Balikosa*), the Committee stated:

> ... where State authorities or others acting in official capacity or under colour of law, know or have reasonable grounds to believe that acts of torture or ill-treatment are being committed by non-State officials or private actors and they fail to exercise due diligence to prevent, investigate, prosecute and punish such non-State officials or private actors consistently with the Convention, the *State bears responsibility and its officials should be considered as authors, complicit or otherwise responsible under the Convention for consenting to or acquiescing in such impermissible acts.* Since the failure of the State to exercise due diligence to intervene to stop, sanction and provide remedies to victims of torture facilitates and enables non-State actors to commit acts impermissible under the Convention with impunity, the State's indifference or inaction provides a form of encouragement and/or de facto permission. The Committee has applied this principle to States parties' failure to prevent and protect victims from

---

430   *Ibid.*

431   *Ibid.*, § 9.6. In the case ComAT, *Bakatu-Bia v. Sweden*, 3 June 2011, no. 379/2009, §§ 3, 5.1, 5.5 and 10.5–11, the Committee also found a violation of Art. 3 CAT because of the expulsion of a single woman to the DRC. The considerations on the merits in both cases are similar with the exception that the Committee does not explicitly refer to its General Comment no. 2 in *Bakatu-Bia* and further notes that the complainant's account of events (political activity, past detention and torture) is consistent with the Committee's knowledge of the present human rights situation in the DRC. However, the main source of the harm alleged by the complainant in this case was of a public nature.

432   Ingelse 2001, p. 225; McAdam 2007, p. 116; Weissbrodt & Hörtreiter 1999, pp. 52 and 70; Wouters 2009, p. 454.

433   Ingelse 2001, p. 225.

gender-based violence, such as rape, domestic violence, female genital mutilation, and trafficking.[434] (Emphasis added)

This comment on Article 2 CAT has had a more general impact on the Committee's practice under Article 3 CAT, which can also be observed in the decision *A.A.M. v. Sweden* adopted in May 2012.[435] The case concerned a Burundian woman who alleged, *inter alia*, that she would be tortured and killed if returned to her country of origin by Hutu militias, because her brother had been a well-known member of the Tutsi militia. The Committee noted that 'the issue of whether a State party has an obligation to refrain from expelling a person who might risk torture or ill-treatment inflicted by a non-governmental entity falls within the scope of Article 3 of the Convention in cases in which there is consent or acquiescence by the State authorities in the country of return to such conduct.'[436] In a footnote, it then referred to its 'jurisprudence' as reflected in its General Comment on Article 2 CAT, according to which 'State parties bear responsibility for acts of torture or ill-treatment committed by private actors on the basis of having consented or acquiesced to such torture where the authorities know or have a reasonable ground to believe that such acts are being committed and fail to exercise due diligence to prevent, investigate, prosecute and punish the perpetrators.'[437] The Committee then added that 'while the complainant alleges that she initially fled Burundi because of her fear of harm by Hutu militias, she has not provided any evidence to support a claim that she would face a risk of harm by such militias if returned at the present time.'[438]

The decisions *Njamba and Balikosa* and *A.A.M.* confirm the views of scholars who have called for or already recognized a broadening by the Committee of its protection from acts of torture perpetrated by private actors, where the state is not able or willing to protect against such acts.[439] This understanding is further confirmed by the decision *K.H. v. Denmark* adopted in November 2012

---

434 General Comment No. 2 on Art. 2 (2008), § 18. See further § 25, according to which states have the obligation to take measures to prevent torture inflicted privately.

435 ComAT, *A.A.M. v. Sweden*, 23 May 2012, no. 413/2010.

436 *Ibid.*, § 9.2.

437 *Ibid.*, fn. 16 to the decision.

438 *Ibid.*, § 9.2.

439 As such see Chetail 2006, pp. 82 and 83; Ingelse 2001, pp. 239–240; Miller 2003, p. 323; Weissbrodt and Hörtreiter 1999, pp. 52, 64 and 70; Wouters 2009, p. 454. See also ComAT, *C.A.R.M. et al. v. Canada*, 18 May 2007, no. 298/2006, § 8.9, in which the Committee rejected the refoulement complaint, *inter alia*, because the complainant had never sought protection from the authorities against the drug traffickers who allegedly persecuted him. See also de Weck 2011, p. 8.

concerning the deportation of an Afghan applicant.[440] The Committee noted that the complainant 'had failed to provide sufficient evidence in support of his claims to the effect that he would be exposed to a real and personal risk of torture by the Taliban if returned to Afghanistan.'[441] However, in November 2010, the Committee was still rejecting complaints concerning risks from private actors at the admissibility stage, arguing simply that pain or suffering inflicted by non-governmental actors without the consent or acquiescence of the government fell outside the scope of Article 3 CAT.[442]

In November 2013, the Committee made a stronger statement in *Dewage v. Australia*.[443] The case concerned a Sri Lankan national of Sinhalese ethnic origin who claimed to be threatened with torture by the authorities because of his past involvement as a profiled trade unionist and political opponent to the government in Sri Lankan. He further alleged to be threatened by the LTTE. With regard to the claimed risk emanating from the LTTE, the Committee recalled 'that it has, in its jurisprudence and in general comment No.2, addressed risk of torture by non-State actors and failure on the part of a State party to exercise due diligence to intervene and stop the abuses that were impermissible under the Convention.'[444] The Committee further confirmed the application of Article 3 CAT in that context in *R.S. et al. v. Switzerland* decided in November 2014.[445] Here the complainants claimed to be threatened by members of another family in Kosovo. The Committee rejected the application by stating that the complainant's reference to the inefficacy of the police and judicial system in Kosovo was of too general a nature and without direct bearing on the case. Hence, it concluded 'that the complainants have not sufficiently substantiated their allegations concerning the failure of the State to protect them from the attacks to which they were subjected.'[446] The Committee did not even mention the Swiss government's objection, according to which the claim fell outside the scope of Article 3 CAT.[447] It reasoned similarly recently in the case

---

440   ComAT, *K.H. v. Denmark*, 23 November 2012, no. 464/2011.

441   *Ibid.*, § 8.7.

442   ComAT, *Güclü v. Sweden*, 11 November 2010, no. 349/2008, § 5.2; ComAT, *Aytulun and Güclü v. Sweden*, 19 November 2010, no. 373/2009, § 6.2.

443   ComAT, *Dewage v. Australia*, 14 November 2013, no. 387/2009.

444   *Ibid.*, § 10.9. The Committe referred to the cases *Njamba and Balikosa* and *Bakatu-Bia*. However, it finally based its conclusion according to which the complainant's removal would violate Article 3 CAT mainly on the danger emanating from governmental powers; *ibid.*, §§ 8.1–8.2. Interestingly, the state party Australia, in its submission, recognizes that, in light of General Comment No. 2, threats from private actors are relevant under Art. 3 CAT.

445   ComAT, *R.S. et al. v. Switzerland*, 21 November 2014, no. 482/2011.

446   *Ibid.*, § 8.4.

447   See *ibid.*, § 4.4.

F.B. v. Netherlands concerning the removal of a victim of female genital mutilation (FGM) who had undertaken a reconstructive plastic surgery and who
claimed to be forced to undergo the genital mutilation again if returned to
Guinea.[448] The Committee observed that 'due to the ineffectiveness of the relevant laws, including impunity of the perpetrators, victims of FMG in Guinea
do not have access to an effective remedy and to appropriate protection by
the authorities.'[449] It then considered that the national asylum authorities
had failed to give due consideration to the complainant's past experience, her
condition as a single woman, the capacity of the authorities in Guinea to provide her with protection, and the severe anxiety that her return to Guinea may
cause her within this context.[450] Accordingly, it concluded that, in the particular circumstances of this case, the complainant was in danger of treatment
contrary to Article 1 CAT such that her removal to Guinea would constitute a
breach of Article 3 CAT.[451]

However, as the case law so far shows, it is rather difficult for complainants
in practice to demonstrate a sufficient risk in cases in which the risks emanates
from non-state actors. This can also be observed in the recent decision *M.S. v.
Denmark* adopted in August 2015.[452] The case concerned an Afghan men from
Kandahar, who had probably been ill-treated by the Taliban in the past and
feared reprisals from them in case of return. The Committee rejected the complaint noting, *inter alia*, that the complainant had not adduced evidence that
the Afghan authorities or the Taliban had been looking for him in the recent
past. It further observed that 'no material on the file permits to establish that
the complainant has been subjected to torture by State authorities or that the
complainant will be unable to obtain the protection of the Afghan authorities against the risk of torture, over six years after the alleged abuse and torture
occurred.'[453] According to the Committee, the complainant had not discharged
his burden of proof.[454] Taking into account the generally rather sensible practice with regard to victims of torture[455] and the terrible human rights situation
in Afghanistan, the burden of proof seems set particularly high in this case.

Looking at the Committee's refoulement practice so far, there are, at the
time of writing, two situations in which the Committee has accepted that a

---

448   ComAT, *F.B. v. Netherlands*, 20 November 2015, no. 613/2014.

449   *Ibid.*, § 8.8.

450   The statement on the relevance of the complainant's anxiety is unusual in the Committe's
       pratice under Art. 3 CAT.

451   *Ibid.*

452   ComAT, *M.S. v. Denmark*, 10 August 2015, no. 571/2013.

453   *Ibid.*, §§ 7.7 and 7.8.

454   *Ibid.*, § 7.9.

455   See Chapter 5 Section 3.3.2.b.

risk of being subjected to torture by private actors is sufficient to prevent a removal:

(1)   In the case *Elmi*, where the risk of torture emanated from quasi-governmental entities and where there was no central government.[456] As a possible alternative scenario in this context, attention is drawn to the case *S.S. v. Netherlands*, in which the Committee noted that risks from non-governmental entities could be relevant under Article 3 CAT if such entities occupied and exercised quasi-governmental authority over the territory to which the complainant would be returned. However, if a central government exists, then its own internal protection is usually considered adequate.[457]

(2)   The other situation is that in *Njamba and Balikosa*, where the risk of torture did not emanate from quasi-governmental entities but private actors, but where the Committee considered that the *government failed to provide adequate protection against severe acts of violence*. In this case, the applicants were women and gender-based violence was, in particular in *Njamba and Balikosa*, part of their claims. It seems that when complainants belong to particularly vulnerable groups, like unmarried women, the Committee is less severe with the requirement of state responsibility.[458]

Generally, in recent years, and in particular since the adoption of its General Comment on Article 2 CAT in 2008, the Committee has become more accepting of the fact that state parties bear the responsibility for acts of torture committed by private actors where the authorities know of these acts but fail to act on them. However, it would be helpful if the Committee *could make a clear declaration and provide explanation when it develops a new practice on such an essential point*. As will be discussed in section 4.3.1 of this chapter, the developments in international law allow the Committee, perhaps even require it, to interpret the terms 'consent or acquiescence of a public official' in Article 1 CAT as including acts by private actors as acts of torture if the state is not willing or able to offer protection from such acts.

---

456   This is also referred to as the *failed state* concept; Nowak & McArthur 2008, p. 201 (§ 185).

457   See in this sense also Wouters 2009, p. 453.

458   This is also intended by paragraph 18 of the Committee's General Comment No. 2 on Art. 2 CAT. In the context of combatting violence against women, Manfred Nowak, in his mandate as a special rapporteur on torture and inhuman treatment, has stated that the concept of 'acquiescence' entails protection obligations and a duty for the state to prevent acts of torture in the private sphere; UN Doc. A/HRC/7/3, 15 January 2008, §§ 68, 70 and 71.

3.4   *Absolute Character of the Prohibition*

The absolute nature of the prohibition of torture is explicitly mentioned in Article 2(2) CAT, which states:

> No exceptional circumstances whatsoever, whether a state of war or a threat of war, internal political instability or any other public emergency, may be invoked as a justification of torture.

The absolute character of the prohibition of torture implies that there can never be a justification for torture, not even in the most exceptional circumstances such as war or terrorist threats.[459] It also implies that no one is excluded from the protection against torture, even criminals and individuals considered a threat to the public.

In the context of refoulement, the absolute prohibition of torture is equally valuable. This means that no exception is allowed for the prohibition on refoulement where there is a risk of torture, no matter the circumstances the state parties face and no matter the background of the person facing expulsion. The Committee has made clear in several decisions that neither criminals nor persons considered a threat to national security can be excluded from the application of Article 3 CAT.[460] It has held that the nature of the activities in which a person is engaged with respect to concerns of domestic state security are not relevant to decisions taken under Article 3 CAT.[461]

This is in marked contrast to the 1951 Geneva Convention, which excludes from its protection certain criminals and people representing a threat to a nation.[462] In the decision on *Abdussamatov and 28 Others* concerning the extradition of 29 individuals who had all been charged with religious extremism in Uzbekistan, the Committee observed that the non-refoulement principle in Article 3 CAT is absolute 'even if after an evaluation under the 1951 Convention relating to the Status of Refugees, a refugee is excluded under article 1 F (c),' which excludes persons guilty of acts contrary to the purposes and principles of the UN.[463] It recalled that 'the fight against terrorism does not absolve the State party from honouring its obligation to refrain from expelling or returning

---

459   ComAT, General Comment No. 2 on Art. 2 (2008), §§ 5 and 7.

460   See, among others, ComAT, *Agiza v. Sweden*, 20 May 2005, 233/2003, § 13.8; ComAT, *Dadar v. Canada*, 23 November 2005, no. 258/2004, § 8.8; ComAT, *Tebourski v. France*, 1 May 2007, no. 300/2006, §§ 8.2 and 8.3; ComAT, *Sogi v. Canada*, 16 November 2007, no. 297/300, §§ 10.2 and 10.4; ComAT, *Abdussamatov and 28 Others v. Kazakhstan*, 1 June 2012, no. 444/2010, § 13.7; ComAT, *Abichou v. Germany*, 21 May 2013, no. 430/2010, § 11.5.

461   ComAT, *Paez v. Sweden*, 28 April 1997, no. 39/1996, § 14.5.

462   See on that Chapter 1 Section 4.

463   ComAT, *Abdussamatov and 28 Others v. Kazakhstan*, 1 June 2012, no. 444/2010, § 13.7.

an individual to another State, where there are substantial grounds for believing that he would be in danger of being subjected to torture.'[464] The Committee has acknowledged that measures taken to fight terrorism, including denial of a safe haven, are both legitimate and important, but that their execution must be carried out with full respect to the CAT.[465] There is no room for balancing a risk of refoulement against the fact that the complainant might be a threat to security in the host state.[466]

4   Comparison

4.1   *Introduction*
This section compares the scope of Article 3 ECHR with that of Article 3 CAT with a focus on what is relevant in the context of refoulement. It explains the practical implications of the fact that the protection against refoulement under Article 3 CAT refers to a risk of *torture* in the sense of Article 1 CAT, while the prohibition on refoulement contained in Article 3 ECHR includes a protection against a risk of torture *and* inhuman or degrading treatment or punishment.

4.2   *The Nature of the Harm*
4.2.1   Torture v. Inhuman Treatment in the Context of Refoulement
The main elements of the definition of torture under the ECHR and CAT are similar: for both the Court and the Committee, an act of torture has (1) a certain level of severity, which is higher than that of other forms of ill treatment. Under both instruments, (2) torture must be intentionally inflicted and is usually committed (3) for a specific purpose, such as obtaining information or inflicting

---

464   *Ibid.* Confirmed in ComAT, *Nasirov v. Kazakhstan*, 14 May 2014, no. 475/2011, § 11.6. See also
        ComAT, *Paez v. Sweden*, 28 April 1997, no. 39/1996, concerning an applicant who had been
        active for Shining Path, and was therefore excluded from refugee status according to Art.
        1 F of the 1951 Refugee Convention.

465   ComAT, *Agiza v. Sweden*, 20 May 2005, 233/2003, § 13.1.

466   See, for example, ComAT, *T.P.S. v. Canada*, 16 May 2000, no. 99/1997, §§ 8.3, 8.5 and 15.3,
        in which the state had argued that 'the examination of possible irreparable harm should
        be a rigorous one, particularly when the individual concerned was found to represent a
        threat.' See also ComAT, *Abichou v. Germany*, 21 May 2013, no. 430/2010, § 11.4, in which
        the Committee noted that 'by arriving at a determination of the existence of foreseeable,
        real and personal risk of torture, the Committee expresses no opinion as to the veracity or
        gravity of the criminal charges' against him at the time of his extradition.'

punishment or intimidating. In short, torture constitutes an *aggravated and deliberate* form of cruel, inhuman or degrading treatment or punishment.[467]

While the distinction between torture and other inhuman treatment is not relevant for a complainant seeking protection from the Court in Strasbourg (as long as the harm falls under the scope of Article 3 ECHR), it may be for a complainant before the Committee in Geneva, where the protection against refoulement refers to acts of torture. When the Committee finds a violation of Article 3 CAT, one has to assume that a complainant expects he will be subjected to an act of torture in the receiving country. This is not the case for refoulement judgments before the Court, in which it is usually unspecified whether the complainant fears acts of torture or other inhuman treatment.

However, in cases before both institutions, information about the expected harm is more often implied by the judgments and decisions rather than being a factor in the decision-making in the judgments themselves. There are only a few refoulement cases in which one can see that the Committee has failed to examine a claim further because of the restriction of its protection to the risk of torture.[468] Ingelse criticizes the distinction between torture and inhuman treatment and the limited application of the principle of non-refoulement of the CAT as a setback, but rightly states that the Committee often ignores the distinction.[469]

As the Committee has itself declared in its General Comment on Article 2 CAT released in 2008, 'experience demonstrates that the conditions that give rise to ill-treatment frequently facilitate torture.'[470] It is further stated in that Comment that the obligations under the CAT to prevent torture and inhuman treatment are 'indivisible, interdependent and interrelated' and that 'in practice' the obligation to prevent inhuman treatment 'overlaps with and is largely congruent with the obligation to prevent torture.'[471] With that, the Committee comes closer to the Human Rights Committee, according to which it is not

---

467   These according to the terms already used in EComHR, *Denmark, Norway, Sweden and Netherlands v. Greek* (the Greek case), report of 5 November 1969, Yearbook 12 (1969), p. 186 referring to Art. 1 of the 1975 United Nations Declaration on the Protection of All Persons from Being Subjected to Torture or Other Cruel, Inhuman or Degrading Treatment or Punishment.

468   As exceptions see ComAT, *Y. v. Switzerland*, 21 May 2013, no. 431/2010, § 7.7 and ComAT, *L.J.R. v. Australia*, 10 November 2008, no. 316/2007. See further Chapter 2 Section 3.2.5, in which it is observed that the admissibility criterion *rationae materia* has not been of particular relevance in the Committee's practice under Art. 3 CAT.

469   Ingelse 2001, pp. 84, 239 and 315.

470   ComAT, General Comment No. 2 on Art. 2 (2008), § 3.

471   *Ibid.*, § 3.

necessary to 'establish sharp distinctions' between torture and other inhuman or degrading treatment.[472] This lack of necessity can for instance be observed in *J.K. v. Canada* adopted in November 2015 concerning the removal of a homosexual LGTB activist, in which the Committee concluded that the complainant would be in 'danger of torture or ill-treatment if returned to Uganda.'[473] Committee member Menendez also confirms in an academic article published in 2015 that in practice, the distinction between torture and inhuman treatment loses relevance.[474]

Generally, the judgments and decisions in refoulement cases of *both bodies pay scant attention to the exact nature of the harm expected in the receiving country,* as long as the harm could *prima facie* fall into the range of acts categorised as torture or inhuman treatment.[475] This is related to the ambiguity of the notions of torture and inhuman treatment, and any distinction between them, particularly in cases in which the risk of ill treatment in the receiving state would be inflicted *intentionally*.[476] Both the Committee and the Court admit that there is no clear line between torture and other inhuman treatment. In addition, the Court has expressed that the distinction between torture and other

---

472   See HRC, General Comment No. 20 on Art. 7 (1992), § 4. With regard to non-refoulement, see also Art. 24 of the Draft Articles on the Expulsion of Aliens by the International Law Commission (ILC), which is inspired by Art. 3 CAT but, following regional and universal developments in international human rights law, includes inhuman or degrading treatment or punishment; see the draft with commentary (UN 2014) at: <http://legal.un.org/docs/?path=../ilc/texts/instruments/english/draft> [16.2.2016].

473   ComAT, *J.K. v. Canada*, 23 November 2015, no. 562/2013, § 10.6. However, normally, the Committee still concludes its decisions by referring to a risk/danger of 'torture.'

474   See Menéndez 2015, p. 68 and 67. He refers to the Committee's practice of accepting inhuman treatment implicitly as a relevant risk and to General Comment No. 2 on Art. 2 CAT, which, as he writes, has perhaps been influenced by the case law of the Court. He further refers to the non-derogable character of Art. 16 CAT as addressed in § 3 of General Comment No. 2, and states that the Committee's jurisprudence has 'yet to clarify' in which manner treatment falling short of torture may trigger a state's obligation to guarantee the principle of non-refoulement. However, so far, Art. 16 CAT has not been applied by the Committee as containing a prohibition on refoulement.

475   However, where the alleged harm in the receiving state is clearly rather of an 'inhuman or degrading nature,' the Court will pay more attention to the analysis of that harm to find out whether the threshold of Art. 3 ECHR is met; see in particular the cases *M.S.S.* and *S.H.H.* discussed in Chapter 3 Section 2.3.2.

476   In ECtHR, *Harkins and Edwards v. UK*, 17 January 2012, nos. 9146/07 and 32650/07, §123, the Court stated it has normally refrained from considering whether the ill treatment in question should be characterised as torture or inhuman or degrading treatment or punishment in cases in which the risk of ill treatment would be *intentionally inflicted* in the receiving state.

forms of ill treatment 'is more easily drawn in the domestic context where, in examining complaints made under Article 3, the Court is called upon to evaluate or characterise acts which have already taken place.'[477] It has held that in the context of refoulement, where a *prospective assessment* is required, 'it is not always possible to determine whether the ill-treatment which may ensue in the receiving State will be sufficiently severe to qualify as torture.'[478] This is surely true for the Committee, too.

However, there are exceptions in which the distinction between torture and inhuman treatment is more clear and in which *even possible future harms can be classified as inhuman treatment and not as torture*, either because of the predictability of their particular nature or because of their particular source. In these cases, the Court offers broader protection.

According to the Court's case law under Article 3 ECHR, bad prison conditions are rather considered inhuman or degrading treatment and not as torture, because the harm caused is usually not inflicted intentionally. This is consistent with the Committee's practice under Article 16 CAT. Meanwhile, the examples in which the Court has condemned extraditions to countries with *poor prison conditions* mark a difference from the practice of the Committee.[479] Refoulement claims based simply on a risk of bad prison conditions in the receiving country hence might have a higher chance of success in Strasbourg than in Geneva.[480] However, where the prison conditions in the receiving state are not known to be 'just' degrading, but where systematic acts of intentional violence against inmates are reported, the distinction between torture and other inhuman treatment is more difficult to draw, as is correspondingly the differentiation between the Court's and the Committee's practice in such extradition cases.[481]

Other situations in which the expected harm may be considered as not constituting torture but rather inhuman treatment or punishment are cases

---

477   ECtHR, *Harkins and Edwards*, § 122.

478   *Ibid.*

479   See in particular the cases in which the Court has prohibited the extradition of ordinary criminals to countries of the former Soviet Union because of inhuman prison conditions, for example, ECtHR, *Ryabikin v. Russia*, 19 June 2008, no. 8320/04, § 120; ECtHR, *Soldatenko v. Ukraine*, 23 October 2008, no. 2440/07, §§ 69–72. See further ECtHR, *Aswat v. UK*, 16 April 2013, no. 17299/12, concerning the risk for the mentally ill applicant of being detained in a maximum-security facility in the United States.

480   See as an illustrative example the Committee's arguments in ComAT, *L.J.R. v. Australia*, 10 November 2008, no. 316/2007, §§ 2.5, 2.6, 2.10 and 7.5.

481   Compare, for example, the very similar cases ComAT, *Abdussamatov and 28 Others v. Kazakhstan*, 1 June 2012, no. 444/2010 and ECtHR, *Abdulkhakov v. Russia*, 2 October 2012, no. 14743/11, both concerning the extradition of Muslims suspected of religious extremism to Uzbekistan.

concerning a risk of the death penalty. The Committee classifies the death penalty as torture if it is carried out in a particularly cruel manner. In this context as well, as will be discussed in section 4.2.3 of this chapter, the Court offers better protection.

In addition, as has been explained in section 2.3.2 of this chapter, there are exceptional cases in which the Court has recognized that a removal may amount to a violation of Article 3 ECHR because of the applicant's health condition and/or the socioeconomic circumstances in the receiving state.[482] In fact, health issues and dire living conditions are unlikely to amount to torture in the sense of Article 1 CAT. Such circumstances, even if causing severe pain or suffering, will hardly constitute torture.[483] The Court has also unmistakably qualified this kind of harm as inhuman or degrading treatment and not as torture. With regard to health issues it explicitly stated that 'the distinction between torture and other forms of ill-treatment can be more easily drawn in cases where the risk of the ill-treatment stems from factors which do not engage either directly or indirectly the responsibility of the public authorities of the receiving State.'[484]

In conclusion, even though the scope of application of the protection against refoulement under the CAT is principally restricted to torture, it is usually difficult to point to a sharp distinction in the practice of the Court and the Committee for this reason. However, where complainants risk detention in *degrading prison conditions*, where they risk the *death penalty*, or where they face *exceptionally poor health or living conditions*, then a distinction in the approach of the Court and the Committee can be seen.

4.2.2   Impact of the Lawful Sanctions Clause

Contrary to the CAT, the ECHR does not contain a 'lawful sanctions clause.' However, in its practice on individual complaints, in general as well as in removal cases, the Committee has never explicitly addressed the clause. Furthermore, there is not one refoulement case in which the clause appears to have been pivotal for the decision of the Committee. Therefore, looking at the Committee and Court's practice up to the present, the effect of the lawful sanction clause can almost be ignored.

There is, however, still some uncertainty about the clause. The Court and the Committee tend to give individual states the freedom to decide on the severity of their penal systems, except when it comes to corporal punishment.

---

482   See, in particular, ECtHR, *D. v. UK*, and ECtHR, *M.S.S.* discussed in Chapter 3 Section 2.3.2.

483   See ComAT, *E.L. v. Canada*, 21 May 2012, no. 370/2009, § 8.6.

484   See ECtHR, *Harkins and Edwards v. UK*, 17 January 2012, nos. 9146/07 and 32650/07, § 122.

Here the Court has practically zero tolerance.[485] For the Committee, in refoulement cases, an analysis must be made to decide whether the pain or suffering
to be caused by an anticipated corporal punishment are severe enough to be
qualify as torture in the sense of Article 1 CAT. One can only speculate whether
the clause would have an impact in such cases. It would be interesting to see
how the Committee would respond to a case like *D. and Others v. Turkey*, in
which the Court decided that the deportation of the complainant would be in
breach of Article 3 ECHR because she would be sentenced to lashes for fornication in Iran.[486] It seems likely that the Committee would take issue with the
severity of the punishment rather than with its character as a legal sanction.
However, this is simply a guess. It should be borne in mind that the Committee,
despite the wording of Article 1 CAT, has classified a 'lawful sanction' like the
stoning of a woman for adultery as torture.[487] However, it is imaginable that
the clause encourages the Committee to set a high threshold on the severity of
a legal sanction, before considering it torture. This is especially likely in cases
in which there is no consensus within the state community about the nature or
permissibility of a particular legal sanction, as for example with the death penalty.[488] A clarification from the Committee on its understanding of the clause
would be desirable.

4.2.3   Death Penalty: Better Protection under the ECHR
According to the Court's latest jurisprudence in the case *Al-Saadoon and Mufdhi v. United Kingdom*, the exposure of a person to a well-founded fear of execution amounts to inhuman treatment in the sense of Article 3 ECHR and is
therefore prohibited. In this judgment, the Court made clear that, despite the
wording of Article 2 ECHR that allows a lawful death penalty, interpreting the
ECHR 'dynamically,' that is, in light of current thinking, the death penalty now
constitutes inhuman treatment.[489] The Court thus offers an all-embracing protection against capital punishment, within and outside the context of refoulement, irrespective of whether a contracting state has ratified the 6th or 13th
Protocol to the ECHR prohibiting the death penalty.

---

485   See Section 2.2.3 of this Chapter.
486   ECtHR, *D. and Others v. Turkey*, 22 June 2006, no. 24245/03, §§ 45–54. The Court further
       observed that the enforcement of the sentence through even a single stroke from a lash
       would already amount to inhuman treatment.
487   See ComAT, *A.S. v. Sweden*, 24 November 2000, no. 149/1999.
488   See Ingelse 2001, p. 280 and 281; Rosati 1998, p. 539.
489   ECtHR, *Al-Saadoon and Mufdhi v. UK*, 2 March 2010, no. 61498/08, §§ 115–145. See Chapter
       3 Section 2.2.5.

The CAT does not offer such protection against capital punishment. This is not surprising: international law does not in principle forbid the death penalty and neither the Human Rights Committee nor the Court consider capital punishment necessarily as a form of torture but, if anything, a form of inhuman treatment or a violation to the right to life.[490] When considering the death penalty in the context of the state reports procedure, the Committee addresses itself to the prohibition of inhuman treatment in Article 16 CAT rather than Article 1 CAT. But even assuming that the Committee did also explicitly protect against refoulement in cases of inhuman treatment, it should be noted that according to the Human Rights Committee, the death penalty does not *per se* constitute an inhuman treatment. It has, for example, considered that an execution by lethal injection is not contrary to the prohibition of inhuman treatment or the right to life.[491] It appears that it would be difficult for the Committee to argue this matter differently. Therefore, in cases where there is a real risk of capital punishment in the receiving state by lethal injection, the applicant should address his complaint to the Court rather than to the Committee. However, according to the Committee, the circumstances or the method of execution can amount to torture and therefore preclude a deportation. The case *A.S. v. Sweden* concerning a removal to Iran, where the complainant risked the death penalty by stoning, is an example of this.[492]

It is finally worth noting that although the CAT does not in principle guarantee the right to life, both the Court and the Committee can protect an individual against removal if there is a real risk of arbitrary or unlawful deprivation of life or forced disappearance.[493]

4.2.4   Excursus: Forced Expulsion as Ill Treatment

The Court and the Committee both recognize that a removal may *per se* constitute cruel, inhuman or degrading treatment, irrespective of whether an individual has grounds to fear a prohibited ill treatment in the country of

---

490   Unless the manner in which the death penalty is executed is particularly violent. It is so far only in the case ECtHR, *Ilaşcu and Others v. Moldova and Russia*, 8 July 2004, no. 48787/99, §§ 409–442 that the Court has specified that the death sentence imposed coupled with the treatment suffered in detention amounted to torture.

491   HRC, *Cox v. Canada*, 31 October 1994, no. 539/1993, § 17.3.

492   ComAT, *A.S. v. Sweden*, 24 November 2000, no. 149/1999. See the similar case ECtHR, *Jabari v. Turkey*, 11 July 2000, no. 40035/98.

493   ComAT, *Kalinichenko v. Morocco*, 25 November 2011, no. 428/2010, §§ 15.5 and 15.6; ComAT, *E.L. v. Canada*, 21 May 2012, no. 370/2009, § 8.6, in which the Committee notes that 'the complainant provided no persuasive evidence to corroborate the allegations, be they of kidnapping, the risk of torture or the risk of violation of the right to life.'

destination. Article 3 and Article 16 CAT can both be used to offer protection against the use of excessive force or degrading treatment in the context of forced deportations.[494] However, in general the excessive use of force in the context of forced removals has rarely been invoked.[495] Potential complainants will probably usually be outside the country responsible for the inhuman or degrading treatment that occurs during a deportation, which is why it may be difficult for them to take legal action. Illustrative of this is the Committee case *Arana v. France*: the complainant, who belonged to the Basque separatist movement, alleged that he had suffered greatly during his transfer from France to Spain because of his extreme weakness and because he had been beaten and thrown on the ground by the French police officers.[496] He claimed that the treatment he was subjected to throughout the journey was contrary to Article 16 CAT.[497] The Committee rejected this part of the complaint, noting that the complainant had not exhausted the domestic remedies available in France in this respect, even though it accepted that the transfer itself had been illegal, since it was made in violation of Article 3 CAT.[498] Delas rightly notes that it does not appear to be realistic for a person having been extradited to a country where there is a risk of his being subjected to torture in detention to exhaust domestic remedies in another state.[499]

Next to the manner in which a forced deportation is carried out, the Court and the Committee have both indicated that, if the applicant has serious health issues, this could also mean that his forced deportation amounts to a prohibited inhuman or degrading treatment in and of itself. However, the threshold seems to be very high for the Committee as well as for the Court. Post-traumatic stress disorders and even a concrete risk of suicide are not as such serious enough to give a forced deportation an inhuman character. The Court has frequently argued that as long as a contracting state provides adequate measures such as medical accompaniment and monitoring, the forced deportation of a complainant at risk of suicide is in accordance with Article 3 ECHR. The Committee argues similarly.

---

494   See ECtHR, *Nasr and Ghali v. Italy*, 23 February 2016, no. 44883/09, §§ 284–287; ComAT, *Agiza v. Sweden*, 20 May 2005, no. 233/2003, § 13.4.

495   See the few cases treated by the Court and the Committee as described in the Sections 2.2.6, 3.2.5 and 4.2.4 above.

496   ComAT, *Arana v. France*, 9 November 1999, no. 63/1997, § 2.8.

497   *Ibid.*, § 2.8.

498   *Ibid.*, § 11.2.

499   Delas 2011, p. 188.

Generally, before the Court as before the Committee, it is difficult to suc-cessfully invoke health issues in the context of forced deportations. The case *D. v. United Kingdom*[500] is the only example of a health issue – the complainant suffering from AIDS was almost dying – that lead to the inadmissibility of an expulsion.[501] In this case, it was not, however, the expulsion as such but the circumstances in the receiving country of St. Kitts that was the relevant factor in the assessment under Article 3 ECHR. The case is thus considered a classic refoulement case in which, *exceptionally,* 'conditions' outside the responsibil-ity of a state in the receiving country are relevant factors. Based on the unusual character of the protection against a harm that is not attributable to the au-thorities in the receiving state, the Court made clear that in the context of de-portations, health problems might only raise an issue under Article 3 ECHR in 'very exceptional' cases where the humanitarian grounds against the removal are 'compelling.'[502] It appears that this high threshold developed in the context of refoulement and health issues has had repercussions on the threshold ap-plied by the Court and the Committee with regard to the question of whether the deportation of an ill applicant may *as such* constitute an inhuman treat-ment. Both have required 'exceptional circumstances' in this context. This is related to the fact that it is not easy to distinguish the two types of cases. How-ever, in a case in which the act of the deportation *as such* is the focus, there is in fact no dogmatic basis in the Court's or Committee's jurisprudence for requesting a particularly high threshold, since the act of the forced deportation falls within the direct responsibility of the contracting state.[503] In fact, there are no legal reasons why contracting states to the ECHR and the CAT should not have the same responsibility to provide humane conditions in the context of forced removals, including the care for the individual's health, as they do for individuals whom they subject to force in other circumstances. Against this background, the UN Human Rights Committee has recently taken the right di-rection in *A.H.G. and M.S. v. Canada,* in which it considered that the deporta-tion of the mentally ill applicant to Jamaica, 'which has effectively resulted in the abrupt withdrawal of the medical and family support on which a person

---

500   See ECtHR, *D. v. UK*, 2 May 1997, no. 30240/96.

501   Worth mentioning is ECtHR, *Aswat v. UK*, 16 April 2013, no. 17299/12, discussed in Sec-tion 2.3.2.a above concerning the extradition of a seriously mentally ill applicant to a maximum-security facility in the United States, in which the Court, however, applied its approach developed with regard to state's responsibilities for the treatment of prisoners.

502   See ECtHR, *N. v. UK*, 27 May 2008 [GC], no. 26565/05, § 42 and the critique in Chapter 3 Section 2.3.2.

503   See Thurin 2012, p. 152, with regard to the Committee; de Weck 2013, p. 8, with regard to the Court. See also the general critique on the Court's practice in that context in Chapter 3 Section 2.3.2 above.

in his vulnerable position is necessarily dependent,' constituted a violation of Article 7 ICCPR. The Human Rights Committee did not refer to a particularly high threshold in that decision but recalled the aim of Article 7 ICCPR, which 'is to protect both the dignity and the physical and mental integrity of the individual.'[504]

4.3   The Source of the Harm

4.3.1   *Rapprochement* of the Committee to the Court's Approach with
         Regard to State Responsibility for Private Actors

The Court and the Committee have recognized that there is an obligation on states to protect individuals against private threats. In the context of refoulement this may lead to a state's obligation not to expose a person to threats by private actors through expulsion or extradition. The practice of the Court in this regard is much more developed than that of the Committee.

Since the mid-90s, the Court has recognized that the prohibition on refoulement applies when there is a real risk of ill treatment by private actors and the complainant is able to show that the authorities of the receiving state are not able or willing to obviate this risk by providing appropriate protection. This approach, having its origins in international refugee law, is called the 'protection view' or the 'protection clause.'[505] The Committee, for a long time, did not accept dangers from private actors as relevant under its non-refoulement obligation anchored in Article 3 CAT. This results from the definition of torture in Article 1 CAT to which Article 3 CAT refers, according to which torture is an act that requires the direct or indirect participation of public actors.

In recent years, the Committee has distanced itself in practice from its traditional understanding of torture. It first accepted that acts committed by powerful clans with control over the territory to which an applicant should be removed and where there is no central government to offer protection may be qualified as torture.[506] In the case *Njamba and Balikosa* decided in May 2010 the Committee accepted violence against women that was not necessarily instigated by quasi-governmental entities as torture, indicating that the government of the DRC did not provide adequate protection from such violence.[507] The Committee thereby referred to its General Comment on Article 2 CAT adopted in January 2008, which shows that it is now more prepared to accept that state parties bear *responsibility for acts of torture committed by private actors on*

---

504   See HRC, *A.H.G. and M.R. v. Canada*, 25 March 2015, no. 2091/2011, § 10.4.

505   Thurin 2012, p. 129; Wouters 2009, p. 554. This view or theory has also been implemented
       to the EU Qualification Directive in Art. 6 and 7.

506   ComAT, *Elmi v. Australia*, 14 May 1999, no. 120/1998.

507   ComAT, *Njamba and Balikosa v. Sweden*, 14 May 2010, no. 322/2007.

the basis of having consented or acquiesced to such torture where the authorities
know or have reasonable grounds to believe that such acts are being committed
and fail to exercise due diligence to protect against such acts.[508]

However, in general, the Committee's practice on private actors remains
scant and the decisions on the issue are poorly reasoned. It would be helpful
if the Committee would make clear and explicit statements with regard to its
understanding of state responsibility for private actors in the context of refoulement, as the Court did in 1997 in *H.L.R. v. France*.[509] Several scholars call
for this. They rightly state, first, that the term 'without ... acquiescence of the
Government' in Article 1 CAT does allow for such an interpretation of torture;
second, that the CAT should be read in conjunction with other human rights
treaties; and third, that for the individual concerned, it makes no difference
whether the party that threatens him is a state agent or not.[510] Ingelse notes on
that subject that the drafters of the CAT cannot have realized the consequences of the limited definition of torture in Article 1 CAT at the time of drafting.[511]

However, it must be noted in this context that even if the Court's practice is clearer on that topic, it is only in few cases in which the alleged harm
emanated from private actors that the Court has held that Article 3 ECHR was
violated.[512] The application of the principle of non-refoulement in this context
is rather exceptional in Strasbourg, too. It is in fact difficult to demonstrate in
practice, first, the existence of a real risk of ill treatment by private actors, and
second, a lack of protection against such harm. Recent cases of the Committee
in which it has adopted the so-called 'protection view' (as already applied for
longer by the Court) confirm this difficulty.[513]

Wouters notes rightly that the issue of what effective protection means has
never been discussed in detail.[514] A lack of state authority in a country or territory is a strong indication of a lack of protection, for the Court as well as for the
Committee. The question of whether individuals are generally able to obtain
redress for ill treatment in a receiving country is of relevance for the Court as
well as for the Committee, when it comes to the question of whether a State is

---

508   ComAT, General Comment No. 2 on Art. 2 (2008), §§ 18 and 25.

509   ECtHR, *H.L.R. v. France,* 29 April 1997, no. 24573/94, § 40.

510   See Chetail 2006, pp. 82 and 83; David 2003, p. 804; Ingelse 2001, pp. 239–240 and 291; Miller 2003, p. 323; Weissbrodt & Hörtreiter 1999, pp. 52, 64 and 70; Wouters 2009, pp. 445–449
and 536.

511   Ingelse 2001, p. 291.

512   See Section 2.3.1 of this Chapter.

513   See, in particular, ComAT, *R.S. et al. v. Switzerland,* 21 November 2014, no. 482/2011, § 8.4.

514   Wouters 2009, p. 555.

able or willing to offer effective protection.[515] It should be noted that the Court has indicated that *protection* from threats from private actors can *also* come from clans or other powerful communities,[516] family members,[517] NGOs[518] or a third state's authorities present in the receiving state.[519]

Summing up, one can state the following: historically, there has been a higher degree of state complicity required under the CAT than under the ECHR for a finding of actual risk. In recent cases, based on its General Comment No.2, the Committee has adopted a similar approach to the Court, according to which the principle of non-refoulement applies when the complainant can demonstrate that there is a real risk of his being submitted to ill treatment and that the receiving state's authorities are either unwilling or unable to offer protection against such acts. However, the Committee's practice remains quite unpredictable.[520] Clear guidelines on the principles applied within non-refoulement decisions would be welcome.

In practice, not only in proceedings before the Committee but also before the Court, it is very difficult to successfully rely on threats from private actors. This is also related to the fact that the Court and the Committee are both more open to relying on the concept of an internal flight alternative when the alleged harm emanates from private actors than when it emanates from a central government.[521]

4.3.2 Socioeconomic and Health Issues in Strasbourg

A clearer distinction between the Court's and the Committee's case law can be drawn with regard to the relevance of socioeconomic and health issues in the refoulement context. The Court's broader protection against inhuman and

---

515 ECtHR, *Salah Sheekh v. Netherlands*, 11 January 2007, § 147; ECtHR, *Abdolkhani and Karimnia v. Turkey*, 22 September 2009, no. 30471/08, § 74; ComAT, *Njamba and Balikosa v. Sweden*, 14 May 2010, no. 322/2007, § 9.5 with referral to the Committee's General Comment No. 2 on Art. 2 CAT (2008).

516 ECtHR, *Salah Sheekh v. Netherlands*, 11 January 2007, § 144; ECtHR, *Auad v. Bulgaria*, 11 October 2011, no. 46390/10, § 103.

517 ECtHR, *A.A. and Others v. Sweden*, 28 June 2012, no. 14499/09, § 83.

518 See ECtHR, *Izevbekhai and Others v. Ireland*, 17 May 2011, no. 43408/08, 80 (decision), in which the Court referred to international NGOs fighting female genital mutilation in Nigeria.

519 ECtHR, *Husseini v. Sweden*, 13 October 2011, no. 10611/09, § 85, in which the presence of US coalition forces in Afghanistan is cited as a risk-lowering element.

520 See also Committee Menéndez 2015, p. 69 noting in an academic article that the Committee jurisprudence is not fully coherent in this context.

521 See on this Chapter 4 Section 3.4.1.

degrading treatment as well as its wider understanding of state responsibility has led to a few successful refoulement complaints in which the harm expected in the receiving state was of a medical or socioeconomic nature.

Making the comparison with the Committee, the approach taken by the Court in *D. v the United Kingdom* and particularly in *M.S.S.* and *Tarakhel* as discussed in section 2.3.2 of this chapter is difficult to conceive with a refoulement protection restricted to torture in the sense of Article 1 CAT. However, as explained in section 3.2.5 of this chapter, the Committee has indicated that under particular circumstances, a forced removal of a seriously ill person can *per se* constitute an inhuman or degrading treatment within the meaning of Article 16 CAT. In a recent inadmissibility decision concerning the removal of two Congolese (DRC) from Switzerland to Spain under the Dublin III regulation, the Committee further vaguely indicated that it is not entirely ignorant with regard to the reception conditions of asylum seekers in the frame of a Dublin transfer.[522] However, in *E.L. v. Canada* decided in 2012 concerning the deportation of an Haitian applicant, who alleged, *inter alia*, that his pacemaker would need to be replaced but that there was no such service in Haiti, the Committee made clear on the merits that the situation did not fall within the scope of Article 1 CAT and cannot 'on its own fall under the scope of Article 16 CAT.'[523] Against this background, it must be stated that with its protection against refoulement including degrading treatment and its particular attention for the standards in Europe, the Court is the better address with regard to dire reception conditions for refugees and asylum seekers in the Dublin context than the Committee.[524] However, in the context of the deportation of individuals suffering from illness, it must be noted that both the Court and the Committee have been extremely severe so far. That said, as has been explained in section 2.3.2a of this chapter, the Court's severe approach on health issues is internally debated and could be overturned. It should be added that on health issues and/or living conditions, the UN Human Rights Committee's recent practice under Article 7 ICCPR has become quite interesting for the individual concerned.[525]

---

522   See ComAT, *M.K. and B.B. v. Switzerland*, 26 November 2015, no. 635/2014, § 7.3 (not published yet), discussed in Chapter 4 Section 3.4.3.b.

523   ComAT, *E.L. v. Canada*, 21 May 2012, no. 370/2009, § 8.6. The Committee nevertheless took note of the fact that the state party had looked into the availability in Haiti of treatment and carried out necessary checks before proceeding with his removal; see Section 3.2.5 above.

524   However, with regard to a risk of indirect refoulement, this is not as clear; see on this Chapter 4 Section 3.4.3.

525   See HRC, *Jasin v. Denmark*, 22 July 2015, no. 2360/2014 (Dublin case Italy) and HRC, *A.H.G. and M.R. v. Canada*, 25 March 2015, no. 2091/2011 (mentally ill to Jamaica), addressed in the Chapter 1 Section 5 and Chapter 3 Sections 2.3.2 and 4.2.4. See also HRC, *A.H. v. Denmark*,

Finally, it should also be kept in mind that even if the Court's statements in *M.S.S.* and *Tarakhel* are of general importance, it has made clear that it is only in particular circumstances that it will find a violation of the principle of non-refoulement in that context. Interestingly, environmental issues have never been considered under Article 3 ECHR or Article 3 CAT. In *Sufi and Elmi* the Court nevertheless indicated that 'if the dire humanitarian conditions in Somalia were solely or even predominantly attributable to poverty or to the State's lack of resources to deal with a naturally occurring phenomenon, such as a drought, the test in *N. v. United Kingdom* may well have been considered to be the appropriate one.'[526]

4.4 *Absolute Character of the Prohibition on Refoulement*

Under both the ECHR and the CAT, a refoulement cannot be justified under any circumstances. The legal status of the individual concerned or his past activities are not relevant for the Committee or the Court. This is an important difference from the 1951 Refugee Convention. While the ECHR and the CAT unconditionally protect each and every individual who is threatened in the event of removal, the prohibition on refoulement in Article 33 of the Refugee Convention excludes certain criminals or persons representing a danger to the security of the host state from its protection.

For contracting states, the obligation not to expel or extradite individuals threatened with torture or inhuman treatment irrespective of offences committed by them and irrespective of the fact that they represent a threat for the citizen can cause legal and political problems. McAdam observes that there is no consistent state practice as to how 'undesirable' but non-removable people should be treated.[527] Wouters and Bruinrightly state that states bound by international human rights law have a responsibility to take all necessary steps to hold suspected criminals, or 'terrorists,' accountable for their actions.[528] However, holding people in detention without a lawful justification is also impermissible under international human rights law. McAdam argues that if persons considered 'undesirable' cannot be detained legally, they have to obtain a permanent status.[529] This may lead to a clash between the state's duty

---

       16 July 2015, no. 2370/2014, § 8.8, concerning a deportation to Afghanistan, in which it is referred, *inter alia*, to the applicant's unstable state of health, which has likely rendered him 'particularly vulnerable.'

526   ECtHR, *Sufi and Elmi v. UK*, 28 June 2011, nos. 8319/07 and 11449/07, § 282.

527   McAdam 2011, p. 728.

528   Wouters & Bruin 2003, p. 29; Wouters 2009, p. 564, claiming that the prohibition on refoulement should never lead to impunity.

529   McAdam 2011, pp. 727–730. See in this sense also ComAT, *Ktiti v. Morocco*, 26 May 2011, no. 419/2010, § 9.

to protect its own citizens on the one hand, and its unconditional obligation to respect the principle of non-refoulement on the other. The Court and the Committee have shown themselves to be aware of that problem, but they do not provide advice to states as how to resolve it.

Certain state parties regularly challenge the principle of the Court and the Committee of unconditionally protecting every human being from a refoulement in an equal way no matter what background a person may have and no matter what danger he may represent to the society of the contracting state. The Court and the Committee have declared in decisions and judgments that they are aware of the difficulties states face when it comes to combating crime and guaranteeing security for their citizens, but that these difficulties should not call into question the absolute nature of the prohibition on torture or inhuman treatment. They both recognize the need for cooperation between states in the fight against crime and particularly terrorism and for effective measures for that purpose. They insist, however, that such measures 'must fully respect the rights and fundamental freedoms of the individuals concerned.'[530] The *Court and the Committee have remained resolute on the absolute validity of their prohibition on refoulement.* It seems that they have both strengthened their steadfastness on this issue that is not easy to defend.[531]

The future will show whether the international human rights instances will remain firm on the absoluteness of the principle of non-refoulement with regard to the deportation of suspected or convicted criminals.[532] In light of the worldwide consensus on the proscription of torture and the fundamental importance of the protection against such harm, the Court and the Committee are fully justified in staying firm on their practice that no matter what the circumstances, no human being should be submitted, either directly or indirectly, to torture or other severe inhuman treatment. Since the prohibition of torture is considered a norm of *jus cogens* character, there is no legitimate argument that the principle of non-refoulement inherent to this prohibition should not have this character, too. It is in fact the *raison d'être* and great strength of international institutions such as the Court and the Committee to resist political pressure at the national level in to defend fundamental values. However, with

---

530   ECtHR, *Abu Qatada v. UK*, 17 January 2012, no. 8139/09, § 184. See further, for example, ComAT, *Arana v. France*, 9 November 1999, no. 63/1997, § 11.5; ComAT, *Abdussamatov and 28 Others v. Kazakhstan*, 1 June 2012, no. 444/2010, § 13.7. See further the Sections 2.4 and 3.4 above.

531   See the respective indications in ComAT, *T.P.S. v. Canada*, 16 May 2000, no. 99/1997, § 15.4; ComAT, *Sogi v. Canada*, 16 November 2007, no. 297/2006, § 10.2 (footnote 11); ECtHR, *Abu Qatada v. UK*, 17 January 2012, no. 8139/09, § 266. See on this also Chapter 5 Section 2.

532   See Delas 2011, p. 412, who notes that one must stay very attentive with regard to that question.

a scope of protection covering an increasingly wide range of harms of a clearly less severe nature than torture, it will be difficult to convince states that the prohibition on refoulement should apply equally to each and every individual no matter the background of the case.[533] States may challenge the Court in Strasbourg on that issue in future cases.

It should be stressed that states also cannot evade their responsibility under Article 3 ECHR or Article 3 CAT by relying on obligations arising out of *bilateral or multilateral agreements*.[534] In the case *Agiza v. Sweden* concerning the extradition of an Egyptian national suspected of terrorist activities, the Committee acknowledged 'that measures taken to fight terrorism, including denial of safe haven, deriving from binding Security Council Resolutions are both legitimate and important.'[535] It noted, however, that their execution 'must be carried out with full respect to the applicable rules of international law, including the provisions of the Convention, as affirmed repeatedly by the Security Council.'[536]

The same principle applies in situations of *mass influx of asylum seekers*. In *Hirsi Jamaa and Others v. Italy*, the Court observed that the 'external borders of the European Union are currently experiencing considerable difficulties in coping with the increasing influx of migrants and asylum seekers. It does not underestimate the burden and pressure this situation places on the States concerned, which are all the greater in the present context of economic crisis.'[537] The Court further held that it is particularly aware of the difficulties related to the phenomenon of migration by sea, involving for states additional complications in controlling the borders in southern Europe.[538] In the *M.S.S.* judgment, it had already noted that it is 'particularly aware of the difficulties involved in the reception of migrants and asylum seekers on their arrival at major international airports and of the disproportionate number of asylum seekers when compared to the capacities of some of these States.'[539] However, the Grand Chamber made also very clear in these judgments that having regard to the absolute character of the rights secured by Article 3 ECHR, this cannot absolve a state of its obligations under that provision.[540]

---

533   See in this sense also Wouters 2009, p. 314.

534   See, for example, ECtHR, *Hirsi Jamaa and Others v. Italy*, 23 February 2012 [GC], no. 27765/09, § 129; ComAT, *D.S.I. v. Hungary*, 8 December 2015, no. 671/2015, § 9.2 (with regard to interim measures).

535   ComAT, *Agiza v. Sweden*, 20 May 2005, no. 233/2003, § 13.1.

536   *Ibid.*

537   ECtHR, *Hirsi Jamaa and Others v. Italy*, 23 February 2012 [GC], no. 27765/09, § 122.

538   *Ibid.*

539   ECtHR, *M.S.S. v. Belgium and Greece*, 21 January 2011 [GC], no. 30696/09, § 223.

540   *Ibid.*, § 223; ECtHR, *Hirsi Jamaa and Others*, § 122.

Assessment of Risk

Torture and other ill treatment usually takes place secretly and is denied by its perpetrators. Even in domestic cases in which complainants allege past torture, it is difficult for them to adduce evidence. In refoulement cases, the Court and the Committee do not assess past violations of human rights but possible future ones. To prove future ill treatment is technically impossible.[1] In its Grand Chamber judgment *Saadi v. Italy*, the Court stated that the risk assessment in refoulement cases is to some degree speculative.[2] To keep the degree of speculation as small as possible, the Court and the Committee have developed principles on how to assess the risk.

The principles established by the Court and the Committee with regard to the risk assessment are continuously being developed. They are non-exhaustive and can only be fully comprehended with the knowledge of individual cases. It is hence mostly with reference to individual cases that they will be discussed in the following pages. To give guidelines for the implementation of Article 3 CAT in the context of individual complaints, at its 19th session in November 1997 the Committee adopted a General Comment that reflects its own approach in assessing individual complaints under that provision.[3] The Court has never published such guidelines but it usually starts its consideration on the merits by summarizing its general principles established in the context of refoulement.[4]

The Court and the Committee have developed principles with regard to the standard and burden of proof (section 1) and the time at which the risk is assessed (section 2). In Strasbourg as well as Geneva, the profile of each complainant is evaluated in light of these principles on a case-by-case basis against

---

1 See judge Zupančič in his concurring opinion to ECtHR, *Saadi v Italy*, 28 February 2008 [GC], no. 37201/06.

2 ECtHR, *Saadi v. Italy*, 28 February 2008 [GC], no. 37201/06, § 142.

3 See ComAT, General Comment No. 1 on Art. 3 CAT (1997). According to Wouters 2009, p. 490, footnote 314, the Comment is not meant to provide guidelines for national asylum procedures but for the international procedure under Art. 22 CAT. Considering that the Comment reflects which criteria it considers important, it nevertheless also constitutes a guideline for national authorities.

4 An illustrative example of this is ECtHR, *Auad v. Bulgaria*, 11 October 2011, no. 46390/10, §§ 95–100.

the human rights situation in the receiving country (section 3.2) and the particular circumstances of the applicant (section 3.3). As will be shown (section 3.1), the quality of the risk assessment at national level also plays a role in the Court's and the Committee's risk assessment.

1   Standard of Proof and the Role of the Actors

To protect an individual against removal, the Court and the Committee must be convinced there is a certain probability that this individual will be exposed to ill treatment in the event of expulsion or extradition. What degree or standard of probability constitutes a sufficient risk to trigger the application of the principle of non-refoulement? Who has the burden of demonstrating this probability and by what means? These questions will be dealt with in this section by analysing the standard and burden of proof required in refoulement procedures before the Court and the Committee. The roles of the actors participating in the international procedure (complainant, decision body, state party) are also discussed.

1.1   *Court*
1.1.1   Standard of Proof
According to the Court's standard formula, the decision by a contracting state to extradite or expel a person may give rise to an issue under Article 3 ECHR 'where substantial grounds have been shown for believing that the person concerned faces a real risk of being subjected to torture or to inhuman or degrading treatment or punishment.'[5] The level of probability required to give rise to a breach of the principle of non-refoulement is indicated by the terms 'real risk.'

There is no precise definition of the concept of real risk. The Court has stated that the risk must be 'personal'[6] and present.[7] In some judgments, the Court has also used the term 'serious risk' instead of 'real risk.'[8] The risk cannot

---

5   For the first time stated in ECtHR, *Soering v. UK*, 7 July 1989, no. 14038/88, § 91.

6   Amongst many others, ECtHR, *Kaboulov v. Ukraine*, 19 November 2009, no. 41015/04, § 112.

7   Amongst many others, ECtHR, *Venkadajalasarma v. Netherlands*, 17 February 2004, no. 58510/00, §§ 66–69.

8   For example, ECtHR, *Soldatenko v. Ukraine*, 23 October 2008, no. 2440/07, § 72; ECtHR, *Kaboulov v. Ukraine*, 19 November 2009, no. 41015/04, § 112.

solely constitute the subjective view of the individual concerned (even if well-founded); it has to be of an objective nature.[9]

The Court has indicated that a 'mere possibility' of ill treatment is not sufficient to give rise to a breach of Article 3 ECHR.[10] It noted recently that it need not be established with 'certitude' that the applicant would be ill-treated if returned home, but that he must be able to show a 'high likelihood that he would be ill-treated' if returned.[11] However, in *Saadi v. Italy* the Court's Grand Chamber noted that the risk must *not* be 'more likely than not.'[12] In *Shamayev and Others v. Georgia and Russia*, the Court concluded that the facts of the case do not support 'beyond any reasonable doubt' that the extradition would expose the applicants to a real and personal risk of inhuman or degrading treatment, within the meaning of Article 3 ECHR.[13] This formulation indicates a very high standard of proof. It has, however, barely been recalled by the Court in the context of refoulement.[14]

However, none of the formulations just cited are very useful in practice. As Thurin rightly states, the concept of a 'real risk' can only be approached in a useful way – if at all – by the study of the case law.[15] The Court decides on a case-by-case basis where substantial grounds indicating a real risk are given. It must examine the 'foreseeable consequences of the removal of an applicant to the receiving country in light of the general situation there as well as his or her personal circumstances.'[16]

---

9   ECtHR, *Shamayev and Others v. Georgia and Russia*, 12 April 2005, no. 36378/02, §§ 340 and 351.

10   ECtHR, *Vilvarajah and Others v. UK*, 30 October 1991, nos. 13163/87, § 111.

11   ECtHR, *Azimov v. Russia*, 18 April 2013, no. 67474/11, § 128; ECtHR, *Rakhimov v. Russia*, 10 July 2014, no. 50552/13, § 93.

12   ECtHR, *Saadi v. Italy*, 28 February 2008 [GC], no. 37201/06, § 140.

13   ECtHR, *Shamayev and Others v. Georgia and Russia*, 12 April 2005, no. 36378/02, § 353.

14   See ECtHR, *Garabayev v. Russia*, 7 June 2007, no. 38411/02, § 76. Wouters (2009, pp. 269 and 270) rightly observes that it remains unclear why the Court refers to a standard of proof that is usually required in Art. 3 ECHR cases outside the context of refoulement. It is interesting to note that both cases cited above concern complainants who had already been extradited when the Court took its decision. However, the Court's case law as a whole does not indicate that it wanted to establish a higher burden of proof in cases in which a transfer had already taken place; see in particular the more recent case ECtHR, *Iskandarov v. Russia*, 23 September 2010, no. 17185/05 in which the Court does not refer to the formulation of 'beyond reasonable doubt.' In general, the practice with regard to the standard of proof in the refoulement context is not always consistent; see in this sense Battjes 2009, p. 609, 610; Rieter 2010, p. 830; Suntinger 1995, p. 217.

15   Thurin 2012, p. 764.

16   See, amongst many others, ECtHR, *Hirsi Jamaa and Others v. Italy*, 23 February 2012 [GC], no. 27765/09, § 117.

Analysts of the early refoulement case law came to the conclusion that the Court had set quite a high standard of proof.[17] They referred to the fact that very few complaints had been successful in Strasbourg. Until the beginning of the year 2000, it was only in four cases that the Court had found a violation of the principle of non-refoulement. The case *Vilvarajah v. United Kingdom* decided in 1991 was often cited to demonstrate the high standard of proof required.[18] It concerned five Tamils expelled to Sri Lanka in 1988. Even though three of the applicants had in fact been ill-treated after their deportation, the Court concluded that, at the time of their removal, no substantial grounds had been established for believing that the applicants would be exposed to a real risk of being subjected to inhuman treatment in Sri Lanka.

In recent times as well, a number of scholars, having analysed the case law as a whole, are of the opinion that the Court is strict in accepting the existence of a real risk.[19] There are judgments that confirm this opinion explicitly: In *Harkins and Edwards* adopted in January 2012, the Court reaffirmed the observation of a member of the House of Lords according to which the Court has so far 'been very cautious in finding that removal from the territory of a Contracting State would be contrary to Article 3 ECHR.' It added that 'it has only rarely reached such a conclusion since adopting the Chahal judgment.'[20] In the case *E.G. v. United Kingdom*, decided in May 2011, the Court found that the applicant's removal to Sri Lanka would not give rise to a violation of Article 3 ECHR despite the fact that the applicant had been detained and ill-treated for his LTTE-membership in the past.[21] In their joint dissenting opinion, the judges *Garlicki* and *Kalaydjeva* criticized the majority for applying too high a standard of proof.[22] The Court appears to apply a particularly high standard of proof depending on the source of the harm feared in case of removal: as has been explained, successful cases in which the harm feared in the receiving country does not emanate from public officials but from non-state actors or where it is related to the applicant's health are rare.[23]

---

17 Einarsen 1990, pp. 373 and 385; Suntinger 1995, p. 219; Weissbrodt & Hörtreiter 1999, p. 36.

18 ECtHR, *Vilvarajah and Others v. UK* 30 October 1991, nos. 13163/87 and further.

19 Chetail 2006, p. 101; Schürmann & Scheidegger 2009, p. 213; Thurin 2012, pp. 179 and 260, Wouters 2009, p. 578.

20 ECtHR, *Harkins and Edwards v. UK*, 17 January 2012, nos. 9146/07 and 32650/07, § 131.

21 ECtHR, *E.G. v. UK*, 31 May 2011, no. 41178/08, §§ 65–81.

22 *Ibid.* See similar the judges Power and Zupančič speaking of 'the high threshold of Art. 3 ECHR as elaborated in the case law of this Court' in their dissenting opinion in ECtHR, *F.H. v. Sweden*, 20 January 2009, 32621/06.

23 See on this Chapter 3 Section 2.3.

In *Bensaid v. United Kingdom*, the Court remarked on 'the high threshold set by Article 3, particularly where the case does not concern the direct responsibility of the Contracting State for the infliction of harm.'[24] As this latter statement indicates, it is generally difficult for failed asylum seekers to be successful under the principle of non-refoulement in Strasbourg. Looking at the Court's case law as a whole and the rather modest number of successfully alleged violations of the principle of non-refoulement compared to the thousands of incoming complaints on that subject,[25] I fully agree with the findings of many scholars that the threshold set by the Court to accept the existence of 'real risk' is high.

1.1.2   Burden of Proof and Supporting Evidence

In the standard formula used since the *Soering* judgment, the Court states that there must be 'substantial grounds' for believing that there is a real risk of ill treatment in case of deportation. The expression 'substantial grounds' is almost as vague as 'real risk.'[26] The terms refer to the risk elements or grounds that can 'make a case' as they will be discussed in section 3 of this chapter. In most refoulement cases in which the Court has found a violation of Article 3 ECHR the 'substantial grounds' consist of a combination of several factors. These can include a complainant's background, the human rights situation in the receiving country or, in general, evidential material for concluding that a risk exists. Most complaints rejected by the Court end with the formulation that no substantial grounds have been established for believing that the applicant would be exposed to a real risk of treatment contrary to Article 3 ECHR if expelled.

The initial burden of presenting such grounds lies with the applicant. According to the Court, it is up to him to adduce evidence capable of proving a risk of ill treatment in case of removal.[27] However, once such evidence is

---

24   ECtHR, *Bensaid v. UK*, 6 February 2001, no. 44599/98, § 40 recited in ECtHR, *A.A. and Others v. Sweden*, 28 June 2012, no. 14499/09, § 93, concerning the risk of domestic violence in case of deportation.

25   See the numbers on the case law in Chapter 1 Section 2.2.2 and the statistics on interim measures in Chapter 2 Section 1.2.

26   Thurin 2012, p. 186.

27   See the illustrative case ECtHR, *Said v. Netherlands*, 5 July 2005, no. 2345/02, § 49, in which the Court summarises that it is up to the applicant 'to adduce, to the greatest extent practically possible, material and information allowing the authorities of the Contracting State concerned, as well as the Court, to assess the risk a removal might entail.'

adduced, it is for the government to dispel any doubts about it.[28] The authorities cannot remain passive. They have the responsibility to respond to any serious allegation and evidence presented.[29] However, the Court has made clear that 'requesting an applicant to produce "indisputable" evidence of a risk of ill-treatment in the requesting country would be tantamount to asking him to prove the existence of a future event, which is impossible, and would place a clearly disproportionate burden on him.'[30] In *Azimov v. Russia* adopted in April 2013, it was noted that allegations under the principle of non-refoulement

> ... always concern an eventuality, something which may or may not occur in the future. Consequently, such allegations cannot be proven the same way as past events. The application must only be required to show, with reference to specific facts relevant to him and to the class of people he belonged to, that there was a high likelihood that he would be ill-treated.[31]

The *presentation of evidence* is an element that may lead to a shift in the burden of proof from the applicant to the respondent state. Depending on the human rights situation, arrest warrants, court summons and other criminal records can be of particular importance. The onus is on the authorities to show that the presented evidence is false or forged if this is what they allege.[32] In the case *R.C. v. Sweden*, the complainant feared an expulsion to Iran.[33] Before the Swedish authorities, he alleged that he had been detained and tortured in 2001 for having participated in demonstrations against the Iranian regime and produced a medical certificate indicating that he might have been ill-treated in the past. Although experts did not establish the authenticity of the

---

28   See, amongst many others, ECtHR, *Saadi v Italy*, 28 February 2008 [GC], no. 37201/06, § 129; ECtHR, *R.C. v. Sweden*, 9 March 2010, no. 41827/07, § 50; ECtHR, *M.A. v. Switzerland*, 18 November 2014, no. 52589/13, §§ 55 and 69.

29   Whether the evidence concerns a complainant's personal background, see, for example, ECtHR, *D. and others v. Turkey*, 22 June 2006, no. 24245/03, §§ 47 and 48, or the general human rights situation; see, for example, ECtHR, *S.H. v. UK*, 15 June 2010, no. 19956/06, § 71; ECtHR, *Iskandarov v. Russia*, 23 September 2010, no. 17185/05, § 129.

30   ECtHR, *Yakubov v. Russia*, 8 November 2011, no. 7265/10, §§ 76 and 77; ECtHR, *Rustamov v. Russia*, 3 July 2012, no. 11209/10, § 117; ECtHR, *Azimov v. Russia*, 18 April 2013, no. 67474/11, § 128.

31   ECtHR, *Azimov v. Russia*, 18 April 2013, no. 67474/11, § 128. See also ECtHR, *Rustamov v. Russia*, 3 July 2012, no. 11209/10, § 117; ECtHR, *Ismailov v. Russia*, 17 April 2014, no. 20110/13, § 81.

32   See, for example, ECtHR, *Hilal v. UK*, 6 March 2001, no. 45276/99, § 63; ECtHR, *M.A. v. Switzerland*, 18 November 2014, no. 52589/13, §§ 64–68.

33   ECtHR, *R.C. v. Sweden*, 9 March 2010, no. 41827/02.

certificate, the Court noted that in such circumstances, it was up to the state authorities to *dispel any doubts* that might have persisted as to the cause of the injuries. The judges held that the Swedish immigration authorities, having the duty to ascertain all relevant facts, should have provided an expert opinion in response to the certificate submitted by the complainant. At the request of the Court, the Swedish authorities mandated an expert to produce a forensic medical report. According to this second report, it was very likely that the complainant had been tortured in the past. The judges noted that 'having regard to its finding that the applicant has discharged the burden of proving that he has already been tortured, the Court considers that the onus rests with the State to dispel any doubts about the risk of his being subjected again to treatment contrary to Article 3 ECHR in the event that his expulsion proceeds.'[34] In light of the worrisome human rights conditions for political opponents in Iran and the fact that the complainant was without valid documents allowing him to enter Iran without coming to the attention of the authorities, the Court eventually found that the complainant's removal thereto would be in violation of Article 3 ECHR.[35] In a dissenting opinion attached to the judgment, judge Fura criticized that the shift in the burden of proof in the present case did not follow the established case law of the Court. Evidence demonstrating past ill treatments or persecution are often taken into account in the Court's risk assessment; but a shift in the burden of proof – as was recognized in this case because the complainant has been ill-treated in the past – is rather exceptional. It can be agreed with Fura that usually, the Court's assessment is more future-orientated.[36]

The human rights situation in the receiving country also has an impact on the complainant's burden of proof.[37] In the case *Muminov v. Russia* for example, the applicant feared extradition to Uzbekistan, where he was charged with involvement in a proscribed Islamic organisation. The applicant alleged that

---

34   *Ibid.,* § 55.

35   *Ibid.,* §§ 23–25 and 52–56.

36   See on this also Section 3.3.3.b of this Chapter. On the importance of past ill treatment in the Court's risk assessment see, in more detail, Section 3.3.1.b of this Chapter (Past ill treatment). However, for a similar approach as taken in *R.C.*, see *Mo.M. v. France*, 18 April 2013, no. 18372/10, §§ 38–44, concerning the expulsion of a Chadian suspected of being part of the opposition movement and who had been ill-treated in the past.

37   See on this Section 3.2.1.a of this Chapter in which it will be shown that, exceptionally, the Court will accept that violent conditions in a receiving state can by themselves trigger the application of the principle of non-refoulement.

he would be threatened with ill treatment as a Muslim detainee. Noting that the applicant had substantiated his claim before the national authorities by referring to the reports of international organisations on the human rights situation in Uzbekistan, in particular regarding the risk of persons being executed on account of their religious beliefs, it was, according to the Court, up to the Russian authorities to dispel any doubt about such a risk.[38] In the case *M.S.S. v. Belgium and Greece*, the Court noted that the Belgian authorities were aware of the deficiencies in the asylum procedures in Greece and that the applicant should therefore 'not be expected to bear the entire burden of proof.'[39] The case *Auad v. Bulgaria* concerned the removal of a stateless person of Palestinian origin to a refugee camp in Lebanon.[40] The Court noted that Palestinian refugee camps were constantly plagued by outbursts of violence and armed clashes between various factions. The Court found therefore that the complainant, with his personal background, had established at least *prima facie* evidence capable of proving that he would be at real risk of ill treatment in the camps and that the burden was therefore on the state to dispel any doubts in that regard.[41] Noting that the government had presented no evidence on that issue and that, on national security grounds, the competent domestic authorities and courts had not even tried to make an assessment of that risk, the Court found a violation of Article 3 ECHR.[42] In *Hirsi Jamaa v. Italy*, the Court considered that faced with several independent reports indicating the systematic ill treatment of irregular migrants and asylum seekers in Gaddafi's Libya, 'it was for the national authorities to find out about the treatment to which the applicants would be exposed after their return,' despite the fact that they had failed to expressly request asylum when they had been intercepted by Italian authorities in the Mediterranean Sea.[43]

It can be concluded that depending on the claim presented by the complainant, the Court may expect the contracting state to participate quite actively in the process. Wouters appropriately speaks of a 'shared responsibility between the individual concerned and the state.'[44]

---

38   ECtHR, *Muminov v. Russia*, 11 December 2008, no. 42502/06, § 87.

39   ECtHR, *M.S.S. v. Belgium and Greece*, 21 January 2011 [GC], no. 30696/09, § 352.

40   ECtHR, *Auad v. Bulgaria*, 11 October 2011, no. 46390/10.

41   *Ibid.*, § 103.

42   *Ibid.*, §§ 104–108.

43   ECtHR, *Hirsi Jamaa and Others v. Italy*, 23 February 2012 [GC], no. 27765/09, §§ 132 and 133.

44   Wouters 2009, p. 274.

1.1.3   The Role of the Court

According to the Court,

> having regard to the fact that Article 3 ECHR enshrines one of the most
> fundamental values of a democratic society and prohibits in absolute
> terms torture or inhuman or degrading treatment or punishment, a 'rig-
> orous scrutiny' must necessarily be conducted of an individual's claim
> that his or her deportation to a third country will expose that individual
> to such treatment.[45]

Article 38 ECHR states that the Court shall examine the case together with
the representatives of the parties and, if needed, undertake an investigation,
for which the states concerned shall furnish all necessary facilities. The Court
regularly states in refoulement judgments that it 'will take as its basis all the
material placed before it or, if necessary, material obtained *proprio motu*.'[46]

In refoulement cases treated on the merits, the Court usually seeks material
proprio motu with regard to the human rights situation in the receiving country. In fact it is quite active in seeking and analysing its own country-specific
information.[47] Also, when an applicant's version is corroborated by a very large
number of credible sources from reputable NGOs or international organisations, the Court is likely to attach more weight to them than to the government's account.[48] It has held that 'in cases concerning aliens facing expulsion
or extradition it is entitled to compare material made available by the government with material from other reliable and objective sources.'[49]

With regard to facts concerning the personal circumstances of the applicant
(for example his past political activities, detention or experiences of ill treatment or persecution), the Court is more reluctant to seek further evidence. It
does recognize, as a general principle, that national authorities 'are best placed
to assess the facts but particularly the credibility of individuals, since it is they

---

45   ECtHR, *Jabari v. Turkey*, 11 July 2000, no. 40035/98, § 39. Recalled for example in ECtHR,
      I.K. v. Austria, 28 March 2013, no. 2964/12, § 71.

46   Amongst many others, ECtHR, *Mamatkulov and Askarov v. Turkey*, 4 February 2005 [GC],
      nos. 46827/99 and 46951/99, § 69.

47   See on this Chapter 4 Section 3.2.1.c.

48   See ECtHR, *M.S.S. v. Belgium and Greece*, 21 January 2011 [GC], no. 30696/09, § 304 (with
      regard to the deficiencies in the Greek asylum system); ECtHR, *Hirsi Jamaa and Others v.
      Italy*, 23 February 2012 [GC], no. 27765/09, § 203 (with regard to the treatment of asylum
      seekers by Italian forces when intercepted at sea).

49   ECtHR, *Kolesnik v. Russia*, 10 June 2010, no. 26876/08, § 71.

who have had an opportunity to see, hear and assess the demeanour of the individual concerned.'[50]

The Court respects the knowledge of state parties in dealing with asylum claims from specific countries.[51] It is not, however, bound by the national authorities' analysis. Concerning its own scrutiny, the Court has summarized its role in recent judgments as follows:

> It must be *cautious in taking the role of a first-instance tribunal of fact*. It has held in various contexts that where domestic proceedings have taken place, it is not its task to substitute its own assessment of the facts for that of the domestic courts and, *as a general rule, it is for those courts to assess the evidence before them*. Although the Court is not bound by the findings of domestic courts, *in normal circumstances it requires cogent elements to lead it to depart from the findings of fact reached by those courts*. At the same time, in accordance with Article 19 of the Convention, the Court's duty is to ensure the observance of the commitments undertaken by the Contracting Parties to the Convention. With reference to extradition or deportation, the Court reiterates that in cases where an applicant provides reasoned grounds which cast doubts on the accuracy of the information relied on by the respondent Government, *the Court must be satisfied that the assessment made by the authorities of the Contracting State is adequate* and sufficiently supported by domestic materials, as well as by materials originated from other reliable sources.[52] (Emphasis added)

In the event that the national authority's procedure appears incomplete or inadequate, the Court will rely to a lesser extent on the government's statements

---

50   See, for example, ECtHR, *Auad v. Bulgaria*, 11 October 2011, no. 46390/10, § 102; ECtHR, *A.A. and Others v. Sweden*, 28 June 2012, no. 14499/09, § 77; ECtHR, *Mo.M. v. France*, 18 April 2013, no. 18372/10, § 35. In addition, as has been explained in Chapter 2 Section 3.2.4 on admissibility, the rule of exhaustion of domestic remedies requires that national authorities are *first* given the opportunity to assess all relevant allegations and related evidence establishing a risk of ill treatment in case of removal.

51   ECtHR, *Cruz Varas and Others v. Sweden*, 20 March 1991, no. 15576/89, § 81; ECtHR, *Vilvarajah and Others v. UK*, 30 October 1991, nos. 13163/87 and further, § 114.

52   ECtHR, *Abdulkhakov v. Russia*, 2 October 2012, no. 14743/11, § 137. See also ECtHR, *Ryabikin v. Russia*, 19 June 2008, no. 8320/04, § 111; ECtHR, *Shakurov v. Russia*, 5 June 2012, no. 55822/10, §§ 125 and 126; ECtHR, *Kozhayev v. Russia*, 5 June 2012, no. 60054/10, §§ 77 and 78; ECtHR, *Umirov v. Russia*, 18 September 2012, no. 17455/11, §§ 97 and 98; ECtHR, *H. and B. v. UK*, 9 April 2013, nos. 70073/10 and 44539/11, § 111; ECtHR, *Sidikovy v. Russia*, 20 June 2013, no. 73455/11, §§ 135 and 136.

and proceed more actively to its own risk assessment.[53] It has held that it 'is in principle prepared to defer to the national authorities in borderline cases, provided that they have addressed all relevant aspects of the case and have given a reasonable interpretation of evidence and facts.'[54] However, it has also made clear that where allegations are made under Article 3 ECHR, it must apply a particularly thorough scrutiny, 'even if certain domestic proceedings and investigations have already taken place.'[55] In *L.M. and Others v. Russia*, the Court recently noted that 'the critical elements' it has to subject 'to a searching scrutiny' in certain cases may be summarized as follows:

> *Firstly*, it has to be considered whether an applicant has presented the national authorities with substantial grounds for believing that he faces a real risk of ill-treatment in the destination country. *Secondly*, the Court will inquire into whether the claim has been assessed adequately by the competent national authorities discharging their procedural obligations under Article 3 of the Convention and whether their conclusions were sufficiently supported by relevant material. *Lastly*, having regard to all of the substantive aspects of a case and the available relevant information, the Court will assess the existence of the real risk of suffering torture or treatment incompatible with Convention standards.[56] (Emphasis added)

As can be seen from the statements cited, the Court's approach combines the assessment of the national authorities' respect for their procedural obligations under Article 3 ECHR with its own substantive risk assessment. The Court has been criticized for imposing its own analysis of evidence instead of relying on the material and analyses submitted by the parties.[57] In a concurring opinion on *D.N.W. v. Sweden*, judge *Lemmens* criticized his colleagues for having examined the credibility of the applicant's account themselves, instead of referring to the findings of the domestic authorities. He postulated that it should not be 'the Court's task to proceed with such an assessment where it appears – as

---

53   See on this Section 3.1.1.a of this Chapter and, for example, ECtHR, *Auad v. Bulgaria*, 11 October 2011, no. 46390/10, § 101; ECtHR, *Al-Husni v. Bosnia and Herzegovina*, 7 February 2012, no. 3727/08, §§ 52–54.

54   ECtHR, *Azimov v. Russia*, 18 April 2013, no. 67474/11, § 143.

55   *Ibid.*, § 115.

56   ECtHR, *L.M. and Others v. Russia*, 15 October 2015, nos. 40081/14, 40088/14 and 40127/14, § 109. The Court referred to its practice in applications lodged against Russia, primarily by applicants originating from the countries of Central Asia, in particular, ECtHR, *Mamazhonov v. Russia*, 23 October 2014, no. 17239/13, §§ 136–137.

57   See in particular Bossuyt 2010, pp. 147–151 and 172–175.

in this case – that the competent domestic authorities heard the applicant, examined his claims carefully, and delivered decisions containing extensive reasons for their conclusions.'[58] Judge Maruste in *N. v. Finland*,[59] judge Fura in *R.C. v. Sweden*[60] and more recently judge Kjølbro in *M.A. v. Switzerland*[61] have made similar statements. Wouters notes that it is only in a few decisions on admissibility that the Court fully relied on the assessment conducted by the state party.[62] It is true that in its published judgments and decisions, the Court does usually proceed to its own, at least minimal, assessment of the facts, whether the domestic proceedings appeared arbitrary or not.[63] It is, however, to be borne in mind that most complaints are rejected at the admissibility stage without the involvement of the representatives of the states concerned.[64] It is a given that in these cases, the Court will usually rely on the government's statement in the national procedure.

1.2 *Committee*

1.2.1 Standard of Proof

According to Article 3 (1) CAT no state party shall return a person to another state where there are 'substantial grounds for believing that he would be in danger of being subjected to torture.' According to the Committee's established case law, this danger of torture must be 'foreseeable, real and personal.'[65] The Committee has further made clear in several decisions that the danger must be present.[66] In most decisions, it uses the term 'risk' rather than

---

58   ECtHR, *D.N.W. v. Sweden*, 6 December 2012, no. 29946/10.

59   ECtHR, *N. v. Finland*, 26 July 2005, no. 38885/02. See further the harsh critique of this judgment in Bossuyt 2010, pp. 105–107.

60   ECtHR, *R.C. v. Sweden*, 9 March 2010, no. 41827/07.

61   ECtHR, *M.A. v. Switzerland*, 18 November 2014, no. 52589/13.

62   Wouters 2009, p. 283.

63   See on this also Section 3.1.1.a of this Chapter.

64   See Chapter 2 Sections 1.1.1 and 3.3.

65   The Committee did not use these terms from the beginning: in its very first decision, the Committee spoke of a 'foreseeable and necessary consequence' of exposing the complainant to a real risk; see ComAT, *Mutombo v. Switzerland*, 27 April 1994, no. 13/1993, § 9.4. In ComAT, *Aemei v. Switzerland*, 9 May 1997, 34/1995, § 9.5, it then skipped the word 'necessary' and spoke of a 'foreseeable consequence.' Since ComAT, *E.A. v. Switzerland*, 10 November 1997, no. 28/1995, § 11.5, the Committee has used the expression 'foreseeable, real and personal' risk, which continues to be its practice today. See also ComAT, General Comment No. 1 on Art. 3 CAT (1997), § 7.

66   See, amongst many others, ComAT, *A.A. et al. v. Switzerland*, 10 November 2008, 285/2006 § 7.5.

'danger.'[67] The Committee is constantly recalling its General Comment on Article 3 CAT, according to which the risk of torture in case of removal must rise 'beyond mere theory or suspicion,' but does not have to be 'highly probable.'[68]

These abstract formulations give little information about the standard of proof required.[69] More instructive for the practice is the fact that the Committee regularly points out in its decisions that its goal is to find out 'whether the individual concerned would be *personally* at risk' of being subjected to torture if expelled.[70] As will be shown in section 3.2.2a of this chapter, even very poor human rights conditions or violent conflicts in a receiving country are not enough by themselves to trigger the protection of Article 3 CAT, although they can alleviate the burden of proof considerably. As the Committee is constantly stating, 'additional grounds must be adduced to show that the individual concerned would be personally at risk.'[71] Specific and different risk factors, in particular evidence demonstrating that the applicant has been tortured or personally persecuted in the past, thus play an important role in determining the line between a relevant and non-relevant risk or danger.[72]

Scholars analysing the Committee's case law as a whole have held that the standard of proof required by the Committee appears to be lower than that required under other relevant treaties such as the ECHR[73] or the ICCPR.[74] It is true that the Committee has taken a particularly cautious approach with regard to certain applicants, in particular victims of torture. However, the Committee's short reasoning makes it difficult to reconstruct its decision-making process in many cases and makes general statements on the required standard of proof difficult. The question of whether the required standard of proof can be considered low in relation to the standard adopted by the Court will be addressed in the comparative section just below.

---

67   Wouters (2009, p. 458 fn. 147) rightly observes that the terms are interchangeable; see also the French version of Art. 3 CAT, in which the term 'risk' ('*risque*') is used.

68   General Comment No. 1 on Art. 3 CAT (1997), § 7. See, amongst many others, ComAT, *E.A. v. Switzerland*, 10 November 1997, no. 28/1995, § 11.3, in which the Committee stated this concept for the first time.

69   See in this sense Goodwin-Gill & McAdam 2007, p. 305.

70   As already stated in the first decision in a refoulement case, ComAT, *Mutombo v. Switzerland*, 27 April 1994, no. 13/1993, § 9.3, and repeated ever since.

71   As a recent example amongst others see ComAT, *B.M.S. v. Sweden*, 25 November 2015, no. 594/2014, § 8.3.

72   Thurin 2012, p. 184. See on this also Section 3.3.2 of this chapter.

73   Chetail 2006, p. 101; Schürmann & Scheidegger, 2009, p. 213; Weissbrodt & Hörtreiter 1999, p. 15.

74   Ingelse 2001, pp. 311–312.

Finally, it should be noted that in the judgment *El Rgeig v. Switzerland*, the Committee caused some confusion by using a formulation indicating a very low standard of proof. The Committee observed that the 'State party had not presented to it sufficiently convincing arguments to demonstrate a complete absence of risk.'[75] Wouters has rightly observed that, while such a statement is certainly not beneficial for the better understanding of the level of risk required, it was probably not the intention of the Committee to indicate a new standard of proof.[76] The Committee has not used this formulation in other decisions and has always come back to its standard phrase according to which the risk or danger must be real, personal and foreseeable and must go beyond mere theory or suspicion but without having to be highly probable.

1.2.2   Burden of Proof and Supporting Evidence

According to the Committee's General Comment on Article 3 CAT, 'the burden is upon the author to present an arguable case. This means that there must be a factual basis for the author's position, sufficient to require a response from the State party.'[77] It is up to the applicant to 'establish that he would be in danger of being tortured and that the grounds for so believing are substantial in the way described, and that such danger is personal and present.'[78] As has been indicated, the 'substantial grounds' that must be present for believing an applicant would be in danger of being subjected to torture must primarily result from the personal situation of the complainant. Most rejections of complaints by the Committee end with the conclusion that the complainant has failed to substantiate or establish his claim that he would face a foreseeable, real and personal risk of being subjected to torture upon his return.[79]

---

75   ComAT, *El Rgeig v. Switzerland*, 15 November 2006, no. 280/2005, § 7.4.

76   Wouters 2009, pp. 460–461.

77   ComAT, General Comment No. 1 on Art. 3 CAT (1997), § 5; see also § 4 of this Comment, according to which a complainant must establish a *prima facie* case for his complaint to be declared admissible. In ComAT, *M.N. v. Switzerland*, 17 November 2006, no. 259/2004, § 6.7, the Committee uses the word 'convincing' instead of 'arguable.'

78   ComAT, General Comment No. 1 on Art. 3 CAT (1997), § 7 and, amongst many others, ComAT, *A.S. v. Sweden*, 24 November 2000, no. 149/1999, § 8.6; ComAT, *A.A. et al. v. Switzerland*, 10 November 2008, 285/2006 §§ 7.3 and 7.4; ComAT, *X. v. Australia*, 30 April 2009, no. 324/2007, § 7.4.

79   As recent examples amongst many others see ComAT, *E.C.B. v. Switzerland*, 26 May 2011, no. 369/2008, §§ 10.9 and 10.13; ComAT, *T.D. v. Switzerland*, 26 May 2011, no. 375/2009, § 7.9; ComAT, *M.B. v. Switzerland*, 31 May 2013, no. 439/2010, § 8.

However, as early as the *traveaux préparatoires* on Article 3 CAT, it was pointed out that the evidentiary requirement should not be too rigorous and that the burden of proof should not fall solely upon the complainant.[80] In this spirit, the Committee has made clear that once the complainant has presented an arguable case, the state must make 'sufficient efforts' to determine whether there are substantial grounds for believing he would be subjected to torture in case of removal.[81] States have a duty under Article 3 CAT to examine carefully and take into account all existing circumstances that may reasonably be considered to indicate a risk of torture.[82] In particular, according to Article 3(2) CAT, the 'competent authorities shall take into account all relevant considerations including, where applicable, the existence in the State concerned of a consistent pattern of gross, flagrant or mass violations of human rights.'

In principle it falls to the complainant to *collect and present evidence* in support of his claim or account of events.[83] A complainant does not have to prove or to submit evidence for all the facts cited, but the Committee must be able to consider them 'sufficiently substantiated and reliable.'[84] The presentation of convincing evidence may provoke a shift in the burden of proof to the government. The case *A.S. v. Sweden* concerned the removal of a woman to Iran who alleged she had been sentenced to death by stoning for adultery in her country.[85] The Committee was of the opinion that the applicant had submitted sufficient details regarding her marriage and alleged arrest (such as names of persons, their positions, dates, addresses) to shift the burden of proof to the state party. Finding that the state party had not made 'sufficient efforts to determine whether there are substantial grounds for believing that the author would be in danger of being subjected to torture,' and considering that she had sufficiently established the risk, the Committee concluded that the removal to Iran would violate Article 3 CAT.[86]

---

80   Nowak & McArthur 2008, p. 134 (§ 20).

81   ComAT, *A.S. v. Sweden*, 24 November 2000, no. 149/1999, § 8.6. See also ComAT, General Comment No. 1 on Art. 3 CAT (1997), § 5.

82   ComAT, *Boily v. Canada*, 14 November 2011, no. 327/2007, § 14.4.

83   Amongst others see ComAT, *A.H. v. Sweden*, 16 November 2006, no. 265/2005, § 11.6; ComAT, *N.Z.S. v. Sweden*, 22 November 2006, no. 277/2005, § 8.6; ComAT, *E.R.K. and Y.K. v. Sweden*, 30 April 2007, no. 270 & 271/2005, §§ 7.4 and 7.5; ComAT, *M.M. et al. v. Sweden*, 11 November 2008, no. 332/2007, § 7.6; ComAT, *M.B. v. Switzerland*, 31 May 2013, no. 439/2010, § 7.9.

84   See for example ComAT, *Aemei v. Switzerland*, 9 May 1997, 34/1995, § 9.6.

85   ComAT, *A.S. v. Sweden*, 24 November 2000, no. 149/1999.

86   *Ibid.*, § 8.4–9. Similar ComAT, *Karoui v. Sweden*, 8 May 2002, no. 185/2001, § 10.

The Committee attaches particular importance to medicolegal reports of past torture. If a complainant presents medical reports proving he has been tortured in the recent past, the burden of proof will likely shift to the government.[87] This can be observed for example in the case *K.H. v. Denmark*, in which an Afghan applicant had presented the national authorities with scars and two medical memoranda as evidence that he had been tortured in the past. The asylum authorities, however, refused to order a specialized medical examination. The Committee noted that 'although it is for the complainants to establish a *prima facie* case to request for asylum, it does not exempt the State party from making substantial efforts to determine whether there are grounds for believing that the complainant would be in danger of being subjected to torture if returned.'[88] It concluded that by rejecting the asylum request without seeking further investigation on his claims of having been tortured or ordering a medical examination, the state party had failed to determine whether there were substantial grounds for the existence of a relevant danger. Accordingly, it found that the applicant's removal to Afghanistan would violate Article 3 CAT.[89]

Evidence showing past detentions, political activities or a current interest by the state authorities in a complainant is also of importance.[90] In a case concerning the removal to Iran of a woman who alleged she would be persecuted by the Iranian authorities as an opponent of the regime, the Committee found that the complainant had not submitted sufficient details or corroborating evidence to shift the burden of proof. She had in particular not adduced satisfactory evidence or details as to her alleged former detention and escape.[91] In the case *M.A.K v. Germany*, the Committee found that, due to lack of evidence proving the complainant's alleged former activities for the PKK, a shift in the burden of proof would not be justified and the complainant could not reasonably claim the benefit of the doubt.[92] The Committee argued similarly with

---

87   On the importance of past ill treatment in the Committee's risk assessment see, in more detail, Section 3.3.2.b of this Chapter (Past torture or ill treatment).

88   ComAT, *K.H. v. Denmark*, 23 November 2012, no. 464/2011, § 8.8.

89   *Ibid.* See similar, ComAT, *F.K. v. Denmark*, 23 November 2015, no. 580/2014, § 7.6.

90   See on this Section 3.3.2b of this Chapter (Political and/or religious background).

91   ComAT, *S.P.A. v. Canada*, 7 November 2005, no. 282/2005, § 7.5.

92   ComAT, *M.A.K. v. Germany*, 12 May 2004, no. 214/2002, § 13.5. In this decision, the Committee noted 'that it is not competent to pronounce itself on the standard of proof applied by German tribunals.' This statement is strange since the Committee has made clear in other decisions that it considers the standard of proof as set by domestic authorities to be too high; see explicitly ComAT, *Tala v. Sweden*, 15 November 1996, no. 43/1996, §§ 5.2, 7.2 and 10.2.

regard to the expulsion to Sri Lanka of a Tamil woman who claimed to be in danger because of her family members' affiliation with the LTTE.[93] It noted that the complainant had not discharged the burden of proof by pointing out, *inter alia*, that she had not presented any evidence that the authorities in Sri Lanka had any interest in her whereabouts in the recent past.[94]

In a number of cases concerning the removal of applicants from Sweden to Azerbaijan, the Committee has held that the burden of proof did not shift to the government, since the applicants had not presented enough reliable evidence with regard to significant political activity or past problems with the Azerbaijani authorities in connection with such activity.[95] In all cases, the Swedish embassy made investigations in Azerbaijan, showing that important allegations by the complainants were false.[96] The Committee attached weight to the government's findings and found no violation of Article 3 CAT in the cases. The Committee generally attaches particular weight to investigations by state embassies on the alleged personal circumstances of a complainant in a receiving country,[97] unless such an investigation is made after the termination of the domestic procedure without the possibility for the complainant to contest it.[98] However, generally, if the state party does not dispute allegations, the Committee will likely consider them established.[99]

The human rights situation in a receiving state can provoke shifts in the burden of proof as well. Nowak and McArthur go as far as to state that if there

---

93   ComAT, *Sivagnanaratnam v. Denmark*, 11 November 2013, no. 429/2010.

94   *Ibid.*, §§ 10.5 and 10.6.

95   ComAT, *A.H. v. Sweden*, 16 November 2006, no. 265/2005, § 11.6; ComAT, *E.R.K. and Y.K. v. Sweden*, 30 April 2007, no. 270 & 271/2005, §§ 7.4 and 7.5; ComAT, *E.V.I. v. Sweden*, 1 May 2007, no. 296/2006, §§ 8.5–8.7; ComAT, *M.M. et al. v. Sweden*, 11 November 2008, no. 332/2007, § 7.6.

96   *Ibid.*

97   See further ComAT, *K.M. v. Switzerland*, 16 November 1999, no. 107/1998, § 6.6; ComAT, *N.Z.S. v. Sweden*, 22 November 2006, no. 277/2005, § 8.6.

98   See ComAT, *E.J. et al. v. Sweden*, 14 November 2008, no. 306/2006, § 8.4, in which the Committee stated that it would not take into account the Swedish embassy's investigations for these reasons. The Committee further criticized the authorities for not revealing the name of the author of the investigation.

99   See, for example, ComAT, *A.S. v. Sweden*, 24 November 2000, no. 149/1999, § 8.7; ComAT, *C.T. and K.M. v. Sweden*, 17 November 2006, no. 279/2005, §§ 7.5 and 7.6; ComAT, *Amini v. Denmark*, 15 November 2010, no. 339/2008, §§ 9.7 and 9.8; ComAT, *Ktiti v. Morocco*, 26 May 2011, no. 419/2010, §§ 8.6 and 8.7.

... exist[s] a consistent pattern of gross, flagrant or mass violations of human rights, above all a systematic practice of torture in the home country, it is up to the government of the host State to provide evidence showing why the applicant would not be at risk of torture. If such a systematic practice does not exist, there is a stronger burden on the applicant to provide evidence.[100]

There are decisions demonstrating a considerable alleviation in the burden of proof on the complainant because of poor human rights conditions in the receiving country.[101] However, the concept of a 'consistent pattern of gross, flagrant or mass violations of human rights' is not clear, and even where the human rights situation in the receiving state is very worrying, the initial burden to show a risk of torture will usually rest with the complainant.[102] It may be added that according to the Committee, the burden of proof might also shift to the government in cases in which diplomatic assurances are sought 'given that such a request demonstrates that the extraditing state harbours concerns about the treatment that may be reserved for the extradited person in the destination country.'[103]

Wouters summarizes that there is a 'combined and co-operative responsibility' with regard to the burden of proof but that the 'exact division of roles between individuals and State is difficult to determine in general and depends on each individual case.'[104] The Committee has stated that, 'even though there may be some remaining doubt as to the veracity of the facts adduced by a complainant, it must ensure that his security is not endangered.'[105] Having the security of the complainant as the main objective, the Committee's approach with regard to the burden of proof seems indeed to be quite flexible. Ingelse and Nowak and McArthur state that the burden of proof is not 'particularly

---

100   Nowak & McArthur 2008, pp. 130–131, 193, 224.

101   For recent examples see ComAT, *Jahani v. Switzerland*, 23 May 2011, no. 357/2008, §§ 9-4-9.10 (Iran); ComAT, *Chahin v. Sweden*, 30 May 2011, no. 310/2007, § 9.6 (Syria); ComAT, *Fadel v. Switzerland*, 14 November 2014, no. 450/2011, § 7.8 (Yemeni prisons); ComAT, *J.K. v. Canada*, 23 November 2015, no. 562/2013, §§ 10.4 and 10.5 (Uganda for LGBTI).

102   See on this Section 3.2.2.a of this chapter.

103   ComAT, *Boily v. Canada*, 14 November 2011, no. 327/2007, § 14.4. See on this Section 3.4.2.b of this chapter.

104   Wouters 2009, p. 487. See in this sense also Ingelse 2001, p. 191.

105   ComAT, *Mutombo v. Switzerland*, 27 April 1994, no. 13/1993, § 9.2; ComAT, *M.P.S. v. Australia*, 30 April 2002, no. 138/1999, § 7.3.

great.'[106] Weissbrodt and Hörtreiter speak of a 'very protective approach' and note that the Committee attaches more weight to a complainant's general credibility than to objective evidence.[107] These considerations are correct. However, the question of whether the requirements of the Committee with respect to the burden of proof are low is easier to address in comparison with the Court's case law.[108]

1.2.3   The Role of the Committee

According to Article 22(4) CAT, the Committee shall consider complaints in light of all information made available to it by or on behalf of the individual and by the state party concerned. Although this provision indicates that the Committee should in principle 'not actively seek further evidence or carry out its own fact finding,' the Committee often refers to information gained through its own procedures when it considers the human rights situation of the country of destination.[109] In exercising its jurisdiction pursuant to Article 3 CAT, the Committee must 'give considerable weight to findings of fact that are made by the organs of the State party concerned'; it is not, however, bound by such findings and instead has the power 'provided by article 22, paragraph 4, of the Convention, of free assessment of the facts based upon the full set of circumstances in every case.'[110] The Committee reminds us from time to time that although it is free to assess the facts, it is not a judicial or appellate body.[111] From 2004 on, the Committee has stated in several decisions that it is not its place to question the evaluation of evidence by the domestic courts or substitute its own findings

---

106   Ingelse 2001, p. 298; Nowak & McArthur 2008, p. 193 (§ 164). Similarly Weissbrodt and Hörtreiter 1999, p. 15.

107   Weissbrodt and Hörtreiter 1999, p. 50.

108   See Section 1.3.2 of this chapter below.

109   Nowak & McArthur 2008, pp. 788 (§ 182) and 790 (§ 186), who speak of a broad interpretation of Art. 22(4) CAT. See further Rule 118(2) RoP CAT (CAT/C/3/Rev.6), according to which the Committee may at any time in the course of the examination obtain documents from UN bodies, specialized agencies, or other sources that may assist in the consideration of the complaint. On the role of country reports in the Committee's risk assessment see Section 3.2.2.c. of this chapter.

110   ComAT, General Comment No. 1 on Art. 3 CAT (1997), § 9; Recalled for example in ComAT, *Abdussamatov and 28 Others v. Kazakhstan*, 1 June 2012, no. 444/2010, § 13.9.

111   See, as recent examples, ComAT, *E.L. v. Switzerland*, 15 November 2011, no. 351/2008, § 9.6; ComAT, *D.Y. v. Sweden*, 21 May 2013, no. 463/2011, § 9.4; ComAT, *T.M. v. Republic of Korea*, 21 November 2014, no. 519/2012, § 9.4. See also General Comment No. 1 on Art. 3 CAT (1997), § 9.

'unless it can be ascertained that the manner in which the evidence was evaluated was clearly arbitrary or amounted to a denial of justice, or that the officers had clearly violated their obligations of impartiality.'[112] However, scholars have rightly observed that this statement is not reflected in the Committee's overall case law.[113] The Committee has drawn conclusions from facts presented which differ from those drawn by national authorities in several cases in which the risk assessment did not seem arbitrary or to amount to a denial of justice. Significantly, in the case *Dadar v. Canada*, the Committee noted that 'the argument submitted by the State party that the Committee is not a so-called fourth instance cannot prevail.'[114] In *Singh v. Canada*, the Committee noted 'that in the case under analysis, most of the facts are undisputed by the parties, however the assessment of the legal consequences of the relevant facts are challenged. In this situation, the Committee should assess the facts in light of the State party's obligations under the Convention.'[115] In *Sonko v. Spain* adopted in 2011, the Committee recalled again that 'it is not its task to weigh the evidence or to reassess the statements made regarding the facts or the credibility of the relevant national authorities.'[116] Committee member Gaer strongly dissented from this declaration in an individual opinion. He noted that the statement conflicts both with the content of the Committee's General Comment No. 1, according to which the Committee can freely assess the facts, and with its practice when assessing individual complaints. He rightly added that in a number of cases, whether the national judicial organs have made relevant findings or not, the Committee has engaged in a 'free assessment' of the facts at issue,

---

112 ComAT, *A.K. v. Australia*, 5 May 2004, no. 148/1999, § 6.4; ComAT, *Rios v. Canada*, 23 November 2004, no. 133/1999, § 8.5; ComAT, *Brada v. France*, 17 May 2005, no. 195/2002, § 13.6; ComAT, *S.P.A. v. Canada*, 7 November 2005, no. 282/2005, § 7.6; ComAT, *Pelit v. Azerbaijan*, 1 May 2007, no. 281/2005, § 7.11; ComAT, *J.A.M.O. v. Canada*, 9 May 2008, no. 293/2006, § 10.5; ComAT, *Ktiti v. Morocco*, 26 May 2011, no. 419/2010, § 8.7.

113 Chetail, 2006, p. 90; Wouters 2009, p. 491, who both further note that this statement is not in accordance with § 9 of the Committee's General Comment on Art. 3 CAT, according to which the Committee has the power to freely assess the facts.

114 ComAT, *Dadar v. Canada*, 23 November 2005, no. 258/2004, § 8.8. See also ComAT, *Minani v. Canada*, 5 November 2009, no. 331/2007, § 7.8.

115 ComAT, *Singh v. Canada*, 30 May 2011, no. 319/2007, § 8.3. See further ComAT, *Boily v. Canada*, 14 November 2011, no. 327/2007, § 14.2, in which the Committee found a violation of Art. 3 CAT although it noted that 'the information before it does not indicate any obvious errors in the State party's consideration of the allegations and evidence provided by the complainant.'

116 ComAT, *Sonko v. Spain*, 25 November 2011, no. 368/2008, § 10.2.

based upon the full set of circumstances.[117] The Committee should be clear on the fact that it *does* reassess the facts in many cases, since this is simply visible. What can be observed, however, is that the more solid, exhaustive and fair the assessment carried out by the national authorities appears, the more reluctant the Committee will be to impose its own assessment.[118]

1.3   *Comparison*

1.3.1   Higher Standard of Proof before the Court

According to the Court's standard formulation used since the *Soering* judgment, the removal of a person is illicit 'where substantial grounds have been shown for believing that the person concerned faces a real risk of being subjected to torture or to inhuman or degrading treatment or punishment in the requesting country.' This formula was inspired by the risk criterion stated in Article 3(1) CAT, according to which no state shall return a person to another state 'where there are substantial grounds for believing that he would be in danger of being subjected to torture.'[119] Article 3(1) CAT was in turn inspired by the case law of the former European Commission on Human Rights.[120] The mutual influence of the Court and the Committee on each other and the similarity in their descriptions of the standard of proof required is evident. The wording of the Court and the Committee in their decisions and judgments when defining the risk or danger is almost identical. While the Court requires a real, personal and foreseeable risk that goes beyond a mere possibility but need not be more likely than not, the Committee requires a real, personal and foreseeable danger, that must go beyond theory or suspicion, but does not have to be highly probable.

In its standard formulation, the Court uses the term 'risk' instead of the term 'danger' from Article 3 CAT. Some scholars have noted that this indicates a lower standard of probability required by the Court than by the Committee.[121]

---

117   *Ibid.*

118   See Section 3.1.2.a of this chapter below and, as examples for this approach ComAT, *S.U.A. v. Sweden*, 22 November 2004, no. 223/2002, § 6.5; ComAT, *N.Z.S. v. Sweden*, 22 November 2006, no. 277/2005, § 8.6; Or, *e contrario*, ComAT, *Tala v. Sweden*, 15 November 1996, no. 43/1996, §§ 10.2–10.5; ComAT, *A.F. v. Sweden*, 8 May 1998, no. 89/1997, §§ 6.4–6.7; ComAT, *M.M.O. v. Denmark*, 12 November 2003, no. 209/2002, § 6.5; ComAT, *Ke Chun Rong v. Australia*, 5 November 2012, no. 416/2010, §§ 7.4 and 7.5; ComAT, *Y.G.H. et al v.' Australia*, 14 November 2013, no. 434/2010, §§ 8.4 and 8.5; ComAT, *B.M.S. v. Sweden*, 25 November 2015, no. 594/2014, § 8.9. Also de Weck 2011, p. 10.

119   ECtHR, *Soering v. UK*, 7 July 1989, no. 14038/88, § 88.

120   See on this Chapter 1 Section 3.2.1.

121   Alleweldt 1996, pp. 30–31; Lorz & Sauer 2010, p. 396; Weissbrodt & Hörtreiter 1999, p. 55.

Suntinger rejects this interpretation, rightly pointing out that the French version of Article 3 CAT also uses the term 'risk' (*'risque'*) and not the term 'danger' (French: *'danger'*).[122] In addition, the Committee usually uses both the term 'risk' and the term 'danger' in its decisions on Article 3 CAT.[123]

The case-by-case approach of the Court and the Committee makes it difficult to make statements of general value with regard to the standard of proof. One case will appear severe, another lenient. Looking simply at the language used by the Court and the Committee, the standard of risk required appears similar.[124] However, in comparative analyses scholars have rightly noted that the standard of proof required by the Court in practice seems higher than that required by the Committee.[125] This conclusion is reaffirmed by the numbers: in 2012, the Court stated that it has 'only rarely reached the conclusion' that a removal would violate the principle of non-refoulement.[126] Compared to the Committee, this statement is true. While around 20 per cent of all complaints assessed under Article 3 CAT have been successful before the Committee,[127] far fewer have been successful before the Court. There are no official statistics, but as has been explained in chapter 1, the Court has dealt with thousands of requests for interim measures but it is in 125 judgments so far that it has found the principle of non-refoulement to have been violated.[128] However, the numbers may only be seen as an indication of the analysis of the case law as a whole since it is impossible to compare the 'quality' of the complaints that have been submitted in Strasbourg and Geneva.

Suntinger sees a basis for a lower standard of proof in Committee proceedings in the wording of Article 3 CAT, which considers illicit any expulsion or extradition of a person to a state where there are 'substantial grounds for believing' that he would be in danger of being subjected to torture, while the standard formula used by the Court since the *Soering* judgments adds that

---

122   Suntinger 1995, p. 217.

123   See, as one recent example among many others, ComAT, *Y.B.F., S.A.Q. and Y.Y. v. Switzerland*, 31 May 2013, no. 467/2011, § 7.2. It should also be noted that the Court occasionally uses the term 'danger'; see, for example, ECtHR, *Mamatkulov and Askarov v. Turkey*, 4 February 2005 [GC], nos. 46827/99 and 46951/99, § 68.

124   Arai-Takahashi 2002, p. 20; McAdam 2011, pp. 722 and 725–726; Suntinger 1995, p. 217.

125   Chetail 2006, p. 101; Schürmann & Scheidegger 2009, p. 213; Suntinger 1995, pp. 224 and 225; Weissbrodt & Hörtreiter 1999, pp. 15–16, 36, 50.

126   ECtHR, *Harkins and Edwards v. UK*, 17 January 2012, nos. 9146/07 and 32650/07, § 131.

127   See the numbers explained in Chapter 1 Section 3.2.2.

128   See the discussion of this in Chapter 1 Section 2.2.2. Generally, as has been explained in Chapter 2 more than 95 per cent of all complaints in Strasbourg are declared inadmissible.

substantial grounds 'must have been shown.'[129] However, in my opinion, the severity of the Court or 'generosity' of the Committee is not a result of the definition of the risk used (which is almost identical), but rather a result of their different practices with regard to the evaluation of risk elements as discussed in this chapter. As Thurin states, both the Court and the Committee draw the line between a relevant and a non-relevant risk depending on the existence or non-existence of risk factors in a particular case.[130] Weissbrodt and Hörtreiter argue that the more generous approach in Geneva is legitimated by the fact that with torture, the Committee provides protection only from the most severe form of persecution.[131] It cannot be excluded that the protection offered under Article 3 ECHR against inhuman and degrading treatment of a broader nature and from varying protagonists has led to a certain severity of the Court with regard to the standard of proof in individual cases. It has been explained for instance that the threshold set by Article 3 ECHR appears particularly high where the risk does not concern the *direct responsibility* of the receiving states in the infliction of harm.[132] However, considering that the distinction between torture and inhuman treatment does not play a major role in many of the Court's and Committee's judgments and decisions, the argument is of limited value.

In sum, when there are two almost identical cases in which both complainants fear acts of torture from their home countries' authorities because of past political activities, a complaint before the Committee *will have more chance of success*. The *Paez* cases concerning two Peruvian brothers who had both been affiliated with Shining Path confirm this in an illustrative way.[133] The brothers had fled to Sweden in the early 90s. After their request for asylum was rejected in Sweden, one of the brothers submitted an individual complaint alleging a

---

129   Suntinger 1995, pp. 218 and 220, who further indicates the French versions, in which the Court speaks of '*motifs sérieux et avérés de croire,*' while Art. 3 CAT solely speaks of '*motifs serieux de croire.*'

130   Thurin 2012, p. 184. See in this sense also Wouters 2009, p. 542.

131   Weissbrodt and Hörtreiter 1999, pp. 15–16 and 64; in their opinion, the more severe the ill treatment a person faces, the lower the required degree of probability should be.

132   See Chapter 3 Sections 2.3.1 and 2.3.2. However, the Grand Chamber has recently proclaimed in *Tarakhel* § 104 that 'the source of the risk does nothing to alter the level of protection guaranteed by the Convention or the Convention obligations of the State ordering the person's removal.' This statement is again, however, in contrast to the Court's approach in the lead case *N. v UK*, discussed and criticized in Chapter 3 Section 2.3.2.a.

133   See EComHR, *Paez v. Sweden*, report of 6 December 1996, no. 29482/95 and ComAT, *Paez v. Sweden*, 28 April 1997, no. 39/1996. Wouters (2009, p. 577) has contrasted the two *Paez* cases in his comprehensive study on prohibitions of refoulement in international law to highlight that non-refoulement is not an unequivocal concept.

violation of the principle of non-refoulement in Geneva. The other one submitted a complaint in Strasbourg. Their risk background appeared identical. However, in contrast to the Committee in Geneva, the former European Commission on Human Rights in Strasbourg found no violation of the principle of non-refoulement. Strasbourg reasoned that the applicant 'had not presented any warrant of arrest or similar evidence which would show that he is wanted by the Peruvian authorities or is otherwise of any particular interest to them' and that 'there are no specific indications that the applicant has ever been singled out as a high profile member of the Sendero Luminoso movement.'[134]

However, it should not be forgotten that the success or failure of a complaint always depends on various factors, in which the standard or burden of proof, as an abstract concept, is often not at the centre of the decision-making bodies' considerations. Before both the Court and the Committee, the probability of success in refoulement cases is not a mathematical concept, but a normative one.[135]

1.3.2   Burden of Proof and Supporting Evidence

Before the Court and the Committee, the complainant has the initial burden of proof. Under both, the burden can shift to the government under specific circumstances. One can distinguish two main situations in which there is such a shift:

1.   The complaint presents reliable evidence indicating a risk of ill treatment.
2.   The human rights situation in the receiving country is extremely poor.

(1) With regard to the presentation of evidence it should be noted that neither the Court nor the Committee require that all facts invoked by a complainant be supported by evidence. However, the absence of evidence may have a negative impact on the credibility of a complainant.[136] The Court seems generally to ask for more evidence.[137] What kind of evidence is pertinent depends on the circumstances of the case. If a complainant presents reliable evidence that he has been tortured in the recent past by perpetrators who are still powerful in the receiving country, the burden of proof will likely shift to the government. The Committee puts particular weight on evidence demonstrating past acts of

---

134   EComHR, *Paez v. Sweden*, report of 6 December 1996, no. 29482/95, §§ 79 and 82. The conclusion was, however, made by 15 votes to 14.

135   See, with reference to the Court, Thurin 2012, p. 162.

136   See Section 3.3.3a of this chapter below on credibility.

137   In this sense also Chetail 2006, p. 101; Weissbrodt and Hörtreiter 1999, p. 55.

torture.[138] Other evidence that can be of importance includes arrest warrants, court summons or documents demonstrating that an applicant has been politically active against powerful actors in the receiving country, provided, however, that practices of ill treatment against political opponents by such actors are known. It is up to the government to demonstrate that evidence presented is not authentic, not reliable or not pertinent.

(2) Under both the Court and the Committee, the Human Rights situation in the receiving country has an impact on the burden of proof. If conditions are extremely poor, fewer distinguishing elements and less evidence demonstrating that a complainant is threatened because of his personal background will be required.

It should be added that the burden of proof on the complainant in the international procedure is further compensated by a strict surveillance of procedural guarantees given in the national deportation procedure. As demonstrated in section 3.1 of this chapter, under both the Court and the Committee an unfair or missing national risk assessment can considerably alleviate the burden on the applicant in proceedings in Strasbourg or Geneva. In addition, when no proper assessment of important allegations is apparent in the national decisions, the government's observations within the framework of the international procedure become particularly important.[139]

In summary, while the complainant has the initial burden of proof before both the Court and the Committee, the state must be fully engaged. Authorities must actively contribute to the process. They have to analyse a complainant's allegations in light of the human rights situation in the receiving country and make sure, through procedural guarantees, that the individual can freely bring his claim before the competent authorities. They further have to counter any serious allegation by a complainant, be it an allegation regarding personal circumstances or the human rights situation, if they want to demonstrate to the Court or the Committee that such allegations are not reliable. If the burden of proof shifts, the state may itself have the obligation to provide evidence to demonstrate that a complainant is lying or is simply not in danger in case of deportation. Under both the Court and the Committee there is a shared responsibility for the procedure between the state and the individual.

It is clear that with a lower standard of proof, the burden of proof on a complainant is also lower. As has been stated by Chetail, the Committee is readier

---

138   See on this Sections 3.3.2.b and 3.3.3.b of this Chapter.

139   See, for example, ComAT, *C.T. and K.M. v. Sweden*, 17 November 2006, no. 279/2005, §§ 5.8, 7.5 and 7.6; ECtHR, *Abdolkhani and Karimnia v. Turkey*, 22 September 2009, no. 30471/08, § 90.

than the Court to attribute the benefit of the doubt to applicants, which in turn leads it to find violations more often.[140] The Court seems to be more reluctant to discharge the applicant from the burden of proof.[141] However, it must be recalled that the Court and the Committee follow a case-by-case approach in which so many different factors may play a role that abstract definitions or statements on the standard or burden of proof are difficult. In addition, the Committee's decisions are often very short, such that it is difficult to determine in many cases on what grounds or due to which evidence the Committee has been persuaded that a real risk of torture has either been established or not.[142]

1.3.3 The Role of the Court and the Committee Compared

The starting point of the Court and the Committee in the risk assessment is the material evaluation of the facts as presented by the parties involved. The Committee postulates that it gives particular weight to government's findings. The Court has stated that it requires cogent elements to lead it to depart from the findings of fact reached by national courts.

However, neither the Court nor the Committee are bound by the national authorities' findings or restrict their assessment to the material submitted by the parties. They regularly seek further information, in particular with regard to the human rights situation in the receiving country. On this matter the Court is particularly active when compared to the Committee.[143] When it comes to the evaluation of the human rights situation in receiving countries, the Court and the Committee, as international institutions, are not necessarily at a disadvantage compared to national courts.[144] This is, however, not the case with regard to the examination of a complainant's personal credibility or the analysis of personal evidence, like medical reports, arrest warrants or testimonies (of which the Court and the Committee usually only see copies). Hence, when it comes to the complainant's personal circumstances, the Court and the Committee are less proactive. They will in principle only seek new evidence with regard to a complainant's personal background if they observe deficiencies

---

140   Chetail 2006, p. 101. See further Schürmann & Scheidegger 2009, p. 213, according to which the Committee is more inclined to make decisions *in dubio pro individuo* than the Court. See also Duffy 2008, p. 380; Ingelse 2001, p. 399; Weissbrodt & Hörtreiter 1999, p. 58.

141   See in this sense also Mole & Meredith 2010, pp. 53–54, and Suntinger 1995, p. 220, speaking of a more active role of the state in the procedure under the CAT.

142   See in this sense also McAdam 2011, p. 717.

143   It is worth noting that the ECHR leaves more room here than the CAT does; read Art. 38 ECHR in comparison with Art. 22(4) CAT.

144   See in this sense also Rieter 2010, p. 830.

in the national procedure or if they realize that important elements have not been taken into account by the national courts.[145]

The Court and the Committee both state that they are sensitive to the *subsidiary nature of their role*. They both recognize that the state party is primarily responsible for the assessment of the facts and evidence. However, in assessing whether the national authorities have correctly applied the principle of non-refoulement in individual cases, they both usually proceed to a risk assessment that includes the substance of a case. Neither the Court nor the Committee shy away from drawing different conclusions from the national authorities on the facts presented in the domestic procedure. Their occasional assertion that they would not substitute their own findings except in case of manifest procedural irregularities is actually not reflected in their case law.[146] With that, the Court and the Committee's approach is distinguished from that of the UN Human Rights Committee which, as a rule, tries only to intervene with its own material risk assessment when manifest deficiencies in the risk assessment at national level are visible.[147] That said, if the Court or the Committee are persuaded of the existence of a real risk, the level of professionalism and the thoroughness of the assessment at national level will not be that relevant in their assessment. However, where the risk assessment at national level appears fair and comprehensive, the Court and the Committee are more reluctant to carry out their own analysis of the facts. Conversely, where deficiencies in the national procedure are striking, this might considerably enhance the complainant's general position and credibility within the risk assessment in the international procedure.[148]

---

145   See the examples ECtHR, *R.C. v. Sweden*, 9 March 2010, no. 41827/02, §§ 23–25 and 53; ECtHR, *Ahmade v. Greece*, 25 September 2012, no. 50520/09, §§ 51, 70–79; ComAT, *Aemei v. Switzerland*, 9 May 1997, 34/1995, §§ 2.5, 2.6, 9.7 and 9.8, ComAT, *Amini v. Denmark*, 15 November 2010, no. 339/2008, § 6.2.

146   For the Court, see ECtHR, *Kaldik v. Germany*, 10 November 2005, no. 28526/06 (decision), in which the Court noted 'as a general rule, that the assessment of the facts and the taking of evidence and its evaluation is a matter which necessarily comes within the appreciation of the national courts and cannot be reviewed by the Court unless there is an indication that the judges have drawn grossly unfair or arbitrary conclusions from the facts before them.' This explicit statement in *Kaldik* remains exceptional.

147   As indicated in Chapter 1 Section 5, it appears 'that the HRC has even intensified the application of this approach in its recent practice. It is, however, not fully consequent in its use.

148   See on this Section 3.1 of this chapter below. As will be explained in this section, there are cases, particularly before the Committee, in which procedural deficiencies at the national level are the main reason for the finding of a violation of the principle of non-refoulement.

The Court's and Committee's independence in the risk assessment provokes the criticism that they have lost their subsidiary character and are acting as a fourth-instance asylum court.[149] However, an effective protection mechanism cannot abstain from imposing its own view on the conclusions that have to be drawn from facts in a particular case, even if no arbitrary procedure is apparent. This is particularly true since the Court and the Committee, by indicating interim measures and making a full up-to-date assessment, take effective responsibility for a possible future human rights violation.[150] Nonetheless, if international institutions draw other conclusions than those of the national authorities that have made a full risk assessment, this requires a special motivation. The Court has reminded us of its subsidiary nature in recent judgments and pointed out that cogent reasons are needed for it to depart from the findings of fact of the national courts.[151] In the great majority of its judgments in which the Court has found that Article 3 ECHR would be violated in case of deportation, it has in fact provided substantive reasoning. In contrast, the Committee's decisions are often extremely short. This makes it hard to trace why the Committee agrees or disagrees with the national examination in many of its decisions.[152] For this reason the Committee's role often appears unclear.

2   Time of the Risk Assessment

In the *Soering* case, the Court held that it is 'not normally for the Convention institutions to pronounce on the existence or otherwise of potential violations of the Convention,' but that 'a departure from this principle is necessary, in view of the serious and irreparable nature of the alleged suffering risked, in order to ensure the effectiveness of the safeguard provided by Article 3 ECHR.'[153]

---

149   See with regard to the Court in particular the critique of Bossuyt 2010, pp. 147–151 and 172–175. Nowak & McArthur 2008, pp. 127–128 (§ 1) note that the practice under Art. 3 CAT has led to criticism that the Committee acted as a kind of fourth instance in asylum proceedings in the North. See also, for example, the governments arguments in ComAT, *Kalonzo v. Canada*, 18 May 2012, no. 343/2008, § 4.1.

150   See in this sense also the interesting comment of judge Villiger in his concurring opinion to ECtHR, *M.S.S.* He notes that 'subsidiarity plays an important part, for instance, in applying the second paragraphs of Articles 8–11 ECHR,' but that 'its role must surely be more restricted in the light of a cardinal provision such as Article 3 and in view of the central importance of the applicant's *refoulement* for this case.'

151   See, for example, ECtHR, *H. and B. v. UK*, 9 April 2013, nos. 70073/10 and 44539/11, § 111.

152   For a critique of the Committee's lack of detailed reasoning see also Chapter 5 Section 3.

153   ECtHR, *Soering v. UK*, 7 July 1989, no. 14038/88, § 90.

With the examination of a future risk, the question arises: which point in time is decisive for the risk assessment of the Court and the Committee – the moment of the national court's final decision, or the moment of the international institution's decision? And what if a person has already been expelled? Is it legitimate to look at how he was treated on his return or should only the information be taken into account that the state parties knew when they expelled this person?

2.1   Court

In the judgment *Cruz Varas* in 1991, the Court established the following principle, which is still relevant today:

> Since the nature of the Contracting States' responsibility under Article 3 in cases of this kind lies in the act of exposing an individual to the risk of ill-treatment, the existence of *the risk must be assessed primarily with reference to those facts which were known or ought to have been known to the Contracting State at the time of the expulsion*; the Court is not precluded, however, from having regard to information which comes to light subsequent to the expulsion. This may be of value in confirming or refuting the appreciation that has been made by the Contracting Party of the well-foundedness or otherwise of an applicant's fears.[154] (Emphasis added)

In the *Chahal* judgment in 1996, the Court made clear that if a complainant has *not been yet deported*, the material point must be that of the Court's consideration of the case. It held that in such situations, although the historical position is of interest insofar as it may shed light on the current situation and its likely evolution, it is the *present conditions that are decisive*.[155] The principle of an *ex nunc* assessment in cases where the applicant has not yet been deported is constantly reiterated in the Court's jurisprudence.[156] In other words, if an expulsion or extradition has already taken place, the Court will base its risk assessment primarily on the facts the state party knew or should have known at the date of the deportation. If the complainant has not yet been deported, a situation that typically arises when the deportation has been stayed as a result of an interim measure, the relevant date is the date of the Court's decision.

---

154   ECtHR, *Cruz Varas and Others v. Sweden*, 20 March 1991, no. 15576/89, § 76.

155   ECtHR, *Chahal v. UK*, 15 November 1996, no. 22414/93, § 86.

156   See, for example, ECtHR, *Sufi and Elmi v. UK*, 28 June 2011, nos. 8319/07 and 11449/07, § 215.

The historical information is only of relevance insofar as it sheds light on the current situation.

In the case *Vilvarajah and Others v. United Kingdom*, the deportation had already taken place when the Court took its decision. Even though there was evidence that some of the complainants had been ill-treated on their return to Sri Lanka, the Court found no violation of Article 3 ECHR. It argued that the United Kingdom's authorities could not have foreseen the ill treatment at the time of the expulsion.[157] However, the Court is not strictly bound by information that was known or ought to have been known by the state when it took its decisions. Events subsequent to the expulsion 'may be of value in confirming or refuting the appreciation that has been made by the Contracting Party or the well-foundedness or otherwise of an applicant's fears.'[158] In *Cruz Varas*, the Court took note of the fact that in the course of his stay in Chile subsequent to his expulsion, the complainant was unable to adduce any evidence corroborating his alleged political activities.[159] In the case *Mamatkulov and Askarov* concerning the extradition of two applicants to Uzbekistan despite interim measures being indicated, the Grand Chamber took into account medical reports produced by the government after the return of the complainants, which did not reveal any pathological symptoms. For this and other reasons, the Court concluded that there had been no violation of Article 3 ECHR.[160] Contrast the case *Ben Khemais v. Italy*, in which the Court found that the extradition of the complainant to Tunisia after his condemnation for membership of a terrorist group had violated Article 3 ECHR, even though there was evidence that he had *not* been tortured on his return.[161] In the case *Y. v. Russia*, the Court held *inter alia* that the complainant moved in with his son after his expulsion to China and that there was no information indicating that he had

---

157   ECtHR, *Vilvarajah and Others v. UK*, 30 October 1991, nos. 13163/87 and further, §§ 104 and 112. See also ECtHR, *Panjeheighalehei v. Denmark*, 13 October 2009, no. 11230/07 (decision); ECtHR, *H.S. and Others v. Cyprus*, 21 July 2015, no. 41753/10 and 13 other applications, § 280.

158   ECtHR, *El-Masri v. Former Yugoslav Republic of Macedonia*, 13 December 2012 [GC], no. 39630/09, §§ 214 and 218.

159   ECtHR, *Cruz Varas and Others v. Sweden*, 20 March 1991, no. 15576/89, § 79.

160   ECtHR, *Mamatkulov and Askarov v. Turkey*, 4 February 2005 [GC], nos. 46827/99 and 46951/99, §§ 34 and 76. Note the partly dissenting opinion of judges Bratza, Bonello and Hedigan criticizing the fact that the medical reports (carried out long after the events in question) could not 'be relied on as refuting the well-foundedness of the applicant's fear at the time of their extradition.'

161   ECtHR, *Ben Khemais v. Italy*, 24 February 2009, no. 246/07, §§ 62–65.

been ill-treated.[162] In the case *Garabayev v. Russia*, the Court first stated that the Russian authorities made no proper risk assessment before the complainant had been extradited to Turkmenistan, but that they were made sufficiently aware of a risk of ill treatment in case of the applicant's return to that country.[163] The Court therefore found that 'at the date of the applicant's extradition to Turkmenistan there existed substantial grounds for believing that he faced a real risk of treatment proscribed by Article 3 ECHR.' It noted then that since the complainant had already been extradited, it was 'able to look beyond the moment of extradition and to assess the situation in view of these later developments.' Finding that the applicant's submissions that he had been ill-treated in Turkmen prisons were not contested by the respondent government, they would 'serve to strengthen the Court's above conclusions about a violation of Article 3 by the authorities' failure to give a proper consideration to the well-grounded fears raised by the applicant.'[164] In *Ermakov v. Russia,* the Court considered that the fact that neither the applicant's lawyers nor his relatives were able to contact him after his illegal transfer to Uzbekistan confirmed the well-foundedness of his fears.[165] However, in the case *Mamazhonov* the Court emphasised that, 'even in the absence of final evidence in some of the cases,' one must not overlook that a serious risk of inhuman treatment is sufficient to trigger the protective mechanisms of the Convention.[166]

It is not clear from the case law when and to what extent the Court will take into account information concerning the situation of an applicant *after* a deportation.[167] It can be observed that the materialisation of the anticipated

---

162   ECtHR, *Y. v. Russia*, 4 December 2008, no. 20113/07, §§ 83 and 89. See comparable considerations in ECtHR, *Cahuas v. Spain*, 10 August 2006, no. 24668/03, § 44; ECtHR, *Al-Moayad v. Germany*, 20 February 2007, no. 35865/03 (decision), § 67.

163   ECtHR, *Garabayev v. Russia*, 7 June 2007, no. 38411/02.

164   *Ibid.*, §§ 77–83. See the similar reasoning in ECtHR, *Iskandarov v. Russia*, 23 September 2010, no. 17185/05, §§ 128–135; ECtHR, *Mannai v. Italy*, 27 March 2012, no. 9961/10, § 41.

165   ECtHR, *Ermakov v. Russia*, 7 November 2013, no. 43165/10, § 206.

166   ECtHR, *Mamazhonov v. Russia*, 23 October 2014, no. 17239/13, § 146.

167   See also Mole & Meredith 2010, pp. 52–53, pointing out that in *Shamayev v. Russia and Georgia*, 12 April 2005, no. 36378/02, § 348–350, the Court judged that the applicants extradited to Russia against the indicated interim measures had not provided sufficient evidence of ill treatment after their extradition, despite the fact that they were not able to freely inform the Court about their situation in Russian detention. The Court found no violation of Art. 3 ECHR with regard to the extradition of theses applicants. In the case *Muminov v. Russia,* 11 December 2008, no. 42502/06, § 98, the Court held in contrast that 'the absence of any reliable information as to the situation of

ill treatment is not a condition for a violation of Article 3 ECHR in cases in which complainants have already been deported when the Court takes its decision. In any event, most cases considered by the Courts on the merits do not concern past expulsions or extraditions, but possible future ones. As has been stated, *if an expulsion has yet not taken place – because of interim measures or other reasons – the material time point for the risk assessment is the time of the Court's decision.* Therefore, the Court finds it 'necessary' in these cases to take into account information that has come to light after the final decision taken by the domestic authorities.[168] Although the national Courts can actually only be held responsible for the risk assessment at the time of their decision, new events that were not known to the state party at the time play a role in the Court's assessment.[169] As the Court states, 'a full and *ex nunc* assessment is called for as the situation in a country of destination may change in the course of time.'[170]

2.2   *Committee*

For a while, the Committee decided the question of a violation of Article 3 CAT 'at the time of its consideration of the complaint, rather than as at the time of the submission of the complaint' without distinguishing between cases in which the deportation had already taken place and those where it had not.[171] In the case *T.P.S. v. Canada*, the complainant was removed to India despite a request for interim measures. When the Committee examined the case, the complainant had spent two years back in India, and had not been subjected to torture. Given the substantial period of time that had elapsed in which the 'fears of the complainant had not been realized,' the Committee concluded that his allegations about a violation of Article 3 CAT were unfounded.[172] Committee member Camara criticised this approach in his individual opinion.

---

the applicant after his expulsion to Uzbekistan' was a matter of grave concern. The Court here found a violation of Art. 3 ECHR.

168   See for, example, ECtHR, *Salah Sheekh v. Netherlands*, 11 January 2007, no. 1948/04, § 136; ECtHR, *I.K. v. Austria*, 28 March 2013, no. 2964/12, § 62.

169   See on this issue the comparative Section 2.3 of this chapter below.

170   ECtHR, *Sufi and Elmi v. UK*, 28 June 2011, nos. 8319/07 and 11449/07, § 215; ECtHR, *Abdulkhakov v. Russia*, 2 October 2012, no. 14743/11, § 135.

171   ComAT, *T.P.S. v. Canada*, 16 May 2000, no. 99/1997, § 15.4; ComAT, *G.K. v. Switzerland*, 7 May 2003, no. 219/2002, § 6.8; ComAT, *J.A.G.V. v. Sweden*, 11 November 2003, no. 215/2002, § 7.4; ComAT, *Attia v. Sweden*, 17 November 2003, no. 199/2002, § 12.1. See also Chetail 2006, p. 74; Nowak & McArthur 2008, p. 202 (§ 186).

172   ComAT, *T.P.S. v. Canada*, 16 May 2000, no. 99/1997, § 15.4.

For him it was clear from the terms of Article 3 CAT that the time for the risk assessment was the moment of the expulsion or extradition. He held that in this particular case, there clearly had been a sufficient risk at this moment and that Canada had therefore violated Article 3 CAT. He stressed that 'the fact that in this case the author was not subsequently subjected to torture has no bearing on whether the State party violated the Convention in expelling him. The question of whether the risk – in this case, of acts of torture – actually materializes is of relevance only to any reparation or damages.' Camara's criticism seemed first to fall on deaf ears and the Committee rejected two other complaints considering, *inter alia*, that the complainants had not been tortured on their return to their respective countries.[173] However, in the landmark case *Agiza v. Sweden* adopted in 2005, the Committee changed its approach.[174] Ahmed Agiza is an Egyptian national who was tried for terrorist activity *in absentia* before a military court in Egypt. In 2000, Mr Agiza and his wife went to Sweden, where they applied for asylum. Because of the political sensitivity of Mr Agiza's case, their applications were remitted to the Swedish government for decision. The government rejected their applications and ordered their deportation on 18 December 2001. Mr Agiza was deported the same day. His wife Ms Attia evaded police custody and stayed in Sweden.[175] On 25 June 2003, Mr Agiza submitted a complaint to the Committee claiming that he had been tortured on his return and that his deportation to Egypt had therefore violated Article 3 CAT.[176] The Committee was presented with a report by the Swedish ambassador who, after visiting Mr Agiza in prison in January 2002, reported that Mr Agiza had complained about ill treatment when apprehended and during his transfer to Egypt, which had been organized by American security personnel in a US aircraft. Mr Agiza had further claimed that he had been blindfolded during interrogations, held in cells of no more than 1.5 × 1.5 meters, deprived of sleep and medical treatments and beaten by prison guards.[177]

---

173   ComAT, *G.K. v. Switzerland*, 7 May 2003, no. 219/2002, § 6.8; ComAT, *J.A.G.V. v. Sweden*, 11 November 2003, no. 215/2002, § 7.4.

174   ComAT, *Agiza v. Sweden*, 20 May 2005, no. 233/2003.

175   Ms Attia submitted a separate complaint under Art. 3 CAT but was not successful; see ComAT, *Attia v. Sweden*, 17 November 2003, no. 199/2002. However, when the Committee took its decision on that case, it did not have all the information about the treatment of her husband on his return to Egypt; see on this ComAT, *Agiza v. Sweden*, 20 May 2005, no. 233/2003, §§ 8.1, 8.2, 12.11, 9.2, 13.5.

176   ComAT, *Agiza v. Sweden*, 20 May 2005, no. 233/2003, §§ 2.5–2.10 and 3.2.

177   *Ibid.*, §§ 8.1, 8.2 and 12.11.

On 20 May 2005, the Committee took its decision on the case. It stated that 'the issue must be decided in light of the information that was known, or ought to have been known, to the State party's authorities at the *time of* the removal.' Subsequent events would only be relevant to 'the assessment of the State party's knowledge, actual or constructive, at the time of the removal.'[178] The Committee then applied this principle and considered that 'it was known or should have been known' to the Swedish authorities at the time of the complainant's removal that there was a widespread use of torture on detainees, and 'that the risk of such treatment was particularly high in the case of detainees held for political and security reasons.'[179] The Committee further noted that the Swedish authorities were aware of the interest in the complainant by the intelligence services of Egypt and the United States. It hence found that the 'natural conclusion from these combined elements' was that the complainant was at risk of torture in Egypt at the time of his removal. This was further confirmed when 'immediately preceding expulsion, the complainant was subjected on the State party's territory to treatment in breach of, at least, article 16 of the Convention by foreign agents but with the acquiescence of the State party's police.'[180] The diplomatic assurances that the Swedish government had provided before expelling Mr Agiza did not suffice to protect 'against this manifest risk.'[181]

It is hard to believe that the Committee did not take into account the events subsequent to the expulsion in this case, or, in other words, that it limited its assessment strictly to the facts that were known or ought to be known by the government at the time of the expulsion.[182] However, compared to its earlier case law, the Committee did not base its risk assessment on the subsequent events. Focusing on what should have been known at the *time of the expulsion*, the Committee indicated its conviction that the actual occurrence of anticipated torture should not be decisive. Several subsequent cases also

---

178   *Ibid.*, § 13.2.

179   *Ibid.*, § 13.4.

180   See on this also Chapter 3 Section 3.2.5.

181   *Ibid.*, §§ 13.2–13.4. The Committee further criticized the Swedish government for not having provided all relevant information in the Attia and Agiza cases, in particular the report of the Swedish ambassador's first visit and the implication of the US agents in that case, and therefore also found a violation of Art. 22 CAT, §§ 13.5 and 13.10.

182   See also the separate opinion of Committee member Yakovlev criticizing the fact that the majority of the information on which the Committee's decision was based 'relates to events transpiring after expulsion, which can have little relevance to the situation at the time of the expulsion.' See on this also Wouters 2009, pp. 488 and 489.

concerning complainants that had already been expelled confirmed this approach: the Committee recalled the formula developed in *Agiza* according to which it must take a decision 'in light of the information which the authorities of the State party had or should have had in their possession at the time of the expulsion' and that 'subsequent events are useful only for assessing the information which the State party actually had or could have deduced at the time of expulsion.'[183]

In the case *Sogi v. Canada* decided in November 2007, the complainant was expelled to India despite interim measures.[184] He was suspected of being a member of a militant Sikh organisation and a number of attacks on Indian political leaders were attributed to him. Concerning the information on the complainant after his removal, according to which he was in detention and had been ill-treated on his return, the Committee noted that this 'is relevant only to assess what the State party actually knew, or could have deduced, about the risk of torture at the time the complainant was expelled.'[185] The Court finally found a violation of Article 3 CAT because of the complainant's background as a suspected member of a terrorist organisation.[186] In *Diaz v. France*, the Committee made clear that 'the fact of torture does not, of itself, necessarily violate article 3 of the Convention, but it is a consideration to be taken into account by the Committee.'[187] In *Abichou v. Germany* decided in May 2013, the Committee noted that the fact that the complainant was ultimately *not* subjected to torture following his extradition to Tunisia could not 'be justifiably used to call into question or minimize, retrospectively, the existence of such a risk at the time of his extradition.'[188] In light of the widespread use of torture against detainees held for political reasons and against detainees charged with ordinary criminal offences *at the time of the complainant's extradition* to Tunisia, the Committee concluded that the complainant had demonstrated a foreseeable, real and personal risk of being subjected to torture such that his extradition had violated Article 3 CAT.[189] As can be observed, the Committee

---

183   See ComAT, *Tebourski v. France*, 1 May 2007, no. 300/2006, § 8.1. See further ComAT, *Brada v. France*, 17 May 2005, no. 195/2002, § 13.1; ComAT, *Chahin v. Sweden*, 30 May 2011, no. 310/2007, § 8.3; ComAT, *Abdussamatov and 28 Others v. Kazakhstan*, 1 June 2012, no. 444/2010, § 13.2.

184   ComAT, *Sogi v. Canada*, 16 November 2007, no. 297/2006.

185   *Ibid.*, § 10.8.

186   *Ibid.*, §§ 10.9–10.11.

187   ComAT, *Diaz v. France*, 3 May 2005, no. 194/2001, § 9.4. This approach is also reflected in ComAT, *Boily v. Canada*, 14 November 2011, no. 327/2007, §§ 14.3-14-5.

188   ComAT, *Abichou v. Germany*, 21 May 2013, no. 430/2010, § 11.7.

189   *Ibid.*, §§ 11.6 and 11.7.

has principally stopped using events subsequent to a deportation as evidence for a violation or non-violation of Article 3 CAT as it did in *T.P.S* described at the beginning of this section. However, in *Alp v. Denmark* adopted in 2014, the Committee appears to have reapplied its previous habit and gave clear weight to the fact that the complainant had submitted no evidence suggesting that, after his return to Turkey, he would have been maltreated.[190] This is regrettable, as will be addressed in the following comparative section.

However, most decisions concern cases in which the complainants have not been deported yet. In these cases, the Committee takes its decision at the time of its considerations rather than on basis of the time when the national authorities took theirs.[191] Needless to say, the Committee has to take into account any change in the relevant human rights situation.[192] In several cases, the Court has excluded a risk of torture for complainants after a change of regime or a positive development in the general human rights situation in the destination country.[193] However, government changes or other political events in a country may also strengthen an applicant's claim that he is in danger in a certain country.[194]

2.3   *Comparison*

The Committee's practice with regard to the time of the risk assessment is less elaborated than the Court's. While until the *Agiza* decision in 2005, the Committee would base its decision on the knowledge available at the time of its consideration of the case, irrespective of whether the expulsion had already

---

190   ComAT, *Alp v. Denmark*, 14 May 2014, no. 466/2011, § 8.6.

191   See, for example, ComAT, *S.S. and S.A. v. Netherlands*, 11 May 2001, no. 142/1999, § 6.7; ComAT, *Chahin v. Sweden*, 30 May 2011, no. 310/2007, §§ 9.4 and 9.6.

192   See ComAT, General Comment No. 1 on Art. 3 CAT (1997), § 8 (d).

193   See, for example, ComAT, *X. Y. and Z. v. Sweden*, 6 May 1998, no. 61/1996, § 11.3 (overthrow of Mobutu in former Zaire in 1997). See further ComAT, *A.D. v. Netherlands*, 12 November 1999, no. 96/1997, § 7.4 (Sri Lanka); ComAT, *A.A. v. Netherlands*, 30 April 2003, no. 198/2002, § 7.6 (Sudan); ComAT, *A.I. v. Switzerland*, 12 May 2004, no. 182/2001, §§ 6.3 and 6.5 (Sri Lanka); ComAT, *M.A.F. v. Sweden*, 23 November 2012, no. 385/2009, §§ 8.6 and 8.7 (Libya following the revolt and Gaddafi's downfall).

194   See ComAT, *Chahin v. Sweden*, 30 May 2011, no. 310/2007, §§ 9.4–9.6 (Syria in spring 2011). See the Iran cases ComAT, *Amini v. Denmark*, 15 November 2010, no. 339/2008, § 9.8; ComAT, *Jahani v. Switzerland*, 23 May 2011, no. 357/2008, 9.4; ComAT, *Faragollah et al. v. Switzerland*, 21 November 2011, no. 381/2009, § 9.4; ComAT, *Eftekhary v. Norway*, 25 November 2011, no. 312/2007, § 7.4, in which the Committee found a violation of Art. 3 CAT. It noted its concern about the deteriorating situation in that country, particularly after the elections held in the country in June 2009.

taken place, it has changed its practice so that where an expulsion has already taken place, it will try to evaluate what the state party knew or should have known at the time of the expulsion. This development is to be welcomed. The Committee's former approach invited one to look at the outcome of a deportation to judge its legality, which would contravene the preventive character and with that the main objective behind the protection against refoulement.[195] Unfortunately, the Committee is still not entirely consistent in applying its new practice.[196] As Addo and Grief have explained, the occurrence of torture that has been correctly anticipated cannot be decisive since 'it is the *risk* of ill-treatment which is sought to be prevented, not the *fact* of ill-treatment.'[197]

Generally, in Strasbourg as well as in Geneva, it is still difficult to identify to what extent subsequent events serve the Court and the Committee as indications in assessing what the national authorities knew or should have known at the time of the deportation in cases in which the complainant has already been removed. Wouters assumes that the Court and the Committee are rather reluctant to take into account subsequent information when they are refuting the national court's assessment.[198] It is true that the cases in which the Court has found a violation of Article 3 ECHR and has explicitly given importance to information that came to light after the deportation are rather rare.[199] The same is true for the Committee's case law.[200]

However, it must be kept in mind that most of the cases decided on the merits by the Court and the Committee do not concern past but rather possible future deportations. In these cases, the practice of the Court and the Committee has always been similar. They both proceed to an *ex nunc* assessment,

---

195   See also the critiques of the Committee's practice in *T.P.S. v. Canada* in Chetail 2006, pp. 73–75; Nowak & McArthur 2008, p. 206 (§ 193); Wouters 2009, pp. 489 and 490.

196   See, in particular, ComAT, *Alp v. Denmark*, 14 May 2014, § 8.6.

197   Addo and Grief 1998, p. 522.

198   Wouters 2009, pp. 282 and 552. In this sense also Delas 2011, pp. 276 and 287.

199   As exceptions see ECtHR, *Garabayev v. Russia*, 7 June 2007, no. 38411/02, §§ 79–83; ECtHR, *Labsi v. Slovakia*, 15 May 2012, no. 33809/08, § 131. See further the very particular cases concerning illegal transfers, for instance, ECtHR, *El-Masri v. Former Yugoslav Republic of Macedonia*, 13 December 2012 [GC], no. 39630/09, §§ 161, 214 and 218; ECtHR, *Ermakov v. Russia*, 7 November 2013, no. 43165/10, § 206.

200   As exceptions see ComAT, *Boily v. Canada*, 14 November 2011, no. 327/2007, § 14.5, in which the Committee took into account the fact that the complainant alleged to have been tortured on his return. It has further been explained that in the case ComAT, *Agiza v. Sweden*, 20 May 2005, no. 233/2003, it is hard to believe that the Committee did not take into account the events subsequent to the complainant's extradition.

which means that they both examine the risk of a refoulement at the time of their decision. This can have problematic effects, in particular when the Court or Committee's decision is taken a long time after the final domestic decision and the situation has changed in between. In case a human rights situation deteriorates in a significant way, it is possible that a state is held responsible for a deportation in a way it would not have been at the time of the national court's judgment.[201] On the other hand, if a situation improves considerably, it is possible that a state is not held responsible for a deportation that, at the time at which it had been ordered, may have been in violation of the principle of non-refoulement.[202] In the Strasbourg case *Venkadajalasarma*, judge Mularoni criticized this and stated in a dissenting opinion that the Court should only take new circumstances into consideration if the human rights situation has detoriated.[203]

With the *ex nunc* examination, more weight is given to guaranteeing the complainant's security than to holding states to account for their actual responsibility in the national procedure. From a human point of view, the principle is logical. From a procedural point of view, situations in which the circumstances change during the international procedure are unsatisfactory since they cause the Court or the Committee to abandon their role as a subsidiary institution controlling national procedures in favour of a role as a first-instance court, one that is confronted with certain facts for the first time.[204] The only way to reduce the negative effects of this tendency would be to accelerate the Court's and the Committee's procedures so that there is no time for situations to change significantly between the consideration of events by the national authorities and the decision by the international authorities.

---

201 It should be noted that the Court and the Committee usually reject governments' arguments that, based on a new human rights situation, a complainant should introduce a fresh asylum claim before the national authorities and that the complainant has therefore failed to exhaust domestic remedies. See on this Chapter 2 Section 3.2.4.c.

202 See, for example, ECtHR, *Müslim v. Turkey*, 26 April 2005, no. 53566/99, § 54, in which the Court explicitly states that, with a view to the fall of the Saddam Hussein regime in 2003, it will not examine whether the Turkish authorities properly assessed the risk to the complainant from agents of Saddam Hussein. As another example see ECtHR, *Al Hanchi v. Bosnia and Herzegovina*, 15 November 2011, no. 48205/09, §§ 11–17, 41 and 44, with regard to the situation for Islamists in Tunisia after spring 2011.

203 ECtHR, *Venkadajalasarma v. Netherlands*, 17 February 2004, no. 58510/00. See in this sense also the separate opinion of judge de Meyer in ECtHR, *Cruz Varas and Others v. Sweden*, 20 March 1991, no. 15576/89.

204 See the indication in the speech given by the former president of the Court Jean-Paul Costa in the Court's 'Annual Report 2011,' p. 40. See in this sense also Delas 2011, p. 271.

3   Elements of the Risk Assessment

To determine whether there is a risk of ill treatment, the Court and the Committee examine the foreseeable consequences of sending the applicant to the receiving country, bearing in mind the general situation there and his personal circumstances. The assessment of the general human rights situation in the receiving state is often referred to in literature as the *objective test* under the principle of non-refoulement. What importance this test plays in the Court's and the Committee's assessment will be discussed in section 3.2 of this chapter. The assessment of the complainant's personal circumstances and the specific risk that may result from his particular background is referred to as the *subjective test*. Which elements are taken into account by the Court and the Committee in this test and how will be discussed in section 3.3. When the Court and the Committee make the objective and subjective assessment of a complaint, which cannot always be separated, they take into account the question of whether the risk assessment at the national level appears to have been fair and exhaustive. As will be discussed in the section 3.1 of this chapter, the quality of the risk assessment at the national level might have a general impact on the scrutiny applied by the Court and the Committee when assessing a risk of refoulement.

In addition, there are other elements that may play an important role in the risk assessment and that will be discussed in section 3.4: the question of whether it is possible for the complainant to find protection within the receiving state outside the region he is originally from (section 3.4.1). The question of whether diplomatic assurances given by the receiving state according to which the applicant's security is guaranteed have an impact on the risk (section 3.4.2). And in certain cases, the Court and the Committee are confronted with the question of whether there is a risk of indirect refoulement in the receiving state (section 3.4.3).

It must be noted that it is rare that only one of the elements just mentioned leads the Court or the Committee to the conclusion that an expulsion or extradition would violate the principle of non-refoulement. It is mostly the *cumulative and combined analysis* of these factors that make a case.

3.1   *Fair and Effective Assessment at National Level*
In their risk assessment under Article 3 ECHR and Article 3 CAT the question of whether the national authorities have properly assessed the risk of refoulement plays an important role. The quality of the assessment made by the national authorities has an impact on the weight the Court or the Committee give

to government statements and affects their activity regarding the evaluation of facts. The relevant question is hence: what kind of risk assessment do the Court and the Committee expect from national authorities for it to be relied upon? Many of the judgments and decisions discussed in the following pages provide answers to this question.

As will be apparent, to provide effective protection against refoulement, states have a duty to provide certain minimum guarantees in non-refoulement procedures at the national level. Hence, even though neither the ECHR nor the CAT contains a right to a fair trial for procedures under the principle of non-refoulement, Article 3 ECHR and Article 3 CAT contain an implied obligation for states to assess allegations of refoulement, which *includes a right to an effective remedy*. The scope and content of this duty and the difference between the Court's and the Committee's practice on that account will also be looked at.

It should be added that the obligation for states to properly assess each alleged violation of the principle of non-refoulement is also referred to as a *procedural or positive obligation*, as opposed to the *negative obligation* not to remove an individual threatened with ill treatment.[205] However, it is recognized that the distinction between negative and positive in this context 'is far from clear.'[206]

3.1.1 Court
a *Assessment by the Domestic Authorities*

The Court attaches weight to the question of whether the domestic authorities have meaningfully assessed the risk of refoulement.[207] The Court requires that the national authorities have carried out a 'rigorous scrutiny' of any claim under Article 3 ECHR.[208] It must be satisfied that their evaluation is 'based on a reasonable assessment of the evidence, that all relevant factors were assessed, and whether inferences made by the domestic courts from the facts of the case

---

205   See, for example, Battjes 2009, p. 603; Ingelse 2001, p. 315; Wouters 2009, p. 571.

206   See Battjes 2009, pp. 600–606. This can also be observed in this section, in which it will be explained that the lack of 'positive' procedural guarantees may in itself trigger the 'negative' obligation not to remove an individual.

207   See illustrative ECtHR, *Garabayev v. Russia,* 7 June 2007, no. 38411/02, § 77, in which the Court states that in line with its case law under Art. 3 ECHR, it 'needs to establish whether there existed a real risk of ill-treatment in case of extradition to Turkmenistan and whether this risk was assessed prior to taking the decision on extradition.'

208   ECtHR, *M.S.S. v. Belgium and Greece,* 21 January 2011 [GC], no. 30696/09, § 293.

were compatible with the letter and spirit of Article 3 ECHR.'[209] Where the risk assessment by the national authorities appears deficient, the Court is more prepared to disagree with their findings.

A risk assessment is only meaningful in the eyes of the Court if it is 'sufficiently supported by domestic materials as well as by materials originating from other reliable and objective sources such as, for instance, other Contracting or non-Contracting States, agencies of the UN and reputable non-governmental organisations.'[210] National authorities and tribunals must further take into account every kind of relevant information known during the entire procedure,[211] including the Court's own case law.[212] In *Khaydarov*, the Court noted that it was struck by the fact that the Russian Courts failed to study carefully the documents produced in the applicant's extradition case. In such circumstances, it was 'unable to conclude that the Russian authorities duly addressed the applicant's concerns with regard to Article 3 ECHR.'[213] Similarly in *Rustamov v. Russia* concerning an extradition to Uzbekistan, the Court noted that the authorities had not carried out a 'proper assessment.' It pointed out the 'lack of thorough and balanced examination of the general human rights situation in Uzbekistan, the unqualified reliance on the assurances provided by the Uzbek authorities and the failure to give meaningful consideration to the applicant's personal circumstances.'[214]

In *N.A. v. United Kingdom*, the Court made a statement with regard to a list of 'risk factors' developed by the United Kingdom migration authorities to evaluate the asylum applications of Tamils fleeing Sri Lanka. The Court held that such lists are legitimate as long as they are not handled as pure 'check lists' or considered exhaustive.[215] It must be apparent to the Court that an *individualized assessment* has taken place.[216] The Court has made clear in several recent judgments that in assessing the quality of the fact-finding by national authorities, it attaches weight to the question of whether the applicant has been heard

---

209   ECtHR, *Azimov v. Russia*, 18 April 2013, no. 67474/11, § 115.

210   ECtHR, *Salah Sheekh v. Netherlands*, 11 January 2007, no. 1948/04, § 136. On this subject see Section 3.2.1.c of this Chapter.

211   Wouters 2009, p. 279.

212   ECtHR, *Dzhurayev v. Russia*, 25 April 2013, no. 71386/10, § 162.

213   ECtHR, *Khaydarov v. Russia*, 20 May 2010, no. 21055/09, §§ 113 and 114. Similar ECtHR, *Abdulkhakov v. Russia*, 2 October 2012, no. 14743/11, § 148.

214   ECtHR, *Rustamov v. Russia*, 3 July 2012, no. 11209/10, § 121.

215   ECtHR, *N.A. v. UK*, 17 July 2008, no. 25904/07, § 129.

216   ECtHR, *Barnic v. Austria*, 13 December 2011, no. 54845/10 (decision).

and legally represented during the procedure.[217] The Court requires a higher level of assessment if the applicant is a minor.[218]

The Court is very sceptical if asylum claims are rejected on purely procedural grounds.[219] It has observed that for asylum seekers

> ... it must be very difficult if not impossible to supply evidence within a short time, especially if such evidence must be obtained from the country from which he or she claims to have fled. Accordingly, procedural rules should not be so strict, or applied so inflexibly, as to deny an applicant for refugee status a realistic opportunity to prove his or her claim.[220]

An eye should always be kept on the merits of the complaint.[221] In the case *Jabari v. Turkey*, the Court criticized the fact that 'the applicant's failure to comply with the five-day registration requirement under the Asylum Regulation 1994 denied her any scrutiny of the factual basis of her fears about being removed to Iran.' It noted that 'the automatic and mechanical application of such a short time-limit for submitting an asylum application must be considered at variance with the protection of the fundamental value embodied in Article 3 of the Convention.'[222]

What are the consequences if no meaningful assessment at the national level is apparent for the Court? The Court will either perform a risk assessment

---

217 ECtHR, *Husseini v. Sweden*, 13 October 2011, no. 10611/09, § 86; ECtHR, *Samina v. Sweden*, 20 October 2011, no. 55463/09, §§ 53–54 and 62–65; ECtHR, *J.H. v. UK*, 20 December 2011, no. 48839/09, § 58; ECtHR, *H.N. v. Sweden*, 15 May 2012, no. 30720/09, § 39; ECtHR, *A.A. and Others v. Sweden*, 28 June 2012, no. 14499/09, § 77; ECtHR, *F.N. v. Sweden*, 18 December 2012, no. 28774/09, § 70; ECtHR, *N.K. v. France*, 19 December 2013, no. 7974/11, § 45.

218 See ECtHR, *Ahmade v. Greece*, 25 September 2012, no. 50520/09, § 79.

219 See, for example, ECtHR, *M.S.S. v. Belgium and Greece*, 21 January 2011 [GC], no. 30696/09, § 392; ECtHR, *Rustamov v. Russia*, 3 July 2012, no. 11209/10, §§ 115 and 116.

220 ECtHR, *Bahaddar v. Netherlands*, 19 February 1998, no. 25894/94, § 45; ECtHR, *Kandomabadi v. Netherlands*, 29 June 2004, nos. 6276/03 and 6122/04 (decision); ECtHR, *I.M. v. France*, 2 February 2012, no. 9152/09, §§ 136–160. See also ECtHR, *F.N. v. Sweden*, 18 December 2012, no. 28774/09, § 72, in which the Court makes clear that it is not always possible for asylum seekers to prove their identity by submitting original documents and that other documents might be used to do this.

221 Spijkerboer 2009, p. 58.

222 ECtHR, *Jabari v. Turkey*, 11 July 2000, no. 40035/98, § 40.

itself[223] or rely on individual assessments made by the UNHCR, if they exist.[224] Particularly grave procedural deficiencies at national level can in themselves indicate a contravention of the prohibition on refoulement under Article 3 ECHR.[225] In *Auad v. Bulgaria* concerning the deportation of a stateless person of Palestinian origin to Lebanon, the Court observed that the Bulgarian authorities had not assessed the risks to which the applicant would be subjected in Lebanese refugee camps. The judges deduced that 'the lack of a legal framework providing adequate safeguards in this domain allows the Court to conclude that there are substantial grounds for believing that the applicant risks a violation of his rights under Article 3 ECHR.'[226] In the case *Mamazhonov v. Russia* adopted in October 2014, the judges made the following interesting statement:

> The Court is mindful of the failure of the national authorities to rigorously review serious and reasoned claims of the applicant, which is in itself an affront to the protection mechanism established under the Convention. It would be normally redundant for an international tribunal to engage in a further detailed substantive review of the relevant matters, since the abovementioned failure even taken alone is sufficient for finding of a violation of Article 3 of the Convention.[227]

---

223   See, for example, ECtHR, *Muminov v. Russia*, 11 December 2008, no. 42502/06, §§ 86–98; ECtHR, *Gaforov v. Russia*, 21 October 2010, no. 25404/09, §§ 118–139; ECtHR, *Rustamov v. Russia*, 3 July 2012, no. 11209/10, §§ 112–132; ECtHR, *Abdulkhakov v. Russia*, 2 October 2012, no. 14743/11, §§ 141–151; ECtHR, *I.K. v. Austria*, 28 March 2013, no. 2964/12, §§ 75–90.

224   See ECtHR, *Jabari v. Turkey*, 11 July 2000, no. 40035/98, § 41; ECtHR, *Abdolkhani and Karimnia v. Turkey*, 22 September 2009, no. 30471/08, §§ 82 83 and 91; ECtHR, *Z.N.S. v. Turkey*, 19 January 2010, no. 21896/08, §§ 47–50 ECtHR, *Khaydarov v. Russia*, 20 May 2010, no. 21055/09, §§ 108–115; ECtHR, *M.B. and Others v. Turkey*, 15 June 2010, no. 36009/08, §§ 32–35; ECtHR, *Dbouba v. Turkey*, 13 July 2010, no. 15916/09, §§ 41–43.

225   See ECtHR, *Klein v. Russia*, 1 April 2010, no. 24268/08, § 48–57; ECtHR, *Khaydarov v. Russia*, 20 May 2010, no. 21055/09, §§ 112–115; ECtHR, *Iskandarov v. Russia*, 23 September 2010, no. 17185/05, §§ 128–135; ECtHR, *Gaforov v. Russia*, 21 October 2010, no. 25404/09, §§ 128–140; ECtHR, *R.J. v. France*, 19 September 2013, no. 10466/11, §§ 40–43. See further the cases ECtHR, *Garabayev v. Russia*, 7 June 2007, no. 38411/02, §§ 77–83; ECtHR, *Ryabikin v. Russia*, 19 June 2008, no. 8320/04, §§ 115–122, in which the Court did almost no substantial risk assessment.

226   ECtHR, *Auad v. Bulgaria*, 11 October 2011, no. 46390/10, § 107.

227   ECtHR, *Mamazhonov v. Russia*, 23 October 2014, no. 17239/13, § 161.

However, despite this redundancy, the Court found itself compelled to further examine the specific circumstances of the case to determine whether the applicant would be exposed to a real risk of ill treatment in the event of his transfer to Uzbekistan.[228]

In the case *Abdulkhakov v. Russia*, the complainant was kidnapped and deported to Tajikistan with the involvement of the Russian authorities.[229] The Court did not assess whether there was a real risk of ill treatment for the applicant in Tajikistan. It noted, however, that it found it 'particularly striking that the applicant's transfer to Tajikistan was carried out in secret and outside any legal framework capable of providing safeguards against his removal to Uzbekistan without an evaluation of the risks of his ill-treatment there.' The Court observed 'that any extra-judicial transfer or extraordinary rendition, by its deliberate circumvention of due process, is an absolute negation of the rule of law and the values protected by the Convention' and therefore amounts to a violation of Article 3 ECHR.[230]

Finally, it is important to note that the Court often justifies the rejection of a complaint by pointing out that the national authorities have conducted a thorough examination of the applicant's case and given extensive reasons for their conclusions.[231] It has even rejected certain complaints by simply stating that the risk assessment conducted by the national authorities appeared to be fair and exhaustive.[232] Generally, extensive reasoning in the national authorities' decisions will enhance the Court's trust in them.[233]

However, the fact that a national procedure appears to have been fair and exhaustive does not mean that the Court automatically relies on its conclusions.[234] As has been mentioned in section 1.1.3 of this chapter above, when allegations are made under Article 3 ECHR the Court will apply 'particularly

---

228   *Ibid.*

229   ECtHR, *Abdulkhakov v. Russia*, 2 October 2012, no. 14743/11, §§ 152–157.

230   *Ibid.*, § 156. See also ECtHR, *Dzhurayev v. Russia*, 25 April 2013, no. 71386/10, § 204.

231   See, for example, ECtHR, *Barnic v. Austria*, 13 December 2011, no. 54845/10 (decision); ECtHR, *Habib v. Sweden*, 4 January 2012, no. 11152/09 (decision); ECtHR, *D.N.W. v. Sweden*, 6 December 2012, no. 29946/10, 40.

232   See ECtHR, *Damla and Others v. Germany*, 26 October 2000, no. 61479/00 (decision); ECtHR, *Sultani v. France*, 20 September 2007, no. 45223/05, §§ 64–68 and ECtHR, *Samina v. Sweden*, 20 October 2011, no. 55463/09, §§ 51–55 and 62–65, in which the Court comes close to this.

233   See, as illustrative examples, ECtHR, *M.O.M. v. France*, 18 April 2013, no. 18372/10, § 41; ECtHR, *Lapitov v. Russia*, 12 December 2013, no. 77658/11, § 94; ECtHR, *N.K. v. France*, 19 December 2013, no. 7974/11, §§ 45–47.

234   See in this sense also Alleweldt 1996, p. 88.

thorough scrutiny, even if certain domestic procedures and investigations have already taken place.'[235] The Court has recently pointed out that the rights guaranteed by the ECHR would be devoid of any substance if it would renounce 'all supervision of the result obtained using domestic remedies.'[236] In recent cases the Court has explicitly noted 'that it finds no indications that the domestic proceedings lacked effective guarantees to protect the applicants against arbitrary refoulement' but added that it will 'therefore continue by examining whether the information presented before this Court leads it to depart from the domestic authorities' conclusion.'[237]

b   *The Right to an Effective Remedy under Article 13 ECHR*

As has been explained, there is a duty for states to conduct a proper assessment of refoulement complaints under Article 3 ECHR, and if they do not, they are likely to be taken to task at international level. In addition, Article 13 ECHR explicitly provides the right to an effective remedy for potential breaches of the ECHR, including the principle of non-refoulement.

It is not easy to draw a line between a state's positive obligations to conduct a proper assessment under Article 3 ECHR as discussed above and an individual's right to an effective remedy under Article 13 ECHR. As Lambert states, 'there clearly is some overlap between the implied State's duty under Article 3 and that under Article 13 ECHR.'[238] This can be observed for example in *Khaydarov v. Russia* concerning the extradition of an ethnic Uzbek charged with membership of an illegal armed group in Tajikistan. The Court held that the Russian authorities had not duly addressed the applicant's concerns in the domestic extradition proceedings and found a violation of Article 3 ECHR. It did not separately examine the alleged violation of Article 13 ECHR, noting that this issue had already been dealt with under the heading of Article 3 ECHR.[239]

---

235   ECtHR, *Azimov v. Russia*, 18 April 2013, no. 67474/11, § 115. See also ECtHR, *El-Masri v. Former Yugoslav Republic of Macedonia*, 13 December 2012 [GC], no. 39630/09, § 155; ECtHR, *Dzhuayev v. Russia*, 25 April 2013, no. 71386/10, § 128.

236   ECtHR, *Dzhurayev v. Russia*, 25 April 2013, no. 71386/10, § 155.

237   See, for example, ECtHR, *A.A. and Others v. Sweden*, 28 June 2012, no. 14499/09, § 77; ECtHR, *Ghali v. Sweden*, 15 November 2012, no. 74467/12 (decision); ECtHR, *F.N. v. Sweden*, 18 December 2012, no. 28774/09, § 70. See further ECtHR, *N. v. Finland*, 26 July 2005, no. 38885/02, §§ 7–8 and 152–157 and the partly dissenting opinion of Maruste.

238   Lambert 2005, p. 47.

239   ECtHR, *Khaydarov v. Russia*, 20 May 2010, no. 21055/09, § 156. See the same line of argument in several recent judgments, for example, ECtHR, *Gaforov v. Russia*, 21 October 2010, no. 25404/09, § 144; ECtHR, *Rustamov v. Russia*, 3 July 2012, no. 11209/10, § 135; ECtHR, *Mamazhonov v. Russia*, 23 October 2014, no. 17239/13, § 211. See further ECtHR, *Shakurov v. Russia*, 5 June 2012, no. 55822/10, § 141 and ECtHR, *Yefimova v. Russia*, 19 February 2013, no. 39786/09, § 214; ECtHR, *K. v. Russia*, 23 May 2013, no. 69235/11, § 74. In the latter three

The purpose of Article 13 ECHR is to secure the availability of a remedy at national level to enforce the substance of the Convention rights and freedoms.[240] It requires the provision of a domestic remedy to deal with the substance of any 'arguable complaint' under the rights guaranteed by the ECHR.[241] Together with the admissibility requirement of the exhaustion of domestic remedies in Article 35(1) ECHR, it articulates the subsidiary character of the machinery of complaint to the Court.[242] Hence, the violation of Article 13 ECHR can only be invoked before the Court in combination with the *potential* violation of another (substantial) right guaranteed by the ECHR. However, the violation or non-violation of the substantial right is not relevant as such for the question of whether Article 13 ECHR has been breached. *Mwanje v. Belgium* can serve as an example for this. In this case, the Court rejected the allegation that the principle of non-refoulement inherent to Article 3 ECHR would be violated should the complainant, who suffered from HIV, be deported to Cameroon.[243] However, it found a violation of Article 3 ECHR in conjunction with Article 13 ECHR, noting that the appeal authority had not examined the complainant's medical condition and needs using a medical expert.[244]

However, Article 13 ECHR does not guarantee the right to an effective remedy against any deportation decision. According to the Court, an individual must have an 'arguable claim' of a potential violation of the principle of non-refoulement. The Court has indicated that to be arguable, a claim must be 'subjectively well-founded and genuinely perceived as such.'[245] The human rights standards in the receiving state will often play an important role in deciding the question of whether a claim is arguable.[246] When the Court rejects a refoulement complaint under Article 3 ECHR at admissibility level for being manifestly ill-founded, it usually also rejects the complaint under Article 13 ECHR as not being arguable.[247] This indicates that arguable complaints are

---

cases, the Court argued that no separate examination is necessary under Art. 13 ECHR by reasoning that the same arguments have already been examined under Art. 3 ECHR, after it had found that the applicant's extradition would *not* be in breach of Art. 3 ECHR.

240 ECtHR, *Vilvarajah and Others v. UK*, 30 October 1991, nos. 13163/87 & further, § 122.

241 ECtHR, *M.S.S. v. Belgium and Greece*, 21 January 2011 [GC], no. 30696/09, § 287.

242 On these admissibility requirements see Chapter 2 Section 3.2.4.

243 ECtHR, *Mwanje v. Belgium*, 20 December 2011, no. 10486/10, §§ 78–86.

244 *Ibid.*, §§ 106–108.

245 ECtHR, *Diallo v. Czech Republic*, 23 June 2011, no. 20493/07, § 70.

246 *Ibid.*, § 64. See also ECtHR, *Mohammed v. Austria*, 6 June 2013, no. 2283/12, § 75.

247 See, amongst others, ECtHR, *O. v. Netherlands*, 17 November 2009, no. 37755/06, §§ 38–44 (decision); ECtHR, *SE v. France*, 15 December 2009, no. 10085/08 (decision); ECtHR, *Izevbekhai and Others v. Ireland*, 17 May 2011, no. 43408/08 (decision).

comparable to complaints that are not manifestly ill founded.[248] However, as the Court has stated, the fact that a substantive claim is declared inadmissible does not necessarily exclude an assessment under Article 13 ECHR.[249] It is interesting to note in that context that the fact that the Court has granted interim measures does not necessarily make a case 'arguable.'[250]

The question remains: When it is established that the complainant has an arguable claim, what are the requirements under the right to an effective remedy in the sense of Article 13 ECHR? First of all, if potential asylum seekers with an arguable claim are simply returned by authorities without being given the possibility of an assessment of their case, this will be in violation of Article 13 ECHR.[251] Hence, the right to an effective remedy includes the *right to a first determination*. In fact, the right to submit a remedy would be meaningless without the right to a first determination.

Article 13 ECHR does not go so far as to require any particular form of remedy against an initial determination, or, in the context of refoulement, a deportation order. The authority referred to in Article 13 ECHR does not 'necessarily have to be a judicial authority.'[252] However, the appeal body should be able to deal 'with the substance of the relevant Convention complaint and to grant appropriate relief,' that is, to quash the first decision.[253] It must be independent from the first decision maker.[254] The competent authority must be available in law as well as in practice.[255]

---

248 See, in particular, ECtHR, *Singh and Others v. Belgium*, 2 October 2012, no. 33210/11, § 84: '... *un grief peut être considéré comme étant défendable dès lors qu'il n'est pas manifestement mal fondé et qu'il nécessite un examen au fond.*' See also quite explicit ECtHR, *H.S. and Others v. Cyprus*, 21 July 2015, no. 41753/10 and 13 other applications, §§ 282 and 283. However, Wouters 2009, pp. 334–336, finds it difficult 'to conclude that manifestly ill-founded complaints cannot be arguable.' See in this sense also Einarsen 1990, pp. 377–378; Mole & Meredith 2010, p. 117. Looking at certain very substantive cases that have been rejected as manifestly ill-founded, I can agree with Wouters; see, for example, ECtHR, *Abdi Ibrahim v. UK*, 18 September 2012, no. 14535/10, (decision), concerning a removal to Somalia.

249 ECtHR, *A.D. and Others v. Turkey*, 22 July 2014, no. 22681/09, §§ 86–88, in which the complaint under Art. 3 ECHR was declared inadmissible for loss of victim status. The Court nevertheless made an assessment under Art. 13 ECHR.

250 See ECtHR, *Kandomabadi v. Netherlands*, 29 June 2004, nos. 6276/03 and 6122/04 (decision).

251 See ECtHR, *Hirsi Jamaa and Others v. Italy*, 23 February 2012 [GC], no. 27765/09, §§ 201–207, in which the complainants had been intercepted in the Mediterranean Sea by the Italian police and directly deported to Libya without access to asylum procedures.

252 ECtHR, *M.S.S. v. Belgium and Greece*, 21 January 2011 [GC], no. 30696/09, § 289.

253 *Ibid.*, § 291.

254 ECtHR, *Isakov v. Russia*, 8 July 2010, no. 14049/08, § 136.

255 ECtHR, *M.S.S. v. Belgium and Greece*, 21 January 2011 [GC], no. 30696/09, § 290.

Contracting States generally have 'a margin of discretion' in conforming to their obligations under Article 13 ECHR.[256] The scope of this margin varies with the nature of the complaint.[257] In view of the importance of Article 3 ECHR and 'the irreversible nature of the damage which may result if the risk of torture or ill-treatment materialises,' the Court has set the following conditions for an effective remedy in circumstances of extradition or expulsion:

> The effectiveness of a remedy within the meaning of Article 13 impera-tively requires *independent* and *rigorous scrutiny of any claim* that there exist substantial grounds for fearing a real risk of treatment contrary to Article 3 as well as a *particularly prompt* response; it also requires that the person concerned should have access to a remedy with *automatic suspensive effect.*[258] (Emphasis added)

As can be seen, the effectiveness of a remedy requires that the person con-cerned have access to a remedy with automatic suspensive effect. It appears from the Court's case law that the requirements with regard to the automatic suspensive effect are met if individuals threatened with deportation have at least the possibility of submitting a request for suspensive effect with the legal guarantee that they will not be deported until the outcome of the appeal.[259] The Court could be clearer on the question of just *how automatic* an automatic suspensive effect should be.[260] However, it has pointed to the risks involved in a system where stays of execution must be applied for and are granted on a case-by-case basis.[261] It has further made very clear that a complainant must

---

256   ECtHR, *Vilvarajah and Others v. UK* 30 October 1991, nos. 13163/87 & further, § 122.

257   ECtHR, *M.S.S. v. Belgium and Greece*, 21 January 2011 [GC], no. 30696/09, § 288.

258   See ECtHR, *Gebremedhin v. France*, 26 April 2007, no. 25389/05, §§ 63–66; ECtHR, *M.S.S. v. Belgium and Greece*, 21 January 2011 [GC], no. 30696/09, § 293; ECtHR, *R.U. v. Greece*, 7 June 2011, no. 2237/08, § 73; ECtHR, *Diallo v. Czech Republic*, 23 June 2011, no. 20493/07, § 74; ECtHR, *Labsi v. Slovakia*, 15 May 2012, no. 33809/08, § 137.

259   ECtHR, *Čonka v. Belgium*, 5 February 2002, no. 51564/99, § 79; ECtHR, *Gebremedhin v. France*, 26 April 2007, no. 25389/05, § 66; ECtHR, *Isakov v. Russia*, 8 July 2010, no. 14049/08, § 136; ECtHR, *Agalar v. Norway*, 8 November 2011, no. 55120/09 (decision); ECtHR, *M.A. v. Cyprus*, 23 July 2013, no. 41872/10, §§ 135–143; ECtHR, *A.C. and Others v. Spain*, 22 April 2014, no. 6528/11, § 94.

260   Spijkerboer (2009, p. 72) notes that it might be sufficient for the applicant concerned not to be deported until a judge has decided on the suspensive effect. Wouters (2009, pp. 342 and 574–575) notes that the terms and practice of the Court indicate that in ordinary proceedings, the suspensive effect should be automatic for the whole procedure.

261   ECtHR, *Čonka v. Belgium*, 5 February 2002, no. 51564/99, § 82; ECtHR, *M.A. v. Cyprus*, 23 July 2013, no. 41872/10, § 137.

be given enough time before being deported to make effective use of the remedy, which must include sufficient time to submit a request for suspensive effect if this is required, with the guarantee that no measure is taken until an arguable claim on that account is properly assessed.[262] The Court itself assesses on a case-by-case basis whether these criteria are met.[263]

According to the Court, 'judicial review proceedings constitute, in principle, an effective remedy within the meaning of Article 13 ECHR in relation to complaints in the context of expulsion and extradition, provided that the courts can effectively review the legality of executive discretion on substantive and procedural grounds and quash decisions as appropriate.'[264] What the Court requires for a remedy to be effective in the sense of Article 13 ECHR may vary with the quality of the first instance's decision-making.[265] In other words, 'even if a single remedy does not by itself entirely satisfy the requirements of Article 13, the aggregate of remedies provided for under domestic law may do so.'[266] Likewise, the requirement for the national authorities scrutiny under Article 13 ECHR may be less strict if a claim is assessed for the second time. In the case *Mohammed v. Austria* the Court held that 'if an asylum claimant has had access to a substantive examination of his asylum claim at first instance, re-examination in an accelerated procedure does not in itself deprive the claimant of rigorous review of his claims in relation to Article 3 ECHR.'[267]

---

262 ECtHR, *Shamayev and Others v. Georgia and Russia*, 12 April 2005, no. 36378/02, §§ 460 and 467; ECtHR, *Garabayev v. Russia*, 7 June 2007, no. 38411/02, § 106; ECtHR, *Labsi v. Slovakia*, 15 May 2012, no. 33809/08, § 139; ECtHR, *A.C. and Others v. Spain*, 22 April 2014, no. 6528/11, §§ 90–105.

263 For an interesting recent case see ECtHR, *A.C. and Others v. Spain*, 22 April 2014, no. 6528/11, §§ 90–105.

264 ECtHR, *Muminov v. Russia*, 11 December 2008, no. 42502/06, § 102. See, for example ECtHR, *Diallo v. Czech Republic*, 23 June 2011, no. 20493/07, §§ 74–85, in which the Court found a violation of Art. 13 in conjunction with Art. 3 ECHR because the judicial review lacked careful scrutiny and automatic suspensive effect.

265 See, for example, ECtHR, *M.S.S. v. Belgium and Greece*, 21 January 2011 [GC], no. 30696/09, §§ 299–322, in which the deficiencies in the Greek asylum system as a whole lead to a violation by Greece of Art. 13 ECHR in conjunction with Art. 3 ECHR. Another good example is ECtHR, *I.M. v. France*, 2 February 2012, no. 9152/09, § 156, in which the Court noted that procedural irregularities in the initial asylum determination procedure (which was a fast-track procedure) had not been offset at the appeal stage.

266 ECtHR, *Budrevich v. Czech Republic*, 17 October 2013, no. 65303/10, § 102.

267 ECtHR, *Mohammed v. Austria*, 6 June 2013, no. 2283/12, § 79. See also ECtHR, *Sultani v. France*, 20 September 2007, no. 45223/05, §§ 65 and 66; ECtHR, *H.R. v. France*, 22 September 2011, no. 64780/09, § 68.

The landmark judgment *M.S.S. v. Belgium and Greece*[268] shows in an exemplary way which kind of deficiencies can contravene Article 13 ECHR in the context of refoulement procedures, specifically for asylum seekers. The case concerned the deportation of an Afghan asylum seeker from Belgium to Greece under the EU Dublin II Regulation and the risk of his further removal therefrom to Afghanistan.[269] Under the head of Article 13 ECHR, the Court observed grave structural deficiencies in the Greek asylum procedures. They included:

> insufficient information for asylum-seekers about the procedures to be followed; ... no reliable system of communication between authorities and asylum-seekers; a shortage of interpreters and lack of training of the staff responsible for conducting the individual interviews; a lack of legal aid effectively depriving asylum seekers of legal counsel; and excessively lengthy delays in receiving a decision.[270]

The Court was 'concerned that almost all first-instance decisions are negative and drafted in a stereotyped manner without any details of the reasons for the decisions being given.'[271] With regard to the applicant's opportunity to apply for judicial review of a rejection of his asylum request before the Greece's Supreme Administrative Court, the Court considered that the authorities' failure to ensure communication with the asylum seeker made it 'very uncertain whether he will be able to learn the outcome of his asylum application in time to react within the prescribed time-limit.'[272] The Court observed moreover that the average duration of appeals to the Supreme Administrative Court was more than five years.[273]

As a general rule, the 'effectiveness' of a remedy within the meaning of Article 13 ECHR does not depend on the certainty of a favourable outcome for the applicant.[274] However, the Court took note of 'the extremely low rate of asylum or subsidiary protection granted by the Greek authorities compared with other European Union member States.'[275] It observed that although 'the

---

268 ECtHR, *M.S.S. v. Belgium and Greece*, 21 January 2011 [GC], no. 30696/09.

269 On the Court's approach with regard to complaints in which a risk of indirect removal is alleged see Chapter 4 Section 3.4.3.a.

270 ECtHR, *M.S.S. v. Belgium and Greece*, 21 January 2011 [GC], no. 30696/09. § 301.

271 *Ibid.*, §302.

272 *Ibid.*, §§ 316–318.

273 *Ibid.*, §§ 190 and 320.

274 *Ibid.*, § 289.

275 *Ibid.*, § 313; UNHCR reports from 2008 and 2009 showed a success rate in Greece at first instance of 0.04 per cent for refugee status under the Geneva Convention (11 people), and

importance to be attached to statistics varies, they tend to strengthen the applicant's argument concerning his loss of faith in the asylum procedure.'[276] In view of all these issues, the Court concluded that the relevant legislation was not being applied in practice so that asylum seekers were not protected against arbitrary removal to their countries of origin.[277] However, it should be stressed that many of the issues criticized in *M.S.S.* taken independently do not necessarily lead to the ineffectiveness of a remedy. Article 13 ECHR does not, for instance, guarantee a right to free legal representation.[278]

In *M.S.S.*, the Court also found a violation of Article 13 in conjunction with Article 3 ECHR by Belgium. The Belgian migration authorities had first expelled the applicant to Greece as a result of an accelerated procedure in the application of the EU Dublin II Regulation. The Court rejected the government's argument that the appeal available to the applicant against the expulsion order before the Belgian Aliens Appeal Board 'under the extremely urgent procedure' was effective.[279] It emphasised the reduced rights of the defence, practical obstacles in exercising the remedy, the increased burden of proof, and the limited examination on the merits in such procedures. It further observed 'that the parties appear to agree to consider that the applicant's appeal had no chance of success in view of the constant case law.'[280]

The Court is sceptical about an automatic assignation of individuals to accelerated procedures. The case *I.M. v. France* concerned a Sudanese asylum seeker who had been registered for a fast-track asylum procedure because he had only applied for asylum after having received a deportation order.[281] The Court criticized the fact that the registration for the accelerated procedure was based on procedural grounds not linked to the circumstances of the case on the merits. It concluded that the automatic registration, the short deadlines imposed (48 hours to submit an appeal) and the practical difficulties for the applicant in producing evidence within these short time-limits, given that he was in detention and applying for asylum for the first time, made the legal

    0.06 per cent for humanitarian or subsidiary protection (18 people) compared to the average success rate of 36.2 per cent in five of the six EU countries that, along with Greece, received the largest number of applications; §§ 125–126.

276   *Ibid.*

277   *Ibid.*, § 300.

278   See ECtHR, *Goldstein v. Sweden*, 12 September 2000, no. 46636/99 (decision) and Chapter 2 Section 3.2.4.b.

279   The 'extremely urgent procedure' suspended the execution of an expulsion measure for a maximum of 72 hours until the Board reached a decision.

280   ECtHR, *M.S.S.*, §§ 385–397.

281   ECtHR, *I.M. v. France*, 2 February 2012, no. 9152/09.

remedies that were available in theory inaccessible in practice.[282] However, in two more recent cases against France, the Court did not criticize the assignation of first asylum requests to the same fast-track procedure under Article 13 ECHR.[283] It noted that, in contrast to *I.M.*, the applicants in these cases had waited particularly long on French territory before submitting their request for asylum. By doing so, they had missed the opportunity of an ordinary asylum procedure by their own delay. Since they had already been on French territory for years before submitting their request for asylum, they would have had all the time needed to collect the necessary evidence, so that the short time-limits within the accelerated procedure did not constitute a breach of Article 13 ECHR in their cases.[284] As can be seen, accelerated procedures are not as such incompatible with Article 13 ECHR.[285] In *Mohammed v. Austria* concerning the deportation of a Sudanese applicant to Hungary under the Dublin system, the Court acknowledged the need for accelerated asylum proceedings as practiced in a number of European countries to deal with repetitive and clearly abusive or manifestly ill-founded applications for asylum.[286] It further recalled that it is only where an applicant has an 'arguable claim' under Article 3 ECHR that he should have access to a remedy that fully satisfies the minimum requirements of Article 13 ECHR.[287] With regard to the transfer of asylum seekers from one European country to the other under the EU Dublin System, the Court indicated that an 'arguable claim' will only be given when it is 'widely known' through international reports, notably from the UNHCR, that the situation for asylum seekers in the receiving European country does not meet the standards of Article 3 ECHR.[288]

When the lack of an effective remedy is claimed in a refoulement case, the Court usually first assesses the risk of refoulement under Article 3 ECHR, and second, a possible violation of Article 13 ECHR in conjunction with Article 3

---

282   §§ 136–160. The Court found a violation of Art. 13 in conjunction with Art. 3 ECHR.

283   ECtHR, *M.E. v. France*, 6 June 2013, no. 50094/10, §§ 65–70; ECtHR, *K.K. v. France*, 10 October 2013, no. 18913/11, §§ 66–71.

284   *Ibid.*

285   See the explicit statement in ECtHR, *M.E. v. France*, 6 June 2013, no. 50094/10, § 67. See also the 'Guidelines on Human Rights Protection in the Context of Accelerated Asylum Procedures,' adopted by the Committee of Ministers on 1 July 2009 at the 1062nd meeting of the Ministers' Deputies.

286   ECtHR, *Mohammed v. Austria*, 6 June 2013, no. 2283/12, §§ 79 and 80.

287   *Ibid.*, § 80.

288   *Ibid.*, § 75. See on this Section 3.4.3.a of this Chapter.

ECHR.[289] This is logical since an individual complaining about the lack of a proper remedy in that context will usually at the same time be afraid of being deported in violation of the principle of non-refoulement. Curiously, in a few recent judgments, the Court did not proceed in this way. In *M.S.S.*, the Court found a violation of the applicant's rights under Article 3 ECHR in conjunction with Article 13 ECHR by Greece. The Court did not, however, make a separate examination under Article 3 ECHR with regard to the risk of refoulement of the applicant from Greece to Afghanistan. In his concurring opinion to *M.S.S.*, Judge Villiger criticized this new approach.[290] He drew attention to the fact that in cases in which the Court finds a violation of Article 13 in conjunction with Article 3 ECHR but does not examine a violation of Article 3 ECHR on its own, the complainant's risk of deportation still persists.[291] With regard to *M.S.S.* in particular, this argument might be not relevant since the Court exceptionally advised Greece under Article 46 ECHR, 'to proceed with an examination of the merits of the applicant's asylum request that meets the requirements of the Convention and, pending the outcome of that examination, to refrain from deporting the applicant.'[292] Villiger, however, rightly drew attention to the implication of the approach for future cases. His objections were very pertinent, as the case *R.U. v. Greece* adopted a few months after *M.S.S.* demonstrates.[293] In this case, the Court found a violation of Article 13 ECHR but did *not* assess the complainant's explicit claim under the principle of non-refoulement. It did not even make an indication to the Greek government that the complainant should not be deported to Turkey, although it noted explicitly that he was still at risk of deportation without a risk assessment despite having established a *prima facie* case.[294]

---

289   See, amongst many others, ECtHR, *Soering v. UK*, 7 July 1989, no. 14038/88; ECtHR, *Auad v. Bulgaria*, 11 October 2011, no. 46390/10; ECtHR, *Hirsi Jamaa and Others v. Italy*, 23 February 2012 [GC], no. 27765/09, unless the Court concludes that issues under Art. 13 ECHR have already been dealt with under the heading of Art. 3 ECHR.

290   The discrepancies with the Court's own practice can be observed within the *M.S.S.* judgment itself: Villiger notes that 'while the Court refuses to examine Art. 3 separately in respect of Greece, it does precisely that in respect of Belgium, where it finds, first, a violation of Art. 3 and then a further one under Art. 13 taken together with Art. 3 of the Convention.'

291   When the Court finds that Art. 13 ECHR has been violated, it may grant compensation. However, it does not require states to annul the deportation.

292   ECtHR, *M.S.S.*, § 402. See the similar approach applied in ECtHR, *A.C. and Others v. Spain*, 22 April 2014, no. 6528/11, § 112.

293   ECtHR, *R.U. v. Greece*, 7 June 2011, no. 2237/08, §§ 79–82.

294   *Ibid.*, §§ 44 and 82.

In a few cases, the Court has exceptionally assessed refoulement cases under Article 13 ECHR in combination with Article 3 ECHR despite the fact that the complainant was no longer threatened with deportation and had therefore lost his victim status under Article 3 ECHR. This might be justified in order to allow the Court to address important procedural issues or indicate minimal guarantees that should be observed by immigration authorities under Article 13 ECHR.[295] However, not to assess the risk of refoulement in cases in which a violation of Article 13 ECHR is alleged, even though applicants are still threatened with expulsion, surely contravenes the Court's principle of unconditional protection against refoulement. Future cases will show whether the Strasbourg judges will follow judge Villiger's reasonable objections.[296]

3.1.2   Committee
a   *Assessment by the Domestic Authorities*
According to the Committee, procedural irregularities in the domestic assessment procedure must be considered to ascertain whether there has been a violation of Article 3 CAT in a particular case.[297] The principle of non-refoulement includes the duty for state authorities 'to examine carefully and take into account all existing circumstances that may reasonably be considered to indicate a risk of torture.'[298] In fact, without the obligation for the state to carry out a risk assessment of a certain standard, Article 3 CAT would be meaningless. Article 3 CAT hence contains an implicit right to an individualized risk assessment satisfying minimum fair trial requirements.[299] Against this background,

---

295   See ECtHR, *I.M. v. France*, 2 February 2012, no. 9152/09, addressing the issue of accelerated asylum procedures; ECtHR, *Gebremedhin v. France*, 26 April 2007, no. 25389/05, addressing the requirement of a suspensive effect; ECtHR, *M.A. v. Cyprus*, 23 July 2013, no. 41872/10, §§ 115–121, addressing the requirement of a suspensive effect. See also ECtHR, *L.T. v. Belgium*, 12 March 2012, no. 31201/11, § 30 (decision), in which the Court held that it does not let escape a question of general interest by striking out the application under Art. 13 ECHR.

296   The Court adopted the same problematic approach in ECtHR, *Ahmade v. Greece*, 25 September 2012, no. 50520/09, §§ 109–116 and ECtHR, *Singh and Others v. Belgium*, 2 October 2012, no. 33210/11, §§ 53–56. However, it acted again according to its previous method in ECtHR, *Mohammed v. Austria*, 6 June 2013, no. 2283/12, §§ 69–111.

297   ComAT, *Sogi v. Canada*, 16 November 2007, no. 297/2006, § 9.2. Similar ComAT, *E.L. v. Canada*, 21 May 2012, no. 370/2009, § 8.7.

298   ComAT, *Boily v. Canada*, 14 November 2011, no. 327/2007, § 14.4.

299   See ComAT, *Abdussamatov & Others v. Kazakhstan*, 1 June 2012, no. 444/2010, § 13.9.

it can be stated that Article 3 CAT also contains a sort of prohibition on collective expulsion.[300]

States have the duty under Article 3 CAT to examine carefully and take into account all existing circumstances that may reasonably be considered to indicate a risk of torture in case of deportation.[301] The Committee is particularly sensible to the question of whether domestic authorities have seriously analysed or taken into account alleged experiences of past torture.[302] It is explicitly stated in paragraph 2 of Article 3 CAT that authorities have to take into account all relevant considerations including the general human rights situation.

In *Sogi v. Canada*, the Committee held that the 'State party is obliged, in determining whether there is a risk of torture under article 3, to give a fair hearing to persons subject to expulsion orders.'[303] States should not rely on information on which complainants have not been given the possibility of taking a position.[304] Generally, the Committee will be more likely to trust a government's findings on a complainant's credibility if he has personally been heard.[305] However, in *Minani v. Canada*, it noted that 'the fact that the complainant was not called to a hearing is not of itself a procedural irregularity insofar as his arguments were considered by the Canadian authorities.'[306]

---

300   See ComAT, *Mopongo and Others v. Morocco*, 7 November 2014, no. 321/2007, concerning 34 immigrants of sub-Saharan origin arrested by Moroccan forces and taken to the desert close to the Algerian border. Having been forced to walk to Algerian territory without any protection and food or water, they were exposed to all sorts of danger. They further had no opportunity to challenge their expulsion before the Moroccan authorities. The Committee, without assessing the situation of the applicants individually, stated that 'the facts as described by the complainants reveal a failure on the part of the State party's authorities to assess the risks involved before sending the complainants to a State where they would risk being subjected to torture, in contravention of the principle of non-refoulement, and thus disclose a violation of article 3, paragraph 1, of the Convention, inasmuch as the complainant's expulsion to Algeria placed them in a situation in which they were in danger of being subjected to torture.' On the prohibition of collective expulsion according to Art. 4 of Protocol No. 4 to the ECHR see Chapter 1 Section 2.2.3.

301   ComAT, *Boily v. Canada*, 14 November 2011, no. 327/2007, § 14.4.

302   See, as recent examples, ComAT, *Fadel v. Switzerland*, 14 November 2014, no. 450/2011, § 7.6; ComAT, *F.K. v. Denmark*, 23 November 2015, no. 580/2014, § 7.6. On the importance given to past experiences of torture see further Section 3.3.2.b of this Chapter.

303   ComAT, *Sogi v. Canada*, 16 November 2007, no. 297/2006, §§ 10.4 and 10.5.

304   ComAT, *E.J. et al. v. Sweden*, 14 November 2008, no. 306/2006, § 8.4.

305   ComAT, *A.M.A. v. Switzerland*, 12 November 2010, no. 344/2008, § 7.7.

306   ComAT, *Minani v. Canada*, 5 November 2009, no. 331/2007, § 7.8.

The Committee will be sceptical when allegations are rejected on purely procedural grounds.[307] In *Aemei v. Switzerland*, the Swiss authorities had refused to assess the risk emanating from the Iranian applicant's political activities in Switzerland, since he had not referred to this in the initial asylum procedure. The Committee held that 'the refusal to take up the author's request for review, based on reasoning of a procedural nature, does not appear justified in light of article 3 of the Convention.'[308] In *Iya v. Switzerland*, the Swiss immigration authorities rejected the complainant's asylum request on the basis of his failure to submit identity documents within the deadline of 48 hours. Noting that the applicant's case had never been examined on the merits, the Committee assessed the risk of refoulement itself. In a short reasoning, it found that his expulsion to the DRC would violate Article 3 CAT.[309]

When the national authorities have made no proper risk assessment, the Committee will freely assess the facts as presented by the complainant. In those circumstances, applicants seem to be given the benefit of the doubt in the international procedure.[310] In certain cases, procedural deficiencies have been the main reason for which the Committee found that Article 3 CAT was violated: the case *Tebourski v. France* concerned the deportation of a Tunisian who had been convicted in France for his connection with a terrorist enterprise. Considering that the applicant was a threat to national security, the French authorities expelled him before the Refugee Appeals Board had taken its decision on the merits.[311] The Committee did not make a single statement on the material risk of torture for the complainant but considered that 'by expelling the complainant to Tunisia under the conditions in which it did' the state party had failed to meet its obligations under Article 3 CAT.[312] A similar approach was taken by the Committee in the case *K.H. v. Denmark* concerning an applicant who claimed to be at risk of being tortured by the Afghan authorities.[313] The Danish immigration authorities had rejected the applicant's request for asylum by referring to inconsistent statements made during his interviews. The complainant's requests for a medical examination to shed light on the possible repeated use of torture had been rejected. The Committee

---

307   Schürmann & Scheidegger 2009, p. 213.

308   ComAT, *Aemei v. Switzerland*, 9 May 1997, 34/1995, § 9.8.

309   ComAT, *Iya v. Switzerland*, 16 November 2007, no. 299/2006, §§ 6.5–7.

310   Along with the case *Iya v. Switzerland* just cited see, for example, ComAT, *Sogi v. Canada*, 16 November 2007, no. 297/2006, §§ 10.2–10.10; ComAT, *Ke Chun Rong v. Australia*, 5 November 2012, no. 416/2010, §§ 7.4–8.

311   ComAT, *Tebourski v. France*, 1 May 2007, no. 300/2006, §§ 8.2–9.

312   *Ibid.*, § 8.7; the Committee also found a violation of Art. 22 CAT.

313   ComAT, *K.H. v. Denmark*, 23 November 2012, no. 464/2011.

held that 'by rejecting the complainant's asylum request without seeking further investigation of his claims nor ordering a medical examination, the State party failed to determine whether there were substantial grounds for believing that the complainant would be in danger of being subjected to torture if returned.'[314] By simply referring to this insufficient assessment at national level, the Committee concluded that the deportation of the applicant would constitute a violation of Article 3 CAT. The Committee itself had not made a risk assessment.[315] In this context, it should be pointed out that the Committee has also rejected complaints by simply arguing that the domestic authorities *have* properly assessed the case.[316] In most cases, however, the Committee proceeds to an at least minimal risk assessment of some sort, whether deficiencies are evident or not. Nonetheless, the examples just described show that the quality of the domestic authorities' risk assessment can have an important, and in some cases even decisive, impact on the Committee's evaluation of the risk.

b   *The Right to an Effective Remedy under Article 3 CAT*
It is apparent from the Committee's case law described in the previous section that Article 3 CAT contains an implicit right to an individualized risk assessment satisfying certain minimum requirements. As will be explained in this section, this duty includes the obligation for states to provide an effective remedy with regard to claims under the principle of non-refoulement.

The CAT does not have a provision explicitly guaranteeing the right to an effective remedy for violations of the principle of non-refoulement. The Committee has nevertheless made clear that 'the prohibition on refoulement should be interpreted to encompass a remedy for its breach.'[317] In *Agiza v. Sweden*, the

---

314   *Ibid.*, § 8.8.

315   See similar ComAT, *Arana v. France*, 9 November 1999, no. 63/1997, §§ 11.4, 11.5; ComAT, *X. v. Russia*, 8 May 2015, no. 542/2013, § 11.8; ComAT, *F.K. v. Denmark*, 23 November 2015, no. 580/2014, § 7.6. See also ComAT, *Ktiti v. Morocco*, 26 May 2011, no. 419/2010, §§ 8.5–8.7 and ComAT, *Agiza v. Sweden*, 20 May 2005, no. 233/2003, §§ 13.6–13.8, in which the Committee carried out a substantial *and* a procedural assessment under Art. 3 CAT and concluded in both that this article had been contravened. In referring to *Arana* it noted that the 'inability to contest an expulsion decision before an independent authority' is a relevant finding of a violation of Art. 3 CAT.

316   See ComAT, *X.Y. v. Switzerland*, 15 May 2001, no. 128/1999, §§ 8.5–9; ComAT, *A.R. v. Netherlands*, 14 November 2003, no. 203/2002, §§ 7.4–7.6; ComAT, *S.U.A. v. Sweden*, 22 November 2004, no. 223/2002, § 6.5; ComAT, *J.A.M.O. v. Canada*, 9 May 2008, no. 293/2006, §§ 10.5-10.7. In this sense also ComAT, *Brada v. France*, 17 May 2005, no. 195/2002, § 13.6; ComAT, *B.M.S. v. Sweden*, 25 November 2015, no. 594/2014, § 8.9.

317   ComAT, *Agiza v. Sweden*, 20 May 2005, no. 233/2003, § 13.6. See also ComAT, *Arana v. France*, 9 November 1999, no. 63/1997, § 11.5; ComAT, *Tebourski v. France*, 1 May 2007, no. 300/2006, §§ 8.2–10; ComAT, *Ke Chun Rong v. Australia*, 5 November 2012, no. 416/2010,

Committee stated that 'the right to an effective remedy contained in article 3 requires an opportunity for effective, independent and impartial review of the decision to expel or remove, once that decision is made, when there is a plausible allegation that article 3 issues arise.'[318] As indicated in this decision, there is only a right to an effective remedy when a 'plausible allegation' under Article 3 CAT has been made. Unfortunately, the Committee has to date not explained what a 'plausible' allegation is.

According to the Committee, the question of whether domestic remedies 'are available and effective, as required by article 22, paragraph 5, of the Convention, [cannot] be determined *in abstracto*, but [has] to be assessed by reference to the circumstances of the particular case.'[319] The Committee has made clear that only a remedy with suspensive effect can be considered effective.[320] Individuals threatened with deportation must further be given sufficient time to make use of that remedy.[321] The authority deciding on the remedy must be independent from the authority that has taken the initial decision and must have the power to review a case on the merits.[322]

The aforementioned case *Agiza* concerned the deportation of an Egyptian suspected of terrorist activities from Sweden to Egypt in December 2001 with the involvement of US agents. Due to national security concerns, the Swedish government took the first and final decision to expel the complainant. There was no possibility for him to review that decision. The Committee found 'that the absence of any avenue of judicial or independent administrative review of the government's decision to expel the complainant does not meet the procedural obligation to provide for effective, independent and impartial review required by article 3 of the Convention.'[323]

---

§ 7.5. Note further ComAT, *Singh v. Canada*, 30 May 2011, no. 319/2007, §§ 4.6 and 7.3, in which the Committee rejected the government's argument that the complainant's allegation of lack of effective remedy should be found inadmissible because this right was not guaranteed by the CAT.

318   ComAT, *Agiza v. Sweden*, 20 May 2005, no. 233/2003, § 13.7.

319   ComAT, *Z.T. (No. 2) v. Norway*, 14 November 2005, no. 238/2003, § 8.1.

320   ComAT, *Brada v. France*, 17 May 2005, no. 195/2002, §§ 7.6–7.9; ComAT, *Tebourski v. France*, 1 May 2007, no. 300/2006, §§ 7.3 and 7.4; ComAT, *Kalonzo v. Canada*, 18 May 2012, no. 343/2008, § 8.3; ComAT, *S.A.C. v. Monaco*, 13 November 2012, no. 346/2008, § 7.2.

321   ComAT, *Arana v. France*, 9 November 1999, no. 63/1997, § 6.1; ComAT, *Diaz v. France*, 3 May 2005, no. 194/2001, § 6.1, in which the complainants were extradited on the same day the deportation order was issued.

322   ComAT, *Kalonzo v. Canada*, 18 May 2012, no. 343/2008, § 8.3.

323   ComAT, *Agiza v. Sweden*, 20 May 2005, no. 233/2003, § 13.8.

In the case *Ke Chun Rong v. Australia*, the Committee observed that the applicant had submitted sufficient details regarding his affiliation with the Falun Gong movement, including evidence corroborating his account of having been detained and ill-treated by the Chinese authorities for that reason.[324] However, the Committee observed that the Australian immigration authorities had 'failed to duly verify the complainant's allegations and evidence, through proceedings meeting the State party's procedural obligation to provide for effective, independent and impartial review as required by article 3 of the Convention.'[325] The Committee thereby noted 'that the review on the merits of the complainant's claims regarding the risk of torture that he faced was conducted predominantly based on the content of his initial application for a Protection visa, which he filed shortly after arriving in the country, without knowledge or understanding of the system.' The complainant was further not interviewed in person and therefore did not have the opportunity to clarify any inconsistencies in his initial statement.[326] The Committee hence noted that 'the complainant has not had access to an effective remedy against the decision to reject his application for a Protection Visa. Accordingly, the Committee concludes that the deportation of the complainant to his country of origin would constitute a violation of Article 3 of the Convention.'[327]

In *Singh v. Canada*, the Committee stated that states should 'provide for judicial review of the merits, rather than merely of the reasonableness, of decisions to expel an individual.'[328] For that reason, it accepted neither the judicial review procedure before the Canadian Federal Court nor the pre-removal risk assessment, in which individuals can submit evidence that has arisen after the rejection of the refugee protection claim, as effective remedies in the instant case.[329] The findings with regard to the Canadian review system in this judgment appear to be in contradiction to other admissibility decisions, in which the Committee explicitly held that 'these remedies are not mere formalities, and the Federal Court may, in appropriate cases, look at the substance of a case.'[330] The Committee's statements in *Singh* regarding the effectiveness of the Canadian review

---

324   ComAT, *Ke Chun Rong v. Australia*, 5 November 2012, no. 416/2010, § 7.4.

325   *Ibid.*, 7.5.

326   *Ibid.*

327   *Ibid.*

328   ComAT, *Singh v. Canada*, 30 May 2011, no. 319/2007, § 8.9.

329   *Ibid.*, §§ 8.8 and 8.9.

330   ComAT, *Aung v. Canada*, 15 May 2006, no. 273/2005, §§ 6.3 and 6.4. See similar ComAT, *R.S.A.N. v. Canada*, 17 November 2006, no. 284/2006, § 6.4; ComAT, *L.Z.B. and J.F.Z. v. Canada*, 8 November 2007, no. 304/2006, § 6.6; ComAT, *Yassin v. Canada*, 4 November 2009, no. 307/2006, §§ 9.3 and 9.4. See further recently ComAT, *Z.H. v. Canada*, 20 November 2015,

system do not seem to be well thought out: the Federal Court's competences as described in this decision seem not to exclude a substantive assessment.[331] It is likely that certain European review systems would also not stand up to the Committee's requirement for an effective remedy if this test were applied.[332] In *Singh*, the Committee further found a violation of Article 22 CAT with regard to the lack of an effective remedy, instead of relying on procedural rights inherent to Article 3 CAT, as it usually does.[333] This gives the impression that the Committee has created a new right within Article 22 CAT, although it stated itself in the same decision that the prohibition on refoulement in Article 3 CAT should be interpreted as including a remedy for its breach.[334] Finally, all that can be said is that the Committee's case law on the right to an effective remedy inherent to Article 3 CAT is not yet very well elaborated.

3.1.3   Comparison
a   *Assessment by the Domestic Authorities*
Although neither the Court nor the Committee guarantee a right to a fair trial in expulsion or extradition procedures, as this is enshrined for instance in Article 6 ECHR for civil and criminal proceedings, they both consider the fairness of a procedure to be an important indication of the quality of 'truth-finding' under the principle of non-refoulement. Gaps in the system lead to a higher risk of a violation of the prohibition on refoulement. It is therefore logical that the Court and the Committee both attribute weight to the quality of the risk

---

no. 604/2014, §§ 2.5 and 7.3, in which the Committee noted that 'in the present case' it does not consider that 'application for leave to apply for a judicial review of the decision would have been an ineffective remedy in the complainant's case, in the absence of any particular circumstances adduced by him in support of such an assumption.'

331   The Committee observed that 'the Federal Court may quash a decision of the Immigration Refugee Board if satisfied that: the tribunal acted without jurisdiction; failed to observe a principle of natural justice or procedural fairness; erred in law in making a decision; based its decision on an erroneous finding of fact; acted, or failed to act, by reason of fraud or perjured evidence; or acted in any other way that was contrary to law.' It then held 'that none of the grounds above include a review on the merits of the complainant's claim that he would be tortured if returned to India'; ComAT, *Singh v. Canada*, 30 May 2011, no. 319/2007, § 8.8.

332   See also the critique of the Canadian government in ComAT, *W.G.D. v. Canada*, 26 November 2014, no. 520/2012, §§ 4.6 and 4.7, in which the Committee confirmed the approach taken in *Singh v. Canada* (see § 7.3). With regard to the ineffectiveness of a *second* pre-removal sisk assessment see ComAT, *Y. v. Canada*, 28 July 2015, no. 512/2012, § 7.2.

333   ComAT, *Singh v. Canada*, 30 May 2011, no. 319/2007, §§ 8.9 and 9.

334   *Ibid.*, § 7.3. The individual complaint mechanism as guaranteed by Art. 22 CAT is in fact not affected when no proper domestic remedies are available.

assessment in the national procedure when assessing whether the principle of non-refoulement has been violated in a particular case. Neither the Court nor the Committee describes exactly how the risk assessment at national level should be set out. Efforts that national authorities should make with regard to the risk establishment under the principle of non-refoulement might vary with the circumstances of each case. It is nevertheless possible to draw guidelines from their case law. The Court and Committee's minimum conditions for proper truth-finding are, with the exception of certain nuances, very similar.[335]

The assessment made by national authorities should include all relevant information submitted by the complainant as well as additional sources concerning the situation in the receiving country. On the latter issue, the Court is particularly demanding. The Committee is instead particularly sensitive to the question of whether national authorities have duly investigated allegations of past ill treatment. It should further be added that immigration authorities should take into consideration gender aspects[336] or other circumstances that may put applicants in particularly vulnerable or difficult situations in the asylum procedure or in case of removal. If the complainant has not been heard or if he has not been given the possibility of having his own materials taken into account by the national authorities in the risk assessment, the Court's and Committee's trust in their findings appears to be considerably weakened.

The Court and the Committee are both sceptical if national authorities or courts reject refoulement applications for purely procedural reasons and if no specific and individualized assessment is apparent.[337] The automatic and mechanical application of provisions such as short time limits for submitting an asylum application or the rejection of applications for not having presented identity papers must be considered as endangering the protection of the rights embodied in Article 3 ECHR and Article 3 CAT. *Accelerated procedures*, for example with regard to clearly unfounded complaints or those concerning removals to states considered safe, are not prohibited but individuals must be given a realistic opportunity to present their claims.[338] However, the abolition of any kind of remedy with regard to certain applicants or destination countries is not in accordance with the two Conventions. No matter what the circumstances are, individuals presenting an 'arguable' (ECHR) or 'plausible'

---

335   See also Wouters 2009, p. 573.

336   See ECtHR, *N. v. Sweden*, 20 July 2010, no. 23505/09, §§ 5.5–6.2; ComAT, *J.A.M.O. v. Canada*, 9 May 2008, no. 293/2006, § 10.7; ComAT, *F.B. v. Netherlands*, 20 November 2015, no. 613/2014, § 8.8.

337   See also Schürmann and Scheidegger 2009, p. 205; Spijkerboer 2009, pp. 57–58.

338   See also Wouters 2009, pp. 572–573.

(CAT) claim under the principle of non-refoulement have a right to an assessment on the merits.

Finally, not only do national authorities have the duty to make a proper examination of the risk, but their assessment has to be apparent to the Court and the Committee.[339] Decisions formally taken at admissibility level are not as such problematic if they contain a visible material risk assessment.[340]

The consequences of procedural irregularities within the national proceedings on the Court and the Committee's risk assessment are variable. The impact depends to some extent on the nature or severity of the deficiencies. It has been stated that the Court and the Committee will generally attach less weight to findings made by domestic authorities if they appear arbitrary or unreasonable. The more time and effort invested in the truth-finding, the better the prediction of future events in their eyes.[341] When serious deficiencies are apparent or the national authorities have simply not done a risk assessment, one of two reactions may be expected from the Court and the Committee:

(1)   They perform the risk assessment themselves, freely assessing the facts as presented by the complainant and collecting further information *proprio motu*. Complainants often have the benefit of the doubt in such cases: a poor human rights situation or past experiences of ill treatment might be enough, together with the lack of an examination, to trigger the application of the principle of non-refoulement.[342] In some cases, the lack of proper investigation by the domestic authorities is *per se* considered a factor enhancing the risk of ill treatment.[343]

---

339   See, as illustrative examples, ECtHR, *Sultani v. France*, 20 September 2007, no. 45223/05, § 66; ComAT, *A.F. v. Sweden*, 8 May 1998, no. 89/1997, § 6.4.

340   ComAT, *R.A. v. Switzerland*, 20 November 2012, no. 389/2009, § 9.4.

341   See also Battjes 2009, p. 604, with regard to the Court.

342   As examples see, for the Court: ECtHR, *Al-Husni v. Bosnia and Herzegovina*, 7 February 2012, no. 3727/08; ECtHR, *Hirsi Jamaa and Others v. Italy*, 23 February 2012 [GC], no. 27765/09; ECtHR, *M.O.M. v. France*, 18 April 2013, no. 18372/10, § 41; ECtHR, *R.J. v. France*, 19 September 2013, no. 10466/11, §§ 40–43; ECtHR, *N.K. v. France*, 19 December 2014, no. 7974/11, §§ 42–47. Committee: ComAT, *Sogi v. Canada*, 16 November 2007, no. 297/2006; ComAT, *Iya v. Switzerland*, 16 November 2007, no. 299/2006; ComAT, *Kalinichenko v. Morocco*, 25 November 2011, no. 428/2010, §§ 14.2 and 15.6; ComAT, *Ke Chun Rong v. Australia*, 5 November 2012, no. 416/2010, §§ 7.4 and 7.5.

343   As examples see, for the Court: ECtHR, *Klein v. Russia*, 1 April 2010, no. 24268/08; ECtHR, *Khaydarov v. Russia*, 20 May 2010, no. 21055/09; ECtHR, *Iskandarov v. Russia*, 23 September 2010, no. 17185/05; ECtHR, *Gaforov v. Russia*, 21 October 2010, no. 25404/09; ECtHR, *Auad v. Bulgaria*, 11 October 2011, no. 46390/10. Committee: ComAT, *Arana v. France*, 9 November 1999, no. 63/1997; ComAT, *Ktiti v. Morocco*, 26 May 2011, no. 419/2010, §§ 8.5–8.7.

(2)   In cases in which irregularities are particularly heavy, the Committee might find a violation of Article 3 CAT without doing a material risk assessment.[344] The Court in contrast is more reluctant to take this approach, that is, to find violations of the principle of non-refoulement simply because no risk assessment has been done at national level. However, it has come very close to this in some cases.[345]

In this context, one must remember that the Court and the Committee have both rejected complaints for the simple reason that the national authorities' assessment did not reveal irregularities. However, among the published decisions and judgments, this remains the exception. In most of theses cases and *in almost all cases treated on the merits, the Court and the Committee carry out their own (at least minimal) risk assessment,* whether procedural irregularities are apparent or not. In other words, even national assessments that fulfil all the requirements with regard to procedural guarantees will not prevent the Court and the Committee from finding a violation of the principle of non-refoulement if they think the conclusions made by the domestic authorities cannot be accepted. Despite their assertions in some verdicts, the Court and the Committee's main concern in refoulement cases is not the quality of the risk assessment at national level or procedural standards; it is the applicant's security. Spijkerboer rightly notes that 'the thoroughness of the national asylum procedure is one factor, but the crucial issue is not a procedural one, but the substance.'[346]

It can nevertheless be concluded that in cases in which no meaningful refoulement assessment by national authorities is apparent, the Court and the Committee will be particularly cautious. If the deficiencies are severe and the

---

344   See, by way of illustration, ComAT, *Tebourski v. France,* 1 May 2007, no. 300/2006, §§ 8.2–9; ComAT, *K.H. v. Denmark,* 23 November 2012, no. 464/2011, § 8.8.

345   See ECtHR, *Garabayev v. Russia,* 7 June 2007, no. 38411/02 and ECtHR, *Ryabikin v. Russia,* 19 June 2008, no. 8320/04; ECtHR, *Mamazhonov v. Russia,* 23 October 2014, no. 17239/13. To highlight as exceptions are further the so-called extraordinary renditions treated in Strasbourg, which have a particular character. The Court has made clear on this subject 'that any extra-judicial transfer or extraordinary rendition, by its deliberate circumvention of due process, is an absolute negation of the rule of law and the values protected by the Convention' and therefore amounts to a violation of Art. 3 ECHR; ECtHR, *Dzhurayev v. Russia,* 25 April 2013, no. 71386/10, § 204.

346   Spijkerboer 2009, p. 66.

human rights situation worrying, the complainants seem more likely to get the benefit of the doubt with regard to the risk of refoulement.[347]

b   *The Right to an Effective Remedy*

Individuals claiming to be threatened with ill treatment if removed to a third country have the right under the principle of non-refoulement for their claim to be assessed and to obtain a formal decision on the issue of refoulement that they can review. Without this right, the protection against refoulement would remain theoretical. Article 3 ECHR and Article 3 CAT therefore contain an implied positive obligation for states to assess allegations of refoulement. Neither the Court nor the Committee have determined how far these positive, procedural obligations under the principle of non-refoulement should reach. Their case law as described in the preceding section sets out some important guidelines. Particularly, the Court and the Committee both recognize that individuals threatened with deportation have the *right to apply for an effective remedy* against their deportation order.

According to the Committee, this right is inherent in Article 3 CAT. The Court indicates in rulings that Article 3 ECHR contains an implicit right to an effective remedy against refoulement decisions. In contrast to the CAT, the ECHR has also a separate norm under Article 13 ECHR that explicitly guarantees the right to an effective remedy with regard to potential violations of all Convention rights. The Court therefore need not necessarily rely on rights inherent to the prohibition on refoulement when assessing whether its effective application could be endangered by a lack of domestic remedies. Having a separate norm guaranteeing the right to an effective remedy, the Court's practice on that matter is richer and much more elaborated than the Committee's. The Court has even examined alleged violations of Article 13 ECHR in the context of refoulement in cases in which applicants were no longer threatened with deportation. Since it examines complaints under Article 3 CAT only if there is an imminent risk of deportation, this approach is unlikely to be taken by the Committee. The Committee has never found a violation of procedural rights inherent to Article 3 CAT without similarly finding that the deportation would in itself violate this guarantee. The lack of a separate norm to address only procedural aspects under the principle of non-refoulement might be the reason for which the Committee, in contrast

---

347   Lorz and Sauer 2010, pp. 395 and 401, who note that risk assessments made by national authorities have an impact on the complainant's burden of proof. See on this also the Sections 1.1.2, 1.2.2 and 1.3.2 of this chapter above.

to the Court, has occasionally found a violation of that principle for *purely procedural reasons.*

States do not have to provide 'effective remedies' against any kind of deportation decision. According to the Court, individuals must have at least an 'arguable claim' in order to benefit from the right to an effective remedy. The Committee speaks of a 'plausible allegation.' There is no indication in the Committee's case law of what 'plausible' means. One can only assume that 'plausibility,' just like 'arguability' in the Court's case law, suggests complaints that pass the admissibility bar of not being manifestly ill-founded.[348] With this approach, given that the lack of substantiation of a complaint must be much more evident in Geneva than in Strasbourg for it to be declared 'manifestly ill-founded,'[349] it may be assumed that the Committee attributes 'plausibility' to a complaint more easily than the Court does. However, the question of what makes an arguable or plausible claim and the relation to manifestly ill-founded complaints is anyway almost impossible to know, since neither of these terms are clear-cut concepts but are decided on a case-by-case basis.

While the Court has indicated that an appeal body need not necessarily be of judicial character, the Committee has made no clear statement on the matter. It is, however, evident that both institutions prefer judicial authorities to administrative ones.[350] In any event, the appeal body must have a 'court-like character in terms of independence and competence.'[351] It must have the power to freely assess the claims on the merits and to quash the lower body's decision. The chance of success a remedy offers is not decisive for its effectiveness but extremely low success rates will be taken as indications of a lack of effectiveness. The Court and the Committee have made clear that a remedy in expulsion or extradition matters is only effective if it has suspensive effect.[352] ›
According to the Court, a remedy should *automatically* lead to the suspension of the enforcement, which implies, as a minimum, that the deposition of a request must have automatic suspensive effect.[353] The Committee has made no pronouncement on how automatic the suspensive effect should be. Both

---

348   See also Wouters 2009, p. 517.

349   See Chapter 2 Section 3.2.6.

350   Wouters 2009, p. 574. See ComAT, *Kalonzo v. Canada*, 18 May 2012, no. 343/2008, § 8.3, speaking quite clearly for this preference.

351   Spijkerboer 2009, p. 50.

352   The Court and the Committee have clearly influenced each other on that matter: see for instance the referral to the Committee's conclusions and recommendations in ECtHR, *Gebremedhin v. France*, 26 April 2007, no. 25389/05, §§ 58 and 65.

353   See, for example, in ECtHR, *M.A. v. Cyprus*, 23 July 2013, no. 41872/10, §§ 131–143.

the Court and the Committee have, however, made clear that complainants must be given sufficient time to submit an appeal. The adequateness of time limits will depend on the circumstances of the case.[354] Finally, the Court and the Committee have also made clear that individuals should not be precluded from submitting complaints at the international level in Strasbourg or Geneva. However, this right is inherent to the right to submit individual complaints under Article 34 ECHR and Article 22 CAT and not to the right to an effective remedy.[355]

Since the Court and the Committee assess each case in light of its particular circumstances, it is possible that a remedy that is considered effective in one case may not be considered effective in another.[356] The Committee's practice on the question of which powers an appeal body should have is quite unpredictable,[357] but this is also related to its scant case law and poor reasoning. A reasoned discussion of the issue is lacking. However, the Court's handling of Article 13 ECHR with regard to refoulement complaints is also not always consistent.[358] It has been mentioned above that the Court has recently, against its previous practice, assessed a refoulement complaint against Greece under Article 13 ECHR in conjunction with Article 3 ECHR without making a separate risk assessment under Article 3 ECHR.[359] Should the Court continue to follow this approach, the Committee could be the better body to address for protection against arbitrary removals in cases in which the national proceedings are considered deficient. Even if the Committee finds a violation of Article 3 CAT simply for procedural reasons, it will still advise the concerned state not to deport the complainant. This is not necessarily the case in a violation of Article 13 ECHR.

In conclusion, it can be stated that the procedural obligations contained in the principle of non-refoulement are not clearly defined.[360] States have a

---

354   See, for example, ECtHR, *I.M. v. France*, 2 February 2012, no. 9152/09, § 151, in which 48 hours were considered too short a time to prepare an application.

355   See on this also Chapter 2 Sections 1.2 and 2.2 on interim measures.

356   See for the Court: ECtHR, *Mwanje v. Belgium*, 20 December 2011, no. 10486/10, §§ 102–107 and ECtHR, *Quraishi v. Belgium*, 12 May 2009, no 6130/08 (decision) with regard to the urgent procedure before the Belgian *Conseil de contentieux des étrangers*.

357   See illustrative the case *Singh v. Canada* discussed above in Section 3.1.2.b of this chapter.

358   See in this sense also Spijkerboer 2009, p. 49.

359   See ECtHR, *R.U. v. Greece*, 7 June 2011, no. 2237/08 discussed in Section 3.1.1.b of this chapter.

360   See on this Battjes 2009, p. 606, who concludes that in contrast to the state obligation not to remove an individual under the principle of non-refoulement, the procedural obligations inherent to this principle are rather 'blurry' and can therefore not really be considered absolute rights.

duty to assess refoulement complaints and to offer an effective remedy against decisions of the authority of first instance. What impact a lack of assessment or a proper assessment has on the Court and the Committee's risk assessment is difficult to predict and seems somehow to depend, before both institutions, on the substantiation of the complaint with regard to the material aspect of the principles of non-refoulement. States do have a certain amount of freedom when it comes to the manner in which they fulfil their procedural obligations under the principle of non-refoulement. Some scholars have therefore noted that the procedural part of the prohibition on refoulement is in danger of threatening the absolute and unconditional character of the substantive part of Article 3 ECHR.[361] It should nevertheless be recalled that according to the Court and the Committee, no situation – be it mass population influx, economic crisis, security concerns, or any bi- or multilateral agreement – can excuse any state from a proper assessment of each and every arguable or plausible refoulement claim that is presented to it.[362] The Court recently held that it is aware of the institutional and administrative challenges states face when confronted with a high number of asylum requests. However, according to the Court, like the right to a fair trial in civil or criminal matters according to Article 6 ECHR (which does not apply to asylum or extradition procedures), Article 13 ECHR obliges them to organise their judicial systems in such a way that their authorities and courts can meet each of its requirements.[363] With that, the Court makes clear that it considers the respect of the minimum standards in asylum proceedings according to Article 13 ECHR as indispensable as fair proceedings in general.

3.2   *General Human Rights Situation*

When the Court and the Committee examine whether an individual faces a real risk of ill treatment in the country to which he is to be removed, they will consider both the general human rights situation in that country and the

---

361   Battjes 2009, pp. 603–606 and 618; Lambert 2005, p. 47.

362   See ECtHR, *M.S.S*, § 223; ECtHR, *Hirsi Jamaa and Others*, §§ 122, 129; ECtHR, *El-Masri v. Former Yugoslav Republic of Macedonia*, 13 December 2012 [GC], no. 39630/09, § 257; ComAT, *Agiza v. Sweden*, 20 May 2005, no. 233/2003, § 13.8; See also Wouters 2009, p. 514.

363   See ECtHR, *A.C. and Others v. Spain*, 22 April 2014, no. 6528/11, § 104: 'La Cour est consciente de la nécessité pour les États confrontés à un grand nombre de demandeurs d'asile de disposer des moyens nécessaires pour faire face à un tel contentieux, ainsi que des risques d'engorgement du système. Toutefois, tout comme l'article 6 de la Convention, l'article 13 astreint les États contractants à organiser leurs juridictions de manière à leur permettre de répondre aux exigences de cette disposition (voir, mutatis mutandis, Süßmann c. Allemagne, 16 septembre 1996, Recueil des arrêts 1996-IV, § 55).'

particular characteristics of the applicant. The role of the Court and the Committee is not to establish whether the receiving country is responsible for human rights violations.[364] The human rights situation in the receiving country is, however, an important element that can corroborate or debilitate an applicant's allegation of a real risk of ill treatment in case of deportation.

How much weight do the Court and the Committee give to general human rights conditions in a receiving country in their risk assessment? Can a situation in a receiving country *per se* be such that any removal thereto is prohibited under the principle of non-refoulement? On what information do the international institutions rely when they want to find out about the conditions in a receiving country? These questions will be dealt with in this section.

3.2.1   Court
a   *The Human Rights Situation and the Individualisation of the Risk*
According to the Court's established case law, the risk assessment in non-refoulement procedures 'inevitably involves an assessment of conditions in the receiving country against the standards of Article 3 ECHR.'[365] The Court must assess the foreseeable consequences of sending a complainant to a receiving country, bearing in mind the general situation there.

The general human rights situation will 'not normally in itself entail a violation of Article 3 ECHR in the event of an expulsion.'[366] As the Court repeatedly states, the 'mere possibility of ill-treatment on account of an unsettled situation in the receiving country does not in itself give rise to a breach of Article 3 ECHR.'[367] In other words, 'reference to a general problem concerning human rights observance in a particular country cannot alone serve as a basis for refusal of extradition.'[368] In principle, where the sources available to the Court

---

364   The Court often states in its judgments that 'there is no question of adjudicating on or establishing the responsibility of the receiving country, whether under general international law, under the Convention or otherwise'; see, amongst many others, ECtHR, *Auad v. Bulgaria*, 11 October 2011, no. 46390/10, § 96. In ComAT, *Aemei v. Switzerland*, 9 May 1997, 34/1995, §§ 9.2, the Committee holds that 'it is by no means its responsibility to determine whether the author's rights as recognized by the Convention have been violated by Iran, the country to which he risks being expelled, regardless of whether or not this State is a party to the Convention.'

365   Stated for the first time by the Court in ECtHR, *Soering v. UK*, 7 July 1989, no. 14038/88, § 91.

366   Amongst many others, ECtHR, *H.L.R. v. France*, 29 April 1997, no. 24573/94, § 41; ECtHR, *N.A. v. UK*, 17 July 2008, no. 25904/07, § 114.

367   See, for example, ECtHR, *Y. v. Russia*, 4 December 2008, no. 20113/07, § 79; ECtHR, *Zokhidov v. Russia*, 5 February 2013, no. 67286/10.

368   ECtHR, *Dzhurayev v. Russia*, 25 April 2013, no. 71386/10, § 153.

describe a general situation only, an applicant's allegations in a particular case require 'corroboration by other evidence, with reference to the individual circumstances substantiating his fears of ill-treatment.'[369] However, with its judgment in the case *N.A. v. United Kingdom* the Court made clear that there might be an exception to that principle. It noted that,

> ... it has *never excluded the possibility that a general situation of violence in a country of destination may be of a sufficient level of intensity as to entail that any removal to it would necessarily breach Article 3* of the Convention. Nevertheless, the Court would adopt such an approach *only in the most extreme cases of general violence*, where there was a real risk of ill-treatment simply by virtue of an individual being exposed to such violence on return.[370] (Emphasis added)

Before this judgment, adopted in 2008, the Court's jurisprudence had given rise to uncertainty around the question of whether extremely poor human rights conditions could in themselves be sufficient to trigger the application of the principle of non-refoulement according to Article 3 ECHR. An unclear statement from the Court in *Vilvarajha and Others v. United Kingdom* adopted in 1991 notably contributed to this uncertainty.[371] This case concerned the removal of five Tamils to Sri Lanka in 1988. Three of the applicants were in fact subjected to ill treatment following their return. Concerning the situation of the applicants in Sri Lanka the Court stated:

> The evidence before the Court concerning the background of the applicants, as well as the general situation, does *not establish that their personal position was any worse than the generality of other members of the Tamil community or other young male Tamils* who were returning to their country. Since the situation was still unsettled there existed the possibility that they might be detained and ill-treated as appears to have occurred previously in the cases of some of the applicants. A mere possibility of ill-treatment, however, in such circumstances, is not in itself sufficient to give rise to a breach of Article 3.[372] (Emphasis added)

---

369   Amongst many others, ECtHR, *Mamatkulov and Askarov v. Turkey*, 4 February 2005 [GC], nos. 46827/99 and 46951/99, § 73.

370   ECtHR, *N.A. v. UK*, 17 July 2008, no. 25904/07, §§ 114.

371   See on this Alleweldt 1996, pp. 43–48; Durieux 2008, pp. 10–13; Thurin 2012, pp. 196–202.

372   ECtHR, *Vilvarajah and Others v. UK*, 30 October 1991, nos. 13163/87 and further, § 111. Similar ECtHR, *H.L.R. v. France*, 29 April 1997, no. 24573/94, § 42, in which the Court held that there were 'no documents to support the claim that the applicant's personal situation would be worse than that of other Colombians, were he to be deported.'

The Court stated in the same judgment that 'there existed no special distinguishing features' in the cases of the applicants that could have enabled the United Kingdom's authorities to foresee that they would be ill-treated in case of return.[373] Scholars having analysed the Court's practice as a whole realized quickly that, although the cited statement and particularly the term 'distinguishing features' could be understood that way, the Court did not mean to establish a requirement that a complainant would always have to demonstrate that he was worse off than others in a receiving country in order to benefit from protection against a removal of Article 3 ECHR. The Court was merely expressing the opinion that the situation in Sri Lanka was not so bad at that time that any Tamil would be subjected to treatment contrary to Article 3 ECHR in case of return.[374] Taking into account the Court's case law after *Vilvarajha*, Wouters stated that the term 'distinguishing features' probably relates to the principle that, except in cases of extreme violence, a complainant normally has to show specific 'risk factors' placing him at real risk of being ill-treated in case of removal.[375] He was not wrong. In the case *Sufi and Elmi v. United Kingdom* adopted in 2011, the Court cleared up any misunderstandings by stating:

> In *Vilvarajah v. the United Kingdom* the Court appeared to suggest that a mere situation of general instability would only give rise to a breach of Article 3 of the Convention if there was evidence to demonstrate that the applicant's personal situation was worse than that of the generality of other members of his group (*Vilvarajah v. the United Kingdom*, cited above, § 111). However, in *N.A. v. the United Kingdom* the Court expressly considered its earlier decision in *Vilvarajah v. the United Kingdom* and concluded that it should *not be interpreted so as to require an applicant to show the existence of special distinguishing features if he could otherwise show that the general situation of violence in the country of destination was of a sufficient level of intensity to create a real risk that any removal to that country would violate Article 3 of the Convention* (*N.A. v. the United Kingdom*, cited above, §§ 115 – 116). *To insist in such cases that the applicant show the existence of such special distinguishing features would render the protection offered by Article 3 illusory* (*N.A. v. the United Kingdom*, cited above, § 116). Moreover, such a finding would call into question the absolute nature of Article 3, which prohibits in absolute terms torture and inhuman or degrading treatment or punishment.[376] (Emphasis added)

---

373   ECtHR, *Vilvarajah and Others v. UK*, 30 October 1991, nos. 13163/87 & further, § 112.

374   Alleweldt 1996, p. 47; Suntinger 1995, p. 216.

375   Wouters 2009, pp. 249–250 and 544.

376   ECtHR, *Sufi and Elmi v. UK*, 28 June 2011, nos. 8319/07 and 11449/07, § 217.

The Court eventually summarized its practice as follows:

> The sole question for the Court to consider in an expulsion case is wheth-
> er, in all the circumstances of the case before it, substantial grounds have
> been shown for believing that the person concerned, if returned, would
> face a real risk of being subjected to treatment contrary to Article 3 of the
> Convention. *If the existence of such a risk were established, the applicant's
> removal would necessarily breach Article 3, regardless of whether the risk
> emanates from a general situation of violence, a personal characteristic of
> the applicant, or a combination of the two.* However, it is clear that not
> every situation of general violence will give rise to such a risk. On the con-
> trary, the Court has made it clear that a *general situation of violence would
> only be of sufficient intensity to create such a risk 'in the most extreme cases'*
> where there was a real risk of ill-treatment simply by virtue of an indi-
> vidual being exposed to such violence on return.[377] (Emphasis added)

The cited case *Sufi and Elmi v. United Kingdom* concerned two men who were
threatened with expulsion to Somalia. The Court made a comprehensive analysis of the situation in Mogadishu and other parts of southern or central Somalia as well as camps for internally displaced persons (IDPs) and refugees in
Somalia and Kenya. With regard to Mogadishu, the Court observed 'that the
large quantity of objective information overwhelmingly indicates that the level of violence in Mogadishu is of sufficient intensity to pose a real risk of treatment reaching the Article 3 threshold to anyone in the capital,' except possibly
those who are 'exceptionally well-connected powerful actors.'[378] With regard
to possible internal flight alternatives in other parts of Somalia, the Court noted that a returnee with no recent experience of Somalia would be at risk of
treatment proscribed by Article 3 ECHR if he had to live in a region controlled
by the al-Shabaab or even if he simply had to travel through such a region to
get home.[379] Concerning the refugee camps or IDP settlements in Somalia and
Kenya in which individuals who have no family connections outside of Mogadishu might seek protection, the Court found that any refugee would be at a
'real risk of Article 3 ill-treatment on account of the dire humanitarian conditions' there.[380] Shortly examining the complainant's personal situation in light

---

377   *Ibid.,* § 218.
378   *Ibid.,* §§ 241–250.
379   *Ibid.,* §§ 268–277.
380   *Ibid.,* §§ 271–292. See on this also Chapter 3 Section 2.3.2.b.

of these considerations, the Court found a violation of Article 3 ECHR in case of removal of the two complainants to Somalia.[381]

It was the first time that the Court acknowledged the existence of general violence of such intensity as to prohibit the return of almost any person. The Court held that the situation of general violence in Mogadishu was sufficiently intense to enable it to conclude that *any returnee* would be at a real risk of Article 3 ill treatment there, unless it could be demonstrated that he was sufficiently well connected to powerful actors in the city.[382] With regard to well-connected individuals, the Court noted, however, that it would be very unlikely that a state could successfully raise such an argument, unless the individual in question would have connections at the highest level, which basically excluded persons who had not recently been in Somalia.[383]

The Court further indicated in *Sufi and Elmi* that it is not persuaded that Article 3 ECHR does not offer comparable protection to that afforded under Article 15(c) of the European Union's Qualification Directive, which offers protection against a 'serious and individual threat to a civilian's life or person by reason of indiscriminate violence in situations of international or internal armed conflict.'[384] It stated that the threshold set by both provisions may, in exceptional circumstances, be attained in consequence of a situation of general violence of such intensity that any person being returned to the region in question would be at risk simply on account of his presence there.[385]

However, the exact overlap between these provisions remains unclear,[386] and this blurriness has not changed with another recent judgment concerning indiscriminate violence, in which the Court refrained from addressing the relation of Article 3 ECHR and Article 15(c) of the Qualification Directive. The judgment *L.M. and Others v. Russia* was adopted in October 2015 and concerned the removal of two Syrians and a stateless Palestinian to Syria.[387] The Court first referred to the principles developed in *Sufi and Elmi*, in which it had

---

381   *Ibid.*, §§ 301–304 and 309–312. See also the summary of the Court's conclusions with regard to the situation in Somalia in §§ 293–296.

382   *Ibid.*, § 293.

383   *Ibid.*, §§ 249–250 and 293.

384   *Ibid.*, §§ 225 and 226. See on this Chapter 1 Section 6 on the EU legislation.

385   The Court referred to ECJ, C-465-07(2009) ECR I-00921, *Elgafaji v. Staatssecretaris van Justitie*, 17 February 2009, §§ 35 and 39, according to which the more an applicant can show that he is specifically affected by reason of factors particular to his personal circumstances, the lower is the level of indiscriminate violence required for him to be eligible for subsidiary protection.

386   See Chapter 1 Section 6 and Peers, Moreno-Lax, Garlick & Guild 2015, pp. 139–143.

387   ECtHR, *L.M. and Others v. Russia*, 15 October 2015, nos. 40081/14, 40088/14 and 40127/14.

regard to 'indiscriminate bombardments and military offensives carried out by all parties to the conflict, the unacceptable number of civilian casualties, the substantial number of persons displaced within and from the city and the unpredictable and widespread nature of the conflict.'[388] The judges indicated that these criteria *were not to be seen as an exhaustive list to be applied to all future cases*, but that they formed an appropriate yardstick in the assessment of such cases. Turning to the applicants, they acknowledged that this was the first case in which they had to evaluate the risk of danger to life or ill treatment in the context of the ongoing conflict in Syria. As the Court notes, this is due to the fact that most European countries do not carry out returns to Syria at the moment, as is also suggested by the UNHCR and UN documentation, which report 'massive violation of human rights and humanitarian law by all parties' and describe the situation as a 'humanitarian crisis.'[389] The Court then held that the applicants originate from Aleppo and Damascus, where particularly heavy fighting was going on. With regard to the applicant who is a stateless Palestinian, the Court specified that he belongs to a group in need of international protection according to the UNCHR. In addition, all three applicants were young men who, according to Human Rights Watch, are in particular danger of detention and ill treatment in Syria. These elements were 'sufficient' for the Court to conclude that their return would be 'in breach of Articles 2 and/or 3 of the Convention.'[390] As can be seen, the Court still mentioned certain special features with regard to the particular risk situation of the three male applicants.[391] However, the judgment made clear that in light of the general situation in Syria, the burden had switched to the authorities to show 'any special circumstances' which could demonstrate sufficient protection for the applicants if returned.[392] With that, the Court's conclusion in *L.M. and Others* is comparable to that in *Sufi and Elmi*.[393]

---

388   *Ibid.*, § 122, referring to *Sufi and Elmi*, § 248.

389   *Ibid.*, §§ 122 and 123.

390   The Court, following its practice in cases in which a violation of Art. 2 *and* 3 ECHR is alleged, assessed the case in light of its principles developed under Art. 3 ECHR (see on this also Chapter 1 Section 2.2.3.).

391   The Court further noted that the national court's approach in this case was 'particularly regretful' as they had failed to adequately assess the risk of ill treatment in Syria, focusing rather on establishing that the applicants' presence in Russia was illegal, *Ibid.*, §§ 114–118.

392   *Ibid.*, §§ 124–126.

393   See ECtHR, *Sufi and Elmi*, § 293, in which the Court indicated that applicants well connected to powerful actors in Mogadishu may still be able to obtain protection.

However, the judgments *Sufi and Elmi* and *L.M. and Others* remain exceptional. In addition, the Court's evaluation of a conflict can change quite quickly, as the judgment *K.A.B. v. Sweden* adopted in September 2013 reveals.[394] In this judgment the Court had already altered its estimation of the risk situation in Mogadishu as declared two years before in *Sufi and Elmi*. The Strasbourg judges held that according to *most recent* information, the new Somali national government had improved security in Mogadishu since al-Shabaab had lost power over the city in August 2011.[395] The Court held that 'it is aware that the human rights and security situation in Mogadishu is serious and fragile and in many ways unpredictable.'[396] It even recognized that al-Shabaab is still present in the city and does perform attacks against specific groups that can also affect ordinary citizens.[397] However, in light of 'the fact that al-Shabaab is no longer in power of the city, there is no front-line fighting or shelling any longer and the number of civilian casualties has gone down,' the Court found that 'the available country information did not indicate that the situation is, at present, of such a nature as to place everyone who is present in the city at a real risk of treatment contrary to Article 3 of the Convention.' Therefore, it had 'to establish whether the applicant's personal situation is such that his return to Somalia would contravene the relevant provisions of the Convention.'[398] The Court then briefly assessed the applicant's personal circumstances in case of removal to Mogadishu.[399] Noting that he allegedly had a home in Mogadishu, where his wife lived, and that he did not belong to any group at risk of being targeted by al-Shabaab,[400] the Court concluded that the applicant had failed to 'make it plausible that he would face a real risk of being killed or subjected to ill-treatment upon return to Somalia.'[401] In their dissenting opinion, Judges

---

394   ECtHR, *K.A.B. v. Sweden*, 5 September 2013, no. 886/11.

395   *Ibid.*, §§ 78–91.

396   *Ibid.*, § 91.

397   *Ibid.*, § 88.

398   *Ibid.*, § 91.

399   It should be noted that the national authorities did not intend to deport the applicant to Mogadishu but to Somaliland, since they considered that no one could be deported to Mogadishu when they took their decision. The Court, however, rejected the possibility of deporting the applicant to Somaliland, since he did not have sufficiently strong connections to gain admittance and settle there and assessed the situation in Mogadishu; §§ 80–84. Judge Power-Forde, joined by judge Zupančič, rightly indicated in a dissenting opinion that it is unusual for the Court to assess a removal to a region to which the national authorities did not intend to send the applicant. See on this also the critique in Section 3.4.1.c of this Chapter.

400   *Ibid.*, §§ 92–96.

401   *Ibid.*, § 97.

Power-Forde and Zupančič expressed surprise that given 'the devasting human rights abuses throughout the twenty year civil war and the ongoing human rights abuses under the current regime,' their colleagues made a significant departure from the Court's relatively recent judgment *Sufi and Elmi*. In light of the very unpredictable nature of the conflict in Mogadishu[402] and the significant numbers of civilians still displaced in Somalia and Kenya,[403] their objection is very appropriate. However, in September 2015, the Court confirmed *K.A.B.* with the very severe judgment *R.H. v. Sweden* concerning the removal of a woman to Mogadishu.[404]

In general, as can be seen from the above and as has been stated by the Court, a human rights situation 'will not normally in itself entail a violation of Article 3 ECHR.'[405] The Court has explicitly rejected the existence of an 'extreme case of general violence' for the eastern part of the Democratic Republic of Congo in 2005,[406] for Iraq[407] and Afghanistan[408] on several occasions, as well as for the Sudan.[409] Hence, even in cases in which the human rights conditions in the receiving state are very disturbing, the Court has usually insisted that the applicant demonstrate individualizing risk elements or, in the words of the Court, 'special distinguishing features' like political activities or other factors, to establish that he would be at risk of being ill-treated. However, as has been explained, in general the human rights situation in the receiving state does have an important impact on the complainant's burden of proof.[410] In other words, if a complainant is supposed to be deported to a country known for systematic human rights violations, the Court will be less demanding on

---

402   See also *Sufi and Elmi*, § 247, in which the Court describes the situation in Mogadishu as unpredictable and capable of changing on a daily basis.

403   See § 90 of *K.A.B. v. Sweden*.

404   ECtHR, *R.H. v. Sweden*, 10 September 2015, no. 4601/14. See the critique on this judgment in the next Section 3.2.1.b.

405   Amongst others, ECtHR, *N.A. v. UK*, 17 July 2008, no. 25904/07, § 114.

406   ECtHR, *Mossi and Others v. Sweden*, 8 March 2005, no. 15017/03 (decision).

407   ECtHR, *Müslim v. Turkey*, 26 April 2005, no. 53566/99, § 70; ECtHR, *F.H. v. Sweden*, 20 January 2009, no. 32621/06, §§ 90–93; ECtHR, *S.A. v. Sweden*, 27 June 2013, no. 66523/10, § 47. Confirmed also in ECtHR, *J.K. and Others v. Sweden*, 4 June 2015, no. 59166/12, §§ 54 and 55 (not in force), which is, however, pending before the Grand Chamber.

408   ECtHR, *Sultani v. France*, 20 September 2007, no. 45223/05, § 67; ECtHR, *Husseini v. Sweden*, 13 October 2011, no. 10611/09, § 84; ECtHR, *H. and B. v. UK*, 9 April 2013, nos. 70073/10 and 44539/11, § 93; ECtHR, *A.G.R. v. Netherlands*, 12 January 2016, no. 13442/08, § 59.

409   ECtHR, *Mohammed v. Austria*, 6 June 2013, no. 2283/12, § 109; ECtHR, *A.A. v. Switzerland*, 7 January 2014, no. 58802/12, § 39.

410   See the cases discussed in Section 1.1.2 of this Chapter above.

the establishment of personal risk factors and the presentation of related evidence.

b   *Protection of Groups Systematically Exposed to Ill Treatment and Vulnerable Individuals*

Complainants can also be exempt from having to show special 'distinguishing risk factors' in a situation where there is no extreme general violence but where they can show that they belong to a *group that is systematically threatened with ill treatment* in the receiving country. In the case *N.A. v. United Kingdom*, the Court held:

> Exceptionally, however, in cases where an applicant alleges that he or she is a *member of a group systematically exposed to a practice of ill-treatment*, the Court has considered that the protection of Article 3 of the Convention enters into play when the *applicant establishes that there are serious reasons to believe in the existence of the practice in question and his or her membership of the group concerned. In those circumstances, the Court will not then insist that the applicant show* the existence of further special distinguishing features if to do so would render illusory the protection offered by Article 3. ...
>
> In determining whether it should or should not insist on further special distinguishing features, it follows that the Court may take account of the general situation of violence in a country. It considers that it is appropriate for it to do so if that general situation makes it more likely that the authorities (or any persons or group of persons where the danger emanates from them) will *systematically ill-treat* the group in question.[411] (Emphasis added)

It is essentially up to the complainant to demonstrate that he is a member of a group systematically exposed to a practice of ill treatment.[412] However, the Court is quite strict in recognizing the existence of such groups. In the case *N.A.*, it did not accept that Tamils being sent back to Colombo in 2008 belonged to such a group and requested the applicants to show 'special distinguishing features' putting them individually at risk.[413] The Court examined the case in light of individual risk factors that could increase the risk of ill treatment such as *inter alia* the age of the applicant, the fact that he was a suspected LTTE

---

411   ECtHR, *N.A. v. UK*, 17 July 2008, no. 25904/07, § 116.
412   ECtHR, *Saadi v. Italy*, 28 February 2008 [GC], no. 37201/06, § 132.
413   ECtHR, *N.A. v. UK*, 17 July 2008, no. 25904/07, § 128.

member, previous criminal records, past detention, the presence of scarring, return from London or other centre of LTTE fundraising, illegal departure from Sri Lanka, lack of ID card, having made an asylum claim abroad or having relatives in the LTTE. The fact that the applicant would have to pass through Colombo airport, where he was likely to be apprehended, was also of relevance. The Court finally found that Article 3 ECHR would be violated in case of the deportation of that particular applicant, because of the cumulative effect of such factors that showed he was of interest to the authorities in Sri Lanka in their efforts to combat the LTTE.[414] In five judgments all decided in January 2011, the Court explicitly maintained its principle established in *N.A. v the United Kingdom* according to which there was *no general risk* of treatment contrary to Article 3 ECHR for Tamils returning to Sri Lanka.[415] After having analysed each case in light of the risk factors established in *N.A. v. United Kingdom*, the Court concluded in all cases that, in contrast to *N.A.*, the particular background of the applicant did not show they would be of interest to the Sri Lankan authorities. The Court found no violations of Article 3 ECHR in these five cases.[416]

In the case *Y. v. Russia*, the Court did not recognize Falun Gong practitioners in China as being members of a group systematically exposed to ill treatment despite international reports showing that they were under threat of persecution.[417] In the case *M.E. v. France* concluded in June 2013, the Court made clear that it was worried about the situation of the Copts in Egypt, but that there was no generalised risk of ill treatment for them there.[418] However, the Court found that the applicant, who was charged with proselytism in Egypt, had established a personal risk of being detained and ill-treated in case of return.[419] In *H. and B. v. United Kingdom* adopted in April 2013, the Court held

---

414   *Ibid.*, §§ 123–147.

415   The Court took into account a slight improvement of the situation for Tamils since the end of the hostilities in May 2009, although this did not seem to be decisive. Except for the examination of the individual risk factors, the five judgments are almost identical: ECtHR, *N.S. v. Denmark*, 20 January 2011, no. 58359/08, §§ 68–97; ECtHR, *P.K. v. Denmark*, 20 January 2011, no. 54705/08, §§ 67–98; ECtHR, *S.S. and Others v. Denmark*, 20 January 2011, no. 54703/08, §§ 80–117; ECtHR, *T.N. and S.N. v. Denmark*, 20 January 2011, no. 36517/08, §§ 84–117; ECtHR, *T.N. v. Denmark*, 20 January 2011, no. 20594/08, §§ 79–109.

416   *Ibid.* With regard to Sri Lanka see also the complaints rejected in ECtHR, *E.G. v. UK*, 31 May 2011, no. 41178/08, §§ 65–81; ECtHR, *S.R. v. France*, 19 June 2012, no. 17859/09 (decision). An exception is ECtHR, *R.J. v. France*, 19 September 2013, no. 10466/11, concerning a torture victim.

417   ECtHR, *Y. v. Russia*, 4 December 2008, no. 20113/07, §§ 80, 84–91. The Court assessed the case on an individual basis and did not find a violation of Art. 3 ECHR.

418   ECtHR, *M.E. v. France*, 6 June 2013, no. 50094/10, § 50.

419   *Ibid.*, §§ 51–52.

that it was 'not persuaded that the applicants have established that everyone with connections to the UN or the US forces, even in Kabul, can be considered to be at real risk of treatment contrary to Article 3 regardless of their profile or whether or not they continue to work for the international community' in Afghanistan.[420] The Court assessed the individual risks for the applicants at the hands of the Taliban in Kabul as a result of their previous work as a driver for the UN and as an interpreter for the US forces respectively. It rejected the complaints.[421]

However, there are cases in which the Court explicitly admitted that certain groups are systematically exposed to a practice of ill treatment, so that Article 3 ECHR entered into play simply because the applicant established that he was a member of the group concerned. In the *Salah Sheek v. Netherlands* adopted in 2007, the Court found that the reported systematic ill treatment of members of the minority Ashraf clan in parts of Somalia, and the fact that the applicant's membership to this clan was not disputed, were sufficient to conclude that his expulsion would be in violation of Article 3 ECHR.[422]

The Court found a violation of Article 3 ECHR in a number of cases concerning the expulsion of convicted or suspected terrorists to Tunisia before the Arab Spring. In the landmark case on this matter *Saadi v. Italy*, the fact that the applicant was prosecuted for terrorists activities, together with reliable sources reporting systematic ill treatment and torture of persons accused of terrorism in Tunisia, was sufficient for the Grand Chamber to conclude that Article 3 ECHR would be violated in case of a deportation.[423] The Court further considered the diplomatic assurances obtained by the Italians from the Tunisian authorities, according to which the complainant would be treated in compliance with international law, to be ineffective.[424] In several similar subsequent cases, the Court contented itself with referring to its conclusions in *Saadi*, according to which individuals accused of terrorism and returned to Tunisia are generally at risk of ill treatment in Tunisia.[425] This approach changed with the fall of the Tunisian regime in spring 2011, after the Ennahda party, which had been considered a terrorist organisation by the regime of Ben Ali, became the most

---

420 ECtHR, *H. and B. v. UK*, 9 April 2013, nos. 70073/10 and 44539/11, § 100. See the dissenting opinion of judge Kalaydjeva.

421 *Ibid.*, §§ 92–116.

422 ECtHR, *Salah Sheekh v. Netherlands*, 11 January 2007, no. 1948/04, §§ 145–149.

423 See ECtHR, *Saadi v. Italy*, 28 February 2008 [GC], no. 37201/06, §§ 132, 143–146.

424 *Ibid.*, § 147–149. On diplomatic assurances see Section 3.4.2 of this Chapter.

425 See, among others, ECtHR, *Ben Khemais v. Italy*, 24 February 2009, no. 246/07, §§ 53–56; ECtHR, *O. v. Italy*, 24 March 2009, no. 37257/06, §§ 36–39; ECtHR, *Trabelsi v. Italy*, 13 April 2010, no. 50163/08, §§ 40–52; ECtHR, *Toumi v. Italy*, 5 April 2011, no. 25716/09, §§ 47–50;

powerful party in the Tunisian government.[426] In Algeria, where no change of regime occurred with the Arab Spring, the situation is still deemed problematic under Article 3 ECHR for people suspected or convicted of terrorist activities.[427]

From 2008 on, the Court found violations of the principle of non-refoulement in a high number of complaints concerning extraditions and expulsions from Russia and the Ukraine to Central Asian states because of torture, ill-treatment or inhuman conditions in those receiving states' prisons.[428] The Court made clear in several judgments that individuals accused of involvement in

---

ECtHR, *Mannai v. Italy*, 27 March 2012, no. 9961/10, §§ 37 and 38. For a comparable case concerning Libya see ECtHR, *A. v. Netherlands*, 20 July 2010, no. 4900/06, §§ 144–151.

426   See the rejection of the application for that reason in ECtHR, *K.A. v. Switzerland*, 17 April 2012, no. 30352/09, §§ 27–31 (decision).

427   Although the Court has not been as explicit as it was in *Saadi*, it appears from a few judgments that it recognizes a generally enhanced risk of ill treatment for such individuals in Algeria; ECtHR, *Daoudi v. France*, 3 December 2009, no. 19576/08, §§ 68–72; ECtHR, *H.R. v. France*, 22 September 2011, no. 64780/09, §§ 54–65; ECtHR, *Labsi v. Slovakia*, 15 May 2012, no. 33809/08, §§ 127 and 129. See similar with regard to individuals suspected of terrorism in Morocco, ECtHR, *Rafaa v. France*, 30 May 2013, no. 25393/10, §§ 40–43; ECtHR, *Ouabour v. Belgium*, 2 June 2015, no. 26417/10, §§ 62–79.

428   As examples for deportations to *Uzbekistan* see, among others, ECtHR, *Ismoilov and Others v. Russia*, 24 April 2008, no. 2947/06; ECtHR, *Garayev v. Azerbaijan*, 10 June 2010, no. 53688/08; ECtHR, *Yakubov v. Russia*, 8 November 2011, no. 7265/10; ECtHR, *Abdulkhakov v. Russia*, 2 October 2012, no. 14743/11; ECtHR, *Ermakov v. Russia*, 7 November 2013, no. 43165/10; ECtHR, *Mamazhonov v. Russia*, 23 October 2014, no. 17239/13; ECtHR, *Nazarov v. Russia*, 11 December 2014, no. 74759/13; ECtHR, *Khalikov v. Russia*, 26 February 2015, no. 66373/13. For deportations to *Tajikistan* see, among others, ECtHR, *Gaforov v. Russia*, 21 October 2010, no. 25404/09; ECtHR, *Abdulkhakov v. Russia*, 2 October 2012, no. 14743/11; ECtHR, *Azimov v. Russia*, 18 April 2013, no. 67474/11. Deportations to *Turkmenistan*: ECtHR *Garabayev v. Russia*, 7 June 2007, no. 38411/02; ECtHR, *Ryabikin v. Russia*, 19 June 2008, no. 8320/04; ECtHR, *Soldatenko v. Ukraine*, 23 October 2008, no. 2440/07; ECtHR, *Kolesnik v. Russia*, 10 June 2010, no. 26876/08. Deportations to *Kazakhstan*. ECtHR, *Kaboulov v. Ukraine*, 19 November 2009, no. 41015/04; ECtHR, *Baysakov and Others v. Ukraine*, 18 February 2010, no. 54131/08. Deportation to *Belarus*: ECtHR, *Koktysh v. Ukraine*, 10 December 2009, no. 43707/07. Deportation to *Kyrgyzstan*: ECtHR, *Saliyev v. Russia*, 17 April 2014, no. 39093/13; ECtHR, *Mamadeliyev v. Russia*, 24 July 2014, no. 5614/13; ECtHR, *Kadirzhanov and Mamashev v. Russia*, 17 July 2014, nos. 42351/13 and 47823/13; ECtHR, *Khamrakulov v. Russia*, 16 April 2015, no. 68894/13; ECtHR, *Abdullayev v. Russia*, 15 October 2015, no. 8474/14; ECtHR, *Turgunov v. Russia*, 22 October 2015, no. 15590/14; ECtHR, *Tadzhibayev v. Russia*, 1 December 2015, no. 17724/14; ECtHR, *R. v. Russia*, 26 January 2016, no. 11916/15.

the activities of Islamic organisations (in particular suspected members of Hizb al-Tahir, a transnational Islamic organisation considered extremist and banned in Uzbekistan and Tajikistan) belonged to a group systematically exposed to the practice of ill treatment in Uzbekistan and Tajikistan. Considering the membership of the applicants to that group as established, the Court did not insist that they show the existence of further special distinguishing features to find a violation of Article 3 ECHR.[429] The Court even established a near-absolute prohibition of extraditions to Kazakhstan and Turkmenistan for a while. In the case *Soldatenko v. Ukraine* concerning an extradition to Turkmenistan, the Court made the following statement in October 2008:

> From the materials considered above it appears that *any criminal suspect held in custody faces a serious risk of being subjected to torture or inhuman or degrading treatment* both to extract confession and as punishment for being a criminal. Despite the fact that the applicant is wanted for a relatively minor and not politically motivated offence, the Court agrees with the applicant's argument *that the mere fact of being detained as a criminal suspect* in such a situation provides sufficient grounds for fearing that he will be at serious risk of being subjected to treatment contrary to Article 3 of the Convention.[430] (Emphasis added)

With regard to the situation in prisons in Kazakhstan the Court held in November 2009 in *Kaboulov v. Ukraine* that 'any criminal suspect held in custody runs a serious risk of being subjected to torture or inhuman or degrading treatment.'[431] However, in February 2011 the Court took a step back with regard to the prison conditions in Kazakhstan in *Dzhaksybergenov v. Ukraine* and noted,

---

429   ECtHR, *Muminov v. Russia*, 11 December 2008, no. 42502/06, §§ 94–96; ECtHR, *Khodzhayev v. Russia*, 12 May 2010, no. 52466/08, §§ 100–102; ECtHR, *Yuldashev v. Russia*, 8 July 2010, no. 1248/09, §§ 83–86; ECtHR, *Isakov v. Russia*, 8 July 2010, no. 14049/08 §§ 109 and 110; ECtHR, *Karimov v. Russia*, 29 July 2010, no. 54219/08, §§ 99 and 100; ECtHR, *Yakubov v. Russia*, 8 November 2011, no. 7265/10, §§ 88 and 89; ECtHR, *Ergashev v. Russia*, 20 December 2011, no. 12106/09, §§ 112–115; ECtHR, *Zokhidov v. Russia*, 5 February 2013, no. 67286/10, §§ 136–142; ECtHR, *Sidikovy v. Russia*, 20 June 2013, no. 73455/11, § 149; ECtHR, *Kasymakhunov v. Russia*, 14 November 2013, no. 29604/12, §§ 122–128. See also a summary of this practice in ECtHR, *Mamazhonov v. Russia*, 23 October 2014, no. 17239/13, §§ 136–146.

430   ECtHR, *Soldatenko v. Ukraine*, 23 October 2008, no. 2440/07, § 72.

431   See ECtHR, *Kaboulov v. Ukraine*, 19 November 2009, no. 41015/04, §§ 112. See also ECtHR, *Baysakov and Others v. Ukraine*, 18 February 2010, no. 54131/08, §§ 49–52, in which the Court examined some individual elements.

... the international documents available demonstrate some improvement in the human rights situation recently and in particular as to conditions of detention. ... Therefore, the Court is called to reassess its previous
findings in the other cases concerning extradition to Kazakhstan, notably
in the cases of *Kaboulov* ... and *Baysakov and Others*. ... It further notes
that international reports still voice serious concerns as to the human
rights situation in Kazakhstan, in particular with regard to political rights
and freedoms. However, *there is no indication that the human rights situation in Kazakhstan at present is serious enough to call for a total ban on
extradition to that country*. ... Reference to a general problem concerning
human rights observance in a particular country cannot alone serve as a
basis for refusal of extradition.[432] (Emphasis added)

Taking into account the fact that the applicant did not belong 'to the political opposition or to any other vulnerable group,' the Court found that he had
failed to substantiate his allegations of a real risk of ill treatment by individualizing evidence. His claim that any criminal suspect in Kazakhstan would be in
danger of ill treatment was considered too general.[433] The Court rejected other
complaints concerning extraditions of ordinary criminals to Uzbekistan,[434]
Belarus[435] and Tajikistan[436] with similar arguments.

As regards applicants who are members of the Hizb ut-Tahrir, the Court still
recognizes that they are generally at an increased risk of ill treatment if extradited to Uzbekistan or Tajikistan. It has nevertheless taken a step back in
the sense that it assessed recent claims concerning such individuals by taking
into account their particular personal situation.[437] In the case *Azimov v. Russia*

---

432   ECtHR, *Dzhaksybergenov v. Ukraine*, 10 February 2011, no. 12343/10, §§ 35–38. Confirmed,
        among others, in ECtHR, *Oshlakov v. Russia*, 3 April 2014, no. 56662/09, §§ 85–92.

433   See ECtHR, *Dzhaksybergenov v. Ukraine*, 10 February 2011, no. 12343/10, §§ 37 and 38.

434   See ECtHR, *Elmuratov v. Russia*, 3 March 2011, no. 66317/09, § 84; ECtHR, *Shakurov v. Rus-
        sia*, 5 June 2012, no. 55822/10, §§ 136 and 137; ECtHR, *Bakoyev v. Russia*, 5 February 2013,
        no. 30225/11, §§ 115–116. See also, however, ECtHR, *F.N. v. Sweden*, 18 December 2012, no.
        28774/09, § 76, in which the Court reaffirmed that torture and inhuman treatment by law
        enforcement remains widespread and endemic in Uzbekistan.

435   See ECtHR, *Kamyshev v. Ukraine*, 20 May 2010, no. 3990/06, § 44; ECtHR, *Kozhayev v. Rus-
        sia*, 5 June 2012, no. 60054/10, § 89 and 90; ECtHR, *K. v. Russia*, 23 May 2013, no. 69235/11,
        §§ 66–73.

436   ECtHR, *Latipov v. Russia,* 12 December 2013, no. 77658/11, §§ 97–106.

437   See, for example, ECtHR, *Gaforov v. Russia*, 21 October 2010, no. 25404/09, §§ 132–140 (Ta-
        jikistan); ECtHR, *Zokhidov v. Russia*, 5 February 2013, no. 67286/10, §§ 138–142 (Uzbekistan).

concerning the extradition of an applicant who had been accused of being an active member of the Islamic Movement of Uzbekistan to Tajikistan, the Court noted that 'being a member of an opposition party or group does not by itself justify a fear of ill-treatment.'[438] It held that it was 'necessary to examine the specific situation of the applicant.'[439] However, in light of the widely reported risk of ill treatment for applicants suspected of membership of banned religious and political organisations in Tajikistan, the burden had shifted to the Russian authorities to 'dispel any doubts' about a possible ill treatment of the applicant, which they were not able to do.[440] In the case *Kasymakhunov v. Russia* decided in November 2013, the Court held that having regard to numerous reports disclosing a real and systematic risk of ill treatment to persons accused, like the applicant, of criminal offences in connection with their membership of Hizb ut-Tahrir, and to the absence of sufficient safeguards presented by the Russian government to dispel this risk, the applicant's forcible return to Uzbekistan exposed him to a real risk of treatment contrary to Article 3 ECHR.[441] The Court confirmed this approach in several judgements adopted in 2014 and 2015. It described the practice of ill treatment and torture on those accused of religious or political crimes in Uzbekistan as 'systematic and indiscriminate' and stated that there is no evidence demonstrating any fundamental improvement in that area.[442] It recalled its 'constant position that the individuals, whose extradition was sought by the Uzbek authorities on charges of religiously or politically motivated crimes, constituted a vulnerable group, running a real risk of treatment contrary' to Article 3 ECHR.[443]

In the context of particular threatened or vulnerable groups, the landmark judgment *M.S.S. v. Belgium and Greece* decided in January 2011 is worth highlighting once again.[444] The Grand Chamber found a violation of Article 3 ECHR on account of the deficiencies in the asylum procedure in Greece as

438   ECtHR, *Azimov v. Russia*, 18 April 2013, no. 67474/11, § 141.

439   *Ibid.*

440   *Ibid.*, §§ 112–143. See similar ECtHR, *Dzhurayev v. Russia*, 25 April 2013, no. 71386/10, §§ 169–176 (Tajikistan).

441   ECtHR, *Kasymakhunov v. Russia*, 14 November 2013, no. 29604/12, §§ 122–128.

442   See, among others, ECtHR, *Ismailov v. Russia*, 17 April 2014, no. 20110/13, §§ 85–89; ECtHR, *Egamberdiyev v. Russia*, 26 June 2014, no. 34742/13, § 47; ECtHR, *Mamazhonov v. Russia*, 23 October 2014, no. 17239/13, §§ 140 and 145; ECtHR, *Nazarov v. Russia*, 11 December 2014, no. 74759/13, § 34; ECtHR, *Eshonkulov v. Russia*, 15 January 2015, no. 68900/13, § 45; ECtHR, *Khalikov v. Russia*, 26 February 2015, no. 66373/13, § 51; ECtHR, *Mukhitdinov v. Russia*, 21 May 2015, no. 20999/14, § 52.

443   See ECtHR, *Eshonkulov v. Russia*, 15 January 2015, no. 68900/13, § 34.

444   ECtHR, *M.S.S. v. Belgium and Greece*, 21 January 2011 [GC], no. 30696/09.

well as the extremely poor living conditions for the applicant as an asylum seeker there.[445] With regard to these living conditions, the Court held that it 'attaches considerable importance to the applicant's status as an asylum seeker and, as such, a member of a particularly underprivileged and vulnerable population group in need of special protection.'[446] The Court noted that 'the fact that a large number of asylum seekers in Greece find themselves in the same situation as the applicant does not make the risk concerned any less individual where it is sufficiently real and probable.'[447] The Grand Chamber judgment *Hirsi Jamaa v. Italy* has also been mentioned.[448] It concerned Somalia and Eritrean migrants travelling from Libya who had been intercepted at sea by Italian authorities and sent back to Libya. The Court observed that numerous organisations reported that irregular migrants and asylum seekers were systematically arrested and detained in conditions described as inhuman in Gaddafi's Libya. The deportation of the asylum seekers to Libya had therefore been in breach of Article 3 ECHR. The Court noted that 'the fact that a large number of irregular immigrants in Libya found themselves in the same situation as the applicants does not make the risk concerned any less individual where it is sufficiently real and probable.'[449] In this context, the judgment *Sufi and Elmi* is also worth mentioning again. When assessing internal flight possibilities for the complainants outside of Mogadishu, the Court noted that any individual forced to seek refuge in camps such as those in the Afgooye Corridor or in a refugee camp such as the Dadaab camps in Kenya would be at real risk of Article 3 ECHR ill treatment on account of the dire humanitarian conditions to be found there.[450] As can be seen from these judgments and has been elaborated in chapter 3 section 2.3.2.b, the Court considers asylum seekers 'and refugees as members of a particularly underprivileged and vulnerable population group and this places special responsibilities on states under Article 3 ECHR. As has further been confirmed with the *Tarakhel* judgment, this concept of vulnerability and state responsibility is enhanced for children.[451]

---

445   See on this Chapter 3 Sections 2.3.2.b and Chapter 4 Sections 3.1.1.b and 3.4.3.a.

446   ECtHR, *M.S.S.*, § 251. See further the similar statement in § 232 with regard to asylum seekers in the context of detention conditions.

447   ECtHR, *M.S.S.*, § 359.

448   ECtHR, *Hirsi Jamaa and Others v. Italy*, 23 February 2012 [GC], no. 27765/09, §§ 122–138.

449   *Ibid.*, § 136.

450   ECtHR, *Sufi and Elmi v. UK*, 28 June 2011, nos. 8319/07 and 11449/07, §§ 279–292 and 296.

451   See ECtHR, *Tarakhel v. Switzerland*, 4 November 2014 [GC], no. 29217/12, §§ 99, 118 and 119.

In this context, the judgment *N. v. Sweden* adopted in July 2010 concerning the expulsion of a woman to Afghanistan must also be mentioned again.[452] In this case, the Court noted that several reports indicated widespread violence against women in Afghanistan, which was accepted by society as well as the authorities. Against this background, the fact that the complainant was a divorced woman who had lived in a Western country put her at a very relevant risk of ill treatment by her husband and by both of their families in the event of a return to Afghanistan.[453] The Court did not establish that any single women would be at risk of ill treatment if deported to Afghanistan. It made clear, though, that women fear particular risks in that country. However, the judgment is rather unique. Astonishingly, in the refoulement context, the Court has *not given significant weight to the particular vulnerability of women or to risks of domestic or gender-based violence* so far. This can also be observed namely in two complaints submitted by women that have been rejected recently: the case *R.H. v. Sweden* decided in September 2015 concerned the removal of a woman to Mogadishu.[454] The Court held that women are generally discriminated against in Somali society and that a single woman returning to Mogadishu without access to protection from a male network would face a real risk of living conditions constituting inhuman or degrading treatment there. However, by indicating that the applicant had retained contacts and had some male family members in Mogadishu and that she would not have to live in camps for refugees or IDPs, the Court rejected the complaint.[455] The case *A.A. and Others*, introduced in chapter 3 section 2.3.1, concerned the expulsion of a mother and her five children to Yemen fearing honour-related crimes and forced marriage.[456] Again, the Court referred to a few family members remaining and NGOs providing help for women in Sana'a.[457] In her dissenting opinion to *A.A. and Others*, judge Power-Forde criticized her colleagues for having disregarded the fact that the female applicants fell within a group of 'vulnerable individuals' entitled to particular state protection.[458] Surely, Article 3 ECHR sets a high threshold in refoulement

---

452　See ECtHR, *N. v. Sweden*, 20 July 2010, no. 23505/09, §§ 55–62, introduced in Chapter 3 Section 2.3.1.

453　*Ibid.*, §§ 55–62.

454　ECtHR, *R.H. v. Sweden*, 10 September 2015, no. 4601/14. A request for referral to the Grand Chamber was denied.

455　*Ibid.*, §§ 70 and 73.

456　See ECtHR, *A.A. and Others v. Sweden*, 28 June 2012, no. 14499/09.

457　*Ibid.*, §§ 77–96.

458　Judge Power-Forde rightly refers to the landmark case on gender-based violence in the domestic context ECtHR, *Opuz v. Turkey*, 9 June 2009, no. 33401/02, in which the Court

cases in which the risk alleged emanates from private actors.[459] However, taking into account the considerable weight the Court has given to the vulnerability of refugees and children in *M.S.S.* and *Tarakhel* and the state's obligations to protect them from degrading living conditions, its severe approach with regard to the general risks of violence and degrading treatment for single women in Mogadishu and Yemen in the two cases described is astonishing. In their dissenting opinion to *R.H. v. Sweden*, the judges Zupančič and de Gaetano note that, whatever family the applicant may still have in Mogadishu, she will find an extremely hostile environment to her life and physical integrity, coming probably also from those male family members the Court suggested could protect her. I agree with them that it is hard to understand why in this case the forced return to Mogadishu and the associated risks do not reach the threshold that was met with regard to living conditions in *Tarakhel*.[460]

Finally, it is noteworthy that the cases in which the Court has *explicitly* recognized that certain groups are systematically exposed to ill treatment are exceptional. In some judgments, the Court will indicate that a complainant belongs to a particular threatened or vulnerable group but then base its conclusions not on the complainant's membership of that group, but on other more individualized risk elements.[461] In most cases, complainants have to show special distinguishing risk elements that put them personally at risk.

It is possible that the Court is reluctant to proclaim general bans on expulsions or extraditions of certain groups of people (or with regard to specific countries or regions) because this practice could lead to diplomatic problems or an increase in the volume of complaints.[462] The Court's withdrawal of the

---

recognized that the applicant may be considered to fall within a group of 'vulnerable individuals' entitled to state protection (see *Opuz* § 160).

459   See on this Chapter 3 Section 2.3.1.

460   One should also take into account that still in *Sufi and Elmi* in 2011, the Court estimated that almost anyone would be at risk of ill treatment in Mogadishu. Similar considerations apply to the chamber judgment ECtHR, *W.H. v. Sweden*, 27 March 2014, no. 49341/10 (not in force), in which the Court found that the removal of a Mandaean woman originally from Baghdad to Iraq, with the possibility to relocate to the Kurdistan region, was in accordance with Art. 3 ECHR. The Grand Chamber later struck out this case; see ECtHR, *W.H. v. Sweden*, 8 April 2015 [GC], no. 49341/10 (striking out).

461   See, for example, ECtHR, *Abdolkhani and Karimnia v. Turkey*, 22 September 2009, no. 30471/08, §§ 78–83; ECtHR, *Keshmiri v. Turkey*, 13 April 2010, no. 36370/08, §§ 26 and 27; ECtHR, *Tehrani and Others v. Turkey*, 13 April 2010, nos. 32940/08, 41626/08, 43616/08, §§ 66 and 67 (all three cases concerning members of the People's Mujahidin Organization and sympathisers in Iran).

462   See in this sense Chetail 2006, pp. 95–96, with regard to ECtHR, *Vilvarajah and Others v. UK*, 30 October 1991, nos. 13163/87 and further, § 105.

general ban on deportations of individuals facing detention in Kazakhstan could be an example of this reluctance.[463] However, the Grand Chamber judgments *M.S.S.* and *Hirsi Jamaa* and the various extradition cases presented in this section show that the Court is not afraid of making statements with a broad impact on member states' practices or of making judgments likely to have a structural and political impact, when it considers this to be necessary for the protection of the rights guaranteed in the ECHR.

It is finally worth reminding ourselves that in assessing whether there is a risk of ill treatment in the receiving country, the Court 'assesses the general situation in that country, taking into account any indications of improvement or worsening of the human-rights situation in general or in respect of a particular group or area that might be relevant to the applicant's personal circumstances.'[464] Hence, as the practice has also shown, with changes in the human rights situation, the classification of groups may change from case to case.

c   *Sources on the Human Rights Conditions*

To examine the general situation in the receiving country, the Court examines all the material placed before it, or, if necessary, material obtained *proprio motu* from international, domestic, governmental and NGO sources.[465] In its judgments on the merits, the Court usually carries out quite an extensive assessment of sources obtained *proprio motu* with regard to the general human rights situation in the receiving country. According to the Court, 'it would be too narrow' If, as an international human rights court, it 'was only to take into account materials made available by the domestic authorities of the Contracting State concerned, without comparing these with materials from other reliable and objective sources.'[466]

The Court takes into consideration reports of *international organisations*, in particular the UN. Often cited are reports of the UN Human Rights Committee, the Committee against Torture and the UN High Commissioner for Human Rights as well as the reports of the UN's Special Rapporteur on torture, or UN Rapporteurs on other human rights violations or specific countries. When referring to the CAT, the Court usually refers to the Committee's concluding

---

463   See in this sense also Lorz and Sauer 2010, p. 401.

464   ECtHR, *Abdulkhakov v. Russia*, 2 October 2012, no. 14743/11, § 135.

465   See, amongst many others, ECtHR, *Kaboulov v. Ukraine*, 19 November 2009, no. 41015/04, § 107.

466   ECtHR, *Salah Sheekh v. Netherlands*, 11 January 2007, no. 1948/04, § 136.

observations in the framework of the state reporting procedure under Article 19 CAT.[467] Exceptionally it refers to decisions adopted by the Committee on individual cases.[468] The Court gives particular weight to country reports, guidelines and other documents from the UNHCR.[469] It considers that this is 'the most authoritative international organisation in the field of refugee law.'[470] The Court also occasionally refers to resolutions, reports and documents from other organs of the Council of Europe like the Parliamentary Assembly or the European Committee for the Prevention of Torture.

The Court also relies on reports from NGOs. The most frequently cited sources are Amnesty International and Human Rights Watch. The Court, however, also refers to reports of smaller NGOs like, for example, the Helsinki Federation for Human Rights or the Medical Foundation for the Care of Victims of Torture. Occasionally, the Court takes into account recent media reports from the BBC or other respectable institutions.[471]

The Court further relies on analyses and state reports of contracting and noncontracting States. It takes into account the domestic reports of the authorities and tribunals of the state party concerned but also country reports of states that are not necessarily involved in the procedure. The human rights reports

---

467   See, amongst many others, ECtHR, *Daoudi v. France*, 3 December 2009, no. 19576/08, §§ 42–48 and 68; ECtHR, *Klein v. Russia*, 1 April 2010, no. 24268/08, §§ 31 and 53; ECtHR, *Khaydarov v. Russia*, 20 May 2010, no. 21055/09, § 103; ECtHR, *B.A. v. France*, 2 December 2010, no. 14951/09, § 29; ECtHR, *N.M. and M.M. v. UK*, 15 January 2011, nos. 38851/09 and 39128/09, §§ 36–37, 61–62; ECtHR, *Labsi v. Slovakia*, 15 May 2012, no. 33809/08, § 179; ECtHR, *MO.M. v. France*, 18 April 2013, no. 18372/10, § 18; ECtHR, *Dzhurayev v. Russia*, 25 April 2013, no. 71386/10, § 174.

468   See ECtHR, *Paez v. Sweden*, 30 October 1997, no. 29482/95 § 29; ECtHR, *Mamatkulov and Askarov v. Turkey*, 4 February 2005 [GC], nos. 46827/99 and 46951/99; ECtHR, *Abu Qatada v. UK*, 17 January 2012, no. 8139/09, §§ 189 (viii) and 194; ECtHR, *Rakhimov v. Russia*, 10 July 2014, no. 50552/13, §§ 65, 86 and 99. See on this also Chapter 5 Section 2.

469   See, among others, ECtHR, *N. v. Finland*, 26 July 2005, no. 38885/02, § 161; ECtHR, *Salah Sheekh v. Netherlands*, 11 January 2007, no. 1948/04, § 139–143; ECtHR, *F.H. v. Sweden*, 20 January 2009, no. 32621/06, § 91; ECtHR, *Abdolkhani and Karimnia v. Turkey*, 22 September 2009, no. 30471/08, §§ 78–83; ECtHR, *M.S.S. v. Belgium and Greece*, 21 January 2011 [GC], no. 30696/09, § 349; ECtHR, *E.G. v. UK*, 31 May 2011, no. 41178/08, § 69; ECtHR, *J.H. v. the UK*, 20 December 2011, no. 48839/09, § 65; ECtHR, *Mohammed v. Austria*, 6 June 2013, no. 2283/12, §§ 74–75 and 97–110.

470   ECtHR, *Azimov v. Russia*, 18 April 2013, no. 67474/11, § 141.

471   See ECtHR, *Salah Sheekh v. Netherlands*, 11 January 2007, no. 1948/04, § 143; ECtHR, *N.A. v. UK*, 17 July 2008, no. 25904/07, § 55; ECtHR, *Sufi and Elmi v. UK*, 28 June 2011, nos. 8319/07 and 11449/07, §§ 190–195; ECtHR, *Auad v. Bulgaria*, 11 October 2011, no. 46390/10, §§ 81–88.

of the US Department of State and the Country of Origin Information Report of the UK Home Office are also often referred to. It is worth mentioning in that context that when examining the human rights situation in a receiving country, the Court takes into account whether other countries in Europe are currently refraining from expulsions or extraditions to that receiving country.[472]

According to the Court itself, states' authorities should not solely rely on their own sources.[473] In the case *Azimov v. Russia*, the Court made the criticism that in the extradition proceedings, the Russian courts did not attach any weight to reports by international organisations and NGOs, qualifying them as mere 'opinions.'[474] It is, however, interesting to mention that it has been noted by judges in separate opinions that the Court itself relies too heavily on reports published by states and not enough on those published by NGOs.[475] The Court has explicitly acknowledged the particular weight it gives to reports from governmental sources and the UN. It has held that:

> States (whether the respondent State in a particular case or any other Contracting or non-Contracting State), through their diplomatic missions and their ability to gather information, will often be able to provide material which may be highly relevant to the Court's assessment of the case before it. It finds the same considerations must apply, *a fortiori*, in respect of agencies of the United Nations, particularly given their direct access to the authorities of the country of destination as well as their ability to carry out on-site inspections and assessments in a manner which States and non-governmental organisations may not be able to do.[476]

---

472 For example ECtHR, *Ben Khemais v. Italy*, 24 February 2009, no. 246/07, § 59; ECtHR, *Salah Sheekh v. Netherlands*, 11 January 2007, no. 1948/04, § 143; ECtHR, *L.M. and Others v. Russia*, 15 October 2015, nos. 40081/14, 40088/14 and 40127/14, § 123.

473 See, for example, ECtHR, *Salah Sheekh v. Netherlands*, 11 January 2007, no. 1948/04, § 136; ECtHR, *Garabayev v. Russia*, 7 June 2007, no. 38411/02, § 74; ECtHR, *N.A. v. UK*, 17 July 2008, no. 25904/07, § 119.

474 ECtHR, *Azimov v. Russia*, 18 April 2013, no. 67474/11, § 136.

475 See the separate opinion of judge Loucaides to ECtHR, *Said v. Netherlands*, 5 July 2005, no. 2345/02, who criticises the use of country reports of the US State Department. Established by a 'purely government agency which promotes and expresses the foreign policy' of the United States, the reports could not be considered credible sources of information. See also the dissenting opinion of judge Mularoni to ECtHR, *Venkadajalasarma v. Netherlands*, 17 February 2004, no. 58510/00 and of judges Power and Zupančič to ECtHR, *F.H. v. Sweden*, 20 January 2009, no. 32621/06.

476 Stated, for example, in ECtHR, *Shakurov v. Russia*, 5 June 2012, no. 55822/10, § 127; ECtHR, *Rakhimov v. Russia*, 10 July 2014, no. 50552/13, §§ 86 and 99. See also ECtHR, *Bajsultanov*

In assessing the weight to be attributed to country material, the Court gives consideration to its source, independence, reliability and objectivity. The authority and reputation of the author as well as the seriousness of the investigations and their corroboration by other sources are other relevant considerations.[477] The Court further notes that consideration must also be given to the presence and reporting capacities of the author of the material in the country in question.[478] In *Sufi and Elmi* concerning the situation in Somalia, the Court recognised that it understood the difficulties faced by governments and NGOs gathering information in dangerous and volatile situations. However, in this particular case, it observed that the description of the sources cited by the government's fact-finding mission was too vague. Most of the sources had simply been described as 'an international NGO,' a 'security adviser' or a 'diplomatic source.'[479] The Court hence found itself unable to attach substantial weight to the government's description of the situation.[480]

The Court recognizes that many reports are, by their very nature, general assessments, but that greater importance must necessarily be attached to reports that directly address the grounds for the alleged risk.[481] In *N. v. Sweden*, concerning a woman who claimed that she was threatened with ill treatment in Afghanistan by her own and her husband's family since she had asked for a divorce, the various reports indicating the systematic violence and repression used against women in Afghan society were crucial in the Court's decision making.[482] In cases in which the Court recognizes the existence of a group systematically exposed to ill treatment, country reports on the situation of these groups will naturally be of particular significance.[483]

---

v. Austria, 12 June 2012, no. 54131/10, § 65, in which the Court gave particular weight to the report of the Danish Immigration Service's fact-finding mission in Chechnya.

477   ECtHR, *Saadi v. Italy*, 28 February 2008 [GC], no. 37201/06, § 143.

478   ECtHR, *N.A. v. UK*, 17 July 2008, no. 25904/07, § 121.

479   ECtHR, *Sufi and Elmi v. UK*, 28 June 2011, nos. 8319/07 and 11449/07, §§ 231–234.

480   See also ECtHR, *S.H. v. UK*, 15 June 2010, no. 19956/06, § 71, in which the fact that very little first-hand information on the situation in Bhutan was available clearly worked in favour of the complainant.

481   ECtHR, *Sidikovy v. Russia*, 20 June 2013, no. 73455/11, § 138.

482   ECtHR, *N. v. Sweden*, 20 July 2010, no. 23505/09, §§ 55–62, see in particular § 58, in which the Court points out that there are 'no specific circumstances sustaining that the applicant will be subjected to ill-treatment' by her husband, but that the Court 'cannot ignore the general risk indicated by statistics and international reports.'

483   See, for example, ECtHR, *Salah Sheekh v. Netherlands*, 11 January 2007, no. 1948/04, §§ 138–149; ECtHR, *Saadi v. Italy*, 28 February 2008 [GC], no. 37201/06, § 143; ECtHR, *Kaboulov v. Ukraine*, 19 November 2009, no. 41015/04, § 110–112; ECtHR, *M.S.S. v. Belgium and Greece*, 21 January 2011 [GC], no. 30696/09, §§ 347–352 & 366.

It is hard to generalise about what type of information is given particular weight by the Court, since the characteristics of any situation will depend on the complainant's personal background. It is logical that the Court appears to favour reports that are 'couched in terms' similar to Article 3 ECHR.[484] There are nevertheless also further elements often pointed out by the Court that are therefore worth mentioning: a culture of impunity for official perpetrators of torture is a sign often highlighted by the Court as enhancing the risk of ill treatment.[485] The Court will take into account whether a receiving state allows the monitoring of detention conditions for applicants by international organisations like the International Committee of the Red Cross or Human Rights Watch or UN special rapporteurs, although such monitoring will not exclude a risk of ill treatment.[486] In *Ahorugeze v. Sweden* concerning the extradition of an applicant charged with genocide to Rwanda, the Court gave particular weight to the fact that the International Criminal Tribunal for Rwanda had confirmed in other extradition cases that the prison conditions for genocide suspects in Rwanda met international standards. The Court further mentioned monitoring carried out by the African Commission on Human and Peoples' Rights as an extra safeguard. In light of these facts and taking into account the fact that the complainant would not be sentenced to life imprisonment in isolation, the Court found that his extradition would not violate Article 3 ECHR.[487] In *Hirsi Jamaa v. Italy*, the Court noted that the presence of an UNHCR office in Tripoli was not of particular relevance for the safety of asylum seekers. It observed that the activity of the UNHCR was never recognised in any way by the Libyan government and that the refugee status granted by the UNHCR did not guarantee the persons concerned any kind of protection against ill treatment or the risk of being further deported.[488] It should also be noted that repatriation programs of the UNHCR or other organisations as well as the voluntary return of refugees have been considered by the Court as strong

---

484   ECtHR, *N.A. v. UK*, 17 July 2008, no. 25904/07, § 122.

485   See, for example, ECtHR, *Chahal v. UK*, 15 November 1996, no. 22414/93, § 104; ECtHR, *Daoudi v. France*, 3 December 2009, no. 19576/08, § 68; ECtHR, *N. v. Sweden*, 20 July 2010, no. 23505/09, § 57.

486   See, for example, ECtHR, *Shamayev and Others v. Georgia and Russia*, 12 April 2005, no. 36378/02, § 364; ECtHR, *Saadi v Italy*, 28 February 2008 [GC], no. 37201/06, § 146; ECtHR, *Ben Khemais v. Italy*, 24 February 2009, no. 246/07, § 54; ECtHR, *Labsi v. Slovakia*, 15 May 2012, no. 33809/08, § 129.

487   ECtHR, *Ahorugeze v. Sweden*, 27 October 2011, no. 37075/09, §§ 91–95.

488   ECtHR, *Hirsi Jamaa and Others v. Italy*, 23 February 2012 [GC], no. 27765/09, § 130.

indicators of an improved human rights situation, in which complainants have to show convincing reasons as to why they are at risk.[489]

Finally, it is worth noting that in order to allow a full *ex nunc* assessment of the situation, reports should be as recent as possible.[490] The Court often relies on reports that the national authorities who decided the case could not have been aware of.[491] The Court is not, however, always completely up to date itself.[492]

d   *Where the Country of Destination is a State Party to the ECHR*
In its assessment, the Court occasionally takes into account whether the receiving state has ratified instruments like the CAT or the ICCPR and has accepted their monitoring mechanisms.[493] Wouters, however, rightly states that such ratifications are of 'limited relevance' in the Court's assessment.[494] They might be an indication for a certain human rights standard, but what finally counts is the *prevailing practice* in the receiving country as reported by credible sources. In *Saadi v. Italy* the Grand Chamber made clear that

> ... the existence of domestic laws and accession to international treaties guaranteeing respect for fundamental rights in principle are not in themselves sufficient to ensure adequate protection against the risk of ill-treatment where, as in the present case, reliable sources have reported practices resorted to or tolerated by the authorities which are manifestly contrary to the principles of the Convention.[495]

---

489   See ECtHR, *Cruz Varas and Others v. Sweden*, 20 March 1991, no. 15576/89, § 80; ECtHR, *Vilvarajah and Others v. UK*, 30 October 1991, nos. 13163/87 and further, § 110; ECtHR, *Müslim v. Turkey*, 26 April 2005, no. 53566/99, § 71; ECtHR, *F.H. v. Sweden*, 20 January 2009, no. 32621/06, § 91.

490   See ECtHR, *Salah Sheekh v. Netherlands*, 11 January 2007, no. 1948/04, § 136.

491   See, for example, ECtHR, *Venkadajalasarma v. Netherlands*, 17 February 2004, no. 58510/00, §§ 63–69 and the dissenting opinion of judge Mularoni; ECtHR, *M.S.S. v. Belgium and Greece*, 21 January 2011 [GC], no. 30696/09 and the partly dissenting opinion of judge Bratza §§ 9 and 10.

492   See, for example, the dissenting opinions of judge Kalaydjeva on ECtHR, *H. and B. v. UK*, 9 April 2013, nos. 70073/10 and 44539/1 and judge Power-Forde in ECtHR, *A.A.M. v. Sweden*, 3 April 2014, no. 68519/10. See also Lorz and Sauer 2010, p. 397; Wouters 2009, p. 273.

493   See, for example, ECtHR, *Mamatkulov and Askarov v. Turkey*, 4 February 2005 [GC], nos. 46827/99 and 46951/99, §§ 76 and 77; ECtHR, *Al Hanchi v. Bosnia and Herzegovina*, 15 November 2011, no. 48205/09, § 44.

494   Wouters 2009, p. 305.

495   ECtHR, *Saadi v Italy*, 28 February 2008 [GC], no. 37201/06, § 147. Confirmed, for example, in ECtHR, *Hirsi Jamaa and Others* v. Italy, 23 February 2012 [GC], no. 27765/09, § 128.

The great majority of the cases dealt with on the merits by the Court concern deportations of persons to states that are not members of the Council of Europe. There are exceptions, though: in a few of them the Court has found a violation of the principle of non-refoulement:[496]

The case *M.S.S. v. Belgium and Greece* decided in January 2011 concerning an expulsion from Belgium to Greece under the EU Dublin Regulation has been mentioned before. In this case the Grand Chamber made clear that the fact that a person is removed to another contracting party to the ECHR does not allow the expelling state to neglect either an assessment of the conditions for a complainant in that country, or of the risk of a chain-refoulement.[497] The Court confirmed this principle in another Grand Chamber judgment, *Tarakhel v. Switzerland*, which concerned a transfer under the Dublin system to Italy.[498]

The judgment *Shamayev and Others* adopted in 2005 concerned the extradition to Russia of several complainants of Chechen origin charged as terrorists. The Court found a violation of Article 3 ECHR with regard to only one of them who, in contrast to the others, had not been extradited at the time of the Court's decision. The Court pointed to NGO reports indicating that individuals like the complainant would likely be subjected to ill treatment in detention in the North Caucasus area. It further noted the new and 'extremely alarming phenomenon' that individuals of Chechen origin who lodged applications with the Court were often persecuted.[499]

---

496   See ECtHR, *Shamayev and Others v. Georgia and Russia*, 12 April 2005, no. 36378/02 (Russia); ECtHR, *M.S.S. v. Belgium and Greece*, 21 January 2011 [GC], no. 30696/09 (Greece); ECtHR, *I.K. v. Austria*, 28 March 2013, no. 2964/12 (Russia); ECtHR, *I v. Sweden*, 5 September 2013, no. 61204/09 (Russia); ECtHR, *M.G. v. Bulgaria*, 25 March 2014, no. 59297/12 (Russia); ECtHR, *M.V. and M.T. v. France*, 4 September 2014, no. 17897/09 (Russia); ECtHR, *Sharifi and Others v. Italy and Greece*, 21 October 2014 (Greece); ECtHR, *Tarakhel v. Switzerland*, 4 November 2014 [GC], no. 29217/12 (Italy); ECtHR, *R.K. v. France*, 9 July 2015, no. 61264/11 (Russia).

497   ECtHR, *M.S.S. v. Belgium and Greece*, 21 January 2011 [GC], no. 30696/09, §§ 323, 353 and 368.

498   The judgments *M.S.S.* and *Tarakhel* are discussed in Chapter 3 Section 2.3.2.b and Chapter 4 Section 3.4.3.a. See also ECtHR, *Sharifi and Others v. Italy and Greece*, 21 October 2014, no. 16643/09 confirming *M.S.S.* with regard to a risk of indirect removal for asylum seekers in Greece.

499   ECtHR, *Shamayev and Others v. Georgia and Russia*, 12 April 2005, no. 36378/02, §§ 356–368. It is not understood why the Court did not take into account the NGO reports on the prison conditions in North Caucasus with regard to the five other applicants who had already been extradited to the same region; see the critique in Thurin 2012, p. 65 fn. 345. In a dissenting opinion the Russian judge Kovler noted his discontent with the majority of judges in the case of an extradition to another member state, particularly if the receiving state, as was the case in this complaint, had given assurances of compliance with the Convention.

In the cases *I.K. v. Austria*[500] and *I. v. Sweden*[501] decided in 2013, the Court found again that deportations to Russia would violate Article 3 ECHR. The case *I.K.* concerned a Chechen applicant who had been persecuted by Russian authorities; security forces had murdered his father. The mother of the applicant had been granted the status of a recognised refugee in Austria.[502] The case *I.* concerned a Chechen applicant who had fresh scars of ill treatment on his body, which could indicate that he took active part in the second war in Chechnya. For this reason he would likely raise the Security Services' interests immediately upon his return.[503] The case *M.G. v. Bulgaria* decided in 2014 concerned the extradition of a Chechen men wanted by the Russian security services for offenses relating to Chechen rebel groups.[504] Based on several sources[505] reporting the frequent ill treatment of detainees suspected of belonging to armed groups operating in the North Caucasus and Chechnya and being held in pre-trial detention there, the Court ruled that, despite diplomatic assurances given by the Russian authorities, the extradition of the applicant from Bulgaria to Russia would violate Article 3 ECHR. It attached much importance to the fact that the applicant, who had fled criminal charges in Russia, had obtained refugee status in Poland and Germany.[506]

However, in a case decided in November 2013 concerning the extradition of a former Chechen rebel convicted in Russia for participation in military operations against the federal forces, the Court found that the applicant's role in the Second Chechen War was not prominent enough to put him in danger of ill treatment.[507] It thereby attached importance to the fact that, in contrast to *I.K. v. Austria* and *I. v. Sweden*, the applicant was not facing a deportation to Chechnya or other areas in the North Caucasus.[508] It further highlighted that the purpose of the extradition was for the applicant to serve a sentence already imposed by the Russian courts in a penal facility for convicted prisoners.

---

500   ECtHR, *I.K. v. Austria*, 28 March 2013, no. 2964/12.

501   ECtHR, *I v. Sweden*, 5 September 2013, no. 61204/09.

502   ECtHR, *I.K. v. Austria*, 28 March 2013, no. 2964/12, §§ 64–90.

503   ECtHR, *I v. Sweden*, 5 September 2013, no. 61204/09, §§ 66–69. See also ECtHR, *M.V. and M.T. v. France*, 4 September 2014, no. 17897/09 §§ 39–48; ECtHR, *R.K. v. France*, 9 July 2015, no. 61264/11, §§ 58–71.

504   ECtHR, *M.G. v. Bulgaria*, 25 March 2014, no. 59297/12.

505   Including its own case law and observations from the Committee.

506   *Ibid.*, §§ 84–96. On the importance of a granted refugee status in the Court's case under Article 3 ECHR see Section 3.3.1.c of this chapter below.

507   ECtHR, *Chankayev v. Azerbaijan*, 14 November 2013, no. 56688/12, §§ 68–82.

508   *Ibid.*, § 71.

Hence, it was not likely that he would be placed in a remand prison or other pre-trial detention facility, where the risks of ill treatment were enhanced.[509]

In 2014 the Court rejected two further complaints of Chechen men opposing their deportation to Russia.[510] One applicant was wanted by the Russian authorities for military activities against the Russian federal forces.[511] The Court observed that he was not facing deportation to Chechnya or other areas in the North Caucasus but that it was likely that he would be placed in a remand prison or pre-trial detention facility. However, they estimated that while remand prisons in Russia remain a matter of serious concern, the general situation could not be described as such to conclude that any extradition of Chechens to Russia would violate Article 3 ECHR. Noting, *inter alia*, that the applicant did not appear to have been a prominent figure in the Second Chechen War, the Court rejected the complaint.[512] In the complaints dismissed, the Court explicitly attached importance to the fact that they concerned deportations to a contracting party to the ECHR.[513] It is quite unpredictable, though, in which circumstances the Court will rely on that criterion in Chechnya cases.[514]

Generally, the fact that a person is sent to another contracting state *is a relevant criterion* in the Court's risk assessment. The burden of proof on the complainant is usually high in such cases. The Court has rejected several complaints stating, *inter alia*, that 'it attaches particular importance to the fact that the case concerns expulsion to a High Contracting Party to the European Convention on Human Rights, which has undertaken to secure the fundamental rights as guaranteed under this provision.'[515] In cases concerning a risk of

---

509   *Ibid.*, §§ 71–74.

510   ECtHR, *Tershiyev v. Azerbaijan*, 31 July 2014, no. 10226/13; ECtHR, *Zarmayev v. Belgium*, 27 February 2014, no. 35/10, § 98, where the complainant's lack of credibility was decisive for the rejection.

511   ECtHR, *Tershiyev v. Azerbaijan*, 31 July 2014, no. 10226/13.

512   *Ibid.*, §§ 52–57. See also ECtHR, *Bajsultanov v. Austria*, 12 June 2012, no. 54131/10, § 65.

513   ECtHR, *Bajsultanov v. Austria*, 12 June 2012, no. 54131/10, § 70; ECtHR, *Chankayev v. Azerbaijan*, 14 November 2013, no. 56688/12, § 80; ECtHR, *Zarmayev v. Belgium*, 27 February 2014, no. 35/10, § 113; ECtHR, *Tershiyev v. Azerbaijan*, 31 July 2014, no. 10226/13, § 61.

514   See also the cases ECtHR, *M.V. and M.T. v. France*, 4 September 2014, no. 17897/09 §§ 39–48; ECtHR, *R.K. v. France*, 9 July 2015, no. 61264/11, §§ 58–71, in which the Court did not give much attention to that fact and concluded that the deportation to Russia of the applicants of Chechen origin would be in violation of Art. 3 ECHR.

515   See, amongst others, ECtHR, *Gasayev v. Spain*, 17 February 2009, no. 48514/06 (decision); ECtHR, *Barnic v. Austria*, 13 December 2011, no. 54845/10 (decision); ECtHR, *Zarmayev v. Belgium*, 27 February 2014, no. 35/10, § 113 and the dissenting opinion of judge Power-Forde. See *e contrario* ECtHR, *Y.P. and L.P. v. France*, 2 September 2010, no. 32476/06,

chain-removal, the fact that the receiving state is a contracting party to the ECHR is of particular importance.[516] The Court also attaches particular weight to that question when it assesses whether diplomatic assurances are reliable.[517] However, as the cases *M.S.S.*, *Tarakhel* and the extraditions cases to Russia have shown, the fact that the receiving state is a member of the Council of Europe does not exclude a risk ill treatment or of chain-removal and does not as such prove the reliability of diplomatic assurances.[518]

3.2.2   Committee
a   *The Human Rights Situation and the Individualisation of the Risk*
Article 3(2) CAT states that for the purpose of determining whether there are grounds for believing an individual would be in danger of being subjected to torture, 'the competent authorities shall take into account all relevant considerations including, where applicable, the existence in the State concerned of a consistent pattern of gross, flagrant or mass violations of human rights.' By the same logic, to assess the risk of a refoulement, the Committee takes into account the personal circumstances of a complainant as well as the general human rights situation in the receiving country. With regard to the relationship between this subjective test and this objective test,[519] the Committee repeats the following statement in *all* its decisions on the merits:

> In assessing whether there are substantial grounds for believing that the complainant would be in danger of being subjected to torture on return, the Committee must take into account all relevant considerations, pursuant to article 3, paragraph 2, of the Convention, including the existence, in the State concerned, of a consistent pattern of gross, flagrant or mass

---

§ 67; ECtHR, *Saliyev v. Russia*, 17 April 2014, no. 39093/13, § 66. See also the Court's rather exceptional statement in ECtHR, *Tatar v. Switzerland*, 14 April 2015, no. 65692/12, § 53, according to which the applicant has the possibility to submit complaints for Convention violations in the receiving state Turkey. This reasoning is in contradiction with the Court's preventive approach in non-refoulement cases.

516   See ECtHR, *K.R.S. v. UK*, 2 December 2008, no. 32733/08 (decision); ECtHR, *Hirsi Jamaa and Others v. Italy*, 23 February 2012 [GC], no. 27765/09, § 147. See on this also Section 3.4.3.a of this chapter.

517   ECtHR, *Abu Qatada v. UK*, 17 January 2012, no. 8139/09, § 189. See on this also Section 3.4.2.a and 3.4.2.b of this chapter.

518   With regard to assurances given by contracting states but considered unreliable by the Court see ECtHR, *M.S.S.*, §§ 347–352; ECtHR, *M.G. v. Bulgaria*, 25 March 2014, no. 59297/12, §§ 93–95.

519   See these terms used by Nowak 2008, p. 114.

violations of human rights. However, the Committee recalls that the aim of its determination is to establish whether the individual concerned would be personally at risk of being subjected to torture in the country to which he or she would return. It follows that the existence of a consistent pattern of gross, flagrant or mass violations of human rights in a country does not as such constitute a sufficient ground for determining that a particular person would be in danger of being subjected to torture upon his or her return to that country. Additional grounds must be adduced to show that the individual concerned would be personally at risk. Conversely, the absence of a consistent pattern of gross violations of human rights does not necessarily mean that a person cannot be considered to be in danger of being subjected to torture in his or her specific circumstances.[520]

It is clear from this formula that the human rights situation in a receiving country must be taken into account in the risk assessment, but that even very poor human rights conditions will not *as such* be enough to trigger the application of the principle of non-refoulement under Article 3 CAT. In its case law, the Committee consistently requires the existence of 'specific,'[521] 'additional'[522] or 'other grounds'[523] indicating that a complainant is *personally* at risk. Conversely, the absence of a consistent pattern of flagrant violations of human rights does not mean that a person might not be subjected to torture in his specific circumstances.

The very first decision on a refoulement complaint, *Mutombo v. Switzerland*, is a good example to demonstrate the interdependence of the human rights situation and the personal background of a complainant in the Committee's risk assessment. The Committee considered that substantial grounds existed for believing that the complainant would be at risk of being subjected to torture because of his ethnic background, alleged political affiliation, detention history, desertion from the army and the fact that he had left Mobutu's Zaire in a clandestine manner and had adduced arguments that could be considered defamatory towards his country when formulating his application for asylum. This observation was 'strengthened' by the 'existence of a consistent pattern of gross, flagrant or mass violations' in Zaire (today the DRC).[524]

---

520   This standard formula is sometimes used with variations.

521   See, for example, ComAT, *M.A.K. v. Germany*, 12 May 2004, no. 214/2002, § 13.3.

522   See, for example, ComAT, *H.M.H.I. v. Australia*, 1 May 2002, no. 177/2001, § 6.5.

523   See, for example, ComAT, *H.D. v. Switzerland*, 30 April 1999, no. 112/1998, § 6.3.

524   ComAT, *Mutombo v. Switzerland*, 27 April 1994, no. 13/1993, § 9.4. The Committee also took into account that Zaire was not a party to the CAT.

It is rare that the Committee explicitly confirms the existence of a 'consistent pattern of gross, flagrant or mass violations of human rights' as explicitly referred to in paragraph 2 of Article 3 CAT and as it did in *Mutombo*.[525] This does not mean that the Committee thinks that there is no such situation in cases in which it does not explicitly mention it. Nowak and McArthur rightly observe that the Committee uses a range of variable formulations in its decisions to describe very poor human rights conditions such as 'ongoing widespread violations of human rights,' 'systematic practice of torture' or simply 'serious human rights situation.'[526] However, even where human rights conditions are not as poor as indicated by the use of such terms, this does not mean that the situation in the receiving state does not play a role in the risk assessment. On the contrary, the Committee's case law clearly shows that the human rights situation generally must be taken into account.[527]

As has been stated, even the most terrible human rights situation will not in itself be sufficient for the establishment of a relevant risk of torture under the CAT. The Committee will in principle always require individualised risk factors. The case *Z.Z. v. Canada* concerned the expulsion of a complainant to Afghanistan while the Taliban ruled the country.[528] The Committee rejected the claim, noting that the complainant had only submitted information on the general situation in Afghanistan. It argued that he had not brought evidence, such as past torture or political or religious activities that could draw the Taliban's attention, showing that he would be personally at risk. His membership of a particular ethnic group could also not substantiate the alleged risk of torture.[529]

525   As exceptions see ComAT, *Elmi v. Australia*, 14 May 1999, no. 120/1998 § 6.6 (Somalia); *A.S. v. Sweden*, 24 November 2000, no. 149/1999, § 8.7 (Iran); ComAT, *S.S. and S.A. v. Netherlands*, 11 May 2001, no. 142/1999, § 6.5 (Somalia); ComAT, *M.C.M.V.F. v. Sweden*, 14 November 2005, no. 237/2003, § 6.4 (El Salvador around 1990); with regard to Uzbekistan for 'individuals practising their Muslim faith outside of the official framework' see ComAT; *Abdussamatov and 28 Others v. Kazakhstan*, 1 June 2012, no. 444/2010, § 13.8; ComAT, *Nasirov v. Kazakhstan*, 14 May 2014, no. 475/2011, § 11.7; ComAT, *Tursunov v. Kazakhstan*, 8 May 2015, no. 538/2013, § 9.8.

526   Nowak & McArthur 2008, pp. 184 and 186–187.

527   See also ComAT, General Comment No. 1 on Art. 3 CAT (1997), § 8 (d), according to which the Committee takes into account whether 'the internal situation in respect of human rights has altered.'

528   ComAT, *Z.Z. v. Canada*, 15 May 2001, no. 123/1998.

529   *Ibid.*, §§ 8.4 and 8.5. See the similar statement in ComAT, *A.A. v. Switzerland*, 1 May 2007, no. 268/2005, § 8.5 (Pakistan).

However, if there is a particularly violent human rights situation, the burden of proof will tend to shift to the government, which will then have to present strong arguments to justify why a complainant is not in danger in his home country.[530] This can be observed for example in *Chahin v. Sweden* concerning a removal to Syria.[531] In the domestic procedure (which ended in 2006), the question of whether restrictions had been imposed on the complainant by the Syrian security service because of his opposition activities constituted an important disputed point. In light of the 'serious deterioration' of the human rights situation in Syria in connection with the government's crackdown on the opposition movements in spring 2011, the Committee did not consider it 'decisive whether or not any restrictions were imposed on the complainant.' The fact that the complainant would be taken into detention upon arrival in Syria and that he had been convicted for anti-state crimes were 'sufficient in the present circumstances' for assuming there were substantial grounds to believe that the complainant would be subjected to torture upon his return.[532]

The fact that the human rights situation can have a considerable impact on the burden of proof can also be observed in decisions concerning deportations to Iran. The Committee noted that the situation there is 'extremely worrisome, particularly since the elections held in the country in June 2009.'[533] Observing the 'repression and arbitrary detention of many reformers, students, journalists and human rights defenders, some of whom have been detained in secret and others sentenced to death and executed,'[534] the Committee found violations of Article 3 CAT in several cases in which the applicant's profile as a political opponent was not particularly high.[535]

In the cases *Njamba and Balikosa* as well as *Bakatu-Bia v. Sweden*, it is hard to believe that the Committee did not take the general human rights situation to be the main factor in its decision-making.[536] Both cases concerned the expulsion of single women to the DRC. The Committee noted in both cases that the

530 Ingelse 2001, pp. 292 and 298; Nowak & McArthur 2008, pp. 193 (§ 164), 207 (196) and 224 (§ 227). See also Chapter 4 Section 1.3.2 on the burden of proof.

531 ComAT, *Chahin v. Sweden*, 30 May 2011, no. 310/2007.

532 *Ibid.*, §§ 2.13, 2.19, 3.2, 4.10, 6.3 and 9.4–9.6.

533 See ComAT, *Jahani v. Switzerland*, 23 May 2011, no. 357/2008, § 9.4; ComAT, *Eftekhary v. Norway*, 25 November 2011, no. 312/2007, § 7.4.

534 ComAT, *Faragollah et al. v. Switzerland*, 21 November 2011, no. 381/2009, § 9.4. Similar ComAT, *Tahmuresi v. Switzerland*, 26 November 2014, no. 489/2012, § 7.5.

535 See on this Section 3.3.1.b of this chapter below on the relevance of political activities.

536 ComAT, *Njamba and Balikosa v. Sweden*, 14 May 2010, no. 322/2007; ComAT, *Bakatu-Bia v. Sweden*, 3 June 2011, no. 379/2009. See also de Weck 2011, p. 9.

precarious human rights situation in the DRC made it impossible to identify particular areas of the country that could be considered safe for the complainants. Looking particularly at *Njamba and Balikosa*, in which the alleged personal risk elements remained disputed,[537] it is apparent that the Committee will, when appropriate, deviate from its standard formula regarding the relevance of the general human rights situation in a receiving country.[538] This is especially so when complainants have characteristics that make them particularly vulnerable, such as their gender. The next section will look at this in more detail. However, to find a violation of Article 3 CAT the Committee will normally request the establishment of individual risk factors like past torture, a detention history or relevant political activity.

As has been mentioned, good human rights conditions in the receiving country do not necessarily exclude a risk of torture in case of deportation, and the Committee adheres to this principle quite consistently. The case *Arana v. France* is an example of this approach in the Committee's case law.[539] It concerned the extradition of an activist of the Basque separatist organisation ETA from France to Spain. The Committee held that the complainant had been convicted in France for his links with ETA and that he had been suspected in the press of holding an important position in the ETA. NGOs had expressed concern that persons in the same circumstances had been subjected to torture in Spain during their incommunicado detention. This and the manner in which the complainant had been deported to Spain, without being able to contact his family or his lawyer, put him 'in a situation where he was particularly vulnerable to possible abuse.' The Committee eventually found a violation of Article 3 CAT.[540] Note that when a complainant opposes his deportation to a country with good human rights standards, he will have

---

537   ComAT, *Njamba and Balikosa v. Sweden*, 14 May 2010, no. 322/2007, § 9.5. In *Bakuta-Bia* the Committee mentioned that the complainant had brought medical evidence of past torture; ComAT, *Bakatu-Bia v. Sweden*, 3 June 2011, no. 379/2009, § 10.5.

538   Note also that if a state party declares a moratorium on the removal of individuals of a certain nationality, but excludes the applicant from this moratorium because of his criminal record, the Committee will be very sceptical; see ComAT, *Kalonzo v. Canada*, 18 May 2012, no. 343/2008, § 9.5; ComAT, *E.L. v. Canada*, 21 May 2012, no. 370/2009, § 1.2. In *Kalonzo*, the Committee noted that in spirit of Art. 3 CAT 'it is to be understood that a moratorium on the removal of persons who would be at risk in their country because of widespread violence should apply to everyone without distinction.'

539   ComAT, *Arana v. France*, 9 November 1999, no. 63/1997.

540   *Ibid.*, §§ 11.5 and 12.

to present particularly strong arguments and evidence demonstrating he is at risk of torture in that country. There have not been many refoulement complaints concerning deportations to Western Europe, North America or Australia. So far, *Arana* is the only one that has been successful with the Committee in any of these areas.[541]

b   *Protection of Vulnerable Individuals and Groups Systematically Exposed to Ill Treatment*

The Committee has indicated in some cases that it may offer a more general protection for members of particularly threatened groups:

In *Elmi v. Australia* decided in May 1999, the Committee gave particular weight to the fact that the complainant belonged to the Shikal, a small, unarmed and vulnerable clan that remained at the 'mercy of the armed factions' in the chaos prevailing in Mogadishu.[512] However, there were also two personal elements that made the complainant appear particularly at risk of torture: first, his family was particularly targeted and second, his case had received wide publicity, which could damage the reputation of his persecutors. The Committee found a violation of Article 3 CAT based on the complainant's membership of the Shikal clan as well as his personal circumstances.[543]

In *S.S. and S.A. v. Netherlands* adopted in 2001 concerning the removal of Tamils to Sri Lanka, the Committee noted that the complainants had 'failed to demonstrate, generally, that their membership of a particular group, and/or, specifically that their individual circumstances give rise to a personal, real and foreseeable risk of being tortured if returned to Sri Lanka at this time.'[544]

---

541   See also two other cases concerning extraditions of convicted ETA activists to Spain that were not successful: ComAT, *G.K. v. Switzerland*, 7 May 2003, no. 219/2002 and ComAT, *Diaz v. France*, 3 May 2005, no. 194/2001.

542   ComAT, *Elmi v. Australia*, 14 May 1999, no. 120/1998, §§ 6.6 and 6.7.

543   *Ibid.*, §§ 6.8. and 6.9.

544   ComAT, *S.S. and S.A. v. Netherlands*, 11 May 2001, no. 142/1999, §§ 6.6 and 6.7. As to the complainant's individual circumstances, the Committee considered 'that the respective detention suffered by the authors does not distinguish the authors' cases from those of many other Tamils having undergone similar experiences, and in particular they do not demonstrate that the respective detentions were accompanied by torture or other circumstances which would give rise to a real fear of torture in the future.' This reasoning demonstrates the Committee's reluctance to accept the general protection of certain groups. It seems to be adopted from the controversial statements made by the Court in ECtHR, *Vilvarajah and Others v. UK*, 30 October 1991, nos. 13163/87 and further, § 111; see the discussion in Section 3.2.1.a of this chapter above.

In the case *T.I. v. Canada* the Committee held that the complainant had 'not provided sufficient information to support his claim that Tatars and therefore, he himself, are discriminated against to the extent that would place him at a particular risk of torture in Uzbekistan.'[545]

The case *Aytulun and Güclü* decided in 2010 concerned the expulsion of a Turkish father and daughter of Kurdish ethnicity.[546] The Committee noted that 'the complainant was a member of the PKK for 14 years; and ... there are strong indications that he is wanted in Turkey, to be tried under anti-terrorist laws and thus is likely to be arrested upon arrival and subjected to a forced confession.'[547] Taking into account these personal circumstances and the fact that various sources indicated that security forces continued to use torture despite the Turkish government's policy of zero tolerance of torture, the Committee considered the risk of torture as sufficiently established for a violation of Article 3 CAT. It pointed to a report quoted by the state party according to which 'members of the PKK should be considered a specific target group for individual civil servants who violate the prohibition on using torture.'[548] However, the Committee does not consider all individuals with relations to the PKK to be at risk.[549]

In *S.M., H.M. and A.M. v. Sweden*, the Committee noted that several sources reported a widespread 'hostile attitude on the part of the general public towards ethnic Armenians living in Azerbaijan.'[550] It held that persons of Armenian origin were at risk of discrimination in their daily life and were frequently harassed or bribed by low-ranking officials. In light of this situation and the fact that the complainants had been tortured in the past, the Committee concluded that their deportation to Azerbaijan would breach Article 3 CAT.

In the case *Mondal v. Sweden*, the fact that the complainant was homosexual and therefore liable to persecution in the receiving state of Bangladesh and additionally belonged to the minority group of Hindus, were important factors

---

545   ComAT, *T.I. v. Canada*, 15 November 2010, no. 333/2007, § 7.4. See similar ComAT, *X v. Switzerland*, 9 May 1997, no. 38/1995, § 10.5, with regard to the deportation of a former journalist who had worked for Sudan's opposition press. The Committee rejected his complaint noting, *inter alia*, that he did 'not belong to a political, professional or social group targeted by the authorities for repression and torture.' See the similar statement with regard to a deportation to China in ComAT, *P.Q.L. v. Canada*, 17 November 1997, no. 57/1996 § 10.4.

546   ComAT, *Aytulun and Güclü v. Sweden*, 19 November 2010, no. 373/2009.

547   *Ibid.*, § 7.7.

548   *Ibid.*, §§ 7.6 and 7.7.

549   See, for example, ComAT, *R.A. v. Switzerland*, 20 November 2012, no. 389/2009, §§ 9.4 and 9.5 and further examples referred to in Section 3.3.1.b of this chapter below (Political and/or religious background).

550   ComAT, *S.M., H.M. and A.M. v. Sweden*, 21 November 2011, no. 374/2009, § 9.7.

in the finding of a violation of Article 3 CAT.[551] However, the Committee also took into account the fact that the complainant had been active in politics and had been tortured in the past. This case demonstrates in an exemplary way that several individual risk factors which, taken alone, would probably not be relevant, can, when taken together, constitute a relevant risk of torture. However, in November 2015, the Committee adopted *J.K. v. Canada* in which the complainant's homosexuality and his involvement in the LGBTI rights movement in Uganda were the key reasons for the violation of Article 3 CAT.[552] The Committee noted that the Constitutional Court in Uganda had nullified an Anti-Homosexuality Act in August 2014, but that this nullification was only based on procedural reasons so that the Act could be resubmitted to the Parliament at any time.[553] Based on NGO reports, it held that 'there was an increase number of cases of arbitrary arrest, police extortion, eviction and attacks on the reputation of lesbian, gay, bisexual, transgender and in the number who became homeless.'[554] The Committee hence considered that, despite certain ambiguities with regard to the applicant's claim in the national procedure, he 'may be at risk of torture or ill-treatment if he is returned to Uganda, taking into account not only his sexual orientation, but also his militancy in lesbian, gay, bisexual, transgender and intersex organisations and the fact that he could be detained pursuant to the criminal charges brought against him.'[555]

In the cases *Njamba and Balikosa* decided in May 2010 and mentioned above, the Committee found that Article 3 CAT would be violated, if the complainants, a single woman with her daughter, were removed to the DRC.[556] The Committee based its decision on recent reports indicating 'alarming levels of violence against women across the country.'[557] Although the Committee does not use the word 'group' in this judgment, it is quite obvious that the complainants do mainly benefit from the protection of Article 3 CAT because of their gender.[558]

---

551   ComAT, *Mondal v. Sweden*, 23 May 2011, no. 338/2008, § 7.7.

552   ComAT, *J.K. v. Canada*, 23 November 2015, no. 562/2013.

553   *Ibid.*, § 10.5.

554   *Ibid.* The Committee referred to information provided by Human Rights Watch, Amnesty International and Chapter Four Uganda. The Committee also referred to information provided by the UK Home Office.

555   *Ibid.*

556   ComAT, *Njamba and Balikosa v. Sweden*, 14 May 2010, no. 322/2007, § 9.5.

557   *Ibid.*, § 9.5.

558   In this context, it is to be noted that a year later, the Committee rejected in quite a rigorous way the complaint of a man opposing his deportation to the DRC. He had been politically active and had presented medical evidence indicating he had been tortured in the past; ComAT, *R.T-N. v. Switzerland*, 3 June 2011, no. 350/2008, §§ 8.5–8.9.

No individual circumstances were relevant in the Committee's considerations on the merits besides the fact that the complainants were a single woman and a girl. The approach was confirmed a year later in *Bakatu-Bia v. Sweden,*[559] in which the Committee took an almost identical decision. Based on the same UN reports indicating widespread sexual violence against women in the DRC, it concluded again that the precarious human rights situation in the DRC 'makes it impossible to identify particular areas of the country which could be considered safe for the complainant.'[560] Contrary to *Njamba and Balikosa*, the Committee did mention some personal elements in its risk assessment. It noted that the complainant had presented medical reports indicating that she had been tortured in the past and that the complainant's account of events appeared credible.[561] In November 2011, the Committee tempered the absolute statements made with regard to the situation of women in the DRC in *Njamba and Balikosa*. In *N.B.-M. v. Switzerland*, it noted:

> The Committee acknowledges the dire human rights situation in the Democratic Republic of the Congo, especially for women, and recalls its jurisprudence on the issue. The Committee observes that the State party has taken this factor into account in evaluating the risk the complainant might face if returned to her country. It concludes, moreover, on the basis of information on the prevailing situation in Kinshasa, where the complainant would be returned, that the weight to be attached to this factor is not sufficient to prevent her removal. The Committee therefore proceeds to an analysis of the personal risk facing the complainant with respect to article 3 of the Convention.[562]

In the analysis of the personal risk in this case, the Committee noted that it was not convinced that the complainant, who had never been politically active in the DRC, was a wanted person. Recalling that the burden of proof is normally on the complainant, it concluded that 'on the basis of all the information submitted to it, including information on the situation in Kinshasa, the Committee is of the view that the complainant has not provided sufficient evidence to allow it to consider that her return' would violate Article 3 CAT.[563]

---

559   ComAT, *Bakatu-Bia v. Sweden*, 3 June 2011, no. 379/2009.

560   *Ibid.*, §§ 10.6 and 10.7.

561   *Ibid.*, §§ 10.5 and 10.8.

562   ComAT, *N.B.-M. v. Switzerland*, 14 November 2011, no. 347/2008, § 9.5. See similar ComAT, *E.L. v. Switzerland*, 15 November 2011, no. 351/2008, § 9.4.

563   ComAT, *N.B.-M. v. Switzerland*, 14 November 2011, no. 347/2008, §§ 9.6–9.9.

With regard to the situation in Kinshasa, the Committee referred in a footnote to guidelines with regard to the situation in the DRC that had been provided by the UNHCR in November 2011. According to these guidelines, individuals coming from the conflict zones in North Kivu, South Kivu, Maniema or Orientale provinces should benefit from international protection. Asylum requests from residents of other areas, including Kinshasa, should be considered on a case-by-case basis to determine their acceptability under the 1951 Refugee Convention.[564] The distinction made between the risk in eastern and other regions in the DRC as described by the UNHCR was a concept that was generally known by asylum experts at the time the decisions *Njamba and Balikosa* as well as *Bakuta-Bia* were adopted.[565] It remains unexplained why the Committee did not take this into account in these two cases, in which neither of the complainants originated from the eastern conflict zones.[566] However, whatever the source for the Committee's statements with regard to a very general risk for single women in the DRC in *Njamba and Balikosa* was, the Committee showed with this decision that it is particularly *sensitive to gender-based violence*.[567] This is also supported by the recent decision *E.K.W. v. Finland*, in which the Committee again found a violation of Article 3 CAT for the removal of a woman originally from Kinshasa to the DRC, though also taking into account the complainant's alleged past ill treatment by military forces and her affiliation with the opposition.[568] The Committee recalled its jurisprudence in *Njamba and Balikosa* and referred to widespread violence against women that is 'mostly inherent in conflict-affected and rural areas of the country, especially in the east.' It added, however, that according to UN reports from 2013, 'such violence is also taking place in other parts of the country.'[569]

The Committee's approach with regard to a general risk for women in the DRC in *Njamba and Balikosa* has also demonstrated that, implicitly, the Committee does not necessarily exclude the membership of a vulnerable group as

---

564   *Ibid.*, footnote 14.

565   It is interesting to note that in the inadmissibility decision *S.M. v. Sweden* taken approximately one year before *Njamba and Balikosa*, the Court in Strasbourg rejected the complaint of an unmarried woman opposing her deportation to the DRC; ECtHR, *S.M. v. Sweden*, 10 February 2009, no. 47683/08, §§ 30–37.

566   See also the Swedish government's arguments on that account in their observations on *Njamba and Balikosa* §§ 8.1–8.4 and *Bakuta-Bia*, § 4.13.

567   Which is also visible in ComAT, General Comment No. 2 on Art. 2 (2008), §§ 18 and 22.

568   See ComAT, *E.K.W. v. Finland*, 4 May 2015, no. 490/2012, §§ 9.5–9.8.

569   *Ibid.*, § 9.7. See the comparable approach taken recently in ComAT, *F.B. v. Netherlands*, 20 November 2015, no. 613/2014, §§ 8.7 and 8.8 on the risk of female genital mutilation in Guinea (introduced in Chapter 3 Section 3.3.).

a possible trigger for Article 3 CAT. This is confirmed by the decision *Abdussamatov and 28 Others v. Kazakhstan* adopted in June 2012, in which the Committee recognized that Muslims charged with religious extremism are specifically targeted for ill treatment in Uzbekistan.[570] The case concerned 27 Uzbek and 3 Tajik nationals who had fled to Kazakhstan for fear of persecution for practising their religion. On request of the Uzbek authorities (and despite the interim measures indicated by the Committee), they had been extradited to Uzbekistan on the basis of their involvement in 'illegal organizations' and 'attempts to overthrow the constitutional order.' Upon their extradition, the French representative lost contact with the detained applicants. The Committee recalled its concluding observations on Uzbekistan's periodic report, in which it had expressed concern about ongoing and consistent allegations of routine use of torture by officials in Uzbekistan, and that persons who had sought refuge abroad and been returned had been kept in detention in unknown places and possibly subjected to breaches of the CAT.[571] It then noted that all 29 complainants were Muslims reportedly practising their religion outside official Uzbek institutions. It further held that they were all extradited pursuant to a request accusing them of serious crimes, including religious extremism. The Committee reiterated the absolute character of the prohibition on refoulement and the concern expressed in its concluding observations about forcible returns to Uzbekistan in the name of regional security including the fight against terrorism.[572] Based on this and on information presented by the applicants' representative, the Committee considered that 'the pattern of gross, flagrant or mass violations of human rights and the significant risk of torture or other cruel, inhuman or degrading treatment in Uzbekistan, in particular for individuals practising their faith outside of the official framework, has been sufficiently established.'[573] The Committee also noted that the complainants had been subjected to religious persecution, in some cases including detention and torture, before they had fled to Kazakhstan.[574] It further stated that the authorities of Kazakhstan had not properly examined the complainants' claims under Article 3 CAT and that they had not provided any sufficiently specific details as to the reliability of the diplomatic assurances provided by the Uzbek authorities.[575] Without

---

570   ComAT, *Abdussamatov and 28 Others v. Kazakhstan*, 1 June 2012, no. 444/2010.
571   *Ibid.*, § 13.6.
572   *Ibid.*, § 13.7.
573   *Ibid.*, § 13.8.
574   *Ibid.*
575   *Ibid.*, §§ 13.9 and 13.10.

assessing each case individually, the Committee found that the extradition of the 29 applicants had violated Article 3 CAT.[576]

As can be concluded from the case law as a whole, the Committee will usually reject complaints in which the alleged risk is of a general nature.[577] Until now, membership of a threatened group must primarily be seen as lightening the burden of proof borne by a complainant. However, as has been shown, the Committee has indicated in some cases that it may offer a more general protection for members of particularly threatened groups. It would be useful if the Committee were more explicit about its acceptance of a more general protection of individuals belonging to a vulnerable group.[578]

c   *Sources on the Human Rights Conditions*

In accordance with Article 22, paragraph 4, CAT, the Committee considers complaints in light of all information made available to it by the parties concerned. In addition, according to its Rules of Procedure, the Committee can at any time in the course of the procedure obtain documents from UN bodies, specialized agencies, or other sources that may be helpful in its consideration of the complaint.[579] The Committee has used this possibility in several cases. It particularly relies on its own findings made in the context of the state reporting procedures under Article 19 CAT or inquiries proceeding under Article 20 CAT.[580] The Committee also cites reports of the UN special rapporteurs and representatives in charge of specific human rights violations or the human rights situation in a specific country.[581] It attaches particular weight to

---

576   See the similar cases ComAT, *Nasirov v. Kazakhstan*, 14 May 2014, no. 475/2011 and ComAT, *Tursunov v. Kazakhstan*, 8 May 2015, no. 538/2013.

577   See the explicit statements of the Committee in ComAT, *L.J.R. v. Australia*, 10 November 2008, no. 316/2007, § 7.5; ComAT, *J.L.L. v. Switzerland*, 18 May 2012, no. 364/2008, § 8.8; ComAT, *M.B. v. Switzerland*, 31 May 2013, no. 439/2010, 7.7.

578   See in this sense also Wouters 2009, p. 462.

579   Rule 118(2) RoP CAT (CAT/C/3/Rev.6).

580   See as a recent example, among many others, ComAT, *Abdussamatov and 28 Others v. Kazakhstan*, 1 June 2012, no. 444/2010, § 13.6; ComAT, *Fadel v. Switzerland*, 14 November 2014, no. 450/2011, § 7.8.

581   In particular the UN Special Rapporteur on extrajudicial, summary or arbitrary executions and the UN Special Rapporteur on torture. See, for example, ComAT, *Jahani v. Switzerland*, 23 May 2011, no. 357/2008, § 9.4 and ComAT, *Chahin v. Sweden*, 30 May 2011, no. 310/2007, § 9.4, in which the Committee attaches particular weight to statements commonly made by all special procedures mandate holders of the UN Human Rights Council on the situation of Iran after the 2009 elections and on the situation in Syria after the beginning of the revolts in 2011.

statements and guidelines from the UNHCR.[582] In the recent years, the Committee has also increasingly cited the concluding observations of the UN Human Rights Committee.[583]

The Committee takes into account the analysis and reports presented by the national authorities in the domestic or international procedure.[584] It is, however, rather rare for the Committee itself to bring up country reports drawn up by states.[585] The Committee deals with reports of NGOs or human rights organisations in a similar manner: if submitted by the complainant it will take them into account,[586] but it is rare for it to bring up such reports by itself.[587]

Examining most of the complaints at the time of its own assessment, the Committee usually relies on recent reports, even though in some cases the

---

582   See ComAT, *Kioski v. Sweden*, 8 May 1996, no. 41/1996, § 9.5; *ComAT, X. Y. and Z. v. Sweden*, 6 May 1998, no. 61/1996, § 11.5; ComAT, *Korban v. Sweden*, 16 November 1998, no. 88/1997, § 6.5; ComAT, *Haydin v. Sweden*, 20 November 1998, no. 101/1997, 6.4; ComAT, *N.B.-M. v. Switzerland*, 14 November 2011, no. 347/2008, § 9.5.

583   See, for example, ComAT, *E.L. v. Switzerland*, 15 November 2011, no. 351/2008, § 9.4; ComAT, *J.L.L. v. Switzerland*, 18 May 2012, no. 364/2008, § 8.5; ComAT, *D.Y. v. Sweden*, 21 May 2013, no. 463/2011, § 9.5. See also ComAT, *S.M., H.M. and A.M. v. Sweden*, 21 November 2011, no. 374/2009, § 9.7, in which the Committee referred to reports of the Committee on the Elimination of Racial Discrimination and the European Commission against Racism and Intolerance.

584   See, for example, ComAT, *Güclü v. Sweden*, 11 November 2010, no. 349/2008, §§ 6.2 and 6.6; ComAT, *G.B.M. v. Sweden,* 14 November 2012, no. 435/2010, §§ 4.8, 4.15 and 7.7.

585   See, as exceptions, ComAT, *V.L. v. Switzerland*, 20 November 2006, no. 262/2005, § 8.7; ComAT, *Y. v. Switzerland*, 21 May 2013, no. 431/2010, § 7.8, in which the Committee refers to recent country reports of the US State Department.

586   See ComAT, *Khan v. Canada*, 15 November 1994, no. 15/1994 §§ 9.1 and 12.4; ComAT, *H.B.H., T.N.T., H.J.H., H.O.H., H.R.H. and H.G.H. v. Switzerland*, 29 April 2003, no. 192/2001, §§ 2.8, 3.2 and 6.9; ComAT, *G.K. v. Switzerland*, 7 May 2003, no. 219/2002, § 6.3; ComAT, *A.A. v. Switzerland*, 1 May 2007, no. 268/2005, §§ 7.1 and 8.5; ComAT, *Sogi v. Canada*, 16 November 2007, no. 297/2006, § 10.9; ComAT, *Khalsa et al. v. Switzerland*, 26 May 2011, no. 336/2008, § 11.4; ComAT, *Gbadjavi v. Switzerland*, 1 June 2012, no. 396/2009, § 7.7.

587   See, as exceptions, ComAT, *Arana v. France*, 9 November 1999, no. 63/1997, § 11.5, in which the Committee refers to 'some NGOs'; ComAT, *A.S. v. Sweden*, 24 November 2000, no. 149/1999, § 8.7, in which the Committee simply refers to 'numerous reports of NGOs'; ComAT, *S.S. v. Netherlands*, 5 May 2003, no. 191/2001, § 6.3 (Amnesty International); ComAT, *X. v. Denmark*, 28 November 2014, no. 458/2011, § 9.6 (Amnesty International); ComAT, *J.K. v. Canada*, 23 November 2015, no. 562/2013, 10.5 (Amnesty International, Human Rights Watch and other NGO documents on LGBTI rights in Uganda).

competent authorities were not able to take them into account in the domestic procedure.[588] As discussed in the previous section with regard to cases concerning the deportation of women to the DRC, it has also happened that the Committee has failed to take into account certain country information.

Reports of practices of torture with the direct or indirect participation of state agents are of particular importance for the Committee. There are, however, also other elements that are occasionally mentioned by the Committee as risk-enhancing. One is the failure of a state to investigate allegations of torture and to punish perpetrators of torture.[589] Ongoing peace processes, the conclusion of ceasefire agreements between conflict parties and amnesties for political opponents are cited as indicators for an improved human rights situations in several decisions.[590] Repatriation programs and the opinion of the UNHCR with regard to the returning of former refugees to a receiving country seem to be highly relevant for the Committee, too.[591]

Finally, it should be stressed that the Committee, being generally short in its decisions, is not in the habit of making detailed country analyses. There are decisions in which the Committee gives brief statements about a situation in a receiving country simply by reference to 'reports from reliable sources' or without even referring to any source.[592]

---

588   See, for example, ComAT, *Njamba and Balikosa v. Sweden*, 14 May 2010, no. 322/2007, § 9.5; ComAT, *Bakatu-Bia v. Sweden*, 3 June 2011, no. 379/2009, §§ 10.5–10.7; ComAT, *Y. v. Switzerland*, 21 May 2013, no. 431/2010, § 7.8.

589   ComAT, *V.L. v. Switzerland*, 20 November 2006, no. 262/2005, §§ 8.4 and 8.10; ComAT, *Güclü v. Sweden*, 11 November 2010, no. 349/2008, § 6.6, ComAT, *Aytulun und Güclü v. Sweden*, 19 November 2010, no. 373/2009, § 7.6; ComAT, *Mondal v. Sweden*, 23 May 2011, no. 338/2008, § 7.5; ComAT, *Khalsa et al. v. Switzerland*, 26 May 2011, no. 336/2008, § 113; ComAT, *Kalinichenko v. Morocco*, 25 November 2011, no. 428/2010, 15.6; ComAT, *Gbadjavi v. Switzerland*, 1 June 2012, no. 396/2009, § 7.7.

590   ComAT, *A.L.N. v. Switzerland*, 19 May 1998, no. 90/1997, § 8.6; ComAT, *U.S. v. Finland*, 1 May 2003, no. 197/2002, § 7.7; ComAT, *S.S. v. Netherlands*, 5 May 2003, no. 191/2001, § 6.3; ComAT, *K.K. v. Switzerland*, 11 November 2003, no. 186/2001, § 6.3; ComAT, *A.I. v. Switzerland*, 12 May 2004, no. 182/2001, § 6.3; ComAT, *M.C.M.V.F. v. Sweden*, 14 November 2005, no. 237/2003, § 6.4; ComAT, *C.M. v. Switzerland*, 14 May 2010, no. 355/2008, § 10.8.

591   ComAT, *X. Y. and Z. v. Sweden*, 6 May 1998, no. 61/1996, § 11.5; ComAT, *H.M.H.I. v. Australia*, 1 May 2002, no. 177/2001, § 6.6; ComAT, *U.S. v. Finland*, 1 May 2003, no. 197/2002, § 7.7; ComAT, *S.S. v. Netherlands*, 5 May 2003, no. 191/2001, § 6.3; ComAT, *K.K. v. Switzerland*, 11 November 2003, no. 186/2001, § 6.3; ComAT, *A.I. v. Switzerland*, 12 May 2004, no. 182/2001, § 6.3; ComAT, *R.T-N. v. Switzerland*, 3 June 2011, no. 350/2008, §§ 8.5 and 8.9.

592   See, for example, ComAT, *Paez v. Sweden*, 28 April 1997, no. 39/1996, §§ 14.1–15; ComAT, *Ayas v. Sweden*, 12 November 1998, no. 97/1997, § 6.4; ComAT, *A. v. Netherlands*, 13 November 1998, no. 91/1997, § 6.4; ComAT, *H.M.H.I. v. Australia*, 1 May 2002, no. 177/2001, §§ 6.4 and 6.5.

d   *Where the Country of Destination is a State Party to the* CAT

The fact that a receiving state has ratified the CAT or even accepted the individual complaint mechanism under Article 22 CAT is not of particular relevance in the Committee's risk assessment under Article 3 CAT. In the case *Alan v. Switzerland* concerning the expulsion of a Kurdish Turk, the Committee stated that 'the main aim of the Convention is to prevent torture, not to redress torture once it had occurred.'[593] It followed from this that 'the fact that Turkey is a party to the Convention and has recognized the Committee's competence under Article 22, does not, in the circumstances of the instant case, constitute sufficient guarantee for the author's security.'[594]

The ratification of the CAT or other human rights treaties is, however, not completely irrelevant either. In a several decisions in which the Committee found a violation of Article 3 CAT, it concluded its risk assessment in stating that, in view of the fact that the receiving state is not a party to the CAT, 'the complainants would be in danger, in the event of expulsion, not only of being subjected to torture but of no longer having the legal possibility of applying to the Committee for protection.'[595] In *A.H. v. Sweden*, the Committee noted that although human rights abuses were still being reported in Azerbaijan, this country 'had made some progress towards improving the human rights situation since it joined the Council of Europe.'[596] In two decisions in which the Committee found no violation of Article 3 CAT, it pointed out the fact that, next to the ratification of the CAT, the receiving state had also accepted the Committee's competence to assess individual complaints under Article 22 CAT.[597] When there is a risk of chain-removal, this latter question is of particular importance, since the risk of a subsequent refoulement by the receiving country can be considerably reduced if it has accepted the individual complaint mechanism.[598]

---

593   ComAT, *Alan v. Switzerland*, 8 May 1996, no. 21/1995, § 11.5.

594   *Ibid.*

595   See, for example, ComAT, *Mutombo v. Switzerland*, 27 April 1994, no. 13/1993, § 9.6 ('Zaire'); ComAT, *Khalsa et al. v. Switzerland*, 26 May 2011, no. 336/2008, § 11.7 (India); ComAT, *K.N., F.W. and S.N. v. Switzerland*, 19 May 2014, no. 481/2011 (Iran); ComAT, *Tahmuresi v. Switzerland*, 26 November 2014, no. 489/2012, § 7.7 (Iran).

596   ComAT, *A.H. v. Sweden*, 16 November 2006, no. 265/2005, § 11.7.

597   ComAT, *S.C. v. Denmark*, 10 May 2000, no. 143/1999, § 6.5; ComAT, *E.J.V.M. v. Sweden*, 14 November 2003, no. 213/2002, § 8.4.

598   See ComAT, *Korban v. Sweden*, 16 November 1998, no. 88/1997, § 7 discussed in Section 3.4.3.b of this Chapter.

However, in most of its decisions, the Committee does not take into account whether the receiving state has ratified the CAT and accepted the individual complaint procedure or not. In fact, most of the cases in which the Committee has found a violation of Article 3 CAT concern removals to states that have ratified the CAT, many of which have even recognized the competence of the Committee to receive individual complaints under Article 22 CAT. Against that background, it is clear that a receiving state's ratification of the CAT or other instruments and its participation in the individual complaint mechanism under Article 22 CAT is not of decisive importance. As the Committee has recently recalled, 'in assessing the risk of torture to which an individual would be exposed in the context of extradition or deportation proceedings, a State cannot base itself solely on the fact that another State is a party to the Convention against Torture.'[599]

3.2.3 Comparison

a *The Human Rights Situation and the Individualisation of the Risk*

It is uncontested before the Court and the Committee that the personal background of a complainant can be sufficient to trigger the application of the principle of non-refoulement, regardless of the general human rights situation in the receiving country. It is worth recalling in that context that the first case in which the Court found a violation of the principle of non-refoulement, *Soering v. United Kingdom*, concerned an extradition to the United States. However, for countries with high human rights standards, it will usually be hard for a complainant to show the existence of a real risk. In January 2012, the Court noted that it has rarely found that there would be a violation of Article 3 ECHR 'if an applicant were to be removed to a State which had a long history of respect for democracy, human rights and the rule of law.'[600] This statement is equally valid for the Committee.

In contrast to the Court, the Committee does not recognize that a particularly high level of violence in a receiving country could as such prohibit any deportation thereto. The Committee has made clear that the human rights situation in the receiving country is 'neither a necessary nor a sufficient' criterion in the risk assessment under Article 3 CAT.[601] Thurin notes that the reason for this approach could be that a generalized risk of inhuman treatment in a country is more probable than a generalized risk of torture.[602]

---

599 ComAT, *R.A.Y. v. Morocco*, 16 May 2014, no. 525/2012, § 7.4.

600 ECtHR, *Harkins & Edwards v. UK*, 17 January 2012, nos. 9146/07 and 32650/07, § 131.

601 Translated from Chetail 2006, p. 94.

602 Thurin 2012, p. 207, footnote 994.

At first sight, the Court seems hence to offer a broader protection than the Committee with regard to extreme situations of general violence. However, it is unusual for the Court to recognise such a situation: until now, the only places to which the Court has indicated that almost *any* removal should be avoided because of extreme violence was Mogadishu in June 2011[603] and Syria in 2015.[604] But even with regard to the terrible situation in Mogadishu, the Court changed its practice two years later in *K.A.B. v. Sweden* and considered that the level of violence in this city was no longer of such intensity as to prohibit any removal there.[605] In addition, although this remains mere speculation, it is most likely that the Committee would have come to the same conclusion with regard to expulsions to Mogadishu in summer 2011 or to Syria in 2015. That said, the Committee would probably not have openly admitted that it drew its conclusion based solely on the human rights situation.

The Court does seem to be more explicit than the Committee in recognising the importance of the general human rights in situations of extreme violence, although this is usually not the sole factor.[606] Given the above, the difference in approach by the Court and the Committee with regard to a general protection against refoulement when there is widespread generalized violence in the receiving state seems to a large extent theoretical for individuals submitting complaints at the international level.[607]

b   *Protection of Vulnerable Individuals and Groups Systematically Exposed to Ill Treatment*

Exceptionally, where an applicant alleges that he is a member of a group systematically exposed to a practice of ill treatment, the Court has considered that the protection of Article 3 ECHR enters into play when the applicant establishes there are serious reasons to believe in the existence of the practice in question and his membership of the group concerned. In those circumstances, the Court will not insist that the applicant show the existence of further special distinguishing features. In contrast to the Court, the Committee has

---

603   ECtHR, *Sufi and Elmi v. UK*, 28 June 2011, nos. 8319/07 and 11449/07.

604   ECtHR, *L.M. and Others v. Russia*, 15 October 2015, nos. 40081/14, 40088/14 and 40127/14.

605   ECtHR, *K.A.B. v. Sweden*, 5 September 2013, no. 886/11, § 91.

606   See also Wouters 2009, p. 545, stating that while the Court has adopted a 'three-pronged approach' (extreme case of general violence, membership of a group systematically exposed to ill-treatment, and individual risk factors) other treaties provide less clarity with regard to the question of what impact the human rights conditions in a receiving country can have on the requirement of individualising risk factors.

607   See in this sense also Schürmann & Scheidegger 2008, p. 208.

not *explicitly* developed a principle of protection of members of groups that are particularly threatened in a receiving country. It has, however, indicated in some decisions that it could make use of such a concept. Its practice has further shown that the membership of a particular threatened group can have a considerable impact on the burden of proof of a complainant with regard to the submission of individual factors substantiating an alleged risk of torture.

The Committee is, as a rule, reluctant to issue sweeping statements. Although exceptions seem to be possible, as the cases *Njamba and Balikosa* and *Abdussamatov and 28 Others* described above demonstrate, the Committee usually focuses on individual risk factors against the background of the general human rights situation. This can be observed in the comparison of the cases *Salah Sheek*[608] before the Court and *Elmi*[609] before the Committee, both concerning removals to Somalia. In both judgments, the international institutions stated that the complainants were particularly threatened because of their membership of a minority clan. They both noted reliable sources indicating that members of minority clans were violently oppressed by more powerful clans controlling the area. For the Court, this information was enough to find that Article 3 ECHR would be violated in case of removal. It noted that the applicant could not 'be required to establish the existence of further special distinguishing features concerning him personally in order to show that he was personally at risk.'[610] The Committee in contrast pointed out two individual factors supporting the complainant's case in its risk assessment; the complainant's family's persecution in the past and the wide publicity that his case had attracted. It was then in light of all these factors that the Committee came to the conclusion that his expulsion to Somalia would violate Article 3 CAT.[611]

We may conclude as follows: under extreme circumstances, the Court recognizes that a situation of violence in a certain location may persist at such a level that almost any removal thereto would be prohibited. Until now, it is only in the judgment *Sufi and Elmi* with regard to the situation in the city of Mogadishu in 2011 and likewise in *L.M. and Others v. Russia* with regard to the current situation in Syria that the Court has acknowledged the existence of such an extreme case of indiscriminate violence. When numerous human rights reports indicate that members of a group are systematically exposed to ill treatment and the complainant has established that he is member of that group,

---

608   ECtHR, *Salah Sheekh v. Netherlands*, 11 January 2007, no. 1948/04.

609   ComAT, *Elmi v. Australia*, 14 May 1999, no. 120/1998.

610   ECtHR, *Salah Sheekh v. Netherlands*, 11 January 2007, no. 1948/04, §§ 145–149.

611   ComAT, *Elmi v. Australia*, 14 May 1999, no. 120/1998, §§ 6.6–7.

the Court will not require special distinguishing features. There are, however, only a few cases in which the Court has *explicitly* recognized the existence of such groups. It did this with regard to:

· suspected Islamic terrorists in Tunisia before the Arab Spring
· members of minority clans in certain parts of Somalia
· the situation of individuals charged with politically and/or religiously mo-tivated criminal offences in custody in Kazakhstan, Kyrgyzstan, Tajikistan, Turkmenistan and Uzbekistan
· the situation of irregular migrants in Libya and asylum seekers in Greece

With its refoulement protection essentially restricted to torture, the Commit-tee is rather unlikely to follow the arguments of the Court concerning living conditions and degrading prison conditions. However, if reliable reports indi-cate that a complainant belongs to a group threatened *with systematic torture* in a receiving country, the Committee will also require very few risk factors. Similarly to the Court, it has recognized a general risk of ill treatment for Mus-lim applicants extradited to Uzbekistan on the basis of religious extremism. The cases *N. v. Sweden*[612] and *Njamba and Balikosa*[613] further demonstrate that the Court and the Committee are both sensitive to removals of women to countries with a known and widespread problem of violence against wom-en. It should be noted in that context that for a long time it seemed that the Court and Committee only considered a risk from private actors as relevant in cases where such actors were organized groups like powerful clans or rebel groups.[614] With the decision of the Committee in *Njamba and Balikosa* and the judgment of the Court in *N. v. Sweden* concerning the deportation of unmar-ried women to the DRC and Afghanistan, the two institutions demonstrated that a threat from private actors does not necessarily have to come from an organized political group to be relevant. In these cases, the threat emanated mainly from society itself.

However, with regard to *gender-based violence*, it must be stated that the Committee, based on its General Comment no. 2 on Article 2 CAT, has adopted a *particularly sensitive* approach in its recent case law, while the vulnerable position of the complainants as women did not receive significant attention in

---

612   ECtHR, *N. v. Sweden*, 20 July 2010, no. 23505/09.

613   ComAT, *Njamba and Balikosa v. Sweden*, 14 May 2010, no. 322/2007.

614   See the statement of the Court in ECtHR, *F.H. v. Sweden*, 20 January 2009, no. 32621/06, § 97; see also Fornerod 2010, p. 321 with references.

recent refoulement judgments of the Court.[615] On this subject, the Committee currently appears more in line with international developments, according to which states have a *particular responsibility* under the prohibition of torture and inhuman treatment to provide protection against gender-based violence, including in the refoulement context.[616]

Finally, under what circumstances the Court (more explicitly) and the Committee (more implicitly) will accept the existence of particularly vulnerable or threatened groups is difficult to predict. The case law has shown that their evaluation of the situation can change from one case to another within short time periods (sometimes even without considerable changes in the human rights situation). The Committee is generally more reluctant to offer global protection to members of particular groups. However, looking at the case law as a whole, the principles developed by the Court should not be considered as rigid categorizations to which one can assign a case. In the end the Court's more developed principles with regard to extreme cases of violence and groups systematically exposed to ill treatment demonstrate a rule that is equally valid under the Committee's case law: the more precarious the human rights situation, the fewer additional or personal elements required to trigger the application of the principle of non-refoulement. Some scholars therefore consider the concepts developed by the Court simply as 'alleviations' of the burden of proof.[617] In most cases before the Court and the Committee, the human rights situation or the membership of a particular group in the receiving country will not in itself be sufficient for the establishment of a real risk of ill treatment in case of return. Complainants will have to adduce additional elements showing they are personally targeted. The judges Power and Zupančič comment that the human

---

615   See the most relevant cases discussed and criticized in Chapter 3 Section 3.3 and Chapter 4 Sections 3.2.1.b and 3.2.2.b and ComAT, General Comment No. 2 on Art. 2 (2008), §§ 18 and 22.

616   See ComAT, General Comment No. 2 on Art. 2 (2008), §§ 18 and 25 and the conclusions and recommendations made by the Special Rapporteur on torture and other cruel, inhuman or degrading treatment or punishment, Manfred Nowak, in UN Doc. A/HRC/7/3, 15 January 2008; see also General recommendation No. 32, § 19 of the UN Committee on the Elimination of Discrimination against Women on the gender-related dimensions of refugee status, asylum, nationality and statelessness of women (UN Doc. CEDAW/C/GC/32, 14 November 2014). Compare further the Strasbourg case law in the *domestic context*, in which more attention appears to be given to the vulnerability of women and related state obligations with regard to risks of gender-based violence; see, for example, ECtHR, *Eremia v. Republic of Moldova*, 28 May 2013, no. 3564/11, §§ 48–66 and the reference to the relevant international material in §§ 32–37.

617   See Fornerod 2010, p. 327; Lorz and Sauer 2010, pp. 399 and 400.

rights situation 'when considered with other factors in relation to alleged risk, *may* be decisive in terms of tipping the balance when it comes to the preponderance of evidence.'[618] This statement is equally valid for the Committee.

c   *Sources on the Human Rights Conditions*

The Court puts much more visible effort into the analysis of the situation in the receiving country than the Committee. The Court clearly consults sources obtained *proprio motu* more often. Moreover, while the Court usually takes into account a vast range of different sources from international organisations, NGOs and governments, the Committee tends to focus on UN sources, in particular its own conclusions in the state reporting procedures under Article 19 CAT. The Court and the Committee both attach weight to analyses made by the UNHCR. Relying mostly on UN documents, it is not surprising that the Committee, in contrast to the Court, has not established guidelines indicating which kind of external sources can be considered reliable. In some cases, the Committee does not mention any reports at all or does not make any explicit pronouncements on the situation in a receiving country.

Before both the Court and the Committee, the more precisely reports describe a danger alleged by a complainant, the more importance they will have in the considerations on the merits. Of course, reports on torture and ill treatment of individuals in comparable circumstances to a complainant will be of particular importance. Reports indicating human rights violations that do not necessarily amount to torture or inhuman treatment, like for example discriminations or oppressions of the freedom of speech, will only be relevant if they appear to indicate an enhanced risk of ill treatment for the applicant. Impunity for perpetrators of ill treatment or repatriation programs allowing the return of former refugees are two elements considered as indicators for an either a higher or lower risk of ill treatment.

The less individualized the alleged source of risk in the receiving country, the more important human rights reports are in the Court's or the Committee's considerations.[619] It may be simply on account of human rights reports that the Court and the Committee recognize that a group of people is particularly threatened in a receiving country. Since the Committee is in principle more reluctant to accept that general risks could trigger the application of the

---

618   See the dissenting opinion of the judges Power and Zupančič in ECtHR, *F.H. v. Sweden*, 20 January 2009, no. 32621/06.

619   See, for example, the importance of the reports in ECtHR, *Sufi and Elmi v. UK*, 28 June 2011, nos. 8319/07 and 11449/07, §§ 80–195, 241–250, 265–277 and 284–292, or in ComAT, *Njamba and Balikosa v. Sweden*, 14 May 2010, no. 322/2007, § 9.5.

principle of non-refoulement, it is not surprising that it pays less attention to general reports than the Court.

It should finally be noted that in many cases, the time elapsed since the national authorities' decisions forces the Court and the Committee to proceed to a new assessment of the human rights situation. It is thus not uncommon for them to base their conclusions on reports that could not have been known by national authorities at the time of the domestic procedure.

d   *Where the Country of Destination is a State Party to the ECHR or the CAT*

For both the Court and the Committee, the accession of the receiving state to international treaties guaranteeing respect for fundamental rights is not in itself sufficient to ensure adequate protection against the risk of ill treatment in case of a removal This is particularly true when reliable sources report practices of ill treatment and torture in that country. Ratifications of human rights treaties are occasionally mentioned in judgments of both bodies as indications for a certain human rights standard, but these considerations are rarely of importance in the risk assessment.

With regard to removals to states that are themselves parties to the ECHR or the CAT the situation is different: Chetail notes that the Committee is more realistic than the Court in such cases, since it does not assume that a member state will not breach the CAT.[620] In that context, he refers to two cases: one assessed in Strasbourg, the other in Geneva, concerning the transfer of active ETA members from France to Spain in 1996 and 1997.[621] Although the circumstances in those cases were very similar and the Court and the former Commission of Human Rights both noted that the UN Human Rights Committee, the Committee against Torture itself and the European Committee for the Prevention of Torture had raised concerns for individuals in the situation of the complainants' in Spanish detention, it was only the Committee who found that the direct handover of the applicant by police forces from France to Spain had violated the principle of non-refoulement. In its decision, the former European Commission held that 'there is a presumption that treatment contrary to Article 3 ECHR does not occur' in a contracting state, but this presumption can be refuted.[622] Although the Court has not explicitly recited this statement in

---

620   Chetail 2006, pp. 92–93.

621   See Chetail 2004, pp. 196–197 referring to EComHR, *Iruretagoyena v. France*, 12 January 1998, no. 32829/96 (decision) and ComAT, *Arana v. France*, 9 November 1999, no. 63/1997.

622   See EComHR, *Iruretagoyena v. France*, 12 January 1998, no. 32829/96 (decision).

its subsequent case law, it is evident that for cases before the Court the burden of proof for complainants is particularly high in cases concerning removals to other member states of the Council of Europe. The Court is unlikely to be convinced that there is a real risk for a complainant to be subjected to ill treatment in its zone of influence unless various independent sources indicate that individuals in similar circumstances to a complainant are treated in that way. So far it has been only in Dublin cases concerning transfers of asylum seekers to Greece and Italy and a few removal cases to Russia related to the violent conflict in Chechnya that applicants have been successful with a refoulement complaint in which the receiving state is part of the Council of Europe.[623] In contrast, most of the successful complaints before the CAT concern removals to contracting states to the CAT.

It could be suggested that – compared to the broad average of states that have ratified the CAT – ill treatment is rare in the states of the Council of Europe. However, the Court, by its own rich experience with Article 3 ECHR in domestic cases, is aware that ill treatment does occur in its domain of influence. In this context, it is interesting to note that while the Committee has found violations of the principle of non-refoulement with regard to deportations to Turkey in several cases,[624] the Court has only once found a violation of the right to an effective remedy in Article 13 ECHR in combination with the principle of non-refoulement inherent to Article 3 ECHR with regard to a removal to Turkey.[625] The comparison of the Turkish cases further demonstrates that the Committee is not necessarily swayed by the fact that a receiving state is subject to the Strasbourg jurisdiction. The same is valid for the Court with regard to receiving states that have ratified the CAT or accepted the Committee's competence under Article 22 CAT.

It is apparent that both the Court and the Committee give more weight to the question of whether the receiving state is part of their jurisdiction or has ratified other international human rights treaties when they assess the risk of a chain-removal. The Court further gives particular weight to that question when it assesses the reliability of diplomatic assurances. However, also in

---

623   See Chapter 4 Section 3.2.1.d.

624   See ComAT, *Alan v. Switzerland*, 8 May 1996, no. 21/1995; ComAT, *Ayas v. Sweden*, 12 November 1998, no. 97/1997; ComAT, *Haydin v. Sweden*, 20 November 1998, no. 101/1997; ComAT, *Dadar v. Canada*, 23 November 2005, no. 258/2004; ComAT, *Pelit v. Azerbaijan*, 1 May 2007, no. 281/2005; ComAT, *Güclü v. Sweden*, 11 November 2010, no. 349/2008; ComAT, *Aytulun and Güclü v. Sweden*, 19 November 2010, no. 373/2009; ComAT, *A.K. v. Switzerland*, 8 May 2015, no. 544/2013.

625   ECtHR, *R.U. v. Greece*, 7 June 2011, no. 2237/08, §§ 79 and 82.

such cases, the fact that the state party is part of a Convention system remains one factor among others; what matters in the end is the existence of a real risk of ill treatment. In summary, no matter where a person might be expelled to and no matter which international instruments are ratified by the receiving country, the domestic authorities will always have to assess individually an 'arguable claim' of a violation of the principle of non-refoulement. Whether a receiving state is a member state or not, what finally counts is not which treaties it has ratified, but the actual human rights practice as it is described by international organisations, in particular the UN, NGOs and credible state sources.

3.3   *Personal Circumstances*

As has been explained, the Court and the Committee assess refoulement complaints on a case-by-case basis in light of the human rights situation in the receiving country and the particular circumstances of the applicant. Mostly, it is the combination of several individual risk elements that, taken together, indicate a sufficient risk to trigger the application of the principle of non-refoulement. It would be impossible to enumerate all the risk elements that the Court or the Committee have taken into account when analysing a complainant's background in their previous assessments. Elements that are highly relevant in some cases may be of less importance in others. In practice, it will often be the overall impression that makes the case. Nonetheless, certain factors reappear in many decisions and judgments and are therefore worth a more detailed discussion: past political or religious activities, a risk of detention and past ill treatment are among such factors. They are looked at individually below.[626]

In addition, the fact that an applicant or individuals with similar backgrounds have been recognized as refugees under the Geneva Convention is considered by the Court and the Committee as a strong indication that there is real risk of being subjected to treatment contrary to Article 3 ECHR or Article 3 CAT in case of removal. The cases in which this has been relevant merit separate discussion since they make particularly visible the material and procedural nexus between the risk assessments under general human rights treaties on the one hand and the Refugee Convention on the other.[627]

A precondition for the Court and the Committee to take facts in the complainant's personal history into account is that they judge them to be credible. The state authorities' conclusions on a person's credibility will usually rely on

---

626   See Sections 3.3.1.b, 3.3.2.b and 3.3.3.b of this chapter.
627   See Sections 3.3.1.c, 3.3.2.c and 3.3.3.c of this chapter.

interrogations made and the assessment of evidence presented by the individual concerned. For the Court and the Committee, which base their assessment on written statements by the parties, it is particularly difficult to assess a complainant's credibility. The Court and the Committee have nevertheless pointed out certain patterns of behaviour or circumstances that allow them either to understand the national authorities' doubts regarding a complainant's credibility or to refute them. These elements will be looked at in the following sections.[628]

3.3.1   Court

a   The Complainant's Credibility

In assessing whether there are substantial grounds for believing an applicant who claims he would be exposed to a real risk of treatment contrary to Article 3 ECHR if expelled, the Court has to take into account whether there are indications or evidence undermining or corroborating the applicant's credibility. Such indications can be of an objective nature, such as evidence presented or the human rights situation. However, they can also lie in the complainant's conduct in the national procedure. Certain circumstances and behaviours have been pointed out by the Court as raising serious doubts as to the credibility of a complainant. One example of such behaviour is where the complainant raises important allegations only at a late stage of the national procedure[629] or only before the Court.[630] It also does not speak in favour of an applicant's credibility if he is continuously changing his story or his account of the origin of the threats in the receiving country.[631] The same can be said of complainants who give only very general information about their past or the events or activities related to the alleged risk of ill treatment.[632]

---

628   See Sections 3.3.1.a, 3.3.2.a and 3.3.3.a.

629   See, for example, ECtHR, *H.R. v. France*, 22 September 2011, no. 64780/09, §§ 52 and 53; ECtHR, *H.N. v. Sweden*, 15 May 2012, no. 30720/09, § 40; ECtHR, *A.A. and Others v. Sweden*, 28 June 2012, no. 14499/09, §§ 79, 81 and 87; ECtHR, *D.N.W. v. Sweden*, 6 December 2012, no. 29946/10, § 43; ECtHR, *R.H. v. Sweden*, 10 September 2015, no. 4601/14, § 72.

630   See ECtHR, *F.H. v. Sweden*, 20 January 2009, no. 32621/06, § 103; ECtHR, *H. and B. v. UK*, 9 April 2013, nos. 70073/10 and 44539/11, §§ 112 and 113; ECtHR, *M.K.N. v. Sweden*, 27 June 2013, no. 72413/10, § 43. The submission of important allegations only to the Court might also lead to the inadmissibility of a complaint for non-exhaustion of domestic remedies; see on this Chapter 2 Section 3.2.4.c.

631   See, for example, ECtHR, *B. v. Sweden*, 26 October 2004, no. 16578/03 (decision); ECtHR, *A.A. v. Sweden*, 2 September 2008, no. 8594/04, §§ 64–68 (decision); ECtHR, *T.N. v. Denmark*, 20 January 2011, no. 20594/08, § 101; ECtHR, *S.P. v. Belgium*, 14 June 2011, no. 12572/08 (decision).

632   See, for example, ECtHR, *Y. v. Russia*, 4 December 2008, no. 20113/07, §§ 87–98; ECtHR, *S.M. v. Sweden*, 10 February 2009, no. 47683/08, § 33 (decision).

The veracity of the applicant's story will also be assessed by the Court on the basis of presented evidence.[633] In principle, though, it is up to the government to challenge the authenticity of documents submitted.[634] The submission of forged or fabricated documents will naturally considerably undermine a complainant's credibility. If a complainant does not submit any evidence to substantiate his allegations, this will not speak in favour of his credibility either.[635]

The Court will be sceptical when complainants do not participate in the fact-finding. In the case *Ahmade*, the complainant rejected being subjected to a radiological test that had been ordered to verify his allegation that he was a minor.[636] In view of this refusal, the Court accepted the government's arguments that the applicant was older than he alleged.[637]

The Court will not in general reject a claim if a complainant seems to be acting irrationally. It has noted as a general principle that 'due to the special situation in which asylum seekers often find themselves, it is frequently necessary to give them the benefit of the doubt when it comes to assessing the credibility of their statements and the documents submitted in support thereof. However, when information is presented which gives strong reasons to question the veracity of an asylum seeker's submissions, the individual must provide a satisfactory explanation for the alleged inaccuracies in those submissions.'[638] According to the Court, a person's failure to apply for refugee status or seek protection in due time does not, as such, refute allegations under Article 3 ECHR, but it may be relevant for the assessment of the credibility.[639] Even the fact that a complainant initially submitted a false identity will not necessarily undermine his credibility with regard to risk encountered in his home country.[640] The Court will always take into account the complainant's particular situation.

---

633   ECtHR, *M.A. v. Switzerland*, 18 November 2014, no. 52589/13, § 62. See also Section 1.1.2 of this chapter on the burden of proof.

634   *Ibid.*, §§ 64–68.

635   See, for example, ECtHR, *Cruz Varas and Others v. Sweden*, 20 March 1991, no. 15576/89, § 79; ECtHR, *J.H. v. UK*, 20 December 2011, no. 48839/09, § 66. See further Section 1.1.2 of this chapter on the burden of proof.

636   ECtHR, *Ahmade v. Greece*, 25 September 2012, no. 50520/09, §§ 70–79.

637   *Ibid.*, § 79.

638   See, for example, ECtHR, *F.H. v. Sweden*, 20 January 2009, no. 32621/06, § 95; ECtHR, *R.C. v. Sweden*, 9 March 2010, no. 41827/07, § 50; ECtHR, *N. v. Sweden*, 20 July 2010, no. 23505/09, § 53; ECtHR, *H.N. v. Sweden*, 15 May 2012, no. 30720/09, § 35; ECtHR, *D.N.W. v. Sweden*, 6 December 2012, no. 29946/10, § 36.

639   See, for example, ECtHR, *Zokhidov v. Russia*, 5 February 2013, no. 67286/10, § 130; ECtHR, *Rakhimov v. Russia*, 10 July 2014, no. 50552/13, § 91.

640   ECtHR, *Mo.M. v. France*, 18 April 2013, no. 18372/10, § 43.

The Court recognizes that it is often difficult to establish precisely the pertinent facts in refoulement cases.[641] It has occasionally accepted that victims of ill treatment might not always be able to present their claim in a coherent way.[642] Generally, the Court has emphasized that the task of the domestic courts in refoulement cases is not to 'search for flaws in the alien's account or to trip him up, but to assess, on the basis of all the elements in their possession, whether the alien's fears as to the possible ill-treatment in the country of destination are objectively justified.'[643] The mere fact that an applicant fails to submit accurate information on 'some points' does not mean that his central claim, namely that he faces a risk of ill treatment, is unsubstantiated.[644] The Court has further shown itself to attach less importance to certain inconsistencies in an applicant's story if they have been produced in an accelerated asylum procedure.[645] The Court will generally be more reluctant to disagree with national immigration authorities regarding a complainant's credibility when it can see that the complainant has been sufficiently heard in interviews and when it appears from their decisions that all the information and evidence presented has been properly examined.[646] Generally, the Court acknowledges that the national authorities are best placed to assess the facts but particularly the credibility of an individual 'since it is they who have had an opportunity to see, hear and assess the demeanour of the individual concerned.'[647] However,

---

641   See ECtHR, *S.A. v. Sweden*, 27 June 2013, no. 66523/10, § 47; ECtHR, *D.N.M. v. Sweden*, 27 June 2013, no. 28379/11, § 51.

642   EComHR, *Hatami v. Sweden*, report of 23 April 1998, no. 3244/96, § 106; ECtHR, *Hilal v. UK* 6 March 2001, no. 45276/99, § 64. See further the Court's statement in ECtHR, *Bello v. Sweden*, 17 January 2006, no. 32213/04 (decision), according to which complete accuracy cannot be expected in all circumstances from a person seeking asylum.

643   ECtHR, *Azimov v. Russia*, 18 April 2013, no. 67474/11, § 121.

644   *Ibid.*

645   See ECtHR, *A.A. v. France*, 15 January 2015, no. 18039/11, § 54.

646   See, for example, ECtHR, *Auad v. Bulgaria*, 11 October 2011, no. 46390/10, § 102; ECtHR, *Samina v. Sweden*, 20 October 2011, no. 55463/09, §§ 51–55 and 62–65; ECtHR, *H.N. v. Sweden*, 15 May 2012, no. 30720/09, § 39 and 40; ECtHR, *A.A. and Others v. Sweden*, 28 June 2012, no. 14499/09, §§ 77–96; ECtHR, *Mo.M. v. France*, 18 April 2013, no. 18372/10, § 41; ECtHR, *K.K. v. France*, 10 October 2013, no. 18913/11, §§ 52 and 53; ECtHR, *N.K. v. France*, 19 December 2013, no. 7974/11, §§ 42–47; ECtHR, *R.H. v. Sweden*, 10 September 2015, no. 4601/14, §§ 71–74.

647   See, amongst many others, ECtHR, *R.C. v. Sweden*, 9 March 2010, no. 41827/07, § 52; ECtHR, *H. and B. v. UK*, 9 April 2013, nos. 70073/10 and 44539/11, § 103.

this does not hinder the Court in disagreeing with the manner or the outcome of the credibility assessment at national level.[648]

b   *The Complainant's Background and History*
        Political and/or Religious Background
As will become apparent in this section, unless the human rights situation in the receiving country is particularly bad, complainants must have quite high political profiles to benefit from the protection of Article 3 ECHR for political reasons.[649] The first asylum case in which the Court found a violation of Article 3 ECHR, *Chahal v. United Kingdom,* concerned the deportation of a leading figure in the Sikh community's fight for the autonomy of the Punjab region of India. The Court stated that the applicant's high profile and the notoriety of his case would likely increase his risk of harm.[650] In several rejection decisions and judgments, the Court pointed out that the applicants did not have a *sufficiently high political profile* to be of interest to the receiving state's authorities or had failed to show distinguishing features that would bring them to their attention.[651] The case *B.A. v. France* decided in 2010 concerned a former sergeant major in the Chadian army who, after a military training course in 2004, remained on French territory unlawfully. The complainant claimed that if he returned to Chad, he would be punished for his desertion with torture and a long detention or even the death penalty.[652] The Court recognized that the Chadian authorities are known for being repressive towards deserters in order to be able to combat multiple rebel groups fighting the government. It further observed that France had attributed subsidiary protection to some Chadian deserters for that reason. In contrast to the complainant, those deserters were, however, of higher military rank or had openly criticized their government in the press or in demonstrations. Noting that the complainant had not produced

---

648   See, for example, ECtHR, *M.A. v. Switzerland,* 18 November 2014, no. 52589/13, §§ 60–69 and the dissenting opinion of judge Kjølbro.

649   See also Chetail 2004, pp. 191–192; Fornerod 2010, p. 321.

650   ECtHR, *Chahal v. UK,* 15 November 1996, no. 22414/93, § 106.

651   See, for example, ECtHR, *Venkadajalasarma v. Netherlands,* 17 February 2004, no. 58510/00, § 68 (LTTE supporter to Sri Lanka); ECtHR, *N.M. and M.M. v. UK,* 15 January 2011, nos. 38851/09 and 39128/09, §§ 63 and 69 (applicants without political connections to Uzbekistan); ECtHR, *H.N. v. Sweden,* 15 May 2012, no. 30720/09, § 41 (isolated activities in Sweden against the government in Burundi); ECtHR, *D.N.W. v. Sweden,* 6 December 2012, no. 29946/10, (lack of political activity in Ethiopia, apart from working as an observer during elections).

652   ECtHR, *B.A. v. France,* 2 December 2010, no. 14951/09, § 30.

evidence that he would be wanted by the Chadian army, the Court rejected the complaint.[653] The Court decided differently in April 2013 with regard to another Chadian, who was suspected of being part of the armed opposition movement.[654] It pointed out that the applicant had already been subjected to torture in the past and that he was still politically active in France.[655] In *Said v. Netherlands* decided in 2005, the fact that the complainant had *deserted the Eritrean* army was sufficient, in the eyes of the Court, to establish that there was a real risk of ill treatment for him in case of return, since trusted government and NGO reports reported the systematic ill treatment of deserters in Eritrea.[656]

When judging the relevance of a complainant's political activities or background, the Court will often look at the fate of individuals with similar backgrounds.[657] However, it has also made clear that if 'certain people in a comparable situation might have been fortunate enough' to avoid ill treatment, this 'may not lessen the weight attached by the national authorities or this Court to well substantiated claims of a real risk of ill-treatment.'[658]

With regard to the situation for political opponents in Iran, the Court noted in March 2010 in *R.C. v. Sweden* that 'it is not only leaders of political organisations or other high profile persons who are detained but anyone who demonstrates or in any way opposes the current regime is at risk of being detained and ill-treated or tortured.'[659]

There are two cases concerning deportations to the DRC in which the Court found a violation of Article 3 ECHR.[660] The case *Z.M. v. France* was decided in November 2013 and concerned a political opponent that had campaigned

.

---

653   *Ibid.*, §§ 39–47.

654   ECtHR, *Mo.M. v. France*, 18 April 2013, no. 18372/10.

655   *Ibid.*, §§ 38–44.

656   ECtHR, *Said v. Netherlands*, 5 July 2005, no. 2345/02, §§ 51–56.

657   See, as an illustrative example, ECtHR, *Iskandarov v. Russia*, 23 September 2010, no. 17185/05, § 131, concerning the extradition of a challenger to the Tajikistan presidency. Noting that another opposition leader had been ill-treated, the Court considered that there 'existed special distinguishing features' in the applicant's case which ought to have enabled the Russian authorities to foresee that the he might be ill-treated.

658   ECtHR, *Mamazhonov v. Russia*, 23 October 2014, no. 17239/13, § 146.

659   ECtHR, *R.C. v. Sweden*, 9 March 2010, no. 41827/07, § 54. Confirmed in ECtHR, *S.F. and Others v. Sweden*, 15 May 2012, no. 52077/10, § 63; ECtHR, *M.A. v. Switzerland*, 18 November 2014, no. 52589/13, § 56.

660   See ECtHR, *N. v. Finland*, 26 July 2005, no. 38885/02 and ECtHR, *Z.N. v. France*, 14 November 2013, no. 40042/11.

against the re-election of the Congolese president Joseph Kabila in 2006.[661] Taking into account the applicant's links with the opposition, his former imprisonment and the existence of a medical certificate corroborating that he had been ill-treated as well as arrest warrants and court summons issued against him on account of his campaigning activities (which stated that he was being prosecuted for crimes punishable by life imprisonment), the Court concluded that his case was of sufficient interest to the Congolese authorities to make it likely that he would be detained and interrogated upon his arrival at the airport and that he would be subjected to treatment contrary to Article 3 ECHR if deported.[662]

When it comes to alleged risks of ill treatment on account of religious beliefs or affiliations, the Court takes into account considerations similar to those with regard to political issues.[663] However, so far there are only few cases in which complainants have successfully invoked a risk of ill treatment mainly because of their religious affiliation (not taking into account the cases concerning the transfer of individuals considered to be Islamic extremists and suspected of terrorist activities). One case concerned the expulsion of a Christian Copt to Egypt in 2013.[664] The Court held that, even though reliable sources reported that members of the Copt minority were frequently subjected to violence and persecution, they were not generally at risk of ill treatment in Egypt. The applicant had, however, established that he was personally at risk of being subjected to ill treatment because he had been subjected to persecution before and because he had been convicted *in absentia* for proselytism. The Court considered therefore that the applicant would be a likely target for persecution by Islamists, whether he were held in detention in Egypt or able to live in liberty. It concluded that the applicant would be at risk of ill treatment by the Egyptian authorities in case of removal.[665] Another case concerned a Pakistani who had converted to the Ahmadiyya religion after he had married.[666] The Court held that the applicant was not perceived as a simple practioner of that religion by the Pakistani authorities but that he was wanted for proselytising. In light of this marked profile and the general situation for Ahmadis in Pakistan, the

---

661   ECtHR, *Z.N. v. France*, 14 November 2013, no. 40042/11.

662   *Ibid.*, § 79.

663   Fornerod 2010, p. 319.

664   ECtHR, *M.E. v. France*, 6 June 2013, no. 50094/10.

665   *Ibid.*, §§ 50–52. The judgment was adopted just before the Muslim Brotherhood lost governmental power in Egypt in July 2013.

666   ECtHR, *N.K. v. France*, 19 December 2013, no. 7974/11, §§ 42–47.

Court concluded that there was a real risk of ill treatment for him in case of re-turn to Pakistan.[667] Two cases concerned Iranian nationals who had converted to Christianity.[668] In the correspondent judgments adopted in 2010, the Court did not explicitly assess the particular situation of Christians in Iran. It based the violation mainly on the fact that the Turkish authorities had not meaning-fully assessed the applicants' claims and that the UNHCR had recognised them as refugees.[669] However, in *F.G. v. Sweden* decided at chamber level in January 2014, the Court appeared not bothered by the fact that the national migration authorities had not paid much attention to risks arising for the applicant in Iran due to his conversion to Christianity, even though they were aware of that risk factor.[670] It rejected the complaint namely with the following reasoning:

> As regards the applicant's conversion, the Court observes that the appli-cant expressly stated, before the domestic authorities, that he did not wish to invoke his religious affiliation as a ground for asylum, since he felt that this was a private matter. The Court notes that the applicant had the op-portunity to raise the question of his conversion during the oral hearing be-fore the Migration Court but chose not to. This stance ultimately changed when the expulsion order against him became enforceable. Moreover, the applicant has claimed that he converted to Christianity only after arrival in Sweden and he has kept his faith a private matter. Against this back-ground, and apart from the possible publication of the applicant's im-age in connection with broadcasted church services, the transmission of which to the Iranian authorities is merely speculative, the Court finds that there is nothing to indicate that the Iranian authorities are aware of his conversion. Consequently, the Court considers that the applicant would not face a risk of ill-treatment by the Iranian authorities on this ground.[671]

In their dissenting opinion, the judges Zupančič, Power-Forde and Lemmens criticized the contradiction to the Court's practice in previous cases with regard to the lack of proper assessment at national level.[672] Moreover, they

---

667   *Ibid.*, §§ 46 and 47.

668   ECtHR, *Z.N.S. v. Turkey*, 19 January 2010, no. 21896/08, §§ 47–50; ECtHR, *M.B. and Others v. Turkey*, 15 June 2010, no. 36009/08, §§ 32–35.

669   *Ibid.*

670   ECtHR, *F.G. v. Sweden*, 16 January 2014, no. 43611/11 (not in force – referral to Grand Chamber).

671   *Ibid.*, § 41.

672   See in particular the contrast to ECtHR, *Z.N.S. v. Turkey* cited just above.

disapproved the fact that with its reasoning on the Iranian authorities' lack of awareness with regard to the applicants' conversion, the majority implicitly endorsed the Swedish government's argument according to which no risk should arise for the applicant as long as he does not bring his religious affiliation to the attention of the Iranian authorities by publicly practicing it. The Luxembourg Court of Justice had in fact rejected this problematical line of reasoning with regard to the definition of a refugee in *Y and Z v. Bundesrepublik Deutschland*.[673] It is indeed awkward for an institution like the Strasbourg Court, whose aim is to protect human rights, to expect individuals to refrain from practicing their religious freedom to avoid ill treatment. The judgment *F.G. v. Sweden* was adopted by four votes to three and a referral to the Grand Chamber was accepted so there is a chance that the Court will correct its approach. However, as discussed in the comparative section 3.3.3b below, Strasbourg has unfortunately taken a similarly problematic direction in a complaint concerning an alleged risk of ill treatment for homosexuality.

The Court has rejected further claims in which persecution on religious grounds was alleged: in the case *Y. v. Russia* decided in December 2008, the Court observed that according to international reports, Falun Gong members were under threat of persecution in China.[674] However, it noted that there were differences in the treatment of active members and ordinary practitioners so that each case should be assessed on an individual basis. Members holding a prominent place in the movement would be particularly at risk. In the instant case, the complainant had failed to adduce any reliable evidence showing that the Chinese authorities knew him as an active member or that his involvement could be regarded as sufficiently deep to put him at a real risk of ill treatment upon his return.[675] In the case *F.H. v. Sweden*, the complainant had alleged, *inter alia*, that he would be persecuted or even killed in Iraq because of his Christian faith.[676] The Court rejected the claim in 2009 noting that the reported attacks directed against Christians in Iraq had been carried out by individuals rather than by organized groups and that the complainant would be able to seek the protection of the Iraqi authorities.[677] In June 2013, the Court rejected six complaints of Christian Iraqis from Baghdad, Mosul and

---

673 See CJEU, Joined Cases C-71/11 and C-99/11, *Y and Z v. Bundesrepublik Deutschland*, 5 September 2012, in the context of refugee status.

674 ECtHR, *Y. v. Russia*, 4 December 2008, no. 20113/07, § 86.

675 *Ibid.*, §§ 83–91.

676 ECtHR, *F.H. v. Sweden*, 20 January 2009, no. 32621/06.

677 *Ibid.*, § 97.

Kirkuk.[678] It observed that the situation for Christians in southern and central Iraq had escalated since 2009. A high number of attacks conducted by organised extremist groups, apparently specifically targeting Christians, had been recorded in recent years. The Court further referred to the UNHCR and other sources stating that Christians form a vulnerable minority in the southern and central parts of Iraq. It even recognized that the authorities in these parts of the country were probably unable to protect Christians and other religious minorities. However, the Court concluded that, irrespective of the question of whether there was a general risk to Christians in southern and central parts of Iraq, the Kurdistan region was a viable alternative for them to seek refuge. Consequently, their deportation to Iraq would not involve a violation of Article 3 ECHR.[679] The Court's problematic approach with regard to 'internal flight alternatives' is discussed in chapter 4 section 3.4.1a.

It is not only personal activities or convictions that can put persons at risk in certain countries but also their social backgrounds and their association with family members. The Court has recognized that 'the situation of the applicant's family in the home country is a relevant factor in assessing the risk of ill-treatment.'[680] In *Y.P. and L.P. v. France* submitted by a Belarusian couple, the Court stated that the wife, being married to a Belarusian political opponent, would be exposed to intimidations or inhuman treatment if deported. On that occasion, the Court cited the EU Council Directive 2004/83/EC of 29 April 2004 on minimum standards for the qualification and status of third-country nationals or stateless persons as refugees[681] and the *Handbook on Procedures and Criteria for Determining Refugee Status* under the 1951 Refugee Convention, according to which 'considerations need not necessarily be based

---

678   ECtHR, *A.G.A.M. v. Sweden*, 27 June 2013, no. 71680/10; ECtHR, *M.Y.H. v. Sweden*, 27 June 2013, no. 50859/10; ECtHR, *M.K.N. v. Sweden*, 27 June 2013, no. 72413/10; ECtHR, *N.A.N.S. v. Sweden*, 27 June 2013, no. 68411/10; ECtHR, *N.M.B. v. Sweden*, 27 June 2013, no. 68335/10; ECtHR, *N.M.Y. and Others v. Sweden*, 27 June 2013, no. 72686/10.

679   With regard to the six judgments see ECtHR, *M.Y.H. v. Sweden*, 27 June 2013, no. 50859/10, §§ 56–73.

680   ECtHR, *Azimov v. Russia*, 18 April 2013, no. 67474/11, § 126. See also ECtHR, *Bajsultanov v. Austria*, 12 June 2012, no. 54131/10, § 66, in which the Court pointed out that the applicant's family continued to live in Chechnya after he had left and had not reported any harassment by security forces in the region.

681   The Court referred to paragraph 27 of this EU directive, according to which 'family members, merely due to their relation to the refugee, will normally be vulnerable to acts of persecution in such a manner that could be the basis for refugee status.' On the EU asylum system see Chapter 1 Section 6.

on the applicant's own personal experience. What, for example, happened to his friends and relatives and other members of the same racial or social group may well show that his fear that sooner or later he also will become a victim of persecution is well-founded.'[682] The Court noted that the husband had been arrested and ill-treated in the past. It took into account that the applicants' son had been harassed and intimidated, which indicated that the authorities would still be interested in the family. The Court also took into account the fact that the application for asylum in France was likely to be seen as 'discrediting Belarus,' an offence punishable by imprisonment in Belarus. It further noted that the French immigration authorities had not considered the alleged continuation of the complainants' political activities in France. For all these reasons the Court found that the couple's removal to Belarus would violate Article 3 ECHR.[683] The weight the Court attributes to family bonds will depend, however, on the particular circumstances of the case[684] and the authorities' awareness of an affiliation.[685]

The Court will take into account a complainant's political activities in the host country (so-called *sur place* activities) and other elements occurring after a flight that could put a complainant in danger upon return.[686] In the case *Muminov v. Russia*, the Court objected to the fact that the domestic authorities had not given any consideration to whether the applicant fell within the definition of a refugee *sur place*.[687] In the case *S.F. and Others v. Sweden* decided in May 2012 concerning the deportation of a family of Kurdish and Persian origin to Iran, the applicant's *sur place* activities and incidents after they arrived in Sweden were the main reason for the Court to find that their deportation would violate Article 3 ECHR.[688] The applicants had expressed their opinions against the Iranian regime on prominent Kurdish Internet sites and had taken

---

682   ECtHR, *Y.P. and L.P. v. France*, 2 September 2010, no. 32476/06, § 73.

683   *Ibid.*, §§ 70–74.

684   In ECtHR, *Nnyanzi v. UK*, 8 April 2008, no. 21878/06, §§ 61–65, the Court rejected the complaint of the daughter of a former Ugandan government minister, who had been in detention since 1998 on treason charges. The Court stated, *inter alia*, that there was no reason to believe that someone who had never been politically active in any way would be at risk merely by association with a relative in Uganda.

685   See ECtHR, *N.S. v. Denmark*, 20 January 2011, no. 58359/08, § 94.

686   See, for example, ECtHR, *Chahal v. UK*, 15 November 1996, no. 22414/93, §§ 19–22 and 106; ECtHR, *Mo.M. v. France*, 18 April 2013, no. 18372/10, § 42; ECtHR, *A.A. v. Switzerland*, 7 January 2014, no. 58802/12, §§ 40–43.

687   ECtHR, *Muminov v. Russia*, 11 December 2008, no. 42502/06, § 88.

688   ECtHR, *S.F. and Others v. Sweden*, 15 May 2012, no. 52077/10, §§ 67–71.

leading roles in an exile committee for the support of Kurdish prisoners. The Court observed that the country information on Iran confirmed that Iranian authorities effectively monitored Internet communications and regime critics both within and outside Iran.[689] The Court reasoned similarly in *A.A. v. Switzerland* decided in January 2014 with regard to a Sudanese regime opponent who was politically active in Switzerland.[690] The judges took note of the fact that the Swiss government disputed the genuineness of his activities. It acknowledged that 'it is generally very difficult to assess in cases regarding *sur place* activities whether a person is genuinely interested in the political cause or has only become involved in it in order to create post-flight grounds.' Hence, it would take factors into account 'such as whether the applicant was a political activist prior to fleeing his home country, and whether he played an active role in making his asylum case known to the public in the respondent State.'[691] However, in this particular case, the general human rights situation in Sudan played a more important role for the Court than these criteria. Noting that it has been acknowledged that the Sudanese government monitors activities of political opponents abroad and that not only leaders and high-profile people but also those merely suspected of supporting opposition movements are at risk of ill treatment in Sudan, it concluded that the removal of the applicant would violate Article 3 ECHR.[692]

In the case *N. v. Finland*, the Court had taken into account the publicity of the applicant's case as a former member of Mobutu's security forces. In that connection, it noted that it was relevant that the applicant himself did not appear to have played any active role in making his asylum case known to the public or other DRC nationals.[693] The Court has made a similar observation in *A.A. v. Switzerland* just described[694] and in the case *Kolesnik* concerning an extradition to Turkmenistan.[695] The statements are surprising since in light of the absolute protection afforded by Article 3 ECHR, it should not be relevant whether a complainant has contributed to the publicity of his case and thus to an enhanced risk of ill treatment.[696] However, a complainant's role in the

---

689   *Ibid.*, §§ 67–71.

690   ECtHR, *A.A. v. Switzerland*, 7 January 2014, no. 58802/12.

691   *Ibid.*, § 41.

692   *Ibid.*, § 43. See also ECtHR, *A.A. v. France*, 15 January 2015, no. 18039/11 and ECtHR, *A.F. v. France*, 15 January 2015, no. 80086/13, in which the Court found that the deportation of the two non-Arabic applicants to Sudan would be in violation of Art. 3 ECHR.

693   ECtHR, *N. v. Finland*, 26 July 2005, no. 38885/02, § 165.

694   ECtHR, *A.A. v. Switzerland*, 7 January 2014, no. 58802/12, § 41.

695   ECtHR, *Kolesnik v. Russia*, 10 June 2010, no. 26876/08, § 70.

696   See the corresponding note in Wouters 2009, p. 266.

publicity of his case could be of relevance if a complainant's attempt to attract the public's attention appears designed merely to assist his case and therefore undermines his general credibility with regard to the seriousness of his fear of ill treatment in his home country.

The fact that the applicant has submitted an asylum claim abroad will sometimes be considered as one risk element amongst others.[697] In *S.H. v. United Kingdom* the Court gave particular weight to that fact.[698] In this case, the applicant alleged that his removal to Bhutan would expose him to a risk of ill treatment on account of his Nepalese ethnicity and his status as a failed asylum seeker. The Court noted that experts on Bhutan had expressed concerns that the applicant would be imprisoned and tortured as a failed asylum seeker who had publicly spoken against the government. Against the background of discriminatory treatment afforded to ethnic Nepalese in Bhutan and a lack of information as to the conditions there, the Court found a violation of Article 3 ECHR if the applicant were to be removed.[699] International procedures can also become a risk element. They usually get more publicity than national procedures and are therefore more likely to be taken note of by the authorities of receiving states.[700] In *Shamayev and Others* the Court observed the 'extremely alarming and new phenomenon' that individuals of Chechen origin who lodged applications with the Court were often persecuted in Chechnya.[701]

It should finally be taken into account that in the majority of the judgments in which the Court found a violation of the principle of non-refoulement, the risk of ill treatment was connected with a certain risk of arrest or detention in the receiving country. Although the Court recognizes that it is difficult for

---

697   See, for example, ECtHR, *Hilal v. UK*, 6 March 2001, no. 45276/99, § 65 (Zanzibar); ECtHR, *N. v. Finland*, 26 July 2005, no. 38885/02, § 165 (DRC); ECtHR, *N.A. v. UK*, 17 July 2008, no. 25904/07, § 146 (Sri Lanka).

698   ECtHR, *S.H. v. UK*, 15 June 2010, no. 19956/06, § 67.

699   *Ibid.*, §§ 69–72. The Court tends to interpret an extensive lack of information with regard to a particular human rights situation in favour of the complainant; see also ECtHR, *Sufi and Elmi v. UK*, 28 June 2011, nos. 8319/07 and 11449/07, § 271.

700   See ECtHR, *T.N. and S.N. v. Denmark*, 20 January 2011, no. 36517/08, § 115, in which the Court noted in the risk assessment that because of the anonymity granted in the international procedure, there was no indication that the Sri Lankan authorities would be aware of the complaints or the failed asylum requests.

701   See ECtHR, *Shamayev and Others v. Georgia and Russia*, 12 April 2005, no. 36378/02, §§ 366. This statement was one main element distinguishing the case of the one applicant in which the Court found a violation of the principle of non-refoulement from those of five other applicants treated within the same judgment, who had been deported years before and for which the Court found no violation.

complainants to obtain direct documentary evidence proving that the authorities of the receiving country are seeking them for arrest or detention, it will attach much weight to documents actually submitted such as warrants or court summonses.[702] The Court will also take into account whether the time elapsed since a complainant's political activities or other actions might have diminished the authorities' interest in him.[703]

Past Ill Treatment

In its risk assessment, the Court will take past ill treatment of a complainant into account.[704] Being focused on the present risk of ill treatment, the Court has nevertheless rejected several complaints in which applicants had been ill treated before their flight, pointing out that the situation in their country had changed meanwhile, or that the time passed since the alleged events would have diminished the perpetrators' interest in the complainant.[705] In the case *D.N.W. v. Sweden* decided in December 2012, the Court accepted that the applicant might have been detained and subjected to ill treatment in Ethiopia.[706] It found, however, 'in agreement with the Swedish authorities, that the main issue at hand is whether it has been substantiated that the applicant would be at a real risk of being subjected to such treatment upon return.'[707] Observing that the applicant appeared to have been travelling and preaching in public 'without the Ethiopian authorities showing any adverse interest in him,' it did not attach much weight to the applicant's past experiences and rejected the

---

702   See ECtHR, *Said v. Netherlands*, 5 July 2005, no. 2345/02, § 49; ECtHR, *Bader and Kanbor v. Sweden*, 8 November 2005, no. 13284/04, § 44; ECtHR, *Karim v. Sweden*, 4 July 2006, no. 24171/05 (decision); ECtHR, *Al-Husni v. Bosnia and Herzegovina*, 7 February 2012, no. 3727/08, § 53; ECtHR, *Mo.M. v. France*, 18 April 2013, no. 18372/10, § 41.

703   See, for example, ECtHR, *N.A. v. UK*, 17 July 2008, no. 25904/07, § 145 (Sri Lanka); ECtHR, *XA. v. France*, 25 May 2010, no. 36457/08 (decision; RDC); ECtHR, *Bajsultanov v. Austria*, 12 June 2012, no. 54131/10, §§ 65–72 (Chechnya); ECtHR, *S.R. v. France,* 19 June 2012, no. 17859/09 (decision; Sri Lanka).

704   See, for example, ECtHR, *Hilal v. UK*, 6 March 2001, no. 45276/99, §§ 61–64; ECtHR, *Nnyanzi v. UK*, 8 April 2008, no. 21878/06, § 58; ECtHR, *Gaforov v. Russia*, 21 October 2010, no. 25404/09, § 135; ECtHR, *Shakurov v. Russia*, 5 June 2012, no. 55822/10, § 130; ECtHR, *Mo.M. v. France*, 18 April 2013, no. 18372/10, §§ 39–44.

705   See, for example, ECtHR, *Cruz Varas and Others v. Sweden*, 20 March 1991, no. 15576/89, §§ 77 and 80; ECtHR, *Vilvarajah and Others v. UK*, 30 October 1991, nos. 13163/87 and further, §§ 104 and 109–110; ECtHR, *Venkadajalasarma v. Netherlands*, 17 February 2004, no. 58510/00, §§ 64 and 66–69.

706   ECtHR, *D.N.W. v. Sweden*, 6 December 2012, no. 29946/10, § 42.

707   *Ibid.*

complaint.[708] In her dissenting opinion, judge Power-Forde (joined by judge Zupančič) criticized this, commenting that to expect an applicant who has already been tortured to prove that he will be tortured again if deported is going too far. In her opinion, and referring to the judgment *R.C. v. Sweden*[709] and the UNHCR's *Handbook on Procedures and Criteria for Determining Refugee Status*, the onus of proof should have shifted to the state authorities in this case.

It is rare that the mere fact that a complainant has been ill-treated in the past has led to a shift in the burden of proof in the Court's practice. To be cited is the case *R.C. v. Sweden* concerning the expulsion of a man to Iran, who alleged that after having participated in demonstrations against the Iranian government in 2001, he had been detained and ill-treated.[710] Medical reports (one of them arranged by the Swedish authorities at the Court's request) strongly indicating that the complainant had been tortured in the past provoked a shift in the burden of proof to the government. According to the Court, the medical evidence substantiated the applicant's claim and outweighed inconsistencies in his story. In light of the current human rights situation in Iran and the fact that the complainant had no documents that would allow him to enter Iran without attracting the authorities' attention, the Court eventually found a violation of Article 3 ECHR.[711] In his dissenting opinion, the Swedish judge Fura criticized the shift in the burden of proof in the case as not following the established case law of the Court. It is true that it is rather unusual for the mere fact of past torture to have provoked such a shift in the Court's practice.[712] However, another such exception is *R.J. v. France* decided in September 2013 concerning a deportation of an ethnic Tamil to Sri Lanka.[713] The Court considered that a medical certificate submitted by the applicant had not adequately

---

708 *Ibid.*, §§ 40–45.

709 ECtHR, *R.C. v. Sweden*, 9 March 2010, no. 41827/07.

710 *Ibid.* This case has also been discussed in Chapter 4 Section 1.1.2 on the burden of proof.

711 *Ibid*, §§ 50–57.

712 For other cases tending in that direction see *Mo.M. v. France*, 18 April 2013, no. 18372/10, §§ 38–44 (Chad); ECtHR, *R.J. v. France*, 19 September 2013, no. 10466/11 (Sri Lanka). For that reason, it does not appear that the Court has introduced an 'important point of principle' in the judgment *R.C.*, as is suggested by the judge Power-Forde joined by judge Zupančič in her dissenting opinion concerning ECtHR, *D.N.W. v. Sweden*, 6 December 2012, no. 29946/10. See in this sense also the analysis of *R.C.* in ECtHR, *I v. Sweden*, 5 September 2013, no. 61204/09, §§ 62–69 (however, in this case, the Court attached much importance to the fact that the applicant had visible scars on his body, which could indicate that he took active part in the second war in Chechnya).

713 ECtHR, *R.J. v. France*, 19 September 2013, no. 10466/11.

been taken into account by the national authorities, despite the fact that the seriousness and the recent character of the injuries described in this certificate constitute a 'strong presumption' of past treatment contrary to Article 3 ECHR in Sri Lanka.[714] Against this background, the Court concluded that the government had not properly objected to the applicant's allegations, and that he had established a real risk of ill treatment in case of removal.[715]

Evidence of past ill treatment is not only relevant for substantiating a claim. Under particular circumstances, it can also constitute as such a risk-enhancing factor: in the lead case *N.A. v. United Kingdom* concerning the expulsion of a Tamil to Sri Lanka, the Court noted that torture-related scars on the body of a person could enhance the likelihood of ill treatment upon return, since they could raise the interest of the Sri Lankan authorities in their fight against the Tamil Tigers.[716] However, the presence of scars was *as such* not sufficient to establish that there was a real risk of the complainant being subjected to ill treatment on return.[717] In conclusion, the fact that a complainant has been ill-treated in the past can be an indication of a future risk of ill treatment, but it will seldom constitute a 'substantial ground' for believing that there is a real risk of ill treatment in case of deportation.[718]

c   *Focus: Recognition as a Refugee*

It has been made clear that the protection against refoulement offered by the Court is wider than that of the Refugee Convention with regard to serious criminals or persons considered a threat to national security.[719] In addition, the Court's protection is not restricted to ill treatment for specific reasons such as the individual's race, religion, nationality or social or political affiliation.

714   *Ibid.*, § 42, 'La Cour considère que ce document constitue une pièce particulièrement importante du dossier. En effet, la nature, la gravité et le caractère récent des blessures constituent une forte présomption de traitement contraire à l'article 3 de la Convention infligé au requérant dans son pays d'origine.'

715   *Ibid.*, § 43.

716   ECtHR, *N.A. v. UK*, 17 July 2008, no. 25904/07, §§ 144 and 147. See similar ECtHR, *I v. Sweden*, 5 September 2013, no. 61204/09, §§ 62–69 (Chechnya).

717   As discussed in the section 3.2.1.b of this Chapter, there were several risk factors that, taken together, led to the Court's conclusion that the complainant's return to Sri Lanka would be contrary to Art. 3 ECHR. This is further confirmed by other complaints concerning the return to Sri Lanka of Tamils who had scars from past ill treatments, but who were not successful before the Court; see, for example, ECtHR, *Venkadajalasarma v. Netherlands*, 17 February 2004, no. 58510/00, §§ 64–69 and the dissenting opinion of judge Mularoni; ECtHR, *T.N. v. Denmark*, 20 January 2011, no. 20594/08, §§ 103–106; ECtHR, *E.G. v. UK*, 31 May 2011, no. 41178/08, §§ 65–81.

718   See also Thurin 2012, pp. 187–190.

719   See Chapter 1 Section 4 and Chapter 3 Section 2.4.

Treatments falling outside 'persecution' for those grounds within the meaning of the Geneva Convention, for example inhuman prison conditions, can amount to ill treatment within the meaning of Article 3 ECHR.[720] The Court has often held that it does not 'itself examine the actual asylum applications or verify how the states honour their obligations under the Geneva Convention.'[721] It has repeatedly stated that the ECHR does not include a right to political asylum.[722]

However, although the scope of protection against refoulement offered by the Refugee Convention is not identical to that offered by the ECHR, it is evident that it overlaps to a large extent.[723] The elements in the Court's assessment under Article 3 ECHR are usually just as relevant in the assessment of the existence of a risk of 'persecution' within the meaning of the Refugee Convention.[724] In its judgments, the Court in fact uses the term 'persecution' as an indicator for a risk of ill treatment in the sense of Article 3 ECHR.[725] In addition, if a complainant has refugee status but is exempt from the protection against removal *only* because of a criminal conviction or because he is considered a threat to national security, the Court is likely to consider the deportation as being in violation of Article 3 ECHR.[726] In cases in which the national authorities have completed no proper risk assessment under the Refugee Convention or Article 3 ECHR, but in which the UNHCR has made an individual risk assessment and recognized the applicant as a refugee, the Court almost

---

720 See the Court's explicit statements in ECtHR, *Ryabikin v. Russia*, 19 June 2008, no. 8320/04, §§ 118 and 120. The Court criticized Russia for having examined the applicant's case only in light of the Refugee Convention and not under Art. 3 ECHR.

721 See, among many others, ECtHR, *T.I. v. UK*, 7 March 2000, no. 43844/98 (decision); ECtHR, *Müslim v. Turkey*, 26 April 2005, no. 53566/99, § 72; ECtHR, *Samina v. Sweden*, 20 October 2011, no. 55463/09, § 48; ECtHR, *A.G.R. v. Netherlands*, 12 January 2016, no. 13442/08, § 54.

722 See, among many others, ECtHR, *Vilvarajah and Others v. UK*, 30 October 1991, nos. 13163/87 and further, § 102; ECtHR, *Salah Sheekh v. Netherlands*, 11 January 2007, no. 1948/04, § 135; ECtHR, *Nnyanzi v. UK*, 8 April 2008, no. 21878/06, § 53; ECtHR, *Yefimova v. Russia*, 19 February 2013, no. 39786/09, § 209.

723 See on this also Chapter 1 Section 4.

724 Thurin 2012, p. 245.

725 See, for example, ECtHR, *Shamayev and Others v. Georgia and Russia*, 12 April 2005, no. 36378/02, §§ 366; ECtHR, *Nnyanzi v. UK*, 8 April 2008, no. 21878/06, § 61; ECtHR, *Ahorugeze v. Sweden*, 27 October 2011, no. 37075/09, § 90; ECtHR, *I.K. v. Austria*, 28 March 2013, no. 2964/12, § 72; ECtHR, *M.E. v. France*, 6 June 2013, no. 50094/10, § 51.

726 See ECtHR, *Chahal v. UK*, 15 November 1996, no. 22414/93, §§ 75–101; ECtHR, *Ahmed v. Austria*, 17 December 1996, no. 25964/94, §§ 42–47; ECtHR, *A.B. v. Sweden*, 31 August 2004, no. 24697/04 (decision); ECtHR, *Baysakov and Others v. Ukraine*, 18 February 2010, no. 54131/08, § 50; ECtHR, *Mawaka v. Netherlands*, 1 June 2010, no. 29031/04, §§ 12, 14 and

automatically relies on the UNHCR's conclusions.[727] Generally, when the UNHCR recognizes an applicant as a refugee, the Court will attach due weight to it.[728] An interesting case is also *I.K. v. Austria* decided in March 2013.[729] It concerned an applicant from Chechnya whose father had worked for a separatist leader and, as a result, had been persecuted by the Russian authorities together with his family. Security forces had eventually murdered the applicant's father. While the mother had obtained refugee status in Austria, the applicant's request had been denied. The Court criticized the fact that the Austrian authorities had not brought forward any argument as regards the discrepancy between the assessment of the applicant's asylum request and his mother's status as a recognised refugee. It found that there was no 'indication that the applicant was at lesser risk of persecution upon a return to Russia than his mother,' who had gained asylum solely because of the former position and murder of her husband.[730] Noting that occurrences of targeted human-rights violations, such as abductions, killings or beatings, still seem to be happening on a regular basis in Chechnya, the Court came to the conclusion that there was a real risk of ill treatment for the applicant if returned to Russia.[731] The Court ruled similarly in *M.G. v. Bulgaria* concerning the extradition of a man accused of offenses relating to an armed Chechen insurgent group.[732] The applicant had fled the criminal charges in Russia and obtained refugee status with his family in Poland and Germany. After being intercepted at the Bulgarian-Romanian border, he was detained pending extradition by the Bulgarian

---

43–51. See also ECtHR, *Bajsultanov v. Austria*, 12 June 2012, no. 54131/10, §§ 64–72, in which no violation was found but in which the Court pointed out that the Austrian authorities had thoroughly examined the applicant's personal circumstances in the proceedings concerning the lifting of his asylum status.

727   See ECtHR, *Abdolkhani and Karimnia v. Turkey*, 22 September 2009, no. 30471/08, §§ 82 83 and 91; ECtHR, *Z.N.S. v. Turkey*, 19 January 2010, no. 21896/08, §§ 47–50 ECtHR, *Khaydarov v. Russia*, 20 May 2010, no. 21055/09, §§ 108–115; ECtHR, *M.B. and Others v. Turkey*, 15 June 2010, no. 36009/08, §§ 32–35; ECtHR, *Dbouba v. Turkey,* 13 July 2010, no. 15916/09, §§ 41–43.

728   See the cases in which the Court found a violation of Art. 3 ECHR by pointing out, *inter alia*, that the complainants had been recognized as refugees by the UNHCR: ECtHR, *Jabari v. Turkey*, 11 July 2000, no. 40035/98, § 41; ECtHR, *Ismoilov v. Russia*, 24 April 2008, no. 2947/06, § 125; ECtHR, *Charahili v. Turkey*, 13 April 2010, no. 46605/07, §§ 21 and 59; ECtHR, *Karimov v. Russia*, 29 July 2010, no. 54219/08, § 100; ECtHR, *Gaforov v. Russia*, 21 October 2010, no. 25404/09, § 137; ECtHR, *Rustamov v. Russia*, 3 July 2012, no. 11209/10, §§ 51 and 129.

729   ECtHR, *I.K. v. Austria*, 28 March 2013, no. 2964/12.

730   *Ibid.*, §§ 73–78.

731   *Ibid.*, §§ 79–83.

732   ECtHR, *M.G. v. Bulgaria*, 25 March 2014, no. 59297/12, § 88.

authorities. The Court stated that it is not entitled to supervise the Geneva Convention or the respect of EU legislation in asylum matters. However, it considered that it must take into account the granted refugee status in Poland and Germany. It considered this as an 'important indication' of sufficient evidence of persecution risk at the time it was granted. However, the Court made clear that this fact remained a 'starting point' for its assessment of the current risk to the applicant.[733] Based on sources reporting frequent ill treatment of detainees suspected of operating in armed groups in the North Caucasus, such as the applicant, the Court ruled that his extradition to Russia would violate Article 3 ECHR.[734] Generally, as has been shown, the fact that an applicant (or individuals with similar backgrounds) is considered persecuted in the sense of the Refugee Convention by national asylum authorities is taken by the Court as a strong indication that there is a real risk of being subjected to treatment contrary to Article 3 ECHR in case of removal.

However, not every form of persecution within the meaning of the Refugee Convention necessarily amounts to treatment contrary to Article 3 ECHR.[735] In other words, the protection offered by Article 3 ECHR is not always broader than that offered by the Refugee Convention.[736] On this topic the case *Y. v. Russia* on the deportation of a Falun Gong member to China is particularly interesting.[737] The Court observed serious violations of human rights in China for individuals identified as Falun Gong practitioners, especially those holding a prominent place in the movement. However, the applicant had not established that the Chinese authorities knew him to be an active member. The Court hence ruled that there was no violation of Article 3 ECHR. Noting the 'difference in scope of protection afforded by Article 3 of the Convention and by the UN Convention on the Protection of Refugees and the particular circumstances of the present case,' the Court did not find that the fact that the complainant had been recognized as a refugee by the UNHCR Office in Moscow 'alone justifies altering its conclusions as to the well-foundedness of the

---

733 *Ibid.*

734 *Ibid.*, §§ 84–87 and 89–96.

735 See Wouters 2009, p. 242, citing the example of a detention of several months for a political and non-violent protest or Chetail 2004, pp. 180–181, naming the cumulative violations of different human rights not amounting to inhuman treatment.

736 See on this also Chapter 1 Section 4. See also the Court's indication in *ECtHR, T.I. v. UK*, 7 March 2000, no. 43844/98 (decision), according to which the 'examination of the English courts will go further than this Court, since under domestic law an applicant may claim a right to asylum which is not guaranteed by the European Convention on Human Rights.'

737 ECtHR, *Y. v. Russia*, 4 December 2008, no. 20113/07.

applicant's claim.'[738] This example shows that an assessment by the UNHCR does not generally disburden the Court from performing an assessment under Article 3 ECHR.[739] However, cases like *Y. v. Russia* are rare in the Court's practice.[740] Looking at the case law as a whole one can say that although the Court consistently points out that it does not supervise the Refugee Convention, the facts that a complainant has been recognized as a refugee by the UNHCR or national authorities, or that he is solely exempt from the protection under the Refugee Convention for security reasons, are elements that considerably increase the applicant's chance of success before the Court.

3.3.2   Committee
a   *The Complainant's Credibility*
The complainant's credibility is often the crux of a case. It might depend on objective elements such as presented evidence or the human rights situation in the applicant's home country. It may, however, also depend on the persuasiveness of the applicant in the national procedure. The Committee in its General Comment on Article 3 CAT addresses the latter when stating that it has to take into account whether there are 'factual inconsistencies in the claim of the author' and, if so, if they are relevant.[741]

Inconsistencies, contradictions and a lack of detail as well as the late submission of important facts can undermine a complainant's credibility in a decisive way.[742] The same is true for the presentation of forged documents.[743] The Committee does not require applicants to prove or to submit evidence

---

738 *Ibid.*, §§ 84–91.

739 See also ECtHR, *N.A. v. UK*, 17 July 2008, no. 25904/07, § 122, in which the Court stated that where the UNHCR's concerns are focused on general socioeconomic and humanitarian considerations, it will accord less weight to them since 'such considerations do not necessarily have a bearing on the question of a real risk to an applicant of ill-treatment within the meaning of Article 3 ECHR.'

740 Cases also going in this direction are ECtHR, *Husseini v. Sweden*, 13 October 2011, no. 10611/09, §§ 95–98; ECtHR, *Yefimova v. Russia*, 19 February 2013, no. 39786/09, § 209.

741 ComAT, General Comment No. 1 on Art. 3 CAT (1997), § 8 (f) and (g).

742 See, for example, ComAT, *X.Y. v. Switzerland*, 15 May 2001, no. 128/1999, §§ 6.7–6.8 and 8.5; ComAT, *E.T.B. v. Denmark*, 30 April 2002, no. 146/1999, § 10; ComAT, *H.K.H. v. Sweden*, 19 November 2002, no. 204/2002, § 6.3; ComAT, *M.O. v. Denmark*, 23 November 2003, no. 209/2002, §§ 6.5–6.6; ComAT, *Zare v. Sweden*, 12 May 2006, no. 256/2004, § 9.6; ComAT, *A.A.M. v. Sweden*, 23 May 2012, no. 413/2010, § 9.6; ComAT, *Y.Z.S. v. Australia*, 23 November 2012, no. 417/2010, § 7.6; ComAT, *D.Y. v. Sweden*, 21 May 2013, no. 463/2011, §§ 9.5–9.9.

743 ComAT, *Zare v. Sweden*, 12 May 2006, no. 256/2004, § 9.5; ComAT, *A.M. v. France*, 5 May 2010, no. 302/2006, §§ 13.5 and 13.6; ComAT, *M.S.G. v. Switzerland*, 30 May 2011, no. 352/2008,

for all the facts stated, but it must consider their claims to be 'sufficiently sub-stantiated and reliable.'[744] However, the absence of *any evidence* pointing to the existence of a risk will not speak in favour of a complainant's credibility.[745] In this context, it should also be noted that a complainant should be able to explain how he came into possession of any evidentiary documents.[746]

Contradictory statements from complainants about their nationality or identity in the asylum procedure can undermine their credibility, since they make it more difficult for the authorities to assess the risk upon return.[747] However, the Committee has been quite generous in accepting explanations on that matter in some cases.[748] The Committee focusses on the 'general ve-racity' of a claim rather than on single inconsistencies or a lack of details in an applicant's presentation of the facts.[749] It is particularly generous in accepting inconsistencies or omissions in cases in which it is established by medical evi-dence that the complainant has been a victim of torture and is still suffering as a result.[750] When state parties invoke inconsistencies in such cases, the Com-mittee frequently replies that 'complete accuracy is seldom to be expected by victims of torture,' especially when the victim suffers from post-traumatic stress syndrome and that inconsistencies that may exist in an applicant's pre-sentation of the facts are only material if they raise doubts about the general

---

§§ 11.4–11.6; ComAT, *E.L. v. Switzerland*, 15 November 2011, no. 351/2008, § 9.6; ComAT, *M.D.T. v. Switzerland*, 14 May 2012, no. 382/2009, § 7.6.

744   See, for example, ComAT, *H.D. v. Switzerland*, 30 April 1999, no. 112/1998, § 6.4; ComAT, *M.P.S. v. Australia*, 30 April 2002, no. 138/1999, § 7.3.

745   See, for example, ComAT, *J.A.M.O. v. Canada*, 9 May 2008, no. 293/2006, § 10.6; ComAT, *T.I. v. Canada*, 15 November 2010, no. 333/2007, §§ 7.5 and 8; ComAT, *M.B. v. Switzerland*, 31 May 2013, no. 439/2010, §§§ 7.7 and 7.9; ComAT, *Y.B.F., S.A.Q. and Y.Y. v. Switzerland*, 31 May 2013, no. 467/2011, § 7.6.

746   See, for example, ComAT, *A.M. v. France*, 5 May 2010, no. 302/2006, § 13.5; ComAT, *A.A.M. v. Sweden*, 23 May 2012, no. 413/2010, § 9.7.

747   ComAT, *Chahin v. Sweden*, 30 May 2011, no. 310/2007, § 8.3. See also ComAT, *D.Y. v. Sweden*, 21 May 2013, no. 463/2011, §§ 9.6–9.9.

748   See ComAT, *A. v. Netherlands*, 13 November 1998, no. 91/1997, §§ 3.2, 5.2 and 6.5, in which the Committee accepted the complainant's explanation that he initially had not given his real name because he was afraid. See further ComAT, *Ayas v. Sweden*, 12 November 1998, no. 97/1997, §§ 2.3, 2.4 and 6.5, in which the Committee did not attach weight to the fact that the complainant had destroyed his passport on arrival.

749   See the Committee's clear statements on this approach in ComAT, *K.N., F.W. and S.N. v. Switzerland*, 19 May 2014, no. 481/2011, § 7.7; ComAT, *X. v. Switzerland*, 24 November 2014, no. 470/2011, § 7.6.

750   See also Weissbrodt and Hörtreiter 1999, p. 15; Wouters 2009, p. 549.

veracity of an applicant's claims.[751] According to the Committee 'torture victims cannot be expected to recall entirely consistent facts relating to events of extreme trauma. But they must be prepared to advance such evidence as there is in support of such a claim.'[752] It is the overall story of a complainant and the elements that are pertinent with regard to the risk of torture that have to be credible.[753]

In the case *V.L. v. Switzerland*, the state party argued that the complainant was not credible because it was only in a request for revision after the ordinary asylum procedure that she had stated that the Belarusian police had raped her.[754] The Committee replied that the complainant had given plausible explanations for her delay. She had explained that her husband, who had been present at the ordinary procedure, had forbade her to talk about the sexual abuse. The Committee noted that as soon as her husband had left her and she was freed from his influence, she immediately mentioned the rapes to the Swiss authorities. The Committee also observed that it is well known that victims of sexual abuse withhold facts about their experiences until it appears absolutely necessary to disclose them. Particularly for women, there is often an additional fear of rejection by partners or family members. The Committee also took into account the fact that the complainant had not been represented in the proceedings. It eventually found that the allegations were credible despite their late delivery.[755]

In *Chahin v. Sweden*, the Committee considered that the complainant had provided satisfactory reasons for his delay in submitting medical reports and a Syrian judgment that convicted him for terrorism since he had explained that his application had been prepared by a non-lawyer and that it was only after receiving funds from Amnesty International that he was able to obtain

---

751   ComAT, *Alan v. Switzerland*, 8 May 1996, no. 21/1995, § 11.3; ComAT, *Kioski v. Sweden*, 8 May 1996, no. 41/1996, § 9.3; ComAT, *Tala v. Sweden*, 15 November 1996, no. 43/1996, § 10.3; ComAT, *Haydin v. Sweden*, 20 November 1998, no. 101/1997, § 6.7; ComAT, *Karoui v. Sweden*, 8 May 2002, no. 185/2001, § 10; ComAT, *C.T. and K.M. v. Sweden*, 17 November 2006, no. 279/2005, §§ 7.5 and 7.6.; ComAT, *Ke Chun Rong v. Australia*, 5 November 2012, no. 416/2010, § 7.5; ComAT, *J.K. v. Canada*, 23 November 2015, no. 562/2013, § 10.4; ComAT, *R.G. et al. v. Sweden*, 25 November 2015, no. 586/2014, § 8.6. See comparable ComAT, *A.F. v. Sweden*, 8 May 1998, no. 89/1997, § 6.5; ComAT, *Rios v. Canada*, 23 November 2004, no. 133/1999, § 8.5.

752   ComAT, *E.T.B. v. Denmark*, 30 April 2002, no. 146/1999, § 10.

753   See, for example, ComAT, *A.D. v. Netherlands*, 12 November 1999, no. 96/1997, § 7.4; ComAT, *K.M. v. Switzerland*, 16 November 1999, no. 107/1998, § 6.5.

754   ComAT, *V.L. v. Switzerland*, 20 November 2006, no. 262/2005, § 6.5.

755   *Ibid.*, § 8.8.

the documents.[756] Generally, the Committee will be rather sceptical if it is only at a late phase of a procedure that a complainant introduces important facts or evidence, in particular if such elements are only introduced in response to rejection decisions[757] or if they are only invoked before the Committee.[758] However, if such new elements indicate that the complainant has been tortured in the past, the Committee will usually not ignore them.[759]

According to its own statements, the Committee will give due weight to findings made by the state authorities with regard to a complainant's credibility as long as they appear reasonable and not arbitrary.[760] However, with its very brief reasoning, the Committee is quite unpredictable in its handling of a complainant's credibility.[761] Unfortunately, the Committee is often not very precise in explaining why it makes a different appraisal of an applicant's credibility from that made by the domestic authorities. It has rightly been criticized for decisions in which it relies on disputed facts without explaining why it is doing so.[762] In its first decision on a refoulement complaint in *Mutombo v. Switzerland*, the Committee stated that although it was aware of concerns that the implementation of Article 3 CAT 'might be abused by asylum seekers,' it considered 'that, even if there are doubts about the truthfulness of the facts

---

756   ComAT, *Chahin v. Sweden*, 30 May 2011, no. 310/2007, § 9.5.

757   See ComAT, *X.Y. v. Switzerland*, 15 May 2001, no. 128/1999, §§ 6.7–6.8 and 8.5; ComAT, *E.T.B. v. Denmark*, 30 April 2002, no. 146/1999, § 10; ComAT, *H.K.H. v. Sweden*, 19 November 2002, no. 204/2002, § 6.3; ComAT, *H.B.H., T.N.T., H.J.H., H.O.H., H.R.H. and H.G.H. v. Switzerland*, 29 April 2003, no. 192/2001, § 6.8.

758   See ComAT, *M.B.B. v. Sweden*, 5 May 1999, no. 104/1998, § 6.6; ComAT, *Chorlango v. Sweden*, 22 November 2004, no. 218/2002, § 5.3; ComAT, *A.M. v. France*, 5 May 2010, no. 302/2006, §§ 11.1, 11.2 and 13.5; ComAT, *N.B.-M. v. Switzerland*, 14 November 2011, no. 347/2008, §§ 9.6 and 9.7; ComAT, *S.K. and R.K. v. Sweden*, 21 November 2011, no. 365/2008, § 11.4; ComAT, *G.B.M. v. Sweden*, 14 November 2012, no. 435/2010, § 7.9.

759   See ComAT, *M.M.K. v. Sweden*, 3 May 2005, no. 221/2002, §§ 6.7, 7.4 and 7.5; ComAT, *Z.K. v. Sweden*, 9 May 2008, no. 301/2006, § 8.4; ComAT, *R.K. et al. v. Sweden*, 16 May 2008, no. 309/2006, §§ 5.3, 6.1, 6.2, 8.4 and 8.5; ComAT, *F.K. v. Denmark*, 23 November 2015, no. 580/2014, §§ 5.1 and 7.6. See further Chapter 4 Section 3.3.2.b.

760   ComAT, *M.O. v. Denmark*, 23 November 2003, no. 209/2002, §§ 6.5–6.6; ComAT, *A.K. v. Australia*, 5 May 2004, no. 148/1999, § 6.4; ComAT, *S.U.A. v. Sweden*, 22 November 2004, no. 223/2002, § 6.5. Similar ComAT, *A.M.A. v. Switzerland*, 12 November 2010, no. 344/2008, §§ 7.6.-7.8; ComAT, *B.M.S. v. Sweden*, 25 November 2015, no. 594/2014, § 8.9.

761   In this sense also Wouters 2009, p. 479–480.

762   See the critique of McAdam 2007, p. 123. See also Goodwin-Gill & McAdam 2007, p. 305. As illustrative example see ComAT, *Boily v. Canada*, 14 November 2011, no. 327/2007, §§ 7.1 and 14.5.

adduced by the author, it must ensure that his security is not endangered.'[763] This statement is clearly reflected in the Committee's practice as a whole.

b   *The Complainant's Background History*
              Political and/or Religious Background

According to the Committee, 'the engagement in political or other activities within or outside the State concerned which would appear to make a complainant particularly vulnerable to the risk of being subjected to torture' has to be taken into account in the risk assessment under Article 3 CAT.[764] The Committee has rejected a number of complaints noting that the applicant has a low political profile or has failed to adduce evidence about any political activity of such significance that would attract the interest of the authorities.[765]

However, the degree of activity or the level of political profile required will always depend on the general human rights situation. Since its early case law, the Committee has been particularly worried about the situation for political opponents in Iran[766] and Kurdish PKK activists in Turkey.[767] The Committee

---

763   ComAT, *Mutombo v. Switzerland*, 27 April 1994, no. 13/1993, § 9.2. See also ComAT, *Khan v. Canada*, 15 November 1994, no. 15/1994, § 12.4.

764   ComAT, General Comment No. 1 on Art. 3 CAT (1997), § 8 (e). Recalled, for example, in ComAT, *Jahani v. Switzerland,* 23 May 2011, no. 357/2008, § 9.3.

765   See as recent examples ComAT, *M.Z.A. v. Sweden*, 22 May 2012, no. 424/2010, § 8.4 (Azerbaijan); ComAT, *R.S.M. v. Canada*, 24 May 2013, no. 392/2009, § 7.4 (Togo); ComAT, *M.B. v. Switzerland*, 31 May 2013, no. 439/2010, § 7.8 (Iran), ComAT, *Y.B.F., S.A.Q. and Y.Y. v. Switzerland*, 31 May 2013, no. 467/2011, § 7.7 (Yemen); ComAT, *R.D. v. Switzerland*, 8 November 2013, no. 426/2010, § 9.7 (Ethiopia); ComAT, *M.A.H. and F.H. v. Switzerland*, 17 November 2013, no. 438/2010 (Tunisia); ComAT, *Sivagnanaratnam v. Denmark*, 11 November 2013, no. 429/2010, § 10.6 (Sri Lanka).

766   See the successful complaints concerning members of opposition movements in Iran: ComAT, *Tala v. Sweden*, 15 November 1996, no. 43/1996; ComAT, *Aemei v. Switzerland*, 9 May 1997, 34/1995; ComAT, *A.F. v. Sweden*, 8 May 1998, no. 89/1997; ComAT, *Amini v. Denmark*, 15 November 2010, no. 339/2008; ComAT, *Jahani v. Switzerland,* 23 May 2011, no. 357/2008; ComAT, *Faragollah et al. v. Switzerland*, 21 November 2011, no. 381/2009; ComAT, *Eftekhary v. Norway*, 25 November 2011, no. 312/2007; ComAT, *Mr. X and Mr. Z v. Finland*, 12 May 2014, no. 483/2011 and 485/2011; ComAT, *K.N., F.W. and S.N. v. Switzerland*, 19 May 2014, no. 481/2011; ComAT, *Khademi et al. v. Switzerland*, 14 November 2014, no. 473/2011; ComAT, *X. v. Switzerland*, 24 November 2014, no. 470/2011; ComAT, *Tahmuresi v. Switzerland*, 26 November 2014, no. 489/2012; ComAT, *Azizi v. Switzerland*, 27 November 2014, no. 492/2012.

767   See the successful complaints concerning PKK activists and affiliated individuals: ComAT, *Alan v. Switzerland*, 8 May 1996, no. 21/1995; ComAT, *Ayas v. Sweden*, 12 November 1998, no. 97/1997; ComAT, *Haydin v. Sweden*, 20 November 1998, no. 101/1997; ComAT,

has protected quite low-level activists from such groups.[768] With regard to Iran, the Committee has confirmed its concerns on the human rights situation in several decisions adopted in 2014, in which it found violations of Article 3 CAT.[769] It held that there are continuing reports of detention, torture and public executions of political opponents and that there would be no information according to which this situation had significantly improved since the change in leadership in 2013.[770] Referring to different UN reports, it noted that even low-level opposition activists, including university students, are monitored by the authorities, and that political opponents, human rights defenders, journalists and members of minorities (particularly individuals of Kurdish ethnicity[771]) are arrested, prosecuted and convicted for crimes of political nature.[772] The Committee considered that this is all the more 'worrying in light of the fact that Iran frequently administers the death penalty and applies it without due process and in cases involving certain crimes not meeting international standards for the "most serious" offences.'[773]

Dadar v. Canada, 23 November 2005, no. 258/2004; ComAT, *Pelit v. Azerbaijan*, 1 May 2007, no. 281/2005; ComAT, *Güclü v. Sweden*, 11 November 2010, no. 349/2008; ComAT, *Aytulun and Guclu v. Sweden*, 19 November 2010, no. 373/2009; ComAT, *A.K. v. Switzerland*, 8 May 2015, no. 544/2013; ComAT, *F.K. v. Denmark*, 23 November 2015, no. 580/2014. In some decisions, however, the Committee found that there was no current risk of torture because of the time elapsed since the applicant's political activities, or because the activities for the PKK were not significant enough, see, as recent examples, ComAT, *N.S. v. Switzerland*, 6 May 2010, no. 356/2008; ComAT, *R.A. v. Switzerland*, 20 November 2012, no. 389/2009; ComAT, *Y. v. Switzerland*, 21 May 2013, no. 431/2010, §§ 7.7 and 7.8; ComAT, *Alp v. Denmark*, 14 May 2014, no. 466/2011, §§ 8.5 and 8.6.

768 See ComAT, *Güclü v. Sweden*, 11 November 2010, no. 349/2008 (Turkey); ComAT, *Amini v. Denmark*, 15 November 2010, no. 339/2008 (Iran); ComAT, *Aytulun and Güclü v. Sweden*, 19 November 2010, no. 373/2009 (Turkey); ComAT, *Eftekhary v. Norway*, 25 November 2011, no. 312/2007, §§ 7.4–8 (Iran); ComAT, *X. v. Switzerland*, 24 November 2014, no. 470/2011, §§ 7.5–8 (Iran).

769 See ComAT, *Mr. X and Mr. Z v. Finland*, 12 May 2014, no. 483/2011 and 485/2011; ComAT, *K.N., F.W. and S.N. v. Switzerland*, 19 May 2014, no. 481/2011; ComAT, *Khademi et al. v. Switzerland*, 14 November 2014, no. 473/2011; ComAT, *X. v. Switzerland*, 24 November 2014, no. 470/2011; ComAT, *Tahmuresi v. Switzerland*, 26 November 2014, no. 489/2012; ComAT, *Azizi v. Switzerland*, 27 November 2014, no. 492/2012.

770 ComAT, *K.N., F.W. and S.N. v. Switzerland*, 19 May 2014, no. 481/2011, § 7.6; ComAT, *X. v. Switzerland*, 24 November 2014, no. 470/2011, § 7.5.

771 ComAT, *Mr. X and Mr. Z v. Finland*, 12 May 2014, no. 483/2011 and 485/2011, § 7.3.

772 ComAT, *X. v. Switzerland*, 24 November 2014, no. 470/2011, § 7.8; ComAT, *Azizi v. Switzerland*, 27 November 2014, no. 492/2012, § 8.5.

773 ComAT, *K.N., F.W. and S.N. v. Switzerland*, 19 May 2014. no. 481/2011, § 7.7.

Article 3 CAT 'does not distinguish between the commission of acts, which might later expose the applicant to the risk of torture, in the country of origin or in the receiving country.'[774] In *Aemei v. Switzerland*, it stated that 'even if the activities of which the author is accused in Iran were insufficient for article 3 to apply, his subsequent activities in the receiving country could prove sufficient for application of that article.'[775] This was not the only case concerning a deportation to Iran in which *activities in the host state* were of particular importance (so-called risk *sur place*). In *Jahani v. Switzerland* decided in May 2011, the Committee noted that the complainant was the regional representative for the Democratic Association for Refugees (which is part of the Iranian opposition movement in Switzerland) and had participated in several demonstrations since his arrival in Switzerland.[776] He had further taken part in radio broadcasts where he had expressed his political opinions against the Iranian regime and had written articles in which his name was published. The Committee also noted that the highest Swiss Court in asylum matters had attributed refugee status to another member of the Democratic Association for Refugees who, like him, held a position as a regional representative. Noting the 'extremely worrisome' situation in Iran particularly after the 2009 elections, the Committee concluded:

> Consequently, and in the light of the general human rights situation in the Islamic Republic of Iran that particularly affects human rights defenders and members of the opposition seeking to exercise their right to freedom of expression, and in view of the complainant's political opposition activities in Switzerland, which could suggest that he has attracted the attention of the iranian authorities, the Committee considers that there are substantial grounds for believing that the complainant risks being subjected to torture if returned to the Islamic Republic of Iran.[777]

In November 2011, the Committee took a similar decision for another regional representative of the Democratic Association for Refugees in Switzerland threatened with deportation to Iran.[778] In this case, an important consideration was the fact that the complainant's son had received refugee status 'on the basis of activities comparable to those carried out by his father in the

---

774   ComAT, *Aemei v. Switzerland*, 9 May 1997, 34/1995, § 9.5.

775   *Ibid*, §§ 9.7–9.10.

776   ComAT, *Jahani v. Switzerland*, 23 May 2011, no. 357/2008, § 9.5.

777   *Ibid.*, § 9.10.

778   ComAT, *Faragollah et al. v. Switzerland*, 21 November 2011, no. 381/2009, §§ 9.4–10.

association, in particular the collection of signatures for petitions, the distribution of its monthly magazine, *Kanoun*, and involvement in a radio project.'[779]

The participation in sporadic demonstrations in the receiving country will not normally be sufficient to trigger the application of Article 3 CAT.[780] In the case *T.D. v. Switzerland* concerning a member of the exiled Ethiopian opposition in Switzerland, the Committee noted 'that the decisive factor in assessing the risk of torture on return is whether the person occupies a position of particular responsibility in a movement opposing the regime and thus poses a threat to it.'[781] It agreed with the Swiss government on the fact that simply holding the position as a regional representative for an exiled unit of an opposition party could not be considered as a threat to the Ethiopian government and that it was unlikely that the complainant's activities would have attracted their attention. As can be seen, the Committee is clearly more demanding with regard to the profile of members of the Ethiopian opposition than it is with regard to Iranian activists. In the case *S.M. v. Switzerland*, the Committee pointed out that the applicant had not claimed to have been arrested or ill-treated in Ethiopia, nor had she claimed that any charges had been brought against her under the Anti-Terrorism law or any other domestic law.[782] It further held that she had not presented evidence to support her claim that the Ethiopian authorities would monitor people like her. It concluded that 'the absence of any political activities in Ethiopia' prior to the applicant's departure from Ethiopia and 'the low level of her political activities in Switzerland' were insufficient to establish that she would personally be exposed to a substantial risk of being subjected to torture if returned to that country.[783]

---

779   *Ibid.*, § 9.5. See the comparable cases ComAT, *Tahmuresi v. Switzerland*, 26 November 2014, no. 489/2012, § 7.6 and ComAT, *Azizi v. Switzerland*, 27 November 2014, no. 492/2012, § 8.6, in which the Committee indicates in the risk *sur place* context that even low-level opposition is closely monitored in Iran and that Iranian authorities effectively monitor Internet communication and regime critics both within and outside of Iran.

780   ComAT, *X. Y. and Z. v. Sweden*, 6 May 1998, no. 61/1996, § 11.4 (DRC); ComAT, *A.A. v. Switzerland*, 17 November 2006, no. 251/2004, §§ 7.6 and 7.7 (Iran); ComAT, *M.B. v. Switzerland*, 31 May 2013, no. 439/2010, § 7.8 (Iran). See further ComAT, *M.A.K. v. Germany*, 12 May 2004, no. 214/2002, §§ 2.3 and 13.5 (Turkey), in which the complainant had participated in a highway blockage organised by sympathisers of the PKK in Germany, and ComAT, *S.G. v. Netherlands*, 12 May 2004, no. 135/1999, §§ 2.8 and 6.8 (Turkey), in which the complainant had occupied the Greek ambassador's residence in The Hague in 1999.

781   ComAT, *T.D. v. Switzerland*, 26 May 2011, no. 375/2009, § 7.8.

782   ComAT, *S.M. v. Switzerland*, 23 November 2012, no. 406/2009, § 7.5.

783   *Ibid.*, §§ 7.5 and 7.6. See the Committee's similar reasoning with regard to Ethiopia in, for example, ComAT, *H.K. v. Switzerland*, 23 November 2012, no. 432/2010, § 7.6; ComAT,

The question of whether the complainant's political activity attracts the interest of the authorities and therefore, in the language of the General Comment, makes him 'particularly vulnerable' to the risk of being subjected to torture is at the core of the Committee's analysis. The publicity of a case can enhance the attention of authorities and powerful actors.[784] The time elapsed since a complainant's political activities can, however, considerably diminish the authorities' interest and with that a risk of torture.[785]

According to the Committee 'family ties, of themselves, are generally insufficient to ground a claim' under Article 3 CAT.[786] There are, however, several cases in which the complainant's affiliation to politically active family members was considered as enhancing a risk of torture.[787] In two decisions concerning the former Zaire, the asylum claim of the applicant, which may be considered defamatory in the receiving state or may lead to an interrogation upon arrival, is mentioned as a risk element.[788] In *Nasirov v. Kazakhstan* concerning an extradition to Uzbekistan, the procedure before the Committee itself was considered one of the risk factors.[789]

Religious and other activities can also put individuals in danger of being subjected to ill treatment in certain countries. In the case *M.B.B. v. Sweden* decided in 1999, the Committee noted that the complainant had failed to substantiate his claims that deserters from the Iranian Revolutionary Guard who leave the country as well as converts to Christianity in general face a risk of being subjected to torture in Iran, especially if they are not prominent members of

---

    R.D. v. Switzerland, 8 November 2013, no. 426/2010, § 9.7; ComAT, *X. v. Denmark*, 28 November 2014, no. 458/2011, § 9.6; ComAT, *E.E.E. v. Switzerland*, 8 May 2015, no. 491/2012, § 7.7.

784   ComAT, *Elmi v. Australia*, 14 May 1999, no. 120/1998, § 6.8.

785   See, for example, ComAT, *V.X.N. and H.N. v. Sweden*, 15 May 2000, no. 130 and 131/1999, § 13.7 (Vietnam); ComAT, *A.A. v. Switzerland*, 17 November 2006, no. 251/2004, § 7.7 (Iran); ComAT, *G.B.M. v. Sweden*, 14 November 2012, no. 435/2010, § 7.7 (Tanzania).

786   ComAT, *Attia v. Sweden*, 17 November 2003, no. 199/2002, § 12.3. See also ComAT, *Y. v. Switzerland*, 21 May 2013, no. 431/2010, § 7.2.

787   ComAT, *Paez v. Sweden*, 28 April 1997, no. 39/1996, §§ 14.3–14.6 (Peru); ComAT, *Elmi v. Australia*, 14 May 1999, no. 120/1998, § 6.8 (Somalia); ComAT, *M.V. v. Netherlands*, 2 May 2003, no. 201/2002, § 7.3 (Turkey); ComAT, *T.A. v. Sweden*, 6 May 2005, no. 226/2003, § 7.3; ComAT, *V.L. v. Switzerland*, 20 November 2006, no. 262/2005, § 8.7 (Belarus). See also, *e contrario*, ComAT, *D.Y. v. Sweden*, 21 May 2013, no. 463/2011, § 9.8 (Uzbekistan).

788   ComAT, *Mutombo v. Switzerland*, 27 April 1994, no. 13/1993, § 9.4 and ComAT, *Kioski v. Sweden*, 8 May 1996, no. 41/1996, § 9.5.

789   ComAT, *Nasirov v. Kazakhstan*, 14 May 2014, no. 475/2011, § 11.9.

the Christian community.[790] However, in the case *Azizi v. Switzerland* decided in 2014, the Committee observed that Christians who have converted from Islam face persecution in Iran and have frequently been arrested, detained and ill-treated over the past few years.[791] In light of these circumstances and the fact that the complainant had converted to Christianity, had been affiliated to Kurdish political activists in Iran and had been active against the Iranian regime in his host state Switzerland, the Committee concluded that he would risk being subjected to torture if returned to the Islamic Republic of Iran.[792] Worth noting is also the case *Ke Chun Rong v. Australia*, in which the Committee found that the deportation of the applicant, who had submitted sufficient details regarding his affiliation with the Falun Gong movement, would violate Article 3 CAT.[793] There are a few further cases in which the Committee found violations of Article 3 CAT with regard to deportations of suspected or convicted Islamic terrorists and members of partly political/partly religious Islamic groups to North African States before the Arab Spring[794] and to Uzbekistan.[795] The desertion of a complainant was a risk factor amongst others in *Mutombo v. Switzerland* concerning a deportation to Mobutu's former Zaire[796] and in *A. v. Netherlands* concerning the deportation to Tunisia.[797]

---

790 ComAT, *M.B.B. v. Sweden*, 5 May 1999, no. 104/1998, § 6.6. See further ComAT, *Z.Z. v. Canada*, 15 May 2001, no. 123/1998, § 8.4, concerning a deportation to Afghanistan before the US invasion. The Committee noted that the complainant had not been involved in any political or religious activities making him of interest for the Taliban.

791 ComAT, *Azizi v. Switzerland*, 27 November 2014, no. 492/2012, § 8.7.

792 *Ibid.*, § 8.8.

793 ComAT, *Ke Chun Rong v. Australia*, 5 November 2012, no. 416/2010, § 7.4, however, procedural deficiencies in the national procedure were of particular importance in the Committee's reasoning. Another case concerning the deportation of an applicant who claimed to be part of Falun Gong to China but was rejected for lack of credibility is ComAT, *Y.Z.S. v. Australia*, 23 November 2012, no. 417/2010. See also the rejected case ComAT, *Y.G.H. et al. v. Australia*, 14 November 2013, no. 434/2010, in which the applicant claimed to be persecuted in China because of his involvement in the underground Christian church in China.

794 ComAT, *Karoui v. Sweden*, 8 May 2002, no. 185/2001 (Tunisia); ComAT, *Agiza v. Sweden*, 20 May 2005, no. 233/2003 (Egypt); ComAT, *El Rgeig v. Switzerland*, 15 November 2006, no. 280/2005 (Libya); ComAT, *Tebourski v. France*, 1 May 2007, no. 300/2006 (Tunisia).

795 ComAT, *Abdussamatov and 28 Others v. Kazakhstan*, 1 June 2012, no. 444/2010; ComAT, *X. v. Russia*, 8 May 2015, no. 542/2013; ComAT, *Tursunov v. Kazakhstan*, 8 May 2015, no. 538/2013; ComAT, *Nasirov v. Kazakhstan*, 14 May 2014, no. 475/2011.

796 ComAT, *Mutombo v. Switzerland*, 27 April 1994, no. 13/1993, § 9.4.

797 ComAT, *A. v. Netherlands*, 13 November 1998, no. 91/1997, § 6.7.

A risk of detention or arrest in the receiving country is not a condition for a violation of Article 3 CAT.[798] In the great majority of the cases in which the Committee has found a violation of Article 3 CAT, the risk of the complainant being subjected to torture was, however, *combined with a risk of being arrested or detained*. When a complainant establishes relevant political activities and the receiving state's authorities are known for the ill treatment of political opponents, evidence such as a court summonses or arrest warrants will be of particular importance.[799] Even the possibility of being questioned upon return might increase the risk of torture.[800] In *Chahin v. Sweden*, the Committee noted that in light of the 'serious deterioration' of the human rights situation in Syria in connection with the government's crackdown on the opposition movement in spring 2011, the facts that the complainant would be taken into detention upon arrival in Syria for having left the country illegally and that he had been convicted for anti-state crimes in 1997 were 'sufficient in the present circumstances' for assuming that he would be subjected to torture upon return.[801] However, the Committee has also made clear that the mere risk of being arrested and interrogated upon arrival is usually not sufficient to indicate that there is also a real risk of being subjected to torture.[802]

For ordinary criminals, it is much more difficult to be successful under Article 3 CAT.[803] There are only a few cases concerning the deportation of

---

798   See ComAT, *V.L. v. Switzerland*, 20 November 2006, no. 262/2005, § 8.10, in which the Committee held that 'sexual abuse by the police in this case constitutes torture even though it was perpetrated outside formal detention facilities.' See further ComAT, *Njamba and Balikosa v. Sweden*, 14 May 2010, no. 322/2007 and ComAT, *Bakatu-Bia v. Sweden*, 3 June 2011, no. 379/2009, concerning sexual abuse of women in general.

799   ComAT, *Khan v. Canada*, 15 November 1994, no. 15/1994 § 12.4; ComAT, *M.S.H. v. Sweden*, 14 November 2005, no. 235/2003, §§ 5.3 and 6.6–6.8; ComAT, *Minani v. Canada*, 5 November 2009, no. 331/2007, §§ 7.7 and 7.8; ComAT, *Eftekhary v. Norway*, 25 November 2011, no. 312/2007, § 7.9; ComAT, *M.Z.A. v. Sweden*, 22 May 2012, no. 424/2010, § 8.4; ComAT, *E.T. v. Switzerland*, 23 May 2012, no. 393/2009, § 7.4; ComAT, *S.M. v. Switzerland*, 23 November 2012, no. 406/2009, § 7.5; ComAT, *Y. v. Switzerland*, 21 May 2013, no. 431/2010, § 7.7.

800   ComAT, *Dadar v. Canada*, 23 November 2005, no. 258/2004, § 8.7 (Iran).

801   ComAT, *Chahin v. Sweden*, 30 May 2011, no. 310/2007, § 9.6.

802   See ComAT, *P.Q.L. v. Canada*, 17 November 1997, no. 57/1996 § 10.5 (China); ComAT, *I.A.O. v. Sweden*, 6 May 1998, no. 65/1997, § 14.5 (Djibouti); ComAT, *V.X.N. and H.N. v. Sweden*, 15 May 2000, nos. 130 and 131/1999, § 13.7 (Vietnam); ComAT, *M.S. v. Australia*, 23 November 2001, no. 154/2000, § 6.5 (Algeria); ComAT, *S.N.A.W. et al. v. Switzerland*, 24 November 2005, no. 231/2003, § 7.6 (Sri Lanka); ComAT, *Y. v. Switzerland*, 21 May 2013, no. 431/2010, § 7.8 (Turkey); ComAT, *M.A.H. and F.H. v. Switzerland*, 17 November 2013, no. 438/2010, § 7.5 (Tunisia).

803   See as illustrative ComAT, *R.A. v. Switzerland*, 20 November 2012, no. 389/2009 (Turkey), in which the Committee points out that the Kurdish applicant has failed to show that the

non-political criminals that have been successful before the Committee so far: one case concerned a French national, Djamel Ktiti, who had been arrested in August 2009 in Morocco to be extradited to Algeria.[804] The Algerian judiciary had issued an international arrest warrant after a certain M.K., who had been arrested for possession of cannabis resin in Algeria, had mentioned the applicant's name during an interrogation. It was reported that while in police custody M.K. had been tortured into confessing he was involved in marijuana trafficking and revealing the names of his accomplices. In January 2010, an Algerian court sentenced Mr Ktiti *in absentia* to life imprisonment.[805] Before the Committee, the complainant alleged he would be subjected to torture if extradited to Algeria.[806] In referring to the last state report on Algeria under Article 19 CAT, the Committee noted that it was concerned about many allegations it had received of cases of torture and ill treatment inflicted on detainees by law-enforcement officers in Algeria. It held that 'despite the complainant's allegation highlighting the potential risks, the Supreme Court of Morocco did nothing to assess those risks but was content to base its decision to extradite on statements which, according to the complainant, were obtained under torture.' In view of this 'evidence, which furthermore, has not been refuted by the State party,' the Committee concluded that the complainant's extradition to Algeria would violate Article 3 CAT.[807] Another case concerned the extradition in summer 2010 of a French citizen from Germany to Tunisia based on a sentence *in absentia* on several counts of smuggling and drug trafficking.[808] The Tunisian authorities provided diplomatic assurances according to which the applicant would be entitled in Tunisia to a retrial in which the rights set out in the ICCPR would be upheld and that, in the event of a conviction, he would serve his

---

criminal proceedings against him in Turkey were politically motivated. See on this also Chetail 2006, p. 80, who indicates that the lawful sanction clause in Art. 1 CAT could have an impact on the severity of the Committee with regard to ordinary criminals.

804   ComAT, *Ktiti v. Morocco*, 26 May 2011, no. 419/2010.

805   *Ibid.*, §§ 2.1–2.4.

806   *Ibid.*, § 3.1.

807   *Ibid.*, § 8.7. According to the Committee, the Moroccan authorities should have verified the complainant's allegations that the statements made by M.K. had been obtained under torture. It eventually found that by using them as evidence in the extradition proceedings, Morocco had further violated its obligation under Art. 15 CAT, which prohibits the use of evidence extracted by torture; *ibid.*, § 8.8. See also ComAT. *R.A.Y. v. Morocco*, 16 May 2014, no. 525/2012, where the alleged factual background is similar to *Ktiti*. However, this complaint was rejected for non-exhaustion of domestic remedies concerning Art. 15 CAT and lack of substantiation under Art. 3 CAT.

808   ComAT, *Abichou v. Germany*, 21 May 2013, no. 430/2010.

sentence in a facility that complied with the UN Standard Minimum Rules for the Treatment of Prisoners.[809] The Committee held that 'notwithstanding the diplomatic assurances that were provided,' it 'must consider the actual human rights situation in Tunisia at the time of the complainant's extradition.'[810] Noting that 'Tunisia routinely resorted to the widespread use of torture against detainees held for political reasons and against detainees charged with ordinary criminal offences,'[811] the Committee considered that the complainant had demonstrated a foreseeable, real and personal risk of being subjected to torture at the time of his extradition to Tunisia.

However, these cases remain exceptional:[812] in most of the cases in which the Committee found a violation of Article 3 CAT, the complainants had been arrested or were likely to be arrested because of their *political* engagement or affiliation. Although the Committee has made clear that even an unjustified or politically motivated detention will not as such amount to torture,[813] one can observe from the case law that the Committee considers political detainees as particularly vulnerable to torture.

Finally, the Committee's continuing obligation to monitor changes in human rights situations should not be forgotten.[814] In this context several complaints concerning the removal of opponents of the former political system in Bangladesh are worth mentioning. The Committee rejected these, since by the time it considered the applications, the applicants' political party had become a participant in the government of Bangladesh.[815]

---

809   *Ibid.*, §§ 2.6 and 6.3.

810   *Ibid.*, §§ 11.6 and 11.7.

811   *Ibid.*, § 11.7.

812   As another exception see ComAT, *Fadel v. Switzerland*, 14 November 2014, no. 450/2011, § 7.8, concerning an applicant who had fled a Yemeni prison. His alleged political activities were not sufficiently established. The Committee nevertheless concluded that he faced a real risk of torture in Yemen, since he was regarded as a fugitive and torture is widespread in Yemeni prisons.

813   See ComAT, *P.Q.L. v. Canada*, 17 November 1997, no. 57/1996 § 10.5; ComAT, *I.A.O. v. Sweden*, 6 May 1998, no. 65/1997, § 14.5; ComAT, *V.X.N. and H.N. v. Sweden*, 15 May 2000, nos. 130 and 131/1999, § 13.7; ComAT, *M.S. v. Australia*, 23 November 2001, no. 154/2000, § 6.5; ComAT, *S.N.A.W. et al. v. Switzerland*, 24 November 2005, no. 231/2003, § 7.6.

814   See ComAT, General Comment No. 1 on Art. 3 CAT (1997), § 8 (d).

815   See ComAT, *T.M. v. Sweden*, 18 November 2003, no. 228/2003, § 7.3; ComAT, *S.A. v. Sweden*, 6 May 2004, no. 243/2004, § 4.2; ComAT, *M.A.M. v. Sweden*, 14 May 2004, no. 196/2002, § 6.5; ComAT, *David v. Sweden*, 2 May 2005, no. 220/2002, § 8.3; ComAT, *M.S.H. v. Sweden*, 14 November 2005, no. 235/2003, §§ 6.5–6.7; ComAT, *A.A.C. v. Sweden*, 16 November 2006, no. 227/2003, §§ 8.3–8.5; ComAT, *M.N. v. Switzerland*, 17 November 2006, no. 259/2004, § 6.6.

Past Torture or Ill Treatment

According to the Committee's case law and its General Comment on Article 3 CAT, the question of whether the complainant has 'been tortured or maltreated in the recent past' is an important element in the risk assessment.[816] Several decisions mention the absence of previous experiences of torture or ill treatment as one of the reasons that there was no real risk of the applicant being subjected to torture in case of return to his home country.[817] If a complainant presents medical reports stating he has been tortured in the past, his case will in principle at least amount to a *prima facie* case to be considered on the merits by the Committee.[818] In more than half of the cases in which the Committee has found a violation of Article 3 CAT, the applicants had established that they had already been subjected to ill treatment in the past.

However, not every case in which the complainant has been previously subjected to torture will automatically be successful. According to the Committee, 'past torture is one of the elements to be taken into account' when examining a claim concerning Article 3 CAT, 'but the aim of the Committee's examination is to find whether the authors would risk being subjected to torture now, if returned.'[819] Events that did not occur in the recent past will not have the same importance. The Committee has rejected complaints pointing out that considerable time had elapsed since the acts of torture had occurred.[820] Time

---

816   ComAT, General Comment No. 1 on Art. 3 CAT (1997), § 8 (b).

817   See, as recent examples, ComAT, *R.S.M. v. Canada*, 24 May 2013, no. 392/2009, § 7.4; ComAT, *M.B. v. Switzerland*, 31 May 2013, no. 439/2010, § 7.7; ComAT, *Y.B.F., S.A.Q. and Y.Y. v. Switzerland*, 31 May 2013, no. 467/2011, § 7.5.

818   See ComAT, *T.M. v. Sweden*, 18 November 2003, no. 228/2003, §§ 2.6 and 6.3; ComAT, *David v. Sweden*, 2 May 2005, no. 220/2002, §§ 2.6 and 7.3; ComAT, *A.A.C. v. Sweden*, 16 November 2006, no. 227/2003, § 7.4; ComAT, *Amini v. Denmark*, 15 November 2010, no. 339/2008, § 6.2. Unless the former perpetrators are clearly not threatening anymore; see ComAT, *S.A. v. Sweden*, 6 May 2004, no. 243/2004, § 4.2.

819   ComAT, *X. Y. and Z. v. Sweden*, 6 May 1998, no. 61/1996, § 11.12; ComAT, *A.L.N. v. Switzerland*, 19 May 1998, no. 90/1997, § 8.3; ComAT, *N.Z.S. v. Sweden*, 22 November 2006, no. 277/2005, § 8.5; ComAT, *M.M. et al. v. Sweden*, 11 November 2008, no. 332/2007, § 7.5; ComAT, *Khalsa et al. v. Switzerland*, 26 May 2011, no. 336/2008, § 11.4; ComAT, *Sivagnanaratnam v. Denmark*, 11 November 2013, no. 429/2010, § 10.5.

820   See, for example, ComAT, *Y. v. Switzerland*, 21 May 2013, no. 431/2010 (Turkey, 15 years); ComAT, *Sivagnanaratnam v. Denmark*, 11 November 2013, no. 429/2010 (Sri Lanka, 10 years); ComAT, *Alp v. Denmark*, 14 May 2014, no. 466/2011 (Turkey, 20 years); ComAT, *X. v. Denmark*, 28 November 2014, no. 458/2011 (Ethiopia, 7 years); ComAT, *M.S. v. Denmark*, 10 August 2015 (Afghanistan, more than 5 years). According to Thurin 2012, pp. 193–194, the Committee sometimes overvalues the time factor. See also Doerfle 2005, pp. 87–88, who

elapsed since past experiences of torture will be of particular relevance if the political situation in the receiving country has changed and former perpetrators are no longer in power[821] or when complainants have not been high-level political activists.[822] The Committee will not only take into account how recently the ill treatment occurred, it will also examine whether it 'occurred in circumstances which are relevant to the prevailing political realities in the country concerned.'[823]

The Committee requires state parties to take into account a complainant's mental illness resulting from past experiences when assessing asylum applications.[824] Generally, past experiences of torture do have an impact on the Committee's appreciation of a complainant's general credibility and therefore on the burden of proof with regard to other possible alleged risk factors like past political activities or detentions[825] or other risk-relevant elements.[826] If evidence of past torture is adduced, the Committee will be particularly generous in accepting inconsistencies or omissions from complainants who have established they are still suffering from a past ill treatment.[827] As stated in

---

indicates that after a complainant has exhausted all domestic remedies, his departure and therefore his experiences of torture are likely to date back several years.

821   See, for example, ComAT, *Y.H.A. v. Australia*, 23 November 2001, no. 162/2000, § 6.2 (Somalia); ComAT, *T.M. v. Sweden*, 18 November 2003, no. 228/2003, § 7.3 (Bangladesh); ComAT, *A.I. v. Switzerland*, 12 May 2004, no. 182/2001, §§ 6.3, 6.5 and 6.7 (Sri Lanka); ComAT, *S.S.S. v. Canada*, 16 November 2005, no. 245/2004, § 8.4 (India).

822   See, for example, ComAT, *A.A.C. v. Sweden*, 16 November 2006, no. 227/2003, § 8.3 and 8.5 (Bangladesh); ComAT, *R.K. et ai. v. Sweden*, 16 May 2008, no. 309/2006, §§ 8.4 and 8.5 (Azerbaijan).

823   ComAT, *A.A.C. v. Sweden*, 16 November 2006, no. 227/2003, § 8.3.

824   ComAT, *I.A.O. v. Sweden*, 6 May 1998, no. 65/1997, § 14.3; ComAT, *Haydin v. Sweden*, 20 November 1998, no. 101/1997, § 6.6; ComAT, *A.A. v. Denmark*, 13 November 2012, no. 412/2010, § 7.10. See also ComAT, General Comment No. 1 on Art. 3 CAT (1997), § 8 (c).

825   See ComAT, *Tala v. Sweden*, 15 November 1996, no. 43/1996, §§ 3.2, 3.4, 5.4, 7.4–7.7 10.3–10.5; ComAT, *A.F. v. Sweden*, 8 May 1998, no. 89/1997, §§ 4.12 and 6.5; ComAT, *Ayas v. Sweden*, 12 November 1998, no. 97/1997, § 6.5; ComAT, *Haydin v. Sweden*, 20 November 1998, no. 101/1997, § 6.7; ComAT, *Rios v. Canada*, 23 November 2004, no. 133/1999, §§ 4.8–4.9 and 8.4–9; ComAT, *C.T. and K.M. v. Sweden*, 17 November 2006, no. 279/2005, §§ 7.4–8; ComAT, *S.M., H.M. and A.M. v. Sweden*, 21 November 2011, no. 374/2009, §§ 9.6 and 9.7; ComAT, *Kalonzo v. Canada*, 18 May 2012, no. 343/2008, §§ 9.6 and 9.7; ComAT, *K.H. v. Denmark*, 23 November 2012, no. 464/2011, §§ 8.5–8.8; ComAT, *J.K. v. Canada*, 23 November 2015, no. 562/2013, § 10.4.

826   See the recent decision ComAT, *F.B. v. Netherlands*, 20 November 2015, no. 613/2014, § 8.8, with regard to an applicant who had been subjected to female genital mutilation.

827   See ComAT, *T.A. v. Sweden*, 6 May 2005, no. 226/2003, § 7.3; ComAT, *C.T. and K.M. v. Sweden*, 17 November 2006, no. 279/2005, §§ 7.4–8; ComAT, *V.L. v. Switzerland*,

the section on credibility, the Committee has held that 'complete accuracy is seldom to be expected by victims of torture,'[828] especially when the victim suffers from post-traumatic stress syndrome.[829]

It is in principle up to the complainant to present evidence of past ill treatment and up to the authorities to take such evidence into account and to respond to it. However, medical reports indicating past experiences of ill treatment should catch 'the attention of the State party and constitute sufficient grounds for investigating the alleged risk more thoroughly.'[830] In *A. v. Netherlands*, the Committee indicated that if the applicant gives substantial signs of having been tortured in the past, the obligation could shift to the government to request a medical examination.[831] It confirmed this in *K.H. v. Denmark*, in which the national authorities considered it unnecessary to examine the Afghan complainant for signs of torture – as the complainant had requested – since his oral statements were considered contradictory.[832] The Committee held that by rejecting the complainant's asylum request without seeking further investigation into his claims or ordering a medical examination, the state party had failed to respect its obligations under Article 3 CAT.[833] Based on this procedural deficiency, it concluded that the applicant's deportation would constitute a violation of Article 3 CAT. The Committee decided similarly in the recent case *F.K. v. Denmark* concerning the removal of an ethnic Kurd to Turkey.[834] It made very clear in this decision that it considers allegations of past torture as a 'fundamental aspect' of an asylum claim, and as such they require adequate examination despite serious credibility concerns.[835]

In *Sivagnanaratnam v. Denmark* concerning the expulsion to Sri Lanka of a Tamil woman who claimed to have been tortured in 2003, the Committee

20 November 2006, no. 262/2005, § 8.8. See also Weissbrodt and Hörtreiter 1999, p. 15; Wouters 2009, p. 549.

828 See, for example, ComAT, *Karoui v. Sweden*, 8 May 2002, no. 185/2001, § 10; ComAT, *Ke Chun Rong v. Australia*, 5 November 2012, no. 416/2010, § 7.5; ComAT, *J.K. v. Canada*, 23 November 2015, no. 562/2013, § 10.4; ComAT, *R.G. et al. v. Sweden*, 25 November 2015, no. 586/2014, § 8.6.

829 ComAT, *Tala v. Sweden*, 15 November 1996, no. 43/1996, § 10.3.

830 ComAT, *Gbadjavi v. Switzerland*, 1 June 2012, no. 396/2009, § 7.8. See also ComAT, *K.H. v. Denmark*, 23 November 2012, no. 464/2011, § 8.8.

831 ComAT, *A. v. Netherlands*, 13 November 1998, no. 91/1997, §§ 5.5-5.7 and 6.6. Similar ComAT, *Fadel v. Switzerland*, 14 November 2014, no. 450/2011, § 7.6.

832 ComAT, *K.H. v. Denmark*, 23 November 2012, no. 464/2011, § 8.8.

833 *Ibid.*

834 ComAT, *F.K. v. Denmark*, 23 November 2015, no. 580/2014.

835 *Ibid.*, § 7.6.

decided differently.[836] It ruled that the complainant had not convinced it that the national authorities' investigation was not adequate. It noted that the responsible organs had thoroughly evaluated all the evidence presented by the complainant, found it to lack credibility and hence did not consider it necessary to order a medical examination. However, and this is probably more decisive in this case, the Committee pointed out that even if the complainant had been subjected to torture in the past, it does not necessarily follow that, several years after the alleged events occurred, she would still be at risk in Sri Lanka. Taking in account that the complainant had not presented evidence or convinced the Committee that the authorities in Sri Lanka currently had an interest in her whereabouts, it rejected the complaint.[837]

However, if the state party does not challenge the applicant's claim of past torture or the authenticity of medical reports, the Committee will usually accept the allegation as established.[838] The Committee is generally very sensitive to the question of whether the state authorities have properly assessed claims of past torture and evidence submitted on that account. It expects state parties to take into account evidence of past torture presented at any stage of the national procedure.[839] The Committee has even taken into account evidence of past torture that had only been presented during the international procedure.[840]

---

836   ComAT, *Sivagnanaratnam v. Denmark*, 11 November 2013, no. 429/2010.

837   *Ibid.*, §§ 10.5. and 10.6. For a similar reasoning in recent cases see ComAT, *Alp v. Denmark*, 14 May 2014, no. 466/2011, § 8.4 (ethnic Kurd to Turkey); ComAT, *Z. v. Denmark*, 10 August 2015, no 555/2013, §§ 7.5–7.7 (China); ComAT, *M.S. v. Denmark*, 10 August 2015, no. 571/2013, §§ 7.5–7.9 (Afghanistan).

838   ComAT, *Rios v. Canada*, 23 November 2004, no. 133/1999, § 8.4; ComAT, *Dadar v. Canada*, 23 November 2005, no. 258/2004, § 8.5; ComAT, *C.T. and K.M. v. Sweden*, 17 November 2006, no. 279/2005, § 7.5; ComAT, *Amini v. Denmark*, 15 November 2010, no. 339/2008, §§ 6.2 and 9.6–9.8; ComAT, *Gbadjavi v. Switzerland*, 1 June 2012, no. 396/2009, § 7.8; ComAT, *Dewage v. Australia*, 14 November 2013, no. 387/2009, 10.6–10.9.

839   See ComAT, *Khan v. Canada*, 15 November 1994, no. 15/1994 § 12.3; ComAT, *A. v. Netherlands*, 13 November 1998, no. 91/1997, §§ 4.12–4.18 and 6.5–6.8; ComAT, *V.L. v. Switzerland*, 20 November 2006, no. 262/2005, §§ 6.5 and 8.8.

840   ComAT, *Z.K. v. Sweden*, 9 May 2008, no. 301/2006, § 8.4, in which the Committee notes that although the medical reports were not presented before the national authorities they could not be 'completely disregarded as they state that the scars on the complainant's body could have occurred as a result of torture.' See aslo ComAT, *M.M.K. v. Sweden*, 3 May 2005, no. 221/2002, §§ 6.7, 7.4 and 7.5; ComAT, *R.K. et al. v. Sweden*, 16 May 2008, no. 309/2006, §§ 5.3, 6.1, 6.2, 8.4 & 8.5; ComAT, *F.K. v. Denmark*, 23 November 2015, no. 580/2014, §§ 5.1 and 7.6.

What kind of evidence does the Committee require to establish that a complainant has been subjected to torture or other ill treatment in the past? In its General Comment on Article 3 CAT, the Committee speaks of 'medical or other independent evidence' supporting the applicant's claim.[841] The Committee attaches particular importance to medicolegal reports carried out by independent medical experts (doctors, psychologists or psychiatrists experienced in the field).[842] They should be precise in their diagnosis and show a causal link between the injuries and the complainant's allegations.[843]

However, the Committee does not expect the medical reports to establish with absolute certainty that a complainant has been ill treated in the past. In *Chahin v. Sweden*, the Committee noted that 'even if the medical reports fail to specify when and where the complainant was tortured, they provide grounds which go beyond mere theory or suspicion for believing that he was tortured in the recent past.'[844] In a case concerning the deportation of a family of Armenian origin to Azerbaijan, the Committee gave considerable weight to reports issued by the Crisis and Trauma Centre in Stockholm, although the government had pointed out that the reports were too vague to substantiate the allegations of past ill treatment since they only indicated that the complainants *might* have been tortured in the past.[845] In other cases, the Committee has refused to give weight to comparable medical reports for the reason that they were not precise enough or did not relate sufficiently to the facts alleged by the

---

841   ComAT, General Comment No. 1 on Art. 3 CAT (1997), § 8 (c).

842   See ComAT, *Karou v. Sweden*, 8 May 2002, no. 185/2001, § 10. See further ComAT, *A.L.N. v. Switzerland*, 19 May 1998, no. 90/1997, § 84; ComAT, *M.S. v. Switzerland*, 13 November 2001, no. 156/2000, § 6.7; ComAT, *M.A.K. v. Germany*, 12 May 2004, no. 214/2002, § 13.7; ComAT, *S.N.A.W. et al. v. Switzerland*, 24 November 2005, no. 231/2003, § 7.5; ComAT, *Z.K. v. Sweden*, 9 May 2008, no. 301/2006, § 8.4; ComAT, *Amini v. Denmark*, 15 November 2010, no. 339/2008, §§ 9.6–9.8.

843   ComAT, *U.S. v. Finland*, 1 May 2003, no. 197/2002, § 7.6; ComAT, *J.A.G.V. v. Sweden*, 11 November 2003, no. 215/2002, §§ 4.7 and 7.5; ComAT, *El Rgeig v. Switzerland*, 15 November 2006, no. 280/2005, § 7.4; ComAT, *M.M. et al. v. Sweden*, 11 November 2008, no. 332/2007, § 7.4; ComAT, *Mondal v. Sweden*, 23 May 2011, no. 338/2008, § 7.6.

844   ComAT, *Chahin v. Sweden*, 30 May 2011, no. 310/2007, §§ 2.16 and 9.5. See similar ComAT, *Z.K. v. Sweden*, 9 May 2008, no. 301/2006, § 8.4 and ComAT, *Amini v. Denmark*, 15 November 2010, no. 339/2008, § 9.8; ComAT, *Gbadjavi v. Switzerland*, 1 June 2012, no. 396/2009, § 7.8.

845   ComAT, *S.M., H.M. and A.M. v. Sweden*, 21 November 2011, no. 374/2009, §§ 4.4, 4.15 and 9.7. See similar ComAT, *Kalonzo v. Canada*, 18 May 2012, no. 343/2008, §§ 2.4, 4.9 and 9.6; ComAT, *Mr. X and Mr. Z v. Finland*, 12 May 2014, no. 483/2011 and 485/2011, § 7.5; ComAT, *Khademi et al. v. Switzerland*, 14 November 2014, no. 473/2011, §§ 4.7 and 7.5.

complainant.[846] In *R.T-N. v. Switzerland*, the Committee noted that the psychological problems the complainant was suffering from were 'attributed by the doctors themselves to other factors, including the anxiety associated with the complainant's separation from his family and precarious status in Switzerland.'[847] It further noted that the complainant had provided no details about the torture he allegedly had suffered. Under these circumstances, the Committee failed to give much weight to the reports submitted on the complainant's mental health, even though they were established by experts and stated that the complainant's symptoms were consistent with his account.[848]

It can be concluded that the Committee attaches considerable weight to experiences of past ill treatment in the risk assessment, such that any kind of evidence of such experiences can be of importance.[849] It is, however, difficult to predict when reports will be treated as decisive in a given case.[850] The Committee appears to act very independently on this account. Sørensen notes that state authorities 'naturally enough express their astonishment at the fact that the Committee based on paper only can arrive at another conclusion than that of national authorities, who have seen the papers, but who have also interviewed the person.' His own explanation, as a former Committee member, is 'that the members of the Committee have a considerable knowledge about torture and the way torture victims often react, a knowledge which perhaps is not sufficiently spread within the national boards.'[851]

c   *Focus: Recognition as a Refugee*

According to the Committee, its 'authority does not extend to a determination of whether or not the claimant is entitled to asylum under the national law of a country, nor can it invoke the protection of the Geneva Convention relating to the Status of Refugees.'[852] However, the fact that a complainant has at

---

846   See ComAT, *R.S. v. Denmark*, 19 May 2004, nb. 225/2003, § 6.2; ComAT, *R.K. et al. v. Sweden*, 16 May 2008, no. 309/2006, § 8.5; ComAT, *M.M. et al. v. Sweden*, 11 November 2008, no. 332/2007, § 7.4; in ComAT, *S.L. v. Sweden*, 11 May 2001, 150/1999 §§ 3.2 and 6.4, the Committee seemed to have given no weight to presented medical reports without arguing why.

847   ComAT, *R.T-N. v. Switzerland*, 3 June 2011, no. 350/2008, § 8.7.

848   *Ibid.*, §§ 2.3 and 8.7. See similar ComAT, *S.U.A. v. Sweden*, 22 November 2004, no. 223/2002, §§ 4.15, 5.1 and 6.5.

849   Bruin & Reneman 2006, p. 95; Wouters 2009, pp. 480 and 543.

850   Bruin & Reneman 2006, p. 97.

851   Sørensen 2001, p. 180.

852   ComAT, *X. v. Spain*, 15 November 1995, no. 23/1995, § 7.3. See further ComAT, *Mohamed v. Greece*, 28 April 1997, no. 40/1996, § 11.2 and ComAT, *Aemei v. Switzerland*, 9 May 1997, 34/1995, § 11.

some point in his past been recognized as a refugee in the sense of the Geneva Convention is not at all irrelevant in the Committee's decisions.[853] In *Pelit v. Azerbaijan*, the Committee noted on the merits that 'in the present case, the complainant was recognised as a refugee in Germany, as it had been concluded that she would be at risk of persecution if she was returned to Turkey.' It recalled Conclusion No 12 of the UNHCR's Executive Committee 'On the extraterritorial effect of the determination of refugee status,' pursuant to whose letter (f) 'the very purpose of the 1951 Convention and the 1967 Protocol implies that refugee status determined by one Contracting State will be recognized also by the other Contracting States.' The Committee eventually found a violation of Article 3 CAT, pointing out that the state party Azerbaijan had 'not shown why this principle was not respected in the complainant's case.'[854]

This is not the only case in which the Committee explicitly made a link between a risk of persecution in the meaning of the Refugee Convention and a risk of torture in the sense of Article 3 CAT. In *Paez v. Sweden*, it noted that the refusal to grant the author asylum in Sweden was based on the exception clause of Article 1 F of the 1951 Refugee Convention because of his activities for Shining Path. The Committee further noted that the 'author's mother and sisters were granted de facto asylum in Sweden, since it was feared that they may be subjected to persecution because they belong to a family which is connected to Sendero Luminoso. The Committee pointed out that 'no ground has been invoked by the State party for its distinction between the author, on the one hand, and his mother and sisters, on the other, other than the author's activities for Sendero Luminoso.'[855] It was hence assumed that the complainant would fear persecution in Peru like his mother and sisters, which was considered an important risk factor under Article 3 CAT.

In *Faragollah v. Switzerland*, the Committee gave weight to the fact that the complainant's son had been granted refugee status. It noted:

> ... given that the State party concluded that the complainant's son could not be returned to the Islamic Republic of Iran on account of his political profile, which would imperil his safety upon return, the Committee finds that there is a difference in treatment, since the same authorities

---

853   See on this also Menéndez 2015, p. 73, noting that the relationship between asylum procedures and protection against refoulement under the CAT is 'obviously intimately linked.'

854   ComAT, *Pelit v. Azerbaijan*, 1 May 2007, no. 281/2005, § 11.

855   ComAT, *Paez v. Sweden*, 28 April 1997, no. 39/1996, § 14.4.

are prepared to send his father back to the Islamic Republic of Iran, even though he carries out similar activities and is exposed to similar risks.[856]

In light of these facts and the worrisome human rights situation in Iran after the 2009 elections, the Committee concluded that the complainant's deportation would violate Article 3 CAT. The fact that the expelling state grants asylum to individuals in similar circumstances to the complainant is generally a relevant factor in the Committee's risk assessment.[857]

In *R.T-N. v. Switzerland*, the Committee gave weight to an individual assessment made by the UNHCR that concluded the complainant was not at risk of persecution in his country of origin, the DRC.[858] In *X. v. Switzerland*, the Committee granted interim measures, explicitly taking into account that the UNHCR had requested the Swiss government not to return the complainant to Sudan since it considered that he would be subject to persecution.[859] However, the Committee eventually rejected the complainant's allegation that he would be subjected to torture on his return to Sudan by pointing out that the complainant had not been tortured in the past and did not belong to a 'political, professional or social group targeted by the authorities for repression and torture.'[860] This demonstrates that persecution in the sense of the Refugee Convention need not necessarily amount to torture. The recent decision *Y. v. Switzerland* also goes in that direction: the case concerned a Turkish national who claimed persecution in Turkey because her family members had engaged in pro-Kurdish activities, in particular her sister, who had obtained asylum in Switzerland.[861] The Committee observed that the complainant claimed 'to have been subjected to continuous surveillance, harassment, short-term arrests and persecution until her escape to Switzerland in 2008, but has failed to provide elements which would show that this would amount to torture.'[862] Yet such statements remain exceptional in the Committee's decisions.[863]

---

856   ComAT, *Faragollah et al. v. Switzerland*, 21 November 2011, no. 381/2009, §§ 9.5 and 9.6.

857   See ComAT, *Jahani v. Switzerland*, 23 May 2011, no. 357/2008, § 9.9.

858   ComAT, *R.T-N. v. Switzerland*, 3 June 2011, no. 350/2008, § 8.5.

859   ComAT, *X. v. Switzerland*, 9 May 1997, no. 38/1995, § 4.1.

860   *Ibid.*, §§ 10.4 and 10.5.

861   ComAT, *Y. v. Switzerland*, 21 May 2013, no. 431/2010.

862   *Ibid.*, § 7.7.

863   See in contrast ComAT, *A.K. v. Switzerland*, 8 May 2015, no. 544/2013, which also concerned a Kurdish activist. The Committee noted that the complainant's brother was granted asylum in Switzerland, which was 'likely to attract the attention and suspicions of the Turkish authorities in relation to the complainant' (§ 9.8). Also worth mentioning are two old inadmissibility decisions in which the Committee noted that the facts submitted related

All in all one can conclude that although persecution in accordance with the Refugee Convention might sometimes embrace a wider scope of harm than torture, the Committee takes it as a important factor indicating a risk of torture.[864] However, an established risk of persecution will not always be decisive in the Committee's assessment.

3.3.3 Comparison
a The Complainant's Credibility

To be considered credible, complainants have to tell their story in the most detailed, comprehensive and consistent way possible. Inconsistencies or omissions in an applicant's claim will be decisive if they are essential for the alleged risk, if the complainant is not able to explain them in a plausible way and if they are not outweighed by reliable evidence demonstrating a real risk of ill treatment.

Neither the Court nor the Committee requires that all facts invoked be proved by evidence. However, the presentation of authentic evidence considerably improves an applicant's credibility. Medical evidence showing that a complainant has been a victim of torture must be taken into consideration when the applicant's credibility is assessed. The Committee is particularly generous with inconsistencies or omissions of applicants who have presented reliable evidence that they are still suffering mentally from their past experiences. Before both the Court and the Committee, the fact that a complainant has been tortured in the past will not excuse all incoherent behaviour or allegations.

If a complainant introduces important facts only at a late stage of the asylum procedure, the Court and the Committee will be sceptical about them. If the complainant can explain his omission and demonstrate that he is in fact at a real risk of being subjected to torture or inhuman treatment in case of removal, his security will be more important for the Court and the Committee than his behaviour in the national procedure. What ultimately matters for the two international authorities is that the general story of the complainant appears truthful with respect to those elements that are essential for the risk of ill treatment.

---

to a claim for asylum but that no evidence has been adduced that the complainants could be personally at risk of being subjected to torture if deported; see ComAT, *X v. Spain*, 15 November 1995, no. 23/1995, § 7.3; ComAT, *X and Y v. Netherlands*, 20 November 1995, no. 31/1995, § 4.2.

864   See also Wouters 2009, p. 469.

When it comes to the complainant's personal credibility, the Committee is particularly generous with victims of torture and, more often than the Court, bases its decision on disputed allegations when finding a violation of the principle of non-refoulement if it considers a general story as credible. The Court is more reluctant to ignore inconsistencies or late submissions for the reason that the complainant suffers from post-traumatic stress syndrome.[865] Although the Court has occasionally used the Committee's words when stating that 'complete accuracy is seldom to be expected from victims of torture' in a few decisions,[866] it has not made this statement in a judgment on the merits.

It should be remembered that according to the Court, as a general principle, the national authorities are best placed to assess not just the facts, but also – and especially – the credibility of the individual concerned.[867] When the Court rejects complaints, it often refers to the national authorities' findings with regard to the applicant's lack of credibility.[868] With this, the Court respects in practice, and not only in theory, the fact that national authorities are usually better placed to judge the credibility of a person they are confronted with in person. Such arguments are also relevant in the Committee's practice, but it seems more lenient than the Court with respect to the complainant's credibility, giving him the benefit of the doubt more readily.[869] However, the Committee's reasoning is often too short to be able to identify for what reasons it agrees or disagrees with the domestic findings.

b   *The Complainant's Personal Background and History*
Neither the Court nor the Committee require that complainants already have been ill treated or were in danger of ill treatment when they left their home country. The circumstances in which a complainant has left his country will, however, indicate the circumstances in which he might be received in that country, unless the situation has fundamentally changed. Hence, the Court

---

865   See also Bruin & Reneman 2006, p. 91.

866   EComHR, *Hatami v. Sweden*, report of 23 April 1998, no. 3244/96, § 106; ECtHR, *Bello v. Sweden*, 17 January 2006, no. 32213/04 (decision). See the words used as in ComAT, *Alan v. Switzerland*, 8 May 1996, no. 21/1995, § 11.3.

867   See this principle recalled, for example, in ECtHR, *A.A. and Others v. Sweden*, 28 June 2012, no. 14499/09, § 77.

868   See also Chetail 2004, p. 194, who notes that the Court occasionally reveals an 'excessive trust' ('*confiance parfois excessive*') when it comes to the immigration authorities' conclusions on an applicant's credibility.

869   See also Chetail 2006, p. 101; Weissbrodt and Hörtreiter 1999, p. 55; Schürmann & Scheidegger 2009, p. 213.

and the Committee will both take into account whether the applicant has lived undisturbed in his home country before leaving.

Past political activities and experiences of ill treatment or detention as well as the possibility of being arrested on return are considered risk-enhancing factors in most of the decisions and judgments in which the Court and the Committee have found that the principle of non-refoulement was violated. Looking at the case law as a whole, *the Committee gives more weight than the Court to past events* to determine a present risk of ill treatment.[870] The Committee has rejected several complaints by pointing out that the complainant has not been detained or tortured in the past.

The great majority of cases before the Court and the Committee that have been successful concern complainants who fear ill treatment for political reasons. Complainants who allege that there is a real risk of being ill-treated upon return because of their political background must be able to demonstrate they have been politically active and explain in a convincing way why a risk of ill treatment arises from their activities or political affiliations.[871] If the human rights record in the receiving country is worrisome but not particularly bad, only important representatives of opposition movements will be considered at risk. Similar considerations apply with regard to religious activities or convictions.

Illustrative are the cases *Chahal*,[872] *Singh*[873] and *Khalsa et al.*,[874] in which the Court and the Committee argued in a similar way. These three complaints concerned the deportation of high-profile figures of the Sikh community to India, where they were persecuted by the authorities because of their militant past in the struggle for the independence of the Punjab region. The Court and the Committee pointed out the complainants' leadership role in the Sikh movement and the fact that they were known and looked for by the Indian authorities. Their high profile made them particularly vulnerable to ill treatment in case of return. Their exposure further made it impossible to find safe flight alternatives within India outside the Punjab region.[875]

As indicated, the human rights situation has an important impact on how demanding the Court and the Committee are with regard to an applicant's

---

870 See in this direction also judge Zupančič's comparative remarks with regard to the Committee's practice in his dissenting opinion to ECtHR, *J.K. and Others v. Sweden*, 4 June 2015, no. 59166/12 (Iraq – not in force – referred to Grand Chamber).

871 Schürmann & Scheidegger 2009, p. 212.

872 ECtHR, *Chahal v. UK*, 15 November 1996, no. 22414/93.

873 ComAT, *Singh v. Canada*, 30 May 2011, no. 319/2007.

874 ComAT, *Khalsa et al. v. Switzerland*, 26 May 2011, no. 336/2008.

875 See further the similar arguments in ComAT, *Sogi v. Canada*, 16 November 2007, no. 297/2006, § 10.10.

political engagement. This can be illustrated by the complaints concerning deportations to the Islamic Republic of Iran. The Court and the Committee both judge the human rights situation there as extremely worrisome. Neither the Court nor the Committee consider that *any* political opponent is under threat of ill treatment or torture or Iran, but they are both sensitive to their situation in the sense that, in the years following the elections in 2009, applicants needed not necessarily have a high political profile to benefit from the protection offered by the principle of non-refoulement and exile activities might be sufficient for the establishment of a real risk.[876]

What is interesting to observe is that the Court and the Committee are not always congruent when evaluating the human rights situation or the existence of particular targeted groups. The most striking example of this is the contrasting evaluation of the situation for Kurdish activists in Turkey. It has been mentioned that in contrast to the Committee, the Court has not found a violation of the principle of non-refoulement with regard to a deportation to Turkey so far. In *Aytulun and Güclü v. Sweden*, the Committee indicated that the complainant, as a PKK member, belonged to a particularly targeted group.[877] The Court rejected this a little later in *R.U. v. Greece*.[878] The different appraisal of the situation in Turkey is likely to be related to the fact that the Court attaches more weight than the Committee to the question of whether the receiving state is a contracting state.[879]

An issue that has been occupying the Court and the Committee for several years and in which they have acted in a more similar way is the removal of Tamils to Sri Lanka. With regard to Sri Lankans of Tamil origin having been part of or affiliated with the LTTE, the Court and the Committee have both been quite strict so far. Although they have both acknowledged that there were massive human rights violations and systematic practices of torture on young male Tamils in Sri Lanka, they both always stuck to the individual assessments of each case.[880] The Court has reaffirmed in recent decisions that only Tamils

---

876   See, in particular, ECtHR, *R.C. v. Sweden*, 9 March 2010, no. 41827/07, §§ 54 and 55; ECtHR, *S.F. and 'Others v. Sweden*, 15 May 2012, no. 52077/10, §§ 67–71; ComAT, *Jahani v. Switzerland*, 23 May 2011, no. 357/2008, § 9.4; ComAT, *Tahmuresi v. Switzerland*, 26 November 2014, no. 489/2012, §§ 7.6 and 7.7.

877   ComAT, *Aytulun and Güclü v. Sweden*, 19 November 2010, no. 373/2009, §§ 7.6 and 7.7. However, the Committee did not base the violation of Article 3 CAT in case of removal to Turkey solely on the complainant's membership of the PKK but also on additional personal risk factors.

878   See ECtHR, *R.U. v. Greece*, 7 June 2011, no. 2237/08, § 81.

879   See on this Section 3.2.3.d of this chapter above.

880   The only two successful complaints decided by the Court concerned Tamils who had been ill-treated in the past; see ECtHR, *N.A. v. UK*, 17 July 2008, no. 25904/07 and *R.J. v. France*,

with a particularly high profile of past LTTE involvement will benefit from protection.[881] The only case concerning a removal to Sri Lanka in which the Committee found a violation of Article 3 CAT is *Dewage v. Australia* decided in November 2013.[882] However, this case concerned a Sri Lankan national of *Sinhalese ethnic origin* who claimed to be persecuted by the authorities because of his past involvement as a profiled trade unionist and political opponent of the government.

It should further be added that the Court and the Committee have also been very demanding regarding Afghan asylum seekers.[883] So far, only one rather particular complaint of an Afghan woman threatened with domestic violence has been successful before the Court[884] and one before the Committee.[885] Also with regard to the level of political exposure of opponents in Ethiopia, the Court and the Committee appear very demanding. So far, all refoulement complaints submitted by Ethiopians have been rejected.[886]

It is not only a complainant's actual political activities or affiliation that can be considered risk-enhancing but also the way the authorities of the receiving state perceive a complainant's background.[887] The core question with regard to the importance of political activities in the risk assessment is the interest of authorities or other powerful actors known for practices of ill treatment

19 September 2013, no. 10466/11. In this latter judgment, the Court based its conclusion mainly on the fact that the complaint's case had not been assessed properly at national level.

881 ECtHR, *E.G. v. UK*, 31 May 2011, no. 41178/08, §§ 65–81 and the joint dissenting opinion of the judges Garlicki and Kalaydjieva. See also ECtHR, *S.R. c. France*, 19 June 2012, no. 17859/09 (decision); ECtHR, *R.J. v. France*, 19 September 2013, no. 10466/11, §§ 39 and 40.

882 ComAT, *Dewage v. Australia*, 14 November 2013, no. 387/2009.

883 For recent examples see ECtHR, *S.H.H. v. UK*, 29 January 2013, no. 60367/10 and the dissenting opinion of the judges Ziemle, Thór Björgvinsson and de Gaetano; ECtHR, *H. and B. v. UK*, 9 April 2013, nos. 70073/10 and 44539/11 and the dissenting opinion of judge Kalaydjeva; ComAT, *M.S. v. Denmark*, 10 August 2015, no. 571/2013; ECtHR, *S.S. v. Netherlands*, 12 Janaury 2016, no. 39575/06.

884 ECtHR, *N. v. Sweden*, 20 July 2010, no. 23505/09. The other successful complaint with regard to Afghanistan did not concern an asylum seeker but an extraordinary rendition with the implication of the US secret services; ECtHR, *El-Masri v. Former Yugoslav Republic of Macedonia*, 13 December 2012 [GC], no. 39630/09.

885 ComAT, *K.H. v. Denmark*, 23 November 2012, no. 464/2011, in which it was, however, the deficiencies in the domestic asylum procedure that were determinant.

886 As recent examples in which the Court and the Committee explicitly based their conclusions on the lack of high political profile see ECtHR, *D.N.W. v. Sweden*, 6 December 2012, no. 29946/10, §§ 40–45; ComAT, *R.D. v. Switzerland*, 8 November 2013, no. 426/2010, § 9.7.

887 Chetail 2006, p. 87, referring to ComAT, *A. v. Netherlands*, 13 November 1998, no. 91/1997, § 6.6.

on individuals having a similar background as the complainant. Arrest warrants and other documents establishing that a complainant is targeted by such actors are hence of particular importance. Depending on the circumstances, family ties can be an important risk factor. There are, however, more cases before the Committee than before the Court in which such ties and affiliations have been considered a risk factor.

The Court and the Committee will both take into account the *political activities of complainants within the host country* and other possible risk elements that have occurred after a complainant's flight like the request for asylum or the publicity surrounding an applicant's case (so-called risk *sur place*). There have, however, been fewer cases before the Court in which political activities in the host country have been of particular relevance compared to the Committee.[888] The importance the Committee attaches to after-flight activities is reflected in a decision adopted in its spring session in 2012 on a deportation to the DRC.[889] The Committee rejected the complaint stating, *inter alia*, that the complainant had not provided any explanation of the reasons for which he had not pursued his political activities against the Kabila regime once he was in exile in Switzerland.[890] There is no similar statement in the Court's jurisprudence.[891] The Court seems to be more sceptical with regard to after-flight activities. In this context, it also attaches weight to the question of whether a complainant has contributed to the publicity of his case or his activities in the host country. The Committee has never addressed this point.

Under both the Court and the Committee, a risk of detention or even unjustified detention is not by itself sufficient to trigger the application of the principle of non-refoulement. Past detentions as well as possible future ones are, however, considered risk-enhancing in many decisions and judgments, particularly when they are politically motivated. Since most acts of torture or inhuman treatment occur in the context of detention and arrest, this is not surprising. Practices of incommunicado detention for individuals with a background similar to the complainant's make the Court and the Committee particularly

---

888   See also Wouters 2009, p. 265, who notes that the concept of risk *sur place* has received little attention from the Court so far. See, however, the case ECtHR, *A.A. v. Switzerland*, 7 January 2014, no. 58802/12, discussed in Section 3.3.1.b of this chapter (Political and/or religious background), which might have a broader impact.

889   ComAT, *M.D.T. v. Switzerland*, 14 May 2012, no. 382/2009.

890   *Ibid.* See similar ComAT, *Y. v. Switzerland*, 21 May 2013, no. 431/2010, § 7.7 (Turkey).

891   In my opinion, this statement is problematic: it cannot be parted from the fact that individuals who had to leave their country because they are politically persecuted continue to be politically active in their host country, even before they are recognized as refugees.

cautious. In this context, it should be recalled that bad prison conditions, for example small prison cells, the lack of sanitary or medical facilities and other miserable circumstances for prisoners, are generally classified as inhuman or degrading treatment and not as torture.[892] Ordinary criminals who fear their extradition 'solely' because of degrading prison conditions and not because they fear being intentionally ill-treated by state actors (which is more likely to occur in the context of political repression) will hence have more chance of success before the Court. It is thus not surprising that while the Court has dealt with quite a few cases concerning the extradition of suspected criminals, the cases submitted before the Committee concerning extraditions of ordinary criminals are more rare.

Under both the Court and the Committee, it is essentially up to the complainant to submit evidence with regard to alleged past ill treatments. The Court and the Committee have, however, indicated that if the complainant has provided serious indications that he has been tortured, the burden can shift to the national authorities to assess this claim, which can include the duty to provide a medical report carried out by experts. In fact, the burden of proof before the Committee is more likely to shift to the government if it is established that the applicant has been tortured. Before the Court this remains rather exceptional. However, if the Court considers the human rights situation as particularly worrying, it might also attach much weight to the fact that the complainant has been ill-treated in the past. The Committee is very sensitive to the question of whether the national authorities have properly assessed alleged past ill treatments. It has made clear that, in principle, medical reports indicating past torture must be taken into account at whatever stage of a procedure they are introduced (even if only at international level). The Court in contrast usually agrees with national authorities, stating that if it is only at a late stage of an asylum procedure that an applicant alleges that he has been tortured in the past, this will weaken his credibility.[893] Looking at the Court's and the Committee's case law as a whole, there is no doubt that *past torture or ill treatment is a risk element that is given more weight by the Committee than by the Court*.[894] It goes without saying that medical evidence has been of particular importance in procedures under Article 22 CAT. Questions remain with regard to the quality and precision required by the Committee on such reports. However, it should be recalled that also before the Committee, the fact that

---

892   See Chapter 3 Section 4.2.1.

893   See in this sense also Bruin & Reneman 2006, p. 91.

894   See also Schürmann & Scheidegger 2009, p. 212; Wouters 2009, p. 543.

a complainant has been tortured in the recent past will not in itself lead to a violation of Article 3 CAT. The Court is generally more focused on objective risk elements showing the possibility of future ill treatment than on the complainant's past experiences.

With regard to risks emanating from an applicant's *sexual orientation*, the non-refoulement case law is still scant in Strasbourg and Geneva, but interestingly, the Committee has shown itself to be rather open to accepting a relevant risk in that context. The homosexual orientation of the applicant was an important risk element in the Geneva case *Mondal v. Sweden* concerning a removal to Bangladesh.[895] In *J.K. v. Canada* adopted by the Committee in November 2015, the complainant's homosexuality and his involvement in the LGBTI rights movement in Uganda were the main reasons for the violation of Article 3 CAT.[896] Before the Court, all cases in which the main risk alleged concerned the complainant's sexual orientation have so far been rejected.[897] The latest judgment was adopted in the case *M.E. v. Sweden* but later struck out by the Grand Chamber.[898] It concerned the removal of a Libyan national who alleged that if he had to go back to his country, where he would apply for family reunion to live with his husband in Sweden, he would be at risk of persecution and ill treatment. The Court rejected the complaint. It held that 'even if the applicant would have to be discreet about his private life' during his temporary return to Libya, 'it would not require him to conceal or supress an important part of his identity permanently or for any longer period of time.'[899] The case was referred to the Grand Chamber at the request of the applicant. However, since he was subsequently granted a permanent residence permit in Sweden on account of the deterioration in the security situation in Libya combined with his circumstances as a homosexual, the Grand Chamber considered the

---

895   ComAT, *Mondal v. Sweden*, 23 May 2011, no. 338/2008, § 7.7 (Bangladesh). See also HRC, *M.I. v. Sweden*, 25 July 2013, no. 2149/2012, in which the Human Rights Committee recently found that the expulsion of a lesbian woman to Bangladesh would violate Art. 7 ICCPR.

896   See ComAT, *J.K. v. Canada*, 23 November 2015, no. 562/2013. The Committee also attached importance to a medical report indicating he had been attacked in the past. This case is also addressed in Section 3.2.2.b of this chapter above. See further ComAT, *K.S.Y. v. Netherlands*, 15 May 2003, no. 190/2001, § 7.4 (Iran); ComAT, *E.J.V.M. v. Sweden*, 14 November 2003, no. 213/2002, § 8.7 (Costa Rica); both cases were rejected for lack of credibility/substantiation.

897   See ECtHR, *F. v. UK*, 22 June 2004, no. 17341/03 (decision; Iran); ECtHR, *I.I.N. v. Netherlands*, 9 December 2004, no. 2035/04 (decision; Iran).

898   See ECtHR, *M.E. v. Sweden*, 8 April 2015 [GC], no. 71398/12, § 32 (striking out).

899   ECtHR, *M.E. v. Sweden*, 26 June 2014, no. 71398/12, § 88 (not in force – struck out on 8 April 2015).

case as resolved and struck it out of the lists of cases.[900] With that, the Grand Chamber missed an opportunity to discuss its current approach with regard to homosexuality in the context of refoulement, which, to use the word of judge Power-Forde in her dissenting opinion on the chamber judgment *M.E.*, does 'not fit the current state of International and European law.'[901] Power-Forde rightly notes that the Court's approach in *M.E.* contradicts the asylum case law of the Court of Justice of the European Union, which does not expect individuals to conceal their homosexuality in their country of origin to avoid persecution.[902] As discussed in section 3.3.1b of this chapter, the Court has made use of a similarly problematic approach in *F.G. v. Sweden* by implicitly requiring the applicant to be discreet in the exercise of his Christian religion in Iran. This case will, however, be treated by the Grand Chamber.[903] As already criticized in this context, freedoms in sexual orientation or religious life are both protected by the ECHR. It is hence awkward that the Court should consider their suppression a legitimate precondition to avoid ill treatment. However, with its consideration in *M.E.* that it was 'only' temporarily that the applicant was forced to supress 'an important part of his identity,'[904] the Court signposts that it might decide differently should such suppression have to be practiced on a long-term basis. It is hence not excluded that the Court would have decided comparably to the Committee if confronted with a case like *J.K. v. Canada* described above concerning a long-term removal to Uganda. In this decision, the Committee did not appear to take into account the applicant's discretion as a possibility to avoid a risk of ill treatment in case of removal. However, the risk discussed in this case did not solely emanate from the applicant's sexual orientation but his militancy in the LGBTI rights movement in Uganda was an important risk element too.[905]

---

900   See ECtHR, *M.E. v. Sweden*, 8 April 2015 [GC], no. 71398/12, §§ 32–38 (striking out). On the problematic aspects of striking out complaints for loss of victim status during the international procedure, see Chapter 2 Section 3.2.7.c.

901   See the dissenting opinion of judge Power-Forde on ECtHR, *M.E. v. Sweden*, 26 June 2014, no. 71398/12, § 88 (not in force – struck out on 8 April 2015).

902   *Ibid.* and see CJEU, Joined Cases C-199/12, C-200/12, C-201/12, *X, Y and Z v Minister voor Immigratie, Integratie en Asiel*, 7 November 2013.

903   See ECtHR, *F.G. v. Sweden*, 16 January 2014, no. 43611/11, § 41 (not in force – referral to Grand Chamber).

904   ECtHR, *M.E. v. Sweden*, 26 June 2014, no. 71398/12, § 88 (not in force – struck out on 8 April 2015).

905   See ComAT, *J.K. v. Canada*, 23 November 2015, no. 562/2013. The Committee further attached importance to a medical report indicating he had been attacked in the past.

Finally, it should be remembered that there are several further elements that have been of relevance in the Court's and the Committee's risk assessment other than those just discussed such as, for example, the applicant's ethnic background. Further relevant elements are the question of whether the complainant has secretly left a country or has no valid exit documentation[906] or the fact that during the asylum procedure, the national authorities have revealed the name of the applicant to the receiving state's embassy.[907] As has been explained, of importance are also the applicant's age and gender.[908] Comparing the case law as a whole and the severe approach taken by the Court in recent cases,[909] it appears that the Committee gives particular attention to gender-based risk.[910]

Interestingly, neither the Court nor the Committee have had the occasion to assess a refoulement complaint submitted by an unaccompanied child.[911] However, their practice shows that the applicant's age is a relevant factor in the risk assessment.[912] As the Grand Chamber has made clear in *Tarakhel*, 'it is important to bear in mind that the child's extreme vulnerability is the decisive factor and takes precedence over considerations relating to the status of illegal immigrant.'[913]

In addition, as the Court has noted, 'due regard should also be given to the possibility that a number of individual factors may not, when considered

---

906   See, for example, ComAT, *Mutombo v. Switzerland*, 27 April 1994, no. 13/1993, § 9.4 (former Zaire); ECtHR, *R.C. v. Sweden*, 9 March 2010, no. 41827/07, § 56 (Iran); ECtHR, *S.F. and Others v. Sweden*, 15 May 2012, no. 52077/10, § 69 (Iran); ECtHR, *K.K. v. France*, 10 October 2013, no. 18913/11, § 53 (Iran). *E contrario*: ComAT, *G.B.M. v. Sweden,* 14 November 2012, no. 435/2010, § 7.8 (Tanzania).

907   See ECtHR, *F.N. v. Sweden*, 18 December 2012, no. 28774/09, §§ 74 and 75, in which the Court also pointed out as a relevant factor that the Uzbek authorities generally view the expelling state Sweden as a safe haven for political opponents from Uzbekistan.

908   See in particular the cases ECtHR, *N. v. Sweden*, 20 July 2010, no. 23505/09; ComAT, *Njamba and Balikosa v. Sweden*, 14 May 2010, no. 322/2007.

909   See, in particular, ECtHR, *A.A. and Others v. Sweden*, 28 June 2012, no. 14499/09 (Yemen) and ECtHR, *R.H. v. Sweden*, 10 September 2015, no. 4601/14 (Mogadishu).

910   See on this Chapter 3 Section 3.3 and Chapter 4 Section 3.2.2.b. and ComAT, General Comment No. 2 on Art. 2 (2008), §§ 18 and 22, which has influenced the Committee's recent case law.

911   See, however, the case *Mayeka and Mitunga v. Belgium*, discussed in Chapter 3 Section 2.2.6, concerning the deportation of an unaccompanied five-year-old from Belgium to the DRC. This case was assessed in the domestic context.

912   See, for example, ECtHR, *Soering v. UK*, 7 July 1989, no. 14038/88, § 111; ECtHR, *M.Y.H. v. Sweden*, 27 June 2013, no. 50859/10, § 70 and *mutatis mutandis* ComAT, *Njamba and Balikosa v. Sweden*, 14 May 2010, no. 322/2007, § 9.5.

913   ECtHR, *Tarakhel*, §§ 99, 118 and 119.

separately, constitute a real risk; but when taken cumulatively and when considered in a situation of general violence and heightened security the same factors may give rise to a real risk.'[914] This approach is equally visible in the Committee's practice. It cannot be overemphasised that the particular circumstances of each complainant have to be looked at on a case-by-case basis in light of the prevailing human rights situation. Finally, all the risk factors described can lose their importance with the passage of time or a change of government. However, if a complainant is able to provide credible evidence demonstrating he has been particularly politically active in his home country and that he has been detained and ill-treated for that reason in the recent past by authorities or actors who are still in power in that country, governments will usually have to present good reasons why such a complainant is not at risk in his home country anymore.

c   *Focus: Recognition as a Refugee*

The Court and the Committee both postulate that they are not responsible for supervising the Refugee Convention. It has been explained that the protection against refoulement offered by the ECHR and the CAT differs from that of the Refugee Convention to some extent: the protection offered by the ECHR and the CAT is broader with regard to individuals with certain criminal backgrounds or those considered a threat to the host state's security. Furthermore, the grounds for which an individual is threatened in his home country are immaterial for the Court and the Committee.[915] In addition, 'persecution' as defined under the Geneva Convention need not necessarily amount to torture or inhuman or degrading treatment. There are complaints that have been rejected by the Court and the Committee in which applicants were not threatened with torture or inhuman treatment, but may have faced persecution in the sense of the Refugee Convention. Such cases are rather rare.[916] However, they show that one cannot argue that, *generally*, a wider protection is provided by the prohibition on refoulement derived from the prohibition of torture and inhuman treatment. The principle of non-refoulement under the Refugee Convention is both *broader and narrower* than the protection offered under the ECHR or the CAT.[917] The fact that the protection against persecution might be broader

---

914   ECtHR, *N.A. v. UK*, 17 July 2008, no. 25904/07, § 130.

915   The Refugee Convention protects people from persecution aimed at the individual's life or freedom on account of his race, religion, nationality, membership of a particular social group, or political opinion.

916   See ECtHR, *Y. v. Russia*, 4 December 2008, no. 20113/07, §§ 84–91 and ComAT, *Y. v. Switzerland*, 21 May 2013, no. 431/2010, § 7.7 discussed in the Sections 3.3.1.c and 3.3.2.c of this Chapter.

917   Nowak & McArthur 2008, p. 195 (§ 171); Trechsel 1996, p. 92.

in certain circumstances then the protection against torture or other inhuman treatment should not be forgotten by national authorities when assessing requests for asylum under the Refugee Convention in light of the Court's or the Committee's case law.

Despite these differences, it is evident that there is substantial common ground between the protection offered by the ECHR and the CAT on the one hand and the Refugee Convention on the other.[918] People fearing persecution in the sense of the Refugee Convention are likely to be threatened with inhuman or degrading treatment or torture and people fearing such inhuman treatment or torture will regularly be persecuted in the sense of the Refugee Convention. It has been explained that the Court and the Committee consider the fact that a complainant has been recognized as a refugee (by the UNHCR or a national authority) as an important risk factor in their own risk assessment. It has further been noted that the Court's and the Committee's awareness is particularly raised in cases in which it is solely for reasons of public security that an individual has been exempt from the refoulement protection offered by the Refugee Convention, or in which close family members of the applicant have been granted refugee status.

The great majority of the refoulement complaints before the Court and the Committee concern rejected asylum seekers. In fact, most of the claims assessed in Strasbourg and Geneva have usually been made within the terms of the Refugee Convention at national level. The fact that a complainant has not been recognized as a refugee is not as such relevant for the Court and the Committee; otherwise no complaint introduced by a rejected asylum seeker would ever be successful. The way national authorities have come to the conclusion that an individual should not be granted refugee status is, however, of importance.

The Court and the Committee do not usually differentiate between an assessment concerning refugee status and one concerning a violation of the principle of non-refoulement as guaranteed by human rights treaties when assessing the respect accorded to Article 3 ECHR or Article 3 CAT by domestic authorities. This is not surprising since national authorities usually jointly examine the risk of persecution and the risk of torture or inhuman treatment.[919] The risk elements addressed in the framework of the international procedure are usually the same as those addressed or disputed in the domestic asylum procedure with regard to the question of whether the individual concerned

---

918   See Lauterpacht & Bethlehem 2003, p. 160.

919   Mandal 2005, p. 37.

should be granted refugee status. When examining whether the domestic remedies have been exhausted, the Court and the Committee generally refer to the national remedies available with regard to the determination of refugee status, unless the complainant is clearly exempt from the protection offered by the Refugee Convention.[920] When observing that the risk assessment made by national authorities was deficient or missing, the Court and the Committee usually refer to the refugee determination procedure. In the lead case *M.S.S.*, the Grand Chamber found a violation of Article 3 ECHR by the Belgian authorities because they had exposed the applicant to risks linked to the deficiencies in the 'asylum procedure' in Greece.[921] All of this accentuates how connected the risk assessment under the Refugee Convention and that made under the human rights treaties really is. In fact, as can be observed in this study and as has been stated with regard to the CAT by Goodwin-Gill and McAdam, the ECHR and the CAT may provide relief for those who are explicitly excluded from the Refugee's Convention's protection, those who are not threatened with ill treatment for one of the five Refugee Convention grounds, and also for those who have been overlooked as refugees due to narrow *interpretations* of the Refugee Convention.[922] In the face of the obvious procedural and material nexus between the risk assessment under Article 33 of the Refugee Convention and the ECHR or the CAT, one can also raise the question of why the Court and the Committee do not explicitly admit that in the majority of the refoulement cases, their risk assessment concerns elements that are just as relevant in refugee matters in the sense of the Refugee Convention. It is interesting to note in that context that In its recent case law, the Court has started to state in judgments that 'the right to political asylum is not *explicitly* protected' by the ECHR.[923]

However, it should be recalled that the ECHR and the CAT do not provide for a right to refugee status with all of its benefits and entitlements, but only guarantee the right not to be deported.[924] McAdam argues that 'differentiating between rights and entitlements on the basis of the source of the non-refoulement

---

920   See on this Chapter 2 Section 3.2.4.b.

921   See ECtHR, *M.S.S.*,§§ 358 and 359. See also Mallia 2011, p. 127 noting with regard to the *M.S.S.* judgment that the two guarantees (protection against refoulement under Art. 3 ECHR and Art. 33 Refugee Convention) 'operate in tandem.'

922   Goodwin-Gill & McAdam 2007, p. 303.

923   See ECtHR, *Gaforov v. Russia*, 21 October 2010, no. 25404/09, § 110. Cited, for example, in ECtHR, *Rustamov v. Russia*, 3 July 2012, no. 11209/10, § 105; ECtHR, *Sidikovy v. Russia*, 20 June 2013, no. 73455/11, § 129; ECtHR, *Akram Karimov v. Russia*, 28 May 2014, no. 62892/12, § 117.

924   See Chapter 2 Section 1.3.2 and 2.3.2.

obligation has no cogent legal justification, and overlooks the substantially similar circumstances and needs of those concerned.'[925] Looking at the *significant substantial overlap* between the protection against refoulement under the Refugee Convention and that under the ECHR and the CAT as explained in this section, this argument becomes very convincing.

3.4   *Further Relevant Factors*

3.4.1   Internal Flight Alternative

a   *Court*

The concept of the *internal flight alternative* (also referred to as the possibility of *internal relocation*) has been developed in the context of refugee status determination procedures. It is the option proposed by states to send an individual to a region in the receiving state where he is not originally from, but where there is no risk of his being ill-treated.

Without explicitly citing it, the Court discussed the concept for the first time in *Chahal v. United Kingdom* concerning the removal of a well-known supporter of the Sikh separatist movement to India.[926] The Court rejected the government's argument that the applicant could hide in other parts of India than the Punjab region, where the local police threatened him with ill-treatment. It noted that the Punjab security forces were also acting outside their state's boundaries and that there were serious human rights violations by police forces all over India.[927] In *Hilal v. United Kingdom*, the Court explicitly addressed the concept of an internal flight option but rejected its existence for similar reasons.[928] The government had argued that if the Court would assume the complainant would be at risk in Zanzibar, where he was part of the government opposition, it should take into account that he could find refuge in Tanzania. Pointing out the institutional link between police forces in both regions as well as the widespread human rights violations on mainland Tanzania, the Court rejected this argument. As can be seen from these two cases, if state forces are persecuting an applicant, it is difficult for governments to successfully

---

925   McAdam 2007, p. 251, concluding her chapter on the legal status of beneficiaries of complementary protection in contrast to individuals recognized as refugees under the 1951 Refugee Convention (pp. 197–255). See in this sense also the concurring opinion of judge Pinto de Albuquerque on ECtHR, *Hirsi Jamaa and Others v. Italy*, 23 February 2012 [GC], no. 27765/09.

926   ECtHR, *Chahal v. UK*, 15 November 1996, no. 22414/93.

927   *Ibid.*, §§ 98–107.

928   ECtHR, *Hilal v. UK*, 6 March 2001, no. 45276/99, §§ 67 and 68.

invoke an internal flight option, unless the applicant has a very low profile[929] or unless the authorities' influence is restricted to a certain region.[930]

However, in its case law of the last years, the Court has made very clear that Article 3 ECHR does not preclude states from relying on the existence of an internal flight or relocation alternative if certain preconditions are fulfilled. In the cases *Salah Sheek v. Netherlands* and *Sufi and Elmi v. United Kingdom*, both concerning expulsions to Somalia, the Court held that

> ... as a precondition of relying on an internal flight alternative, certain *guarantees* have to be in place: the person to be expelled must be *able to travel* to the area concerned, *gain admittance and settle there*, failing which an issue under Article 3 may arise, the more so if in the absence of such guarantees there is a *possibility of his ending up in a part of the country* of origin where he may be subjected to ill-treatment.[931] (Emphasis added)

This statement has been recited by the Court as a general principle in subsequent judgments.[932] The Court has also made clear that the same considerations apply to the situation where the applicant will not be sent to the area he originates from but directly to another area within his country of origin.[933] In the cases *Salah Sheek* and *Sufi and Elmi*, the Court rejected the government's arguments according to which there was a possibility for the complainants to hide and find safety in areas outside the region of Mogadishu. In *Salah Sheek* decided in January 2007, the Court assessed the situation in Somaliland and Puntland. The Dutch government considered these northern regions as 'relatively safe.' The Court held that it was most unlikely that the complainant, being a member of a minority clan from another region, would obtain

---

929   See, for example, ECtHR, *Kaldik v. Germany*, 22 September 2005, no. 28526/05 (decision; Turkey); ECtHR, *Karim v. Sweden*, 4 July 2006, no. 24171/05 (decision; Bangladesh).

930   See, for example, ECtHR, *Thampibillai v. Netherlands*, 17 February 2004, no. 61350/00, § 67, in which the Court noted that 'should the applicant remain fearful of the Sri Lankan authorities, he might be expected to settle in LTTE-controlled areas.' See also ECtHR, *Jeltsujeva v. Netherlands*, 1 June 2006, no. 39858/04 (decision), in which the Court suggests that the applicant can settle elsewhere in Russia than Chechnya.

931   ECtHR, *Salah Sheekh v. Netherlands*, 11 January 2007, no. 1948/04, § 141; ECtHR, *Sufi and Elmi v. UK*, 28 June 2011, nos. 8319/07 and 11449/07, § 266.

932   See, among others, ECtHR, *H. and B. v. UK*, 9 April 2013, nos. 70073/10 and 44539/11, § 91; ECtHR, *M.Y.H. v. Sweden*, 27 June 2013, no. 50859/10, § 62.

933   ECtHR, *K.A.B. v. Sweden*, 5 September 2013, no. 886/11, § 82.

protection from a local clan there.[934] It eventually rejected the flight option, however, for the reason that the authorities of Puntland and Somaliland had made clear that the applicant would not be allowed to settle there, which meant that he would have to leave for other parts of the country considered unsafe by the government and the UNHCR.[935]

In *Sufi and Elmi* decided in June 2011, the Court considered whether there was an internal flight alternative for the two complainants in southern and central Somalia. It observed that in view of the humanitarian crisis and the importance of the traditional clan structure in Somalia, it 'does not consider that a returnee could find refuge or support in an area where he has no close family connections.'[936] The Court considered that individuals who had no recent experience of living in Somalia could not travel or settle safely in regions under control of the al-Shabaab. Even if they had family connections in such regions, they could not avoid coming to the attention of the al-Shabaab and becoming victims of their repressive regime.[937] The Court further noted that if a complainant had no family connections or if those connections were in an area that he could not safely reach, there was a likelihood that he would have to have recourse to either a camp for internally displaced persons in Somalia or a refugee camp in Kenya.[938] With regard to these camps, the Court observed that 'any returnee forced to seek refuge in either camp would be at real risk of Article 3 ill-treatment on account of the dire humanitarian conditions.'[939] Looking at the background of the complainants, one having no family connection in the region and both having either to live under the al-Shabaab regime or in dire humanitarian conditions in refugee camps, the Court concluded that no valuable flight alternatives from Mogadishu were available.[940]

The situation was deemed different in *Abdi Ibrahim v. United Kingdom* for an applicant from the northern region of Somaliland, whose complaint was rejected in September 2012.[941] As a member of the majority Isaaq clan who was born in what is now Somaliland, the applicant fulfilled the criteria set out in a memorandum of understanding concluded in 2003 between the British and Somaliland authorities on the readmission of individuals originating from

---

934   ECtHR, *Salah Sheekh v. Netherlands*, 11 January 2007, no. 1948/04, §§ 139 and 140.

935   *Ibid.*, §§ 142–143. See the similar arguments with regard to some islands off the coast of southern Somalia; § 144.

936   ECtHR, *Sufi and Elmi v. UK*, 28 June 2011, nos. 8319/07 and 11449/07, §§ 267 & 294.

937   *Ibid.*, §§ 272–277 and 296.

938   *Ibid.*, § 294.

939   *Ibid.*, §§ 278–292.

940   *Ibid.*, §§ 301–304 and 309–312.

941   ECtHR, *Abdi Ibrahim v. UK*, 18 September 2012, no. 14535/10, (decision).

Somaliland. Relying on this memorandum, the Court saw it as established that the applicant would be permitted entry by the Somaliland authorities and would thus not be forced to remain in Mogadishu or elsewhere in Somalia.[942] The Court referred to *Salah Sheek* and observed that Somaliland can be categorised as 'relatively safe' for those originating from the area and having links to the majority clan. It noted that unlike south and central Somalia, Somaliland has a functioning system of government and has remained stable for many years and does not suffer from a high level of general violence. The Court further recalled its findings in *Sufi and Elmi* that there was no real risk of ill treatment for a person simply transiting through Mogadishu airport. It eventually noted that although the applicant had lived in the United Kingdom since he was a child, it was likely from his background that he had some knowledge of the Somali language and of the behaviour required to blend into Somali communities. Pointing out that the applicant was young, healthy and physically strong with certain skills, such as knowledge of English, it did not find it established that he will 'inevitably be excluded from all forms of economic activity.' The Court noted that there was no evidence demonstrating the existence of exceptionally compelling humanitarian grounds against the removal. The complaint was rejected for being manifestly ill-founded.[943]

Precarious living conditions will not as such exclude the possibility of internal relocation. This was made clear in *Husseini v. Sweden* concerning the deportation of a male to Afghanistan.[944] The Court observed that if the complainant could not be sent back to his hometown in the Ghazni province because of violent Taliban operations, he could reasonably be expected to resettle elsewhere in Afghanistan, such as, for example, in Kabul or Mazar-e Sharif. The Court referred to UNHCR guidelines from 2010 on Afghanistan according to which internal flight alternatives are reasonable where protection is available from an individual's own family or tribe. In certain circumstances, however, single males may subsist without family or community support in

---

942 The Court observed that according to the memorandum, the UK had undertaken to return, at its own expense, every individual denied entry to Somaliland.

943 *Ibid.*, §§ 33–37. See also ECtHR, *A.A. and Others v. Sweden*, 24 July 2014, no. 34098/11, §§ 55–71, in which the applicants belong to the Sheikal clan. The Court notes that 'if the applicants do not gain admittance to Somaliland, a fresh assessment would have to be made by the Swedish migration authorities.' See further ECtHR, *K.A.B. v. Sweden*, 5 September 2013, no. 886/11, §§ 80–84, in which the Court rejected the possibility of deporting the applicant to Somaliland, since he did not have sufficiently strong connections to be able to gain admittance and settle there. However, the Court considered that the applicant could live in Mogadishu; see on this case Chapter 4 Section 3.2.1.a.

944 ECtHR, *Husseini v. Sweden*, 13 October 2011, no. 10611/09.

urban areas with established infrastructure and under effective government control. The Court then reiterated a statement made in *Salah Sheekh* according to which socioeconomic and humanitarian considerations do not 'necessarily have a bearing, and certainly not a decisive one' on the question of whether the persons concerned would face a real risk of ill-treatment in areas considered as an alternative flight option.[945] Without assessing the particular situation of the complainant as suggested by the UNHCR guidelines, the Court eventually rejected Husseini's complaint. It noted that it was not convinced by the applicant's submission that no matter where in Afghanistan he were to resettle he would be exposed to a real risk of being subjected to treatment proscribed by Article 3 ECHR.[946] The Court confirmed it considers Kabul an admissible internal flight alternative for young men in subsequent decisions.[947]

Generally, the Court is more open to accepting the existence of an internal flight alternative in cases in which the risk emanates primarily from non-state actors or/and where a state is fragmented into zones controlled by different actors. This can be observed in eight cases decided in June 2013 concerning the deportation to Iraq of failed asylum seekers originally from Baghdad, Mosul and Kirkuk. Two of those applicants alleged that they would be at risk of becoming victims of honour-related crimes following their relationships with women of whom their families had disapproved.[948] The applicants in the other six cases alleged they would be at risk of persecution on account of belonging to the Christian minority.[949] Even though the Court recognized that all the applicants would be exposed to a real risk to their lives or of inhuman or degrading treatment if removed to their home regions in Iraq, it considered that the Iraqi Christians could reasonably relocate to other regions in Iraq such as Kurdistan in the north, and the applicants confronted with a risk of honour-related crime to southern or central Iraq. With regard to the two applicants persecuted because of their former relationships, the Court noted that there was no evidence that the clans or families of the women by whom they were persecuted were particularly influential or powerful or that they had connections with the authorities or militia in Iraq. More importantly,

---

945   *Ibid.*, §§ 48 and 95–98.

946   *Ibid.*, § 98. See the dissenting opinion of judge Zupančič.

947   ECtHR, *S.S. v. UK*, 24 January 2012, no. 12096/10 (decision) and ECtHR, *H. and B. v. UK*, 9 April 2013, nos. 70073/10 and 44539/11, § 114.

948   ECtHR, *D.N.M. v. Sweden*, 27 June 2013, no. 28379/11; ECtHR, *S.A. v. Sweden*, 27 June 2013, no. 66523/10.

949   ECtHR, *A.G.A.M. v. Sweden*, 27 June 2013, no. 71680/10; ECtHR, *M.Y.H. v. Sweden*, 27 June 2013, no. 50859/10; ECtHR, *M.K.N. v. Sweden*, 27 June 2013, no. 72413/10; ECtHR, *N.A.N.S. v. Sweden*, 27 June 2013, no. 68411/10; ECtHR, *N.M.B. v. Sweden*, 27 June 2013, no. 68335/10; ECtHR, *N.M.Y. and Others v. Sweden*, 27 June 2013, no. 72686/10.

according to the Court, there was nothing to indicate it would be particularly difficult for them as Sunni Muslims, which make up one-third of the population of Iraq, to find a place to settle where they would constitute a majority or, in any event, be able to live in relative safety.[950]

In the other six cases concerning the Iraqi Christians, the Court considered it likely that they could relocate to the three northern governorates (Dahuk, Erbil and Sulaymaniyah) forming the Kurdistan region. Referring to international sources, the Court indicated that this region was a relatively safe area. Large numbers of members of the Christian group had found refuge there. It further did not appear that the applicants would be unable to travel or settle there. The Court recognized that various sources attested that people who relocate to the Kurdistan region might face difficulties, for instance, in finding proper jobs and housing, not the least if they do not speak Kurdish. However, it indicated that there are jobs available in the Kurdistan region and that settlers have access to health care as well as financial and other support from the UNHCR and local authorities.[951] In any event, according to the Court, there was no indication in all cases that 'the general living conditions in the Kurdistan Region for a Christian settler would be unreasonable or in any way amount to treatment prohibited by Article 3 ECHR.' Nor was there a real risk of the applicant's ending up in other parts of Iraq. The Court hence concluded that relocation to the Kurdistan region was a viable alternative for a Christian fearing persecution or ill treatment in other parts of Iraq and that the reliance by a contracting state on such an alternative would thus not, in general, give rise to an issue under Article 3 ECHR.[952]

The Court noted in all eight judgments that internal relocation 'inevitably involves certain hardship.'[953] In one case, the Court observed 'that the applicant is a young man who has an education and is apparently fit for work. In these circumstances, the fact that he does not have a social network in the Kurdistan Region and is not familiar with the culture and traditions there cannot be given any weight in the Court's determination under Articles 2 and 3 of the Convention.'[954] In another judgment, the Court noted that it had not been suggested that any of the applicants would suffer from health

---

950 ECtHR, *D.N.M. v. Sweden*, 27 June 2013, no. 28379/11, §§ 54–60; ECtHR, *S.A. v. Sweden*, 27 June 2013, no. 66523/10, §§ 53–59.

951 See, representative for the six judgments, ECtHR, *M.Y.H. v. Sweden*, 27 June 2013, no. 50859/10, §§ 63–67.

952 *Ibid.*, §§ 66 and 67.

953 See, representative for the six judgments, ECtHR, *M.Y.H. v. Sweden*, 27 June 2013, no. 50859/10, §§ 62–67.

954 ECtHR, *N.A.N.S. v. Sweden*, 27 June 2013, no. 68411/10, § 42.

problems that would affect their ability to work.[955] In a third case in which the applicants pointed out that they were elderly and in bad health, the Court replied that the medical certificates submitted during the proceedings did not suggest that they had such medical problems that they could not return to Iraq, nor were they of such an advanced age as to render their deportation unreasonable.[956]

The fact that the Court will tend to accept an internal flight alternative in the context of threats from private actors can also be observed in inadmissibility decisions concerning the risk of female genital mutilation for the applicants or their daughters if deported to Nigeria. In *Izevbekhai v. Ireland*, the Court noted that notwithstanding the applicants' considerable familial and financial resources, they made no attempt to protect their daughters by relocating to northern Nigeria, where the rate of female genital mutilation is very low.[957] In *Omeredo v. Austria*, the Court accepted that the applicant's fear of being forced to undergo female genital mutilation in Nigeria was well founded, but it found that she disposed of an internal flight alternative within the country.[958] Noting that the 37-year-old applicant had obtained school education for at least 13 years and had worked as a seamstress for 8 years, the Court considered she would be able to build up her life in another area of Nigeria outside her home region even without the support of her family members.[959]

This latter decision clearly shows that family bonds are not the determining factor for the Court's approval of an internal flight alternative. The Court's remark on the applicant's education and ability to build up her life indicates, in contrast, that it does not completely ignore socioeconomic issues when assessing flight alternatives.[960] As Wouters notes, the rights to be assured in the alternative region must go beyond what is guaranteed as a minimum standard under Article 3 ECHR.[961] Thurin rightly observes that although the real risk of a violation of Article 3 ECHR is the principal criterion for the question of whether a complainant can be expelled to a certain region, the Court uses a

---

955   ECtHR, *N.M.Y. and Others v. Sweden*, 27 June 2013, no. 72686/10, § 42.

956   ECtHR, *M.Y.H. v. Sweden*, 27 June 2013, no. 50859/10, § 70.

957   ECtHR, *Izevbekhai and Others v. Ireland*, 17 May 2011, no. 43408/08, §§ 75 and 80–81 (decision).

958   ECtHR, *Omeredo v. Austria*, 20 September 2011, no. 8969/10 (decision).

959   *Ibid.*

960   Similarly the statement of the Court in ECtHR, *Abdi Ibrahim v. UK*, 18 September 2012, no. 14535/10, § 36 (decision) cited above, according to which the complainant will not inevitably be excluded from economic activity in Somaliland.

961   Wouters 2009, p. 558.

slightly lower standard of proof with regard to the risk in regions suggested by the expelling state as flight alternatives.[962] However, as particularly the cases above concerning removals to Iraq show, the Court accepts 'hardship' as a result of internal relocation. Strasbourg generally places a great deal of trust in the concept of internal relocation in its recent case law. Especially in countries that are politically and/or socially fragmented like Iraq and Afghanistan, this kind of trust can provoke an unduly hard burden on applicants to establish a real risk of ill treatment in *any* part of the territory. This problematic will be readdressed in the comparative section below.[963]

b   *Committee*

The first time the Committee made a statement with regard to the concept of an internal flight alternative was in 1996 in *Alan v. Switzerland* concerning the deportation of a Kurdish activist to Turkey.[964] The Committee noted that it was not likely that a 'safe' area would exist for the applicant in Turkey, since the police were looking for him.[965] In *Haydin v. Sweden*, the Committee referred to views of the UNHCR according to which no place of refuge is available within Turkey for persons who risk being suspected of being active in or sympathizers of the PKK.[966] In *Singh v. Canada* and *Khalsa et al. v. Switzerland*, both cases decided in May 2011 and concerning the deportation of high-profile Sikh activists to India, the Committee rejected the government's arguments that the complainants could find refuge in parts of India outside the Punjab region, pointing out that they were still wanted by the police.[967] The Committee had come to a different conclusion in two cases decided a few years before concerning the deportation of two other Sikhs with slightly lower profiles.[968] In *B.S.S. v. Canada*, it observed the following:

---

962   Thurin 2012, p. 212.

963   See the critical remarks on that issue in Chapter 4 Section 3.4.1.c below and the dissenting opinions of judge Spielmann joined by judge Zupančič and of judge Power-Forde on ECtHR, *M.Y.H. v. Sweden*, 27 June 2013, no. 50859/10. For a critical analysis of the Court's case law, see also Schultz in Gauci, Giuffré & Tsourdi, 2015, pp. 31–49.

964   ComAT, *Alan v. Switzerland*, 8 May 1996, no. 21/1995.

965   *Ibid.*, § 11.4.

966   ComAT, *Haydin v. Sweden*, 20 November 1998, no. 101/1997, §§ 4.14 and 6.4. See also ComAT, *Ayas v. Sweden*, 12 November 1998, no. 97/1997, § 6.4.

967   ComAT, *Singh v. Canada*, 30 May 2011, no. 319/2007, §§ 8.5 and 8.6 and ComAT, *Khalsa et al. v. Switzerland*, 26 May 2011, no. 336/2008, § 11.5 and 11.6.

968   ComAT, *B.S.S. v. Canada*, 12 May 2004, no. 183/2001; ComAT, *S.S.S. v. Canada*, 16 November 2005, no. 245/2004.

Insofar as the complainant claims that he currently remains at risk of being tortured in India, the Committee notes that, while confirming the risk of him being subjected to torture, as well as his family's continuing harassment, by the Punjabi police, the evidence produced by the complainant, including affidavits, letters and a document which is said to contain a resolution adopted by the municipal council of his home village, merely refers to his risk of being tortured in Punjab. The Committee considers that the complainant has failed to substantiate that he would be unable to lead a life free of torture in another part of India.[969]

The Committee further held that 'although resettlement outside Punjab would constitute a considerable hardship for the complainant, the mere fact that he may not be able to return to his family and his home village does not as such amount to torture' within the meaning Article 1 CAT.[970] In the case *S.S.S. v. Canada*, the Committee noted that some of the available evidence suggests that high-profile persons may be at risk in other parts of India, but that the complainant had not shown that he fit into that particular category. Considering further the time elapsed and political changes since the complainant's departure from India, the Committee concluded he would be able to lead a life free of torture in other parts of India.[971]

As has been explained, it is still rather new for the Committee to assess cases in which the alleged risk emanates from non-state actors.[972] If it addresses the issue of non-state actors, the concept of the internal flight alternative is likely to be of relevance since threats from private entities are less likely to extend across the whole state territory than threats from state authorities.[973] However, if gross, flagrant or mass violations of human rights are widely committed in the receiving country and no state authorities exist that can offer protection, the Committee will reject the objection of an internal flight option.[974] The latter

---

969   ComAT, *B.S.S. v. Canada*, 12 May 2004, no. 183/2001, § 11.5.

970   *Ibid.* The background of *B.S.S.* appears not that strikingly different from that of *Singh*. For a critique of the lack of reasoning in these decisions see the comparative Section 3.4.1.c just below.

971   ComAT, *S.S.S. v. Canada*, 16 November 2005, no. 245/2004, § 8.5.

972   See the cases discussed in Chapter 3 Section 3.3.

973   See illustrative ComAT, *S.S. v. Netherlands*, 5 May 2003, no. 191/2001, § 6.4 (LTTE-controlled area of Sri Lanka); ComAT, *C.A.R.M. et al. v. Canada*, 18 May 2007, no. 298/2006, § 8.9 (Mexico).

974   See with regard to the situation in Somalia the case ComAT, *Elmi v. Australia*, 14 May 1999, no. 120/1998, §§ 6.5–6.6 compared to ComAT, *H.M.H.I. v. Australia*, 1 May 2002, no. 177/2001, §§ 6.4–6.6.

can be observed in *Njamba and Balikosa* and *Bakatu-Bia v. Sweden*. In those two cases, the Committee considered that the precarious human rights situation for single women in the DRC, as documented in recent UN reports, made it impossible 'to identify particular areas of the country which could be considered safe for the complainants in their current and evolving situation.'[975] However, in a subsequent decision, the Committee indicated that the removal of a woman to Kinshasa was not problematic under Article 3 CAT.[976]

In *Mondal v. Sweden*, the Committee noted it would be impossible for the complainant to prove that the death *fatwa* issued against him by fundamentalist Islamists was not only of local character. It added that 'the notion of "local danger" does not provide for measurable criteria and is not sufficient to dissipate totally the personal danger of being tortured.'[977] The Committee recalled this latter sentence in subsequent decisions in which the alleged risk of ill treatment emanated from state actors.[978] The case *Kalonzo v. Canada* concerned a deportation to the DRC.[979] In this case, the Committee first held that, as the son of an opposition leader and being an ethnic Luba from Kasaï who had already been the victim of violence during a detention in Kinshasa in 2002, there was a real risk of the applicant being subjected to torture in case of removal to the DRC. In addition, the Committee considered that 'the State party's argument that the complainant could resettle in Kinshasa, where the Luba do not seem to be threatened by violence (as they are in the Katanga region), does not

---

975   ComAT, *Njamba and Balikosa v. Sweden*, 14 May 2010, no. 322/2007, § 9.6; ComAT, *Bakatu-Bia v. Sweden*, 3 June 2011, no. 379/2009, § 10.7. See also recently ComAT, *F.B. v. Netherlands*, 20 November 2015, no. 613/2014, §§ 4.14, 8.7 and 8.8 on the risk of female genital mutilation in Guinea (introduced in Chapter 3 Section 3.3.). The Committee did not even address the government's argument according to which the applicant could settle in a different area from where she lived when she was submitted to female genital mutilation (the applicant had undergone a reconstructive plastic surgery).

976   See ComAT, *N.B.-M. v. Switzerland*, 14 November 2011, no. 347/2008, §§ 9.5 and 9.9. However, in 2015, the Committee again found a violation of Art. 3 CAT because of the risk of gender-based violence for a woman originally from Kinshasa, who had however sufficiently alleged to be at risk of ill treatment from the *official military forces* that are present and active in the entire territory. The Committee noted that there was 'widespread violence against women' which was 'mostly inherent in conflict-affected and rural areas of the country, especially in the east,' but that this violence is 'also taking place in other parts of the country.' See ComAT, *E.K.W. v. Finland*, 4 May 2015, no. 490/2012, §§ 9.5–9.8. Both cases are discussed in Chapter 4 Section 3.3.2.b.

977   ComAT, *Mondal v. Sweden*, 23 May 2011, no. 338/2008, §§ 2.6 and 7.4.

978   ComAT, *Kalonzo v. Canada*, 18 May 2012, no. 343/2008, § 9.7 (DRC); ComAT, *A.K. v. Switzerland*, 8 May 2015, no. 544/2013, § 9.5 (PKK activist in Turkey).

979   ComAT, *Kalonzo v. Canada*, 18 May 2012, no. 343/2008.

entirely remove the personal danger for the complainant.' In this regard, the Committee confirmed that, 'in accordance with its jurisprudence, the notion of "local danger" does not provide for measurable criteria and is not sufficient to entirely dispel the personal danger of being tortured.'[980]

The Committee's case law of the last years indicates that it has generally become more sceptical towards the concept of 'local danger.' However, the Committee's case law is still scant and the reasoning in the decisions so brief that statements of a general nature should be made with caution. It can nevertheless be concluded that the Committee is reluctant to accept the concept of an internal flight alternative when complainants have a high profile and are of particular interest to the police or other authorities, or when it observes a widespread and systematic practice of ill treatment towards individuals with similar backgrounds as the applicant.[981] Since these circumstances often constitute the basis of a violation of Article 3 CAT, it is exceptional for internal flight options to play a decisive role in the Committee's case law.

c   *Comparison*

The Court's case law on the concept of the internal flight alternative is more elaborated than the Committee's. According to the Court, an internal flight alternative is only considered an option compatible with Article 3 ECHR if it is established that the complainant

- is able to travel safely to the suggested region,
- has the right to settle there and
- is not threatened with being further removed to a place where he may be subjected to ill treatment.

Hardships like having to live outside the region of origin without family members or having to build a new life in an unknown region are in principle not as such able to dismiss the possibility of an internal flight alternative. However, the Court has occasionally taken such elements as well as economic possibilities into account when assessing the admissibility of internal flight alternatives proposed by governments. In principle, the human rights standard that must be fulfilled in the suggested alternative region is the non-violation of Article 3 ECHR or Article 1 CAT respectively. In *Sufi and Elmi*, the Court considered that refugee camps in Kenya or the settlements for internally displaced people in Somalia did not meet the standards of Article 3 ECHR on account of

---

980   *Ibid.*, § 9.7.
981   See also Nowak & McArthur 2008, p. 208 (§ 197).

dire humanitarian conditions. It is to be assumed that the Committee would be stricter on the question since, also with regard to the alternative region, its protection is restricted to acts of torture. However, it is only in exceptional circumstances that socioeconomic considerations give rise to a breach of Article 3 ECHR.[982] Also before the Court, it is hence difficult for applicants to show that because of hard living conditions, their relocation to a particular area is not permissible.[983]

With regard to the judgment *Sufi and Elmi* it is worth pointing out that it is new for the Court to assess a flight possibility *outside the country of origin* as it did with regard to the refugee camps in Kenya. Flight options *outside* the receiving state should not be taken into account when assessing refoulement complaints, otherwise the expelling state could always claim that individuals should first seek protection in the neighbouring countries. In addition, with regard to refugee camps in general, the criterion of a *permanent settlement* opportunity should also be of relevance. Unfortunately, the Court did not address this question in *Sufi and Elmi*.

When a risk emanates from state authorities such as police agents or other security forces, the Court and the Committee are usually reluctant to accept a flight alternative as guaranteeing the complainant's security, unless the state agent's powers are restricted to a certain territory. Against this background, the Committee's statements in the two Sikh cases *B.S.S.* and *S.S.S.* appear problematic.[984] The Committee suggested that the complainants could find refuge outside the Punjab region, although they seemed to be wanted by the police. In contrast, in the cases *Singh* and *Khalsa et al.*, both decided in 2011 and concerning the deportation of high-profile Sikh activists to India, it was exactly for that reason that the Committee rejected the existence of an internal flight alternative.[985] The Committee did not explain why the Punjab police's influence would be restricted in *B.S.S. and S.S.S.*[986] It did, however, refer to the complainant's lower profile in *S.S.S.*[987] It is not convincing to consider an internal flight option as more relevant if the complainant has a high profile in a case where the risk emanates from state agents who have powers all over

---

982   See on this Chapter 3 Section 2.3.2.

983   As a recent example see ECtHR, *H. and B. v. UK*, 9 April 2013, nos. 70073/10 and 44539/11, § 114 (Afghanistan).

984   ComAT, *B.S.S. v. Canada*, 12 May 2004, no. 183/2001; ComAT, *S.S.S. v. Canada*, 16 November 2005, no. 245/2004.

985   ComAT, *Singh v. Canada*, 30 May 2011, no. 319/2007, §§ 8.5 and 8.6 and ComAT, *Khalsa et al. v. Switzerland*, 26 May 2011, no. 336/2008, § 11.5 and 11.6.

986   See also Chetail 2006, p. 98 and Wouters 2009, p. 494.

987   ComAT, *S.S.S. v. Canada*, 16 November 2005, no. 245/2004, § 8.5.

the country. If the Committee was simply not convinced that the complainants had a sufficiently high profile to attract the Indian authorities' attention in *S.S.S.* and *B.S.S.*, it should have based its decision only on this and not on the internal flight alternative as well.

Chetail noted in 2006 that the Committee lacks coherence and reflection on the subject.[988] This statement is still valid.[989] The only decision in which the Committee has mentioned the issue of the *accessibility* of an internal flight alternative is *Khalsa et al. v. Switzerland*, in which it noted that Sikhs suspected of terrorism had been arrested upon arrival at the airport.[990] In the two cases in which the Committee accepted that the Sikh complainants could live safely outside the Punjab region, the Committee remained silent on any risks on arrival in India.[991] Moreover, the Committee has not addressed the question of *to what extent* a complainant must be able to settle in an alternative flight region. However, in its very recent case law, the Committee appears to have become more reluctant to rely on the concept of an internal flight alternative and has repeatedly stated that 'the notion of local danger' did not provide for a measurable criteria and was not sufficient to dissipate the personal danger of torture for the applicant.[992]

The Court and the Committee are more open to the possibility of an internal flight alternative if the risk emanates from private actors. The approach is logical since the power of state authorities will usually extend across the whole territory of a country, while the threat of private actors, for example rebel groups or powerful clans or families, will tend to be restricted to a certain region.[993]

However, if the Court or the Committee are of the opinion that there are endemic practices of ill treatment all over the receiving state with regard to individuals with a similar background to the complainant, neither will be willing to accept an internal flight alternative.[994] The question of whether the harm

---

988   Chetail 2006, p. 98.

989   It also applies to the HRC; see on this HRC, *B.L. v. Australia*, 16 October 2014, no. 2053/2011 and the respective individual opinions attached to this view.

990   ComAT, *Khalsa et al. v. Switzerland*, 26 May 2011, no. 336/2008, § 11.5 and 11.6. See on this also Wouters (2009, pp. 495-496 and 559), who rightly criticizes that the Committee has not discussed this point when referring to an internal flight alternative in ComAT, *H.M.H.I. v. Australia*, 1 May 2002, no. 177/2001 (Somalia).

991   See ComAT, *B.S.S. v. Canada*, 12 May 2004, no. 183/2001 and ComAT, *S.S.S. v. Canada*, 16 November 2005, no. 245/2004.

992   See lastly ComAT, *A.K. v. Switzerland*, 8 May 2015, no. 544/2013, § 9.5.

993   See in this sense also UNHCR, *Guidelines on International Protection*, 'Internal Flight or Relocation Alternative' within the context of Art. 1(2) of the 1951 and/or 1967 Protocol relating to the Status of Refugees, 23 July 2004, HCR/GIP/03/04, §§ 13 and 14.

994   Schürmann & Scheidegger 2009, p. 207.

emanates from private or public actors becomes less relevant in such cases. This can be observed in *N. v. Sweden* as well as in *Njamba and Balikosa v. Sweden*, in which the Court and the Committee held that there was a real risk of ill treatment for the complainants as single women in Afghanistan and the DRC respectively because of a general and endemic culture of violence against women and abuse in those countries.[995] The cases further make clear that the existence of an internal flight alternative not only depends on the protection offered by state authorities there. The presence of private entities, clans, family members or simply the status accorded by marriage can amount to a protection capable of reducing the risk of ill treatment in a decisive manner in certain regions.

The Court and the Committee have both indicated that it should principally be up to the government to show that an internal flight alternative is safe and to make the respective assessment of the situation there.[996] However, neither of them is very consistent on this question. In *B.S.S. v. Canada*, for instance, the Committee rejected the complaint by noting that the applicant had failed to substantiate that he would be unable to lead a life free of torture in another part of India.[997] In recent cases concerning removals to Iraq and Afghanistan, the Court relied on an internal flight alternative in the international procedure without the respective regions having been assessed in detail by the state authorities or the Court itself.[998] In *K.A.B. v. Sweden*, the national authorities wanted to remove the applicant to Somaliland but the Court judged that he would not be able to gain admittance and settle there.[999] The Court hence, on its own motion, assessed whether the applicant could be removed to Mogadishu, even though the national authorities did not intended to remove him there.[1000] This approach is very problematic. In taking it, the Court effectively puts the applicant in the situation in which the internal flight alternative is

---

995   See ECtHR, *N. v. Sweden*, 20 July 2010, no. 23505/09 (Afghanistan); ComAT, *Njamba and Balikosa v. Sweden*, 14 May 2010, no. 322/2007 (DRC).

996   ECtHR, *Sufi and Elmi v. UK*, 28 June 2011, nos. 8319/07 and 11449/07, § 311; ComAT, *Mondal v. Sweden*, 23 May 2011, no. 338/2008, §§ 2.6 and 7.4; ComAT, *Kalonzo v. Canada*, 18 May 2012, no. 343/2008, 9.7.

997   ComAT, *B.S.S. v. Canada*, 12 May 2004, no. 183/2001, § 11.5.

998   See ECtHR, *Husseini v. Sweden*, 13 October 2011, no. 10611/09 and the dissenting opinion of judge Spielmann joined by judge Zupančič. See further the dissenting opinions of judge Power-Forde in ECtHR, *M.Y.H. v. Sweden*, 27 June 2013, no. 50859/10; ECtHR, *B.K.A. v. Sweden*, 19 December 2013, no. 11161/11 and ECtHR, *A.A.M. v. Sweden*, 3 April 2014, no. 68519/10.

999   ECtHR, *K.A.B. v. Sweden*, 5 September 2013, no. 886/11, §§ 80–84.

1000   *Ibid.*, §§ 85–97.

only assessed at international level,[1001] without even having the possibility to be heard on that subject at national level. Generally, it is felt that the Court and the Committee should be stricter in their insistence on the principle that the state authorities have the obligation to demonstrate that the alternatives they propose are accessible and safe and present a realistic long-term solution. Otherwise applicants have the *disproportionate burden* of demonstrating the existence of a real risk of ill treatment in each and every possible region of their country of origin, even though they might not even know those regions.

3.4.2   Diplomatic Assurances
a   *Court*

It is a common practice of European states to obtain assurances or guarantees from states to which a person is to be extradited or expelled, to the effect that that person will be treated in accordance with fundamental human rights. Such assurances exist in various forms. They can be a simple correspondence between two states, memorandums of understanding or detailed agreements. Diplomatic assurances have been of relevance throughout the Court's case law, particularly in extradition cases.

The Court has attached particular importance to assurances in respect of the death penalty. It has rejected several complaints of individuals charged with murder in the United States, noting that the extraditing state had obtained assurances according to which the prosecution would not seek the death penalty.[1002] The Court has pointed out that a presumption of good faith 'should be applied to a requesting State which has a long history of respect for democracy, human rights and the rule of law, and which has longstanding extradition arrangements with Contracting States.'[1003] Also in highly political cases concerning the extradition of individuals suspected of terrorism, the Court has considered assurances from the US authorities that applicants

---

1001   See the dissenting opinion of judge Power-Forde joined by judge Zupančič.

1002   See, for example, ECtHR, *Nivette v. France,* 3 July 2001, no. 44190/98 (decision); ECtHR, *Babar Ahmad and Others v. UK,* 6 July 2010, nos. 24027/07, 11949/08 and 36742/08 (decision), § 119; ECtHR, *Harkins and Edwards v. UK,* 17 January 2012, nos. 9146/07 and 32650/07; ECtHR, *Rrapo v. Albania,* 25 September 2012, no. 58555/19. See further ECtHR, *Cahuas v. Spain,* 10 August 2006, no. 24668/03, §§ 37 and 43, concerning assurances with regard to the non-imposition of the death penalty obtained by Peru and ECtHR, *Gasayev v. Spain,* 17 February 2009, no. 48514/06 (decision), concerning such assurances obtained by Russia.

1003   ECtHR, *Harkins and Edwards v. UK,* 17 January 2012, nos. 9146/07 and 32650/07, §§ 85, 86 and 91.

would not be subjected to the death penalty or other inhuman treatment as reliable.[1004] The Court has attached importance to the fact that 'in the context of an extradition request, there have been no reported breaches of an assurance given by the United States government to a Contracting State.'[1005]

It is not only in the context of the death penalty that assurances are of relevance but also where there is a risk of other ill treatment or poor prison conditions. However, the Court has made clear that the existence of assurances does not absolve the deporting state or the Court from 'the obligation' to examine whether such assurances, in their practical application, provide a sufficient guarantee that the applicant would be protected against treatment prohibited by Article 3 ECHR.[1006] According to the Court, 'the weight to be given to assurances from the receiving State depends, in each case, on the circumstances prevailing at the material time.'[1007]

The Court has indicated in its early case law that reported practices of systematic ill treatment in the receiving state weaken the reliability of assurances.[1008] However, with the judgment *Abu Qatada v. United Kingdom* adopted in January 2012,[1009] the Court made clear that even if the assurances come from states known for ill treatment, they are not necessarily ineffective. The case concerned a Jordanian applicant who had been recognized as a refugee by the United Kingdom in 1994. In 1999 and 2000, the applicant was tried *in absentia* in Jordan for conspiracies to cause explosions at Western and Israeli targets in Jordan. In 2005, he was served with a notice of intention to deport him to Jordan under the British Prevention of Terrorism Act. The complainant appealed this order claiming that he would be ill-treated and retried in a grossly unfair procedure based on evidence obtained by the torture of his co-defendants. The British Special Immigration Appeals Commission dismissed

---

1004 See ECtHR, *Al-Moayad v. Germany*, 20 February 2007, no. 35865/03 (decision), §§ 65–71. This case concerned the extradition of a Yemeni citizen suspected of working with al-Qaeda. The Court found the diplomatic assurances given by the US that the applicant would not be detained in Guantanamo Bay or prosecuted by a military tribunal to be satisfactory. Similarly ECtHR, *Babar Ahmad and Others v. UK*, 6 July 2010, nos. 24027/07, 11949/08 and 36742/08 (decision), § 104–110, assurance that the complainants will not be designated as enemy combatants.
1005 ECtHR, *Rrapo v. Albania*, 25 September 2012, no. 58555/19, § 73.
1006 ECtHR, *Saadi v. Italy*, 28 February 2008 [GC], no. 37201/06, § 148.
1007 *Ibid.*
1008 ECtHR, *Chahal v. UK*, 15 November 1996, no. 22414/93, §§ 104 and 105.
1009 ECtHR, *Abu Qatada v. UK*, 17 January 2012, no. 8139/09.

the complainant's appeal. It held that the complainant would be protected against ill treatment by a memorandum of understanding negotiated between the United Kingdom and Jordan, which set out a detailed series of assurances. The House of Lords upheld this finding in 2009. In its judgment adopted unanimously in January 2012, the Court recapitulated its principles with regard to diplomatic assurances. It reminded us that assurances constitute *a relevant factor* within the Court's risk assessment under Article 3 ECHR, even though they are 'not in themselves sufficient to ensure adequate protection against the risk of ill-treatment.'[1010] The Court then held that when assessing the practical application of assurances and in determining what weight is to be given to them, 'the preliminary question is whether the general human rights situation in the receiving State excludes accepting any assurances whatsoever.'[1011] It noted, however, that it is only in 'rare cases that the general situation in a country will mean that no weight at all can be given to assurances.'[1012] It thereby referred to several judgments adopted between 2008 and 2010 concerning extraditions of suspected Islamic activists from Russia to Uzbekistan and Tajikistan, in which it had rejected the trustworthiness of diplomatic assurances since reliable sources reported practices tolerated by the authorities of those states that were manifestly contrary to the ECHR.[1013] The Court then stated that, *more usually*, it will assess 'first, the quality of assurances given and, second, whether, in light of the receiving State's practices they can be relied upon.'[1014] The Court then elaborated a non-exhaustive list of elements it will take into account when assessing the quality of assurances. In referring to its previous case law, it noted that it would have regard to the following factors:

(i)   whether the terms of the assurances have been disclosed to the Court;
(ii) whether the assurances are specific or are general and vague;
(iii) who has given the assurances and whether that person can bind the receiving State

---

1010 *Ibid.*, § 187.

1011 *Ibid.*, § 188.

1012 *Ibid.*

1013 The Court referred to the following examples: ECtHR, *Ismoilov v. Russia*, 24 April 2008, no. 2947/06; ECtHR, *Yuldashev v. Russia*, 8 July 2010, no. 1248/09; ECtHR, *Gaforov v. Russia*, 21 October 2010, no. 25404/09; ECtHR, *Sultanov v. Russia*, 4 November 2010, no. 15303/09.

1014 ECtHR, *Abu Qatada*, § 189.

(iv)   if the assurances have been issued by the central government of the receiving State, whether local authorities can be expected to abide by them

(v)   whether the assurances concern treatment which is legal or illegal in the receiving State

(vi)   whether they have been given by a Contracting State

(vii) the length and strength of bilateral relations between the sending and receiving States, including the receiving State's record in abiding by similar assurances

(viii) whether compliance with the assurances can be objectively verified through diplomatic or other monitoring mechanisms, including providing unfettered access to the applicant's lawyers

(ix)   whether there is an effective system of protection against torture in the receiving State, including whether it is willing to cooperate with international monitoring mechanisms (including international human rights NGOs), and whether it is willing to investigate allegations of torture and to punish those responsible

(x)   whether the applicant has previously been ill-treated in the receiving State; and

(xi)   whether the reliability of the assurances has been examined by the domestic courts of the Contracting State.[1015]

Assessing the instant case in light of these principles, the Court first referred to the Committee against Torture's Concluding Observations of May 2010 on Jordan's state report, according to which torture remains 'widespread and routine' in that country.[1016] In view of the situation of detained Islamists as reported by several credible sources and the complainant's high profile, the Court recognized that 'without assurances from the Jordanian government, there would be a real risk of ill-treatment of the present applicant if he were returned.'[1017] The Court, however, explicitly rejected the applicant's assumption that in its previous case law, it had established a prohibition on seeking assurances when there is a systematic problem of torture and ill treatment in the receiving state.[1018]

It then assessed the assurances given by Jordan.[1019] The Court pointed out that the memorandum of understanding was specific and comprehensive.

1015 *Ibid.*
1016 *Ibid.*, § 191.
1017 *Ibid.*, § 192.
1018 *Ibid.*, § 193.
1019 *Ibid.*, §§ 193–207.

A government with strong bilateral relations with the United Kingdom had given them in good faith. It further observed that the assurances had been approved at the highest levels of the Jordanian government with the express approval of the king himself. The applicant's high profile would further make the Jordanian authorities careful to ensure he was properly treated; any ill treatment would have serious consequences for Jordan's relationship with the United Kingdom. In addition, the assurances would be monitored by an independent human rights organisation in Jordan, which would have full access to the applicant in prison. The Court gave further weight to the fact that the agreement had withstood the extensive examination carried out by an independent British tribunal. It also observed that the agreement was superior in both its detail and its formality to any assurances that had previously been examined by itself, the UN Committee Against Torture and the UN Human Rights Committee.[1020] In view of these factors, the Court concluded that the applicant was sufficiently protected by the memorandum of understanding and that his deportation to Jordan would therefore not violate Article 3 ECHR. The Court, however, found that the complainant's deportation would violate Article 6 ECHR, since there were no assurances that the Jordanian authorities, when re-trialing the complainant, would not use the evidence obtained from his codefendants under torture.[1021]

The factors enumerated in *Abu Qatada* are a useful summary of what the Court has taken into account when assessing the quality of assurances in earlier cases.[1022] Particularly the vagueness of assurances and the question of whether the authorities who give the assurances have the factual power to ensure their observance have led the Court to reject the reliability of assurances in several cases.[1023] However, it appears that the Court gave more weight to the

---

1020   *Ibid.*, § 194. The Court referred to ComAT, *Agiza v. Sweden*, 20 May 2005, no. 233/2003; ComAT, *Pelit v. Azerbaijan*, 1 May 2007, no. 281/2005 and the Human Rights Committee decision in *Alzery v. Sweden*, 25 October 2006, no. 1416/2005.

1021   ECtHR, *Abu Qatada*, §§ 258–287. See on this part of the claim under the prohibition on refoulement inherent to Art. 6 ECHR Chapter 1 Section 2.2.3.

1022   In ECtHR, *Abdulkhakov v. Russia*, 2 October 2012, no. 14743/11, § 150, the Court indicates that state parties should use the standards elaborated in that judgment when assessing the reliability of diplomatic assurances.

1023   See, for example, ECtHR, *Soldatenko v. Ukraine*, 23 October 2008, no. 2440/07, §§ 73 and 74; ECtHR, *Kaboulov v. Ukraine*, 19 November 2009, no. 41015/04, § 113; ECtHR, *Baysakov and Others v. Ukraine*, 18 February 2010, no. 54131/08, § 51; ECtHR, *Klein v. Russia*, 1 April 2010, no. 24268/08, § 55; ECtHR, *Khodzhayev v. Russia*, 12 May 2010, no. 52466/08, § 103; ECtHR, *M.S.S. v. Belgium and Greece*, 21 January 2011 [GC], no. 30696/09, §§ 353 and 354; ECtHR, *Yefimova v. Russia*, 19 February 2013, no. 39786/09, §§ 202 and 203; ECtHR,

prevailing human rights situation previous to *Abu Qatada*. As Qatada's lawyer pointed out, it seemed that the Court had established a principle according to which guarantees do not offer adequate protection if reliable sources report systematic practices of torture in the country of destination.[1024] The endemic practice of torture and a culture of impunity as well as the lack of independent monitoring of the treatment of detainees were the main reason for which the Court rejected the relevance of assurances in several cases concerning deportations of suspected or convicted Islamic terrorists to Tunisia before the Arab Spring.[1025] The most famous of these cases was *Saadi v. Italy*, in which the Grand Chamber held that diplomatic assurances are 'not in themselves sufficient to ensure adequate protection against the risk of ill-treatment where reliable sources have reported practices resorted to or tolerated by the authorities which are manifestly contrary to the principles of the Convention.'[1026] As the Court itself indicated in *Qatada*, in some cases concerning extraditions from Russia to Uzbekistan and Tajikistan, the systematic practice of torture as described by reputable sources was the only explicit reason for which the Court considered the assurances given as not reliable.[1027] In fact, cases in which the Court accepts assurances from states as effective when independent sources report systematic practices of ill treatment are rare in the Court's case law.[1028] This is logical since such states do not seem to feel bound by the most fundamental rules of international law. The Court has made an important statement in this context in the judgment *Azimov v. Russia* that was adopted in April 2013 and concerned the extradition of an applicant accused of being a member of several opposition movements including the Islamic Movement of

K. v. Russia, 23 May 2013, no. 69235/11, § 65; ECtHR, Saliyev v. Russia, 17 April 2014, no. 39093/13, §§ 65–69.

1024 See also the interpretation of the Court's case law before Qatada by Delas 2011, p. 314 and Thurin 2012, pp. 227–229.

1025 See, among others, ECtHR, Ben Khemais v. Italy, 24 February 2009, no. 246/07, §§ 57–61; ECtHR, O. v. Italy, 24 March 2009, no. 37257/06, §§ 36–39; ECtHR, Sellem v. Italy, 5 May 2009, no. 12584/08, §§ 39–44; ECtHR, Trabelsi v. Italy, 13 April 2010, no. 50163/08, §§ 43–48; ECtHR, Toumi v. Italy, 5 April 2011, no. 25716/09, §§ 50–55.

1026 ECtHR, Saadi v. Italy, 28 February 2008 [GC], no. 37201/06, § 147.

1027 See the cases referred to in fn. 2354. As a recent example of this practice see also ECtHR, Sidikovy v. Russia, 20 June 2013, no. 73455/11, § 150.

1028 Alongside Abu Qatada see ECtHR, Shamayev and Others v. Georgia and Russia, 12 April 2005, no. 36378/02, §§ 340–353, concerning extraditions of males of Chechen origin to Russia and ECtHR, Mamatkulov and Askarov v. Turkey, 4 February 2005 [GC], nos. 46827/99 and 46951/99, § 76, concerning extraditions to Uzbekistan. For a critique of the reliance on the assurances in these cases see Wouters 2009, pp. 295–303.

Uzbekistan.[1029] It held that 'in the modern world there is virtually no State that would not proclaim that it adheres to the basic international human rights norms, such as the prohibition of torture, and which would not have at least some protecting mechanism at domestic level.'[1030] In *Qatada*, however, the Court explicitly rejected the argument that states that are known for systematically practicing torture and that do not comply with multilateral obligations cannot be relied on to comply with bilateral assurances.[1031] As mentioned, it held that is it only in 'rare cases that the general situation in a country will mean that no weight at all can be given to assurances.'[1032] The Court confirmed this line in subsequent judgments.[1033]

However, as the Court stated in *Qatada*, the quality of the agreement reached between the United Kingdom and Jordan was very unique, as was the wider political context in which it had been negotiated. To achieve these standards will not be easy for states in every case. The relevance of diplomatic assurances was nevertheless enhanced with that judgment. It shows that the Court is taking a different direction from, for instance, the former UN Special Rapporteur on torture Manfred Nowak, who excludes the effectiveness and with that the legitimacy of assurances given by states that practice torture.[1034] The Court in contrast does not exclude their effectiveness categorically but requests that 'where reliable sources have reported practices resorted to or tolerated by the authorities which are manifestly contrary to the principles of the Convention, the domestic courts should have a somewhat critical approach to diplomatic assurances.'[1035]

b   *Committee*
The Committee has been confronted with the issue of diplomatic assurances on several occasions and has shown itself to be becoming more and more sceptical towards that instrument.[1036] Of note are the two cases of *Attia v. Sweden*,

---

1029   ECtHR, *Azimov v. Russia*, 18 April 2013, no. 67474/11.

1030   *Ibid.*, § 133.

1031   ECtHR, *Abu Qatada*, § 193.

1032   *Ibid.*, § 188.

1033   See ECtHR, *M.S. v. Belgium*, 31 January 2012, no. 50012/08, §§ 126–132 concerning an Iraqi applicant; ECtHR, *Kozhayev v. Russia*, 5 June 2012, no. 60054/10, § 84, in which the Court summarizes that it has simply 'cautioned against reliance on diplomatic assurances against torture from states where torture is endemic or persistent.'

1034   See on this the comparative Section 3.4.2.c just below.

1035   ECtHR, *Azimov v. Russia*, 18 April 2013, no. 67474/11, § 133.

1036   See ComAT, *Attia v. Sweden*, 17 November 2003, no. 199/2002; ComAT, *Agiza v. Sweden*, 20 May 2005, no. 233/2003; ComAT, *Pelit v. Azerbaijan*, 1 May 2007, no. 281/2005; ComAT,

decided in 2003, and *Agiza v. Sweden*, decided in 2005.[1037] Hannan Attia and Ahmed Agiza were married. They were both Egyptian nationals. Ahmed Agiza was tried *in absentia* for terrorist activity before a military court in Egypt. In 2000, after having lived in Pakistan, Syria and Iran, Ms Attia and her husband went to Sweden, where they applied for asylum. Because of the political sensitivity of Mr Agiza's case, their applications were remitted to the Swedish government for decision. The government rejected their applications and ordered their deportation on 18 December 2001. Mr Agiza was deported on the same day. Ms Attia evaded police custody and stayed in Sweden.[1038] The same month, she submitted a complaint to the Committee, claiming that because of her husband's activities she would be of great interest to the Egyptian authorities, with a serious risk of being subjected to torture.[1039] In the context of Ms Attia's procedure, the Swedish government informed the Committee that Mr Agiza had been regarded as a serious security threat by their security services and that his request for recognition as a refugee had been refused for that reason. To be able to expel Mr Agiza and Ms Attia, the Swedish government obtained diplomatic assurances from Egypt, according to which Mr Agiza and his family would be treated in accordance with international law.[1040] The government further informed the Committee that the Swedish ambassador regularly visited Mr Agiza in prison. The ambassador reported that he did not show signs of physical abuse.[1041] Ms Attia, however, submitted that her parents-in-law, who had also visited Mr Agiza, had the impression that he had been ill-treated.[1042]

In November 2003, the Committee decided on Ms Attia's case. It noted that her family ties were insufficient to ground a claim under Article 3 CAT. Taking

---

L.J.R. v. Australia, 10 November 2008, no. 316/2007; ComAT, *Boily v. Canada*, 14 November 2011, no. 327/2007; ComAT, *Kalinichenko v. Morocco*, 25 November 2011, no. 428/2010; ComAT, *Abdussamatov and 28 Others v. Kazakhstan*, 1 June 2012, no. 444/2010, § 13.10; ComAT, *Abichou v. Germany*, 21 May 2013, no. 430/2010, §§ 11.5–11.7; ComAT, *Tursunov v. Kazakhstan*, 8 May 2015, no. 538/2013; ComAT, *X. v. Russia*, 8 May 2015, no. 542/2013; ComAT, *R.A.Y. v. Morocco*, 16 May 2014, no. 525/2012; ComAT, *X. v. Kazakhstan*, 3 August 2015, no. 554/2013.

1037 ComAT, *Attia v. Sweden*, 17 November 2003, no. 199/2002; ComAT, *Agiza v. Sweden*, 20 May 2005, no. 233/2003. These cases have been discussed under another angle in Section 2.2 of this chapter on the time of the risk assessment.

1038 ComAT, *Attia v. Sweden*, 17 November 2003, no. 199/2002, §§ 2.1–2.5.

1039 *Ibid.*, § 3.1.

1040 *Ibid.*, §§ 4.5 and 4.6.

1041 *Ibid.*, §§ 4.8–4.10 and 6.1–6.4.

1042 *Ibid.*, §§ 7.1–7.3.

into account the Swedish ambassador's regular visits to her husband and the diplomatic assurances obtained by the Egyptian authorities, the Committee came to the conclusion that Ms Attia's removal to Egypt would not constitute a violation of Article 3 CAT. It considered it as relevant that Egypt, a state party to the CAT, is 'directly bound properly to treat prisoners within its jurisdiction.'[1043] Meanwhile, on the 25 June 2003, Ms Attia's husband Mr Agiza also submitted a complaint to the Committee, claiming that he had in fact been tortured on his return and that his deportation to Egypt had been in violation of Article 3 CAT.[1044] At a later stage of this procedure (in May 2004, after the Attia decision had been taken), the Committee was presented with a report of the Swedish ambassador's first visit to Mr Agiza in January 2002, which contained different information from that submitted by the Swedish government in the Attia case. According to this report, Mr Agiza had complained about ill treatment when apprehended and during his transfer to Egypt. American security personnel in a US aircraft had organized the transfer. Agiza further claimed that he had been blindfolded during interrogations, held in cells of only 1.5 by 1.5 meters, deprived of sleep and medical treatments for certain periods and beaten by prison guards.[1045]

On 20 May 2005, the Committee took its decision on the *Agiza* case. It considered that 'it was known or should have been known' to the Swedish authorities at the time of the complainant's removal that there was a widespread use of torture on detainees, and 'that the risk of such treatment was particularly high in the case of detainees held for political and security reasons.'[1046] The Swedish authorities had been aware of the interest in the complainant by the intelligence services of Egypt and the United States. The Committee hence found that the 'natural conclusion from these combined elements' was that the complainant was at risk of torture in Egypt when he was deported. This was further confirmed by the fact that, preceding expulsion, the complainant 'was subjected on the State party's territory to treatment in breach of, at least, article 16 of the Convention by foreign agents but with the acquiescence of the State party's police.'[1047] The Committee concluded that 'the procurement of diplomatic assurances, which, moreover, provided no mechanism for their enforcement, did not suffice to protect against this manifest risk.'[1048] Article 3

1043   *Ibid.,* § 12.3.
1044   ComAT, *Agiza v. Sweden*, 20 May 2005, no. 233/2003, §§ 2.5–2.10 and 3.2.
1045   *Ibid.,* §§ 8.1, 8.2 and 12.11.
1046   *Ibid.,* § 13.4.
1047   *Ibid.,* §§ 13.2–13.4.
1048   *Ibid.,* § 13.4.

CAT had hence been violated by the applicant's deportation.[1049] The Committee moreover criticized the Swedish government for not having provided all relevant information in the *Agiza* and *Attia* cases.[1050] It pointed out that in the *Attia* case, where it had been satisfied with the guarantees provided, it did not have before it the actual report of mistreatment provided by the complainant to the Swedish ambassador at his first visit; the involvement and mistreatment by a foreign intelligence service; the expanding information on the state practicing extraordinary renditions; the breach by Egypt of the assurances to guarantee a fair trial and the unwillingness of the Egyptian authorities to conduct an independent investigation with regard to alleged ill treatments.[1051]

Unfortunately neither decision, *Attia* or *Agiza*, gives us much information about what causes particular diplomatic assurances to be considered reliable or otherwise.[1052] However, the *Agiza* decision does indicate that assurances will be considered *less reliable when practices of torture are known*. It further made clear that assurances should have an *effective enforcement mechanism*. The latter was confirmed by subsequent decisions, including *Pelit v. Azerbaijan* concerning the extradition of a woman of Kurdish origin from Azerbaijan to Turkey.[1053] The complainant had been sentenced *in absentia* in Turkey for 'subversive activities' for the PKK. Azerbaijan had obtained assurances from Turkey containing provisions for monitoring the complainant's situation after surrender.[1054] The Committee was not convinced by the assurances. It made the following interesting statements:

> The Committee further notes that the Azeri authorities received diplomatic assurances from Turkey going to issues of mistreatment, *an acknowledgment that, without more, expulsion of the complainant would raise issues of her mistreatment.* While a certain degree of post-expulsion monitoring of the complainant's situation took place, the State party has not supplied the assurances to the Committee in order for the Committee

1049 See the separate opinion of Committee member Yakovlev according to which the Committee should have attached more weight to the assurances and the risk as it could be perceived by the Swedish state at the time of the deportation.

1050 *Ibid.*, §§ 13.5 and 13.10.The Committee found that by not disclosing the relevant information, Sweden had also breached its obligation under Art. 22 CAT to fully cooperate with the Committee.

1051 *Ibid.*, § 13.5.

1052 As has been mentioned in Section 2.2 of this chapter on the time of the risk assessment, the fact that Mr Agiza had in fact been tortured in Egypt will have had a certain impact on his case.

1053 ComAT, *Pelit v. Azerbaijan*, 1 May 2007, no. 281/2005.

1054 *Ibid.*, §§ 7.12 and 9.1–9.4.

to perform its *own independent assessment of their satisfactoriness or otherwise* (see its approach in *Agiza v Sweden*), nor did the State party detail with sufficient specificity the monitoring undertaken and the steps taken to ensure that it both was, *in fact and in the complainant's perception, objective, impartial and sufficiently trustworthy*. In these circumstances, and given that the State party had extradited the complainant notwithstanding that it had initially agreed to comply with the Committee's request for interim measures, the Committee considers that the manner in which the State party handled the complainant's case amounts to a breach of her rights under article 3 of the Convention.[1055] (Emphasis added)

The indispensability of an enforceable monitoring system is further confirmed in *Boily v. Canada*, decided in November 2011, concerning the extradition of a Canadian citizen to Mexico.[1056] The complainant had been sentenced to 14 years in prison in Mexico for marijuana trafficking. In 1999 he had organized an escape during which one of the two guards was killed. In 2005 he was arrested in Canada under a warrant for his extradition to Mexico. In the framework of the extradition procedure before the Canadian court, the complainant provided medical evidence corroborating his allegation that he had been tortured in a Mexican prison in the past.[1057] The Canadian Minister of Justice requested assurances from the government of Mexico, according to which Mexico would take reasonable precautions to guarantee the safety of the complainant and would ensure that his lawyer and officials from the Canadian embassy could visit him. Referring to another case in which Canada had requested such assurances, the government pointed out that Mexico's international reputation was at stake if such assurances were not observed. It further emphasized before the Committee that it had put in place a mechanism for monitoring the complainant's situation.[1058] After the Committee had decided to withdraw interim measures that had initially been granted, the complainant was deported to the same prison facility in Mexico, where he was accused of having killed a guard. The complainant alleged before the Committee that prison guards had tortured him immediately upon his return and that he was refused contact with the Canadian embassy and his lawyer.[1059] When assessing the claim, the

---

1055   *Ibid.*, § 11.
1056   ComAT, *Boily v. Canada*, 14 November 2011, no. 327/2007.
1057   *Ibid.*, §§ 2.2 and 2.3.
1058   *Ibid.*, § 5.3.
1059   *Ibid.*, § 2.4.

Committee first recalled that the relevant time of the risk assessment was the time of the extradition. The Committee then interestingly indicated that in cases in which diplomatic assurances are requested, the burden of proof might shift to the government to dispel any doubt with regard to the risk of torture. It made the following statement:

> Article 3 of the Convention obliges the State that decides whether or not to extradite a person under its jurisdiction to another State to take all necessary steps to prevent torture from occurring. This obligation means that it has the duty to examine carefully and take into account all existing circumstances that may reasonably be considered to indicate a risk of torture as previously defined. *The standards that must be met to ensure prevention are still more stringent when the State decides to request diplomatic assurances before proceeding with extradition (or any other type of handover), given that such a request demonstrates that the extraditing State harbours concerns about the treatment that may be reserved for the extradited person in the destination country.* Even when the evidence does not clearly indicate the existence of a risk of such nature, the circumstances of the case may demonstrate that *there is a reasonable doubt that the receiving State would comply with the obligation to prevent torture under articles 1 and 2 of the Convention.* In the instant case it is uncontested that the complainant had been previously subjected to torture. In these circumstances, *the Committee must determine whether the diplomatic assurances in the specific case were of a nature to eliminate all reasonable doubt* that the complainant would be subjected to torture upon his return. In this context the Committee must take into account whether the obtained diplomatic assurances include follow-up procedures that would guarantee their effectiveness.[1060] (Emphasis added)

The Committee decided that in the instant case, the assurances were not able to eliminate any reasonable doubt that the complainant would be subjected to torture in Mexican prisons. It hence found that the complainant's extradition had violated Article 3 ECHR.[1061] The Committee based its decision on two reasons: First, it observed that the Canadian authorities

---

1060 *Ibid.*, § 14.4.
1061 *Ibid.*, §§ 14.5 and 14.6. The Committee strangely further found that Art. 22 CAT was violated. It does not explain why.

... gave no consideration to the fact that the complainant would be sent to the same prison in which a guard had died during his escape, and that the guard's death too was a subject of the extradition request. Second, the agreed system of diplomatic assurances was not carefully enough designed to effectively prevent torture. The diplomatic and consular authorities of the State party were not given due notice of the complainant's extradition and not informed of the need to stay in close and continuous contact with him from the moment he was handed over.[1062]

The Committee held that 'the assurances and the foreseen consular visits failed to anticipate the likelihood that the complainant had the highest risk of being tortured during the initial days of his detention.' It finally added that this lack of anticipation had proven to be true by the complainant's allegation of having been tortured right after his return.[1063]

The importance of an effective monitoring system and the scepticism of the Committee towards diplomatic assurances was reconfirmed in *Kalinichenko v. Morocco* concerning the extradition of a suspected criminal to Russia.[1064] The Committee observed that the assurances provided by Russia were insufficient to protect the complainant 'in the light of their general and non-specific nature and the fact they did not establish a follow-up mechanism.'[1065] In this case again, the Committee found a violation of Article 3 CAT. The Committee argued similarly in *Abdussamatov and 28 Others* concerning the extradition of 29 Muslim applicants to Uzbekistan accused of religious extremism.[1066] It held that the state party had 'failed to provide any sufficiently specific details as to whether it has engaged in any form of monitoring and whether it has taken any steps to ensure that the monitoring is objective, impartial and sufficiently trustworthy.' It further noted that 'diplomatic assurances cannot be an instrument to avoid the application of the principle of non-refoulement.'[1067]

The importance the Committee gives to the prevailing human rights situation when assessing diplomatic assurances is apparent in the recent decision *Abichou v. Germany*.[1068] The case concerned the extradition of a French citizen

---

1062   *Ibid.* § 14.5.

1063   *Ibid.*, § 14.5, which however remained disputed by the Canadian government.

1064   ComAT, *Kalinichenko v. Morocco*, 25 November 2011, no. 428/2010.

1065   *Ibid.*, §§ 4.4 and 15.6.

1066   ComAT, *Abdussamatov and 28 Others v. Kazakhstan*, 1 June 2012, no. 444/2010.

1067   *Ibid.*, § 13.20.

1068   ComAT, *Abichou v. Germany*, 21 May 2013, no. 430/2010.

from Germany to Tunisia based on a sentence *in absentia* to life imprisonment on several counts of large-scale smuggling and drug trafficking. On the German authorities' request, the Tunisian Ministry of Foreign Affairs provided diplomatic assurances that, *inter alia*, the applicant would be entitled to a retrial in Tunisia in which the rights set out in the ICCPR would be upheld and that, in the event of a conviction, he would serve his sentence in a facility that complies with the UN Standard Minimum Rules for the Treatment of Prisoners.[1069] The state party informed the Committee that subsequent to his extradition, the Tunisian courts had acquitted the complainant and he had been released. The German government noted that these facts demonstrate that the Tunisian authorities honoured their diplomatic assurances.[1070] However, the Committee recalled that 'diplomatic assurances cannot be used as a justification for failing to apply the principle of non-refoulement as set forth in article 3 of the Convention.'[1071] It then added that 'notwithstanding the diplomatic assurances that were provided,' it 'must consider the actual human rights situation in Tunisia at the time of the complainant's extradition,' which was in August 2010.[1072] Referring to its own and the Human Rights Committee's concluding observations issued in connection with periodic state reports on Tunisia, it held that the German authorities 'knew or should have known' at the time of the complainant's extradition 'that Tunisia routinely resorted to the widespread use of torture against detainees held for political reasons and against detainees charged with ordinary criminal offences.'[1073] The Committee further took note of the fact that two other defendants in the same case had lodged complaints of torture with the Tunisian courts, and their complaints were dismissed without investigation. The Committee held:

> The fact that diplomatic assurances were obtained was not sufficient grounds for the State party's decision to ignore this obvious risk, especially since none of the guarantees that were provided related specifically to protection against torture or ill-treatment. The fact that Onsi Abichou was ultimately not subjected to such treatment following his extradition

---

1069 *Ibid.*, §§ 2.6 and 6.3.

1070 *Ibid.*, §§ 7.1 and 7.2.

1071 *Ibid.*, § 11.5. Confirmed recently in ComAT, *Tursunov v. Kazakhstan*, 8 May 2015, no. 538/2013, § 9.10; ComAT, *X. v. Russia*, 8 May 2015, no. 542/2013, § 11.9. ComAT, *X. v. Kazakhstan*, 3 August 2015, no. 554/2013, § 12.8.

1072 ComAT, *Abichou*, §§ 11.6 and 11.7.

1073 *Ibid.*, § 11.7.

cannot be justifiably used to call into question or minimize, retrospectively, the existence of such a risk at the time of his extradition.[1074]

The Committee hence concluded that the extradition constituted a violation of Article 3 CAT. In *R.A.Y. v. Morocco*, the Committee recalled in 2014 that, 'in assessing the risk of torture to which an individual would be exposed in the context of extradition or deportation proceedings, a State cannot base itself solely on the fact that another State is a party to the Convention against Torture, or that it has provided diplomatic assurances.'[1075]

A case that should also be mentioned is *L.J.R. v. Australia* concerning the extradition of a suspected murderer to California.[1076] The complainant alleged, *inter alia*, that he would be sentenced to death despite assurances given by the United States. The responsible district attorney as well as the US embassy in Australia had provided assurances that no death penalty would be imposed on the complainant. The Committee did not assess the assurances and rejected the claim with regard to the death penalty as falling outside the scope of the CAT.[1077] It nevertheless took up the issue again in its consideration on the merits with regard to other claims of the complainant and noted: 'Furthermore, the State party considered that the United States was bound by the assurances it provided to the effect that the author, if found guilty, would not be sentenced to the death penalty.'[1078] This statement indicates that the Committee is ready to accept that assurances can be an effective instrument to prevent ill treatment in particular circumstances.[1079]

The case law described demonstrates that the Committee has become very sceptical towards diplomatic assurances. This is not surprising since in two of its cases, *Agiza* and *Boily*, assurances have been revealed to be ineffective. In its recent case law, the Committee has made clear that assurances may even be seen as an *indication for a risk of ill treatment*. When assurances are given

---

1074 *Ibid.*

1075 ComAT, *R.A.Y. v. Morocco*, 16 May 2014, no. 525/2012, § 7.4.

1076 ComAT, *L.J.R. v. Australia*, 10 November 2008, no. 316/2007.

1077 *Ibid.*, § 6.2. See on this Chapter 3 Section 3.2.4 on the death penalty under the CAT.

1078 *Ibid.*, §§ 7.4 and 7.5.

1079 In this context, two cases outside the context of the death penalty are also worth a mention. In both of them the Committee explicitly noted it could review its decision to grant interim measures on the basis of guarantees and assurances furnished by the receiving states' authorities with regard to the complainant's security; see ComAT, *G.K. v. Switzerland*, 7 May 2003, no. 219/2002, § 1.2, concerning the extradition of an ETA member to Spain; ComAT, *J.A.G.V. v. Sweden*, 11 November 2003, no. 215/2002, § 1.3, concerning the deportation of a FARC member to Colombia.

with regard to complainants who have been tortured in the past or who belong to groups whose members are often subjected to ill treatment in the receiving state, the burden of proof will shift to the government to dispel any doubt about the risk of torture. The case law further demonstrates that assurances have to provide an independent and sufficiently trustworthy monitoring system. Such a system must include close and continuous contact from the moment of the hand-over. The Committee should be given the opportunity to assess both the reliability of the assurances and the monitoring system.

In its recent decisions concerning extraditions to states with a certain record of ill treatment, the Committee has further emphasized that diplomatic assurances should not be used as a justification for failing to apply the principle of non-refoulement under Article 3 CAT.[1080] Against this background, it is not established that the Committee accepts assurances from states known for systematic practices of torture *at all*.[1081] In its concluding observations on the United Kingdom adopted in May 2013, the Committee noted,

> the more widespread the practice of torture or other cruel, inhuman or degrading treatment, the less likely the possibility of the real risk of such treatment being avoided by diplomatic assurances, however stringent any agreed follow-up procedure may be. Therefore, the Committee considers that diplomatic assurances are unreliable and ineffective and should not be used as an instrument to modify the determination of the Convention.[1082]

c   *Comparison*

There are two main areas in which European states make use of diplomatic assurances: extraditions to countries with lower human rights standards (in particular in the context of the death penalty), and cases concerning the expulsion or extradition of suspected or convicted terrorists considered a threat to national security. Assurances are rarely relevant in complaints concerning failed asylum seekers without a criminal background.[1083] It is generally up to the government to demonstrate that the assurances are effective.

1080 ComAT, *Abichou v. Germany*, 21 May 2013, no. 430/2010, § 11.5. ComAT, *Abdussamatov and 28 Others v. Kazakhstan*, 1 June 2012, no. 444/2010, § 13.20; ComAT, *Tursunov v. Kazakhstan*, 8 May 2015, no. 538/2013, § 9.10; ComAT, *X. v. Russia*, 8 May 2015, no. 542/2013, § 11.9; ComAT, *X. v. Kazakhstan*, 3 August 2015, no. 554/2013, § 12.8.

1081 In this sense Nowak & McArthur 2008, p. 150 (§ 80); Wouters 2009, pp. 353 and 560.

1082 See ComAT, 'Annual Report 2012/2013,' p. 171 (A/68/44).

1083 See also Wouters (2009, p. 559), who rightly notes that assurances are 'difficult to reconcile with the refugee's fear of being persecuted and his subsequent unwillingness to avail himself of the protection of his country of origin.'

In the context of the death penalty, assurances have proven to be a useful tool permitting states to extradite criminals without subjecting them to a punishment considered inhuman treatment in their own legal system.[1084] Outside this context, the Court and the Committee are both rather cautious of accepting assurances as effective instruments, particularly when given by states known for practices of torture.[1085] The Committee has indicated in decisions that assurances from countries that practice torture appear unreliable and must necessarily contain a strict and independent monitoring mechanism.[1086] In *Boily v. Canada*, the Committee even suggested it considers the request of diplomatic assurances as an *indication for a risk of torture*.[1087] The Court has not taken such a position. In *Abu Qatada*, it made clear that it is only in very exceptional cases that the human rights situation in the receiving country will as such exclude the effectiveness of any assurance.[1088] According to the Court, the reliability of the assurances will usually have to be assessed against the background of the human rights situation and in light of the criteria enumerated in the *Abu Qatada* judgment. In contrast to the Committee, it also attaches considerable weight to the question of whether the assurances are provided by a contracting state to its own convention.[1089]

How much weight the Court will give to the different criteria is difficult to predict. So far, it has paid particular attention to the specificity of assurances as well as the competence of the authority giving them to guarantee their enforcement. Those criteria have not been of particular relevance in the Committee case law. The Committee has focused on the human rights situation

---

1084   See on this also Nowak 2008, p. 122, and Nowak & McArthur 2008, pp. 216–217 (§ 211), who rightly note that the supervision of such assurances is not a difficult task since executions will always come to light.

1085   See in this sense also Schürmann & Scheidegger 2009, p. 207.

1086   The Committee's approach is similar to that of the Human Rights Committee in *Alzery v. Sweden*, 25 October 2006, no. 1416/2005, §§ 11.2–11.5. This case concerned the extradition of a complainant to Egypt with a similar background as Agiza. The HRC found that the principle of non-refoulement inherent to Art. 7 ICCPR was violated. It referred to the *Agiza* decision. See also HRC, *Pirmatov and Others*, 16 July 2008, nos. 1461/2006, 1462/2006, 1476/2006 and 1477/2006, §§ 12.5 and 12.6.

1087   ComAT, *Boily v. Canada*, 14 November 2011, no. 327/2007, § 14.4.

1088   ECtHR, *Abu Qatada v. UK*, 17 January 2012, no. 8139/09, § 189.

1089   See ECtHR, *Abu Qatada*, § 189 (vi); see on this also ECtHR, *Zarmayev v. Belgium*, 27 February 2014, no. 35/10, § 113, concerning an extradition to Russia and the dissenting opinion of judge Power-Forde. An indication in that sense by the Committee in *Attia v. Sweden*, 17 November 2003, no. 199/2002, § 12.3 has not been retaken in subsequent decisions that concerned receiving states that have ratified the CAT (some even having recognized the competence of the Committee to assess individual complaints).

at the time of the deportation and the question of whether there was an effective monitoring mechanism in place to enforce the assurances, without giving a precise definition of how such a mechanism should be constituted.[1090] In *Abu Qatada*, the Court explicitly referred to the Committee's decisions in *Agiza v. Sweden* and *Pelit v. Azerbaijan* when stating that the question of whether assurances can be verified through an independent monitoring mechanism is a factor to take into account when assessing the reliability of assurances.[1091] In recent extradition judgments as well as in *Abu Qatada* itself, the Court gave particular attention to the existence of an effective and independent monitoring mechanism.[1092] In the Court's case law as a whole, it does not, however, appear to be an unconditional criterion for the effectiveness of assurances.[1093] The Committee, since *Agiza*, appears stricter on that matter.[1094]

All the case law indicates that the Court is more willing to rely on diplomatic assurances than the Committee.[1095] This is illustratively confirmed by the case *Abichou v. Germany* in which the Committee held that the complainant's extradition to Tunisia had violated the principle of non-refoulement notwithstanding diplomatic assurances provided by the Tunisian Foreign Ministry, while the Court had even refused to accord interim measures when it was confronted with the same complaint.[1096] While in cases in which practices of ill treatment by the receiving country's authorities are known, the Court requires 'a critical approach'[1097] towards diplomatic assurances, the Committee considers assurances to be an actual indication of an enhanced risk of torture. However, that does not necessarily mean that the Committee would have accepted

---

1090 However, the Court and the Committee have both recognized the first few days following an extradition as a high-risk period in which there should be close and continuous contact with the monitoring body.

1091 ECtHR, *Abu Qatada*, § 189 (viii).

1092 See ECtHR, *Zokhidov v. Russia*, 5 February 2013, no. 67286/10, § 141, in which the Court, in referring to *Abu Qatada*, considered that the assurances were 'couched in general terms and no evidence has been put forward to demonstrate that they were supported by any enforcement or monitoring mechanism.' See also ECtHR, *Yefimova v. Russia*, 19 February 2013, no. 39786/09, § 203.

1093 See on this also Wouters 2009, pp. 304 and 560, referring to *Shamayev* and *Mamatkulov*, in which the Court relied on assurances without a monitoring system.

1094 See in this sense Delas 2011, pp. 322 and 326; Thurin 2012, p. 225 fn. 1082; Wouters 2009, p. 560.

1095 In this sense also Rieter 2010, p. 837; Wouters 2009, p. 560.

1096 The complaint before the Court had been withdrawn after the request for interim measures had been denied; see ComAT, *Abichou v. Germany*, 21 May 2013, no. 430/2010, §§ 4.4, 8.2–8.4 and 9.1–11.7.

1097 ECtHR, *Azimov v. Russia*, 18 April 2013, no. 67474/11, § 133.

Abu Qatada's claim that the assurances provided by Jordan were not reliable. The case-by-case approach of both institutions (and the brief reasoning of the Committee) makes it difficult to make reliable predictions. A statement that can nevertheless be made with regard to both human rights institutions is that the worse the ill treatment record in the receiving state, the slimmer the chances that assurances will be considered reliable or, if the situation does not render assurances completely ineffective, the higher the requirements on their quality (particularly with regard to the establishment of a monitoring system).

In *Abu Qatada*, the applicant pointed out that the 'international consensus was that assurances undermined the established international legal machinery for the prohibition on torture and, if a country was unwilling to abide by its international law obligations, then it was unlikely to abide by bilateral assurances.'[1098] This statement is not taken from thin air. In a report to the UN General Assembly of August 2005, the former UN Special Rapporteur on torture Manfred Nowak referred to cases like *Agiza v. Sweden* and stated that diplomatic assurances have proven to be unreliable and ineffective in the protection against torture and ill treatment.[1099] He noted that assurances are usually sought from states where the practice of torture is systematic. The observance of assurances by such states would therefore be illusory; even post-return monitoring mechanisms had proven to be no guarantee against torture.[1100] He further observed that diplomatic assurances are 'nothing but an attempt by European and other States to circumvent their obligation to respect the principle of non-refoulement.'[1101] It is worth pointing out that Nowak is not alone in this opinion. The current Special Rapporteur on torture Juan E. Méndez has explicitly reconfirmed this opinion on diplomatic assurances.[1102] Several NGOs have also emphasised the ineffectiveness and contradictory character of assurances given by states that practice torture.[1103] In academic articles on the issue, Nowak stated that the request for assurances is in itself evidence of systematic

---

1098 ECtHR, *Abu Qatada v. UK*, 17 January 2012, no. 8139/09, § 168.

1099 UN Doc. A/60/316, 30 August 2005, §§ 42–50.

1100 *Ibid.*, § 51.

1101 UN Doc. E/CN.4/2006/6, 23 December 2005, § 32; see also Nowak 2005, p. 687.

1102 UN Doc. A/HRC/16/52, 3 February 2011, §§ 60–63.

1103 For NGOs see in particular Human Rights Watch (2005); Amnesty International, (2005); Amnesty International, (2010). See further Nowak's predecessor as Special Rapporteur on torture Theo van Boven, who noted that the use of diplomatic assurances is 'increasingly undermining the principle of non-refoulement,' although in contrast to Nowak, he did not categorically reject their effectiveness; see UN Doc. A/59/324, 1 September 2004, §§ 30–31, 37 and 40–42. For scholars see, for example, Delas 2011, pp. 331–338; Wouters 2009, p. 562.

torture in a receiving country. He made the criticism that by requesting assurances, a few individuals might be protected while the state in question might feel free to treat others without respecting the prohibition of torture and inhuman treatment. He further pointed out that both states involved have an interest in denying that a person has in fact been tortured after return, which makes that person even more vulnerable.[1104] In 2008, Nowak therefore disagreed with the Court's and the Committee's case law that, in some decisions and judgments, has accepted that diplomatic assurances received from states with a torture record are reliable.[1105] It would be interesting to see if Nowak still upholds his critique with regard to the Committee after taking into account its recent case law, which seems to reflect his general doubts about diplomatic assurances. However, the Committee has not generally ruled out their effectiveness.

3.4.3   Risk of Indirect Refoulement
a   *Court (Focus 'Dublin cases')*
Contracting states to the ECHR have the responsibility not to deport a person to another country where there is a real risk of his being subjected to ill treatment. It is further established in the case law of the Court that they have the responsibility not to deport a person to a country from which there is a real risk of his being deported in turn in violation of the principle of non-refoulement.[1106] The deportation to such an intermediary country is referred to as submitting individuals to a risk of *indirect removal* or *chain-refoulement*, which is in itself incompatible with the principle of non-refoulement.

In cases in which complainants allege a risk of chain-refoulement, the Court usually proceeds to a two-step assessment: first it assesses whether the complainant can arguably claim the removal to his home country would breach Article 3 ECHR.[1107] Second, it assesses whether 'the intermediary country offers sufficient guarantees to prevent the person concerned being removed to his country of origin without an assessment of the risks faced.'[1108]

The Court asks national authorities to proceed in this way, too, when assessing complaints in which a risk of indirect removal is claimed. Domestic courts should take into account whether,

---

1104   Nowak 2005, p. 687.

1105   Nowak 2008, p. 133.

1106   The first case in which the Court made this statement explicitly is ECtHR, *T.I. v. UK*, 7 March 2000, no. 43844/98 (decision).

1107   On the notion of an 'arguable claim,' see Chapter 4 Section 3.1.1.b.

1108   See ECtHR, *Hirsi Jamaa and Others v. Italy*, 23 February 2012 [GC], no. 27765/09, §§ 147–158; ECtHR, *M.S.S. v. Belgium and Greece*, 21 January 2011 [GC], no. 30696/09, §§ 344 and 345; ECtHR, *Sharifi and Others v. Italy and Greece*, 21 October 2014, no. 16643/09, §§ 231–235.

... after his arrival in the intermediary country, the applicant would be informed in a language he understands about the asylum or other procedures to be followed, would be allowed to apply to a competent national authority in order to voice his fears of ill-treatment, that such an application would automatically have suspensive effect, and that the merits of his fears would be subjected to independent and rigorous scrutiny.[1109]

According to the Court, this assessment 'is all the more important' when the intermediary country is not a state party to the ECHR.[1110]

Most of the cases in which the Court has assessed a risk of chain-refoulement so far concern asylum seekers who were removed from one European State to another under the EU Dublin System. This system is based on an EU Council Regulation[1111] that is today applied by 31 European states.[1112] The Dublin Regulation is at the core of the EU's common policy on asylum matters. It lays down criteria and mechanisms for determining the member state responsible for examining an application for asylum lodged within the EU by a third-country national. It provides that, in principle, the country in which third-country nationals first arrive bears the responsibility for examining their asylum applications. If it is established that individuals have passed through the territory of another member state before having submitted an application for asylum, they will be returned to that state. The Dublin system is aimed at avoiding multiple asylum applications within the EU and guaranteeing that each asylum seeker's case is dealt with by a single member state. It is based on the presumption

---

1109 ECtHR, *Abdulkhakov v. Russia*, 2 October 2012, no. 14743/11, § 155.

1110 ECtHR, *Hirsi Jamaa and Others v. Italy*, 23 February 2012 [GC], no. 27765/09, § 147; ECtHR, *Abdulkhakov v. Russia*, 2 October 2012, no. 14743/11, § 154. See, however, ECtHR, *Singh and Others v. Belgium*, 2 October 2012, no. 33210/11, §§ 78–105, concerning the risk of a chain removal from Russia to Afghanistan in which no such presumption was addressed.

1111 Today Regulation No 604/2013 of the European Parliament and of the Council of 26 June 2013 Establishing the Criteria and Mechanisms for Determining the Member State Responsible for Examining an Application for International Protection Lodged in One of the Member States by a Third-country National or a Stateless Person OJ L 180/31 (recast). The cases referred to in this study mostly concern previous versions of this so-called Dublin III Regulation, which entered into force in January 2014, in particular the so-called *Dublin II* Regulation: Council Regulation No 343/2003 of 18 February 2003 Establishing the Criteria and Mechanisms for Determining the Member State Responsible for Examining an Asylum Application Lodged in One of the Member States by a Third-country National OJ L 50/1.

1112 The regulation applies to the 28 member states of the European Union and to Norway, Iceland, and Switzerland.

that each member state respects the principle of non-refoulement.[1113] However, even before the system was established, the question was raised whether it would be compatible with Article 3 ECHR in conjunction with Article 13 ECHR.[1114] The criticism has been made that the system might enable states to decline their responsibility for asylum seekers by blindly relying on a presumption that might not always be justified.[1115]

As the Strasbourg case law under Article 3 ECHR in Dublin cases since the M.S.S. judgment has evidenced, the scepticism was justified.[1116] In December 2011, the Court of Justice of the European Union in Luxembourg (CJEU) also had to instruct the states not apply the Dublin Regulation blindly.[1117] It clarified that the Dublin system cannot operate on the basis of a 'conclusive presumption' that all participating states 'observe the fundamental rights of the European Union,'[1118] including the Refugee Convention and the ECHR.[1119] This approach is today codified in Article 3(2) of the Dublin III Regulation. The Strasbourg case law under Article 3 ECHR was a crucial factor for this development.[1120]

In *T.I. v. United Kingdom*, the Court in Strasbourg addressed the issue for the first time.[1121] The case concerned the transfer of a Sri Lankan asylum seeker from the United Kingdom to Germany within the framework of the Dublin system. The Court made clear that the transfer of an asylum-seeker to an

---

1113 For an overview and analysis of the Dublin III Regulation and the development of the Dublin system, see Peers, Moreno-Lax, Garlick & Guild 2015, p. 28.

1114 Einarsen 1990, p. 386.

1115 Goodwin-Gill & McAdam 2007, pp. 399–403.

1116 See ECtHR, *M.S.S. v. Belgium and Greece*, 21 January 2011 [GC], no. 30696/09, discussed in this section as well as in Chapter 3 Section 1.3.2.b. This section puts the focus on a risk of *indirect* removal, while Section 2.3.2.b of Chapter 3 has treated the risk of being *directly* submitted to degrading living conditions in the European state responsible.

1117 See CJEU, Joined Cases C-411/10 and C-493/10, *N.S. v. Secretary of State for the Home Department and M.E. and Others v. Refugee Applications Commissioner & Minister for Justice, Equality and Law Reform*, 21 December 2011.

1118 *Ibid.*, § 105.

1119 *Ibid.*, §§ 86–89, 94, 106. Reaffirmed in CJEU, C-4/11, *Kaveh Puid v. Bundesrepublik Deutschland*, 14 November 2013. According to the Luxembourg court, if national authorities *are aware of systemic deficiencies* in the asylum procedure and reception conditions in the receiving state that amount to inhuman treatment, these authorities shall not transfer an asylum seeker in applying the sovereignty clause included in Article 3 (2) of the Dublin Regulation; see on this also Chapter 3 Section 2.3.2.b.

1120 See the numerous references to *M.S.S.* in CJEU, Joined Cases C-411/10 and C-493/10, *N.S. v. Secretary of State for the Home Department and M.E. and Others v. Refugee Applications Commissioner & Minister for Justice, Equality and Law Reform*, 21 December 2011.

1121 ECtHR, *T.I. v. UK*, 7 March 2000, no. 43844/98 (decision).

intermediary country that is a contracting state to the ECHR does not affect the responsibility of the expelling state to ensure the applicant is not exposed to treatment contrary to Article 3 ECHR. It would be incompatible with the purpose and object of the ECHR if states were absolved of all responsibility vis-à-vis the Convention by cooperating in an area where there might be implications as to the protection of fundamental rights. The Court hence stated that contracting states *could not automatically* rely on the arrangements made within the Dublin system. It then assessed whether there was a risk of chain refoulement for the complainant in Germany. Noting that there were no reasons to believe that, in the particular case, Germany would fail to honour its obligations under Article 3 ECHR, the Court rejected the complaint as manifestly ill-founded.[1122]

The next case related to the issue addressed by the Court, *K.R.S. v. United Kingdom*, concerned a risk of chain-refoulement under the EU Dublin system of an Iranian applicant transferred from the United Kingdom to Greece in 2008.[1123] The Court took into account that the UNHCR had recommended that EU member states refrain from returning asylum seekers to Greece, where they would not have access to an effective asylum procedure. However, it observed that Greece currently did not return asylum seekers to Iran. It further noted that the presumption must be that Greece would abide by its obligations under Article 3 ECHR and legal acts from the EU guaranteeing minimum standards in asylum procedures. It further took into account the fact that the Greek government had provided reassurances that the applicant would have the possibility of lodging an application with the Court and requesting interim measures should his deportation to Iran be ordered in Greece.[1124] This possible protection against chain-refoulement offered by the Strasbourg mechanism itself was an important factor in the Court's findings that the applicant's transfer to Greece would not violate Article 3 ECHR.

Although the decisions in *T.I.* and *K.R.S.* already made clear that state parties have a duty to assess a risk of indirect removal when deporting an individual to another contracting state under the EU Dublin system, they also demonstrated that it is difficult for complainants to overturn the presumption that the receiving state will abide by its obligations under the ECHR.[1125] However, as the subsequent case law has shown, it is not impossible.

1122 *Ibid.*

1123 ECtHR, *K.R.S. v. UK*, 2 December 2008, no. 32733/08 (decision).

1124 *Ibid.*

1125 See in this sense Wouters 2009, pp. 566–567.

The lead case *M.S.S. v. Belgium and Greece* has been mentioned at several points in this study.[1126] It concerned the transfer of an Afghan asylum seeker from Belgium to Greece under the EU Dublin system. In the Grand Chamber judgment decided in January 2011, the Court first observed that numerous reports and materials had been added to the available information since its decision in *K.R.S.* in 2008. It noted that these reports, 'based on field surveys, all agree as to the practical difficulties involved in the application of the Dublin system in Greece, the deficiencies of the asylum procedure and the practice of direct or indirect refoulement on an individual or a collective basis.'[1127] The Court concluded from the reports that individuals seeking refuge in Greece do not currently have access to effective asylum procedures.[1128] It further attached critical importance to a letter sent by the UNHCR to the Belgian government in 2009 expressing concerns with regard to transfers to Greece under the Dublin Regulation.[1129] Referring to these numerous sources, the Court considered that the general situation was known or ought to have been known by the Belgian authorities and that the applicant should not have been expected to bear the entire burden of proof. The Court furthermore did not accept the government's argument that the applicant would be able to seek protection against a removal by Greece through the Court itself by requesting interim measures. It observed that only few asylum seekers in Greece actually had access to the Court.[1130] Having regard to these observations, it held

> ... it was in fact up to the Belgian authorities, faced with the situation described above, not merely to assume that the applicant would be treated in conformity with the Convention standards but, on the contrary, to first verify how the Greek authorities applied their legislation on asylum in

---

1126 ECtHR, *M.S.S. v. Belgium and Greece*, 21 January 2011 [GC], no. 30696/09. See in particular Chapter 3 Section 2.3.2.b and Chapter 4 Section 3.1.1.b.

1127 ECtHR, *M.S.S.*, §§ 347 and 348. The authors of these documents are the UNHCR and the European Commissioner for Human Rights, international NGOs like Amnesty International, Human Rights Watch, Pro-Asyl and the European Council on Refugees and Exiles, and non-governmental organisations present in Greece such as Greek Helsinki Monitor and the Greek National Commission for Human Rights.

1128 See on this also the discussion of the *M.S.S.* judgment in Section 3.1.1.b of this chapter on the right to an effective remedy.

1129 ECtHR, *M.S.S.*, §§ 194–195 and 349. See also ECtHR, *Sharifi v. Austria*, 5 December 2013, no. 60104/08, § 36, in which the Court confirms that it 'attached critical importance to that letter when establishing Belgium's awareness of the seriousness of the deficiencies in Greece.'

1130 ECtHR, *M.S.S.*, §§ 352–358.

practice. Had they done this, they would have seen that the risks the applicant faced were real and individual enough to fall within the scope of Article 3. The fact that a large number of asylum seekers in Greece find themselves in the same situation as the applicant does not make the risk concerned any less individual where it is sufficiently real and probable.[1131]

The Court concluded therefore that the transfer of the applicant under the Dublin Regulation had violated the principle of non-refoulement under Article 3 ECHR. It further observed that the extremely urgent procedure for stay of execution to which the complainant was subjected in the framework of Dublin transfers in Belgium did not meet the standards of Article 13 ECHR. It observed, *inter alia*, that the burden of proof in this accelerated procedure was increased to such an extent as to hinder the examination on the merits of the alleged risks.[1132]

However, the Court stressed that the Dublin mechanism was not incompatible with the ECHR. It pointed out that Article 3(2) of the Dublin II Regulation provides that, by derogation from the general rule, each state can decide to examine an application for asylum lodged with it by a third-country national, even if such examination is not its responsibility under the criteria laid down in the Regulation. In view of this so-called sovereignty clause, the Court considered that Belgium's decision to transfer the applicant to Greece did not strictly fall within its international legal obligation under the Dublin Regulation.[1133] In other words, the Regulation does not hinder states from refraining from a transfer if they decide to do so in order to act in accordance with their obligation under Article 3 ECHR and Article 13 ECHR.

The Court made clear that when applying the regulation, *states cannot blindly trust the presumption that each member state respects the principle of non-refoulement*. They must give asylum seekers a fair chance to object to their transfer in light of Article 3 ECHR and refrain from it if a real risk of chain-refoulement is established. It is clear that this statement was not without effect for the application of the Dublin mechanism by member states. States changed their practice with regard to transfers to Greece subsequent to the *M.S.S.* judgment.[1134] The judgment was understood as a call to the EU and its

---

1131   *Ibid.*, § 359.

1132   *Ibid.*, §§ 385–396.

1133   *Ibid.*, §§ 339 and 340.

1134   Which can be observed by the hundreds of cases that have been struck out of the Court's list subsequent to new decisions taken at the national level following the release of *M.S.S.* See, amongst many others, ECtHR, *Shakor and 48 other applications v. Finland*, 28 June 2011, no. 10941/10 (decision); ECtHR, *Z.K. and 27 other applications v. Denmark*, 23 August 2011, no. 37199/10 (decision); ECtHR, *Ali Gedi v. Austria* and 3 other applications, 4 October

member states not just to shift the responsibility for asylum seekers to the southern European states but also to share their burden.[1135] Given that it is through these southern territories that most asylum seekers arrive in Europe, the southern states have become responsible for a disproportionate number of asylum applications under the Dublin system. The *M.S.S.* judgment also had a very important impact on the EU's discussions on further amendments to the Regulation.[1136] As mentioned, the CJEU and the Dublin III Regulation later endorsed the approach developed in Strasbourg to some extend.[1137] In the recent Grand Chamber judgment in *Tarakhel*, the Court further clarified that the presumption according to which a contracting state will comply with Article 3 ECHR can generally be rebutted where the existence of a real risk of ill treatment is proven, irrespective of the existence of systemic deficiencies.[1138] However, even if the Court has made clear that states have a duty not to impose too severe a burden of proof on applicants opposing their transfer under the Dublin system, it remains difficult for individuals concerned to establish a real risk of chain-refoulement in this context.[1139] The deficiencies in Greece were striking, systematic and widely documented. The Court's statement that the assessment of an alleged risk of indirect removal 'is all the more important'[1140] when the intermediary country is not a state party to the ECHR further demonstrates that a certain presumption towards receiving states being part of the Council of Europe is still valid.[1141] It also demonstrates that the Court accepts accelerated procedures in this domain.

These two points can be observed in the judgment *Mohammed v. Austria* adopted in June 2013 concerning a Sudanese applicant who opposed his transfer to Hungary under the Dublin Regulation.[1142] He claimed that he would lack an effective avenue of appeal in any asylum proceedings in Hungary and that he

---

2011, no. 61567/10 (decision); ECtHR, *Ahmed Ali v. Netherlands and Greece*, 24 January 2012, no. 26494/09 (decision).

1135 Von Arnaud 2011, p. 242.

1136 See on this Mallia, 2011, pp. 107–128.

1137 See CJEU, Joined Cases C-411/10 and C-493/10, *N.S. v. Secretary of State for the Home Department and M.E. and Others v. Refugee Applications Commissioner & Minister for Justice, Equality and Law Reform*, 21 December 2011 and Art. 3(2) Dublin III.

1138 See ECtHR, *Tarakhel v. Switzerland*, 4 November 2014 [GC], no. 29217/12, §§ 103 and 104 discussed in Chapter 3 Section 2.3.2.b.

1139 See also Thurin 2012, p. 234.

1140 ECtHR, *Hirsi Jamaa and Others v. Italy*, 23 February 2012 [GC], no. 27765/09, § 147.

1141 See also ECtHR, *Tarakhel*, §§ 103 and 104 speaking of a rebuttable presumption.

1142 ECtHR, *Mohammed v. Austria*, 6 June 2013, no. 2283/12.

would be detained in inhuman conditions there.[1143] The Court first reiterated that when a transferring state is applying the Dublin Regulation, 'it must make sure that the intermediary country's asylum procedure affords sufficient guarantees to avoid an asylum-seeker being removed, directly or indirectly, to his country of origin without any evaluation of the risks he faces from the standpoint of Article 3 of the Convention.'[1144] The Court then acknowledged the alarming nature of reports published, in particular by the UNHCR in 2011 and 2012, in respect of Hungary as a country of asylum and as regards the detention of asylum-seekers under conditions raising serious concern.[1145] However, it also observed that the UNHCR had, in contrast to the situation in Greece, never issued a position paper requesting that EU states refrain from transferring asylum-seekers to Hungary. Furthermore, it referred to most recent notes issued by the UNHCR in which it appreciatively acknowledged the intention of the Hungarian authorities to change their law and practice with regard to detention of asylum seekers.[1146] With regard to the risk assessment made by Austria, the Court observed:

> ... the procedure under the Dublin Regulation does not require the transferring State to conduct any analysis of the underlying flight reasons of an asylum-seeker, but only to establish whether another EU Member State has jurisdiction under the Regulation and to examine whether there are any general reasons or other obstacles concerning the Member State with jurisdiction that would require a stay of the transfer of application of the sovereignty clause.[1147]

Noting that, in contrast to *M.S.S.*, the applicant could not arguably claim that his removal to Sudan would violate Article 3 ECHR and that in any event, according to the most recent information of the UNHCR, it would appear that transferees now have sufficient access to asylum proceedings in Hungary, it concluded that the applicant's transfer would not violate Article 3 ECHR.[1148] However, the Court nevertheless made clear that considering the widely known alarming situation for asylum seekers in Hungary at the time (December 2011), the complainant had an arguable claim under Article 3 in the context

---

1143   *Ibid*, § 86.

1144   *Ibid.*, § 93.

1145   *Ibid.*, §§ 102, 103 and 32–50.

1146   *Ibid.*, §§ 105 and 106.

1147   *Ibid.*, § 108.

1148   *Ibid.*, §§ 109 and 110.

of the examination under Article 13 ECHR, such that his second request for asylum should had been examined according to the minimal standards laid down by this right to an effective remedy.[1149]

The Court's Grand Chamber judgment *Tarakhel* adopted in 2014 did not treat the question of a risk of chain removal but of the reception conditions for asylum seekers in Italy, that is, the direct consequences of the Dublin removal.[1150] The Court did, though, bring to light another constraint on the automatic application of the Dublin system with that judgment,[1151] by clarifying that it is not exclusively in a situation of a complete breakdown of an asylum system that Article 3 ECHR may act as a bar to a removal from one Dublin state to another.[1152] The Grand Chamber cleared up in that judgment that, generally, the transfer of an asylum seeker to a contracting state under the EU Dublin system does not exempt the sending state from carrying out a *thorough and individualised examination* of the situation of the person concerned and from suspending enforcement of the removal order should a real risk of inhuman or degrading treatment be established.[1153] The approach in *Tarakhel* is in line with the Court's early case law on Dublin cases, such as the famous *T.I.* decision, where the Court held that it would be incompatible with the purpose of the ECHR for states to be absolved of responsibility under Article 3 ECHR by cooperating in an area where there might be implications as to the protection of fundamental rights.[1154] The Court nevertheless shows a certain goodwill for the continuation of the EU Dublin-cooperation with Italy in *Tarakhel* in the sense that, in contrast to *M.S.S.*, it did not proclaim that any removal of asylum seekers to that state was prohibited under Article 3 ECHR, but only that particularly vulnerable asylum seekers were affected. In addition, states may even transfer such vulnerable asylum seekers to Italy, where they have obtained sufficiently detailed assurances from the Italian authorities guaranteeing their safety.[1155]

As explained, the Court in Strasbourg has no general objections on how the Dublin system is applied. However, since *M.S.S.* and reinforced by *Tarakhel*, European states cannot ignore the fact that they have a legal obligation under Article 3 ECHR to apply the 'sovereignty clause' under the Dublin Regulation

1149   *Ibid.*, §§ 76–85.
1150   Accordingly, in *Tarakhel*, the Court did not apply the two-step assessment as described at the beginning of this section. On *Tarakhel* see Chapter 3 Section 2.3.2.b.
1151   Costello & Mouzourakis 2014, p. 411.
1152   See on this Chapter 3 Section 2.3.2.b.
1153   See ECtHR, *Tarakhel*, § 104.
1154   See ECtHR, *T.I. v. UK*, 7 March 2000, no. 43844/98 (decision).
1155   See on this Chapter 3 Section 2.3.2.b.

where a real risk of ill treatment or indirect removal is established. It is clear that these judgments represent *important obstacles* to the application of the Dublin system as it was originally designed. With that, Strasbourg was – and continues to be – an important human rights monitoring body with regard to the EU Dublin system. The judgments *M.S.S.* and *Tarakhel* are strong warnings to the EU institutions to correct EU norms or practices that are incompatible with the ECHR. They are further powerful findings for the numerous voices calling for a rethinking of the Dublin system.[1156] Noteworthy in that context is also the case *Sharifi and Others v. Italy and Greece*, concerning a group of Afghans who were immediately deported back to Greece by Italian authorities after they had arrived with an illegal vessel from Greece at the ports of Bari, Ancona and Venice in a period between 2008 and 2009.[1157] Under Article 3 ECHR, the Court basically reapplied the principles developed in *M.S.S.*[1158] In addition, it found that the Italian authorities' action had violated the prohibition on collective expulsion in Article 4 of Protocol No. 4 to ECHR.[1159] The Court recalled on that occasion that no form of collective and indiscriminate returns or other violations of the Convention could be justified by reference to the EU cooperation through the Dublin system or to problems with managing migration flows or the reception of asylum seekers.[1160]

The question remains under what circumstances an *M.S.S.* or *Tarakhel* situation might arise again.[1161] Judgments indicated that a *complete ban* on Dublin

---

1156 See, for example, Peers, Moreno-Lax, Garlick & Guild 2015, p. 382. Another case that could have significant consequences for the functioning of the Dublin system is ECtHR, *V.M. and Others v. Belgium*, 7 July 2015, no. 60125/11, which is not in force as it will be treated by the Grand Chamber; read in particular the dissenting opinions of the judges Keller and Kjølbro on the Court's handling of Art. 13 ECHR in this judgment, which in practice could be understood as imposing an obligation on Dublin states to assess an alleged risk of ill treatment in the country of origin, even when there is no basis for criticising the proper functioning of the asylum procedure or the conditions of reception for asylum seekers in the intermediary EU member state.

1157 ECtHR, *Sharifi and Others v. Italy and Greece*, 21 October 2014, no. 16643/09.

1158 *Ibid.*, § 234.

1159 *Ibid.*, §§ 210–2015. See on this Chapter 1 Section 2.2.4.

1160 ECtHR, *Sharifi*, §§ 223 and 224. ECtHR, *Hirsi Jamaa and Others v. Italy*, 23 February 2012 [GC], no. 27765/09, § 179.

1161 The difficulty in predicting a situation in which states would have the obligation to make use of the sovereignty clause can be observed in comparing *M.S.S.* with the decision *K.R.S.*, which also concerned a transfer to Greece under the Dublin Regulation but was declared inadmissible by the Court. The *K.R.S.* decision was taken less than six months prior to the expulsion of M.S.S. to Greece. In his partly dissenting opinion to *M.S.S.*, judge

transfers as required with regard to Greece according to *M.S.S.* could to a large extent depend on the UNHCR's evaluation of the situation in the receiving state. In *Sharifi v. Austria*, in which no violation was found, the Court noted that at the time of the applicant's transfer to Greece in autumn 2008, the UNHCR *had not* addressed a letter to the Austrian authorities unequivocally asking them to refrain from transferring asylum seekers to Greece, as it had done with Belgium in April 2009. The Court then stated that it 'has attached critical importance to that letter when establishing Belgium's awareness of the seriousness of the deficiencies in Greece.'[1162] Also in *Mohammadi v. Austria* adopted in July 2014, the Court's main argument for the rejection of an Afghan applicant opposing his transfer to Hungary was 'that the UNHCR never issued a position paper requesting EU member States to refrain from transferring asylum-seekers to Hungary under the Dublin II or Dublin III Regulation.'[1163] However, as the *Tarakhel* judgment has demonstrated, it is not only where the deficiencies in the asylum system are systemic that Article 3 ECHR might apply. However, in this case as well, the Court attached much importance to *numerous sources* reporting important failings with regard to the treatment of asylum seekers in Italy in general, including the UNCHR.[1164] It further attached particular importance to the unique vulnerability of the applicants as a family with children.[1165]

The risk of chain removal has been of relevance in a few judgments concerning expulsions to receiving states outside the European Union or the Council of Europe: *Hirsi Jamaa v. Italy* concerned Somali and Eritrean refugees travelling by boat from Libya to Europe.[1166] They had been intercepted at sea and directly returned to Gaddafi's Libya by Italian security forces. With regard to a risk of indirect removal of the complainants by Libyan authorities, the Court first observed that all the information in its possession showed that there was widespread insecurity in Somalia (the Court referred to the judgment *Sufi and Elmi* on that account) and that individuals having left Eritrea regularly faced torture and detention in inhuman conditions on their return. Consequently, the applicants could arguably claim that their repatriation would breach Article 3 ECHR. The Court then noted that Libya had not ratified the 1951 Refugee

---

Bratza criticizes the fact that the Court could not have expected Belgium to change their practice towards Greece after the *K.R.S.* decision.

1162   ECtHR, *Sharifi v. Austria*, 5 December 2013, no. 60104/08, § 36. Confirmed in ECtHR, *Safaii v. Austria*, 7 May 2014, no. 44689/09, § 48. With regard to the situation for asylum seekers in Hungary, see also ECtHR, *Mohammed v. Austria*, 6 June 2013, no. 2283/12, §§ 74 and 75.

1163   ECtHR, *Mohammadi v. Austria*, 3 July 2014, no. 71932/12, § 69.

1164   See ECtHR, *Tarakhel*, §§ 107–113.

1165   See on this Chapter 3 Section 2.3.2.b.

1166   ECtHR, *Hirsi Jamaa and Others v. Italy*, 23 February 2012 [GC], no. 27765/09.

Convention.[1167] It observed the absence of any form of asylum and protection procedure for refugees in that country. The Court could further not subscribe to the government's argument that the UNHCR's activities in Tripoli represented a guarantee against arbitrary repatriation, since the Libyan authorities did not recognise the refugee status granted by this organisation. It held that it was known that Libya forcibly returned refugees to high-risk countries. Accordingly, it concluded that the Italian authorities could not reasonably expect Libya to offer sufficient guarantees against arbitrary repatriation and found that the applicant's removal to Libya had violated Article 3 ECHR.[1168]

b   *Committee*

In its first decision on the merits, *Mutombo v. Switzerland*, the Committee indicated that the principle of non-refoulement in Article 3 CAT includes the prohibition of indirect removal.[1169] This approach was confirmed in subsequent decisions and has been recalled in the Committee's General Comment No. 1 on Article 3 CAT, according to which the phrase 'another State' in Article 3(1) CAT refers 'to the State to which the individual concerned is being expelled, returned or extradited, as well as to any State to which the author may subsequently be expelled, returned or extradited.'[1170]

It is only in two decisions on the merits that the risk of an indirect removal has been of relevance so far: *Z.T. v. Australia* concerned an Algerian who had left his country for South Africa, from which he continued his travel to Australia.[1171] After the Australian authorities had rejected the complainant's application for refugee status, he was removed to South Africa. Before the Committee, the complainant alleged that, by this deportation, the Australian authorities had subjected him to a real risk of being further removed to his home country Algeria, where he would be threatened with torture because of his support for armed Islamic groups. The Committee did not assess whether South Africa would in fact expel the applicant to Algeria. It observed, however, that the complainant had not presented substantial grounds for believing he would be in danger of being subjected to torture in Algeria. His alleged activities for Islamic groups dated back more than 10 years and he had never been tortured or prosecuted for his alleged connections while still living in Algeria.

1167   See similar ECtHR, *Abdolkhani and Karimnia v. Turkey*, 22 September 2009, no. 30471/08, 84–89, with regard to a risk of chain-removal from Iraq to Iran.

1168   ECtHR, *Hirsi Jamaa and Others*, §§ 153–158.

1169   ComAT, *Mutombo v. Switzerland*, 27 April 1994, no. 13/1993, § 10.

1170   ComAT, General Comment No. 1 on Art. 3 CAT (1997), § 2.

1171   ComAT, *Z.T. v. Australia*, 11 November 2003, no. 153/2000.

For those reasons, the Committee found that the complainant's deportation to South Africa did not entail a breach of Article 3 CAT.[1172]

The case *Korban v. Sweden* decided in 1998 concerned an Iraqi citizen threatened with deportation from Sweden to Jordan.[1173] The complainant had left his country in 1991 for Jordan, his wife's country of nationality. In Jordan, he was refused a residence permit. Afraid of being deported to Iraq, the complainant went to Sweden where he applied for refugee status. His wife remained in Jordan. Before the Committee, the applicant claimed that there was a real risk that he would be arrested and subjected to torture in Iraq for his past activities against Saddam Hussein's regime and that he would be held responsible for his son's defection from the army. He claimed that he would be sent back to Iraq from Jordan because he had no residence permit there and the Jordanian police would work closely with the Iraqi authorities. In support of his claim, he provided the Committee with documents in which the UNHCR informed the Swedish Aliens Appeals Board that marriage to a Jordanian citizen was not grounds for being granted residence permits in Jordan and that Iraqis had been denied entry or re-admission into Jordan.[1174] The Swedish government replied that Jordan 'can be characterized as a rather safe country for Iraqi refugees,' although 'their situation may change from time to time depending on the political situation.' It noted that even if Jordan had not ratified the 1951 Refugee Convention, it had expressed its willingness to follow the principle of non-refoulement contained in that Convention. The Jordanian authorities seemed further to have a particular understanding for the difficult situation of the Iraqis. According to the government, this was confirmed by the fact that Jordan and the UNHCR had recently agreed on a memorandum of understanding regarding the rights of refugees in Jordan.[1175] With regard to the alleged risks for the complainant in Iraq, the Committee noted that the presentation of the facts by the applicant did not raise significant doubts as to the general veracity of his claims and observed that the Swedish government had not expressed doubts in this respect either. It therefore found that the complainant had established that there was a real risk of his being subjected to torture in Iraq.[1176] With regard to the risk of being removed to Iraq by Jordanian authorities, the Committee observed the following:

1172 *Ibid.*, §§ 6.2–6.5.

1173 ComAT, *Korban v. Sweden*, 16 November 1998, no. 88/1997.

1174 *Ibid.*, §§ 3.1 and 3.2.

1175 *Ibid.*, §§ 4.9 and 4.12.

1176 *Ibid.*, § 6.4.

The Committee notes that the Swedish immigration authorities had ordered the author's expulsion to Jordan and that the State party abstains
from making an evaluation of the risk that the author will be deported
to Iraq from Jordan. It appears from the parties' submissions, however,
that such risk cannot be excluded, in view of the assessment made by different sources, including UNHCR, based on reports indicating that some
Iraqis have been sent by the Jordanian authorities to Iraq against their
will, that marriage to a Jordanian woman does not guarantee a residence
permit in Jordan and that this situation has not improved after the signature of a Memorandum of Understanding between the UNHCR and the
Jordanian authorities regarding the rights of refugees in Jordan. The State
party itself has recognized that Iraqi citizens who are refugees in Jordan,
in particular those who have been returned to Jordan from a European
country, are not entirely protected from being deported to Iraq.[1177]

In light of these observations, the Committee concluded that Sweden had an
obligation to refrain from returning the author to Iraq or Jordan. It added that
although Jordan was a party to the CAT, it had 'not made the declaration under
article 22. As a result, the author would not have the possibility of submitting a
new communication to the Committee if he was threatened with deportation
from Jordan to Iraq.'[1178]

The elements of relevance to the Committee in these two cases can be summarized as follows: *first*, the establishment of the real risk of torture in case of
deportation to the home country; *second*, the general practice of the intermediary state with regard to deportations to that home country; and *third*, the
possibility for the applicant to submit a complaint to the Committee under
Article 22 CAT against the intermediary state in case of deportation.

It is difficult to say what weight the Committee gives to the third factor. In
Korban, the Committee first concluded that Article 3 CAT would be violated
in case of the deportation of the applicant to Jordan and noted 'furthermore'
that Jordan had not made a declaration under Article 22 CAT. Against this
background, it seems that the question of whether the intermediary state has
recognized the Committee's competence to assess individual complaints is in
itself not decisive for the establishment of a risk of chain-refoulement.[1179] It is
also interesting to note that the Committee only referred to general information regarding the treatment of Iraqi refugees in Jordan. The fact that those

---

1177 *Ibid.*, § 6.5.
1178 *Ibid.*, § 7.
1179 See in this sense Thurin 2012, p. 237 fn. 1131; Wouters 2009, p. 510.

refugees were not 'entirely protected from being deported' was sufficient for it to find that the risk of chain-refoulement was established. I can agree with Wouters who notes that this indicates that the risk of removal by the intermediary state need not be particularly high or personal.[1180] However, one recent inadmissibility decision indicates that applicants claiming a risk of indirect removal must be able to present at least some concrete information on an intermediary state's failure with regard to the respect of the principle of non-refoulement in general, in order to be considered on the merits. The case *M.K. and B.B. v. Switzerland* decided in November 2015 concerned the removal to Spain of two Congolese (DRC), one of them pregnant, under the Dublin III Regulation.[1181] It is in fact the first decision in which the Committee dealt with a so-called *Dublin removal*. The Committee held that the applicants had not submitted evidence to justify their claim that the Spanish authorities would not assess their request for asylum with due respect for the principle of non-refoulement. It further added that the applicants had not submitted information demonstrating that the reception conditions for asylum seekers in Spain were such that they entailed a violation of their rights under the Convention.[1182] This latter statement is particularly interesting since it demonstrates that the Committee is not uncaring as to the reception conditions of asylum seekers in the frame of a Dublin transfer, although Article 3 CAT is principally restricted to torture. However, the Committee chose to declare this complaint manifestly unfounded, which is rare in its practice.[1183] As heard from practice, other Dublin cases are currently pending. One hopes they will lead to further clarifications. Generally, in face of the scant case law, it remains difficult to predict how the Committee will proceed in future cases.

c   *Comparison*

When assessing the risk of a chain-refoulement, the Court and the Committee proceed in a similar way: as a first step they assess whether there is a risk of ill treatment for the complainant in the state to which he might be subsequently removed, usually the complainant's country of origin. When doing this, the Court does not ask the complainant to establish that there is a real risk of ill treatment in this country. The complainant does, however, have to have an arguable claim. As a second step, if the risk as described in the first step is

---

1180   Wouters 2009, p. 510.

1181   See ComAT, *M.K. and B.B. v. Switzerland*, 26 November 2015, no. 635/2014 (not published yet).

1182   *Ibid.*, § 7.3.

1183   See on this Chapter 2 Section 3.2.6.

established, the Court and the Committee assess the intermediary state's practice with regard to the principle of non-refoulement.

In *Korban v. Sweden*, the Committee did not explicitly take into account the complainant's argument that the intermediary state Jordan has not ratified the 1951 Refugee Convention. However, the possibility that this played a role when the Committee members took their decision, as it did for the Court in *Hirsi Jamaa,* cannot be excluded. The question of which Conventions have been ratified by the intermediary state or what legal mechanisms are foreseen to protect refugees is of importance in the second step of the assessment, but it is not necessarily decisive. The determining question is whether the protection against refoulement in the intermediary state is effective in practice. Examples of individuals who have been deported from an intermediary state in violation of the principle of non-refoulement will hence be of particular importance. The Court and the Committee are not particularly demanding with regard to the individualization of the risk of refoulement by the intermediary state. What has to be established is a general practice of disrespect with regard to the principle of non-refoulement. However, as has been explained, it remains difficult for complainants in Strasbourg to demonstrate that a member state of the Council of Europe does not provide effective refugee protection in practice. As a recent inadmissibility decision by the Committee on a Dublin case has shown, this might be similar before the Committee.[1184] However, the Geneva practice on that subject is simply too scant at the moment to make general statements.

What has also been of relevance for both is the question of whether the applicant has the possibility of preventing an eventual deportation by the intermediary state in submitting another complaint against this state to the Court or the Committee itself (with a request for interim measures). The Court gave considerable weight to this point when rejecting the complaint against a transfer under the Dublin Regulation to Greece in *K.R.S. v. United Kingdom*. It did not mention this element when rejecting a similar complaint in *T.I. v. United Kingdom*. In *M.S.S.*, the Court rejected the government's argument on that account in referring quite generally to the lack of access of asylum seekers in Greece to the Court itself. It is difficult to make a general statement on the weight given to this element by the Court and the Committee. Given the subsidiary nature of the international authorities' protection, in my opinion the question of whether they can themselves lower a risk of refoulement should be of subsidiary importance. The Committee appears aligned with this view in *Korban*.

1184   See ComAT, *M.K. and B.B. v. Switzerland*, 26 November 2015, no. 635/2014 (not published yet).

CHAPTER 5

Summary and Concluding Remarks

This chapter concludes this study with a summary of the findings gained through the comparison of the Court's and the Committee's case law on the principle of non-refoulement, a description of the mutual influence of the Court and the Committee on each other and a critical look at the impact and persuasiveness of their judgments and decisions on the principle of non-refoulement.

1 Summary

This study has compared the practice and case law of the European Court of Human Rights (the Court) with that of the UN Committee against Torture (the Committee) in the assessment of individual complaints submitted under the principle of non-refoulement under Article 3 ECHR and Article 3 CAT. The main similarities and differences are summarized in the following.

Procedural Aspects
In General
The individual complaint mechanisms before the Court in Strasbourg and the Committee in Geneva are very similar: the procedures are mainly written and free of charge. The Court and the Committee are both overburdened, so that the procedures with regard to non-refoulement complaints take on average between one and three years. There are two differences in procedure that are of importance in practice:

(1) The Court has a filter mechanism by which it may handle obviously inadmissible complaints in a simplified procedure without the involvement of the government concerned. The great majority of the cases dealt with by the Court in Strasbourg are rejected as being manifestly inadmissible in this simplified procedure. The Committee does *not* have a simplified procedure. All complaints registered in Geneva are transmitted to the respondent government for observations.
(2) The threshold for obtaining *interim measures* is clearly lower before the Committee than before the Court.

Admissibility

The criteria for the admissibility of complaints as laid down in Article 35 ECHR, Article 22 CAT and Rule 113 of the Committee's Rules of Procedure are almost identical:

– The alleged violation must be imputable to a state that has ratified the ECHR or the CAT, and that has accepted the individual complaint mechanism under Article 22 CAT.
– Under the ECHR and the CAT, states can only be held responsible for the violation of rights occurring under their jurisdiction, which is normally on their territory. However, according to the Court and the Committee, the notion of jurisdiction must also include situations where a state party exercises *de facto* or *de jure* control over persons outside its territory. They have both made clear that this includes any transfer of detainees within a state party's effective custody in the context of military or other actions operated outside the respondent state's territory. It further includes the responsibility of states for migrants they have intercepted in foreign or international waters.
– The same complaint shall not be pending or have been examined by another international forum. The Committee in Geneva will not assess complaints examined on the merits by the Court in Strasbourg and vice versa.
– All accessible effective remedies at domestic level must be exhausted.
– The claim must be compatible with the provisions of the relevant convention.
– The complaint shall not be abusive or manifestly ill-founded.
– The complainant must have victim status, which means that he must be personally affected by the alleged violation. In the context of non-refoulement, this means that there must be an enforceable deportation order against the applicant, unless it can be demonstrated that a *de facto* threat of deportation exists without a formal order. Before the Court as well as before the Committee, the assessment of many complaints concerning the principle of non-refoulement is discontinued because the complainants lose their victim status during the course of the procedure.

A difference with regard to admissibility according to the provisions in the conventions is that Article 35(1) ECHR requires that any complaint must be submitted within a period of six months from the date on which the final decision at national level was taken. The CAT does not impose such a time limit. However, according to the Court's recent case law, in complaints concerning

non-refoulement, the six-month period only starts to run with the enforcement of the removal.

Even though the admissibility criteria are similar on paper, passing the bar
of admissibility is much more difficult for complainants before the Court than
before the Committee: while around 95 per cent of complaints submitted to
the Court are declared inadmissible, this only happens in about 20 per cent
of complaints before the Committee. Why is that so? There are no official statistics demonstrating for which reason exactly the Court declares complaints
inadmissible. However, it is known that the most common reason for inadmissibility in Strasbourg is that applications are considered to be 'manifestly
ill-founded.' In the Committee's practice, this criterion only plays a minor role.
Against this background, it is obvious that the Court's wide understanding
of the criterion of 'ill-foundedness' is the main reason that more complaints
are declared inadmissible in Strasbourg than in Geneva. The assessment of
whether a complaint is manifestly ill-founded amounts to a preliminary test
on the merits. With that, it leaves much more room for divergent interpretations than the other admissibility criteria, which are of a formal and not of a
substantive nature.

Legal Nature and Effect of the Judgments and Decisions with Regard to Non-refoulement Complaints

According to Article 34 ECHR, the judgments of the Court are *legally binding*
for the contracting state concerned. This is not the case for the decisions adopted by the Committee. However, the state parties to the CAT that have made
a declaration under Article 22 CAT have explicitly mandated the Committee to
supervise the CAT's provisions by taking decisions on individual cases. There is
a consensus that the Committee's decisions are more than mere recommendations, otherwise the supervisory mechanism would be superfluous. However,
*the exact legal nature and force of the Committee's decisions, being more than
pure recommendations but less than legally binding judgments, remains controversial.* In my opinion, the designation of the Committee's decisions as 'authoritative interpretations' of the Convention obligations applies best to describe
their nature.[1]

In practice, in those decisions in which the Committee has concluded that
an expulsion or extradition would be incompatible with Article 3 CAT, the

---

1   See Nowak & McArthur 2008, p. 797 (§ 199).

states concerned have almost always refrained from the deportation: of the 45 decisions in which the Committee found a violation of Article 3 CAT prior to the end of 2012, there are only two cases in which the state party refused to follow the Committee's decision. Both cases concerned the deportations of individuals considered a threat to national security from Canada. Generally, the Court's and the Committee's verdicts with regard to non-refoulement are respected. However, before both, there have been cases in which interim measures have not been respected. These cases remain exceptional, though, for both institutions. In summary, with regard to individual complaints concerning the principle of non-refoulement submitted against European states by failed asylum seekers, the lack of legal force of the Committee's decisions has made *no significant difference in practice* for the individuals concerned. Applicants who have been successful in Strasbourg or Geneva have usually been granted long-term residence permits. Some have obtained refugee status. However, the Court and the Committee pronounce a bar to removal rather than asking states to attribute a certain status to applicants. Neither Article 3 ECHR nor Article 3 CAT contains a right to political asylum.

Finally, in those exceptional cases in which the complainant has *already been removed* when the Court or the Committee conclude that the principle of non-refoulement is violated, states have the obligation to take diplomatic steps to assure the complainant's security and, eventually, to grant compensation. The implementation of the respective judgments and decisions has shown to be more problematic under both institutions in such cases, since the complainant is not no longer under the contracting state's jurisdiction.

The Scope of the Principle of Non-refoulement under Article 3 ECHR and Article 3 CAT
The Nature of the Harm: Torture vs. Inhuman or Degrading Treatment

The main difference between the protection offered against refoulement by the ECHR and the CAT is that the application of Article 3 CAT is in principle limited to acts that meet the definition of *torture* in Article 1 CAT, while Article 3 ECHR provides protection from *torture and inhuman or degrading treatment or punishment*. What impact has this had in practice?

Torture is an aggravated and deliberate form of inhuman treatment. A main criterion for distinguishing torture from inhuman treatment is the *intensity* of the inflicted harm. Only acts that cause severe pain or suffering will be considered torture. In addition to the severity of a treatment, the Court and the Committee both define torture as a harm *intentionally* inflicted on a person for certain purposes such as the extraction of information, punishment, intimidation or coercion. However, both the Committee and the Court recognize that there is no clear line between torture and other forms of inhuman treatment. The Court has further expressed the view that the distinction between torture and other forms of ill treatment is particularly hard to draw in the context of refoulement, where a prospective assessment is required.[2] This applies for the Committee, too. Hence, in most non-refoulement cases, neither the Court nor the Committee put much effort into categorising the exact nature of the alleged possible future harm as long as it could *prima facie* fall into the range of acts categorised as torture or inhuman treatment. Consequently, in the majority of cases, *the theoretically narrower protection offered under the CAT has made no visible difference for complainants in practice.* However, there are certain types of applications that have been dealt with by the Court in which, because of its particular character, the expected harm in case of deportation may *clearly* be classified as inhuman or degrading treatment and *not* as torture. With regard to these applications, the protection offered under Article 3 ECHR is visibly broader than that under Article 3 CAT. However, these types of complaints still remain rather exceptional in the Court's case law:

- One type concerns cases in which applicants allege the risk of being detained in degrading or inhuman prison conditions in case of deportation. The detention of individuals in deplorable prison conditions is typically considered inhuman or degrading treatment and rarely torture because the harm caused is usually not inflicted intentionally. Hence, in non-refoulement cases in which the expected harm refers to a deficient prison system in the receiving state, the Court might offer better protection than the Committee. However, as soon as the deficiencies in the receiving state's prison system are not 'just' restricted to degrading or inhuman living conditions, but acts of intentional violence or ill treatment are reported against detainees, the differentiation between torture and inhuman treatment in the risk assessment becomes almost impossible and it is therefore hardly done either by the Court or the Committee.
- A distinction can be made with regard to the death penalty. While the Court generally considers capital punishment an inhuman treatment prohibited by Article 3 ECHR, the Committee only classifies the death penalty as torture if it is carried out in a particularly cruel manner. It should be added that the two situations just described, inhuman prison conditions and the death penalty, are often relevant in extradition cases. In extradition cases,

---

2   ECtHR, *Harkins & Edwards v. UK*, 17 January 2012, nos. 9146/07 & 32650/07, § 122.

the expected harm and the exact nature of the harm are generally easier to assess than in expulsion cases.

– Another situation in which the principle of non-refoulement under the CAT does *not* apply when it might apply under the ECHR concerns the removal of individuals suffering from grave illnesses. In the famous judgment *D. v. United Kingdom*[3] adopted in 1997, the Court applied the principle of non-refoulement in a situation where the source of the harm risked in the receiving state stemmed from a naturally occurring illness. The case concerned the deportation of an applicant who was terminally ill with AIDS to St Kitts, where he could not count on any support or shelter. However, the Court made clear in the subsequent case law that the principle of non-refoulement only applies in very exceptional circumstances in the context of medical issues.[4] As was the situation for the complainant from St Kitts, individuals must already be close to death. The case *D. v the United Kingdom* in fact remains the only one in which a petitioner successfully argued that his expulsion violated the principle of non-refoulement because of his illness and the lack of treatment available in the receiving state.[5] The Court's unduly severe approach in this field is in contradiction with its general practice under Article 3 ECHR. The Committee does not apply the principle of non-refoulement with regard to risks emanating from the applicant's health status. It is unlikely that it would consider that a lack of medical treatment for a natural illness amounted to torture. However, the Committee has not excluded the possibility that the deportation of a gravely ill individual might *as such* be considered to be an inhuman treatment prohibited by Article 16 CAT, which applies in the domestic context.

– In the Court judgments *M.S.S.*,[6] *Sufi and Elmi*[7] and *Tarakhel*,[8] the Court has accepted that under particular circumstances *dire living conditions* in

---

3   ECtHR, *D. v. UK*, 2 May 1997, no. 30240/96.

4   See, in particular ECtHR, *N. v. UK*, 27 May 2008 [GC], no. 26565/05.

5   There is one judgment in which the Court concluded that the *extradition* of an applicant suffering from paranoid schizophrenia to a maximum-security facility with a highly restrictive regime in the US would violate Article 3 ECHR; see ECtHR, *Aswat v. UK*, 16 April 2013, no. 17299/12. However, the Court did not apply the high threshold set in *D. v. the UK* in this case. It referred to its principles developed with regard to the appropriate medical care for mentally ill persons held in detention and noted their particular vulnerability. With that, individuals suffering from illnesses appear to have a better chance of being protected from *extradition* than from *expulsion*.

6   ECtHR, *M.S.S. v. Belgium and Greece*, 21 January 2011 [GC], no. 30696/09.

7   ECtHR, *Sufi and Elmi v. UK*, 28 June 2011, nos. 8319/07 and 11449/07.

8   ECtHR, *Tarakhel v. Switzerland*, 4 November 2014 [GC], no. 29217/12.

combination with an uncertain situation may amount to *degrading or inhuman treatment* and may therefore trigger the application of the principle of non-refoulement under Article 3 ECHR. However, such circumstances will *only* be considered a breach of Article 3 ECHR if state authorities have a special responsibility for the individuals concerned because of their particular vulnerability (see the situation for asylum seekers in *M.S.S.* and *Tarakhel*), or when they are predominantly due to the direct and indirect actions of parties to a violent conflict (see the situation for refugees in *Sufi and Elmi*). It is rather difficult to determine when an applicant may fall under these categories. The Court has made clear that 'Article 3 ECHR cannot be interpreted as obliging the State parties to provide everyone within their jurisdiction with a home, and that this provision does not entail any general obligation to give refugees financial assistance to enable them to maintain a certain standard of living.'[9] Making the comparison with the Committee, it is evident that the approach taken by the Court with regard to a risk of *degrading or inhuman living conditions* would hardly be conceivable under Article 3 CAT, with its refoulement protection restricted to torture in the sense of Article 1 CAT.

> ### The Source of the Harm: Rapprochement of the Committee to the Court's Approach with Regard to State Responsibility for Private Actors

According to the Court's established case law, individuals who claim a threat from non-state actors under the principle of non-refoulement must be able to demonstrate *first* that a real risk exists of being subjected to torture or other inhuman treatment by such private actors in the receiving state and *second* that the authorities from the receiving state are not willing or able to provide appropriate protection against the harm expected from these actors.

For a long time, the Committee did not protect individuals from removal when the alleged ill treatment feared in the receiving country emanated from private actors. It followed a narrow interpretation of the definition of torture in Article 1 CAT, according to which an act can only be considered as torture if it is 'inflicted by or at the instigation of or with the consent or acquiescence of a public official or other person acting in an official capacity.' Cases in which the alleged harm emanated from private actors were rejected. An exception was only made in a case concerning a removal to Somalia in 1999: the Committee noted that in a state without a central government in which quasi-governmental factions exercise *de facto* powers comparable to those

---

9   ECtHR, *M.S.S*, § 249.

normally exercised by governments, the members of those factions can fall, for the purposes of the application of the CAT, within the phrase 'public officials or other persons acting in an official capacity' contained in Article 1 CAT.[10]

However, in recent years, the Committee has adopted an approach with regard to the protection against harms inflicted from private actors that resembles that of the Court in Strasbourg. It has made clear that states *bear responsibility for acts of torture committed by private actors where the authorities have reasonable grounds to believe that such acts are being committed but fail to offer protection*.[11] The Committee has shown itself to be particularly cautious if states fail to offer protection against gender-based violence committed by private actors and has applied the principle of non-refoulement in that context.[12] Unfortunately, the Committee's case law on the protection against refoulement based on the risk of harm from non-state actors is still vague. A clear guideline on this essential question in a *revised* General Comment on Article 3 CAT would be welcome. However, it should be borne in mind that even before the Court in Strasbourg with its more established practice, it has proven to be difficult for petitioners to successfully establish a risk of ill treatment from private actors.

Absolute Character of the Prohibition on Refoulement

According to the Court and the Committee, the prohibition on refoulement under Article 3 ECHR and Article 3 CAT is absolute. This means that the protection against refoulement is applied to each and every human being, no matter his background, and that no exceptional circumstances whatsoever may be accepted to justify a derogation of any kind from that prohibition. The absolute character of the prohibition from refoulement under the ECHR and the CAT is the *main difference from the protection offered against refoulement under the 1951 Refugee Convention*, which excludes individuals who have a certain criminal background or who are considered a threat to the security of the host state. The Court and the Committee have both shown to be resistant to any arguments or pressure applied by states against the absolute and equal validity

---

10   ComAT, *Elmi v. Australia*, 14 May 1999, no. 120/1998.

11   See in particular ComAT, *A.A.M. v. Sweden*, 23 May 2012, no. 413/2010, § 9.2; ComAT, *Dewage v. Australia*, 14 November 2013, no. 387/2009, § 109. As can be seen in these decisions, the Committee's General Comment No. 2 on Art. 2 CAT released in 2008 has contributed to this development.

12   See in particular ComAT, *Njamba and Balikosa v. Sweden*, 14 May 2010, no. 322/2007; ComAT, *F.B. v. Netherlands*, 20 November 2015, no. 613/2014 and ComAT, General Comment No. 2 on Art. 2 (2008), §§ 18 and 22.

of the principle of non-refoulement in cases that involved the deportation of individuals considered to be a terrorist threat. They have both made clear that the obligation to respect non-refoulement cannot be weighed against interests of states such as the countries' national security, public order or economic well-being.

In principle, Article 3 ECHR prohibits torture as well as other forms of inhuman or degrading treatment equally regardless of whether these acts occur in the domestic context or a risk of such acts is invoked in the context of refoulement. However, it has been shown to be difficult for complainants to establish that there is a real risk of degrading treatment in case of deportation. In its recent case law, the Court even appears to establish a double standard as to when devastating living conditions may amount to degrading or inhuman treatment or not depending on whether the individual concerned lives inside or outside Europe.[13] Generally, the more the Court widens the protection under Article 3 ECHR to harms of a socioeconomic nature, the more difficult it appears for it not to take into account considerations of a socioeconomic nature when defining the limits of the protection against refoulement. This somehow challenges the equal and absolute nature of the prohibition of inhuman and degrading treatment and the prohibition on refoulement based on that.

The Risk Assessment
Standard and Burden of Proof
To assess whether there is a risk of ill treatment, the Court and the Committee examine the foreseeable consequences of the removal of an applicant to the receiving country in light of the general situation there as well as his personal circumstances. The Court and the Committee use similar terms to describe the standard of proof and burden of proof required under the principle of non-refoulement: applicants must be able to present *substantial grounds* for believing that they face *a real and foreseeable risk or danger* of being subjected to ill treatment in the receiving country. The risk must be *more than a simple possibility* but *does not have to be highly probable or more likely than not.*

It is *in principle for the applicant to adduce evidence* capable of proving that there is such a real and foreseeable risk. Where such evidence is adduced, it is for the national authorities to 'dispel any doubts' about the risk. According to the Court's as well as the Committee's practice, the burden of proof may shift to the government if the complainant presents reliable evidence indicating a risk of ill treatment or if the human rights situation in the receiving country is extremely worrying. In addition, if the national authorities have not properly

---

13   See ECtHR, *S.H.H. v. UK*, 29 January 2013, no. 60367/10, § 90.

examined an applicant's claim, the burden might shift to the respondent state's government to demonstrate within the international procedure why the applicant is not at risk in case of removal.

What can be observed is that even though the terms used by the Court and the Committee to describe the standard and burden of proof are almost the same, *the Court is principally more reluctant than the Committee to recognise the existence of a 'real risk' in practice.* All in all the Committee is less demanding than the Court when it comes to the presentation of evidence or the exposure of complainants as political activists. This is apparent from the case law as a whole and the statistics available. Even though there is no exact data on refoulement cases from the Court, it is evident that the success rate in Strasbourg, where generally less than 10 per cent of all complaints submitted pass the bar of admissibility, is much lower than in Geneva, where approximately 20 per cent of the complaints concerning the principle of non-refoulement assessed have been successful. It has rightly been observed by scholars that the Court has set a remarkably 'high threshold' under the principle of non-refoulement.[14] However, the success or failure of a complaint always depends on various factors, among which the standard or burden of proof, as an abstract normative concept, is often not at the centre of the decision-making process.

Time of the Risk Assessment

With regard to the relevant time of the risk assessment, the Court and the Committee both apply the same principles:

Because the Court and the Committee rarely assess complaints on the merits in which they have refused to grant interim measures, the great majority of the complaints they deal with concern individuals who have not yet been deported. In these cases, the Court and the Committee proceed to a full *ex nunc* risk assessment. This means that the relevant time of the risk assessment is that of the consideration of the case by the international authority. If the human rights situation has changed during the long international procedure, they might be confronted with a different factual background from that considered by the national courts when they took their decision.

Once a deportation has taken place, the focus is primarily on those facts that were known or ought to have been known to the contracting state at the time of the deportation. Subsequent facts will in principle only be taken into account as indications of what the state party knew or should have known at the time of the deportation.

---

14   Chetail 2006, p. 101; Schürmann & Scheidegger 2009, p. 213; Suntinger 1995, p. 219; Thurin 2012, pp. 179 and 260; Wouters 2009, p. 578.

Elements of the Risk Assessment

When the Court and the Committee find a violation of the principle of non-refoulement, it is because they disagree with *at least* one of the following tests as applied by national authorities: the way the human rights situation in the receiving state has been analysed or the assessment of the individual risk factor arising from the complainant's particular background. Generally, in cases in which it is apparent to the Court and the Committee that the assessment at national level was comprehensive and fair, they will be more reluctant to disagree with the national authorities' findings. It is typically the cumulative and combined evaluation of these elements that lead the Court and the Committee to the conclusion that a removal would be in violation of the principle of non-refoulement.

(1)   *Fair and Effective Assessment at National Level*

Fair and Comprehensive Assessment by the Domestic Authorities

Article 3 ECHR and Article 3 CAT contain a *positive obligation* on state parties to provide individuals with a realistic opportunity to substantiate their claims under the principle of non-refoulement. Without this obligation, the protection against refoulement remains theoretical. When assessing whether the principle of non-refoulement has been violated in a particular case, the Court and the Committee hence both take into account the *quality of the risk assessment* at national level. They must be satisfied that the assessment made by the national authorities has included all relevant factors including the human rights situation in the receiving state and that it is based on a reasonable evaluation of the claims and evidence presented by the applicant. The Court and the Committee are both sceptical if no individualized assessment is apparent from the national decisions and judgments, or if claims under the principle of non-refoulement have been rejected for purely procedural reasons.

The *impact of procedural irregularities* within the national proceedings on the Court and the Committee's risk assessment is variable: in cases in which no meaningful assessment by national authorities is visible, the Court and the Committee will be particularly sceptical with regard to the national authorities' findings. If the deficiencies are severe and the human rights situation in the receiving state worrying, the complainant will usually be given the benefit of the doubt with regard to the alleged risk of refoulement. The Committee has occasionally even concluded that the principle of non-refoulement under Article 3 CAT was violated on mainly procedural grounds. However, if the procedure before the national authorities does appear exhaustive, fair and reasonable, the Court and the Committee will attach more weight to their findings. Nevertheless, in almost all cases treated on the merits, the Court and the

Committee usually do their own – at least minimal – assessment of the substance of the risk, whether procedural irregularities in the national risk assessment are apparent or not.[15]

The Right to an Effective Remedy

According to the Court and the Committee a meaningful assessment under the principle of non-refoulement also includes the right of individuals to an effective remedy before an appeal body against the decision to remove, when there is an *arguable* (Court) or a *plausible* (Committee) allegation that issues arise under the principle of non-refoulement. This right is inherent to the principle of non-refoulement under Article 3 ECHR and Article 3 CAT.

In contrast to the CAT, the ECHR explicitly guarantees the right to an effective remedy in Article 13 ECHR with regard to potential violations of all substantive rights of the ECHR including the principle of non-refoulement. With this separate norm, the Court's practice on the right to an effective remedy is richer than the Committee's. The lack of a separate norm to address only procedural aspects under the principle of non-refoulement might be the reason for which the Committee, in contrast to the Court, has occasionally concluded that a violation of that principle existed on mainly procedural grounds.

When assessing whether a complainant has had access to an effective remedy at national level, the Court and the Committee proceed using a case-by-case approach. Unfortunately, their case law on this is somewhat unpredictable and sometimes inconsistent. However, they have developed analogous *general principles*: individuals must be given the possibility of using the remedy before a (preferably judicial) authority that is independent of the authority that has taken the initial decision on the deportation. The appeal body must have the power to effectively review the legality of the initial decision on substantive and procedural grounds and it must have the power to quash that decision. Before the Court and the Committee, only appeals with suspensive effect are considered effective. The individual concerned must be given sufficient time to file such an appeal with the legal guarantee that he will not be deported until the outcome of that appeal.

(2)   *General Human Rights Situation*

In assessing whether there is a risk of ill treatment in the receiving country, the Court and the Committee assess the general human rights situation in that

---

15   With that, they both attach less weight to the question of the quality of the risk assessment at national level than the UN Human Rights Committee does in its recent practice on individual non-refoulement cases.

country, taking into account any improvement or worsening of the human rights situation in general or in respect of a particular group or area that could be relevant to the applicant's personal circumstances.[16]

The Individualisation of the Risk and Protection of Groups Systematically Exposed to Ill Treatment

Neither the Court nor the Committee have a safe country concept according to which the risk of ill treatment may *per se* be excluded for a list of selected countries. At the same time, both the Court and the Committee do *not* in principle generally ban deportations to specific states or regions in which the human rights situation is particularly worrying. References to widespread practices of ill treatment in the receiving state cannot normally alone serve as a basis for relying on the principle of non-refoulement under Article 3 ECHR or Article 3 CAT. According to the Court and the Committee, the applicant's allegations require corroboration by additional grounds by which the individual concerned is able to establish that he is *personally* at a real risk of being subjected to ill treatment in the country to which he would be returned.

However, in contrast to the Committee, the Court in Strasbourg will make an exception to that approach 'where the situation of violence in the country of destination is of such intensity as to create a real risk that any removal to that country would necessarily violate Article 3 ECHR.'[17] However, this will only apply 'in the most extreme cases' of general violence.[18] So far, it has only been in the judgment *Sufi and Elmi*[19] decided in June 2011 with regard to the situation in the city of Mogadishu at the time and likewise in *L M. and Others v. Russia*[20] with regard to the situation in Syria in 2015 that the Court has acknowledged the existence of such an extreme case of indiscriminate violence.

The Court has further developed the principle that a complainant will not be required to present evidence related to an individualised risk if he is able to establish that he is a member of a group that is systematically exposed to ill treatment in the receiving state. However, here again, it has been rare for the Court to explicitly recognize that members of certain groups are systematically subjected to ill treatment. The Committee does not *explicitly* recognise the concept of a general protection of members of certain threatened groups

---

16 See the words used in ECtHR, *Dzhurayev v. Russia*, 25 April 2013, no. 71386/10, § 152.

17 ECtHR, *Sufi and Elmi v. UK*, 28 June 2011, nos. 8319/07 & 11449/07, §§ 218 and 241.

18 *Ibid.*

19 *Ibid.*

20 ECtHR, *L.M. and Others v. Russia*, 15 October 2015, nos. 40081/14, 40088/14 and 40127/14.

or the protection against removal based on extreme cases of general violence. However, there are decisions adopted in Geneva in which it is not evident to the reader that the Committee has in fact relied on grounds additional to the human rights situation for individuals belonging to a certain group when concluding that a removal would be incompatible with Article 3 CAT.[21] Interestingly, the Committee has developed a very sensitive approach with regard to risks of gender-based violence, while the vulnerable position of women has not received particular attention in the Court's recent non-refoulement case law.[22]

In practice, the Court's and the Committee's approach with regard to the relevance and weight given to the human rights situation in the receiving country is comparable: The more worrying the human rights situation in the receiving country – in general or with regard to a particular group that the applicant may be associated with – the less demanding they will be with regard to the establishment of additional personal risk factors.

Assessment of the Human Rights Situation by the Court and the Committee

The assessment and evaluation of the human rights situation in the Court's judgments is much more in-depth than in the Committee's decisions. The Court usually refers to several sources ranging from state reports and judgments from national courts, reports from notable NGOs such as Amnesty International or Human Rights Watch and reports from international organisations, in particular the UNHCR. The Committee in contrast only briefly addresses the human rights situation in the receiving country in two or three sentences. If at all, it usually only refers to its own concluding observations established within the state reporting procedures under Article 19 CAT.

Even if the Court and the Committee mostly coincide in their general estimation of the human rights situation, differences can be observed: in particular, the Court has shown itself to be hard to convince that there is a real risk of complainants being subjected to ill treatment in member states of the Council of Europe unless various independent sources prove that there are widespread practices of ill treatment in those member states or the applicants concerned

---

21   See ComAT, *Njamba and Balikosa v. Sweden*, 14 May 2010, no. 322/2007; ComAT, *Abdussamatov and 28 Others v. Kazakhstan*, 1 June 2012, no. 444/2010.

22   See in particular ComAT, *Njamba and Balikosa*; ComAT, *F.B. v. Netherlands*, 20 November 2015, no. 613/2014 and ComAT, General Comment No. 2 on Art. 2 (2008), §§ 18 and 22 in contrast to ECtHR, *A.A. and Others v. Sweden*, 28 June 2012, no. 14499/09 (Yemen) and ECtHR, *R.H. v. Sweden*, 10 September 2015, no. 4601/14 (Mogadishu).

appear particularly vulnerable. The Committee does not display such a preference towards receiving states that have ratified the CAT or accepted its competence to assess individual complaints.

(3)   *Personal Circumstances*
         The Complainant's Credibility
To establish a real risk of ill treatment, complainants must be able to tell their
story in a detailed, comprehensive and consistent manner. Presentations of
authentic evidence will strengthen their credibility. It is the complainant's
claim as a whole that must be credible, not necessarily each and every statement made. In cases in which applicants have presented reliable evidence (in
particular medical reports) proving that they are torture victims, the Committee has shown itself to be particularly generous with regard to inconsistencies or omissions in the applicant's claim. However, neither the Court nor the
Committee require that all facts cited be proved by evidence. Both institutions
recognize that it is difficult for individuals having fled their country to collect
evidence.

According to the Court, national authorities are better placed to assess not
just the facts but also the personal credibility of the individual concerned.
This doctrine is borne out by practice in Strasbourg. In general, the Committee
tends to give the applicant the benefit of the doubt more easily in individual
cases than the Court.[23]

                    The Complainant's History and Background
Unless the human rights situation in the receiving state has fundamentally
changed, the Court and the Committee will consider the circumstances in
which the applicant has left his country of origin as an important indication
of what he might expect should he be returned there. Past political activities,
experiences of ill treatment or detention as well as the possibility of being arrested on return are considered risk-enhancing factors in most of the decisions
and judgments in which the Court and the Committee have found that the
principle of non-refoulement was violated.

The great majority of the cases that have been successful in Strasbourg and
Geneva have concerned complainants who feared ill treatment for political
reasons. The core question with regard to the importance of political activities in the risk assessment is the interest of authorities or other powerful
actors who are known for practices of ill treatment in individuals having a
similar background as the complainant. Arrest warrants and other documents

---

23   See also Chetail 2006, pp. 100–101; Schürmann & Scheidegger 2009, p. 213.

establishing that a complainant is targeted by such actors are given particular weight. Depending on the circumstances, family ties can also be an important risk factor. The Court and the Committee also take into account whether applicants have been politically active *after* they have left their country of origin. However, so far, after-flight risk elements have played a more important role in the Committee's case law than in the Court's.

If the applicant has established that he has been tortured in the recent past, the burden of proof is likely to shift to the government under the Committee. The Committee has been shown to be particularly sensitive towards applicants with this background. Looking at the Court's and the Committee's case law as a whole, there is no doubt that past torture or ill treatment is a risk element that is given *more weight* by the Committee than by the Court.[24] It goes without saying that medical evidence has been of particular importance in procedures under Article 22 CAT. Questions remain with regard to the quality and precision required by the Committee.

Finally, there are several further risk elements that have been of relevance in the Court's and the Committee's assessments, including the applicant's ethnic background, religion, his age or gender, the question of whether he left his country in secret, his sexual orientation[25] or circumstances that may be unique to a case. It cannot be overemphasised that *the particular background of each complainant is looked at on a case-by-case basis in light of the prevailing human rights situation*. It is very rare that only one of the elements discussed leads the Court or the Committee to the conclusion that an expulsion or extradition would violate the principle of non-refoulement.

In addition, all the risk factors described may lose their importance with the passage of time or a change of power in the receiving state. However, if a complainant is able to provide credible evidence demonstrating he has been politically targeted in his home country and detained and ill-treated for that reason in the recent past by authorities or actors who are still in power, governments will usually have to present good reasons why such a complainant is no longer at risk in his home country.

---

24   See also Schürmann & Scheidegger 2009, p. 212; Wouters 2009, p. 543.

25   Until now, one case before the Committee has been successful for mainly that reason; see ComAT, *J.K. v. Canada*, 23 November 2015, no. 562/2013 (Uganda). It has been shown that when it comes to risks related to the applicant's sexual orientation or religious practice, Strasbourg's current approach appears in tension with that of the CJEU in asylum cases, which found it was not reasonable to expect people to refrain from their religious practice or open display of their sexual orientation to avoid persecution. However, the Court's case law on that subject is not very elaborated yet.

Focus: Recognition as a Refugee as a Risk Element

The risk elements dealt with under Article 3 ECHR and Article 3 CAT are usually the same as those that were assessed or disputed in the domestic asylum procedure with regard to the question of whether the individual concerned should be granted refugee status. Despite certain differences, it is evident that there is substantial common ground between the protection offered by the ECHR and the CAT against torture and inhuman treatment on the one hand and against persecution under the 1951 Refugee Convention on the other. People fearing persecution as set out in the Refugee Convention are likely to be threatened with inhuman or degrading treatment or torture and people fearing such inhuman treatment or torture will in many cases be persecuted in the sense described in the Refugee Convention.

Against this background, it is not surprising that in cases examined by the Court and the Committee in which the UNHCR has attributed refugee status to the applicant, the burden of proof has shifted to the government to demonstrate that this applicant is *not* at risk of ill treatment in case of removal. The Court's and the Committee's awareness has further been particularly raised in cases in which it was solely for reasons of public security that an individual was denied the protection offered by the Refugee Convention, or in which close family members of the applicant have been granted refugee status. In its recent case law, the Court has stated more than once that 'the right to political asylum is not *explicitly* protected' by the ECHR,[26] which indicates that, to a certain degree, it is protected implicitly. However, it should not be forgotten that persecution in the sense of the Refugee Convention does not necessarily amount to torture or inhuman or degrading treatment.

Finally, it must be recalled that the ECHR and the CAT do not provide for a right to asylum or refugee status with its inherent benefits and entitlements or similar, but merely prohibit the deportation. However, looking at the *substantial overlap* between the protection against refoulement under the Refugee Convention and that under the ECHR and the CAT, a differentiation in the status attributed is hard to justify in many cases.

Further Relevant Factors

Internal Flight Alternative

The concept of the *internal flight alternative* (also referred to as the possibility of *internal relocation*) has been developed in the context of refugee status determination procedures. It is the practice used by states to send an

---

26   For example, ECtHR, *Gaforov v. Russia*, 21 October 2010, no. 25404/09, § 110. Emphasis added.

individual to a region in the receiving state where he is not originally from, but where there is no real risk of his being ill-treated. This concept has played a more important role in the Court's case law so far than in the Committee's. The Committee's practice with regard to internal flight alternatives is as yet not very developed.

According to the Court, an internal flight alternative is considered an option compatible with Article 3 ECHR if three guarantees are in place: *First*, the person to be expelled must be able to travel safely to the alternative area. *Second*, the person concerned must be able to gain admittance to the area and have the right to settle there. *Third*, the person must not be threatened with being returned to his place of origin.

The fact that through relocation, the individual concerned has to live without his family members or to build a new life in an unknown region is not in itself reason to dismiss that possibility. According to the Court internal relocation inevitably involves certain hardships. However, the rights to be assured in the alternative region must go beyond what is guaranteed as a minimum standard under Article 3 ECHR.[27]

When a risk emanates from state authorities such as police agents, the Court and the Committee are usually reluctant to accept a flight alternative as guaranteeing the complainant's security, unless the state agent's powers are restricted to a certain region. They are more open to the possibility of an internal flight alternative if the risk emanates from private actors, unless practices of ill treatment by private or quasi-governmental actors are widespread all over the receiving state.

Neither the Court nor the Committee are consistent with regard to the question of *who* has to demonstrate and guarantee that an internal flight alternative is a legitimate option. Even though they have both stated that it is in principle up to the national authorities to demonstrate the existence of a valuable relocation alternative, they have both rejected complaints on the basis that the complainant is able to relocate internally in cases where the respondent states had not evaluated the accessibility and conditions in the relevant regions. This presents some dangers: the burden put on the applicant is far too weighty if he has to demonstrate the existence of a real risk of ill treatment in each and every possible region of his country of origin, even though he might not even be familiar with these regions. The Court's recent practice with regard to this issue is particularly worrying.

---

27   Wouters 2009, p. 558.

Diplomatic Assurances

It is a common practice of European states to request assurances or guarantees from other states requiring the extradition of a person, according to which that person will be treated in accordance with fundamental human rights if delivered. The Court in Strasbourg has made clear that diplomatic assurances have proven to be a useful tool to reduce a risk of ill treatment in the context of extraditions if the states giving them have a long history of the rule of law. It has repeatedly considered that diplomatic assurances given by US authorities to the effect that the applicant will not be subjected to capital punishment are reliable.[28] Outside the context of extraditions to the United States, the Court and the Committee have both been cautious of accepting diplomatic assurances as reliable instruments for reducing the risk of ill treatment, particularly when given by states known for practices of ill treatment.

According to the Court, the reliability of diplomatic assurances must be assessed against the background of the human rights record of the state giving the assurance and in light of the criteria enumerated in the leading judgment *Abu Qatada v. United Kingdom*.[29] This judgment adopted in January 2012 summarizes the Court's case law with regard to diplomatic assurances. Among the criteria it takes into account when assessing the reliability of diplomatic assurances, the Court has placed a particular focus on the questions of whether the assurances are specific or vague, whether the authority that has given the assurance can bind the receiving state, whether the assurances have been given by a contracting state to the ECHR and whether compliance with the assurances can be verified through diplomatic or other monitoring mechanisms.

The Committee's case law on diplomatic assurances is not as elaborated as the Court's. However, the case law as a whole demonstrates that it is less willing to rely on assurances than the Court. Ever since the Committee had negative experiences with the reliability of diplomatic assurances in the famous case *Agiza v. Sweden*,[30] it has considered them as constituting rather an *indication* that a risk of torture is *augmented* than an element that lowers that risk. The experts in Geneva have further made clear that the establishment of an independent and sufficiently trustworthy monitoring system by which the extraditing state will be able to closely follow the applicant's fate after

---

28 The Committee has indicated a similar approach in ComAT, *L.J.R. v. Australia*, 10 November 2008, no. 316/2007. However, the death penalty is not in itself considered a treatment prohibited by the CAT.

29 ECtHR, *Abu Qatada v. UK*, 17 January 2012, no. 8139/09.

30 ComAT, *Agiza v. Sweden*, 20 May 2005, no. 233/2003.

deportation is an indispensable condition for it to take into consideration the effectiveness of diplomatic assurances. The Court requires 'a critical approach' towards diplomatic assurances in cases in which the receiving country's authorities are known for systematic practices of ill treatment.[31] It has, however, made clear that it is only in exceptional circumstances that the human rights record in the receiving country will *per se* exclude the fact that assurances may be considered as reliable. The Committee in its recent case law in contrast appears to consider that if states in which there is a routine use of torture by law enforcement officials give assurances, this might just be in order to *circumvent the principle of non-refoulement.*[32]

Risk of Indirect Removal

The principle of non-refoulement in Article 3 ECHR and Article 3 CAT includes the prohibition of indirect removal. *Indirect removal* (also called *chain-removal*) means the removal to a state where there is no risk of ill treatment itself, but where there is a risk for the individual concerned to be subsequently removed in violation of the principle of non-refoulement. The Court's case law on that topic is much richer. The Committee has only adopted two decisions on the merits on that matter. However, despite the Committee's scant case law, it can be seen that the two institutions proceed with a similar three-step evaluation when assessing whether there is a risk of indirect removal:

As a *first step* they assess whether there is a risk of ill treatment for the complainant in the state to which he might be subsequently removed, usually the complainant's country of origin. While before the Court, it is sufficient if the complainant has an 'arguable claim' with regard to a risk of ill treatment in that country, the Committee has made a full 'real risk' assessment on that question in the two cases assessed on the merits, which is, however, no adequate basis to deduce a general guideline.

As a *second step*, if the arguable or real risk of ill treatment in the country of origin is established, the Court and the Committee assess the intermediary state's practice with regard to the respect of the principle of non-refoulement. The determining question here is whether the protection against refoulement in that intermediary state is effective in practice on a general basis. The judges in Strasbourg have made clear that the requirements of this assessment are higher when the intermediary state is not a party to the ECHR. So far, it has

---

31   ECtHR, *Azimov v. Russia*, 18 April 2013, no. 67474/11, § 133.

32   Among others ComAT, *Abichou v. Germany*, 21 May 2013, no. 430/2010, § 11.5.

rejected most complaints in which applicants alleged a risk of chain-removal if deported to another European state under the EU Dublin system. However, as the famous exceptions in *M.S.S.* and *Tarakhel* have proven, it is not impossible to establish that a member state of the Council of Europe fails to respect the principle of non-refoulement on a regular basis or in individual cases if this is confirmed by reports from NGOs and, in particular, the UNHCR.

A *third issue* that has been of relevance in the Court's as well as the Committee's case law is the question of whether the applicant has the possibility of preventing an eventual second deportation by the intermediary state in submitting another individual complaint including a request for interim measures against this state to the Court or the Committee itself. This possibility must not only be a legal one but must also be realistic in practice.

Concluding Remarks to the Summary

The risk assessment under the principle of non-refoulement by the Court and the Committee is very similar. However, while the protection offered under Article 3 ECHR covers in principle a greater scope of harms than Article 3 CAT, the Court is more reluctant to find a violation of the principle of non-refoulement in individual cases than the Committee. The fact that the Committee is less severe than the Court in granting interim measures and in declaring applications admissible already indicates this. From the case law as a whole, it can also be concluded that the Committee is less demanding on questions of evidence and credibility. It also occasionally finds violations of the principle of non-refoulement based on purely procedural grounds and gives particular weight to past torture or ill treatment. In addition, it is more reluctant than the Court to rely on diplomatic assurances.

However, it cannot be overemphasised that the Court and the Committee assess complaints in a *combined and cumulative analysis of the various factors on a case-by-case basis*, which makes it very difficult to anticipate the results of individual proceedings before either body.[33] In addition, their case law is in constant evolution. Each individual seeking protection has an individual story. Each non-refoulement complaint may therefore contain elements that are decisive but unique to the case. This description of the Court's and the Committee's risk assessment remains therefore a description of the most common risk elements that have been taken into account in Geneva and Strasbourg to date. Just as the human history of seeking protection from refoulement is not exhaustive, neither is the description of the circumstances under which protection from refoulement is guaranteed.

---

33   Schürmann & Scheidegger 2009, p. 205.

2   Mutual Influence

According to the Court, the principles underlying the ECHR cannot be interpreted and applied in a vacuum. The Court, 'in defining the meaning of terms
and notions in the text of the Convention, can and must take into account
elements of international law other than the Convention.'[34] It has stated that
the ECHR should be interpreted in 'harmony with other rules of public international law of which it forms part. Account should be taken, as indicated in
Article 31 § 3 (c) of the 1969 Vienna Convention on the Law of Treaties, of "any
relevant rules of international law applicable in the relations between the
parties", and in particular the rules concerning the international protection of
human rights.'[35] The role of other rules of international law for the Committee
is less clear.[36] However, it is evident that other international law instruments
including the ECHR have had an impact on the CAT and the Committee's
practice.

There was and is a two-way influence when it comes to the definition of
torture. To some extent, the definition of torture in Article 1 CAT incorporated
the existing Strasbourg jurisprudence.[37] The main elements of the definition
of torture in Article 1 CAT are primarily based on the case law of the European Commission and the Court of Human Rights at the time of drafting of
the CAT.[38] The Court in Strasbourg for its part has also been inspired by the
definition of torture in Article 1 CAT.[39] When characterizing torture or further
obligations deriving from that prohibition, the Court has explicitly referred to
the CAT.[40]

---

34   ECtHR, *Demir and Baykara v. Turkey* [GC], 12 November 2008, no. 34503/97, § 85.

35   For example, ECtHR, *A.G.R. v. Netherlands*, 12 January 2016, no. 13442/08, § 52.

36   On the rules of interpretation under the CAT see Wouters 2009, pp. 433–434. He notes that
       in interpreting the CAT the Committee has explicitly referred neither to the general rules
       of interpretation of treaties, including the *travaux préparatoires*, nor to other human
       rights treaties covering the same subject matter in their case law.

37   Ingelse 2001, p. 70.

38   Nowak & McArthur 2008, p. 28 (§ 2).

39   In the famous *Ireland v. UK* case, it explicitly referred to Article 1 of the 1975 United
       Nations Declaration on the Protection of All Persons from Being Subjected to Torture or
       Other Cruel, Inhuman or Degrading Treatment or Punishment, which was the primary
       inspiration for the drafters of the CAT; see ECtHR, *Ireland v. UK*, 18 January 1978, no. 531/71,
       § 167 and Burger & Danelius 1988, pp. 1, 16 and 33.

40   See, for example, ECtHR, *Selmouni v. France*, 28 July 1999, no. 25803/94, §§ 97–101; ECtHR,
       Akkoç v. Turkey, 10 October 2000, nos. 22947/93 and 22948/93, § 115; ECtHR, *Salman v.
       Turkey*, 27 June 2000, no. 21986/93, § 114; ECtHR, *Mahmut Kaya v. Turkey*, 28 March 2000,

As has been mentioned in the introductory chapter 1, there was also an important mutual influence between the Strasbourg institutions and the CAT with regard to the establishment of the principle of non-refoulement. The formulation of the principle of non-refoulement in Article 3 CAT was inspired by the case law of the former European Commission on Human Rights in Strasbourg.[41] On the other hand, the Court referred to Article 3 CAT in its first judgment on refoulement in the famous case *Soering v. United Kingdom.* In this judgment, adopted two years after the entry into force of the CAT in 1987, the Court for the first time dealt with the question of whether the extradition of a fugitive to another state would itself engage the responsibility of a contracting state under Article 3 ECHR. It answered this question in the affirmative by stating, *inter alia,* '[t]hat the abhorrence of torture has such implications is recognised' in Article 3 CAT.[12] The judges further held that the fact that 'a specialised treaty should spell out in detail a specific obligation attaching to the prohibition of torture does not mean that an essentially similar obligation is not already inherent in the general terms of Article 3 ... of the European Convention.'[43]

Having said that, it is rare that the Court refers to decisions adopted by the Committee on individual complaints. The judgment *Abu Qatada v. United Kingdom* is an exception.[44] In this judgment the Court held that when assessing the reliability of diplomatic assurances, the existence of an independent monitoring mechanism is an important factor to take into account.[45] It thereby explicitly referred to the Committee's decisions in *Pelit v. Azerbaijan*[46]

---

no. 22535/93, § 117; ECtHR, *Mammadov v. Azerbaijan,* 11 January 2007, no. 34445/04, § 68; ECtHR, *Gäfgen v. Germany,* 1 June 2010 [GC], no. 22978/05, § 90; ECtHR, *Abu Qatada v. UK,* 17 January 2012, no. 8139/09, § 266; ECtHR, *Al Nashiri v. Poland,* 24 July 2014, no. 28761/11, § 508.

41 Burger and Danelius 1988, pp. 125–162.

42 ECtHR, *Soering v. United UK,* 7 July 1989, no. 14038/88, § 88.

43 *Ibid.*

44 As other exceptions see ECtHR, *Paez v. Sweden,* 30 October 1997, no. 29482/95 § 29, in which the Court refers to the Committee's decision taken with regard to the applicant's brother in ComAT, *Paez v. Sweden,* 28 April 1997, no. 39/1996; ECtHR, *Mamatkulov and Askarov v. Turkey,* 4 February 2005 [GC], nos. 46827/99 and 46951/99, with regard to interim measures; ECtHR, *Rakhimov v. Russia,* 10 July 2014, no. 50552/13, §§ 65 and 99, in which the Court refers to ComAT, *Abdussamatov and 28 Others v. Kazakhstan,* 1 June 2012, no. 444/2010.

45 ECtHR, *Abu Qatada v. UK,* 17 January 2012, no. 8139/09, §§ 189 (viii) and 194. See further § 266 referring to individual complaints in the context of refoulement where there has been an issue under Art. 15 CAT.

46 ComAT, *Pelit v. Azerbaijan,* 1 May 2007, no. 281/2005.

and *Agiza v. Sweden*[47] as well as the Human Rights Committee's decision in *Alzery v. Sweden*.[48] It is also obvious that the Court has borrowed the Committee's wording when stating occasionally that 'complete accuracy is seldom to be expected from victims of torture.'[49]

As can be seen, the Court takes international law into account; however, it clearly follows an autonomous interpretation of human rights including the principle of non-refoulement. In *H.L.R. v France*, the Court did *not* take up the reference made to Article 1 CAT by the French government to argue that the principle of non-refoulement could not be applied in cases in which the risk of ill treatment emanated exclusively from private individuals.[50] In the case *Harkins and Edwards v. United Kingdom*, the Court held that its interpretation according to which the prohibition on refoulement in Article 3 ECHR *includes inhuman treatment* is in accordance with the CAT, particularly since the latter provides that its provisions are 'without prejudice to the provisions of any other international instrument or national law which prohibits cruel, inhuman or degrading treatment or punishment or which relates to extradition or expulsion.'[51] The independent interpretation of human rights also becomes apparent with regard to the death penalty. In referring to European human rights standards, the Court has declared that capital punishment is today prohibited under Article 3 ECHR despite the fact that this form of punishment is not *per se* considered inhuman under the CAT or ICCPR.[52]

Generally, with regard to the *scope of the harms* against which Article 3 ECHR offers protection under the principle of non-refoulement, the Court's case law has shown to be more dynamic than the Committee's. Since the ECHR contains no explicit definition of torture, it is easier for the Court to develop its own interpretation of torture or other inhuman treatment and to adapt it to global or regional developments as they occur. Indeed, as Thurin notes, this was the intention of the drafters of Article 3 ECHR.[53] According to Ingelse, the detailed

---

47   ComAT, *Agiza v. Sweden*, 20 May 2005, no. 233/2003.

48   HRC, *Alzery v. Sweden*, 25 October 2006, no. 1416/2005.

49   See EComHR, *Hatami v. Sweden*, report of 23 April 1998, no. 3244/96, § 106; ECtHR, *Bello v. Sweden*, 17 January 2006, no. 32213/04 (decision) compared to ComAT, *Alan v. Switzerland*, 8 May 1996, no. 21/1995, § 11.3.

50   ECtHR, *H.L.R. v. France*, 29 April 1997, no. 24573/94, §§ 32–44.

51   ECtHR, *Harkins and Edwards v. UK*, 17 January 2012, nos. 9146/07 and 32650/07, § 127. Similar ECtHR, *Babar Ahmad and Others v. UK*, 10 April 2012, nos. 24027/07, 11949/08, 36742/08, 66911/09 and 67354/09, § 175.

52   See Chapter 3 Sections 2.2.5, 3.2.4 and 4.2.3.

53   Thurin 2012, p. 14.

definition of torture in the CAT had a 'restrictive effect' since it leaves less room for the Committee to develop its mandate.[54]

Generally, it is rare that the Committee refers explicitly to other human rights treaties, be they other UN human rights treaties such as the ICCPR or regional human rights conventions such as the ECHR.[55] Applicants as well as state parties frequently invoke the Strasbourg Court's case law in their observations to give weight to their arguments, but these references are never recited explicitly in the Committee's assessment. In addition, while the Court often refers to the Committee's concluding observation in the context of the state reporting procedure under Article 19 CAT when it evaluates the human rights situation in receiving states, it never refers (at least not explicitly) to a human rights analysis made by the Court with regard to the human rights standards in receiving countries.

It is understandable that the Committee, as a universal body, prefers not to refer openly to the case law established by a regional body. An exception is the decision *T.P.S. v. Canada* concerning the deportation of a Sikh who was convicted of highjacking an Indian aeroplane.[56] In its considerations on the merits, the Committee explicitly referred to a case in which the Court in Strasbourg had maintained that the scrutiny of a claim 'must be carried out without regard to what the person may have done to warrant expulsion or to any perceived threat to the national security of the expelling State.'[57] It appears that with regard to the absolute character of the prohibition on refoulement, there is a mutual empowerment between the Court and the Committee. By adopting a common stance, they both clearly raise the authority of their findings. This is quite important in this domain in which they are both under strong political pressure from member states.

In fact, even if the Committee seldom explicitly declares this, it is evident that it has been influenced by the Strasbourg case law and practice.[58] The Court and the Committee have in fact influenced each other on many aspects. The risk assessment, even though usually much more detailed in the Court's judgments than in the Committee's decisions, is made according to more or

---

54   Ingelse 2001, pp. 240.

55   See also Wouters 2009, p. 434.

56   ComAT, *T.P.S. v. Canada*, 16 May 2000, no. 99/1997.

57   *Ibid.*, § 15.3.

58   See in this sense also Chetail 2006, pp. 100–101. See, for example, ComAT, *S.S. and S.A. v. Netherlands*, 11 May 2001, no. 142/1999, § 6.7, compared to ECtHR, *Vilvarajah and Others v. UK*, 30 October 1991, nos. 13163/87 and further, § 111, with regard to the situation of Tamils in Sri Lanka.

less the same criteria. The terms and formulae used to describe the standard and burden of proof are almost identical. According to the Court's standard formulation used since the *Soering* judgment, the removal of a person is illicit 'where substantial grounds have been shown for believing that the person concerned faces a real risk of being subjected to torture or to inhuman or degrading treatment or punishment in the requesting country.' This formula was inspired by Article 3(1) CAT, according to which no state shall return a person to another state 'where there are substantial grounds for believing that he would be in danger of being subjected to torture'.[59] Article 3(1) CAT was in turn inspired by the case law of the former European Commission on Human Rights.[60] Also, the Committee today has the same approach as the Court with regard to the relevant time of the risk assessment. With regard to the harm against which the two institutions offer protection, there has been a rapprochement of the Committee to the Court's practice with regard to private actors as well. However, the Committee here is also following a practice that has been established in national and international law for many years, in particular under the 1951 Refugee Convention,[61] and not solely under the ECHR.

The Court and the Committee have also influenced each other with regard to procedural aspects: in the lead judgment *Mamatkulov*, the Court explicitly relied on the Committee's reasoning with regard to interim measures when it stated that non-observance of interim measures would nullify the end result of the proceedings.[62] Referring to the view expressed in this matter by the Committee in Geneva and other international bodies, the Grand Chamber established a legal obligation on states to comply with an interim measures order based on the right to submit individual applications in Article 34 ECHR.[63] Only a few months later, in May 2005, the Committee also for the first time found that a state's failure to respect interim measures constituted a breach of the right to effectively submit individual applications under Article 22 CAT.[64]

In conclusion, since it is mainly European countries that have accepted the competence of the Committee to assess individual complaints, the Court and the Committee often have to deal with comparable cases, although it is rare

---

59   See ECtHR, *Soering v. UK*, 7 July 1989, no. 14038/88, § 88.

60   See Burger and Danelius 1988, pp. 125–162 and Chapter 1 Section 3.2.1.

61   See UNHCR *Handbook*, 1992, § 65 on private forms of persecution.

62   ECtHR, *Mamatkulov and Askarov v. Turkey*, 4 February 2005 [GC], nos. 46827/99 and 46951/99, §§ 115 and 124.

63   *Ibid.*, §§ 108–129. See Chapter 2 Section 1.2.

64   ComAT, *Brada v. France*, 17 May 2005, no. 195/2002, § 13.4.

that they *explicitly* refer to each other's case law.[65] Nevertheless, it is evident that they have influenced each other in their practice and case law with regard to the principle of non-refoulement. There are in fact more similarities in the Court's and Committee's handling of individual complaints with regard to the principle of non-refoulement than there are differences.[66]

3 Persuasiveness and Impact of the Verdicts

3.1 *Broader Impact and Power of Persuasion*

The fact that the Committee's decisions are not binding under international law is considered in the literature as the *major weakness* of the UN complaint mechanism.[67] In general, with regard to the UN human rights conventions including the CAT, 'the national implementation of findings by human rights treaty bodies in case of individual complaints faces immense difficulties.'[68] Interestingly, as has been explained, with regard to individual complaints concerning the principle of non-refoulement handled by the Committee, this has not been the case.[69] In practice, the Committee in Geneva has not shown to be a less effective tool for applicants fighting their refoulement from Europe than the Court in Strasbourg so far. Implementation in the context of non-refoulement might be facilitated by the fact that states are usually not required to take active measures or grant compensations, but *are simply requested to refrain from taking a measure*.[70] In addition, most decisions on refoulement adopted by the Committee so far have concerned states with a functioning constitutional democracy, a good human rights record and a tradition of support for UN institutions.

---

65   Schürmann & Scheidegger 2009, p. 213.

66   Burns 2001, p. 412; Chetail 2006, pp. 100–101; Schürmann & Scheidegger 2009, p. 213.

67   Boulesbaa 1999, p. 293; Chetail 2006, p. 101; McAdam 2007, p. 126; Nowak & McArthur 2008, p. 796 (§ 199).

68   Inter-committee Meeting of Human Rights Treaty Bodies, Follow-up Procedures on Individual complaints, UN Doc. HRI/ICM/WGFU/2011/3, 7 December 2010, § 25. For interesting reading on the subject: Van Alebeek & Nollkaemper 2012, pp. 356–362, estimating that roughly 70 per cent of the HRC's views are not implemented.

69   On the respect of the decision with regard to Art. 3 CAT see Chapter 2 Section 2.3.2.

70   See as an indication in that direction the Inter-committee Meeting of Human Rights Treaty Bodies, Follow-up Procedures on Individual complaints; UN Doc. HRI/ICM/WGFU/2011/3, 7 December 2010, § 25, in which it is stated that the reasons that state parties fail to implement decisions do often relate to, *inter alia*, the lack of understanding by state parties of their obligations under the respective treaties.

However, in the end, neither the Court nor the Committee have the means to implement a decision by force. While the political and legal authority of the Committee of Ministers in Strasbourg is stronger than that of the Committee against Torture in Geneva, after all, both institutions have to rely on the member states' good faith and on diplomatic pressure.[71] Still, as Heffernan rightly notes, 'the stature of the Court in the international community places it in a better position than most international bodies to effect a mobilization of shame.'[72] She refers to the high regard generally afforded to the Court's judgments among European states. In fact, even though the judgments of the Court are in principle only legally binding on the state concerned, they have a significant importance for other parties to the ECHR. In the context of refoulement, Einarsen summarizes this broader effect of the Court's judgments as follows:

> The importance of the Convention with respect to asylum seekers arriving in Europe cannot be confined to the perspective of individual cases. The primary function of the Convention is to provide a *general* and necessary 'safety-net' in order to ensure respect for certain human rights and traditions within each of the Contracting States. It is a part of this system that jurisprudence under the Convention may be invoked by parties in every State. *A single decision of the Court can have implications for the scope of discretion concerning national asylum law and policies among the several States of the Council of Europe.* Whether or when an appropriate asylum case will be referred to the Court is not easy to predict, but it will not likely be an indifferent issue when it appears.[73] (Emphasis added)

The Court's jurisprudence in the context of refoulement has in fact been of substantial importance for domestic European law and practice as well as for EU legislation.[74] The Court has released several judgments of principle that were clearly meant to resolve a large number of comparable cases and have

---

71   White and Ovey 2010, p. 63. See also Heffernan 1997, p. 109, who compares the Court's judgments with the UN Human Rights Committee's views and summarizes: 'In fact, the nature of international law is such that the distinction between the two systems may be more apparent than real. ... Neither body can step into the domestic system and, for example, remove an offending law or nullify an unacceptable practice.'

72   Heffernan 1997, p. 109, comparing the authority of the Strasbourg supervisory mechanism with that of the UN Human Rights Committee. See also Burns 2001, p. 413.

73   Einarsen 1990, p. 385.

74   Goodwin-Gill & McAdam 2007, pp. 299 and 310 with references; Thurin 2012, p. 2.

in fact received broad attention.[75] The Grand Chamber judgment *M.S.S. v. Belgium and Greece* concerning the transfer of an asylum seeker under the EU Dublin Regulation is an evident example.[76]

The Committee's case law under Article 3 CAT has also contributed in an important way to the development and authority of the principle of non-refoulement worldwide.[77] However, it is particularly challenging to measure the UN treaty bodies' impact on the general practice of states.[78] Compared to the judgments adopted in Strasbourg, it is rare that the Committee's decisions appear to be designed to resolve a whole range of comparable cases. It is rather exceptional that they do receive broad attention in national or international case law or doctrine. One such exception is provided by the case *Agiza v. Sweden* in which the Committee addressed the controversial topic of extraordinary renditions and the use of diplomatic assurances in the fight against terrorism following the September 11 attacks on the World Trade Center in New York.[79]

The individual complaint mechanisms under UN human rights treaty bodies are generally little known outside academic circles and the professional circles of civil servants, specialized lawyers and NGOs.[80] A reason for which

---

75   See, in particular, ECtHR, *N.A. v. UK*, 17 July 2008, no. 25904/07 (return of Tamils to Sri Lanka); ECtHR, *M.S.S. v. Belgium and Greece*, 21 January 2011 [GC], no. 30696/09 (EU Dublin Regulation) ECtHR, *Sufi and Elmi v. UK*, 28 June 2011, nos. 8319/07 and 11449/07 (situation for refugees and internally displaced persons in Somalia); ECtHR, *Hirsi Jamaa and Others v. Italy*, 23 February 2012 [GC], no. 27765/09 (interception of asylum seekers at sea).

76   It is hardly imaginable that national courts would have had the power or interest to denounce the dysfunction of EU law with regard to the risk of indirect refoulement of refugees transferred to Greece under the EU Dublin II Regulation with the same authority and impact as the Court in *M.S.S.* In fact, the more internationalised human rights violations become, the more the international and institutionalised character of human rights supervision becomes important and necessary for the authority of the judgments. This is also apparent from the cases handled by the Court and the Committee concerning extraordinary renditions made at the request of US authorities in the aftermath of the attacks on the World Trade Center in September 2001; see ECtHR, *El-Masri v. Former Yugoslav Republic of Macedonia*, 13 December 2012 [GC], no. 39630/09; ComAT, *Agiza v. Sweden*, 20 May 2005, no. 233/2003.

77   Chetail 2006, pp. 101–104; Gorlick 1999, pp. 479, 481, 490 and 490; McAdam 2007, p. 125; Schürmann & Scheidegger 2009, p. 213; Wouters 2009, p. 528.

78   Ulfstein 2012, p. 104.

79   ComAT, *Agiza v. Sweden*, 20 May 2005, no. 233/2003.

80   See report by the OHCHR, 'Strengthening the United Nations Human Rights Treaty Body System,' June 2012, pp. 34, in which the High Commissioner for Human Rights Navanethem Pillay notes that the UN treaty bodies 'remain largely unknown to the majority of the general public whose rights they are designed to uphold.' See also Inter-commitee

they receive less attention in Europe is probably that, compared to the Court's judgments, their decisions are not legally binding. However, this is not the only reason: acceptance and reception of international jurisprudence will not only depend on the legal authority of the institution but also on the quality, clarity and coherence of its reasoning.[81] As *Andrysek* notes, while states are expected to cooperate and implement their obligations in good faith, they should also have good reasons to feel that judgments or requests for interim measures are justified. Otherwise, the issuing authority will ultimately lose authority.[82] Ulfstein notes that since the UN treaty bodies cannot rely on the binding character of their findings, they are even 'more dependent on the persuasiveness of their reasoning.'[83] In this respect the Committee has room for improvement.[84] It is frequently criticized for its poor, standardized and sometimes inconsistent reasoning in decisions on individual complaints.[85] In fact, the lack of detail or explanation in the decisions repeatedly leaves the impression of the type of superficial assessment that the Committee itself would not accept from national authorities. As Wouters has rightly noted, the Committee's brief and poor reasoning makes it 'difficult to understand why and how the Committee comes to its conclusion in a specific case and to deduce general guidelines on how to interpret and apply Article 3.'[86] Compared to the Court, the Committee also rarely refers to its own case law or explains why it evaluates one case differently from another.[87] It appears that the experts in Geneva sometimes intentionally avoid making legal statements of general value.[88] In fact, to deduce

---

Meeting of Human Rights Treaty Bodies, Follow-up Procedures on Individual Complaints, UN Doc. HRI/ICM/WGFU/2011/3, 7 December 2010, § 26.

81   Keller & Ulfstein 2012, p. 425; Ulfstein 2012, p. 106.

82   Andrysek 1997, p. 414.

83   Ulfstein 2012, p. 113. In this sense also Van Alebeek & Nollkaemper 2012, p. 413.

84   In this sense also Kashgar 2011, p. 73. With regard to the UN human rights treaty monitoring mechanisms in general see Van Alebeek & Nollkaemper 2012, pp. 373–374, 380–382 and 413.

85   See Goodwin-Gill & McAdam 2007, pp. 301 and 305; Gorlick 1999, pp. 490–491; Kashgar 2011, p. 73; Wouters 2009, p. 433.

86   Wouters 2009, p. 433. In this sense also Gorlick 1999, pp. 490–491.

87   See, for example, ComAT, *Khalsa et al. v. Switzerland*, 26 May 2011, no. 336/2008, in which the Committee did not explain why it took a different decision from in ComAT, *T.P.S. v. Canada*, 16 May 2000, no. 99/1997, although the complainants belonged to the same group of Sikhs convicted for highjacking an Indian aeroplane.

88   Consider, for example, the question of whether Art. 3 CAT applies to the risk of harm emanating from private actors.

guidelines under the Article 3 CAT, the case law must be followed as a whole as it has been done in this research. Single decisions are rarely instructive.[89] This does not contribute to the Committee's authority among domestic authorities and the doctrine in general.[90]

However, a helpful guideline is the Committee's General Comment on Article 3 CAT, which was, however, adopted almost 20 years ago in 1997. At its 55th session in 2015, the Committee decided to revise its General Comment No. 1 on Article 3 CAT.[91] Taking into account the developments in the Committee's case law as described in this study and the Committee's reluctance to announce or explain them explicitly in its decisions on individual cases, this revision is strongly to be welcomed.[92]

It may be argued that it is easier for a permanent regional instrument such as the Court to find consensus on legal rules of general value than for a non-permanent organ composed of worldwide experts having very diverse legal backgrounds.[93] It may further be argued that the Committee has the state reporting procedure in Article 19 CAT to provide more general statements and guidelines on how the CAT should be implemented at national level. Indeed, the individual complaint mechanism under Article 22 CAT is designed for the assessment of single cases and not general practices. However, I think that the aim of a universal complaint mechanism must go beyond the assessment of individual cases. International institutions such as the Court and the Committee are not accessible to all individuals in need of protection.[94] Hence, as Ulfstein puts it, their decisions 'should serve as precedents not only for their own practice, but for other treaty bodies as well as for international and national courts.'[95]

---

89   In this sense also Chetail 2006, pp. 66–67.

90   Kashgar 2011, p. 73.

91   Statement of the Chairperson of the Committee Against Torture to the 70th session of the General Assembly, New York, 20 October 2015, accessible on the Committee's website under <http://www.ohchr.org/EN/NewsEvents/Pages/DisplayNews.aspx?NewsID=16624& LangID=E> [15.2.2016].

92   See also the suggestion of Wouters 2009, p. 524. See further Section 4 of this chapter (Concluding remarks), summarizing the main issues to be elucidated.

93   Boulesbaa 199, p. 302; Ingelse 2001, p. 84, according to which the CAT sometimes cannot go as far as regional instruments like the ECHR because of its universal status.

94   As has been explained in Chapter 1 Section 3.2.2, the procedure under Article 22 CAT is largely unknown and often inaccessible for those whose rights they are designed to uphold.

95   Ulfstein 2012, p. 79.

In addition, with due respect for each and every assessment the Court and the Committee have made with regard to the principle of non-refoulement (and in particular for the individuals concerned in those decisions), the more the international bodies focus on questions that are '*solely*' relevant for a particular case, the less they appear persuasive. As the Court and the Committee recognize themselves, national authorities are best placed to assess the facts and, more particularly, the credibility of the individual concerned. International bodies are not designed for the assessment of the personal credibility of individuals they have never seen or spoken to in person.

In my opinion, the Court's and the Committee's key force lies in the establishment and reinforcement of legal principles and procedural standards, and of course in the supervision of the observance of these principles and standards by lower instances – as is also the main function of higher appeal tribunals at national level. For this reason it is important that they provide guidelines of general value for the lower instances.[96] Hence, in my opinion, in the long run, the most sustainable contribution the Court and the Committee can make for the protection against refoulement through their verdicts is the establishment and reinforcement of case-independent legal principles and standards that aim to guarantee that, generally, the assessments made at national level will have a certain minimum quality.

This role is better exercised by the Court than by the Committee. As *McAdam* has noted, the 'flow-on effect of ECHR principles into domestic law may ultimately secure protection for individuals at an earlier stage.'[97] As the case law of the Court shows, sometimes one well-reasoned judgment can have a more important impact than several thinly reasoned individual cases. The preventive effect of international human rights conventions becomes more powerful if the standards to be respected have been explained clearly by the international jurisprudence. In this manner international instances may even be able to discharge themselves from new or pending applications.

In my opinion, in the context of the assessment of individual complaints concerning the principle of non-refoulement, the main weakness of the Committee is not the lack of binding force behind its decisions, which is inherent to the system, but the Committee's lack of detailed reasoning. It may be recalled that the CAT's main objective is to make more effective the general struggle against torture, including the principle of non-refoulement, *throughout the*

---

96   De Weck 2011, p. 11.
97   McAdam 2007, p. 126.

world and not solely in those rather few states that have been concerned with the most individual complaints.

However, as this study has shown, the Court does not always give clear guidelines either. At present, it is particularly hard to anticipate in which direction it will develop the dynamic approach it adopted in *M.S.S.* and *Tarakhel* according to which dire living conditions may, under particular circumstances, be capable of triggering the principle of non-refoulement.[98] On a general basis, the Court is criticized for applying too dynamic approaches in its case law, creating new obligations under the ECHR that states might not have agreed to.[99] It is clear that no jurisprudence, be it national or international, remains persuasive if it is not oriented towards present-day conditions as the Court's practice clearly is.[100] However, a case law that becomes too innovative may not only challenge the state's political will to abide by it, it may also simply exhaust their capacity to follow it.[101]

Finally, it would not be fair to require the Committee to apply exactly the same standards as the Court with regard to the extent and quality of their verdicts. There is certainly a *marge de manoeuvre* for the Committee for more profoundness. However, it simply does not have sufficient resources to allow it to undertake extended jurisprudential analysis similar to that of the Court.[102] While the Committee is composed of ten experts meeting twice or three times a year only, the Court is composed of 47 permanent judges. The Committee's secretariat is far smaller and has fewer linguistic capacities than the Court's registry.[103] Ulfstein notes that in the long run a system of part-time experts 'has no chance of coping with a large influx of cases from all over the world.'[104] The Committee would probably be unable to cope with an increasingly extensive use of the individual complaints procedure that would result from any increased visibility and clarity.[105]

---

98   See the critique in Chapter 3 Section 2.3.2.b-d.

99   Specifically with regard to the Court's case law under the principle of non-refoulement see Bossuyt 2012, pp. 203–245.

100   See, amongst many others, ECtHR, *Soering v. UK*, 7 July 1989, no. 14038/88, § 102, recalling that the ECHR is a 'living instrument.'

101   See in this sense the critique on the case law subsequent to *M.S.S.* in Chapter 3 Section 2.3.2.c and d.

102   In this sense Kashgar 2011, p. 73; Van Alebeek & Nollkaemper 2012, p. 406, with regard to the HRC.

103   Bayefsky 2003, p. 147.

104   Ulfstein 2012, p. 115.

105   Ulfstein 2012, p. 104, with regard to the UN treaty bodies in general. See also the statement by Claudio Grossman, 67th session of the General Assembly, New York, 23 October 2012.

3.2   *Overburden*

The lack of coherence and scarcity of well-reasoned judgments is a generally recognized problem for the underresourced UN human rights treaty monitoring mechanisms, although there appears to be little support for larger budgets.[106] In fact, the problem of lack of resources is topical for the Court in Strasbourg as well. The former president of the Court Sir Nicolas Bratza made clear in 2012 that additional financial support for Strasbourg will be necessary if the volume of incoming cases continues to increase.[107] Towle notes that unless international bodies are given adequate resources to keep pace they are likely to suffer from the same afflictions suffered by national instances.[108] In fact this is already the case. The Court and the Committee both demonstrate practices that they criticise at national level: procedures that take too long and cases rejected without proper reasoning, or, with regard to the Court in Strasbourg, dismissed through an opaque filtering mechanism.[109]

Despite tight financial and personal means, effective reforms and efforts have been made and are continuously pursued to enhance the productivity and quality of the decision-making at international level.[110] However, it is still a fact that overburdening puts the effectiveness and credibility of the Court and the Committee at risk. The long duration of the international procedures has particularly problematic effects in the context of refoulement: when interim measures are attributed, the individual concerned may have to wait for years in a legal limbo and states will have to accept the individual's presence on their territory. In addition, with the many years likely to have elapsed since the last national decision, the Court and the Committee are often confronted with new circumstances, which puts them in the role of first-instance courts even though they are not designed for that.

The problem is aggravated by the fact that the practice of using the international complaints mechanism in the context of refoulement is still an

---

106   Alebeek & Nollkaemper 2012, p. 381.

107   ECtHR, 'Annual Report 2012,' p. 36.

108   Towle 2000, p. 34.

109   It should not be forgotten that even if the published decisions of the Court might be well-reasoned, in contrast to the Committee, it allows itself to filter out the majority of cases and reject them as inadmissible in a non-contradictory procedure and without proper reasoning. See also Keller, Fischer & Kühne 2010, pp. 1043, who note that 'given the very high proportion of manifestly ill-founded applications, the Court's practice of rejecting them without giving reasons leads the Court into a legitimacy problem.'

110   See on this the Chapter 1 Sections 2.1 and 3.1 and the information provided under 'Reform of the Court' on the Strasbourg website under <http://www.echr.coe.int/Pages/home.aspx?p=court/reform&c=> [15.2.2016].

emerging one.[111] There is still a lack of awareness among the general public and even lawyers on how international complaints proceedings are applied.[112] The Committee's procedure in particular is little known – this is highlighted by the fact that there are several European countries that have made the declaration under Article 22 CAT but that have never had to defend a complaint. The number of complaints concerning the principle of non-refoulement submitted under the Geneva procedure has been rising.[113] In Strasbourg as well, a remarkable rise of complaints concerning the principle of non-refoulement in the last 10 years is visible.[114] In 2009, the Court had released 48 judgments on the merits with regard to the principle of non-refoulement in total. Today there are more than 200 such judgments.[115] It should further be taken into account that the fact that asylum lawyers use both mechanisms does not necessarily mean that one international body will be discharged. This can be observed with the Swedish example, where much use is made of both mechanisms.[116] Once lawyers are familiar with the different mechanisms at international level, they make their selection depending on the particular circumstances of their case – which is the logical approach from the perspective of the lawyer and indeed the applicant.

Nowak and McArthur note that the material overlap between the Refugee Convention and general human rights treaties, as well as the lack of an international individual complaints procedure against domestic asylum decisions, 'will continue to prompt refugees, whose asylum requests were rejected, to submit individual non-refoulement complaints to international human rights monitoring bodies, including the CAT Committee.' They argue that 'in times in which many States (particularly in the North) tend to adopt increasingly restrictive asylum policies, this trend will probably continue.'[117] In fact, it is only logical that if political pressure is put on national asylum systems to become increasingly restrictive, the quality of proceedings suffers and higher appeal bodies, at national or international level, will have to intervene more often. With the rising number of asylum seekers in Europe provoked by the current

---

111   ECRE/ELENA Research on ECHR Rule 39 Interim Measures, April 2012, p. 21.

112   See Resolution 1788(2011) of the Parliamentary Assembly of the Council of Europe of January 2011, § 12. See also Nowak & McArthur 2008, p. 128 (§ 1); Rieter 2010, p. 266.

113   Information obtained by the OHCHR, 3 October 2013.

114   See on this also Chapter 2 Section 1.2 on the rise of requests for interim measures.

115   As can be seen from the table of cases on the non-refoulement cases treated on the merits (XXXII), more and more judgments concern Eastern European countries.

116   Before the Human Rights Committee as well there is a comparatively remarkable number of complaints concerning the principle of non-refoulement submitted against Sweden.

117   Nowak & McArthur 2008, pp. 212 (§ 204).

conflicts in the Middle East, it is evident that the factual and the political pressure on migration authorities is rising. However, as Einarsen rightly noted as
early as 1990, if politicians are not ready to take the necessary responsibility with regard to the principle of non-refoulement, 'there is no more well-
equipped institution for striking a balance between human rights and other
interests than the European Court of Human Rights. Such leadership would be
entirely legitimate, and is unlikely to lead to any extreme position.'[118] However,
while many scholars argue that the workload of the Court and the Committee is for a large part the product of an overly restrictive application of the
Refugee Convention at national level,[119] other voices claim that it is instead
related to the international mechanisms' too generous practice with regard to
failed asylum seekers.[120] Particularly the Court's and the Committee's interim
measures practice has come under fire by member states. They have expressed
their fear that based on the possibility of obtaining interim measures, international institutions are systematically used as fourth-instance courts for failed
asylum seekers.[121] It cannot be denied that the chance of obtaining interim
measures for one year or more might also be attractive for individuals whose
fear of ill treatment in case of removal is not well-founded. The Committee is
still much more generous in attributing interim measures than the Court. It
has been criticized for the attribution of interim measures in unsubstantiated
cases.[122] It would not be surprising if, with a rising number of complaints, the
Committee will become stricter in the attribution of interim measures in the
future, as the Court has done in recent years.[123]

However, a system providing protection against refoulement *must* provide
for interim measures, otherwise it is useless.[124] In addition, on a general basis,

---

118   Einarsen 1990. p. 388.

119   In this sense also Andrysek 1997, pp. 410–411; Gorlick 1999, p. 495; Mandal 2005, pp. 8–10;
       Towle 2000, pp. 32 and 33. Chetail 2004, p. 207, observes that the Court in Strasbourg actu-
       ally compensates for the institutional deficit of the Refugee Convention.

120   See Marc Bossuyt's critique in his study published in 2010, 'Strasbourg et les demandeurs
       d'asile: des juges sur un terrain glissant.' See also Bayefsky 2003, p. 87, noting that the Com-
       mittee has been largely unresponsive to concerns by state parties that Art. 3 CAT might be
       'abused' by asylum seekers. See on this subject with regard to the Committee also Nowak
       & McArthur 2008, pp. 208–212.

121   See Chapter 2 Section 1.2 and 2.2.

122   See Chapter 2 Section 2.2.

123   The Committee has already become stricter; in its early practice, it granted interim mea-
       sures almost automatically.

124   First and foremost, the ill treatment cannot be prevented without interim measures. In
       addition, as has been explained in Chapter 2 Section 1.3.2 and 2.3.2, implementating judg-

as this study has shown, the chances for a failed asylum seeker to gain protection at international level are still very low. As I have observed in my own country, Switzerland, asylum lawyers and human rights advocates are very aware of the fact that it is only with very well-founded cases that the international path will be an effective option, particularly in Strasbourg.

However, as Pirjola has put it, the debate on the content of the principle of non-refoulement is ultimately a political one.[125] So is the debate on the institutions guaranteeing the respect of that principle, the persuasiveness of their findings and the reasons for their overburden. It is beyond the scope of this study to discuss the possible sources and solutions for the overburdening of the Court in Strasbourg or the Committee in Geneva. However, it should be taken into account that, in the long run, the effectiveness and credibility of the complaint mechanisms lies not only in the hands of the international human rights institutions and their powers of persuasion; it is also related to the will of the state parties to support and maintain these mechanisms in such a manner that they are able to do their job convincingly. On this background, the most precious contribution states can and should make is not just to provide financial or other resources and to respect the decisions taken at international level, but to ensure the respect for human rights including the principle of non-refoulement at national level, so that recourse to international mechanisms remains the exception.

4   Concluding Remarks

The Court's and Committee's handling of individual complaints concerning the principle of non-refoulement is very similar. This is true for procedural matters as well as for the substantive assessment of the complaints.

The main differences with regard to procedural aspects are, firstly, the Court's filter mechanism by which it dismisses a great number of complaints in a simplified procedure without the involvement of the respondent government (most of them for reasons on the merits); and, secondly, the fact that the Court is less generous than the Committee in according interim measures.

While the judgments of the Court are legally binding under international law, this is not the case for the decisions of the Committee. However, in

---

ments and decisions with regard to complainants who are outside the contracting state's jurisdiction has shown to be very difficult.

125   Pirjola 2007, p. 659.

practice, European states have respected the Committee's decisions with regard to the principle of non-refoulement.

Despite the fact that the Committee's protection against refoulement is restricted to acts of torture and does not encompass inhuman or degrading treatment, the differences this restriction has created in practice remain limited since it is impossible in most cases to distinguish whether the alleged possible future harm can be classified as torture or inhuman treatment. The circumstances in which this distinction is possible and where the protection in Strasbourg is broader concern complaints in which the alleged risk in case of removal is clearly related to inhuman or degrading prison conditions, the risk of the death penalty or the exceptional cases in which the Court has recognized that harm of a socioeconomic nature may amount to degrading or inhuman treatment (medical issues or degrading living conditions for refugees). In addition, the Committee's practice with regard to the application of the principle of non-refoulement to harms emanating from private actors today resembles that of the Court. Hence, in most cases submitted by failed asylum seekers, a complaint prepared for Strasbourg could equally well be submitted to Geneva.

The risk factors taken into account by the Court and the Committee in the risk assessment are essentially the same although they are often evaluated differently. Generally, a comparison of the respective practices shows that the Court is more reluctant than the Committee to recognize the existence of a real risk of ill treatment in individual cases. In light of this and the fact that the Committee's decisions with regard to non-refoulement are normally respected by European states despite their lack of legally binding force, Geneva will often be the more effective option at international level for individuals threatened with refoulement from Europe. It is not surprising that in my country of origin, Switzerland, asylum lawyers have increasingly chosen to apply to Geneva rather than to Strasbourg – one of the reasons I embarked on this study.

However, it is clear that the Committee's institutional framework is weaker than the Court's and the fact that its decisions are not binding will always leave applicants with a certain sense of insecurity. In addition, it is vital to bear in mind the common practice of both the Court and the Committee of considering each case on its own merits, which makes it extremely difficult to anticipate the results of individual proceedings before either body. In its Grand Chamber judgment *Saadi v. Italy*, the Court stated that the risk assessment in refoulement cases is to some degree speculative.[126] As the judges in Strasbourg have stated, there is 'no strict test' for deciding refoulement cases and where

---

126   ECtHR, *Saadi v. Italy*, 28 February 2008 [GC], no. 37201/06, § 142.

domestic courts are called to evaluate the probability of a future event 'there is always room for uncertainty.'[127] This is clearly true for national as well as international organs such as the Court and the Committee.

The shortness and lack of legal reasoning in the Committee's decisions make its case law particularly unpredictable. Key issues with regard to the principle of non-refoulement are treated with ambiguity or vagueness: these include in particular the question of protection against non-state actors, the pertinence and practicability of differentiating between torture and inhuman treatment in the context of refoulement, the application of Article 16 CAT with regard to individuals suffering from illnesses (and generally, its relation to Article 3 CAT), the scope of the right to an effective remedy inherent to Article 3 CAT, the concept of the internal flight alternative, the requirements on medical reports with regard to torture victims and the conditions for group-based protection.[128] Illumination on the Committee's general approach with regard to these and other issues addressed in this study in a revised General Comment on Article 3 CAT would be welcome.

The Strasbourg Court's jurisprudence under the principle of non-refoulement is more elaborated than the Committee's. However, this does not mean the Court is always clear: at present, it is particularly hard to foresee in which direction it will develop its approach on living conditions adopted in *M.S.S.* and *Tarakhel*. In addition, there are also incoherencies in the Court's practice, in particular with regard to non-refoulement and health issues and the Court's concept of internal relocation.

Finally, looking at the Court's and the Committee's case law as a whole, I agree wholeheartedly with the conclusion of other authors that the Court and the Committee, through their assessment of individual complaints, have made an important contribution to the authority, development and strengthening of the principle of non-refoulement in national and international law and practice.[129] While the Court in Strasbourg tends to be more disposed towards establishing legal principles under the principle of non-refoulement than toward holding states accountable in individual cases,[130] the Committee in Geneva is more often prepared to find violations in individual cases than to give guidelines of general application.

---

127 ECtHR, *Azimov v. Russia*, 18 April 2013, no. 67474/11, § 128.

128 See also Chetail 2006, p. 100 and Wouters 2009, p. 524.

129 Chetail 2006, pp. 101–104; McAdam 2007, p. 125; Schürmann & Scheidegger 2009, p. 213; Wouters 2009, p. 528.

130 As Alleweldt observed in 1996 (p. 91).

Bibliography

Addo Michael K. and Grief Nicholas, Does Article 3 of the European Convention on Human Rights Enshrine Absolute Rights? European Journal of International Law 1998, pp. 510–524.

Allain Jean, The Jus Cogens Nature of Non-refoulement, International Journal of Refugee Law 2001, pp. 533–558.

Van Alebeek Rosanna and Nollkaemper André, The Legal Status of Decisions by Human Rights Treaty Bodies in National Law, in: UN Human Rights Treaty Bodies – Law and Legitimacy, H. Keller and G. Ulfstein (Editors), Cambridge 2012, pp. 356–413.

Alleweldt Ralf, Schutz vor Abschiebung bei drohender Folter oder unmenschlicher oder erniedrigender Behandlung oder Strafe, Heidelberg 1996.

Andrysek Oldrich, Gaps in International Protection and the Potential for Redress through Individual Complaints Procedures, International Journal of Refugee Law 1997, pp. 392–414.

Arai-Takahashi Yutaka, 'Uneven, But In The Direction Of Enhanced Effectiveness' – A Critical Analysis of 'Anticipatory Ill-Treatment' Under Article 3 ECHR, Netherlands Quarterly of Human Rights 2002, pp. 5–27.

Arai-Yokoi Yutaka, Grading Scale Of Degradation: Identifying The Threshold of Degrading Treatment Or Punishment Under Article 3 ECHR, Netherlands Quarterly of Human Rights 2003, pp. 385–421.

Von Arnauld Andreas, Konventionsrechtliche Grenzen der EU-Asylpolitik / Neujustierungen durch das Urteil des EGMR im Fall M.S.S./Belgien und Griechenland, Europäische Grundrechte Zeitschrift 2011, pp. 238–242.

Battjes Hemme, In Search of a Fair Balance: The Absolute Character of the Prohibition of Refoulement under Article 3 ECHR Reassessed, Leiden Journal of International Law 2009, pp. 583–621.

Bayefsky Anne F., How to Complain to the UN Human Rights Treaty System, The Hague/London/New York 2003.

Bossuyt Marc, Strasbourg et les demandeurs d'asile: des juges sur un terrain glissant, Bruxelles 2010.

Bossuyt Marc, The Court of Strasbourg Acting as an Asylum Court, European Constitutional Law Review 2012, pp. 203–245.

Boulesbaa Ahcene, Analysis and Proposals for the Rectification of the Ambiguities Inherent in Article 1 of the U.N. Convention on Torture, Florida International Law Journal 1990, pp. 293–326.

Boulesbaa Ahcene, The U.N. Convention on Torture and the Prospects for Enforcement, The Hague/Boston/London 1999.

Bruin René and Reneman Marcelle, Supervising Bodies and Medical Evidence, in: Medico-legal Reports and the Istanbul Protocol in Asylum Procedures, Bruin René, Reneman Marcelle and Bloement Evert (Editors), Amsterdam/Utrecht 2006, pp. 87–109.

Burns Peter, The United Nations Committee Against Torture And Its Role In Refugee Protection, Georgetown Immigration Law Journal 2001, pp. 403–413.

Cherubini Francesco, Asylum Law in the European Union, Abingdon/New York 2015.

Chetail Vincent, Le droit des réfugiés à l'épreuve des droits de l'homme: Bilan de la jurisprudence de la Cour Européenne des Droits de l'Homme sur l'interdiction du renvoi des étrangers menaces de torture et de traitements inhumains ou dégradants, Revue belge de droit international 2004, pp. 155–210.

Chetail Vincent, Le Comité des Nations Unies contre la torture et l'éloignement des étrangers: dix ans de jurisprudence (1994–2004), Revue Suisse de droit international et européen 2006, pp. 63–104.

Clayton Gina, Asylum Seekers in Europe: M.S.S. v. Belgium and Greece, Human Rights Law Review 2011, pp. 758–773.

Coracini Celso Eduardo Faria, The Lawful Sanctions Clause in the State Reporting Procedure Before the Committee Against Torture, Netherlands Quarterly of Human Rights 2006, pp. 305–318.

Costello Cathryn and Mouzourakis Minos, Reflections on Reading Tarakhel: Is 'How Bad is Bad Enough' Good Enough? Asiel&Migrantenrecht 2014, pp. 404–411.

Danelius Hans, Protection Against Torture in Europe and the World, in: The European System for the Protection of Human Rights, S. St. J. Macdondald, F. Matscher, H. Petzold (Editors), Boston/Leiden 1993, pp. 263–275.

Danelius Hans and Burgers Herman, The United Nations Convention against Torture, Dordrecht/Boston/London 1988.

David Samuel L., A Foul Immigration Policy: U.S. Misinterpretation of the Non-Refoulement Obligation under the Convention against Torture, New York Law School Journal of Human Rights 2003, pp. 769–806.

Delas Olivier, Le principe de non-refoulement dans la jurisprudence internationale des droits de l'homme – De la consecration à la contestation, Brussels 2011.

Doerfel Jan, The Convention Against Torture and the Protection of Refugees, Refugee Survey Quarterly 2005, pp. 89–97.

Droege Cordula, Transfers of Detainees: Legal Framework, Non-refoulement and Contemporary Challenges, Review of the Red Cross 2008, pp. 669–701.

Duffy Aoife, Expulsion to Face Torture? Non-refoulement in International Law, International Journal of Refugee Law 2008, pp. 373–390.

Durieux Jean-François, Salah Sheekh Is a Refugee – New Insights into Primary and Subsidiary Forms of Protection, Refugee Studies Centre, Working Paper Series No. 49, October 2008.

Einarsen Terje, The European Convention on Human Rights and the Notion of an Implied Right to de facto Asylum, International Journal of Refugee Law 1990, pp. 361–389.

Fabbricotti Alberta, The Concept of Inhuman or Degrading Treatment in International Law and its Application in Asylum Cases, International Journal of Refugee Law 1998, pp. 637–661.

Fornerod Anne, L'article 3 de la Convention Européenne des droits de l'homme et l'éloignement forcé des étrangers: Illustrations récentes, Revue trimestrielle des Droits de l'Homme n 82 2010, pp. 315–339.

Frumer Philippe, Le transfert de détenus dans le cadre d'opérations militaires multinationales – la peine de mort dans le collimateur de la Cour Européenne des droits de l'homme, Revue trimestrielle des Droits de l'Homme, n 84 2010, pp. 858–885.

Goodwin-Gill Guy S., Opinion – The Right to Seek Asylum: Interception at Sea and the Principle of Non-Refoulement, International Journal of Refugee Law 2011, pp. 443–457.

Goodwin-Gill Guy S. & McAdam Jane, The Refugee in International Law, Oxford 2007.

Gorlick Brian, The Convention and the Committee against Torture: A Complementary Protection Regime for Refugees, International Journal of Refugee Law 1999, pp. 479–495.

Gorlick Brian, Common Burdens and Standards: Legal Elements in Assessing Claims to Refugee Status, International Journal of Refugee Law 2003, pp. 357–376.

Haeck Yves, Burbano Herrera Clara & Zwaak Leo, Non-Compliance With a Provisional Measure Automatically Leads To a Violation of the Right of Individual Application ... or Doesn't It?, European Constitutional Law Review 2008, pp 41–63,

Haeck Yves, Burbano Herrera & Zwaak Leo, Strasbourg's Interim Measures Under Fire: Does the Rising Number of State Incompliance with Interim Measures Pose a Threat to the European Court of Human Rights?, European Yearbook on Human Rights 2011, pp. 375–403.

Heffernan Liz, A Comparative View of Individual Petition Procedures under the European Convention on Human Rights and the International Covenant on Civil and Political Rights, Human Rights Quarterly 1997, pp. 78–112.

Ingelse Chris, The Committee Against Torture: One Step Forward, One Step Back, Netherlands Quarterly of Human Rights 2000, pp. 307–327.

Ingelse Chris, The UN Committee against Torture, An Assessment, The Hague/London/Boston 2001.

Kälin Walter, Das Prinzip des Non-Refoulement. Das Verbot der Zurückweisung, Ausweisung und Auslieferung von Flüchtlingen in den Verfolgerstaat im Völkerrecht und im schweizerischen Landesrecht, Bern, 1982.

Kälin Walter, Genf oder Strassburg? Die Rechtsprechung des UNO-Menschenrechtsausschusses und des Europäischen Gerichtshofes für Menschenrechte im

Vergleich, Studie des Schweizerischen Kompetenzzentrums für Menschenrechte, 9. January 2012.

Kälin Walter and Künzli Jörg, Universeller Menschenrechtsschutz – Der Schutz des Individuums auf globaler und regionaler Ebene, 3. Auflage, Basel 2013.

Kashgar Maral, Art. 3 im Rahmen des Individualbeschwerdeverfahrens gemäß Art. 22 des Übereinkommens gegen Folter und andere grausame, unmenschliche oder erniedrigende Behandlung oder Strafe, Menschenrechtsmagazin 2011, pp. 52–73.

Keller Helen and Ulfstein Geir, Conclusions, in: UN Human Rights Treaty Bodies – Law and Legitimacy, H. Keller and G. Ulfstein (Editors), Cambridge 2012, pp. 414–425.

Keller Helen, Fischer Andreas, Kühne Daniela, Debating the Future of the European Court of Human Rights after the Interlaken Conference. Two Innovative Proposals, European Journal of International Law, 2010 pp. 1025–1048.

Lambert, Hélène, Protection Against Refoulement from Europe: Human Rights Law Comes to the Rescue, International and Comparative Law Quarterly 1999, pp. 515–544.

Lambert Hélène, The European Convention on Human Rights and the Protection of Refugees: Limits and Opportunities, Refugee Survey Quarterly 2005, pp. 39–55.

Lambert Hélène, The Position of Aliens in relation to the European Convention on Human Rights, Human Rights Files – Council of Europe Publishing 2007.

Lauterpacht Elihu and Bethlehem Daniel, The Scope and Content of the Principle of Non-refoulement: Opinion, in: Refugee Protection in International Law – UNHCR's Global Consultations on International Protection, E. Feller, V. Türk and F. Nicholson (Editors), Cambridge 2003, pp. 87–177.

Leach Philip, Taking a Case to the European Court of Human Rights, third edition, Oxford 2011.

Lorz Ralph Alexander and Sauer Heiko, Wann genau steht Art. 3 EMRK einer Auslieferung oder Ausweisung entgegen? / Eine Systematisierung der Rechtsprechung des EGMR zu den Beweisanforderungen, Europäische Grundrechte Zeitschrift 2010, pp. 389–407.

Mallia Patricia, Case of M.S.S. v. Belgium and Greece: A Catalyst in the Re-Thinking of the Dublin II Regulation, Refugee Survey Quarterly 2011, pp. 107–128.

Mandal Ruma, Protection Mechanisms Outside of the 1951 Convention („Complementary Protection"), Legal and Protection Policy Research Series, Department of International Protection UNHCR 2005.

Mantouvalou Virginia, N. v UK: No Duty to Rescue the Nearby Needy? The Modern Law Review, 2009, pp. 815–827.

Matthey Fanny, Cour européenne des droits de l'homme (CourEDH), Affaire Tarakhel c. Suisse, du 4 novembre 2014, requête no 29217/12, Schweizerische Zeitschrift für Asylrecht und -Praxis 1/2015, pp. 26–28.

McAdam Jane, Complementary Protection in International Refugee Law, Oxford 2007.

McAdam Jane, Australian Complementary Protection: A Step-By-Step Approach, Sydney Law Review 2011, pp. 686–734.

Menéndez Fernando M. Mariño, The Convention against Torture and its Optional Protocol, in: International Protection of Human Rights: Achievements and Challenges, Isa Felipe Gómez and de Feyter Koen (Editors), Bilbao 2006, pp. 186–215.

Mendéndez Fernando M. Mariño, Recent Jurisprudence of the United Nations Committee against Torture and the International Protection of Refugees, Refugee Survey Quarterly 2015, pp. 61–78.

Miller Dawn J., Holding States to their Convention Obligations: The United Nations Convention against Torture and the Need for a Broad Interpretation of State Action, Georgetown Immigration Law Journal 2003, pp. 299–323.

Mole Nuala and Meredith Catherine, Asylum and the European Convention on Human Rights, Strasbourg 2010.

Moreno-Lax Violeta, Hirsi Jamaa and Others v Italy or the Strasbourg Court versus Extraterritorial Migration Control?, Human Rights Law Review 2012, pp. 1–25.

Nowak Manfred, Challenges to the Absolute Nature of the Prohibition of Torture and Ill-treatment, Netherlands Quarterly of Human Rights 2005, pp. 674–688.

Nowak Manfred, 'Extraordinary Renditions,' Diplomatic Assurances and the Principle of Non-Refoulement, in: International Law, Conflict and Development, The Emergence of a Holistic Approach in International Affairs, Kälin Walter, Kolb Robert, Spenlé Christoph A. and Voyaume Maurice D. (Editors), Dordrecht/Boston/London 2008, pp. 107–134.

Nowak Manfred and McArthur Elizabeth, The United Nations Convention Against Torture, A Commentary, Oxford 2008.

Peers Steve, Moreno-Lax Violeta, Garlick Madeline and Guild Elspeth, EU Immigration and Asylum Law (Text and Commentary): Second Revised Edition, Leiden/Boston 2015.

Pirjola Jari, Shadows in Paradise – Exploring Non-Refoulement as an Open Concept, International Journal for Refugee Law 2007, pp. 639–660.

Reidy Aisling, The Prohibition of Torture, Human Rights Handbook No. 6, Council of Europe, Strasbourg 2002.

Rieter Eva, Preventing Irreparable Harm. Provisional Measures in International Human Rights Adjudication, Intersentia, Antwerp/Oxford/Portland 2010.

Rosati Kirsten B., The United Nations Convention Against Torture: A Self-Executing Treaty that Prevents the Removal of Persons Ineligible for Asylum and Withholding of Removal, Denver Journal of International Law and Policy 1998, pp. 533–577.

Schabas A. William, The European Convention on Human Rights, A Commentary, Oxford 2015.

Schultz Jessica, The European Court of Human Rights and Internal Relocation: An Unduly Harsh Standard, in: Exploring the Boundaries of Refugee Law – Current

Protection Challenges, Gauci Jean-Pierre, Giuffré Mariagiulia and Tsourdi Evangelia (Lilian) (Editors), Leiden 2015, pp. 31–49.

Schürmann Frank and Scheidegger Adrian, Individualbeschwerde bei drohender Verletzung des Non-Refoulement Prinzips, Schweizerisches Jahrbuch für Europarecht 2009, pp. 201–213.

Sørensen Bent, CAT and Articles 20 and 22, in: International Human Rights Monitoring Mechanisms, Alfredsson Gudmundur, Grimheden Jonas, Ramcharan Bertram G. and de Zayas Alfred (Editors), Hague/Boston/London 2001, pp. 167–183.

Spijkerboer Thomas, Subsidiarity and 'Arguability': The European Court of Human Rights' Case Law on Judicial Review in Asylum Cases, International Journal of Refugee Law 2009, pp. 48–74.

Suntinger Walter, The Principle of Non-Refoulement: Looking Rather to Geneva than to Strasbourg? Austrian Journal of Public and International Law 1995, pp. 203–225.

Thurin Oliver, Der Schutz des Fremden vor rechtswidriger Abschiebung, Das Prinzip des Non-Refoulement nach Artikel 3 EMRK, 2., aktualisierte Auflage, Wien 2012.

Towle Richard, Human Rights Standards: A Paradigm For Refugee Protection? in: Human Rights and Forced Displacement, Bayefsky Anne F. and Fitzpatrick Joan (Editors), The Hague 2001.

Trechsel Stefan, Artikel 3 EMRK als Schranke der Ausweisung, in: Aktuelle asylrechtliche Probleme der gerichtlichen Entscheidungspraxis in Deutschland, Österreich und der Schweiz, Barwig Klaus and Brill Walter (Editors), Baden-Baden 1996, pp. 83–101.

Ulfstein Geri, Individual Complaints, in: UN Human Rights Treaty Bodies: Law and Legitimacy, H. Keller and G. Ulfstein (Editors), Cambridge 2012, pp. 73–115.

Vedsted-Hansen Jens, The European Convention on Human Rights, Counter-Terrorism, and Refugee Protection, Refugee Survey Quarterly 2011, pp. 45–62.

De Weck Fanny, Die EMRK und die Todesstrafe, Schweizerisches Jahrbuch für Europarecht 2011, pp. 341–358.

De Weck Fanny, Die Praxis des Ausschlusses der Vereinten Nationen gegen die Folter in Individualmitteilungsverfahren zum Non-Refoulement-Prinzip, Schweizerische Zeitschrift für Asylrecht und -Praxis 2/2011, pp. 4–11.

De Weck Fanny, Das Rückschiebungsverbot aus medizinischen Gründen nach Art. 3 EMRK, Jusletter, 18. März 2013.

Weissbrodt David and Hörtreiter Isabel, The Principle of Non-Refoulement: Article 3 of the Convention Against Torture and Other Cruel, Inhuman or Degrading Treatment or Punishment in Comparison with the Non-Refoulement Provisions of Other International Human Rights Treaties, Buffalo Human Rights Law Review 1999, pp. 1–73.

White Robin and Ovey Clare, The European Convention on Human Rights, fifth edition, Oxford 2010.

Wouters Kees, International Legal Standards for the Protection from Refoulement, Antwerp/Oxford/Portland 2009.

Index

Printed in the United States
By Bookmasters